The Ultimate Scene Study Series
Volume IV

104 Scenes for Four Actors

Smith and Kraus *Books For Actors*
THE MONOLOGUE SERIES
The Best Men's / Women's Stage Monologues of 1998
The Best Men's / Women's Stage Monologues of 1997
The Best Men's / Women's Stage Monologues of 1996
The Best Men's / Women's Stage Monologues of 1995
The Best Men's / Women's Stage Monologues of 1994
The Best Men's / Women's Stage Monologues of 1993
The Best Men's / Women's Stage Monologues of 1992
The Best Men's / Women's Stage Monologues of 1991
The Best Men's / Women's Stage Monologues of 1990
One Hundred Men's / Women's Stage Monologues from the 1980s
2 Minutes and Under: Character Monologues for Actors
Street Talk: Character Monologues for Actors
Uptown: Character Monologues for Actors
Ice Babies in Oz: Character Monologues for Actors
Monologues from Contemporary Literature: Volume I
Monologues from Classic Plays 468 B.C. to 1960 A.D.
100 Great Monologues from the Renaissance Theatre
100 Great Monologues from the Neo-Classical Theatre
100 Great Monologues from the 19th C. Romantic and Realistic Theatres
A Brave and Violent Theatre: 20th C. Irish Monologues, Scenes & Hist. Context
Kiss and Tell: Restoration Monologues, Scenes and Historical Context
The Great Monologues from the Humana Festival
The Great Monologues from the EST Marathon
The Great Monologues from the Women's Project
The Great Monologues from the Mark Taper Forum
The Ultimate Audition Book Vol.I: 222 Monologues, 2 Minutes and Under
The Ultimate Audition Book Vol.II: 222 Monologues from Non-Dramatic Sources
SCENE STUDY SERIES
The Ultimate Scene Study Series Vol.I: 101 Scenes for Groups
The Ultimate Scene Study Series Vol.II: 102 Scenes for Two Actors
The Ultimate Scene Study Series Vol.III: 103 Scenes for Three Actors
Scenes From Classic Plays 468 B.C. to 1970 A.D.
The Best Stage Scenes of 1998
The Best Stage Scenes of 1997
The Best Stage Scenes of 1996
The Best Stage Scenes of 1995
The Best Stage Scenes of 1994
The Best Stage Scenes of 1993
The Best Stage Scenes of 1992
The Best Stage Scenes for Men / Women from the 1980s

If you require pre-publication information about upcoming Smith and Kraus books, you may receive our semi-annual catalogue, free of charge, by sending your name and address to *Smith and Kraus Catalogue, 4 Lower Mill Road, North Stratford, NH 03590. Or call us at (800) 895-4331, fax (603) 643-1831.*

The Ultimate
Scene Study Series
Volume IV

104 Scenes for Four Actors

edited by Wilma Marcus Chandler

SCENE STUDY SERIES

A SMITH AND KRAUS BOOK

For my family: John, Jana, Valerie, Karin, and David

Published by Smith and Kraus, Inc.
177 Lyme Road, Hanover, NH 03755
www.SmithKraus.com

First Edition: May 2001
10 9 8 7 6 5 4 3 2 1

Library of Congress cataloguing in publication data
The ultimate scene study series / edited by Wilma Marcus Chandler
p. cm. — (Scene study series)
Includes bibliographical references.
Contents: v.1. 101 scenes for groups — v.2. 102 short scenes for two actors —
v.3. 103 scenes for three actors — v.4. 104 scenes for four actors.
ISBN 1-57525-153-1 (v.2)
1. Acting. 2. English drama. 3. American drama. 4. Drama—Translations into English.
I. Chandler, Wilma Marcus II. Series.

PN2080.U49 1999
808.82—dc21 99-089197

NOTE: These scenes are intended to be used for audition and class study; permission is not required to use the material for those purposes. However, if there is a paid performance of any of the scenes included in this book, please refer to the permission acknowledgment pages 562–566 to locate the source who can grant permission for public performance.

Contents

PART THREE: SCENES FOR TWO MEN/TWO WOMEN

PART FOUR: SCENES FOR THREE MEN/ONE WOMAN

PART FIVE: SCENES FOR THREE WOMEN/ONE MAN

All of us, I believe, are capable of everything. We have inside ourselves all the extremes of emotion and desire, and it is that capacity that I think the actor brings, in the last analysis, to the making of his part. That is the Self.

Morris Carnovsky
The Actor's Eye

Foreword

Four-person scenes provide unique opportunities for actors and directors to explore increasingly complex and subtle dramatic situations.

As you begin working on a four-person scene, keep in mind that not all the actors will have the same number of lines to speak, yet all will have action and focus.

Unlike a film, where the camera can zero in on one or two actors as they speak their lines and virtually eliminate others in the scenes, the stage reveals all the characters all the time, and unless you make an exit, your character is visible, vivid, and an integral part of the situation.

Whether your character is pouring cocktails, gearing up for a fight, or sitting at a table drinking coffee, he or she is unique and has a history and a full life.

Stay alive to each moment. Remember your objectives.

For the brief moments of your scene you are offering your audience a glimpse into another realm. Some realms are realistic, others absurd or surreal or expressionistic, but your task is to find the truth within the realm of the scene.

Note that there will be a shift of power, even within a short scene. All scenes, as well, have an arc—rising and then falling energy. As you rehearse, determine the path of that arc, including the introductory rhythm, the climax, and the closing rhythm. Even an excerpt must follow that arc in order to make the truth emerge.

Ideas and attitudes in a four-person scene often fall into two-against-two or three-against-one patterns. Seldom do we see four distinct points of view in one scene. Analyze the distinctions according to patterns and degrees of allegiance. This will help create contrast and texture within the scene because the degree of each character's allegiance is different.

Remember that the script is only the beginning of your work. The vitality of your performance depends on your interpretation and the energy that you use to devote yourself to that interpretation. Try to avoid "standing around," or becoming a group of "talking heads."

Find the movement in the scenes and think of using levels to create visual groupings that will enhance the scenes. Employ stage business whenever possible.

Have a great time with your work!

PART ONE:

SCENES FOR
FOUR MEN

Oedipus the King

Sophocles
430 B.C.

Dramatic

Setting: Outside the palace of Oedipus and Queen Jocasta.

Scene: The Chorus entreat the Gods to heal Thebes of the plague that is destroying it. The old King Laius, Jocasta's first husband, was murdered and only when his murder is solved will the plague end. Creon, Jocasta's brother, suggests they hear testimony from the aged, blind prophet Teiresias.

Oedipus: King of Thebes, 40's, a proud man, beloved by the citizenry.

Chorus I and II: The elders of Thebes (lines divided between two chorus leaders).

Teiresias: The elderly, blind prophet 60's-90's (he is led in by a boy, who has no lines).

LEADER: How sweet is the message of Zeus!
 What word do you bring me from Delphi?
 From Pytho's gold-rich temple?
 What word do you bring here to Thebes?
 To Thebes, my glorious city?
 Healer of Delos, I tremble!
 God of the rapturous cry,
 My heart is shaken with terror!
 Reveal to me, god, your demands!

CHORUS: What do you ask me?
 What is your will?
 What new doom
 Do you bring upon me?
 Or is it renewed
 With the circling years?

CHORUS: Raise up your voice, immortal daughter!
 Child of Golden Hope, give us hope!

LEADER: Athena, first I summon you;
 Daughter of Zeus; eternal maiden!
 And then your sister, throned in the market;
 Splendid Artemis, land's guardian!

And Apollo, archer of the unfailing aim!
Triple defenders against doom, appear!
Rise before me! Let me see you!
You who shielded me once!
CHORUS: Appear!
LEADER: You who averted my ruin!
CHORUS: Appear!
LEADER: You who defended my city!
CHORUS: Appear!
LEADERS: Gods who banished the fires of doom!
CHORUS: Hear me!
LEADER: You the triple defenders of Thebes!
CHORUS: Help me!
LEADER: Unnumbered the miseries that beat me down;
Unnumbered the lives Plague drags into the darkness.
Where is the sword of the mind to protect me?
My glorious fields are barren of fruit;
My women in labor cannot give birth.
CHORUS: Lives take wing like
birds in flight:
sparks that rise
when fire rages;
hastening into
darkening death.

(The Chorus' tone grows hushed, ominous, and its ranks begin to disintegrate as one member after another darts with increasing speed from one area of the orchestra to another in a frenzied choreography, their voices gradually rising to a frantic pitch at the end, and their phrases wildly overlapping.)

CHORUS: —The city wavers, stumbles, falls!
Unnumbered dead, graveless bodies, heavy with death, unmourned!
Young wives, ancient mothers, herd around steps of altars
from all directions!
Grieving! Raising prayers to Apollo! Cries!
Laments! Golden child of Zeus, Athena, send lovely Strength!
Ares, fire-raging god! Ares, god of war, storms among us!
Fever-bringing, feverous god! Unarmored he comes!
Unshielded he comes! He burns me! Burns me!
Bruiting his clamorous song!

Drive him, drive him back from my borders!
Cast him out into the vast sea of Amphitrite!
Or into the turbulent harbor of Thrake!
If tonight I escape him, the fiery god, the god of death,
his fever returns with the sun, and I die! —Zeus!
Father! Ruler of stormwind! Whose bolts are lightning!
Destroy! Destroy the invader! Crush him with the thunder of
  your brow!
—Apollo Lykeios! Lord of light! Be my defender!
String your bow with the sun's golden threads!
Shoot with unerring aim against my enemy!
Let your arrows stand guard before Thebes!
—And, Artemis, you, racing with fiery torches over Lykeian hills!
Drive harsh death from our land!
—And I call now upon you, Bakkhos! Bakkhos! God of wine-
  dark eyes!
Hair bound back with golden band!
Who bears our city's name! Master of maenads who cry eüoi!
Descend with your torch upon Ares! The fiery god!
The feverous god! God of death! Burn him!
Burn him! Burn him whom all the gods hate!

*(The Chorus' frenzy suddenly freezes into icy silence. The music
then faintly reasserts itself as Oedipus enters through the large
doors of the palace and addresses the Theban Elders. The music
fades out.)*

OEDIPUS: My people, listen to me. I have heard your prayers
  And supplications, and I am moved by your plight.
  Now here is an answer; but you must do your part, too.
  Help me to your cure, do as required,
  And soon you will be relieved of all your pains.

  Until today, I knew nothing of this tale.
  How could I have know of Laios' death,
  Or of the murder, without some link with you?
  How could I have tracked the murderer
  Without a clue? I was a stranger here,
  A stranger to the crime as to the city,
  Arriving only after your king's death,
  Made a Theban only then.

But hear me out.
There is one among you knows who killed King Laios,
Son of Labdakos; one among you
Who knows the man whose hand did the deed,
Who held the instrument. Who is he? I ask you
To tell me now. I command you by my authority,
Step forward and speak. And fear is no excuse.
Even if he incriminates himself,
Let him speak and clear himself of the charge.
I assure him that he will not be harmed,
He will not be stumbling into exile,
But leave the land in good and proper health.
(Silence: no response.)
If anyone knows the murderer to be a stranger,
A foreigner from an alien land, let him speak,
For he will have a reward as well as my gratitude.
(Silence: no response.)
If, however, you keep your silence, refusing
To speak in hope of shielding yourself,
Or a friend or loved one from my edict, then hear this:
I command every citizen of the land
Where I hold throne and power to give no shelter
Or word to him, whoever he may be!
Shut your doors against him! Deny him place
In your prayers and sacrifices and lustrations!
Drive him from every hearth, from every house,
Drive him out of Thebes, out of the land,
For he is our pollution, our corruption,
Our disease, as the god's Pythian Oracle,
God's word of prophecy, has revealed to me!
And I, as god's own ally, Apollo's warrior,
Take up arms now in defense of the dead man.

As for the murderer, whether he acted alone,
A single man and unknown, or one of many,
I pray that his evil life be ground down
To miserable and wretched days!

As for me,

If I have given shelter and shared my hearth,
Knowingly, with that man, may the same curse
Turn back to haunt me. These are my orders:
Do it for me, do it for Apollo,
Do it for the land that withers barren
Under pitiless heavens. Even had the gods
Never thrown you into such misery,
You should never have given up your search
To seek out the culprit and wipe the land
Free of the stain. He was your king who died,
First among men! But now, holding the power
That he once held, holding his marital bed
And wife, the wife who now bears me children
That might have been his had Chance not denied him a son,
A son who would have been my children's brother,
Sharing blood between us: I say now:
I will take up his cause as son to father,
And vow not to give up the fight till the hand
That murdered Laios son of Labdakos,
Sprung from Polydoros and Kadmos before him
And from Agenoros long ago, Is brought to light!
And to those who will not listen,
Who refuse to help, may the gods light your fields
Till you die of hunger, and may they infect the wombs
Of your wives with stony barrenness!
May you perish
Of the plague that ravages us now, or one more terrible!

As for you men of Thebes, loyal citizens
Of Kadmos' city who support me in this, may Justice,
Our ally, and all the gods stand by and protect us
In the battle still to come!

LEADER: In light of your curse, my lord, I can only say
That I am not the murderer, nor can I point
To the one who is. Apollo ordered the search,
Apollo should properly tell us where to find him.

OEDIPUS: A man force a god to speak?

LEADER: Then may I suggest the next best thing?

OEDIPUS: Even if it is a third, let us hear it.

(Teiresias, an aged, blind prophet, enters, right, from the city, led by a Boy along with Attendants. Because of the prophet's age their progress in the cross is slow and tortuous.)

LEADER: The prophet Teiresias, sir.
   Next to Apollo, he has the keenest sight
   Where truth is concerned.
   We could learn from him.

OEDIPUS: Teiresias, yes! On Kreon's advice,
   I have sent for him already.
   Twice, in fact.
   Where could he be?

LEADER: Except for him, there are only rumors.

OEDIPUS: Such as? I will consider everything.

LEADER: That Laios was killed by bandits.

OEDIPUS: I've heard; but where is the murderer now?

LEADER: If he has any fear in him,
   And has heard your curses,
   He's not in Thebes now.

OEDIPUS: Words won't frighten a killer of kings!

LEADER: Here is the only man who knows:
   The holy, inspired prophet. God's truth
   Lives as day in his dark eyes.

OEDIPUS: Teiresias, seer who knows all things,
   Master of omens earthly and divine,
   Of things that can be learned, and things mysterious:
   Though your eyes are blind, you see and know
   The plague that sears our city.
   You alone, my lord,
   Can save us from this destruction. You may have heard;
   If not, then I will tell you.

   Apollo has sent us word through his Pythian Oracle,
   That if Thebes is ever to raise its head from this pestilence,
   We must first find the murderers of Laios,
   And then either kill them or send them into exile.
   Share your gifts now, old man, your powers
   Of divination; read the flights of birds,
   Or else use other means, but spare us nothing—
   Nothing. Pull us from danger. Care for yourself,
   Care for your city, for me; rescue us

From the vile pollution the dead man brings upon us.
There can be nobler act for a man
Than to use every means in helping others.

TEIRESIAS: How terrible truth can be when all it brings
To the one who knows is pain! I knew this once,
I knew it well, but I drove it out. I forgot.
No, I should never have come.

OEDIPUS: Never have come?
Why so bleak, so despairing?

TEIRESIAS: Let me go home!
You bear your fate, I will bear mine;
It is better this way.

OEDIPUS: Who are you to say such things to Thebes
That gave you life! Tell us what you know!

TEIRESIAS: Be careful: your own words
Are not as well-aimed as you may think.
I won't have the same be said of mine.

OEDIPUS: We beg you in the god's name!
Tell us what you see!

TEIRESIAS: You're blind—all of you; you know nothing.
Leave me my sorrow;
I will leave you yours!

OEDIPUS: Know and not tell?
Are you set on betraying Thebes?
Destroying the city?

TEIRESIAS: Why grieve myself or you?
Why insist? I will tell you nothing!

OEDIPUS: Despicable, villainous old man!
You could inflame a stone to anger!
Won't talk, eh? Well, I say *talk!*

TEIRESIAS: You rant against *my* temper?
You don't know the one *you* live with!

OEDIPUS: Who could listen to your insults and not be angry!
You shame your city!

TEIRESIAS: Speech or silence, what will be will be

OEDIPUS: If what will be will be, then tell me!

TEIRESIAS: No! Nothing! Rage on!
I have nothing to say!

OEDIPUS: And rage I will! For I *will* speak!

Yes, and in anger, too! All I suspect!
Hear me now!
I say that *you* helped plot the death of Laios!
Plotted it in every way you could,
Even though your hand never struck a blow!
Oh, and if you had eyes, I would even say
You did that, too!

TEIRESIAS: Aha!
Then take responsibility for your own words
And carry out your edict to the letter:
Never to speak another word to me
Or to anyone here in Thebes:
For you yourself
Are this land's curse, you are this land's corruption!
You! The plague is you!

OEDIPUS: And you really think to get by with this?

TEIRESIAS: I have already. My strength is truth.

OEDIPUS: Who taught you this? Your prophet's craft?

TEIRESIAS: You! In forcing me to speak.

OEDIPUS: Then say it again so I will understand!

TEIRESIAS: Did I make no sense? Are you testing me now?

OEDIPUS: Not so I know it clearly! Again!

TEIRESIAS: You, you are the murderer you're hunting.

Lysistrata

Aristophanes

Setting: The Akropolis

Chorus of Old Men
Leader

(Enter a Chorus of Old Men, poorly dressed, exhausted by their load, coughing, wheezing. Each carries two logs, a torch, and a bucket of live coals. The Chorus's sentences are spoken individually.)

MEN'S LEADER: Onward Drakës!
　　　Onward and upward, old friend!
　　　Watch your shoulders, don't skin them
　　　With those infernal big olive-tree branches.
　　　Ah, what a life!
OLD MEN'S CHORUS: Onward and upward, old cockers! Ooooo!
　　　The awful things age does to you!
　　　You, Strymodoros, who would have thought it?
　　　Right where it hurts, that's where we've caught it—
　　　And from women what's more!
　　　The shameless whores!
　　　The wives we wed,
　　　The wives we fed,
　　　The wives we dragged off to bed have fled!
　　　They've taken the Akropolis of my favorite metropolis!
　　　And why? I ask why?
　　　They've barred the gates and bolted the doors!
　　　The ladies from Hades!
　　　The devious whores!
MEN'S LEADER: That's right, Philourgos!
　　　When we get up there we'll pile our branches
　　　Next to the wall in a heaven-high pyre!
　　　We'll burn the bitches, traitors to Athens,
　　　Burn them to cinders and rout the conspiracy!
　　　And the first one will be that Lysistrata!
　　　No one gets the better of us!

OLD MEN'S CHORUS: Not even that Spartan,
　　　The great Kleomenês, all stuffed full of pride and riding his
　　　high-horse,
　　　Got the better of us.
　　　Six hundred men he marched up here,
　　　Six hundred Spartans.
　　　They stayed six years.
　　　The swell and the swagger,
　　　The puff and the pride of those
　　　Six hundred men was doomed to subside.
　　　We slept at the gate.
　　　Sixteen ranks deep.
　　　That sealed their fate.
　　　We protected our state!
MEN'S LEADER: He came out a wreck,
　　　Old King Kleomenês, with
　　　Scarcely a rag to cover his penis.
　　　Starved and unshaved and unwashed for six years!
　　　I remember his smell!
OLD MEN'S CHORUS: We remember it well.
MEN'S LEADER: But he learned his lesson.
OLD MEN'S CHORUS: He learned it well.
MEN'S LEADER: And now these women, these
　　　Pests out of Hades!
　　　These frivolous ladies!
　　　These whores out of Hell!
　　　Have taken the Akropolis of my favorite metropolis!
　　　Down with the ladies!
　　　These pests of Hades!
　　　All the world hates them!
　　　The gods and Euripides!
OLD MEN'S CHORUS: We fought the Medes at Marathon.
　　　So we will not be put upon.
　　　We won it there!
　　　We'll win it here!
MEN'S LEADER: But first let's haul these logs on up there!
OLD MEN'S CHORUS: My legs are wobbly.
　　　My knees a bit quaky.
　　　A good stiff drink would make them less shaky.

A team of oxen would lighten this load.
Steady on, men, it's right up the road.

MEN'S LEADER: Careful there!
Don't drop your pots.
They hold the only fire we've got.
So blow on the embers! Blow as you go!

OLD MEN'S CHORUS: Hoo! Hoo!
What a stench! The smoke makes me choke!
This smoke is a wench that tears at my eyes!
Hoo! Hoo! How fiercely it flies!
Flies straight to my eyes!
This fire is a bitch to make my eyes itch!

MEN'S LEADER: Steady on, men! We've almost arrived!
Another few steps and we'll get there alive!

OLD MEN'S CHORUS: One more step.
Another step onward.
Courage, men, we're almost there.
Just short of despair.
We're almost there.
At the cost of our lives
We'll rescue the goddess from our
miscreant wives.

MEN'S LEADER: We're here, men! Halt!
Lower your loads!
Pile them about!
We'll make us a pyre
To fire the fools out!

MEN'S CHORUS: Ah, my old back!
What a misery I'm in!
My shoulders are slack with that weight off my back.
My arms are undone.
My fingers are numb.
What a misery I'm in!
What a misery we're in!

MEN'S LEADER: Blow on your embers!
Let's make them glow bright.

OLD MEN'S CHORUS: Miserable smoke!
Came right off of Lemnos!
Hoo! Hoo!

Miserable stench!

MEN'S LEADER: Bring the pots over.
Set them down here.
Now dip in your torches.
Let them catch fire.
Then straight to the pyre.

OLD MEN'S CHORUS: Hoo! Hoo!
Miserable stench!
Attacking my eyes like a rabid bitch!
Hoo! Hoo!
How fiercely it flies!
Straight to my eyes!

MEN'S LEADER: There! They're burning!
And now we're already!
Steady there, steady!
We've set them alight!
And now we'll charge the gates like rams!
If that doesn't teach these women what's right,
We'll fire the doors and smoke them to Hades,
The miscreant ladies!
What we really need is that famous general
Who sits on his duff all day on Samos.

Lady Luck! Help us! We need it!
We'll kick the living shit from these bitches,
Or die trying!
Down with women!
Up with men!
Onward to victory!

The Girl from Andros

Terence
166 B.C.

Comic
Setting: In a suburb of Athens. On a street.
Scene: Charinus is in love with Philumena. However, Pamphilus is being married off to her unwillingly by his Father on this day. His father hates Pamphilus' mistress, Glycerium, the girl from Andros, and is trying to force his son into a loveless marriage with a "better class" of woman. Here, Charinus comes down the street, talking to his slave and confidant Byrria.

Charinus: A young man of Athens in love with Philumena, 20's.
Byrria: His slave, 20's.
Pamphilus: A young man of Athens, 20's, in love with Glycerium who is pregnant with his child.
Davos: Slave to Pamphilus' father but attendant upon Pamphilus, 20's.

CHARINUS: What's that, Byrria? Did you say Philumena was to be married to Pamphilus today?
BYRRIA: That's right.
CHARINUS: How do you know?
BYRRIA: I met Davos in town just now, and he told me.
CHARINUS: Oh, it's terrible! Up to now I've been torn between hope and fear—now all hope's lost and—left with a mind numbed by anxiety, worn out and exhausted.
BYRRIA: Good heavens, sir, if you can't have what you want, do try to want what you can have.
CHARINUS: *(Despondently.)* I don't want anything but Philumena.
BYRRIA: You'd do far better to make an effort to rid yourself of this passion, instead of saying things which only add fuel to the fire and do no good.
CHARINUS: It's easy for us all when we're healthy to give good advice to a sick man. If you were in my place you'd think differently.
BYRRIA: All right, have it your own way.
CHARINUS: Look, there's Pamphilus. I must try everything before I accept defeat.

BYRRIA: *(Aside.)* What's he up to?

CHARINUS: I'll appeal to him in person, fall at his knees, tell him of my love—I believe that'll persuade him at least to postpone the wedding for a few days. Meanwhile something'll turn up—I hope.

BYRRIA: *(Aside.)* "Something"? Nothing, more like.

CHARINUS: What do you think, Byrria; shall I go up to him?

BYRRIA: You might as well; at least you'll succeed in giving him the idea that you're all set to be his wife's lover, if he marries her.

CHARINUS: Oh go to hell, you and your insinuations, you rascal!

PAMPHILUS: *(Waking up to their presence.)* Why, here's Charinus. Hullo.

CHARINUS: Hullo, Pamphilus. I come to you in search of hope, salvation, help, and counsel.

PAMPHILUS: I'm in no position to give counsel, and I've no means of helping you. But what's the matter?

CHARINUS: Are you getting married today?

PAMPHILUS: So they say.

CHARINUS: *(Dramatically.)* Pamphilus, if you do so, this is the last time you will set eyes on me.

PAMPHILUS: *(Genuinely surprised.)* Why on earth?

CHARINUS: Alas, I dare not to say. Byrria, you tell him.

BYRRIA: All right.

PAMPHILUS: Then what is it?

BYRRIA: He's in love—with the girl you're to marry.

PAMPHILUS: Well then, our tastes differ . . . *(Hopefully.)* Now tell me, Charinus, has there been anything more between you?

CHARINUS: No, Pamphilus, nothing at all.

PAMPHILUS: If only there had!

CHARINUS: In the name of our friendship and my love for Philumena, I beseech you: Don't marry her. That would be best.

PAMPHILUS: I'll certainly *try* not to.

CHARINUS: But if that proves impossible, or your heart is set on this marriage—

PAMPHILUS: *Set* on it!

CHARINUS: — do at least postpone it for a few days so that I can go away somewhere and not see it.

PAMPHILUS: Now listen to me, Charinus. I don't want credit when none is deserved. I don't think any gentleman should expect it.

And in the case of this marriage—I'm much more anxious to get out of it than you are to take it on.

CHARINUS: Oh, I can breathe again!

PHAMPHILUS: Now you and Byrria here do all you can, plot and plan and devise some means of getting the girl for yourself. On my side I'll do my best not to have her.

CHARINUS: I'm willing.

PAMPHILUS: *(Looking along the street.)* Splendid, I can see Davos. I can count on him for some good suggestions.

CHARINUS: *(To Byrria.)* While you, damn you, are no good at all except to provide useless information. You can go.

BYRRIA: *(Rudely.)* That suits me!

(He goes off left as Davos hurries on right, too excited to see the young men.)

DAVOS: Good heavens, good news! Now where's Pamphilus? I'll rid him of his fears and fill his heart with joy!

CHARINUS: *(Dubiously.)* Something's made him happy.

PAMPHILUS: Nothing in it. He hasn't heard our present troubles.

DAVOS: *(Still to himself.)* If he's heard by now there's a wedding prepared for him I expect he's—

CHARINUS: There, did you hear him?

DAVOS: Hunting wildly for me all over the town. Where can he be? Where shall I look first?

CHARINUS: Quick, speak to him.

DAVOS: *(Beginning to move off.)* I know—

PAMPHILUS: Davos, here, stop!

DAVOS: Who's that? Oh sir, the very man I want! And Charinus, hurrah! The two of you, how splendid! I need you both.

PAMPHILUS: Davos, I'm lost.

DAVOS: Just you listen to this—

CHARINUS: I'm finished.

DAVOS: *(To Charinus.)* I know what you're afraid of.

PAMPHILUS: My life hangs in the balance.

DAVOS: *(To Pamphilus.)* And you too: I know.

PAMPHILUS: That wedding for me—

DAVOS: I know.

PAMPHILUS: —Today—

DAVOS: Why go on and on when I keep telling you I *know*? *(To*

Pamphilus.) You're afraid you'll have to marry the girl. *(To Charinus.)* And you're afraid you can't.

CHARINUS: You've got it.

PAMPHILUS: Absolutely.

DAVOS: And there's absolutely no danger. Trust me.

PAMPHILUS: I implore you, free me quickly from my wretched fears.

DAVOS: All right, I'm freeing you. Chremes isn't giving you his daughter now.

PAMPHILUS: How do you know?

DAVOIS: I know all right. Your father stopped me just now, told me you were to be married today, and a whole lot more things I haven't time to repeat now. I ran off at once into town to tell you. When I couldn't find you anywhere I climbed up a hill and looked all round—no sign of you. Then I caught sight of your friend's man Byrria and asked him. He said he hadn't seen you. I was worried and wondered what to do. On my way back I had a sudden suspicion: "Why, there was very little bought for dinner, the master was in a bad temper, and the wedding was all very sudden: it doesn't make sense."

PAMPHILUS: What are you getting at?

DAVOS: I went straight along to Chremes'. Not a soul outside the house when I got there. I was delighted.

CHARINUS: *(Eagerly.)* You're right.

PAMPHILUS: Go on.

DAVOS: I waited. During this time I saw no one go in, no one come out. There were no married women about the house, no preparations, no excitement. I went up and peeped in—

PAMPHILUS: I see. That's good proof.

DAVOS: *(Triumphantly.)* Does this look like a wedding?

PAMPHILUS: No, I don't think it does.

DAVOS: Only "*think*", sir? You can't have understood me. It's certain. What's more, as I came away I ran into Chremes' boy, and all he was carrying was a penn'orth of greens and a few scraps of fish for the old man's supper.

CHARINUS: I'm saved too, Davos, thanks to you.

DAVOS: Indeed you're not!

CHARINUS: Why not? He isn't marrying her to him *(Indicating Pamphilus.)* after all.

DAVOS: Don't be so silly. It doesn't follow that *you'll* marry here if

Pamphilus doesn't. You'll have to watch out, go round and can-
vass the old man's friends.

CHARINUS: You're right. I'll go, though heaven knows my hopes have
come to nothing more often than not. Good-bye. *(He goes off,
left.)*

PAMPHILUS: What does my father mean by this play-acting?

DAVOS: I can tell you. If he shows annoyance now at Chremes' refusing to give you his daughter, before he finds out your attitude to
the match, he thinks he'll put himself in the wrong—and rightly.
But if you're the one who refuses to marry the girl, he can shift
the blame on to you—and then there'll be the usual scene.

PAMPHILUS: I can face anything.

DAVOS: But he's your father, sir, that's the problem; and besides, your
lady hasn't anyone to stand up for her. He'll find a pretext to
throw her out of the town, no sooner said than done.

PAMPHILUS *(Horrified.)* Throw her out?

DAVOS: In no time.

PAMPHILUS: Then tell me what I can do.

DAVOS: Agree to marry.

PAMPHILUS: What!

DAVOS: What's the matter?

PAMPHILUS: How can I do that?

DAVOS: Why not?

PAMPHILUS: I absolutely refuse.

DAVOS: I shouldn't do that, sir.

PAMPHILUS: I don't want any of your advice.

DAVOS: Think of the effect—

PAMPHILUS: I know. Cut off from *her* and shut up in *there.* *(Indicating
Glycerium's and Simo's houses.)*

DAVOS: No, no, you're wrong. What'll happen I'm sure is that your
father will say he wants the wedding today. You'll say you're
ready. He can't quarrel with that, and then you'll be able to upset
all his well-laid plans without any risk to yourself, for it's quite certain that Chremes will refuse to give you his daughter. Only don't
alter your present behavior, or there's the danger he'll change his
mind. Tell your father you're willing, so that he can't be angry
with you whenever he wants. You may hope it'll be easy to fend
off a wife—"with a character like mine no one will give me one"
is what you'll say, but he's more likely to produce a penniless

bride for you than leave you to go to the bad. But if he finds you take it calmly he'll fuss less and take his time to look for someone else for you. Meanwhile your luck may turn.

PAMPHILUS *(Dubiously.)* Do you really think so?

DAVOS: I'm positive, sir.

PAMPHILUS: Think where you may land me.

DAVOS: Now, don't argue.

PAMPHILUS: All right, I'll agree. But he mustn't know about Glycerium's child, for I've promised to acknowledge it as mine.

DAVOS: *That* was rash!

PAMPHILUS: It was a promise she begged of me, to make sure I wouldn't abandon her.

DAVOS: We'll keep it. But here's your father. Take care he doesn't see you looking worried.

(Simo comes on right, not seeing the others as they draw back.)

SIMO: I'm back to see what they're up to and what plans they're laying.

DAVOS: *(To Pamphilus.)* You see he's quite certain you'll refuse to marry. He's been rehearsing his speech in some lonely spot and now he comes hoping it'll make mincemeat of you. Mind you keep your wits about you.

PAMPHILUS: I only hope I can!

DAVOS: Believe me, sir, just say you'll agree to take a wife and your father won't breathe another word.

(Byrria comes on left, and stands unseen by the other three.)

BYRRIA: Young Charinus told me to drop everything and spend the day watching Pamphilus, to find out his intentions about this marriage. That's why I'm trailing this one now. *(Indicating Simo)*. Why, there *is* Pamphilus with Davos—watch it, Byrria. *(Moving nearer.)*

SIMO: *(Turning to see Pamphilus and Davos.)* There they are, the pair of them.

DAVOS: *(To Pamphilus.)* Now, remember!

SIMO: Pamphilus!

DAVOS: Turn round as if you hadn't seen him.

PAMPHILUS: *(With marked surprise.)* Why, father, is that you?

DAVOS: *(Aside.)* Well done!

SIMO: *(Watching him closely.)* Today, as I told you before, is the day on which I wish you to take a wife.

BYRRIA: *(Aside.)* What'll he answer? I'm nervous on our behalf.

Paphnutius

Hrotsvitha
circa 965

Dramatic

Setting: A neutral acting area. The location might be outdoors, in the monastery, or anywhere of the actors' choosing.

Scene: Paphnutius is sharing both his philosophy and his sorrow with some of his disciples. He appears very unhappy.

Of Note: Since there is no description of the nature of any of the disciples, it is for the actor to define his character traits in the way he deems most appropriate.

Father Paphnutius: A hermit priest, 30's – 60's.
The Disciples of Paphnutius: three young priests, 20's

DISCIPLES: Why are you so unhappy, why not the serene countenance to which we are accustomed, Father Paphnutius?

PAPHNUTIUS: He whose heart is sad wears a sorrowful countenance.

DISCIPLES: Why are you so sad?

PAPHNUTIUS: Because of the ingratitude shown to my Creator.

DISCIPLES: What is this ingratitude of which you speak.

PAPHNUTIUS: That which He suffers from His own creatures, creatures made to His image and likeness.

DISCIPLES: You frighten us by your words.

PAPHNUTIUS: It is understood that the eternal majesty of God cannot be injured by any wrong, nevertheless, if it were permitted to transfer by a metaphor the weakness of our frail nature to God, what greater wrong could be conceived than this—that while the greater part of the world is subject to His will, one part rebels against His law?

DISCIPLES: Which part rebels?

PAPHNUTIUS: Man.

DISCIPLES: Man?

PAPHNUTIUS: Yes.

DISCIPLES: What man?

PAPHNUTIUS: All men.

DISCIPLES: How can this be?

PAPHNUTIUS: It so pleases our Creator.

DISCIPLES: We do not understand.

PAPHNUTIUS: All of us do not understand.

DISCIPLES: Do explain it to us.

PAPHNUTIUS: Listen then, to what I say.

DISCIPLES: We are listening.

PAPHNUTIUS: Accordingly, the greater part of the world is made up of four contrary elements, but the will of the Creator, the contraries are adjusted according to harmonious rule, and man possesses not only these same elements, but has more varying components.

DISCIPLES: And what then is more varying than the elements?

PAPHNUTIUS: The body and the soul, because one can understand that they are contrary, yet they are both in one person; the soul is not mortal like the body, and the body is not spiritual like the soul.

DISCIPLES: So!

PAPHNUTIUS: If, moreover, we follow the logicians, we will not admit these to be contrary.

DISCIPLES: And who can deny it?

PAPHNUTIUS: He who can argue logically; because nothing is contrary to Essence, for she is the receptacle of all contraries.

DISCIPLES: What did you mean when you said "according to harmonious rule"?

PAPHNUTIUS: I meant that, as low and high sounds are joined together harmoniously to make a certain music, thus discordant elements, being brought together harmoniously, make one world....

DISCIPLES: Where did you acquire all this knowledge with which you have just wearied us?

PAPHNUTIUS: I wish to share with you the small drop of knowledge which flowed from the full well of learning; this I found, passing by chance rather than by seeking it.

DISCIPLES: We appreciate your goodness, but we are terrified by the word of the Apostle saying: "God chooses the foolish of the world to confound the wise."

PAPHNUTIUS: Whether a foolish man or a wise man does wrong, he deserves punishment from God.

DISCIPLES: Indeed he does.

PAPHNUTIUS: Knowledge does not offend God, but the wrong doing of him who has knowledge offends Him.

DISCIPLES: True, indeed!

PAPHNUTIUS: To whom may the knowledge of the arts be more worthily and rightly referred than to Him who made things which are knowable and gave us the capacity to understand them?

DISCIPLES: To none other.

PAPHNUTIUS: The more man sees by what marvelous law God has arranged all things by number, by measure, and by weight, the more intensely he will love Him.

DISCIPLES: And rightly so!

PAPHNUTIUS: But why do I dwell upon these things which afford so little pleasure?

DISCIPLES: Tell us the cause of your grief, that we may no longer be burdened by the weight of our curiosity.

PAPHNUTIUS: If ever you do find it out, you will not be happy in that knowledge.

DISCIPLES: A man is often sadder when he has satisfied his curiosity, yet he is unable to overcome this fault because it is a part of our weak nature.

PAPHNUTIUS: A certain infamous woman lives in this neighborhood.

DISCIPLES: This is dangerous to the people.

PAPHNUTIUS: Her beauty is unsurpassed, her wickedness is unspeakable.

DISCIPLES: Horrible! What is her name?

PAPHNUTIUS: Thais.

DISCIPLES: That harlot!

PAPHNUTIUS: Yes, that one.

DISCIPLES: Her wickedness is known to everyone.

PAPHNUTIUS: And no wonder, because she is not satisfied to go to destruction with a few, but she is ready to ensnare all men by the enticements of her beauty and to drag them to ruin with her.

DISCIPLES: How tragic!

PAPHNUTIUS: Not only do wastrels squander their substance by wooing her, but even respectable citizens lay their wealth at her feet, enriching her to their own undoing.

DISCIPLES: Terrible to hear!

PAPHNUTIUS: Crowds of lovers flock to her.

DISCIPLES: They destroy themselves.

PAPHNUTIUS: These lovers, in blindness of heart, quarrel and fight for access to her.

DISCIPLES: One vice begets another.

PAPHNUTIUS: When the struggle begins, sometimes fist fights result in broken noses and jaws; other times they attack with weapons so shamelessly that the threshold of the vile house is drenched with blood.

DISCIPLES: O detestable sin!

PAPHNUTIUS: This is the insult to the Creator which I mourn; this is the cause of my grief.

DISCIPLES: We do not doubt that you rightly grieve aloud about this; and that the heavenly citizens mourn with you.

PAPHNUTIUS: What if I were to approach her in the disguise of a lover; might she by chance turn from her wayward life?

DISCIPLES: He Who has inspired you with this idea is able to bring about its fulfillment.

PAPHNUTIUS: Support me, meanwhile, with your fervent prayers that I may not be overcome by the wiles of the wicked serpent.

DISCIPLES: May He Who laid low the king of darkness give you victory against the enemy!

The Second Shepherd's Play

Anonymous
Fourteenth Century

Dramatic
Setting: In the fields, wintertime. Night.
Scene: Mak enters with a cloak over his tunic. He has a plan to trick the shepherds.

First Shepherd.
Second Shepherd: 20's, ill-clothed, wretchedly poor.
Third Shepherd.
Mak: A rogue; poor but sly, 20's – 30's.

MAK: Now, Lord, for Thy names seven, that made both beast and bird,
        Well more than I can mention, Thy will leaves me unstirred.
        I am all uneven; that upsets my brains.
        Now would God I were in heaven, for there weep no bairns.
        So still.
FIRST SHEPHERD: Who is that pipes so poor?
MAK: Would God ye knew how I were!
        Lo, a man that walks on the moor, and has not all his will.
SECOND SHEPHERD: Mak, where hast thou gone? Tell us tiding.
THIRD SHEPHERD: Is he come? Then each one take heed to this thing.
    (He takes the cloak from Mak.)
MAK: What! Ich be a yeoman, I tell you, of the king,
        The self and the same, agent of a lording,
        And sich. Fie on you! Go hence
        Out my presence! I must have reverence.
        Why, who be Ich?
FIRST SHEPHERD: Why make ye it so quaint? Mak, ye do wrong.
SECOND SHEPHERD: Mak, play ye the saint? I think not for long.
THIRD SHEPHERD: I think the rogue can feign, may the devil him hang!
MAK: I shall make complaint, and make you all to thwang.
        At a word, and tell even how ye doth.
FIRST SHEPHERD: But, Mak, is that truth?
        Now take out that Southern tooth,
        And put in a turd!
SECOND SHEPHERD: Mak, the devil in your eye! A stroke would I beat you.

THIRD SHEPHERD: Mak, know ye not me? By God, I could grieve you.
MAK: God save you all three! Me thought I had seen you.
     Ye are a fair company.
FIRST SHEPHERD: What is it that mean you?
SECOND SHEPHERD: Shrew, peep!
     Thus late as thou goes,
     What will men suppose?
     Thou hast a good nose
     For stealing a sheep.
MAK: And I am true as steel, all men state;
     But a sickness I feel that will not abate:
     My belly fares not well; it is out of estate.
THIRD SHEPHERD: Seldom lies the devil dead by the gate.
MAK: Therefore,
     Full sore am I and sick;
     May I stand like a stick
     If I've had a bit
     For a month and more.
FIRST SHEPHERD: How fares they wife? By the hood, what say you?
MAK: Lies wallowing—by the rood—by the fire, lo!
     And a house full of brood. She drinks well, too;
     There's no other good that she will do!
     But she
     Eats as fast as may be,
     And every year that we see
     She brings forth a baby—
     And, some years, two.

     Were I even more prosperous and richer by some,
     I were eaten out of house and even of home.
     Yet is she a foul souse, if ye come near;
     There is none that goes or anywhere roams
     Worse than she.
     Now will ye see what I proffer?
     To give all in my coffer
     Tomorrow early to offer
     Her head-masspenny.
SECOND SHEPHERD: I know so forwaked is none in this shire;
     I would sleep, if I taked less for my hire.

THIRD SHEPHERD: I am cold and naked, and would have a fire.
FIRST SHEPHERD: I am weary, all ached, and run in the mire,
>   Watch, thou.
>   *(Lies down.)*
SECOND SHEPHERD: Nay, I will lie near by,
>   For I must sleep, truly.
>   *(Lies down beside him.)*
THIRD SHEPHERD: As good a man's son was I
>   As any of you.
>   *(Lies down.)*
>   But, Mak, come thou here. Between us you'll stay.
MAK: Then could I stop you if evil you'd say,
>   No dread.
>   From my top to my toe,
>   *Manus tuas commendo,*
>   *Poncio Pilato;*
>   May Christ's cross me clear
>   *(Then he gets up, the shepherds still sleeping, and says:)*
>   Now's the time for a man that lacks what he would
>   To stalk privily then into a fold,
>   And nimbly to work then, and be not too bold,
>   For he might pay for the bargain, if it were told
>   At the end. Only time now will tell;
>   But he needs good counsel
>   Who fain would fare well,
>   And has little to spend.
>   *(Mak casts a spell over them.)*
>   Here about you a circle, as round as a moon
>   Till I have done what I will, till that it be noon,
>   May ye lie stone-still till that I have done;
>   And I shall say theretil a few good words soon:
>   A height,
>   Over your heads, my hand I lift.
>   Out go your eyes! Black out your sight!
>   But yet I must make better shift
>   If it go right.
>   *(The shepherds begin to snore.)*
>   Lord, how they sleep hard. That may ye all hear.
>   I was never a shepherd, but now will I lere.

Though the flock be scared, yet shall I draw near.
How! Draw hitherward! Now mends our cheer
From sorrow;
A fat sheep, I dare say,
A good fleece, dare I lay.
Pay back when I may,
But this will I borrow.
(He takes the sheep home.)

Benkei on the Bridge

Hiyoshi Sa-ami Yasu
circa fifteenth century

Dramatic
Setting: Near the Western Pagoda.
Scene: Outdoors Benkei and his Follower prepare to travel to the Temple for ritual prayers.
Of Note: The Follower accompanies Benkei but can later become part of the Chorus.

Benkei: A priest, disciplined and honorable.
Ushiwaka: A Prince, young, gives the appearance of a sprite, or elf.
Follower: Benkei's assistant, a younger priest.
Chorus: Voice commenting on the story.

BENKEI: I am one who lives near the Western Pagoda. My name is Musashi-bo Benkei. In fulfillment of a certain vow I have been going lately by night at the hour of the Ox to worship at the Gojo Temple. Tonight is the last time; I ought soon to be starting. Hie! Is any one there?

FOLLOWER: Here I am.

BENKEI: I sent for you to tell you that I shall be going to the Gojo Temple tonight.

FOLLOWER: I tremble and listen. But there is a matter that I must bring to your notice. I hear that yesterday there was a boy of twelve or thirteen guarding the Gojo Bridge. They say he was slashing round with his short sword as nimble as a bird or butterfly. I beg that you will not make your pilgrimage tonight. Do not court this peril.

BENKEI: That's a strange thing to ask! Why, were he demon or hobgoblin, he could not stand along against many. We will surround him and you shall soon see him on his knees.

FOLLOWER: They have tried surrounding him, but he always escapes as though by magic, and none is able to lay hands on him.

BENKEI: When he seems within their grasp.

FOLLOWER: From before their eyes.

BENKEI: Suddenly he vanishes.

CHORUS: This strange hobgoblin, elfish apparition,

Into great peril may bring
The reverend limbs of my master.
In all this City none can withstand the prowess
Of this unparalleled monster.

BENKEI: If this is as you say, I will not go tonight; and yet . . . No. It is not to be thought of that such a one as Benkei should be affrighted by a tale. Tonight when it is dark I will go to the bridge and humble this arrogant elf.

CHORUS: And while he spoke,
Evening already to the western sky had come;
Soon the night-wind had shattered and dispersed
The shapes of sunset.
Cheerless night
Came swiftly, but with step too slow
For him who waits.

(A comic interlude played by a bow-master is sometimes used here to fill in the time while Benkei is arming himself.)

USHIWAKA: I am Ushiwaka. I must do as my mother told me; "Go up to the Temple at daybreak," she said. But it is still night. I will go to Gojo Bridge and wait there till suddenly
Moonlight mingles with the rising waves;
No twilight closes
The autumn day, but swiftly
The winds of night bring darkness.

CHORUS: *(Speaking for Ushiwaka.)*
Oh, beauty of the waves! High beats my heart,
High as their scattered pearls!
Waves white as dewy calabash at dawn,
By Gojo Bridge.
Silently the night passes,
No sound but my own feet upon the wooden planks
clanking and clanking; still I wait
And still in vain.

BENKEI: The night grows late. Eastward the bells of the Three Pagodas toll.
By the moonlight that gleams through leaves of these thick cedar-trees
I gird my armor on;
I fasten the black thongs of my coat of mail.

I adjust its armored skirts.
By the middle I grasp firmly
My great halberd that I have loved so long.
I lay it across my shoulder; with leisurely step stride forward.
Be he demon or hobgoblin, how shall he stand against me?
Such trust have I in my own prowess. Oh, how I long
For a foreman worthy of my hand!

USHIWAKA: The river-wind blows keen;
The night is almost spent,
But none has crossed the Bridge.
I am disconsolate and will lie down to rest.

BENKEI: Then Benkei, all unknowing,
Came towards the Bridge where white waves lapped.
Heavily his feet clanked on the boards of the Bridge.

USHIWAKA: And even before he saw him Ushiwaka gave a whoop of joy.
"Some one has come," he cried, and hitching his cloak over his shoulder
Took his stand at the bridge-side.

BENKEI: Benkei discerned him and would have spoken . . .
But when he looked, lo! it was a woman's form!
Then, because he had left the World, with troubled mind he hurried on.

USHIWAKA: Then Ushiwaka said,
"I will make game of him," and as Benkei passed
Kicked at the button of his halberd so that it jerked into the air.

BENKEI (Cries out in surprise.) Ah! fool, I wil teach you a lesson!

CHORUS: Then Benkei while he retrieved his halberd
Cried out in anger,
"You shall soon feel the strength of my arm," and fell fiercely upon him.
But the boy, not a jot alarmed,
Stood his ground and with one hand pulled aside his cloak,
While with the other he quietly drew his sword from the scabbard
And parried the thrust of the halberd that threatened him.
Again and again he parried the halberd's point.
And so they fought, now closing, now breaking.
What shall Benkei do? For when he thinks that he has conquered,

With his little sword the boy thrusts the blow aside.
Again and again Benkei strikes.
Again and again his blows are parried,
Till at last even he, mighty Benkei,
Can do battle no longer.
Dishearted he steps back the space of a few bridge-beams.
"Monstrous," he cries, "that this stripling . . . No, it cannot be.
He shall not outwit my skill."
And holding out his halberd at full length before him
He rushed forward and dealt a mighty blow.
But Ushiwaka turned and dived swiftly to the left.
Benkei recovered his halberd and slashed at the boy's skirts;
But *he*, unfaltering, instantly leapt from the ground.
And when he thrust at the boy's body,
Then Ushiwaka squirmed with head upon the ground.
Thus a thousand, thousand bouts they fought,
Till the halberd fell from Benkei's weary hands.
He would have wrestled, but the boy's sword flashed before him,
And he could get no hold.
Then at his wits' end, "Oh, marvelous youth!"
Benkei cried, and stood dumbfounded.

CHORUS: Who are you that, so young and frail, possess such daring?
Tell us your name and state.

USHIWAKA: Why should I conceal it from you? I am Minamoto Ushiwaka.

CHORUS: Yoshitomo's son?

USHIWAKA: I am. And your name . . ?

CHORUS: *(Speaking for Benkei.)* "I am called Musashi Benkei of the
Western Pagoda.
And now that we have told our names,
I surrender myself and beg for mercy;
For you are yet a child, and I a priest.
Such are your rank and lineage, such your prowess
That I will gladly serve you.
Too hastily you took me for an enemy; but now begins
A three lives' bond; henceforward as slave I serve you."
So while the one made vows of homage, the other girded up
his cloak.
Then Benkei laid his halberd across his shoulder
And together they went on their way
To the Palace of Kujo.

Much Ado about Nothing

William Shakespeare

1598

Comic

Setting: Messina. A room in the Governor's palace.

Scene: Don Pedro plans to leave Messina for Aragon as soon as Claudio and Hero are married. They are all trying to interest Benedick in falling in love and marrying, too, but he will have no part of the idea.

Don Pedro: Prince of Aragon, friend to the Governor, 40's – 50's.

Claudio: A young nobleman, 20's, in love with Hero, daughter of the Governor.

Benedick: A young nobleman, 20's, Claudio's good friend.

Leonato: Governor of Messina, 40's – 50's.

DON PEDRO: I do but stay till your marriage be consummate, and then go I toward Arragon.

CLAUDIO: I'll bring you thither, my lord, if you'll vouchsafe me.

DON PEDRO: Nay, that would be as great a soil in the new gloss of your marriage, as to show a child his new coat, and forbid him to wear it. I will only be bold with Benedick for his company; for, from the crown of his head to the sole of his foot, he is all mirth: he hath twice or thrice cut Cupid's bow-string, and the little hangman dare not shoot at him; he hath a heart as sound as a bell, and his tongue is the clapper—for what his heart thinks, his tongue speaks.

BENEDICK: Gallants, I am not as I have been.

LEONATO: So say I: methinks you are sadder.

CLAUDIO: I hope he be in love.

DON PEDRO: Hang him, truant! there's no true drop of blood in him, to be truly toucht with love: if he be sad, he wants money.

BENEDICK: I have the toothache.

DON PEDRO: Draw it.

BENEDICK: Hang it!

CLAUDIO: You must hang it first, and draw it afterwards.

DON PEDRO: What! sigh for the toothache?

LEONATO: Where is but a humour or a worm?

BENEDICK: Well, everyone can master a grief but he that has it.

CLAUDIO: Yet say I he is in love.

DON PEDRO: There is no appearance of fancy in him, unless it be a fancy that he hath to strange disguises; as, to be a Dutchman today, a Frenchman tomorrow; or in the shape of two countries at once, as, a German from the waist downward, all slops, and a Spaniard from the hip upward, no doublet. Unless he have a fancy to his foolery, as it appears he hath, he is no fool for fancy, as you would have it appear he is.

CLAUDIO: If he be not in love with some woman, there is no believing old signs: a' brushes his hat o' mornings; what should that bode?

DON PEDRO: Hath any man seen him at the barber's?

CLAUDIO: No, but the barber's man hath been seen with him; and the old ornament of his cheek hath already stuft tennis-balls.

LEONATO: Indeed, he looks younger than he did, by the loss of a beard.

DON PEDRO: Nay, a' rubs himself with civet: can you smell him out by that?

CLAUDIO: That's as much as to say, the sweet youth's in love.

DON PEDRO: The greatest note of it is his melancholy.

CLAUDIO: And when was he wont to wash his face?

DON PEDRO: Yea, or to paint himself? for the which, I hear what they say of him.

CLAUDIO: Nay, but his jesting spirit; which is now crept into a lute-string, and new-govern'd by stops.

DON PEDRO: Indeed, that tells a heavy tale for him. Conclude, conclude he is in love.

CLAUDIO: Nay, but I know who loves him.

DON PEDRO: That would I know too: I warrant, one that knows him not.

CLAUDIO: Yes, and his ill conditions; and, in despite of all, dies for him.

DON PEDRO: She shall be buried with her face upwards.

BENEDICK: Yet is this no charm for the toothache. —Old signior, walk aside with me: I have studied eight or nine wise words to speak to you, which these hobby-horses must not hear.

(Exeunt Benedick and Leonato.)

DON PEDRO: For my life, to break with him about Beatrice.

CLAUDIO: 'Tis even so. Hero and Margaret have by this play'd their parts with Beatrice; and then the two bears will not bite one another when they meet.

Hamlet

William Shakespeare
1600

Dramatic
Setting: On the battlements of the castle of the King of Denmark.
Scene: The dead King Hamlet, murdered, he claims, by his brother, the new King, cannot rest until his murder is avenged. Here, on the fog-enshrouded battlements he appears to the guards and Horatio.

Marcellus: A Danish Officer on guard at the Palace, 20's.
Horatio: A friend to Hamlet, 30's.
Bernardo: An officer, 20's.
Ghost of Hamlet's Father, the old King Hamlet.

MARCELLUS: Holla, Bernardo!
BERNARDO: Say,
   What, is Horatio there?
HORATIO: A piece of him.
BERNARDO: Welcome, Horatio. Welcome, good Marcellus.
HORATIO: What, has this thing appeared again tonight?
BERNARDO: I have seen nothing.
MARCELLUS: Horatio says 'tis but our fantasy,
   And will not let belief take hold of him
   Touching this dreaded sight twice seen of us.
   Therefore I have entreated him along
   With us to watch the minutes of this night,
   That, if again this apparition come,
   He may approve our eyes and speak to it.
HORATIO: Tush, tush, 'twill not appear.
BERNARDO: Sit down awhile,
   And let us once again assail your ears,
   That are so fortified against our story,
   What we two nights have seen.
HORATIO: Well, sit we down,
   And let us hear Bernardo speak of this.
BERNARDO: Last night of all,
   When yond same star that's westward from the pole

Had made his course t' illume that part of heaven
Where now it burns, Marcellus and myself,
The bell then beating one—
(Enter Ghost.)
MARCELLUS: Peace, break thee off. Look where it comes again.
BERNARDO: In the same figure like the king that's dead.
MARCELLUS: Thou art a scholar; speak to it, Horatio.
BERNARDO: Looks 'a not like the king? Mark it, Horatio.
HORATIO: Most like. It harrows me with fear and wonder.
BERNARDO: It would be spoke to.
MARCELLUS: Speak to it, Horatio.
HORATIO: What art thou that usurp'st this time of night
Together with that fair and warlike form
In which the majesty of buried Denmark
Did sometimes march?
By heaven I charge thee, speak.
MARCELLUS: It is offended.
BERNARDO: See, it stalks away.
HORATIO: Stay. Speak, speak. I charge thee, speak.
(Exit Ghost.)
MARCELLUS: 'Tis gone and will not answer.
BERNARDO: How now, Horatio? You tremble and look pale.
Is not this something more than fantasy?
What think you on't?
HORATIO: Before my God, I might not this believe
Without the sensible and true avouch
Of mine own eyes.
MARCELLUS: Is it not like the king?
HORATIO: As thou art to thyself.
Such was the very armor he had on
When he th' ambitious Norway combated.
So frowned he once when, in an angry parle,
He smote the sledded Polacks on the ice.
'Tis strange.
MARCELLUS: Thus twice before, and jump at this dead hour,
With martial stalk hath he gone by our watch.
HORATIO: In what particular thought to work I know not;
But, in the gross and scope of my opinion,
This bodes some strange eruption to our state.

MARCELLUS: Good now, sit down, and tell me he that knows,
        Why this same strict and most observant watch
        So nightly toils the subject of the land,
        And why such daily cast of brazen cannon
        And foreign mart for implements of war,
        Why such impress of shipwrights, whose sore task
        Does not divide the Sunday from the week.
        What might be toward that this sweaty haste
        Doth make the night joint-laborer with the day?
        Who is't that can inform me?
HORATIO: That can I
        At least the whisper goes so. Our last king,
        Whose image even but now appeared to us,
        Was as you know by Fortinbras of Norway,
        Thereto pricked on by a most emulate pride,
        Dared to the combat; in which our valiant Hamlet
        (For so this side of our known world esteemed him)
        Did slay this Fortinbras; who, by a sealed compact
        Well ratified by law and heraldry,
        Did forfeit, with his life, all those his lands
        Which he stood seized of to the conqueror;
        Against the which a moiety competent
        Was gagèd by our king, which had returned
        To the inheritance of Fortinbras
        Had he been vanquisher, as, by the same comart
        And carriage of the article designed,
        His fell to Hamlet. Now, sir, young Fortinbras,
        Of unimprovèd mettle hot and full,
        Hath in the skirts of Norway here and there
        Sharked up a list of lawless resolutes
        For food and diet to some enterprise
        That hath a stomach in't; which is no other,
        As it doth well appear unto our state,
        But to recover of us by strong hand
        And terms compulsatory those foresaid lands.
        So by his father lost; and this, I take it,
        Is the main motive of our preparations
        The source of this our watch, and the chief head
        Of this posthaste and romage in the land.

BERNARDO: I think it be no other but e'en so.
 Well may it sort that this portentous figure
 Comes armèd through our watch so like the king
 That was and is the question of these wars.
HORATIO: A mote it is to trouble the mind's eye.
 In the most high and palmy state of Rome,
 A little ere the mightiest Julius fell,
 The graves stood tenantless and the sheeted dead
 Did squeak and gibber in the Roman streets;
 As stars with trains of fire and dews of blood,
 Disasters in the sun; and the moist star
 Upon whose influence Neptune's empire stands
 Was sick almost to doomsday with eclipse.
 And even the like precurse of feared events,
 As harbingers preceding still the fates
 And prologue to the omen coming on,
 Have heaven and earth together demonstrated
 Unto our climatures and countrymen.
 (Enter Ghost.)
 But soft, behold, lo where it comes again!
 I'll cross it, though it blast me. —Stay, illusion.
 (He spreads his arms.)
 If thou hast any sound or use of voice,
 Speak to me.
 If there be any good thing to be done
 That may to thee do ease and grace to me.
 Speak to me.
 If thou art privy to the country's fate,
 Which happily foreknowing may avoid,
 O, speak!
 Or if thou hast uphoarded in thy life
 Extorted treasure in the womb of earth,
 For which, they say, you spirits oft walk in death,
 (The cock crows.)
 Speak of it. Stay and speak. Stop it, Marcellus.
MARCELLUS: Shall I strike at it with my partisan?
HORATIO: Do, if it will not stand.
BERNARDO: 'Tis here.
HORATIO: 'Tis here.

(Exit Ghost.)

MARCELLUS: 'Tis gone.
    We do it wrong, being so majestical,
    To offer it the show of violence,
    For it is as the air invulnerable,
    And our vain blows malicious mockery.

BERNARDO: It was about to speak when the cock crew.

HORATIO: And then it started, like a guilty thing
    Upon a fearful summons. I have heard
    The cock, that is the trumpet to the morn,
    Doth with his lofty and shrill-sounding throat
    Awake the god of day, and at his warning,
    Whether in sea or fire, in earth or air,
    Th' extravagant and erring spirit hies
    To his confine; and of the truth herein
    This present object made probation.

MARCELLUS: It faded on the crowing of the cock.
    Some say, that ever 'gainst that season comes
    Wherein our Saviour's birth is celebrated,
    The bird of dawning singeth all night long:
    And then, they say, no spirit dare stir abroad;
    The nights are wholesome; then no planets strike,
    No fairy takes, nor witch hath power to charm;
    So hallow'd and so gracious is the time.

HORATIO: So have I heard, and do in part believe it.
    But, look, the morn, in russet mantle clad,
    Walks o'er the dew of yon high eastern hill:
    Break we our watch up: and, by my advice,
    Let us impart what we have seen tonight
    Unto young Hamlet; for, upon my life,
    This spirit, dumb to us, will speak to him:
    Do you consent we shall acquaint him with it,
    As needful in our loves, fitting our duty?

MARCELLUS: Let's do't, I pray; and I this morning know
    Where we shall find him most convenient.
    (Exeunt.)

Hamlet

William Shakespeare
1601

Dramatic
Setting: A graveyard.
Scene: Hamlet and Horatio come upon two peasant gravediggers digging a grave in the churchyard. Comic interlude preceding a dramatic scene, the funeral of Hamlet's love Ophelia.

Hamlet: Prince of Denmark, 33.
Horatio: his true friend, 30's.
Clown
Other clown

CLOWN: Is she to be buried in Christian burial when she willfully seeks her own salvation?

OTHER: I tell thee she is. Therefore make her grave straight. The crowner hath sate on her, and finds it Christian burial.

CLOWN: How can that be, unless she drowned herself in her own defense?

OTHER: Why, 'tis found so.

CLOWN: It must be *se offendendo*; it cannot be else. For here lies the point: if I drown myself wittingly, it argues an act, and an act hath three branches—it is to act, to do, and to perform. Argal, she drowned herself wittingly.

OTHER: Nay, but hear you, Goodman Delver.

CLOWN: Give me leave. Here lies the water—good. Here stands the man—good. If the man go to this water and drown himself, it is, will he nill he, he goes, mark you that. But if the water come to him and drown him, he drowns not himself. Argal, he that is not guilty of his own death shortens not his own life.

OTHER: But is this law?

CLOWN: Ay marry, is't—crowner's quest law.

OTHER: Will you ha' the truth on't? If this had not been a gentlewoman, she should have been buried out o' Christian burial.

CLOWN: Why, there thou say'st. And the more pity that great folk should have count'nance in this world to drown or hang themselves more than their even-Christian. Come, my spade. There is no ancient gentlemen but gard'ners, ditchers, and grave-makers. They hold up Adam's profession.

OTHER: Was he a gentleman?

CLOWN: 'A was the first that ever bore arms.

OTHER: Why, he had none.

CLOWN: What, art a heathen? How dost thou understand the Scripture? The Scripture says Adam digged. Could he dig without arms? I'll put another question to thee. If thou answer me not to the purpose, confess thyself—

OTHER: Go to.

CLOWN: What is he that builds stronger than either the mason, the shipwright, or the carpenter?

OTHER: The gallows-maker, for that frame outlives a thousand tenants.

CLOWN: I like thy wit well, in good faith. The gallows does well. But how does it well? It does well to those that do ill. Now thou dost ill to say the gallows is built stronger than the church. Argal, the gallows may do well to thee. To't again, come.

OTHER: Who builds stronger than a mason, a shipwright, or a carpenter?

CLOWN: Ay, tell me that, and unyoke.

OTHER: Marry, now I can tell.

CLOWN: To't.

OTHER: Mass, I cannot tell.

CLOWN: Cudgel thy brains no more about it, for your dull ass will not mend his pace with beating. And when you are asked this question next, say "a grave-maker." The houses he makes last till doomsday. Go, get thee in, and fetch me a stoup of liquor.
(Exit Other Clown.) (Enter Hamlet and Horatio as Clown digs and sings.)
(Song.)
In youth when I did love, did love,
Methought it was very sweet
To contract—O—the time for—a—my behove,
O, methought there—a—was nothing—a—meet.

HAMLET: Has this fellow no feeling of his business, that 'a sings at grave-making?

HORATIO: Custom hath made it in him a property of easiness.

HAMLET: 'Tis e'en so. The hand of little employment hath the daintier sense.

CLOWN:

(Song.)

But age with his stealing steps

Hath clawed me in his clutch,

and hath shipped me intil the land,

As if I had never been such.

(Throws up a skull.)

HAMLET: That skull had a tongue in it, and could sing once. How the knave jowls it to the ground, as if 'twere Cain's jawbone, that did the first murder! This might be the pate of a politician, which this ass now o'erreaches; one that would circumvent God, might it not?

HORATIO: It might, my lord.

HAMLET: Or of a courtier, which could say Good morrow, sweet lord! How dost thou, sweet lord? This might be my Lord Such-a-one, that priased my Lord such-a-one's horse when 'a meant to beg it, might it not?

HORATIO: Ay, my lord.

HAMLET: Why, e'en so, and now my Lady Worm's, chapless, and knocked about the mazzard with a sexton's spade. Here's fine revolution, an we had the trick to see't. Did these bones cost no more the breeding but to play at loggets with 'em? Mine ache to think on't.

CLOWN:

(Song.)

A pickaxe and a space, a spade,

For and a shrouding sheet;

O, a pit of clay for to be made

For such a guest is meet.

(Throws up another skull.)

HAMLET: There's another. Why may not that be the skull of a lawyer? Where be his quiddities now, his quillities, his cases, his tenures, and his tricks? Why does he suffer this mad knave now to knock him about the sconce with a dirty shovel, and will not tell him of his action of battery? Hum! This fellow might be in's time a great buyer of land, with his statutes, his recognizances, his fines, his double vouchers, his recoveries. [Is this the fine of his fines, and the recovery of his recoveries,] to have his fine pate full of fine dirt? Will his vouchers vouch him no more of his purchses, and double ones too, than the length and breadth of a pair of indentures? The very conveyances of his lands will scarcely lie in this box, and must th' inheritor himself have no more, ha?

HORATIO: Not a jot more, my lord.

HAMLET: Is not parchment made of sheepskins?

HORATIO: Ay, my lord, and of calveskins too.

HAMLET: They are sheep and calves which seek out assurance in that. I will speak to this fellow. Whose grave's this, sirrah?

CLOWN: Mine, sir.

(Sings.) O, a pit of clay for to be made
For such a guest is meet.

HAMLET: I think it be thine indeed, for thou liest in't.

CLOWN: You lie out on't, sir, and therefore 'tis not yours.
For my part, I do not lie in't, yet it is mine.

HAMLET: Thou dost lie in't, to be in't and say it is thine.
'Tis for the dead, not for the quick; therefore thou liest.

CLOWN: 'Tis a quick lie, sir; 'twill away again from me to you.

HAMLET: What man dost thou dig it for?

CLOWN: For no man, sir.

HAMLET: What woman then?

CLOWN: For none neither.

HAMLET: Who is to be buried in't?

CLOWN: One that was a woman, sir; but, rest her soul, she's dead.

HAMLET: How absolute the knave is! We must speak by the card, or equivocation will undo us. By the Lord, Horatio, this three years I have taken note of it, the age is grown so picked that the toe of the peasant comes so near the heel of the courtier he galls his kibe. —How long hast thou been a grave-maker?

CLOWN: Of all the days i' th' year, I came to't that day that our last king Hamlet overcame Fortinbras.

HAMLET: How long is that since?

CLOWN: Cannot you tell that? Every fool can tell that. It was the very day that young Hamlet was born—he that is mad, and sent into England.

HAMLET: Ay, marry, why was he sent into England?

CLOWN: Why, because 'a was mad. 'A shall recover his wits there; or, if 'a do not, 'tis no great matter there.

HAMLET: Why?

CLOWN: 'Twill not be seen in him there. There the men are as mad as he.

HAMLET: How came he mad?

CLOWN: Very strangely, they say.

HAMLET: How strangely?

CLOWN: Faith, e'en with losing his wits.

HAMLET: Upon what ground?

CLOWN: Why, here in Denmark. I have been sexton here, man and boy, thirty years.

HAMLET: How long will a man lie i' th' earth ere he rot?

CLOWN: Faith, if 'a be not rotten before 'a die (as we have many pocky corses now-a-days that will scarce hold the laying in), 'a will last you some eight year or nine year. A tanner will last you nine year.

HAMLET: Why he more than another?

CLOWN: Why, sir, his hide is so tanned with his trade that 'a will keep out water a great while, and your water is a sore decayer of your whoreson dead body. Here's a skull now hath lien you i' th' earth three-and-twenty years.

HAMLET: Whose was it?

CLOWN: A whoreson mad fellow's it was. Whose do you think it was?

HAMLET: Nay, I know not.

CLOWN: A pestilence on him for a mad rogue! 'A poured a flagon of Rhenish on my head once. This same skull, sir, was—sir—Yorick's skull, the king's jester.

HAMLET: This?

CLOWN: E'en that.

HAMLET: Let me see. *(Takes the skull.)* Alas, poor Yorick! I knew him, Horatio, a fellow of infinite jest, of most excellent fancy. He hath borne me on his back a thousand times. And now how abhorred in my imagination it is! My gorge rises at it. Here hung those lips that I have kissed I know not how oft. Where be your gibes now? Your gambols, your songs, your flashes of merriment that were wont to set the table on a roar? Not one now to mock your own grinning? Quite chapfall'n? Now get you to my lady's chamber, and tell her, let her paint an inch thick, to this favor she must come. Make her laugh at that. Prithee, Horatio, tell me one thing.

HORATIO: What's that, my lord?

HAMLET: Dost you think Alexander looked o' this fashion i' th' earth?

HORATIO: E'en so.

HAMLET: And smelt so? Pah!

(Puts down the skull.)

HORATIO: E'en so, my lord.

HAMLET: To what base uses we may return, Horatio! Why may not imagination trace the noble dust of Alexander till 'a find it stopping a bunghole?

HORATIO: 'Twere to consider too curiously, to consider so.

HAMLET: No, faith, not a jot, but to follow him thither with modesty enough, and likelihood to lead it;

King Lear

William Shakespeare

Dramatic

Setting: Near an old hut on the heath.

Scene: Lear and his Fool discover Edgar, still pretending to be mad. Gloucester, searching for Lear, comes upon them in the hut. Lear has been sent away from the homes of his older daughters and is wandering the heath in a storm with his Fool by his side. Edgar, attempting to unmask his own treacherous half-brother, has put on the mask of insanity.

King Lear: Elderly and befuddled King of Britain, at the end of his reign, trying to make equitable division of his lands among his three daughters.

Edgar: Son of the Earl of Gloucester, 20's.

Fool: Attendant of the King and of his Court—the fool often jokes but speaks the truth.

Kent: The Earl of Kent, devoted retainer to King Lear, 50's – 60's.

(Enter Lear, Edgar, and Fool.)

EDGAR: Frateretto calls me, and tells me Nero is an angler in the lake of darkness. Pray, innocent, and beware the foul fiend.

FOOL: Prithee, nuncle, tell me whether a madman be a gentleman or a yeoman.

LEAR: A king, a king.

FOOL: No, he's a yoeman that has a gentleman to his son; for he's a mad yeoman that sees his son a gentleman before him.

LEAR: To have a thousand with red burning spits
    Come hizzing in upon 'em.

EDGAR: The foul fiend bites my back.

FOOL: He's mad that trusts in the tameness of a wolf, a horse's health, a boy's love, or a whore's oath.

LEAR: It shall be done; I will arraign them straight. *(To Edgar.)* Come, sit thou here, most learned justice. *(To the Fool.)* Thou, sapient sir, sit here. Now, you she foxes—

EDGAR: Look, where he stands and glares. Want'st thou eyes at trial, madam? Come o'er the bourn, Bessy, to me.

FOOL: Her boat hath a leak,

And she must not speak
Why she dares not come over to thee.

EDGAR: The foul fiend haunts poor Tom in the voice of a nightingale.
Hoppedance cries in Tom's belly for two white herring. Croak not,
black angel; I have no food for thee.

KENT: How do you, sir? Stand you not so amazed.
Will you lie down and rest upon the cushions?

LEAR: I'll see their trial first. Bring in their evidence.
(To Edgar.) Thou, robèd man of justice, take thy place.
(To the Fool.) And thou, his yokefellow of equity,
Bench by his side. *(To Kent.)* You are o' th' commission;
Sit you too.

EDGAR: Let us deal justly.
Sleepest or wakest thou, jolly shepherd?
Thy sheep be in the corn;
And for one blast of thy minikin mouth
Thy sheep shall take no harm.
Purr, the cat is gray.

LEAR: Arraign her first. 'Tis Goneril, I here take my oath before this
honorable assembly, kicked the poor King her father.

FOOL: Come hither, mistress. Is your name Goneril?

LEAR: She cannot deny it.

FOOL: Cry you mercy, I took you for a joint-stool.

LEAR: And here's another, whose warped looks proclaim
What store her heart is made on. Stop her there!
Arms, arms, sword, fire! Corruption in the place!
False justicer, why hast thou let her 'scape?

EDGAR: Bless thy five wits!

KENT: O pity! sir, where is the patience now
That you so oft have boasted to retain?

EDGAR: *(Aside.)* My tears begin to take his part so much
They mar my counterfeiting.

LEAR: The little dogs and all,
Tray, Blanch, and Sweetheart—
See, they bark at me.

EDGAR: Tom will throw his head at them. Avaunt, you curs.
Be thy mouth or black or white,
Tooth that poisons if it bite;
Mastiff, greyhound, mongrel grim,

Hound or spaniel, brach or lym,
Or bobtail tike, or trundle-tail—
Tom will make him weep and wail;
For, with throwing thus my head,
Dogs leaped the hatch, and all are fled.

Do, de, de, de. Sessa! Come, march to wakes and fairs and market towns. Poor Tom, thy horn is dry.

LEAR: Then let them anatomize Regan. See what breeds about her heart. Is there any cause in nature that makes these hard hearts? *(To Edgar.)* You, sir, I entertain for one of my hundred; only I do not like the fashion of your garments. You will say they are Persian; but let them be changed.

KENT: Now, good my lord, lie here and rest awhile.

LEAR: Make no noise, make no noise; draw the curtains.

So, so. We'll go to supper i' th' morning.

FOOL: And I'll go to bed at noon.

The Changeling

Thomas Middleton and William Rowley

1622

Comic

Scene: The mental hospital where Dr. Alibius works. The Doctor confides in Lollio of his fears concerning his young wife.

Dr. Alibius: An elderly and jealous doctor with a young wife.
Lollio: The doctor's servant and confidant, 40's – 60's.
Antonio: A young man acting insane—in order to attract young women.
Pedro: His friend.

LOLLIO: I was ever close to a secret, Sir.
ALIBIUS: The diligence that I have found in thee,
    The care and industry already past,
    Assures me of thy good continuance.
    Lollio, I have a wife.
LOLLIO: Fie, sir, 'tis too late to keep her secret, she's known to be married all the town and countrey over.
ALIBIUS: Thou goest too fast, my Lollio, that knowledge
    I allow no man can be bar'd it;
    But there is a knowledge which is neerer,
    Deeper and sweeter, Lollio.
LOLLIO: Well, sir, let us handle that between you and I.
ALIBIUS: 'Tis that I go about, man; Lollio,
    My wife is young.
LOLLIO: So much the worse to be kept secret, sir.
ALIBIUS: Why now thou meet'st the substance of the point, I am old, Lollio.
LOLLIO: No, sir, 'tis I am old Lollio.
ALIBIUS: Yet why may not this concord and sympathize?
    Old trees and young plants often grow together,
    Well enough agreeing.
LOLLIO: I, sir, but the old trees raise themselves higher and broader than the young plants.
ALIBIUS: Shrewd application: there's the fear, man!
    I would wear my ring on my own finger;
    Whilst it is borrowed it is none of mine,

But his that useth it.

LOLLIO: You must keep it on still then; if it but lye by,
    one or other will be thrusting into't.

ALIBIUS: Thou conceiv'st me, Lollio; here thy watchful eye
    Must have imployment, I cannot always be
    At home.

LOLLIO: I dare swear you cannot.

ALIBIUS: I must look out.

LOLLIO: I know't, you must look out, 'tis every mans case.

ALIBIUS: Here I doe say must thy imployment be,
    To watch her treadings, and in my absence
    Supply my place.

LOLLIO: I'le do my best, Sir, yet surely I cannot see who you should
    have cause to be jealous of.

ALIBIUS: Thy reason for that, Lollio? 'Tis
    A comfortable question.

LOLLIO: We have but two sorts of people in the house, and both
    under the whip, that's fools and mad-men; the one has not wit
    enough to be knaves, and the other not knavery enough to be
    fools.

ALIBIUS: I, those are all my Patients, Lollio.
    I do profess the cure of either sort:
    My trade, my living 'tis, I thrive by it;
    But here's the care that mixes with my thrift,
    The daily Visitants, that come to see
    My brainsick Patients, I would not have
    To see my wife: Gallants I do observe
    Of quick entising eyes, rich in habits,
    Of stature and proportion very comely:
    These are most shrewd temptations, Lollio.

LOLLIO: They may be easily answered, Sir; if they come to see the
    Fools and Mad-men, you and I may serve the turn, and let my
    Mistress alone, she's of neither sort.

ALIBIUS: 'Tis a good ward, indeed come they to see
    Our Man-men or our Fools, let 'um see no more
    Then what they come for; by that consequent
    They must not see her, I'm sure she's no fool.

LOLLIO: And I'm sure she's no mad-man.

ALIBIUS: Hold that Buckler fast, Lollio; my trust

Is on thee, and I account it firm and strong.

What hour is't, Lollio?

LOLLIO: Towards belly-hour, Sir.

ALIBIUS: Dinner time? Thou mean'st twelve a'clock

LOLLIO: Yes, Sir, for every part has his hour; we wake at six and look about us, that's eye-hour; at seven we should pray, that's knee-hour; at eight walk, that's leg-hour; at nine gather flowers, and pluck a Rose, that's nose-hour; at ten we drink, that's mouth-hour; at eleven lay about us for victuals, that's hand-hour; at twelve go to dinner, that's belly-hour.

ALIBIUS: Profoundly, Lollio! It will be long

Ere all thy Scholars learn this Lesson, and

I did look to have a new one entered—stay,

I think my expectation is come home.

(Enter Pedro and Antonio like an Idiot.)

PEDRO: Save you, sir, my business speaks it self,

This sight takes off the labour of my tongue.

ALIBIUS: I, I, Sir, 'tis plain enough you mean

Him for my patient.

PEDRO: And if your pains prove but commodious, to give but some little strength to his sick and weak part of Nature in him, these *(Gives him money.)* are but patterns to shew you of the whole pieces that will follow to you, beside the charge of diet, washing, and other necessaries fully defrayed.

ALIBIUS: Believe it, sir, there shall no care be wanting.

LOLLIO: Sir, an officer in this place may deserve something; the trouble will pass through my hands.

PEDRO: 'Tis fit something should come to your hands then, sir. *(Gives him money.)*

LOLLIO: Yes, sir, 'tis I must keep him sweet, and read to him; what is his name?

PEDRO: His name is Antonio; marry, we use but half to him, onely Tonie.

LOLLIO: Tonie, Tonie, 'tis enough, and a very good name for a fool; what's your name, Tonie?

ANTONIO: He, he, he! well, I thank you, cousin, he, he, he!

LOLLIO: Good Boy! hold up your head: he can laugh, I perceive by that he is no beast.

PEDRO: Well, sir,

If you can raise him but to any height,
And degree of wit, might he attain
(As I might say) to creep but on all four
Towards the chair of wit, or walk on crutches,
'Twould add an honour to your worthy pains,
And a great family might pray for you,
To which he should be heire, had he discretion
To claim and guide his own; assure you, sir,
He is a Gentleman.

LOLLIO: Nay, there's no body doubted that; at first sight I knew him for a Gentleman, he looks no other yet.

PEDRO: Let him have good attendance and sweet lodging.

LOLLIO: As good as my Mistress lies in, sir, and as you allow us time and means, we can raise him to the higher degree of discretion.

PEDRO: Nay, there shall no cost want, sir.

LOLLIO: He will hardly be stretcht up to the wit of a *Magnifico*.

PEDRO: Oh no, that's not to be expected, far shorter will be enough.

LOLLIO: I'le warrant you [I'le] make him fit to bear office in five weeks; I'le undertake to wind him up to the wit of Constable.

PEDRO: If it be lower then that it might serve turn.

LOLLIO: No, fie, to levell him with a Headborough, Beadle, or Watchman, were but little better than he is; Constable I'le able him: if he do come to be a Justice afterwards, let him thank the Keeper. Or I'le go further with you, say I do bring him up to my own pitch, say I make him as wise as my self.

PEDRO: Why, there I would have it.

LOLLIO: Well, go to, either I'le be as errant a fool as he, or he shall be as wise as I, and then I think 'twill serve his turn.

PEDRO: Nay, I doe like thy wit passing well.

LOLLIO: Yes, you may, yet if I had not been a fool, I had had more wit then I have too; remember what state you find me in.

PEDRO: I will, and so leave you: your best cares, I beseech you.

ALIBIUS: Take you none with you, leave 'um all with us.
      (Exit Pedro.)

ANTONIO: Oh, my cousin's gone, cousin, cousin, oh!

LOLLIO: Peace, Peace, Tony, you must not cry, child, you must be whipt if you do; your cousin is here still, I am your cousin, Tony.

ANTONIO: He, he, then I'le not cry, if thou bee'st my cousin, he, he, he.

LOLLIO: I were best try his wit a little, that I may know what Form to place him in.

ALIBIUS: I, doe Lollio, doe.

LOLLIO: I must ask him easie questions at first; Tony, how many true fingers has a Taylor on his right hand?

ANTONIO: As many as on his left, cousin.

LOLLIO: Good, and how many on both?

ANTONIO: Two less then a Dewce, cousin.

LOLLIO: Very well answered; I come to you agen, cousin Tony: How many fools goes to a wise man?

ANTONIO: Fourty in a day sometimes, cousin.

LOLLIO: Fourty in a day? How prove you that?

ANTONIO: All that fall out amongst themselves, and go to a Lawyer to be made friends.

LOLLIO: A parlous fool! He must sit in the fourth Form at least, I perceive that: I come again, Tony: How many knaves make an honest man?

ANTONIO: I know not that, cousin.

LOLLIO: No, the question is too hard for you: I'le tell you, cousin, there's three knaves may make an honest man, a Sergeant, a Jaylor, and a Beadle; the Sergeant catches him, the Jaylor holds him, and the Beadle lashes him; and if he be not honest then, the Hangman must cure him.

ANTONIO: Ha, ha, ha! that's fine sport, cousin.

ALIBIUS: This was too deep a question for the fool, Lollio.

LOLLIO: Yes, this might have serv'd your self, tho I say't; once more, and you shall goe play, Tony.

ANTONIO: I, play at push-pin, cousin, ha, he.

LOLLIO: So thou shalt; say how many fools are here.

ANTONIO: Two, cousin, thou and I.

LOLLIO: Nay, y'are too forward there; Tony, mark my question: how many fools and knaves are here? A fool before a knave, a fool behind a knave, between every two fools a knave; how many fools, how many knaves?

ANTONIO: I never learnt so far, cousin.

ALIBIUS: Thou putst too hard questions to him, Lollio.

LOLLIO: I'le make him understand it easily; cousin, stand there.

ANTONIO: I, cousin.

LOLLIO: Master, stand you next the fool.

ALIBIUS: Well, Lollio.

LOLLIO: Here's my place: mark now, Tony, there a fool before a knave.

ANTONIO: That's I, cousin.

LOLLIO: Here's a fool behind a knave, that's I, and between us two fools there is a knave, that's my Master; 'tis but we three, that's all.

ANTONIO: We three, we three, cousin. Alexander died, Alexander was buried, Alexander returneth to dust; the dust is earth; of earth we make loam; and why of that loam whereto he has converted might they not stop a beer barrel?

Imperious Caesar, dead and turned to clay,

Might stop a hole to keep the wind away.

O, that that earth which kept the world in awe

Should patch a wall t' expel the winter's flaw!

But soft, but soft awhile! Here comes the king—

The Tragedy of Jane Shore

Nicholas Rowe
1714

Dramatic
Setting: The Tower of London
Scene: The Duke has usurped the British Throne and locked all potential threats and rivals in the Tower to be executed. The Lord Chamberlain comes on behalf of Jane Shore. She is in the Tower.

Duke of Gloster: Soon to be Richard III, brother to Edward, 30's.
Sir Richard Ratcliffe: The Duke's supporter, 30's – 40's.
Lord Hastings: Suspected of still being loyal to the dead King Edward. At present, the Lord Chamberlain to the Court, 40's.
Catesby: The Duke's supporter, 20's – 30's.

GLOST: Thus far success attends upon our councils,
    And each even has answer'd to my wish;
    The queen and all her upstart race are quell'd;
    Dorset is banish'd and her brother Rivers
    Ere this lies shorter by the head of Pomfret.
    The nobles have with joint concurrence nam'd me
    Protector of the realm. My brother's children,
    Young Edward and the little York, are lodg'd
    Here, safe within the Tower. How say you, Sirs,
    Does not this business wear a lucky face?
    The scepter and the golden wreath of royalty
    Seem hung within my reach.
RATCL: Then take 'em to you
    And wear them long and worthily; you are
    The last remaining male of princely York:
    (For Edward's boys, and the state esteems not of 'em)
    And therefore on your sovereignty and rule
    The commonweal does her dependence make,
    And leans upon your Highness' able hand.
CAT: And yet tomorrow does the council meet
    To fix a day for Edward's coronation:
    Who can expound this riddle?
GLOST: That can I.

Those lords are each one my approv'd, good friends,
Of special trust and nearness to my bosom;
And howsoever busy they may seem,
And diligent to bustle in the state,
Their zeal goes on no farther than we lead,
And at our bidding stays.

CAT: Yet there is one,
And he amongst the foremost in his power,
Of whom I wish your highness were assur'd:
For me, perhaps it is my nature's fault,
I own, I doubt of his inclining, much.

GLOST: I guess the man at whom your words would point: Hastings—

CAT: The same.

GLOST: He bears me great good will.

CAT: 'Tis true, to you, as to the Lord Protector
And Gloster's duke, he bows with lowly service:
But were he bid to cry, "God save King Richard,"
Then tell me in what terms he would reply.
Believe me, I have prov'd the man and found him:
I know he bears a most religious reverence
To his dead master Edward's royal memory,
And whither that may lead him is most plain;
Yet more, one of that stubborn sort he is
Who, if they once grow fond of an opinion,
They call it honour, honesty, and faith,
And sooner part with life than let it go.

GLOST: And yet, this tough, impracticable heart
Is govern'd by a dainty-fingered girl;
Such flaws are found in the most worthy natures;
A laughing, toying, wheedling, whimpering she
Shall make him amble on a gossip's message,
And take the distaff with a hand as patient
As e'er did Hercules.

RATCL: The fair Alicia,
Of noble birth and exquisite of feature,
Has held him long a vassal to her beauty.

CAT: I fear he fails in his allegiance there;
Or my intelligence is false, or else
The dame has been too lavish of her feast,

And fed him 'till he loathes.

GLOST: No more, he comes.

(Enter Lord Hastings.)

L. HAST: Health and the happiness of many days attend upon your
grace.

GLOST: My good Lord Chamberlain!
We're much beholden to your gentle friendship.

L. HAST: My Lord, I come an humble suitor to you.

GLOST: In right good time. Speak out your pleasure freely.

L. HAST: I am to move your Highness in behalf of Shore's unhappy
wife.

GLOST: Say you? of Shore?

L. HAST: Once a bright star held her place on high:
The first and fairest of our English dames
While royal Edward held the sovereign rule.
Now sunk in grief, and pining with despair,
Her waning form no longer shall incite
Envy in woman, or desire in man.
She never sees the sun but through her tears,
And wakes to sigh the livelong night away.

GLOST: Marry! the times are badly chang'd with her
From Edward's days to these. Then all was jollity,
Feasting and mirth, light wantonness and laughter,
Piping and playing, minstrelsy and masquing,
Till life fled from us like an idle dream,
A show of mommery without a meaning.
My brother, rest and pardon to his soul,
Is gone to his account; for this his minion.
The revel-rout is done. —But you were speaking
Concerning her. —I have been told that you
Are frequent in your visitation to her.

L. HAST: No farther, my good Lord, than friendly pity
And tender-hearted charity allow.

GLOST: Go to. I did not mean to chide you for it.
For, sooth to say, I hold it noble in you
To cherish the distressed. —On with your tale.

L. HAST: Thus is it, gracious Sir, that certain officers,
Using the warrant of your mighty name,
With insolence unjust and lawless power

Have seiz'd upon the lands which late she held
By grant from her great master Edward's bounty.
GLOST: Somewhat of this, but slightly, have I heard;
And though some counsellors of forward zeal,
Some of most ceremonious sanctity
And bearded wisdom, often have provok'd
The hand of justice to fall heavy on her,
Yet still in kind compassion of her weakness
And tender memory of Edward's love,
I have withheld the merciless, stern law
From doing outrage on her helpless beauty.
L. HAST: Good heav'n, who renders mercy back for mercy,
With open-handed bounty shall repay you:
This gentle deed shall fairly be set foremost,
To screen the wild escapes of lawless passion
And the long train of frailties flesh is heir to.
GLOST: Thus far, the voice of pity pleaded only;
Our father and more full extent of grace
Is given to your request. Let her attend,
And to ourself deliver up her griefs.
She shall be heard with patience, and each wrong
At full redress'd. But I have other news
Which much import us both, for still my fortunes
Go hand in hand with yours; our common foes,
The queen's relations, our new-fangl'd gentry,
Have fall'n their haughty crests. —That for your privacy.
(Exeunt.)

Jeppe of the Hill

Ludvig Holberg
1722

Comic
Setting: Baron Nilus' Palace.
Scene: Jeppe, instead of going to market for his wife, spent all his
    money on drink and was found drunk in a ditch by the Baron and
    his men. They decide to play a trick on him and take him to the
    Palace, put him to bed in the Baron's chambers and when he
    wakes, see what happens. He wakes to beautiful music, gor-
    geous clothes and splendid furnishings, and begins to weep.

Jeppe: a lazy drunk, 30's – 40's.
The Baron's valet.
Doctor #1.
Doctor #2.

JEPPE: Probably I drank too much once again at Jacob Skoemager's,
    died and went straight to heaven. Dying isn't so hard as people
    make it out. I for one didn't feel a single thing. Perhaps at this
    very minute the pastor is standing in the pulpit and delivering a
    funeral sermon over me saying: "That is the end of Jeppe of the
    Hill. He lived like a soldier and died like a soldier." They could
    argue whether I died on land or sea. I know I was quite wet when
    I left the world. Aha, Jeppe, that's very different from running
    four miles to town to buy soap. It's different from sleeping on
    straw, getting beatings from your wife and horns from the dea-
    con. Oh, into what a happy life your hardships and misery have
    turned! I could cry from sheer joy, particularly when I think how I
    didn't deserve it. But one thing bothers me: I'm so thirsty my lips
    are glued together. If I desired to live again it'd be only to get a
    pitcher of beer. For what's the good of all the finery before my
    eyes and ears if I'm going to suffer of thirst. I remember the pas-
    tor used to say: "In heaven there is neither hunger nor thirst, and
    you'll meet there all your dead friends." But I am drying of thirst
    and I'm all alone—I don't see a soul. I thought I'd find at least my
    grandfather here; he was so fine a man that he died, and didn't
    owe a shilling to his lordship. I also know that other people lived

as honest as I. Then why am I the only one in heaven? It can't be heaven. Then what is it? I'm not asleep; I'm not awake; I'm not dead; I'm not alive; I'm not crazy, I am not sane; I'm Jeppe of the Hill; I am not Jeppe of the Hill. I am poor; I am rich; I am a miserable peasant; I am an emperor. *(Roaring.)* O . . o . . . ah . . . Help! Help! Help!

(At his shouting Eric, the Valet, and many others enter to watch the fun.)

VALET: I wish your lordship a happy morning. Here is your dressing-gown—if your worship desires to rise. Eric, fetch quickly the towel and washbasin.

JEPPE: Oh, most worthy chamberlain, I'd very much like to get up, only I beg you please don't do me any harm.

VALET: God forbid that we should harm your lordship!

JEPPE: Oh, before you kill me, won't you please just tell me who I am.

VALET: Does not your lordship know who he is?

JEPPE: Yesterday I was Jeppe of the Hill, today . . . oh, I don't really know what to say.

VALET: We are happy indeed to see his lordship in such fine humor for jesting. But God save us! Why does your worship weep?

JEPPE: I am not your worship. I swear on my blessed soul that I am not. As far as I can remember, I am Jeppe Nielsen of the Hill. If you call my wife she'll tell you the same. But don't permit her to bring Master Eric along.

VALET: That is strange! What does that mean? Perhaps your lordship is not quite awake yet; he has never joked like this before.

JEPPE: Whether I am awake or not, I cannot tell; but this I do know, and I can say it too: I am one of our baron's peasants, called Jeppe of the Hill, and never in my life have I been baron or count.

VALET: Eric, I wonder what this means? I fear our master is falling sick.

ERIC: I think he has turned sleepwalker; it often happens that people get up, dress, read, eat and drink while they are asleep.

VALET: No, Eric, now I understand—our master has hallucinations, brought about by illness. Quick, call a few doctors . . . Oh, your worship, drive these thoughts from your mind. Your lordship is frightening the whole household. Doesn't my lord recognize me?

JEPPE: I don't know myself, so how can I know you?

VALET: Oh, is it possible that I hear such words from your gracious lordship, and see him in such a plight! Alas; the unfortunate house! to be visited by such misfortune! Doesn't my lord remember what he did yesterday when he went out hunting?

JEPPE: I was never a hunter—and no poacher; I know that means prison. No living soul can prove that I hunted even a hare in my lord's lands.

VALET: Why, it was only yesterday that I myself was out hunting with your gracious lordship.

JEPPE: Yesterday I was at Jacob Skoemager's and drank twelve shillings' worth of brandy. How could I have been hunting?

VALET: Oh, on bended knees I beg your worship to stop talking such nonsense. Eric, have the doctors been summoned?

ERIC: They will soon be here.

VALET: Then let us put on his lordship's dressing-gown. Perhaps when he gets some fresh air he'll feel better. Will your worship kindly put on his dressing-gown?

JEPPE: Sure. Do with me what you like, so long as you don't kill me, for I am as innocent as an unborn babe.

(Two doctors enter.)

FIRST DOCTOR: We heard with the very deepest sorrow that your lordship is ill.

VALET: Yes, master doctor, he is in a very serious condition.

SECOND DOCTOR: How do you feel, gracious lord?

JEPPE: Fine, only I am still thirsty from the brandy I drank yesterday at Jacob Skoemager's. If I could get a pitcher of beer and they let me go, you and the other doctor can go hang so far as I'm concerned. I don't need any medicines.

FIRST DOCTOR: That is what I call delirious raving, my colleague!

SECOND DOCTOR: The more violent the fever the quicker it runs its course. Now we will feel his lordship's pulse. *Quid Tibi videtur, domine frater?*

FIRST DOCTOR: *(Feeling Jeppe's pulse.)* I think he should be bled immediately.

SECOND DOCTOR: I do not agree with you; such diseases are cured in a different manner. His lordship had a strange, ugly, dream which so excited his blood and put his brain in such a turmoil that he imagines himself a peasant. We must now divert his attention with such amusements as usually give him the greatest pleasure. We must serve him the wines and foods he likes best and play for him the kind of music he most enjoys.

(Lively music commences to play.)

VALET: This is my lord's favorite piece.

JEPPE: Maybe. —Is there always such fun in the castle?

VALET: Whenever your lordship desires it, for he gives us our board and wages.

JEPPE: It's strange I can't remember the things that I used to.

SECOND DOCTOR: The disease from which my lordship suffers brings with it forgetfulness of what he used to do. I remember a few years ago one of my neighbors drank so much that he became deranged and thought he was minus his head.

JEPPE: I wish that would happen to Judge Christoffer; he has an illness that seems to work the other way. He believes he has a great big head. From the way he judges he really hasn't any at all.

(All laugh.)

SECOND DOCTOR: It is a joy to see his lordship jest, but to get back to my story. The same man went through the whole town asking everyone if they had found the head he had lost. After a time he recovered it; he is now a sexton in Jutland.

JEPPE: He could have been that even if he had never found his head again.

(Everyone laughs.)

FIRST DOCTOR: Does my honored colleague recollect what happened ten years ago to a man who thought his head was full of flies? He couldn't get that delusion out of his mind until a very clever doctor cured him in his fashion: He covered his whole head with plaster which he covered in turn with dead flies. After a time he took the plaster off, showing the patient the flies he believed had come from his head. This cured him. I also heard of another man who after a long fever got the idea that if he made water, the whole country would be flooded. No one could get this out of his head. He said he was ready to die for the common welfare. This is how he was cured. They brought him a message, supposedly from a commander, that the town was threatened with siege, and since there was no water in the moat, he was to fill it and thus keep the enemy from entering. The sick man was delighted that he could serve his country and himself as well, and in this manner got rid of both his water and his sickness.

SECOND DOCTOR: I can cite another case that happened in Germany. A nobleman one day came to an inn. After dining, and getting ready to retire he hung a golden chain which he wore around his neck, on the wall in his sleeping chamber. The innkeeper noted this carefully as he accompanied the gentleman to the bedroom and wished him goodnight. No sooner did he hear that the nobleman was asleep, than he stole into the chamber, took off sixty links from the chain and hung it back again. The guest rose in the morning, ordered his horse saddled, and dressed himself. When he came to putting on the chain he noticed that it was only half its former length. He began to shout that he had been robbed. The host who had been at the door listening ran in at once and putting on an air of great consternation exclaimed: "Lord! What an awful change in you." The traveller asked what he meant by that. "Oh my Lord," replied the innkeeper, "your head is twice as big as it was yesterday." And with that he held before him one of these mirrors that are so made that you appear twice the ordinary size. When the nobleman saw how big his head looked in the mirror, he burst into tears and said: "Now I understand how the chain has become too small." Then he mounted his horse and covered his head so that none could see him on the road. They say he kept a long time to his house, unable to get the silly idea out of head, to wit, that it was not the chain that had become short but that his head had become large.

FIRST DOCTOR: There are endless examples of such obsessions. I remember hearing of a man who convinced himself that his nose was ten feet long and warned everyone not to come near him.

SECOND DOCTOR: Domine Frater has, I am sure, heard the story of the man who thought himself dead. A young man got the notion that he was dead, laid himself in a coffin and would neither eat nor drink. His friends did their utmost to show him how absurd this was. They tried every means to make him eat, but it was useless. In the end a very experienced doctor undertook to cure him by the most unusual method. He had a servant also pretend that he was dead and brought him with great ceremony to the place where the sick man was. At first the two looked at each other in silence. Finally the patient asked the other why he had come. The new arrival answered he was there because he was dead. Then they questioned each other as to how they had died and both explained in full. Later the same people who had been instructed what to do brought supper to the second man who sat up in his coffin and ate heartily. Said he to the sick man: "Don't you want a bite too?" The patient was surprised and asked if it was really proper for dead men to eat. "No one who doesn't eat," replied the other, "can remain dead for any length of time." In this way he allowed himself to be persuaded first to eat, then to rise and dress himself, in short he imitated the counterfeit sick man in every way until in the end he was all well and became normal like the one who set the example. I could tell endless tales of such delusions. That is just what has happened to his gracious lordship. He imagines himself a peasant, but if my lordship will get it out of his head, he will be immediately well again.

JEPPE: Is it really possible that I only imagine it?

FIRST DOCTOR: Certainly. My lord has heard from these stories what delusions can do.

JEPPE: Then I am not Jeppe of the Hill?

FIRST DOCTOR: Certainly not.

JEPPE: Then that cursed Nille is not my wife?

SECOND DOCTOR: Absolutely not, my lord is a widower.

JEPPE: And the whip called Master Erick is only something I imagine?

FIRST DOCTOR: Purely an illusion.

JEPPE: It isn't true either that I was to go to town yesterday to buy soap?

SECOND DOCTOR: No.

JEPPE: Nor that I drank up the money at Jacob Skoemager's?

VALET: Why, your lordship was yesterday with us on the hunt.

JEPPE: Nor that I am a cuckold?

VALET: Her ladyship has been dead for many years.

JEPPE: Oh now I am beginning to see my foolishness. I won't think about the peasant any more. Now I see that it was only a dream that put this silliness into my head. Funny what stupid notions a man can believe.

VALET: Will it please your lordship to take a little walk in the garden before breakfast in prepared.

JEPPE: Very good, you'd better hurry up, for I am hungry and thirsty. *(They go out as the curtain drops.)*

School for Scandal

Richard Brinsley Sheridan
1777

Comic

Setting: Sir Peter's home. London

Scene: Disguising himself as Mr. Stanley, a poor relation, Sir Oliver will be able to test the generosity and morals of his two nephews. Rowley has come up with a plan. Mr. Moses, the moneylender, comes to discuss the financial affairs of Joseph and Charles.

Sir Peter Teazle: A wealthy gentleman married to a young bride, 40's – 50's.

Sir Oliver Surface: The wealthy benefactor to Charles and Joseph Surface who has been travelling in the East for some years. Both Charles and Joseph are wooing Maria, Sir Peter's ward. 50's – 60's.

Mr. Moses: A kindly moneylender, 50's.

Master Rowley: His kindly friend for many years, 40's – 50's.

SIR PETER: Well, then, we will see this fellow first and have our wine afterwards. But how is this, Master Rowley? I don't see the jet of your scheme.

ROWLEY: Why, sir, this Mr. Stanley, whom I was speaking of, is nearly related to them by their mother. He was once a merchant in Dublin but has been ruined by a series of undeserved misfortunes. He has applied by letter, since his confinement, to both Mr. Surface and Charles. From the former he has received nothing but evasive promises of future service, while Charles has done all that his extravagance has left him power to do; and he is at this time endeavoring to raise a sum of money, part of which, in the midst of his own distresses, I know he intends for the service of poor Stanley.

SIR OLIVER: Ah! he is my brother's son.

SIR PETER: Well, but how is Sir Oliver personally to—

ROWLEY: Why, sir, I will inform Charles and his brother that Stanley has obtained permission to apply personally to his friends; and, as they have neither of them ever seen him, let Sir Oliver assume his character and he will have a fair opportunity of judging at least of the benevolence of their dispositions. And, believe me, sir, you will find in the youngest brother one who, in the midst of folly and dissipation, has still, as our immortal bard expresses it,

A tear for pit and a hand,
Open as day for melting charity.

SIR PETER: Psha! What signifies his having an open hand or purse either when he has nothing left to give? Well, well, make the trial, if you please. But where is the fellow whom you brought for Sir Oliver to examine relative to Charles's affairs?

ROWLEY: Below, waiting his commands, and no one can give him better intelligence. This, Sir Oliver, is a friendly Jew, who, to do him justice, has done everything in his power to bring your nephew to a proper sense of his extravagance.

SIR PETER: Pray, let us have him in.

ROWLEY: *(Calls to Servant.)* Desire Mr. Moses to walk upstairs.

SIR PETER: But why should you suppose he will speak the truth?

ROWLEY: Oh, I have convinced him that he has no chance of recovering certain sums advanced to Charles but through the bounty of Sir Oliver, who, he knows, has arrived, so that you may depend on his fidelity to his own interests. I have also another evidence in my power, one Snake, whom I have detected in a matter little short of forgery and shall speedily produce him to remove some of your prejudices, Sir Peter, relative to Charles and Lady Teazle.

SIR PETER: I have heard too much on that subject.

ROWLEY: Here comes the honest Israelite.

(Enter Moses.) —This is Sir Oliver.

SIR OLIVER: Sir, I understand you have lately had great dealings with my nephew Charles.

MOSES: Yes, Sir Oliver. I have done all I could for him; but he was ruined before he came to me for assistance.

SIR OLIVER: That was unlucky, truly, for you have had no opportunity of showing your talents.

MOSES: None at all. I hadn't the pleasure of knowing his distresses till he was some thousands worse than nothing.

SIR OLIVER: Unfortunate, indeed! But I suppose you have done all in your power for him, honest Moses?

MOSES: Yes, he knows that. This very evening I was to have brought him a gentleman from the city, who does not know him and will, I believe, advance him some money.

SIR PETER: What, one Charles has never had money from before!

MOSES: Yes. Mr. Premium, of Crutched Friars, formerly a broker.

SIR PETER: Egad, Sir Oliver, a thought strikes me! —Charles, you say, does not know Mr. Premium?

MOSES: Not at all.

SIR PETER: Now then, Sir Oliver, you may have a better opportunity of satisfying yourself than by an old, romancing tale of a poor relation. Go with my friend Moses and represent Mr. Premium, and then, I'll answer for it, you'll see your nephew in all his glory.

SIR OLIVER: Egad, I like this idea better than the other, and I may visit Joseph afterwards as old Stanley.

SIR PETER: True—so you may.

ROWLEY: Well, this is taking Charles rather at a disadvantage, to be sure. However, Moses, you understand Sir Peter and will be faithful?

MOSES: You may depend upon me. This is near the time I was to have gone.

SIR OLIVER: I'll accompany you as soon as you please, Moses. But hold! I have forgot one thing—how the plague shall I be able to pass for a Jew?

MOSES: There's no need. The principal is Christian.

SIR OLIVER: Is he? I'm sorry to hear it; but then, again, an't I rather too smartly dressed to look like a moneylender?

SIR PETER: Not at all; 'twould not be out of character, if you went in your own carriage, would it, Moses?

MOSES: Not in the least.

SIR OLIVER: Well, but how must I talk? There's certainly some cant of usury and mode of treating that I ought to know.

SIR PETER: Oh, there's not much to learn. The great point, as I take it, is to be exorbitant enough in your demands. Hey, Moses?

MOSES: Yes, that's a very great point.

SIR OLIVER: I'll answer for 't I'll not be wanting to that. I'll ask him eight or ten per cent, on the loan at least.

MOSES: If you ask him no more than that, you'll be discovered immediately.

SIR OLIVER: Hey! what the plague! how much then?

MOSES: That depends upon the circumstances. If he appears not very anxious for the supply, you should require only forty or fifty per cent; but if you find him in great distress and want the moneys very bad, you may ask double.

SIR PETER: A good honest trade you're learning, Sir Oliver!

SIR OLIVER: Truly, I think so—and not unprofitable.

MOSES: Then you know, you haven't the moneys yourself but are forced to borrow them for him of an old friend.

SIR OLIVER: Oh! I borrow it of a friend, do I?

MOSES: Yes, and your friend is an unconscionable dog; but you can't help that.

SIR OLIVER: My friend is an unconscionable dog, is he?

MOSES: Yes, and he himself has not the moneys by him but is forced to sell stock at a great loss.

SIR OLIVER: He is forced to sell stock at a great loss, is he? Well, that's very kind of him.

SIR PETER: I'faith, Sir Oliver—Mr. Premium, I mean—you'll soon be master of the trade. But, Moses, wouldn't you have him run out a little against the annuity bill? That would be in character, I should think.

MOSES: Very much.

ROWLEY: And lament that a young man now must be at years of discretion before he is suffered to ruin himself?

MOSES: Ay, great pity!

SIR PETER: And abuse the public for allowing merit to an act whose only object is to snatch misfortune and imprudence from the rapacious gripe of usury and give the minor a chance of inheriting his estate without being undone by coming into possession.

SIR OLIVER: So, so—Moses shall give me further particulars as we go together.

SIR PETER: You will not have much time, for your nephew lives hard by.

SIR OLIVER: Oh, never fear! My tutor appears so able that though Charles lived in the next street, it must be my own fault if I am not a complete rogue before I turn the corner. *(Exit with Moses.)*

SIR PETER: So, now, I think Sir Oliver will be convinced. You are partial, Rowley, and would have prepared Charles for the other plot.

ROWLEY: No, upon my word, Sir Peter.

SIR PETER: Well, go bring me this Snake, and I'll hear what he has to say presently. I see Maria and want to speak with her. *(Exit Rowley.)* I should be glad to be convinced my suspicions of Lady Teazle and Charles were unjust. I have never yet opened my mind on this subject to my friend Joseph. I am determined I will do it; he will give me his opinion sincerely.

The Second Mrs. Tanqueray

Arthur Wing Pinero
1893

Dramatic

Setting: The rooms of Aubrey Tanqueray, richly and tastefully decorated, in November. A fire is burning in the fireplace.

Scene: Aubrey, Jayne and Misquith are seated around the dinner table. Morse has just placed a cabinet of cigars on the table and exited unobtrusively.

Jayne: Gordon Jayne, M.D., 44, soft-spoken and precise, a physician.
Aubrey Tanqueray: 42, handsome, youthful, wealthy and refined.
Cayley Drummle: 45, small, neat, bright and debonair.
Misquith: 47, portly and friendly.
Brief entrance of Morse, the butler.

MISQUITH: Aubrey, it is a pleasant yet dreadful fact to contemplate, but it's nearly fifteen years since I first dined with you. You lodged in Piccadilly in those days, over a hat-shop. Jayne, I met you at that dinner, and Cayley Drummle.

JAYNE: Yes, yes. What a pity it is that Cayley isn't here tonight.

AUBREY: Confound the old gossip! His empty chair has been staring us in the face all through dinner. I ought to have told Morse to take it away.

MISQUITH: Odd, his sending no excuse.

AUBREY: I'll walk round to his lodgings later on and ask after him.

MISQUITH: I'll go with you.

JAYNE: So will I.

AUBREY: *(Opening the cigar-cabinet.)* Doctor, it's useless to tempt you, I know. Frank—*(Misquith and Aubrey smoke.)* I particularly wished Cayley Drummle to be one of us tonight. You two fellows and Cayley are my closest, my best friends—

MISQUITH: My dear Aubrey!

JAYNE: I rejoice to hear you say so.

AUBREY: And I wanted to see the three of you round this table. You can't guess the reason.

MISQUITH: You desired to give us a most excellent dinner.

JAYNE: Obviously.

AUBREY: *(Hesitatingly.)* Well—I— *(Glancing at the clock.)* Cayley won't turn up now.

JAYNE: H'm, hardly.

AUBREY: Then you two shall hear it. Doctor, Frank, this is the last time we are to meet in these rooms.

JAYNE: The last time?

MISQUITH: You're going to leave the Albany?

AUBREY: Yes. You've heard me speak of a house I built in the country years ago, haven't you?

MISQUITH: In Surrey.

AUBREY: Well, when my wife died I cleared out of that house and let it. I think of trying the place again.

MISQUITH: But you'll go raving mad if ever you find yourself down there alone.

AUBREY: Ah, but I sha'n't be alone, and that's what I wanted to tell you. I'm going to be married.

JAYNE: Going to be married?

MISQUITH: Married?

AUBREY: Yes—tomorrow.

JAYNE: Tomorrow?

MISQUITH: You take my breath away! My dear fellow, I—I—of course, I congratulate you.

JAYNE: And—and—so do I—heartily.

AUBREY: Thanks—thanks.

(There is a moment or two of embarrassment.)

MISQUITH: Er—ah—this is an excellent cigar.

JAYNE: Ah—um—your coffee remarkable.

AUBREY: Look here; I dare say you two old friends think this treatment very strange, very unkind. So I want you to understand me. You know a marriage often cools friendships. What's the usual course of things? A man's engagement is given out, he is congratulated, complimented upon his choice; the church is filled with troops of friends, and he goes away happily to a chorus of good wishes. He comes back, sets up house in town or country, and thinks to resume the old associations, the old companionships. My dear Frank, my dear good doctor, it's very seldom that it can be done. Generally, a worm has begun to eat its way into those hearty, unreserved, prenuptial friendships; a damnable constraint sets in and acts like a wasting disease; and so, believe me, in nine cases out of ten a man's marriage severs for him more close ties than it forms.

MISQUITH: Well, my dear Aubrey, I earnestly hope—

AUBREY: I know what you're going to say, Frank. I hope so, too. In the meantime let's face dangers. I've reminded you of the *usual* course of things, but my marriage isn't even the conventional sort of marriage likely to satisfy society. Now, Cayley's a bachelor, but you two men have wives. By-the-bye, my love to Mrs. Misquith and to Mrs. Jayne when you get home—don't forget that. Well, your wives may not—like—the lady I'm going to marry.

JAYNE: Aubrey, forgive me for suggesting that the lady you are going to marry may not like our wives—mine at least; I beg your pardon, Frank.

AUBREY: Quite so; then I must go the way my wife goes.

MISQUITH: Come, come, pray don't let us anticipate that either side will be called upon to make such a sacrifice.

AUBREY: Yes, yes, let us anticipate it. And let us make up our minds to have no slow bleeding-to-death of our friendship. We'll end a pleasant chapter here tonight, and after tonight start afresh. When my wife and I settle down at Willowmere it's possible that we shall all come together. But if this isn't to be, for Heaven's sake let us recognise that it is simply because it *can't* be, and not wear hypocritical faces and suffer and be wretched. Doctor, Frank— *(Holding out his hands, one to Misquith, the other to Jayne.)* —good luck to all of us!

MISQUITH: But, but, do I understand we are to ask nothing? Not even the lady's name, Aubrey?

AUBREY: The lady, my dear Frank, belongs to the next chapter, and in that her name is Mrs. Aubrey Tanqueray.

JAYNE: *(Raising his coffee-cup.)* Then, in an old-fashioned way, I propose a toast. Aubrey, Frank, I give you "The Next Chapter!" *(They drink the toast, saying, "The Next Chapter!")*

AUBREY: Doctor, find a comfortable chair; Frank, you too. As we're going to turn out by-and-bye, let me scribble a couple of notes now while I think of them.

MISQUITH AND JAYNE: Certainly—yes, yes.

AUBREY: It might slip my memory when I get back.
(Aubrey sits at a writing table at the other end of the room, and writes.)

JAYNE: *(To Misquith in a whisper.)* Frank— *(Misquith quietly leaves his chair, and sits nearer to Jayne.)* What is all this? Simply a morbid crank of Aubrey's with regard to ante-nuptial acquaintances?

MISQUITH: H'm! Did you notice *one* expression he used?

JAYNE: Let me think—

MISQUITH: "My marriage is not even the conventional sort of marriage likely to satisfy society."

JAYNE: Bless me, yes! What does that suggest?

MISQUITH: That he has a particular rather than a general reason for anticipating estrangement from his friends, I'm afraid.

JAYNE: A horrible *mésalliance!* A dairymaid who has given him a glass of milk during a day's hunting, or a little anaemic shopgirl! Frank, I'm utterly wretched!

MISQUITH: My dear Jayne, speaking in absolute confidence, I have never been more profoundly depressed in my life.
(Morse enters.)

MORSE: *(Announcing.)* Mr. Drummle.
(Cayley Drummle enters briskly. He is a neat little man of about five-and-forty, in manner bright, airy, debonair, but with an undercurrent of seriousness. Morse retires.)

DRUMMLE: I'm in disgrace; nobody realises that more thoroughly than I do. Where's my host?

AUBREY: *(Who has risen.)* Cayley.

DRUMMLE: *(Shaking hands with him.)* Don't speak to me till I have tendered my explanation. A harsh word from anybody would unman me.
(Misquith and Jayne shake hands with Drummle.)

AUBREY: Have you dined?

DRUMMLE: No—unless you call a bit of fish, a cutlet, and a pancake dining.

AUBREY: Cayley, this is disgraceful.

JAYNE: Fish, a cutlet, and a pancake will require a great deal of explanation.

MISQUITH: Especially the pancake. My dear friend, your case looks miserably weak.

DRUMMLE: Hear me! hear me!

JAYNE: Now then!

MISQUITH: Come!

AUBREY: Well!

DRUMMLE: It so happens that tonight I was exceptionally early in dressing for dinner.

MISQUITH: For which dinner—the fish and cutlet?

DRUMMLE: For *this* dinner, of course—really, Frank! At a quarter to eight, in fact, I found myself trimming my nails, with ten minutes to spare. Just then enter my man with a note—would I hasten, as fast as cab could carry me, to old Lady Orreyed in Bruton Street?— "sad trouble." Now, recollect, please, I had ten minutes on my hands, old Lady Orreyed was a very dear friend of my mother's, and was in some distress.

AUBREY: Cayley, come to the fish and cutlet!

MISQUITH AND JAYNE: Yes, yes, and the pancake!

DRUMMLE: Upon my word! Well, the scene in Bruton Street beggars description; the women servants looked scared, the men drunk; and there was poor old Lady Orreyed on the floor of her boudoir like Queen Bess among her pillows.

AUBREY: What's the matter?

DRUMMLE: *(To everybody.)* You know George Orreyed?

MISQUITH: Yes.

JAYNE: I've met him.

DRUMMLE: Well, he's a thing of the past.

AUBREY: Not dead!

DRUMMLE: Certainly, in the worst sense. He's married Mabel Hervey.

MISQUITH: What!

DRUMMLE: It's true—this morning. The poor mother showed me his letter—a dozen curt words, and some of those ill-spelt.

MISQUITH: *(Walking up to the fireplace.)* I'm very sorry.

JAYNE: Pardon my ignorance—who *was* Mabel Hervey?

DRUMMLE: You don't—? Oh, of course not. Miss Hervey—Lady Orreyed—as she now is—was a lady who would have been, perhaps has been, described in the reports of the Police or the Divorce Court as an actress. Had she belonged to a lower stratum of our advanced civilisation she would, in the event of judicial inquiry, have defined her calling with equal justification as that of a dressmaker. To do her justice, she is a type of a class which is immortal. Physically, by the strange caprice of creation, curiously beautiful; mentally, she lacks even the strength of deliberate viciousness. Paint her portrait, it would symbolize a creature perfectly patrician; lance a vein of her superbly-modelled arm, you would get the poorest *vin ordinaire!* Her affections, emotions, impulses, her very existence—a burlesque! Flaxen, five-and-twenty, and feebly frolicsome; anybody's in less gentle society I should say everybody's property! That, doctor, was Miss Hervey who is the new Lady Orreyed. Dost thou like the picture?

MISQUITH: Very good, Cayley! Bravo!

AUBREY: *(Laying his hand on Drummle's shoulder.)* You'd scarcely believe it, Jayne, but none of us really know anything about this lady, our gay young friend here, I suspect, least of all.

DRUMMLE: Aubrey, I applaud your chivalry.

AUBREY: And perhaps you'll let me finish a couple of letters with Frank and Jayne have given me leave to write. *(Returning to the writing-table.)* Ring for what you want, like a good fellow! *(Aubrey resumes his writing.)*

MISQUITH: *(To Drummle.)* Still, the fish and cutlet remain unexplained.

DRUMMLE: Oh, the poor old woman was so weak that I insisted upon her taking some food, and felt there was nothing for it but to sit down opposite her. The fool! the blackguard!

MISQUITH: Poor Orreyed! Well, he's gone under for a time.

DRUMMLE: For a time! My dear Frank, I tell you he has absolutely ceased to be. *(Aubrey, who has been writing busily, turns his head towards the speakers and listens. His lips are set, and there is a frown upon his face.)* For all practical purposes you may regard him as the late George Orreyed. Tomorrow the very characteristics of his speech, as we remember them, will have become obsolete.

JAYNE: But surely, in the course of years, he and his wife will outlive—

DRUMMLE: No, no. doctor, don't try to upset one of my settled beliefs. You may dive into many waters, but there is *one* social Dead Sea—!

JAYNE: Perhaps you're right.

DRUMMLE: Right! Good God! I wish you could prove me otherwise! Why, for years I've been sitting, and watching and waiting.

MISQUITH: You're in form tonight, Cayley. May we ask where you've been in the habit of squandering your useful leisure?

DRUMMLE: Where? On the shore of that same sea.

MISQUITH: And, pray, what have you been waiting for?

DRUMMLE: For some of my best friends *to come up. (Aubrey utters a half-stifled exclamation of impatience; then he hurriedly gathers up his papers from the writing-table. The three men turn to him.)* Eh?

AUBREY: Oh, I—I'll finish my letters in the other room if you'll excuse me for five minutes. Tell Cayley the news. *(He goes out.)*

DRUMMLE: *(Hurrying to the door.)* My dear fellow, my jabbering has disturbed you! I'll never talk again as long as I live!

MISQUITH: Close the door, Cayley.

(Drummle shuts the door.)

JAYNE: Cayley—

DRUMMLE: *(Advancing to the dinner table.)* A smoke, a smoke, or I perish! *(Selects a cigar from the little cabinet.)*

JAYNE: Cayley, marriages are in the air.

DRUMMLE: Are they? Discover the bacillus, doctor, and destroy it.

JAYNE: I mean, among our friends.

DRUMMLE: Oh, Nugent Warrinder's engagement to Lady Alice Tring. I've heard of that. They're not to be married till the spring.

JAYNE: Another marriage that concerns us a little takes place tomorrow.

DRUMMLE: Whose marriage?

JAYNE: Aubrey's.

DRUMMLE: Aub—! *(Looking towards Misquith.)* Is it a joke?

MISQUITH: No.

DRUMMLE: *(Looking from Misquith to Jayne.)* To whom?

MISQUITH: He doesn't tell us.

JAYNE: We three were asked here tonight to receive the announcement. Aubrey has some theory that marriage is likely to alienate a man from his friends, and it seems to me he has taken the precaution to wish us good-bye.

MISQUITH: No, no.

JAYNE: Practically, surely.

DRUMMLE: *(Thoughtfully.)* Marriage in general, does he mean, or *this* marriage?

JAYNE: That's the point. Frank says—

MISQUITH: No, no, no; I feared it suggested—

JAYNE: Well, well. *(To Drummle.)* What do you think of it?

DRUMMLE: *(After a slight pause.)* Is there a light there? *(Lighting his cigar.)* He—wraps the lady—in mystery—you say?

MISQUITH: Most modestly.

DRUMMLE: Aubrey's—not—a very—young man.

JAYNE: Forty-three.

DRUMMLE: Ah! *L'age critique!*

MISQUITH: A dangerous age—yes, yes.

DRUMMLE: When you two fellows go home, do you mind leaving me behind here?

MISQUITH: Not at all.

JAYNE: By all means.

DRUMMLE: All right. *(Anxiously.)* Deuce take it, the man's second marriage mustn't be another mistake! *(With his head bent he walks up to the fireplace.)*

The Rising of the Moon

Lady Gregory
1907

Dramatic

Setting: On the side of a wharf in a seaport town. Some posts and chains and a large barrel are nearby.

Scene: The Sergeant looks all around and down a set of steps. The others put down a pastepot and a roll of "wanted" placards.

Sergeant: 30's – 40's.
Policeman B: 20's – 30's.
Policeman X: 20's – 30's.
Man: 20's – 30's.

POLICEMAN B: I think this would be a good place to put up a notice. *(He points to barrel.)*

POLICEMAN X: Better ask him. *(Calls to Sergeant.)* Will this be a good place for a placard?
(No answer.)

POLICEMAN B: Will we put up a notice on the barrel?

SERGEANT: There's a flight of steps here that leads to the water. This is a place that should be minded well. If he got down here, his friends might have a boat to meet him; they might send it in here from outside.

POLICEMAN B: Would the barrel be a good place to put up a notice?

SERGEANT: It might; you can put it there.
(They paste the notice up.)

SERGEANT: *(Reading it.)* Dark hair—dark eyes, smooth face, height, five feet five—there's not much to take hold of in that. It's a pity I had no chance of seeing him before he broke out of jail. They say he's a wonder, that he makes all the plans for the whole organization. There isn't another man in Ireland would have broken jail the way he did. He must have some friends among the jailers.

POLICEMAN B: A hundred pounds is little enough for the Government to offer for him. You may be sure any man in the force that takes him will get promotion.

SERGEANT: I'll mind this place myself. I wouldn't wonder at all if he came this way. He might come slipping along there *(Points to side* of wharf.) and his friends might be waiting for him there (Points down steps.) and once he got away it's little chance we'd have of finding him; it's maybe under a load of kelp he'd be in a fishing boat, and not one to help a married man that wants it to the reward.

POLICEMAN X: And if we get him itself, nothing but abuse on our heads for it from the people, and maybe from our own relations.

SERGEANT: Well, we have to do our duty in the force. Haven't we the whole country depending on us to keep law and order? It's those that are down would be up and those that are up would be down, if it wasn't for us. Well, hurry on, you have plenty of other places to placard yet, and come back here then to me. You can take the lantern. Don't be too long now. It's very lonesome here with nothing but the moon.

POLICEMAN B: It's a pity we can't stop with you. The Government should have brought more police into the town, with *him* in jail, and at assize time too. Well, good luck to your watch.

(They go out.)

SERGEANT: (Walks up and down once or twice and looks at placard.) A hundred pounds and promotion sure. There must be a great deal of spending in a hundred pounds. It's a pity some honest man not to be the better of that.

(A ragged man appears at left and tries to slip past. Sergeant suddenly turns.)

SERGEANT: Where are you going?

MAN: I'm a poor ballad-singer, your honor. I thought to sell some of these (Holds out bundle of ballads.) to the sailors.

(He goes on.)

SERGEANT: Stop! Didn't I tell you to stop? You can't go on there.

MAN: Oh, very well. It's a hard thing to be poor. All the world's against the poor.

SERGEANT: Who are you?

MAN: You'd be a wise as myself if I told you, but I don't mind. I'm Jimmy Walsh, a ballad-singer.

SERGEANT: Jimmy Walsh? I don't know that name.

MAN: Ah, sure, they know it well enough in Ennis. Were you ever in Ennis, sergeant?

SERGEANT: What brought you here?

MAN: Sure, it's to the assizes I came, thinking I might make a few shillings here or there. It's in the one train with the judges I came.

SERGEANT: Well, if you came so far, you may as well go farther, for you'll walk out of this.

MAN: I will, I will; I'll just go on where I was going. *(Goes toward steps.)*

SERGEANT: Come back from those steps; no one has leave to pass down them tonight.

MAN: I'll just sit on the top of the steps till I see will some sailor buy a ballad off me that would give me my supper. They do be late going back to the ship. It's often I saw them in Cork carried down the wharf in a handcart.

SERGEANT: Move on, I tell you. I won't have anyone lingering about the wharf tonight.

MAN: Well, I'll go. It's the poor have the hard life! Maybe yourself might like one, sergeant. Here's the good sheet now. *(Turns one over.)* "Content and a Pipe"—that's not much. "The Peeler and the Goat"—you wouldn't like that. "Johnny Hart"—that's a lovely song.

SERGEANT: Move on.

MAN: Ah, wait till you hear it.

(Sings.) There was a rich farmer's daughter lived near the town of Ross;

She courted a Highland soldier, his name was Johnny Hart;

Says the mother to her daughter, "I'll go distracted mad if you marry that Highland soldier dressed up in Highland plaid."

SERGEANT: Where are you going?

MAN: Sure you told me to be going, and I am going.

SERGEANT: Don't be a fool. I didn't tell you to go that way; I told you to go back to the town.

MAN: Back to the town, is it?

SERGEANT: *(Taking him by the shoulder and shoving him before him.)* Here, I'll show you the way. Be off with you. What are you stopping for?

MAN: *(Who has been keeping his eye on the notice, points to it.)* I think I know what you're waiting for, sergeant.

SERGEANT: What's that to you?

MAN: And I knew well the man you're waiting for—I know him well—I'll be going.

(He shuffles on.)

SERGEANT: You know him? Come back here. What sort is he?

MAN: Come back is it, sergeant? Do you want to have me killed?

SERGEANT: Why do you say that?

MAN: Never mind. I'm going. I wouldn't be in your shoes if the reward was ten times as much. *(Goes offstage to left.)* Not if it was ten times as much.

SERGEANT: *(Rushing after him.)* Come back here, come back. *(Drags him back.)* What sort is he? Where did you see him?

MAN: I saw him in my own place, in the County Clare. I tell you you wouldn't like to be looking at him. You'd be afraid to be in the one place with him. There isn't a weapon he doesn't know the use of, and as to strength, his muscles are as hard as that board. *(Slaps barrel.)*

SERGEANT: Is he as bad as that?

MAN: He is then.

SERGEANT: Do you tell me so?

MAN: There was a poor man in our place, a sergeant from Ballyvaughan. —It was with a lump of stone he did it.

SERGEANT: I never heard of that.

MAN: And you wouldn't, sergeant. It's not everything that happens gets into the papers. And there was a policeman in plain clothes, too. . . It is in Limerick he was. . . It was after the time of the attack on the police barrack at Kilmallock. . . Moonlight. . . just like this. . . waterside. . . Nothing was known for certain.

SERGEANT: Do you say so? It's a terrible country to belong to

MAN: That's so, indeed! You might be standing there, looking out that way, thinking you saw him coming up this side of the wharf, *(Points.)* and he might be coming up this other side, *(Points.)* and he'd be on you before you knew where you were.

SERGEANT: It's a whole troop of police they ought to put here to stop a man like that.

MAN: But if you'd like me to stop with you, I could be looking down this side. I could be sitting up here on this barrel.

SERGEANT: And you know him well, too?

MAN: I'd know him a mile off, sergeant.

SERGEANT: But you wouldn't want to share the reward?

MAN: Is it a poor man like me, that has to be going the roads and singing in fairs, to have the name on him that he took a reward? But you don't want me. I'll be safer in the town.

SERGEANT: Well, you can stop.

MAN: *(Getting up on barrel.)* All right, sergeant. I wonder, now, you're not tired out, sergeant, walking up and down the way you are.

SERGEANT: If I'm tired I'm used to it.

MAN: You might have hard work before you tonight yet. Take it easy while you can. There's plenty of room up here on the barrel, and you can see farther when you're higher up.

SERGEANT: May be so. *(Gets up beside him on barrel, facing right. They sit back to back, looking different ways.)* You made me feel a bit queer with the way you talked.

MAN: Give me a match, sergeant. *(He gives it, and man lights pipe.)* Take a draw yourself? It'll quiet you. Wait now till I give you a light, but you needn't turn round. Don't take your eye off the wharf for the life of you.

SERGEANT: Never, fear, I won't *(Lights pipe. They both smoke.)* Indeed, it's a hard thing to be in the force, out at night and no thanks for it, for all the danger we're in. And it's little we get but abuse from the people, and no choice but to obey our orders, and never asked when a man is sent into danger, if you are a married man with a family.

MAN: *(Sings.)* As through the hills I walked to view the hills and shamrock plain,

I stood awhile where nature smiles to view the rocks and streams,

On a matron fair I fixed my eyes beneath a fertile vale,

As she sang her song it was on the wrong of poor old Granuaile.

SERGEANT: Stop that; that's no song to be singing in these times.

MAN: Ah, sergeant, I was only singing to keep my heart up. It sinks when I think of him. To think of us two sitting here, and he creeping up the wharf, maybe, to get to us.

SERGEANT: Are you keeping a good lookout?

MAN: I am; and for no reward too. Amn't I the foolish man? But when I saw a man in trouble, I never could help trying to get him out of it. What's that? Did something hit me?

SERGEANT: *(Patting him on the shoulder.)* You will get your reward in heaven.

MAN: I know that, I know that, sergeant, but life is precious.

SERGEANT: Well, you can sing if it gives you more courage.

MAN: *(Sings.)* Her head was bare, her hands and feet with iron bands were bound,

    Her pensive strain and plaintive wail mingled with the evening gale,

    And the song she sang with mournful air, I am old Granuaile.

    Her lips so sweet that monarchs kissed. . .

SERGEANT: That's not it. . . "Her gown she wore was stained with gore. . . " That's it—you missed that.

MAN: You're right, sergeant, so it is; I missed it. *(Repeats the line.)* But to think a man like you knowing a song like that.

SERGEANT: There's many a thing a man might know and might not have any wish for.

MAN: Now, I daresay, sergeant, in your youth, you used to be sitting up on a wall, the way you are sitting up on this barrel now, and the other lads beside you, and you singing "Granuaile"?

SERGEANT: I did then.

MAN: And the "Shan Bhean Bhocht"?

SERGEANT: I did then.

MAN: And the "Green on the Cape"?

SERGEANT: That was one of them.

MAN: And maybe the man you are watching for tonight used to be sitting on the wall, when he was young, and singing those same songs. . . It's a queer world. . .

SERGEANT: Whisht!. . . I think I see something coming. . . It's only a dog.

MAN: And isn't it a queer world? . . . Maybe it's one of the boys you used to be singing with that time you will be arresting today or tomorrow, and sending into the dock. . .

SERGEANT: That's true indeed.

MAN: And maybe one night, after you had been singing, if the other boys had told you some plan they had, some plan to free the country, you might have joined them, and maybe it is you might be in trouble now.

SERGEANT: Well, who knows but I might? I had great spirit in those days.

MAN: It's a queer world, sergeant, and it's a little mother knows when she sees her child creeping on the floor what might happen to it before it has gone through its life, or who will be who in the end.

SERGEANT: That's a queer thought now, and a true thought. Wait now till I think it out. If it wasn't for the sense I have, and for my wife and family, and for me joining the force the time I did, it might be myself now would be after breaking jail and hiding in the dark, and it might be him that's hiding in the dark and that got out of jail would be sitting up where I am on this barrel. . . And it might be myself would be creeping up trying to make my escape from himself, and it might be himself would be keeping the law, and myself would be breaking it, and myself would be trying maybe to put a bullet in his head, or to take up a lump of stone the way you said he did. . . no, that myself did. . . Oh! *(Gasps. After a pause.)* What's that? *(Grasps man's arm.)*

MAN: *(Jumps off barrel and listens, looking out over water.)* It's nothing, sergeant.

SERGEANT: I thought it might be a boat. I had a notion there might be friends of his coming about the wharfs with a boat.

MAN: Sergeant, I am thinking it was with the people you were, and not with the law you were when you were a young man.

SERGEANT: Well, if I was foolish then, that time's gone.

MAN: Maybe, sergeant, it comes into your head sometimes, in spite of your belt and your tunic, that it might have been as well for you to have followed Granuaile.

SERGEANT: It's no business of yours what I think.

MAN: Maybe, sergeant, you'll be on the side of the country yet.

SERGEANT: *(Gets off barrel.)* Don't talk to me like that. I have my duties and I know them. *(Looks round.)* That was a boat; I hear the oars.

(Goes to the steps and looks down.)

MAN: *(Sings.)* O, then, tell me, Shawn O'Farrell,
Where the gathering is to be.
In the old spot by the river
Right well known to you and me!

SERGEANT: Stop that! Stop that! I tell you!

MAN: *(Sings louder.)* One word more, for signal token,
Whistle up the marching tune,
With your pike upon your shoulder,
At the Rising of the Moon.

SERGEANT: If you don't stop that, I'll arrest you.

(A whistle from below answers, repeating the air.)

SERGEANT: That's a signal. *(Stands between him and steps.)* You must not pass this way. . . Step farther back. . . Who are you? You are no ballad-singer.

MAN: You needn't ask who I am; that placard will tell you.

(Points to placard.)

SERGEANT: You are the man I am looking for.

MAN: *(Takes off hat and wig. Sergeant seizes them.)* I am. There's a hundred pounds on my head. There is a friend of mine below in a boat. He knows a safe place to bring me to.

SERGEANT: *(Looking still at hat and wig.)* It's a pity! It's a pity. You deceived me. You deceived me well.

MAN: I am a friend of Granuaile. There is a hundred pounds on my head.

SERGEANT: It's a pity, it's a pity!

MAN: Will you let me pass, or must I make you let me?

SERGEANT: I am in the force. I will not let you pass.

MAN: I thought to do it with my tongue. *(Puts hand in breast.)* What is that?

(Voice of Policeman X outside.) Here, this is where we left him.

SERGEANT: It's my comrades coming.

MAN: You won't betray me. . . the friend of Granuaile. *(Slips behind the barrel.)*

(Voice of Policeman B.) That was the last of the placards.

POLICEMAN X: *(As they come in.)* If he makes his escape it won't be unknown he'll make it.

(Sergeant puts hat and wig behind his back.)

POLICEMAN B: Did anyone come this way?

SERGEANT: *(After a pause.)* No one.

POLICEMAN B: No one at all?

SERGEANT: No one at all.

POLICEMAN B: We had no orders to go back to the station; we can stop along with you.

SERGEANT: I don't want you. There is nothing for you to do here.

POLICEMAN B: You bade us to come back here and keep watch with you.

SERGEANT: I'd sooner be alone. Would any man come this way and you making all that talk? It is better the place be quiet.

POLICEMAN B: Well, we'll leave you the lantern anyhow.

(Hands it to him.)

SERGEANT: I don't want it. Bring it with you.

POLICEMAN B: You might want it. There are clouds coming up and you have the darkness of the night before you yet. I'll leave it over here on the barrel.

(Goes to barrel.)

SERGEANT: Bring it with you, I tell you. No more talk.

POLICEMAN B: Well, I thought it might be a comfort to you. I often think when I have it in my hand and can be flashing it about into every dark corner *(Doing so.)* that it's the same as being beside the fire at home, and the bits of bogwood blazing up now and again.

(Flashes it about, now on the barrel, now on Sergeant.)

SERGEANT: *(Furious.)* Be off the two of you, yourselves and your lantern!

(They go out. Man comes from behind barrel. He and Sergeant stand looking at one another.)

SERGEANT: What are you waiting for?

MAN: For my hat, of course, and my wig. You wouldn't wish me to get my death of cold?

(Sergeant gives them.)

MAN: *(Going toward steps.)* Well, goodnight comrade, and thank you. You did me a good turn tonight, and I'm obliged to you. Maybe I'll be able to do as much for you when the small rise up and the big fall down. . . when we all change places at the Rising *(Waves his hand and disappears.)* of the Moon.

SERGEANT: *(Turning his back to audience and reading placard.)* A hundred pounds reward! A hundred pounds! *(Turns toward audience.)* I wonder now, am I as great a fool as I think I am?

A Cry in the Streets

Rolf Lauckner
1922

Dramatic

Setting: The streets outside the Institution where the three men live. New Year's Eve.

Scene: The men have run away from the Home for the Blind and want to celebrate.

Sasha: Blind man, 20's – 60's.
Wolf: Blind man 20's – 60's.
Konzel: Blind man 20's – 60's.
A drunk: Any age.

SASHA: We're free! . . . Just think, we're free! Then why do we stay here? Let's clear out! Dance over the fence and celebrate New Year's on the town.

WOLF: But where? . . . They know us here in the neighborhood. . . And further down?. . .

KONZEL: Between the houses? Us?. . .

SASHA: Then let's look for someone to guide us. . .

WOLF: And rob us snugly around the next corner! . . . You can't even yell for help! . . . Listen to me, Shorty, stay with us.

SASHA: But not alone! . . . Naturally, only together!

WOLF: You always get carried away! Fidgety and excited like someone out there on the street! As if you had eyes. . .

SASHA: Well, once I did see. . .

WOLF: What you saw in those few years couldn't amount to very much. . . The sluice with the little stretch of woods behind it, and the red fence around your yard, right?. . .

SASHA: And yet I won't ever explain to you these two—the only visual impressions that have remained with me! They certainly make me richer than either of you, and I'd rather give away anything but this bit of light behind the veils. . .

KONZEL: How long could you see?. . .

SASHA: Until I was four. . .

WOLF: And that keeps you hopped up all the rest of your life! . . . An old fence dangles in your mind, luring you beyond your limitations! Better to have been born blind like the two of us.

KONZEL: Well, properly speaking, I'm not. Now and then a tinge of light flashes through my brain.

WOLF: Then drives you completely out of your mind! On your "light days" you're not good for anything at all!

KONZEL: The nerves take the toll!

WOLF: That's what I mean! With you it's the nerves, and with Sasha it's the memory that blinds! . . . So which is the healthy one?. . .

SASHA: Oh, Wolf, let's live tonight! . . . I never felt better! . . . Without walls! And all around, life, brimming over!. . .

KONZEL: The city celebrates—you feel it. . . A cloud of lust hovers over the beds of stone!. . .

WOLF: Lust five flights high breaks loose on all the streets, until the New Year is sweated out! The muscles are taut with life. . .

SASHA: The whole world swells up. . . at the bountiful tables of the night. . .

KONZEL: Secret guests. . . the three of us.

SASHA: Out of a sleepy shaft, moon-crazy, and free as a bird, strangely awakened, suddenly plopped into light! . . . Thousand-fold life foaming up! The year staggers by bawling at the night. . . We break the fence and swirl after it! Space is lust! Out into space. . .

WOLF: Are you being carried away again?. . . Just don't forget, Shorty, you walk with a cane! We blind ones. . .

SASHA: We blind ones. . .

KONZEL: We blind have it all over the others in the dark! They see only the small halos around the lamps out there! But we shovel out long stretches with our ears and find things where no beam of light ever falls!. . .

WOLF: But they find their way about town!. . .

KONZEL: And us they hide in cramped holes! . . . We should sleep during the day, and at night, lights out—*our* realm. Before long, we'd serve as guides to the seeing!. . .

SASHA: The town will never be ours. Town is light. Town is like water gurgling over an abyss constantly threatening us without eyes. Town is glass-thin skin over blood-filled veins that cracks under crutches, that needs dancers!

WOLF: Well, let it crack! . . . Blood is warm! Blood shouldn't scare us, worms housed in the world's intestines!

KONZEL: Shorty is scared. . .

WOLF: And therefore he brags. Liberty makes him anxious.

SASHA: It's just that I have better ears for the night. And every breeze brings me images. . .

KONZEL: Not us?. . .

SASHA: Then they don't grow so big in your brain. . .

WOLF: As if our ears weren't good enough!

SASHA: Psst!. . . Well, what do you hear?. . .

KONZEL: Now? . . . Nothing!

SASHA: I hear footsteps!

WOLF: Sure! He's right! . . .

(A "loaded gentlemen" comes through the passageway. The Blind Men listen.)

KONZEL: Well, who's that?. . .

SASHA: He's looking in every corner. . .

WOLF: Too much celebrating. *He* doesn't see us. Let's just stand silent here!. . .

KONZEL: Let's scare him! And line up quietly along the fence. . .

SASHA: He'll think it's a spook. . .

KONZEL: Maybe this will sober him up. . .

(They line up in a row; the Drunk approaches. When he's about to pass them, they gently clear their throats. He stares at them, but is by no means frightened.)

THE DRUNK: Dear folks. . . dear folks, tonight is New Year's Eve, my dear people. . . *(He throws up.)* The New Year has just come in! . . . For the third time, now! . . . A damnable year! . . . Oh, pardon me! . . . I'm just about done in! . . . I'm a Bolshist. . . . You'll treat me kindly, gentlemen! *(He hands them a bottle he has taken out of his overcoat.)* Here! Take it! I can't any more. . . . It solves troubles, it's rather strong. . . Take it, man, don't you want to?

SASHA: He wants to give us something?. . .

WOLF: Hand it over here! We're blind!. . .

KONZEL: You see, we can't see!. . .

(Wolf has seized the bottle.)

THE DRUNK: *(Not noticeably impressed even by this.)* I see, I see. . . That's fine. . . Very pleasant. . . I see exactly what's coming. . . I'm done for. . . Tonight—still a little drugged. . . Tomorrow—hangover gray! . . . No, tomorrow—holiday! Day after tomorrow—finished. . . I'm a Bolshist. . . What good's wailing? . . . You don't know the latest waltz? . . . *Pas mexicain or cowboy trot.* . . You've seen it already? . . . I'll show you the steps. . . Watch! . . . *(Tries to dance a few steps for his own amusement.)*

SASHA: Simply break off the neck. . .

KONZEL: Careful. . .

WOLF: I have a knife. . .

(Uncorks the bottle. They drink.)

KONZEL: Excellent! Fire in the bones! . . .

THE DRUNK: Simply botched. . . More or less like that. . . A rather intricate feel to it, the latest dance. . . And the key to it lies in the stomach. . . A rather intricate— *(He throws up again.)* Everything's going topsy-turvy! . . . Nothing doing. . . Hangover gray, as far as you can see. . . But let 'em make their own furniture. I'm a Bolshist. . . The entrepreneur is the pulse-beat of the body of culture, gentlemen. . . You've cut open the arteries. . . The blood is tapped. . . The taxes and wages will trumpet us to the grave. . . I'm finished! Now let them make the furniture themselves! They won't sell a single table or chest! I'm running the business for eighteen years, and I know my way. . . Fair and square, with ten per cent! Just work, gentlemen! . . . That's finished. . . Drowned by the overhead. . . Gone under little by little! . . . And nothing more to pour in! We haven't pocketed the jacked-up profits! . . . The result? . . . Bankruptcy! . . . After eighteen years of honest labor! . . . Taken over from father! . . . That's the end! . . . Gone to the devil! . . . Even though you've done your duty! . . . Built up by the father! . . . And by the son. Now comes the great misery. . . Hangover gray. . . *(Exits weeping. The Blind Men laugh.)*

WOLF: So drunk, he's lost his memory!

KONZEL: Full of sweet melancholy. . .

WOLF: The bottle bought here and lost. Nothing, knows nothing any more. . .

(Drinks.)

SASHA: The good Lord sent him to us!

KONZEL: So tastes sweetness too. . . And strong as arrack. Happy New Year!

If Men Played Cards as Women Do

George S. Kaufman
1923

Comic

Setting: John's home. The living room, a card table with four chairs has been set up. The house is comfortable and well decorated.

Scene: John calls through the open door to an unseen servant.

John: The host. 30's – 60's.
Bob: A guest, any age.
George: A guest, any age.
Marc: A guest, any age.

JOHN: And don't forget, I want things served very nicely. Use the best china and the filigree doilies. *(He starts to close the door, remembers another instruction.)* And at eleven o'clock just put the cigars and drinks right on the table and we'll stop playing. *(He closes the door and advances into the room. He looks the place over; rubs a suspecting finger along the table top in a quest for dust. He moves one chair a fraction of an inch and seems to think that makes a difference in the appearance of the room. Then there comes a knock on the outer door. John darts to the mirror and takes a quick look at himself; adjusts his tie.)* Come in! *(Bob enters.)* Hello, Bob!

BOB: Hello, John! I thought I'd run over early to see if I could help you with the lunch.

JOHN: Thanks—everything is ready. I baked a cake. Oh, say! That's a new hat, isn't it?

BOB: Why, no—don't you remember? It's the one I got at Knox's in the Spring. Then when they began wearing the bands higher, I said to myself, why should I buy a new hat when I can have a man in and get him to put on another band for me, just as easily as not? Do you like it?

JOHN: Very attractive. I wonder how it would look on me? *(Takes it; starts to try it on, then smooths his hair before he finally puts it on. He looks at himself in the mirror; turns.)* What do you think?

BOB: Lovely! Makes your face look thinner. *(Looks at the card table.)* Who's playing tonight?

JOHN: George and Marc.

BOB: Really? *(He takes his seat.)* Tell me—don't you think George is looking older these days? How are he and Ethel getting along? Any better?

JOHN: Not as good.

BOB: Funny what she saw in him.

(There is a knock on the door.)

JOHN: Come in!

(George enters.)

GEORGE: *(Greatly surprised, as though they were the last people he had expected to see.)* Hello, boys!

JOHN: Hello, George! Well, well, well!

BOB: *(Rises.)* Hello, George! Never saw you look so young!

GEORGE: *(In great excitement.)* Say, I just met Ed Jennings down the street and what do you think? He says Jim Perkins told him that Will Harper's wife may leave him!

BOB: You don't say so! *(Sits again.)*

GEORGE: What do you think of that? *(His excitement dies a little; he looks around.)* The room looks lovely, John. You've changed things around, haven't you? Awfully nice. But if you don't mind just a little suggestion, I'm not sure that I like that table up there where you've got it. *(Another critical look.)* And if you had these chairs re-upholstered in blue—

JOHN: Well, what do you think of a plain chintz?

GEORGE: That would be nice. Oh, say! I've got a T.L. for you, Bob.

BOB: Oh, good! What is it?

GEORGE: Well, you owe me one first.

BOB: Oh, tell me mine! Don't be mean!

GEORGE: Well, all right. Frank Williams said you looked lovely in your dinner coat.

BOB: This *is* nice.

JOHN: How's the baby, George?

GEORGE: Awfully cranky lately. He's teething. I left him with the nurse tonight—first chance I've had to get out. *(Takes a seat at the table.)* Who else is coming?

JOHN: Just Marc.

GEORGE: *(With meaning.)* Oh, is he? I want to speak to you boys about Marc. Don't you think he's been seeing a lot of that Fleming woman lately?

BOB: He certainly has. He was at the Biltmore, having tea with her yesterday—I know because a cousin of Tom Hennessey's saw him.

JOHN: Which cousin is that?

BOB: I don't know whether you know him—Ralph Wilson. He married that Akron girl—they have two children.

GEORGE: *You* remember, one of them is backward.

JOHN: Oh yes! I heard that *(Another knock on the door.)* Come in! *(Marc enters.)*

MARC: Hello, everybody!

GEORGE, JOHN and BOB: Hello, Marc!

MARC: I'm sorry to be the last, but we have a new maid, and you know what that means.

JOHN: That's all right. Say, I like the cut of that vest, Marc. Look, boys! Don't you like that vest?

MARC: It is nice, isn't it?

GEORGE: Oh, lovely! Turn around and let's see the back.
(George and John both get up and examine his clothes, pull down his trousers, etc.)

MARC: I had it made right in the house—I have a little tailor that comes in. Four dollars a day.

GEORGE: Excuse me—there's a little spot— *(He moistens a finger and rubs Marc's lapel.)*

JOHN: Well, shall we play a little poker?

MARC: *(Sitting.)* Yes, sure. Oh, John, may I trouble you for a glass of water?

JOHN: Why, of course, Marc. *(George and Bob sit again.)*

MARC: I'll get it myself if you'll tell me where—

JOHN: Oh, no—that's all right. *(He goes out. A pause. The men look at each other, meaningly. Their heads come together.)*

MARC: John doesn't look well, does he?

BOB: No. Did you notice those lines? He can't hide them much longer.

MARC: He was very good-looking as a boy.

GEORGE: Isn't this room the most terrible thing you ever saw?
(Marc goes to the table upstage; picks up a cigar and shows it to the others. They are scornful.)

MARC: Huh! Ten cents. *(Pause.)* I really wanted to get that water myself. I'd like to see his kitchen. *(John re-enters with the water.)* Oh, thanks, John. *(Marc drinks.)*

JOHN: Is it cold enough, Marc?

MARC: *(Indicating that it isn't.)* Oh, yes. Of course, I generally put ice in, myself. *(Sits.)*

GEORGE: Say, we had the loveliest new dessert tonight!

BOB: Oh! What was it! It's awfully hard to find a new dessert.

MARC: *(With emphasis.)* Is it?

GEORGE: Well, it was a sort of prune whip. You make it out of just nothing at all. And then, if company comes when you don't expect them—

BOB: I want the recipe.

MARC: How many eggs? *(John up at the rear table. Turns on this speech.)*

JOHN: Does it take much butter?

GEORGE: Oh, no—very little. I'll bring you the recipe Tuesday afternoon.

(Marc feels a rough place on his chin. Rubs it, then takes a good sized mirror out of his pocket and stands it on the table. Examines his chin. Then takes out a safety razor and starts to shave. After that he takes out two military brushes and combs his hair. The others pay no attention to this. John is at the rear table, with his back to the audience; Bob is seated, fooling with the cards; George is seated, calmly smoking. After Marc has put everything away, Bob breaks the silence.)

BOB: Are we ready?

JOHN: No! Wait just a minute. *(He brings down the fancy table cover, which he spreads on the table.)* There we are!

MARC: *(Feeling it.)* That's nice, John. Where'd you get it?

JOHN: Why, I bought a yard of this plain sateen down at Macy's—

GEORGE: Really, How much was it?

JOHN: A dollar sixty-three. It was reduced. Then I had this edging in the house.

BOB: Awfully nice!

MARC: Oh, say! Walter Sharp just got back from Paris—

GEORGE: He did?

MARC: Yes. And *he* says they're wearing trousers longer over there.

GEORGE: Really? *(There is quite a fuss about it.)*

JOHN: *(Brings chips and takes his seat.)* What'll we play for?

BOB: Oh, what's the difference? One cent limit?

GEORGE: Does it matter who deals? *(Takes the cards from Bob.)*

MARC: Say, did you hear about Eddie Parker?

JOHN: No.

MARC: Well, it seems he saw these advertisements about how to get thin, and he thought he'd try them. You know Eddie's taken on a lot of weight since his marriage.

GEORGE: Twenty pounds—absolutely.

MARC: Well, they sent him some powders and he began taking them, and what do you think?

GEORGE: Well? *(Marc whispers to him.)* You don't say so?

JOHN and BOB: *(Excited.)* What was it? What was it?
(George whispers to John, who whispers to Bob; great excitement.)

MARC: Who has the cards?

GEORGE: Here they are. *(Starts to deal—poker hands.)*

MARC: I don't want to play late. I've been shopping all day.

GEORGE: And I have an appointment at the barber's tomorrow. I'm going to try a new way of getting my hair cut.
(The deal is completed.)

BOB: *(Picking up a few cards.)* Which is higher—aces or kings?

GEORGE: Now, who bets first?

JOHN: Are these funny little things clubs?

MARC: What are the chips worth?

JOHN: Let's have them all worth the same thing.

BOB: A penny apiece. . .

GEORGE: Say, Lord & Taylor are having a wonderful sale of nightgowns!

MARC: What do you pay your maid?

BOB: Sixty-five, but she isn't worth it.
(The three start talking at once about maids, and John has a hard time being heard.)

JOHN: *(Excited.)* Boys! Boys! Listen to this! Boys!

ALL: Well?

JOHN: *(Excited.)* I *knew* there was something I wanted to tell you!

ALL: *(They must not speak together.)* What is it?

JOHN: Well, now in the first place you must promise not to breathe a word of it to anybody, because I got it in absolute confidence and I promised I wouldn't tell.

GEORGE: What is it?

MARC: Well?

BOB: Well?

JOHN: It's about Sid Heflin! Now, you won't tell anybody? At least, don't let on you got it from me!

ALL: No!

JOHN: Well, I'm told— and I got this pretty straight, mind you—I'm told that he's going to—ah— *(He puts the message across with this eyes.)*

MARC: I don't believe it!

BOB: What do you mean?

GEORGE: When?

JOHN: In April!

MARC: April!

(They count on their fingers, up to four.)

GEORGE: What do you mean?

JOHN: Exactly! They were married late in January!

(They all throw down their hands and begin talking at once.)
(Curtain.)

Waiting for Godot

Samuel Beckett
1954

Comic
Setting: A country road. A tree. No one around. Evening.
Scene: Estragon (Gogo) and Vladimir (Didi) are waiting for a gentle-
man named Godot to arrive at the place under the tree. Vladmir
seems to feel it is vital to wait for his arrival. He has just offered
Estragon a carrot to enjoy while they wait.

Estragon: A man on the road of life, uncertain age.
Vladimir: His companion on the road, a bit taller, uncertain age.
Pozzo: A landowner, uncertain age.
Lucky: Pozzo's slave, attached by a long rope; carrying many bags and
items for Pozzo—uncertain age.

ESTRAGON: *(Chews, swallows.)* I'm asking you if we're tied.
VLADIMIR: Tied?
ESTRAGON: Ti-ed.
VLADIMIR: How do you mean tied?
ESTRAGON: Down.
VLADIMIR: But to whom? By whom?
ESTRAGON: To your man.
VLADIMIR: To Godot? Tied to Godot! What an idea! No question of
it. *(Pause.)* For the moment.
ESTRAGON: His name is Godot?
VLADIMIR: I think so.
ESTRAGON: Fancy that. *(He raises what remains of the carrot by the
stub of leaf, twirls it before his eyes.)* Funny, the more you eat the
worse it gets.
VLADIMIR: With me it's the opposite.
ESTRAGON: In other words?
VLADIMIR: I get used to the muck as I go along.
ESTRAGON: *(After prolonged reflection.)* Is that the opposite?
VLADIMIR: Question of temperament.
ESTRAGON: Of character.
VLADIMIR: Nothing you can do about it.
ESTRAGON: No use struggling.

VLADIMIR: One is what one is.

ESTRAGON: No use wriggling.

VLADIMIR: The essential doesn't change.

ESTRAGON: Nothing to be done. *(He proffers the remains of the carrot to Vladimir.)* Like to finish it? *(A terrible cry, close at hand. Estragon drops the carrot. They remain motionless, then together make a sudden rush towards the wings. Estragon stops halfway, runs back, picks up the carrot, stuffs it in his pocket, runs to rejoin Vladimir who is waiting for him, stops again, runs back, picks up his boot, runs to rejoin Vladimir. Huddled together, shoulders hunched, cringing away from the menace, they wait. Enter Pozzo and Lucky. Pozzo drives Lucky by means of a rope passed round his neck, so that Lucky is the first to enter, followed by the rope which is long enough to let him reach the middle of the stage before Pozzo appears. Lucky carries a heavy bag, a folding stool, a picnic basket, and a greatcoat, Pozzo a whip.)*

POZZO: *(Offstage.)* On! *(Crack of whip. Pozzo appears. They cross the stage. Lucky passes before Vladimir and Estragon and exit. Pozzo at the sight of Vladimir and Estragon stops short. The rope tautens. Pozzo jerks at it violently.)* Back! *(Noise of Lucky falling with all his baggage. Vladimir and Estragon turn towards him, half wishing half fearing to go to his assistance. Vladimir takes a step towards Lucky, Estragon holds him back by the sleeve.)*

VLADIMIR: Let me go!

ESTRAGON: Stay where you are!

POZZO: Be careful! He's wicked. *(Vladimir and Estragon turn towards Pozzo.)* With strangers.

ESTRAGON: *(Undertone.)* Is that him?

VLADIMIR: Who?

ESTRAGON: *(Trying to remember the name.)* Er . . .

VLADIMIR: Godot?

ESTRAGON: Yes.

POZZO: I present myself: Pozzo.

VLADIMIR: *(To Estragon.)* Not at all!

ESTRAGON: He said Godot.

VLADIMIR: Not at all!

ESTRAGON: *(Timidly, to Pozzo.)* You're not Mr. Godot, Sir?

POZZO: *(Terrifying voice.)* I am Pozzo! *(Silence.)* Pozzo! *(Silence.)* Does that name mean nothing to you? *(Silence.)* I say does that name mean nothing to you? *(Vladimir and Estragon look at each other questioningly.)*

ESTRAGON: *(Pretending to search.)* Bozzo . . . Bozzo . . .

VLADIMIR: *(Ditto.)* Pozzo . . . Pozzo . . .

POZZO: PPPOZZZO!

ESTRAGON: Oh! Pozzo . . . let me see . . . Pozzo . . .

VLADIMIR: Is it Pozzo or Bozzo?

ESTRAGON: Pozzo . . . no . . . I'm afraid I . . . no . . . I don't seem to . . . *(Pozzo advances threateningly.)*

VLADIMIR: *(Conciliating.)* I once knew a family called Gozzo. The mother had the clap.

ESTRAGON: *(Hastily.)* We're not from these parts, Sir.

POZZO: *(Halting.)* You are human beings none the less. *(He puts on his glasses.)* As far as one can see. *(He takes off his glasses.)* Of the same species as myself. *(He bursts into an enormous laugh.)* Of the same species as Pozzo! Made in God's image!

VLADIMIR: Well you see—

POZZO: *(Peremptory.)* Who is Godot?

ESTRAGON: Godot?

POZZO: You took me for Godot.

VLADIMIR: Oh no, Sir, not for an instant, Sir.

POZZO: Who is he?

VLADIMIR: Oh he's a . . . he's a kind of acquaintance.

ESTRAGON: Nothing of the kind, we hardly know him.

VLADIMIR: True . . . we don't know him very well . . . but all the same.

ESTRAGON: Personally I wouldn't even know him if I saw him.

POZZO: You took me for him.

ESTRAGON: *(Recoiling before Pozzo.)* That's to say . . . you understand . . . the dusk . . . the strain . . . waiting . . . I confess . . . I imagined . . . for a second . . .

POZZO: Waiting? So you were waiting for him?

VLADIMIR: Well you see—

POZZO: Here? On my land?

VLADIMIR: We didn't intend any harm.

ESTRAGON: We meant well.

POZZO: The road is free to all.

VLADIMIR: That's how we looked at it.

POZZO: It's a disgrace. But there you are.

ESTRAGON: Nothing we can do about it.

POZZO: *(With magnanimous gesture.)* Let's say no more about it. *(He jerks the rope.)* Up pig! *(Pause.)* Every time he drops he falls asleep. *(Jerks the rope.)* Up hog! *(Noise of Lucky getting up and picking up his baggage. Pozzo jerks the rope.)* Back! *(Enter Lucky backwards.)* Stop! *(Lucky stops.)* Turn! *(Lucky turns. To Vladimir and Estragon, affably.)* Gentlemen, I am happy to have met you. *(Before their incredulous expression.)* Yes yes, sincerely happy. *(He jerks the rope.)* Closer! *(Lucky advances.)* Stop! *(Lucky stops.)* Yes, the road seems long when one journeys all along for . . . *(He consults his watch.)* . . . yes . . . *(He calculates)* . . . yes, six hours, that's right, six hours on end, and never a soul in sight. *(To Lucky.)* Coat! *(Lucky puts down the bag, advances, gives the coat, goes back to his place, takes up the bag.)* Hold that! *(Pozzo holds out the whip. Lucky advances and, both his hands being occupied, takes the whip in his mouth, then goes back to his place. Pozzo begins to put on his coat, stops.)* Coat! *(Lucky puts down the bag, basket and stool, advances, helps Pozzo on with his coat, goes back to his place and takes up bag, basket, and stool.)* Touch of autumn in the air this evening. *(Pozzo finishes buttoning his coat, stoops, inspects himself, straightens up.)* Whip! *(Lucky advances, stoops, Pozzo snatches the whip from his mouth, Lucky goes back to his place.)* Yes, gentlemen, I cannot go for long without the society of my likes *(He puts on his glasses and looks at the two likes.)* even when the likeness is an imperfect one. *(He takes off his glasses.)* Stool! *(Lucky puts down bag and basket, advances, opens stool, puts it down, goes back to his place, takes up bag and basket.)* Closer! *(Lucky puts down bag and basket, advances, moves stool, goes back to his place, takes up bag and basket. Pozzo sits down, places the butt of his whip against Lucky's chest and pushes.)* Back! *(Lucky takes a step back.)* Further! *(Lucky takes another step back.)* Stop! *(Lucky stops. To Vladimir and Estragon.)* That is why, with your permission, I propose to dally with you a moment, before I venture any further. Basket! *(Lucky advances, gives the basket, goes back to his place.)* The fresh air stimulates the jaded appetite. *(He opens the basket, takes out a piece of chicken and a bottle of wine.)* Basket! *(Lucky advances, picks up the basket and goes back to his place.)* Further! *(Lucky takes a step back.)* He stinks. Happy days! *(He drinks from the bottle, puts it down and begins to eat.*

Silence. Vladimir and Estragon, cautiously at first, then more boldly, begin to circle about Lucky, inspecting him up and down. Pozzo eats his chicken voraciously, throwing away the bones after having sucked them. Lucky sags slowly, until bag and basket touch the ground, then straightens up with a start and begins to sag again. Rhythm of one sleeping on his feet.)

ESTRAGON: What ails him?

VLADIMIR: He looks tired.

ESTRAGON: Why doesn't he put down his bags?

VLADIMIR: How do I know? *(They close in on him.)* Careful!

ESTRAGON: Say something to him.

VLADIMIR: Look!

ESTRAGON: What?

VLADIMIR: *(Pointing.)* His neck!

ESTRAGON: *(Looking at the neck.)* I see nothing.

VLADIMIR: Here. *(Estragon goes over beside Vladimir.)*

ESTRAGON: Oh I say!

VLADIMIR: A running sore!

ESTRAGON: It's the rope.

VLADIMIR: It's the rubbing.

ESTRAGON: It's inevitable.

VLADIMIR: It's the knot.

ESTRAGON: It's the chafing. *(They resume their inspection, dwell on the face.)*

VLADIMIR: *(Grudgingly.)* He's not bad looking.

ESTRAGON: *(Shrugging his shoulders, wry face.)* Would you say so?

VLADIMIR: A trifle effeminate.

ESTRAGON: Look at the slobber.

VLADIMIR: It's inevitable.

ESTRAGON: Look at the slaver.

VLADIMIR: Perhaps he's a halfwit.

ESTRAGON: A cretin.

VLADIMIR: *(Looking closer.)* Looks like a goiter.

ESTRAGON: *(Ditto.)* It's not certain.

VLADIMIR: He's panting.

ESTRAGON: It's inevitable.

VLADIMIR: And his eyes!

ESTRAGON: What about them?

VLADIMIR: Goggling out of his head.

ESTRAGON: Looks at his last gasp to me.

VLADIMIR: It's not certain. *(Pause.)* Ask him a question.

ESTRAGON: Would that be a good thing?

VLADIMIR: What do we risk?

ESTRAGON: *(Timidly.)* Mister . . .

VLADIMIR: Louder.

ESTRAGON: *(Louder.)* Mister . . .

POZZO: Leave him in peace! *(They turn towards Pozzo who, having finished eating, wipes his mouth with the back of his hand.)* Can't you see he wants to rest? Basket! *(He strikes a match and begins to light his pipe. Estragon sees the chicken bones on the ground and stares at them greedily. As Lucky does not move Pozzo throws the match angrily away and jerks the rope.)* Basket! *(Lucky starts, almost falls, recovers his senses, advances, puts the bottle in the basket, and goes back to his place. Estragon stares at the bones. Pozzo strikes another match and lights his pipe.)* What can you expect, it's not his job. *(He pulls at his pipe, stretches out his legs.)* Ah! That's better.

ESTRAGON: *(Timidly.)* Please Sir . . .

POZZO: What is it, my good man?

ESTRAGON: Er . . . you've finished with the . . . er . . . you don't need the . . . er . . . bones, Sir?

VLADIMIR: *(Scandalized.)* You couldn't have waited?

POZZO: No no, he does well to ask. Do I need the bones? *(He turns them over with the end of his whip.)* No, personally I do not need them any more. (Estragon takes a step towards the bones.) But . . . *(Estragon stops short)* . . . but in theory the bones go to the carrier. He is therefore the one to ask. *(Estragon turns toward Lucky, hesitates.)* Go on, go on, don't be afraid, ask him, he'll tell you. *(Estragon goes towards Lucky, stops before him.)*

ESTRAGON: Mister . . . excuse me, Mister . . .

POZZO: You're being spoken to, pig! Reply! *(To Estragon.)* Try him again.

ESTRAGON: Excuse me, Mister, the bones, you won't be wanting the bones? *(Lucky looks long at Estragon.)*

POZZO: *(In raptures.)* Mister! *(Lucky bows his head.)* Reply! Do you want them or don't you? *(Silence of Lucky. To Estragon.)* They're yours. *(Estragon makes a dart at the bones, picks them up, and begins to gnaw them.)* I don't like it. I've never known him to refuse a bone before. *(He looks anxiously at Lucky.)* Nice business it'd be if he fell sick on me! *(He puffs at his pipe.)*

VLADIMIR: *(Exploding.)* It's a scandal! *(Silence. Flabbergasted, Estragon stops gnawing, looks at Pozzo and Vladimir in turn. Pozzo outwardly calm. Vladimir embarrassed.)*

POZZ: *(To Vladimir.)* Are you alluding to anything in particular?

VLADIMIR: *(Stutteringly resolute.)* To treat a man . . . *(Gesture toward Lucky)* . . . like that . . . I think that . . . no . . . human being . . . no . . . it's a scandal!

ESTRAGON: *(Not to be outdone.)* A disgrace! *(He resumes his gnawing.)*

POZZO: You are severe. *(To Vladimir.)* What age are you, if it's not a rude question? *(Silence.)* Sixty? Seventy? *(To Estragon.)* What age would you say he was?

ESTRAGON: Eleven.

POZZO: I am impertinent. *(He knocks out his pipe against the whip, gets up.)* I must be getting on. Thank you for your society. *(He reflects.)* Unless I smoke another pipe before I go. What do you say? *(They say nothing.)* Oh I'm only a small smoker, a very small smoker, I'm not in the habit of smoking two pipes one on top of the other, it makes *(Hands to heart, sighing.)* my heart go pit-a-pat. *(Silence.)* It's the nicotine, one absorbs it in spite of one's precautions. *(Signs.)* You know how it is. *(Silence.)* But perhaps you don't smoke? Yes? No? It's of no importance. *(Silence.)* But how am I to sit down now, without affectation, now that I have risen? Without appearing to—how shall I say—without appearing to falter. *(To Vladimir.)* I beg you pardon? *(Silence.)* Perhaps you didn't speak? *(Silence.)* It's of no importance. Let me see . . . *(He reflects.)*

ESTRAGON: Ah! That's better. *(He puts the bones in his pocket.)*

VLADIMIR: Let's go.

ESTRAGON: So soon?

The Deputy

Rolf Hochhuth
1963

Dramatic

Setting: The reception room of the Papal Legation in Berlin, 1942.

Scene: Thus far in the war, the Pope, Pope Pius the Twelfth has not
    interceded on behalf of persecuted Jews or Catholics. Riccardo
    asks a question of the Nuncio.

Nuncio: His Excellency Cesare Orsenigo, 69, vigorous, self-disciplined
    from Milan now living in Berlin during Hitler's reign. Head of the
    Papal delegation in Berlin.

Father Riccardo Fontana: A priest, 27.

Lt. Kurt Gerstein: 37, Hitler's SS Armed Forces.

Father: A priest of the Papal Legation.

RICCARDO: You think then, Your Excellency,
    that Herr Hitler will *have to* listen to reason?
NUNCIO: Oh yes! He will even prefer to.
    We saw that at Dunkirk, after all.
    He left the British make their getaway. His policy
    was obviously moderation in victory.
    I grant you, Mr. Churchill gave him no thanks for it . . .
    Please do have some more cake . . .
    With the Spaniards and the French,
    the Balkan nations and the Italians,
    the Belgians and above all his own Catholics
    here in Germany, all of them
    willingly or not supporting his crusade
    against Moscow—with half of Europe
    Catholic, even Hitler cannot risk a schism.
    If he should brand us enemies of state,
    the Rome-Tokyo-Berlin Axis would fall apart.
    It's fortunate that at this very moment
    Japan is making every effort
    to sign a Concordat with us.
    The efforts of the White House to prevent it
    only serve to prove

how eagerly both sides are courting us.
On Sunday in St. Hedwig's,
during the bishop's ordination ceremonies,
I saw a lieutenant of the SS. He went to confession,
took Communion—oh no,
where the Church is concerned, Herr Hitler
remains a realist.
He wants the nations helping him in Russia
to go on backing him when he is forced
to negotiate with England and the U.S.A.
Consider how in the United States
day by day the Catholics power grows—
Herr Hitler has to reckon with that, too.
He will discover what his friends, Franco
and Mussolini, learned long ago:
Fascism is invincible only *with* us,
when it stands with the Church and not against it.
Molotov saw that ten years ago;
in 1934 Molotov admitted
that if the Church in Germany
should strike up an accord with the Hitlerites—
and at the time there were some signs of that;
a promising beginning had been made—
then Communism in Europe would be finished . . .
What's that, what's the commotion?
What's going on out there?
(The Nuncio rises, remains standing and listening a moment, then goes toward the door to the waiting room, murmuring to himself. There is an excited altercation backstage; people begin to shout. The Father is heard, his dialect thickening as his voice grows louder. Amid fragmentary phrases, only half intelligible, sounds the insistent, pleading voice of a man who is obviously holding himself in check with difficulty in the effort to remain polite.)

BOTH: *(Backstage.)* You're in uniform!
But—you *must* announce me!
The Legation is extraterritorial—be off with you
or I'll send for the police.
Please, give me five minutes with His Excellency.

The Nuncio has a visitor from Rome.
He *must* hear me.
Anything the likes of you may want to say
is no affair of ours.
(Riccardo, intrigued, has moved back against the wall, while the Nuncio opens the door to the waiting room. The SS officer, Kurt Gerstein, bursts in, cap in hand. The Father tries to block his way and then to push him out again.)

GERSTEIN and FATHER: *(Simultaneously.)* Your Excellency, isn't this the limit?
I must speak with Your Excellency, just for
two minutes—please—I beg you!
Shall I call the police?
Pushing his way in like this . . . who every heard . . . ?

NUNCIO: What's going on? Whatever are you thinking of?

GERSTEIN: Gerstein is my name, Your Excellency—please
hear me out. I have a message
for the Vatican that . . .

NUNCIO: Sir, I am astounded
that you invade this building in this manner . . .
I suppose your headquarters
are on Prinz Albrecht Strasse . . .
(The Father has hurried across the room to a telephone. He lifts the receiver. Gerstein dashes after him, saying.)

GERSTEIN: Your Excellency, please, no phone calls.
If headquarters were to hear of this visit . . .

NUNCIO: *(Gesturing to the Father to put down the telephone.)*
You call this scene a visit?

FATHER: *(Quickly.)* Go now, just get out of here.

GERSTEIN: *(Just as quickly.)* Your Excellency, a message for the Vatican.
It will not bear a single day's delay,
not one single hour. I have just come from Poland—
from Belzec and Treblinka, northeast of Warsaw.
Your Excellency, daily,
every single day in those places,
ten thousand Jews, *more*
than ten thousand,
are being murdered, put to death with gas. . .

NUNCIO: For God's sake, hold your tongue!

Tell that to Herr Hitler, not to me.
Leave this place.
In the German Government's view
I am not authorized
to say a word about these . . .
these conditions in Poland.

GERSTEIN: *(A shout.)* Your Excellency!

NUNCIO: Who are you, anyhow? I am not authorized,
I tell you, to have any dealings
with members of the German Armed Forces . . .
Are you Catholic? In any case I request you
to leave at once . . . Go, go.

(His Excellency is determined not to hear confirmation of such monstrous crimes. For he is basically a man of deep humanity, and official acknowledgment of this message would make it difficult for him to continue to deal with Weizsäcker as he has done in the past, "indifferently, without much distinction, in a calm spirit and friendly manner.")

FATHER: *(Has gone to the door, holds it open and says very mildly.)*
Well now, will you be off at last.

GERSTEIN: *(Loses his temper, shuts the door violently and strides up to the Nuncio. He speaks jerkily, under great stress.)*
Your Excellency, every hour I see trains pull in
bringing fresh loads from all of Europe to those death factories. . .
No, I am not Catholic. But Pastor Buchholz
who cares for the condemned in Plötzensee
is my friend. Another reference I can give
is Superintendent Otto Dibelius and Church Councilman
Hermann Ehlers. Before he was arrested,
Pastor Niemöller of Dahlem. . .

NUNCIO: *(Politely but very firmly.)* All very well, but I regret
I must now terminate this . . .
I'm very sorry, but you'll have to go.

GERSTEIN: Speak to von Otter
of the Swedish Embassy, Your Excellency.
At this point, only the Vatican can intervene.
You must help, sir!

NUNCIO: *(Indignant, since he does not know what to do.)*
Why do you come to *me*?

You yourself are wearing the uniform of the murderers.

I tell you, I have no authority to interfere.

GERSTEIN: *(Shouting.)* Authority! Here in Berlin you represent
the—the Deputy of Christ,

and you can close your eyes to the worst horror

that man has ever inflicted upon man.

You hold your peace while every hour . . .

NUNCIO: Control yourself . . . keep your voice down . . .
we don't shout here.

I am terminating this conversation now . . .

GERSTEIN: *(Pleading.)* No, please, I beg your pardon.

I know very well, Your Excellency—you can't do anything.

But the Holy Father must take action,

must speak for the world's conscience. . .

*(The Nuncio withdraws; he does not go all the way through the
door to his study only because Riccardo resists following him.
Riccardo stands listening in fascination to Gerstein.)*

GERSTEIN: Your Excellency, please, listen to me;

(As if in a trance.) I can't bear it any more—I've seen it—I see it
all the time—it haunts me right to this room.

Listen . . . the. . . I must tell you about it . . .

*(Covering his eyes, Gerstein drops into a chair. He rises to his feet
at once, not looking at any of the others in the room; his gaze is
turned inward and his eyes have a wild, restlessly flickering
expression. [Thus Frau Bälz described him in her report to the
Institute for Contemporary History. His nocturnal conversation
with Frau Bälz took place at about the same time as his ineffec-
tual call on the Nuncio. Baron von Otter, the Secretary of the
Swedish Embassy, writes that Gerstein told his tale to him in the
aisle of the train "weeping and in a broken voice."]*

*The following passage is spoken in a great variety of tones. At
times Gerstein's sentences taper off into inarticulate murmurs;
then again he speaks loudly, distraughtly, or in a series of brief
outcries, like someone crying out in his sleep. After the first few
sentences the Nuncio takes several steps toward him. The Father
closes the door, but stays in the room, while Riccardo keeps his
eyes on the Nuncio so probingly that his look verges on the insult-
ing.)*

GERSTEIN: *(abruptly.)* So far they've been running the gas chambers
on carbon monoxide, common exhaust gas.
But many times the motors will not start
In Belzec recently I had to watch—
this was on August 20—
while the victims waited two hours and forty-nine minutes
until the gas came on.
Seven hundred and fifty persons
in each of four chambers—
each room with a volume of sixty cubic yards—
three thousand human beings.
Some pray, some weep, some shriek.
The majority keep silent.
The gassing operation takes twenty-five minutes.
Now they want to speed it up,
and so they've brought me in for consultation.
I am an engineer and medical man.
(Screams.) I will not do it, I will not do it . . .
Like marble columns the naked corpses stand.
You can tell the families, even after death
convulsed in locked embrace—with hooks
they're pulled apart. Jews have to do that job.
Ukrainians lash them on with whips.
(He can no longer concentrate, loses himself in details, his eyes vacant.)
There was the manager of Berlin's biggest store . . .
There was a violinist, too, decorated in World War I . . .
Fought at the front for Germany.
And bodies of dead children. A young girl
ahead of the procession, naked like the rest.
Mothers, all stripped, babies at their breasts.
Most of them know the worst—the smell of gas . . .
NUNCIO: *(Starting to leave.)* Enough—I cannot listen any more.
You Germans, why! Why . . .
My dear man, my heart is with the victims.
GERSTEIN: Your Excellency, the Vatican
has made a pact with Hitler!
Yet you can see it in the streets, here in Berlin,
in Oslo, Paris, Kiev—for more than a year

you have seen, *every* priest has seen
how they're rounding up the Jews. The Allied radio
reports that thousands upon thousands
are being exterminated.
When, Your Excellency, when
will you tear up the Concordat?
RICCARDO: *(Overwhelmed.)* Your Excellency, all this agrees completely
with the reports my Order has received,
but no one could quite credit them.
NUNCIO: *(With genuine concern, deeply moved but helpless.)*
My dear Father, please keep out of this . . .
Why doesn't this man go to Herr Hitler!
(Gerstein gives a terrible laugh.)
RICCARDO: *(Pleading.)* But he is not an agent provocateur,
Your Excellency . . . Count Ledochowsky has received
the same sort of reports from Poland . . .
NUNCIO: *(Tried beyond his patience, losing composure.)*
Why does he come to *me*? The Curia
is not here to aggravate strife.
God has charged it with the mission
to work for peace . . .
GERSTEIN: Peace with murderers too? Your Excellency!
(He points to the painting of the Crucified Christ and exclaims.)
Cursed are the peacemakers!
He felt He was authorized, Your Excellency—
but His Deputy does not?
NUNCIO: *(Deeply moved and paternal.)*
Herr Ger—stensteiner, compose yourself!
I share your sorrow for the victims.
GERSTEIN: *(Screaming.)* Every *hour*, Your Excellency, *every* hour
thousands more are killed—those are factories
for killing. Factories, won't you understand?
NUNCIO: Please, sir—whatever my own feelings in this matter,
I cannot simply take account of them.
I intervened, in private, as far back as
nineteen thirty-nine. But I am charged
by my position not to involve myself
in any cause of conflict between Rome
and your authorities. I should not even have

to talk with you—please,
you must go. Go now, please.
God bless you, God help you.
I shall pray for the victims.
(He beckons to Riccardo to follow him, walks to the backstage door and opens it.)
Father, please come—I must insist.

RICCARDO: Your name is Gerstein—I will find you.
(Gerstein pays no attention to these words; he sees only that he has accomplished nothing. The Nuncio has returned to Riccardo, puts his hand on his shoulder and propels him almost forcibly through the door to the study. Before the Nuncio can close the door, Gerstein follows him once more, passionate, beside himself.)

GERSTEIN: Your Excellency, listen you must hear
the dying words of an old Jewish woman—
as she was driven on by whips into the gas
she called down on the murderers' heads
the blood they're spilling there. That blood guilt,
Excellency, falls upon us all
if we keep silent!

NUNCIO: *(Turning once more, softly.)* Compose yourself. Pray!
(Exit. The Father closes the door behind him and speaks mildly.)

FATHER: Have some sense, man, how can you
come at His Excellency like this?
Can he help it? Now please, take yourself off.
There isn't anything one of us can do.

GERSTEIN: *(Has realized that he has lost. One more pointless attempt; he reaches into his coat pocket, takes out a batch of papers, and tries to interest the Father in them.)*
Here is more proof—look at them!
Orders from the camp commandants
of Belzec and Treblinka
for the delivery of hydrocyanide.

In New England Winter

Ed Bullins
1967

Dramatic

Setting: Cliff's room, 1960.

Scene: Cliff has served time for robbery. Now, he is out and the four friends are planning an elaborate robbery and have met to go over the plan.

Steve: 24, a brooding, rational man—a dark-complexioned black man.
Cliff: 29, his half-brother; large, husky, lighter-complexion; worldly.
Bummie: 27, a loyal friend; a bully, athletic, black.
Chuckie: 27, a follower, quiet, fears for his future, black.

BUMMIE: It's too goddam hot to do anything . . . even fuck.

STEVE: *(Stares at Cliff.)* So you're going out tonight?

CHUCKIE: Aww, Steve. Ain't nothin' gonna happen if Cliff takes his . . .

STEVE: I was talking to Cliff.

CLIFF: Chuckie didn't mean nothin', Steve. Besides . . . he's right.

BUMMIE: Chuckie right?

CHUCKIE: Nawh, man . . . I was just . . .

STEVE: All of us, especially you and me. Cliff, have to be sharp for the scene we gonna make tomorrow. We're not kids . . .

CLIFF: I know that!

BUMMIE: Hey . . . why don't we get started?

STEVE: I said we're not kids, anymore. We're not knocking over a candy store like in our junior flip days. This . . .

CLIFF: Yeah, I know as much about the job as you do, Steve.

BUMMIE: *(Under his breath.)* That goddamn Chuckie . . .

STEVE: Then you know how important it is to have everything perfect?

CHUCKIE: But we been rehearsing for days.

BUMMIE: Shut up, Chuckie . . . let's get . . .

CHUCKIE: Lissen, man!

STEVE: Yeah, and we gonna rehearse tonight. A dress rehearsal.

CHUCKIE: I ain't gonna take anymore . . .

CLIFF: Quiet! Everybody! *(Pause.)* Steve . . . you still going through with it, huh?

STEVE: What do you think?

CLIFF: What about tonight?

STEVE: The rehearsal and everything else.

CHUCKIE: Aww . . . sheet.

STEVE: Just like we planned.

BUMMIE: Well, man . . . you guys don't need me.

STEVE: Get into your costume, Chuckie . . . And you help him, Bummie.

BUMMIE: Look Steve!

CLIFF: Bummie!

CHUCKIE: Aww, man, it's too hot to wear all that stuff. *(Appeals to Cliff.)* Aww, man, do I got to do that?
(Pause. Sounds of music and traffic come through the window. A neon sign goes on outside and casts colored shadows.)

STEVE: Yeah.

CHUCKIE: *(protesting.)* Look, man I don't like this . . . I ain't funny or nothin' like that.

BUMMIE: Ain't nobody said you was . . . you coppin'out?

CLIFF: He don't have to dress up, do he, Steve?

CHUCKIE: I ain't gonna take no more of your shit, Bummie!

BUMMIE: I ain't gonna help this mathafukker, man!

STEVE: That's what I said, Cliff. I want a sense of realism brought into this room.

CLIFF: Ain't we real enough? Ain't this heat real enough for you?

STEVE: We can't rely upon distorted senses of reality to . . .

CLIFF: Okay, Professor . . . can the textbook speeches. *(Abrupt.)* Chuckie, go get ready.

BUMMIE: But, man . . .

CLIFF: You too, Bummie.

CHUCKIE: Cliff, you not gonna make me . . .

STEVE: Chuckie! . . . We're waiting.
(Chuckie mutters, picks up a small suitcase and enters the bathroom. Bummie follows, muttering.)

STEVE: Why do you keep them around, Cliff?

CLIFF: Chuckie? . . . Bummie? . . . They're good boys, that's why. Chuckie's one of my best boys, and we need a good driver for this job.

STEVE: Good boy . . . Good flunky . . .

CLIFF: *(Correcting.)* Good driver.

STEVE: Good flunky driver.

CLIFF: Suit yourself, Steve. Suit yourself.

STEVE: And Bummie?

CLIFF: That's your department, ain't it, brother? Guns and things?

STEVE: It didn't have to be Bummie. He's your boy.

CLIFF: That was a long time ago, Steve.

STEVE: *(Iintense.)* No . . . it was yesterday . . . *yesterday*.

CLIFF: But you know how good he is . . . we need him. And we all grew up together, didn't we? We all fought each other. Bummie didn't hassle no more than you . . . He's even aimed at us on occasion . . . just like . . .

STEVE: At me, not you!

CLIFF: *(Insincere.)* Ha ha . . . it's still in the family.

STEVE: *(Disgust.)* A fool . . . a thug . . . and two . . .

CLIFF: Well, we have different tastes, brother, don't we?

STEVE: That nigger knocked me down, put his foot on my chest and aimed a .38 at my head.

CLIFF: It's over.

STEVE: Cops and niggers . . . that's what it was.

CLIFF: It was a long time ago.

STEVE: In his monkey mind he was playin' white cop . . . and I was just a nigger he could . . .

CLIFF: Let it ride, Steve. It's waited this long.

STEVE: Let it ride? . . . Yeah . . . let it ride.

CLIFF: Steve?

STEVE: Humm . . . ?

CLIFF: We are only half brothers but what do you think makes us so different and still be brothers?

STEVE: *(Joking.)* Our mother.

CLIFF: Huh?

STEVE: Forget it. *(Cliff lifts his beer.)* Do you have to drink so much?

CLIFF: It's good for fighting off my distorted sense of reality. *(Silence. Music plays. Steve looks at his watch and walks to the window.)* You still think about Liz, don't you?

STEVE: Liz? . . . Yeah.

CLIFF: That's been a long time too, Steve.

STEVE: Less long.

CLIFF: But you're about as far away from it as you can get.

STEVE: *(Regret.)* You know . . . I think about her all the time.

(Reminiscing.) It's snowing up there now. Snowing . . . Big white white flakes. Snow. Silent like death must be.

CLIFF: Our deaths will be roaring hot.

STEVE: The dying will . . . not the death . . .

CLIFF: Red and orange and blue . . .

STEVE: Death must be still and black and deep.

CLIFF: . . . with white heat reaching all around us.

STEVE: Deathly cold.

CLIFF: Hell is a safe place for black boys.

STEVE: And Christians.

CLIFF: But private.

STEVE: Well . . . it's hot enough here. I don't even know what I'm doing here . . . This place . . . heat, smog, cars, Freeways . . . in January. I don't even know wha . . .

CLIFF: For me when a broad is out of sight . . . you know how the saying says, man . . . The only time I worry about a broad is when I can't get another one.

STEVE: Which is hardly ever, right, Cliff?

CLIFF: And you like that cold ass New England.

STEVE: I'm not so crazy about the place.

CLIFF: That's why you doin' this job, ain't it? . . . so you can get back up there. How you say it? "I need some travelin' money."

STEVE: Yeah, so I can go and see my woman. What's the matter with that? I'm not like you. I don't have a different board for every day of the month.

CLIFF: (Casual.) Oh . . . I strike out sometimes . . . Like tonight, for instance . . . (Chuckles.) I had to go and make a date with my ole faithful . .

STEVE: Sandy?

CLIFF: Who else? Sandra.

(Pause. Steve changes position. He saunters about and looks out front as if he were looking for someone beyond the window. Cliff finishes his beer, snuffs out his cigarette and goes for another drink.)

STEVE: Are you gonna marry her?

CLIFF: Sandy?

STEVE: Yeah, Sandra.

CLIFF: Are you joking?

STEVE: You think so? You been using her all these years and treating here like a puppy . . . I thought you might marry her.

CLIFF: *(Annoyed.)* Aww . . . Come off that bullshit, man! Have you been marryin' all those bitches you been fuckin' around with?

STEVE: But they don't mean nothin' to me . . . they're just fillin' in time.

CLIFF: Oh, that's the new name for it.

STEVE: Sandy loves you. You like her . . . You'd . . .

CLIFF: Look . . . you know better than to even ask me somethin' like am I gonna get married.

STEVE: Lou was a good while ago.

CLIFF: If it was a thousand years it would be like this morning . . . I sat in a cell . . . I sat in a cell one day draggin' it's behind after the other . . . waitin' to get out . . . waitin' to see her, to touch her . . . smell and taste her.

STEVE: But you were in prison for years, Cliff.

CLIFF: So? *(Mocking.)* And I was in prison for years . . . Hahh! . . . She didn't even send me a letter to tell me . . . I got home and found you had moved into the bedroom . . . she and my baby gone . . . and you . . . the master bedroom, *brother*.

STEVE: How can you expect someone to wait for you forever when you're in the slammers? You were sent up for murder.

CLIFF: It wasn't but for five years. I was out in three and then some.

STEVE: She only did what was human.

CLIFF: *(Ridicule.)* Human?

STEVE: You're not easy to live with, you know. And she had your kid to take care of after you were gone.

CLIFF: Human . . . you call leavin' me up there and takin' my son human?

STEVE: You know how Lou is. You know she'll never take relief.

CLIFF: But she took my blood . . . And then what did she do?

STEVE: She did what she had to do . . . I know . . . I was there.

CLIFF: What did she do then?

STEVE: She had that other baby . . . but . . .

CLIFF: *(Accusing.)* You were there . . . *brother* . . . you were there. Was that necessary?

STEVE: She got lonely. That guy started comin' around . . . She was a grown woman . . . what could I say to her?

CLIFF: You could have cut his throat . . . you could have cut his nuts off . . . that's what I would have done in your place.

STEVE: Cliff!

CLIFF: *(Hate.)* You won't even tell me his name . . . you bastard!

STEVE: *(Softer.)* Cliff.

CLIFF: Does he have a name, Steve?

STEVE: It's been a long time, Cliff.

CLIFF: You should have reminded her of where I was an . . . and why I was there.

STEVE: You didn't kill that boy Red because of her . . . It was . . .

CLIFF: Oh, shut up, Steve!

STEVE: *(Angry.)* Like she did . . . like Lou did because you beat the sound out of her?

CLIFF: You're all knowledge you learned from some books you borrowed from the library and never returned.

STEVE: You won't listen . . . you want to hear everything except the reason why you think everything happens to you!

CLIFF: You're the always filled second seat in the second row of some second-rate night course.

STEVE: Attacking me won't get you your wife and son back.

CLIFF: Then if I talk pretty to you, brother, dear . . . you might whistle for them and they might come trotting back?

STEVE: Can't we talk sense sometime?

CLIFF: *(Angry.)* I know why I killed a man . . . and she knows why I was in that jail and she has a debt that she hasn't even begun to pay off to me yet.

STEVE: And will it be paid?

CLIFF: You're fuckin' "A" right it will, Steve . . . Fuckin' "A" . . . in blood . . . in blood.

(Expressionless, Steve looks at him for a while then turns to the bathroom door.)

STEVE: CHUCKIE . . . BUMMIE . . . get the hell out of here!

(The door cracks.)

CHUCKIE: *(Mutters.)* Just wait a minute . . . We'll be out.

STEVE: We've waited long enough . . . c'mon!

(Chuckie enters followed by Bummie; Chuckie wears a dress and pink female mask with blond wig. As Chuckie moves into the room, Bummie shoves him, causing him to stumble.)

CHUCKIE: Sonna a bitch!

(Chuckie turns and shoves Bummie in the chest. Bummie falls back; angered, he regains his balance and rushes Chuckie, launching a haymaker that misses. In fear, Chuckie pushes out a weak jab that connects upon Bummie's nose, squirting blood in several directions. As they both realize their shock and predicament, Steve and Cliff grab them and wrestle them to different sides of the room.)

BUMMIE: LET ME GO! GODDAMMIT! . . . CLIFF . . . LET ME GO SO I CAN KILL HIM!

CLIFF: Come on, Bummie, babe. Forget it.

BUMMIE: Forget hell! I'm gonna kill that mathafukker! . . . Turn me loose so I can kill that sonna bitch.

(Steve has released Chuckie.)

CHUCKIE: *(Calm and confident.)* That's okay, Cliff . . . let him go if he's that much a fool.

BUMMIE: *(Scared, his nose bleeding profusely.)* I'm gonna kill him . . . you black mathafukker!

STEVE: Take him in the bathroom so he can clean up, Cliff!

CLIFF: *(Pulls Bummie half-heartedly toward the bathroom.)* C'mon . . . Bummie . . . you need some cold compresses on that nose. It might be broke.

BUMMIE: *(half-heartedly resisting.)* Mathafukker! I'm gonna take this out of your ass, Chuckie!

CHUCKIE: Yeah, man . . . yeah . . . I know . . . You gonna do numbers and shit cucumbers . . . I know.

(Cliff maneuvers Bummie into the bathroom; the door slams. Sound of water from faucets and muffled cursing. Steve laughs.)

STEVE: You better straighten your wig, man.

CHUCKIE: *(Distracted by noises in bathroom.)* Yeah . . . yeah . . .

(Chuckie looks in mirror and fixes his mask and wig.)

STEVE: And, Chuckie . . .

CHUCKIE: *(Engrossed.)* Ahuh?

STEVE: Your seams could stand straightening.

(Cliff comes out of the bathroom.)

CHUCKIE: *(Perceiving.)* Hey, wait a minute, man . . . look . . .

(Cliff and Steve laugh.)

CLIFF: Ha ha . . . ole bad Bummie the Bruiser walked into a one-man windmill.

STEVE: Man . . . ha ha . . . man, I wouldn't have missed this for any-
thing.
(They laugh more.)
CLIFF: Did you see the look on Bummie's face?
STEVE: Yeah . . . pure shock and terror . . . ha ha . . .
CLIFF: Wait till I tell everybody . . . Bummie's rep will be lower than
whale shit . . . ha ha ha . . .
CHUCKIE: *(Muffled behind the mask.)* Hey, you guys . . . don't laugh
at me.
CLIFF: Bummie . . . smashed by a little blond girl.
STEVE: *(Smiles.)* It's okay, Chuckie. You look just fine.
CLIFF: *(Laughs.)* Yeah . . . you look so sweet, honey.
CHUCKIE: *(Turns.)* Awww, man . . . I ain't goin' for this.
STEVE: C'mon . . . take your places. Knock it off, Cliff. And turn off
that radio.
CLIFF: It's a good station, Steve. And maybe girlie here will want to
kick up her legs and dance some.
CHUCKIE: Fuck you, Cliff! *(Chuckie moves toward Cliff.)*
CLIFF: *(Mimics John Wayne.)* Now look'a here boy . . . don't get car-
ried away cause you smashed Bummie with a sucker punch. I'm
still twice the man that both of you are together . . . if you don't
believe it . . . I'll turn you over mah knee, young lady.
STEVE: Lighten up, Cliff.
CHUCKIE: Just stop laughin' at me . . . that's all.
STEVE: Let's go you guys. This is our last night.
CLIFF: Okay . . . okay . . . but that girlie sure looks nice. Ha ha ha . . .
You gonna let me take you out tonight, baby?
*(Chuckie mutters a curse. He turns off the radio. They move into
place; Chuckie pulls out the table and stands behind it. Cliff and
Steve walk into the closet.)*
CLIFF: Man, I don't like walkin' into this closet . . . it's too much like
jail.
STEVE: Get in place and concentrate on the character.
CLIFF: Sure is funky.
*(The door is shut. Pause. The closet door opens. Steve steps out,
followed by Cliff; they wear black sunglasses, and guns are in
their hands.)*
STEVE: *(To Chuckie.)* All right, Miss. Don't say anything and keep your
hands where I can see them. (*He moves around the table and*

takes Chuckie by the arms and maneuvers him to the center of the room. Cliff walks around them and pantomimes the action of someone taking money from a safe, stuffing it in a briefcase.) Okay, Miss. Now lay down on the floor and put your arms behind you. C'mon, now! I ain't gonna hurt you if you do like I say. Lay down like I said!

(Chuckie lays down on his stomach and puts his hands behind his back. Quickly, Steve ties his hands with a nylon cord taken from his pocket. To Cliff.)

STEVE: Okay, Cliff. *(Cliff pantomimes the action of someone taking money from a safe and stuffs it in his briefcase.)* Okay, Miss. Now lay down on the floor . . .

CHUCKIE: I'm already . . .

STEVE: Okay, skip that part! *(He pantomimes the action of tying Chuckie. To Cliff.)* Okay? *(Cliff nods and closes his briefcase.)* Then go. *(Cliff walks around the front of the table, out of the sight of Chuckie, takes off his sunglasses and walks into the closet. Steve kneels beside Chuckie and twists the ropes about his wrists.)* Now, Miss, I'm going to leave you like this. No gag. Nothin' . . . I don't want you gettin' choke before your boss comes back from lunch. But if I hear any noise out of you before five minutes . . . I'm going to come back here and stomp that nice face of yours . . . Understand?

(Chuckie nods. Steve stands, walks around the table and enters the closet.)

CHUCKIE: Hey, Cliff . . . Steve . . . How bout getting' me loose? Hey! *(Bummie emerges from the bathroom with a wet towel held to his nose and a switchblade knife in his hand.)*

BUMMIE: You goddamn mathafukker . . .

CHUCKIE: *(Apprehensive.)* Hey, man . . . I'm tied . . .

(Steve and Cliff enter from the closet.)

CLIFF: What you gonna do, Bummie . . . carve up the fatted calf?

CHUCKIE: I'm gonna cut this mathafukker's throat.

STEVE: But his hands are tied, killer.

BUMMIE: I don't care . . . I'm gonna cut his eyes out and send them home to his mama . . .

CHUCKIE: *(Scared.)* Hey . . . get this crazy sonna bitch away from me . . . he's gonna kill me.

CLIFF: Nawh . . . I don't think he's gonna kill ya, Chuckie.

STEVE: Cut you up some, maybe . . . but not kill ya.

CHUCKIE: Well . . . don't just stand there . . . keep him away from me!

BUMMIE: *(Bending over Chuckie.)* Shut up, mathafukker! It ain't gonna do you no good to holler.

CLIFF: *(Soft.)* Bummie.

CHUCKIE: Pleez, you guys . . .

CLIFF: *(Threatening.)* Bummie!

STEVE: The man said Bummie, Bummie.

BUMMIE: You guys keep out of this . . . this is between me and Chuckie.

CLIFF: Put the knife on the table, Bummie.

BUMMIE: *(Belligerent.)* Who's gonna make me?

STEVE: On the table, Bummie.

BUMMIE: *(Doubtful.)* Don't try and stop me.

CLIFF: You lookin' to die . . . friend.

STEVE: Slow.

BUMMIE: He's got it comin'.

CLIFF: The table.

(Bummie puts the knife on the table; he raises his foot above Chuckie's face.)

BUMMIE: I should step on your head, punk!

CLIFF: Why don't you go get some beer, Bummie?

STEVE: *(Untying Chuckie.)* Wait until I get Chuckie loose . . . he can go with you.

CHUCKIE: Hey . . . man . . . you shouldn't tie up a guy helpless like that. Anything could happen to him.

The Ceremony of Innocence

Ronald Ribman

1967

Dramatic

Setting: Christmas Day, 1013. A room in the monastery.

Scene: The King, Ethelred, has retired to a remote monastery just as the Danes are about to invade England. Here, two of the Earls seek to hold counsel with the King.

The Earl of Sussex: 30's – 40's, landowner and soldier.
The Earl of Kent: 30's – 40's, landowner and soldier.
Aelfhun: Bishop of London, 40's – 50's.
Abbot Oswald: Head of the monastery on the Isle of Wight.

SUSSEX: I come from the king this once and then I come no more. I am not a man that begs. If he will not of his own return with us, then I have done with him.

KENT: Really?

SUSSEX: *(Emphatically.)* Once I have done, I have done.

KENT: And having done with him, what will you do, Sussex? Return to your shire?

SUSSEX: I will defend my shire. I will do as my men expect of me.

KENT: Then I take it your men expect to die.

SUSSEX: If it comes to that.

KENT: Oh, rest assured, my dear Sussex, it will come to that. You will not keep the Danes out of your shire three months.

SUSSEX: Then I will not keep the Danes out three months!

KENT: *(To the Bishop.)* Listen to the logic of this.

SUSSEX: I am a soldier.

KENT: Your military credentials are always in our mind.

SUSSEX: The thought of death does not frighten me so much that I am content to grow blind imagining Ethelred will return. I come this once for the king, and then no more. If he will not defend his lands, then let the Danes have them. When they come to Sussex, they will find the land burnt beneath their feet.

KENT: Wonderful.

SUSSEX: No Danish plow will ever furrow my land.

KENT: Brilliant. *(To the Bishop.)* Sussex imagines that once his imperial skull has hit the earth the entire universe shall wind down. The spring will not come round again. The rain will not fall again. Birds will of a sudden develop black tongues and fail to offer seasonal twitterings. *(To Sussex.)* Well, you may burn your land as you will, but the land will be washed clean again, the spring will come again, and the Danes will plant your land, eat at your table, and if they find your bed sufficiently comfortable they will lift their dirty boots upon it and sleep in it.

SUSSEX: No man sleeps in Sussex's bed, but Sussex! Before they touch what is mine it will be burnt to the ground.

KENT: *(To the Bishop.)* There you have it, Your Grace, the military mind in all its pristine intricacy. Chop down the trees. Poison the wells. Fire the crops. *(To Sussex.)* Burn less and keep more! I do not find spite so delicious that I am willing to substitute my possessions for it.

SUSSEX: Then let Ethelred act. Let that goddamn marshmallow quit this monastery. I am ready to fight. I am ready to kill these bastard Danes.

KENT: Yes, Sussex. Yes! Yes!

SUSSEX: We waste our time coming here. Place is colder than an Irish tit. *(Walks a few feet away. The Bishop speaks to Kent.)*

BISHOP: There is a monastery at Jarrow like to this one, a place where for want of leather to make shoes the monks go barefoot, or if they are fortunate, they find a piece of cloth and cord and bind them about their feet. All the winter long the wind blows along the floor freezing the stones you kneel upon, icing even as you pray.

KENT: Pray for what?

BISHOP: The death of the man who prays beside me, for when he dies I shall steal his blanket, yea, and if they think to bury him in his woolen habit, to cheat me, to rob me of my expectations, I pray they die as well, or that Christ gave me the cunning to steal the wool from out the grave. I never saw a monk die at Jarrow, but that the brothers stripped him naked and thought themselves blessed to fall into such a profit of clothes.

KENT: Then you are well out of such a place.

BISHOP: I have grown used to serving God in London. Though saints and fanatics may think otherwise, I have never served God better than I do today with pitchy fires burning in the sacristy and velvet padding stuffed beneath the kneeling rail. I pray Ethelred remembers his comforts as well.

SUSSEX: *(Overhearing some of the conversation.)* Or maybe Ethelred'll sit with his ass against a stone wall and a blanket hanging over his head. That's more likely, isn't it?

KENT: You think so, Sussex? Well, with a little patience we'll find out, won't we?

SUSSEX: The son of a bitch never had the guts it takes to pull a herring out of the water.

KENT: The trouble with you, Sussex, is that you tend to judge people by the size of their mouths. I should assure you that there are some men smaller than their mouths. As a matter of fact, I should assure you that there are some men who, if they did not vent upon the void a steady stream of foul air, we should be great danger of losing sight of entirely.

SUSSEX: You saying something to me, rosebush?

KENT: Nobody ever really says anything to you, Sussex. Haven't you ever noticed that?

SUSSEX: What's that supposed to mean? *(Kent in exasperation raises his eyes to the ceiling. Sussex imitates him.)* What's that supposed to mean?

KENT: Nothing. Absolutely nothing.

SUSSEX: What's nothing supposed to be? Some kind of philosophy? *(Raises his eyes again.)* You talking to somebody in the woodwork? *(Stares at Kent.)* Well, you can take your philosophy and piss on some flower with it, Kent. You and Ethelred make a real pack. You know what I mean, Kent? A real pack. Two fuddies without enough piss in their skirts to water a geranium.

KENT: If you'll bring your face over here, I'll water that.

BISHOP: I think it would be best if we found a way to be less argumentative.

SUSSEX: Then tell him to shut his mouth. *(Returns to his corner of the room.)* Half the men in my sire are dead because of him and that pansy-bush of a king.

KENT: They're dead because you marched them to Grimsby without any orders.

SUSSEX: They were my men, not yours, not Ethelred's. What were we supposed to do? The truce was violated. The Danes were at Grimsby. Were we supposed to wait until they walked into

London? Where were you and Ethelred when we were fighting one man to six at Grimsby? Where were you when we were dying? *(To the Bishop.)* They were sitting on their ass in London. That's where they were.

KENT: You don't look any the worse for it.

SUSSEX: *(Deeply enraged; his voice grows ominously calm.)* Sometime, Kent, when your back is to the wall, call for me.

KENT: As a matter of fact, it strikes me as somewhat odd that you have come back from Grimsby at all. Half his men lost at Grimsby, but Sussex, sworn by a blood oath to stand by these men to the death, somehow, miraculously, returns. Miracle of miracles.

SUSSEX: I could not save them.

KENT: Of course.

SUSSEX: I would have given my life to save those men.

KENT: Doubtless. *(Sussex moves toward Kent. The Bishop steps between.)*

BISHOP: There is no man here, Sussex, that doubts your courage in the face of death. You have proven yourself too many times for that. *(Kent turns away. They stand for a moment in silence until Abbot Oswald enters. He goes over to the Bishop and kisses his ring.)*

ABBOT: Your Grace. *(Turning to Kent and Sussex.)* My lords.

BISHOP: How does King Ethelred fare today, Abbot Oswald?

ABBOT: He holds to his cell, Your Grace.

SUSSEX: *(With over sarcasm.)* At his prayers?

ABBOT: He remains at confession.

SUSSEX: So much to confess? Is there so much to confess?

ABBOT: His Majesty finds it so, my lord.

SUSSEX: Well, we find it extraordinary. Those of us closest to Ethelred have always found him so full of grace and piety that confession always seemed more a matter of form than necessity.

ABBOT: Nevertheless His Majesty is still in confession.

SUSSEX: Well, let him get done confessing. The Danes don't give a damn about his confessing.

KENT: The military situation is delicate, Reverend Father. The Danish fleet sits at Grimsby waiting only a favorable turn in the weather to sail up the Humber. Once that is accomplished England lies split in two. If the king does not move the army north within the week, King Sweyn will be in London before spring. The Danish king will take the throne of England.

SUSSEX: Then we'll all be out on our ass. Even those of us fingering beads in monasteries.

ABBOT: What you say may be true, my lords, but I cannot alter these military matters. This island sits of itself in the ocean, and we within the confines of the monastery sit walled within our devotions. We may not concern ourselves with political disputations.

SUSSEX: You may not concern yourself with political disputations? Well, you may. You may! What the hell else does the Church concern itself with if not political disputations?

ABBOT: What is it you wish of me?

KENT: Access to the king. We must speak with him.

ABBOT: He will not quit his cell, my lord; beyond the confessor he permits no one to enter.

BISHOP: Reverend Father, will you tell the king that we have come upon matters most urgent, and that we are content to wait until it pleases him to see us? We do not desire to interfere with his confession, save only that the needs of England . . .

SUSSEX: Now! We have to see him now! Tell him now!

ABBOT: I will do what I can. *(Bows to the Bishop and Earls.)* Your Grace. My lords. *(Exits.)*

SUSSEX: *(Imitating the Abbot.)* We may not concern ourselves with political disputations.

KENT: *(Violently angry.)* Why don't you shut your mouth?

SUSSEX: Who the hell do you think you're talking to?

KENT: You! I'm talking to you! Save your brilliant retorts for your horse. I'm sure your horse lives for them.

BISHOP: *(Futilely.)* We quarrel too much. *(They both stare at the Bishop. Lights out.)*

Streamers

David Rabe
1977

Dramatic

Setting: The barracks room of Roger, Richie, and Billy. Basic Training. The men know they may be shipped out to Vietnam.

Scene: Richie has been flirting with Carlyle, inviting him to their room, hinting about having sex. Roger and Billy are horrified and do not want to leave their room. Richie is taunting them, especially Billy, whom he believes is in denial about his homosexuality.

Carlyle: Late teens, 20's, black, wild, frightened, a drinker and a fighter.

Roger: Late teens, 20's, black, neat, orderly, plays by the rules, smart and loyal.

Richie: Late teens, early 20's, white, effeminate, outspoken, flirtatious, honest, fun-loving.

Billy: Late teens, 20's, white, straight, afraid he might have gay tendencies, good friends with Roger, tries to always do the right thing.

CARLYLE: (*Shifting now for a more comfortable position, he moves his head to the pillow at the top of the bed.*) Richie first saw me, he didn't like me much nohow, but he thought it over now, he changed his way a thinkin'. I can see that clear. We gonna be one big happy family.

RICHIE: Carlyle likes me, Billy; he thinks I'm pretty.

CARLYLE: (*Sitting up a little to make his point clear.*) No, I don't think you pretty. A broad is pretty. Punks ain't pretty. Punk—if he good-lookin'—is cute. You cute.

RICHIE: He's gonna steal me right away, little Billy. You're so slow, Bill. I prefer a man who's decisive. (*He is lying down now on the floor at the foot of his bed.*)

BILLY: You just keep at it, you're gonna have us all believin' you are just what you say you are.

RICHIE: Which is more than we can say for you. (*Now Roger rises on his elbow to light a cigarette.*)

BILLY: Jive, jive.

RICHIE: You're arrogant, Billy. So arrogant.

BILLY: What are you—on the rag?

RICHIE: Wouldn't it just bang your little balls if I were!

ROGER: *(To Richie.)* Hey, man. What's with you?

RICHIE: Stupidity offends me; lies and ignorance offend me.

BILLY: You know where we was? The three of us? All three of us, earlier on? To the wrong side of the tracks, Richard. One good black
upside-down whorehouse you get what you buy, no jive along
with it—so if it's a lay you want and need, you go! Or don't they
have faggot whorehouses?

ROGER: IF YOU GUYS DON'T CUT THIS SHIT OUT I'M GONNA BUST
SOMEBODY'S HEAD! *(Angrily he flops back on his bed. There is
a silence as they all lie there.)*

RICHIE: "Where we *was,*" he says. Listen to him. "Where we *was.*"
And he's got more school, Carlyle, than you have fingers and . . .
*(He has lifted his foot onto the bed; it touches, presses, Carlyle's
foot.)* . . . toes. It's this pseudo-earthy quality he feigns—but
inside he's all cashmere.

BILLY: That's a lie. *(Giggling, he is staring at the floor.)* I'm polyester,
worsted, and mohair.

RICHIE: You have a lot of school, Billy; don't say you don't.

BILLY: You said "fingers and toes"; you didn't say "a lot."

CARLYLE: I think people get dumber the more they put their butts
into some schoolhouse door.

BILLY: It depends on what the hell you're talkin' about. *(Now he looks
at Carlyle, and sees the feet touching.)*

CARLYLE: I seen cats on the block, they knew what was shakin'—then
they got into all this school jive and, man, every year they went,
they come back they didn't know nothin'.

*(Billy is staring at Richie's foot pressed and rubbing Carlyle's foot.
Richie sees Billy looking. Billy cannot believe what he is seeing. It
fills him with fear. The silence goes on and on.*

RICHIE: Billy, why don't you and Roger go for a walk?

BILLY: What? *(He bolts to his knees. He is frozen on his knees on the
bed.)*

RICHIE: Roger asked you to go downtown, you went, you had fun.

ROGER: *(Having turned, he knows almost instantly what is going on.)*
I asked you, too.

RICHIE: You asked me; you begged Billy. I said no. Billy said no. You

took my ten dollars. You begged Billy. I'm asking you a favor now—
go for a walk. Let Carlyle and me have some time. *(Silence.)*

CARLYLE: *(He sits up, uneasy and wary.)* That how you work it?

ROGER: Work what?

CARLYLE: Whosever turn it be.

BILLY: No, no, that ain't the way we work it, because we don't work it.

CARLYLE: See? See? There it is—that goddamn education showin'
through. All them years in school. Man, didn't we have a good
time tonight? You rode in my car. I showed you a good cathouse,
all that sweet black pussy. Ain't we friends? Richie likes me. How
come you don't like me?

BILLY: 'Cause if you really are doin' what I think you're doin', you're a
fuckin' animal!
*(Carlyle leaps to his feet, hand snaking to his pocket to draw a
weapon.)*

ROGER: Billy, no.

BILLY: NO, WHAT?!

ROGER: Relax, man; no need. *(He turns to Carlyle; patiently, wearily,
he speaks.)* Man, I tole you it ain't goin' on here. We both tole
you it ain't goin' on here.

CARLYLE: Don't you jive me, nigger. You goin' for a walk like I'm
askin', or not? I wanna get this clear.

ROGER: Man, we live here.

RICHIE: It's my house, too, Roger; I live here, too. *(Richie bounds to
his feet, flinging the blanket that has been covering him so it flies
and lands on the floor near Roger's footlocker.)*

ROGER: Don't I know that? Did I say somethin' to make you think I
didn't know that? *(Standing, Richie is removing his trousers and
throwing them down on his footlocker.)*

RICHIE: Carlyle is my guest. *(Sitting down on the side of his bed and
facing out, he puts his arms around Carlyle's thigh. Roger jumps
to his feet and grabs the blanket from the foot of his bed.
Shaking it open, he drops onto the bed, his head at the foot of
the bed and facing off as he covers himself.)*

ROGER: Fine. He your friend. This your home. So that mean he can
stay. It don't mean I gotta leave. I'll catch you all in the mornin'.

BILLY: Roger, what the hell are you doin'?

ROGER: What you better do, Billy. It's gettin' late. I'm goin' to sleep.

BILLY: What?

ROGER: Go to fucking bed, Billy. Get up in the rack, turn your back and look at the wall.

BILLY: You gotta be kiddin'.

ROGER: DO IT!

BILLY: Man . . . !

ROGER: Yeah . . . !

BILLY: You mean just . . .

ROGER: It been goin' on a long damn time, man. You ain't gonna put no stop to it.

CARLYLE: You . . . ain't . . . serious.

RICHIE: *(Both he and Carlyle are staring at Roger and then Billy, who is staring at Roger.)* Well, I don't believe it. Of all the childish . . . infantile . . .

CARLYLE: Hey! *(Silence.)* HEY! I got to say this a little weird, but if this the way you do it . . . *(And he turns toward Richie below him.)* . . . it the way I do it. I don't know.

RICHIE: With them right there? Are you kidding? My God, Carlyle, that'd be obscene. *(Pulling slightly away from Carlyle.)*

CARYLE: Ohhh, man . . . they backs turned.

RICHIE: No.

CARLYLE: What I'm gonna do? *(Silence. He looks at them, all three of them.)* Don't you got no feelin' for how a man feel? I don't understand you two boys. Unless'n you a pair of motherfuckers. That what you are, you a pair of motherfuckers? You slits, man. DON'T YOU HEAR ME!? I DON'T UNDERSTAND THIS SITUTION HERE. I THOUGHT WE MADE A DEAL! *(Richie rises, starts to pull on his trousers. Carlyle grabs him.)* YOU GET ON YOUR KNEES, YOU PUNK, I MEAN NOW, AND YOU GONNA BE ON MY JOINT FAST OR YOU GONNA BE ONE BUSTED PUNK. AM I UNDER-STOOD? *(He hurls Richie down to the floor.)*

BILLY: I ain't gonna have this going on here; Roger, I can't

ROGER: I been turnin' my back on one thing or another all my life.

RICHIE: Jealous, Billy?

BILLY: *(Getting to his feet.)* Just go out that door, the two of you. Go. Go on out in the bushes or out in some field. See if I follow you. See if I care. I'll be right here and I'll be sleepin', but it ain't gonna be done in my house. I don't have much in this goddamn army, but *here* is mine. *(He stands beside his bed.)*

Streamers

David Rabe
1977

Dramatic

Setting: The barracks room of Roger, Richie, and Billy. Basic Training. The men know they may be shipped out to Vietnam.

Scene: Richie has been flirting with Carlyle, inviting him to their room, hinting about having sex. Roger and Billy are horrified and do not want to leave their room. Richie is taunting them, especially Billy, whom he believes is in denial about his homosexuality.

Carlyle: Late teens–20's, black, wild, frightened, a drinker and a fighter.

Roger: Late teens–20's, black, neat, orderly, plays by the rules, smart and loyal.

Richie: Late teens–early 20's, white, effeminate, outspoken, flirtatious, honest, fun-loving.

Billy: Late teens–20's, white, straight, afraid he might have gay tendencies, good friends with Roger, tries to always do the right thing.

CARLYLE: I WANT MY FUCKIN' NUT! HOW COME YOU SO UPTIGHT? HE WANTS ME! THIS BOY HERE WANTS ME! WHO YOU TO STOP IT?

ROGER: *(Spinning to face Carlyle and Richie)* That's right, Billy. Richie one a those people want to get fucked by niggers, man. It what he know was gonna happen all his life—can be his dream come true. Ain't that right, Richie! *(Jumping to his feet, Richie starts putting on his trousers.)* Want to make it real in the world, how a nigger is an animal. Give 'em an inch, gonna take a mile. Ain't you some kinda fool, Richie? Here me, Carlyle.

CARLYLE: Man, don't make me no nevermind what he think he's provin' an' shit, long as I get my nut. I KNOW I ain't no animal, don't have to prove it.

RICHIE: *(Pulling at Carlyle's arm, wanting to move him toward the door.)* Let's go. Let's go outside. The hell with it. *(But Carlyle tears himself free; he squats furiously down on the bunk, his hands seizing it, his back to all of them.)*

CARLYLE: Bullshit. Bullshit! I ain't goin' no-fuckin' where—this jive ass ain't runnin' me. Is this you house or not? *(He doesn't know what is going on; he can hardly look at any of them.)*

ROGER: *(Bounding out of bed, hurling his pillows across the room.)* I'm goin' to the fuckin' john, Billy. Hang it up, man; let 'em be.

BILLY: No.

ROGER: I'm smarter than you—do like I'm sayin'.

BILLY: It ain't right.

ROGER: Who gives a big rat's ass!

CARLYLE: Right on, bro? That boy know; he do. *(He circles the bed toward them.)* Hear him. Look into his eyes.

BILLY: This fuckin' army takin' everything else away from me, they ain't takin' more than they got. I see what I see—I don't run, don't hide.

ROGER: *(Turning away from Billy, he stomps out the door, slamming it.)* You fuckin' well better learn.

CARLYLE: That right. Time for more schoolin'. Lesson number one. *(Stealthily he steps and snaps out the only light, the lamp clamped to Richie's bed.)* You don't see what you see so well in the dark. It dark in the night. Black man got a black body—he disappear. *(The darkness is so total they are all no more than shadows.)*

RICHIE: Not to the hands; not to the fingers. *(Moving from across the room toward Carlyle.)*

CARLYLE: You do like you talk, boy, you gonna make me happy. *(As Billy, nervously clutching his sneaker, is moving backward.)*

BILLY: Who says the lights go out? Nobody goddamn asked me if the lights go out. *(Billy, lunging to the wall switch, throws it. The overhead lights flash on, flooding the room with light. Carlyle is seated on the edge of Richie's bed, Richie kneeling before him.)*

CARLYLE: I DO, MOTHERFUCKER, I SAY! *(And the switchblade seems to leap from his pocket to his hand.)* I SAY! CAN'T YOU LET PEOPLE BE? *(Billy hurls his sneaker at the floor at Carlyle's feet. Instantly Carlyle is across the room, blocking Billy's escape out the door.)* Goddamn you, boy! I'm gonna cut your ass, just to show you how it feel—and cuttin' can happen. This knife true.

RICHIE: Carlyle, now c'mon.

CARLYLE: Shut up, pussy.

RICHIE: Don't hurt him, for chrissake.

CARLYLE: Goddamn man throw a shoe at me, he don't walk around clean in the world thinkin' he can throw another. He get some shit come back at him. *(Billy doesn't know which way to go, and then Carlyle, jabbing the knife at the air before Billy's chest, has Billy running backward, his eyes fixed on the moving blade. He stumbles, having run into Richie's bed. He sprawls backward and Carlyle is over him.)* No, no; no, no. Put your hand out there. Put it out. *(Slight pause; Billy is terrified.)* DO THE THING I'M TELLIN'! *(Billy lets his hand rise in the air and Carlyle grabs it, holds it.)* That's it. That's good. See? See? *(The knife flashes across Billy's plam; the blood flows. Billy winces, recoils, but Carlyle's hand still clenches and holds.)*

BILLY: Motherfucker. *(Again the knife darts, cutting, and Billy yelps. Richie, on his knees beside them, turns away.)*

RICHIE: Oh, my God, what are you—

CARLYLE: *(In his own sudden distress, Carlyle flings the hand away.)* That you blood. The blood inside you, you don't ever see it there. Take a look how easy it come out, and enough of it come out— you in the middle of the worst goddamn trouble you ever gonna see. And know I'm the man can deal that kinda trouble, easy as I smile. And I smile . . . easy. Yeah. *(Billy is curled in upon himself, holding the hand to his stomach as Richie now reaches tentatively and shyly out as if to console Billy, who repluses the gesture. Carlyle is angry and strangely depressed. Forlornly he slumps onto Billy's footlocker as Billy staggers up to his wall locker and takes out a towel.)* Bastard ruin my mood, Richie. He ruin my mood. Fightin' and lovin' real different in the feelin's I got. I see blood come outa somebody like that, it don't make me feel good—hurt me—hurt on somebody I thought was my friend. But I ain't sup- posed to see. One dumb nigger. No mind, he thinks, no heart, no feelings a gentleness. You see how that ain't true, Richie. Goddamn man threw a shoe at me. A lotta people woulda cut his heart out. I gotta make him know he throw shit, he get shit. But I don't hurt him bad, you see what I mean? *(Billy's back is to them, as he stands hunched at his locker, and suddenly his voice, hissing, erupts.)*

BILLY: Jesus . . . H . . . Christ . . . ! Do you know what I'm doin'? Do you know what I'm standin' here doin'? *(He whirls now; he holds a straight razor in his hand. A bloody towel is wrapped around the hurt hand. Carlyle tenses, rises, seeing the razor.)* I'm a twenty-four-year-old goddamn college graduate—intellectual goddamn scholar type—and I got a razor in my hand. I'm thinkin' about comin' up behind one black human being and I'm thinkin' nigger this and nigger that—I wanna cut his throat. THAT IS RIDICULOUS. I NEVER FACED ANYBODY IN MY LIFE WITH ANY-THING TO KILL THEM. YOU UNDERSTAND ME? I DON'T HAVE A GODDAMN THING ON THE LINE HERE! *(The door opens and Roger rushes in, having heard the yelling. Billy flings the razor into his locker.)* Look at me, Roger, look at me. I got a cut palm—I don't know what happened. Jesus Christ, I got sweat all over me when I think a what I was near to doin'. I swear it. I mean do I think I need a reputation as a killer, a bad man with a knife?

(He is wild with the energy of feeling free and with the anger at what these others almost made him do. Carlyle slumps down on the footlocker; he sits there.) Bullshit! I need shit! I got sweat all over me. I got the mile record in my hometown. I did forty-two in high school and that's the goddamn record in Windsor County. I don't need approval from either one of the pair of you. *(And he rushes at Richie.)* You wanna be a goddamn swish—a goddamn faggot-queer—go! Suckin' cocks and takin' it in the ass, the thing of which you dream, go! AND YOU— *(Whirling on Carlyle.)* You wanna be a bad-assed animal, man, get it on, go, but I wash my hands. I am not human as you are. I put you down, I put you down— *(He almost hurls himself at Richie.)* You gay little piece a shit cake—SHIT CAKE. AND YOU, *(Hurt, confused, Richie turns away, nearly pressing his face into the bed beside which he kneels, as Billy has spun back to tower over the pulsing, weary Carlyle.)* —you are your own goddamn fault, SAMBO! SAMBO! *(And the knife flashes up in Carlyle's hand into Billy's stomach, and Billy yelps.)* Ahhhhhhhhhhh. *(And pushes at the hand. Richie is still turned away.)*

RICHIE: Well, fuck you, Billy.

BILLY: *(He backs off the knife.)* Get away, get away.

RICHIE: *(As Roger, who could not see because Billy's back is to him, is approaching Carlyle and Billy goes walking up towards the lockers as if he knows where he is going, as if he is going to go out the door and to a movie, his hands holding his belly.)* You're so-o messed up.

ROGER: *(To Carlyle.)* Man, what's the matter with you?

CARLYLE: Don't nobody talk that weird shit to me, you understand?

ROGER: You jive man. That's all you do—jive! *(Billy, striding swiftly, walks flat into the wall lockers; he bounces, turns. They are all looking at him.)*

RICHIE: Billy! Oh, Billy! *(Roger looks at Richie.)*

BILLY: Ahhhhhhhh. Ahhhhhh. *(Roger looks at Carlyle as if he is about to scream, and beyond him, Billy turns from the lockers, starts to walk again, now staggering and moving toward them.)*

RICHIE: I think . . . he stabbed him. I think Carlyle stabbed Billy. Roger! *(Roger whirls to go to Billy, who is staggering downstage and angled away, hands clenched over his belly.)*

BILLY: Shut up! It's just a cut, it's just a cut. He cut my hand, he cut gut. *(He collapses onto his knees just beyond Roger's footlocker.)* It took the wind out of me, scared me, that's all. *(Fiercely he tries to hide the wound and remain calm.)*

ROGER: Man, are you all right? *(He moves to Billy, who turns to hide the wound. Till now no one is sure what happened. Richie only "thinks" Billy has been stabbed. Billy is pretending he isn't hurt. As Billy turns from Roger, he turns toward Richie and Richie sees the blood. Richie yelps and they all begin talking and yelling simultaneously. Overlapping:)*

CARLYLE: You know what I was learnin', he was learning' to talk all that weird shit, cuttin', baby, cuttin', the ways and means a shit, man, razors.

ROGER: You all right? Or what? He slit you?

BILLY: Just took the wind outa me, scared me.

RICHIE: Carlyle, you stabbed him; you stabbed him.

CARLYLE: Ohhhh, pussy, pussy, pussy, Carlyle know what he do.

ROGER: *(Trying to lift Billy.)* Get up, okay? Get up on the bed.

BILLY: *(Irritated, pulling free.)* I am on the bed.

ROGER: What?

RICHIE: No, Billy, no, you're not.

BILLY: Shut up!

RICHIE: You're on the floor.

BILLY: I'm on the bed. I'm on the bed. *(Emphatically. And then he looks at the floor.)* What?

ROGER: Let me see what he did. *(Billy's hands are clenched on the wound.)* Billy, let me see where he got you.

BILLY: (Recoiling.) NO-O-O-O-O-O-O, you nigger!

ROGER: (He leaps at Carlyle.) What did you do?

CARLYLE: (Hunching his shoulders, ducking his head.) Shut up.

ROGER: What did you do, nigger, you slit him or stick him? (And then he tries to get back to Billy.) Billy, let me see.

BILLY: (Doubling over till his head hits the floor.) N-O-O-O-O-O! Shit, Shit, Shit.

RICHIE: (Suddenly sobbing and yelling.) Oh, my God, my God, Ohhhh, ohhhh, ohhhh. (Bouncing on his knees on the bed.)

CARLYLE: FUCK IT, FUCK IT, I STUCK HIM. I TURNED IT. This mother army break my heart. I can't be out there where it pretty, don't wanna live! Wash me clean, shit face!

RICHIE: Ohhhh, ohhhh, ohhhhhhhhhhh. Carlyle stabbed Billy, oh, ohhhh, I never saw such a thing in my life. Ohhhhh. (As Roger is trying gently, fearfully, to straighten Billy up) Don't die, Billy; don't die.

ROGER: Shut up and go find somebody to help. Richie, go!

RICHIE: Who? I'll go, I'll go. (Scrambling off the bed.)

ROGER: I don't know. JESUS CHRIST! DO IT!

RICHIE: Okay. Okay. Billy, don't die. Don't die. (Backing for the door, he turns and runs.)

ROGER: The sarge, or C. Q.

BILLY: (Suddenly doubling over, vomiting blood. Richie is gone.) Ohhhhhhhhhhh. Blood. Blood.

Stopwatch

Jon Jory
1983

Dramatic
Setting: A locker room.
Scene: The team has just lost a race in a dual meet with the USSR.
    They are dressing. Donny sits with his head in his hands.

The mile relay team at UCLA, late teens–early 20's:
    Don
    Art
    Arnie
    Todd

TODD: I love it, man. I mean, I wouldn't trade it for diamonds, man.
    You see the look on Kostilyoff's face? I'm tellin' ya his damn eye-
    brows just kept archin' up 'til they got lost in his hairline, man. He
    twisted around tryin' to see if you dropped it or not, like this, see,
    and he shortened up on his stride 'til he looked like he was doin'
    Swan Lake an' when you burned past him he drained so white he
    looked like a bleach commercial! I mean it was the best, man, we
    went in without a chance and we came out *immortal*.

ART: We came out second. In a dual meet, that's dead last.

TODD: We ran a mile, we got there first, right?

ART: We got there first without the baton, Todd. If there is something
    dumber you can do in the mile relay, perhaps you'd like to point
    it out to me?

TODD: So?

ART: You're joking with me, right?

TODD: You run against yourself or you run against the opposition,
    man?

ART: You oughta send out for a red nose and a funny hat.

TODD: Personal bests. Am I right? Every single quarter. Every single
    one of us, man. I carved two-eighths. You carved a one-sixteenth.
    Arnie carved a mother one-half, man. He carved one-half! And
    my man, my man, Don the Juan, he gets a *full second*, burns the
    best quarter-miler in the world by ten feet, and makes me fall
    down laughing flat on my butt in front of forty thousand people.

ARNIE: We lost the race, Todd. You comprende? The Russians won the race; we lost the race. Personal best and fifty cents will buy you a cup of coffee.

TODD: So?

ARNIE: It was the last go. The last year. The last meet. We will never, ever, ever run together again and we blew it! We ran up to five hours a day for four years. We trained thousands of miles, thousands. We got cramps, we got tendonitis, we pulled hamstrings. We ran one hundred an' sixty races, and when it was showtime, we screwed up. Now stop making the story of the century out of it. Pull up your pants and let's get on with our lives. *(A pause.)*

ART: *(To Don.)* Hey. Hey. Forget it. Hey. You dropped it. That doesn't matter. What matters is why you dropped it. If you know *why* you dropped it, it doesn't matter that you dropped it.

DON: *(Looking at him.)* It was the Russians.

ART: Who cares who it was.

DON: *I* care.

ART: Wrong.

DON: I *care*.

ART: And I say it's wrong. You didn't drop it because it was the Russians. Get it straight. Learn from it. That's what it's for. *(He extends his left hand, thumb straight up, fingers relaxed and slightly curved up.)* Were you flexed one hundred eighty?

DON: Yeah, no. I don't know.

ART: You were flexed one-eighty. It was copasetic. Then what?

DON: He burned me.

ART: That's right. He blazed out off the pass and you thought, "He doesn't run the quarter like that. That ain't in the films. What the heck's going on here?" He made you *think*, fella. And where'd the thumb go?

DON: *(Softly.)* Dropped it down.

ART: Did what?

DON: *(Angrily.)* Dropped it down. You heard me.

ART: You dropped it down, right. So where the stick should of hit joint, it hit tip. But you still had it, you still had it, except for one thing . . . you were up the track after your man with no concentration on the stick. So what did you do wrong?

TODD: Hey, slack up, Art.

ART: You got competitive. You tried to beat the man instead of run your race.

TODD: This is a pretty scene. Four ex-runners who just finished their college careers, having broken their own U.S. record seven times, and just ate the Soviets in their own event thus closing out *outstanding* athletic careers and will be long remembered passed on in song and story, proved, proved beyond a shadow of a doubt, that the baton no longer has any place in a mile relay. In other words are no longer going to run like maniacs in short pants. Perhaps these retired runners should stop beating a dead horse.

ART: It's all technique and strategy, Todd. We spent all this time trying to go *faster*. Refined ourselves. And what we did it for, which you've had a very hard time keeping straight, was not to win races, or get dates, or to restore the national honor, it was to learn how to go faster. So what counts to Don is not that he should be cheered up, or find screwing-up amusing, or forget the whole thing. He should close out trying to see how to go faster. The point is not that we lost the race. The point is he *dropped* his *thumb*. The point is he should go out with that habit in mind.

ARNIE: No.

ART: That isn't the point?

ARNIE: No. The point is we prepared for one thing spring, summer, winter, fall. We prepared for the *last* time we'd do it. The point *was* for the last time to be the best. The best! The point was to see if we could put it together at a point we chose to say it *would* be together.

TODD: *(Declaiming.)* To be masters of our fate and captains of our soul!

ARNIE: You think that's funny?

TODD: *(Not particularly defensive.)* No, but I think you're funny.

ARNIE: *(Simply.)* I wanted to see if I could do one thing in my life exactly right. Something sizable, you know? Something so hard I could like myself for it for the rest of my life. I wanted to burn, man. Pure flame. I'm going to be a schoolteacher, Todd. Where do you think I'll find fire then?

TODD: You ran the best quarter you ever ran by a full one-half second against the best mile relay team in the world, in front of the biggest crowd you ever saw, with your Daddy watching, man. Now is that right or not?

ARNIE: One guy can't be right in a mile relay.

DON: Boy-howdy!

ARNIE: I don't mean it's your fault, buddy. I really don't. I just mean it makes me sad, okay?

DON: Yeah. Yeah, sure.

TODD: Boy-o-boy-o- boy-o-boy-o-boy! You don't run for time, you don't run for style, you don't run for some perfect, incomparable, unforgettable moment. You run for the goddamn fun of it! You run 'cause it feels good and if you forget how to feel good, brothers, then it don't matter what else you're runnin' for, 'cause you just turned the whole damn thing into *work*. You keep that up, you won't even be able to screw 'cause you'll be too busy readin' sex manuals! *(There is a pause.)*

DON: You know, when I dropped that baton, I was already at stride . . .

ART: Yeah.

DON: And I knew, I mean I didn't think it or anything, but I knew if I went back for it, he'd have me by twenty yards, maybe twenty-five, and all I could think was how I'd wanted to run anchor with that sucker for three years, every since he wiped me out in the European Games when I was a freshman. I mean twenty-five yards on me was a wrap for him, right?

TODD: Right.

DON: So I went. See what I mean? I mean there's four of us he was the only one out there. Right?

ART: Right.

DON: And it was the end. The last forty seconds. The last time I'd ever feel that float. And it hit me that you don't drive the legs *down* with the burst like I'd always done, you burst *up* off the cinders into the stride. You put the energy into the lift. So I did that, and I was on his shoulder like that— *(He snaps his fingers.)* It was Kostilyoff who never lost a lead in an anchor in eleven years, and I picked up on him like that . . . *(He snaps his fingers again.)* And what I knew was that he had lots of time. He'd be back in the fall and back in the spring and back in the fall, and all I had was twenty mother seconds and I started laughin' 'cause my momma used to say, "You want somethin' done, you get a busy man to do it 'cause he doesn't have the time to waste!" And I looked over at Kostilyoff an' he was only runnin' from the waist up and I said, I said, "Look ma, no baton." And he smiled and bore down but I ate him 'cause he was runnin' for another five years and I was runnin' for another ten seconds. And you know the funny thing, there wasn't any blur. Everything moved right along with me at my rate of speed, so I had a long time to look at it. A real long time. So what I think is . . . anybody interested? *(Slowly they all raise their hands as if they were in a classroom and a vote was being taken.)* I can't believe it's just the style, even though the style gets you there, or getting better. I mean, look at the work-to-reward ratio. And fun? I don't know, feels like it hurts too much to be fun. And it's not the competition, and you guys know nobody likes the competition better than I do. It's making ten seconds last longer than any year you ever lived. See, you can't stop the time but you can slow it down so there's no blur. You can take all the effort out of your life for forty seconds and concentrate on the scenery. Effort-less. Effortless. That's what you do it for. *(A pause.)* Anyway, that's what I think. and hell with the baton. *(A brief pause. Then Todd holds out his hand. Don shakes it.)*

TODD: Hell with the baton.

ART: *(Shaking Don's hand.)* Hell with the baton. *(Don looks at Arnie. Arnie looks at Don. Arnie picks up his flight bag and leaves the stage without shaking hands. The lights dim.)*

Glengarry Glen Ross

David Mamet

1982

Dramatic

Setting: A real estate office. Robbed and ransacked. Glass everywhere. The plateglass front window has been boarded up.

Scene: The police have arrived to investigate the break-in. Baylen has
taken over an inner room to question each man individually.
Aaronson and Williamson are standing around, smoking cigarettes.

Of Note: The mood in the office is always tense, competitive, and
pressured. The men work with hounds of hell at their backs.

Richard Roma: 40's, a real estate salesman.
George Aarnow: 50's, a real estate salesman.
John Williamson: 40's, a real estate salesman.
Baylen: 30's – 40's, a detective.

AARONOW: People used to say that there are numbers of such mag-
nitude that multiplying them by two made no difference. *(Pause.)*
WILLIAMSON: Who used to say that?
AARONOW: In school. *(Pause.)*
(Baylen, a detective, comes out of the inner office.)
BAYLEN: Alright . . . ? *(Roma enters from the street.)*
ROMA: *Williamson . . . Williamson,* they stole the *contracts* . . . ?
BAYLEN: Excuse me, sir . . .
ROMA: Did they get my contracts?
WILLIAMSON: They got . . .
BAYLEN: Excuse me, fella.
ROMA: . . . did they . . .
BAYLEN: Would you excuse us, please . . . ?
ROMA: Don't *fuck* with me, fella. I'm talking about a fuckin' Cadillac
car that you owe me . . .
WILLIAMSON: They didn't get your contract. I filed it before I left.
ROMA: They didn't get my contracts?
WILLIAMSON: They, excuse me . . . *(He goes back into inner room
with the Detective.)*

ROMA: Oh, *fuck. Fuck. (He starts kicking the desk.)* FUCK FUCK FUCK! WILLIAMSON!!! WILLIAMSON!!! *(Goes to the door Williamson went into, tries the door; it's locked.)* OPEN THE FUCKING . . . WILLIAMSON . . .

BAYLEN: *(Coming out.)* Who are you? *(Williamson comes out.)*

WILLIAMSON: They didn't get the contracts.

ROMA: Did they . . .

WILLIAMSON: They got, listen to me . . .

ROMA: Th . . .

WILLIAMSON: Listen to me: They got *some* of them.

ROMA: Some of them . . .

BAYLEN: Who told you . . . ?

ROMA: Who told me wh . . . ? You've got a fuckin', you've . . a . . . who is this . . ? You've got a board-up on the window . . . *Moss* told me.

BAYLEN: *(Looking back toward the inner office.) Moss* . . . Who told him?

ROMA: How the fuck do *I* know? *(To Williamson.) What . . . talk* to me.

WILLIAMSON: They took *some* of the con .. .

ROMA: . . . some of the contracts . . . Lingk. James Lingk. I closed . . .

WILLIAMSON: You closed him yesterday.

ROMA: *Yes.*

WILLIAMSON: It went down. I filed it.

ROMA: You did?

WILLIAMSON: Yes.

ROMA: Then I'm over the fucking top and you owe me a Cadillac.

WILLIAMSON: I . . .

ROMA: And I don't want any fucking shit and I don't give a shit, Lingk puts me over the top, you filed it, that's fine, any other shit kicks out *you* go back. You . . . *you* reclose it, 'cause I *closed* it and you . . . you owe me the car.

BAYLEN: Would you excuse us, please.

AARONOW: I, um, and may . . . maybe they're in . . . they're in . . . you should, John, if we're ins . . .

WILLIAMSON: I'm sure that we're insured, George . . . *(Going back inside.)*

ROMA: Fuck insured. You owe me a car.

BAYLEN: *(Stepping back into the inner room.)* Please don't leave. I'm going to talk to you. What's your name?

ROMA: Are you talking to me? *(Pause.)*

BAYLEN: Yes. *(Pause.)*

ROMA: My name is Richard Roma. *(Baylen goes back into the inner room.)*

AARONOW: I, you know, they should be insured.

ROMA: What do *you* care . . . ?

AARONOW: Then, you know, they wouldn't be so ups . . .

ROMA: Yeah. That's swell. Yes. You're right. *(Pause.)* How are you?

AARONOW: I'm fine. You mean the *board*? You mean the *board* . . .?

ROMA: I don't . . . yes. Okay, the board.

AARONOW: I'm, I'm, I'm, I'm fucked on the board. *You*. You see now . . . I . . . *(Pause.)* I can't . . . my mind must be in other places. 'Cause I can't do any . . .

ROMA: *What*? You can't do any *what*? *(Pause.)*

AARONOW: I can't close 'em.

ROMA: Well, they're old. I saw the shit that they were giving you.

AARONOW: Yes.

ROMA: Huh?

AARONOW: Yes. They are old.

ROMA: They're ancient.

AARONOW: Clear . . .

ROMA: Clear Meadows. That shit's dead. *(Pause.)*

AARONOW: It *is* dead.

ROMA: It's a waste of time.

AARONOW: Yes. *(Long pause.)* I'm no fucking good.

ROMA: That's . . .

AARONOW: Everything I . . . *you* know . . .

ROMA: That's not . . . Fuck that shit, George. You're a, *hey*, you had a bad month. You're a good man, George.

AARONOW: I am?

ROMA: You hit a bad streak. We've all . . . look at this: fifteen units Mountain View, the fucking things get stole.

AARONOW: He said he filed . . .

ROMA: He filed half of them, he filed the *big* one. All the little ones, I have, I have to go back and . . . ah, *fuck,* I got to go out like a fucking schmuck hat in my hand and reclose the . . . *(Pause.)* I mean, talk about a bad streak. That would sap *anybody's* self confi . . . I got to go out and reclose all my . . . Where's the phones?

AARONOW: They stole . . .

ROMA: They stole the . . .

AARONOW: What. What kind of outfit are we running where . . . where anyone . . .

ROMA: *(To himself.)* They stole the phones.

AARONOW: Where criminals can come in here . . . they take the . . .

ROMA: They stole the phones. They stole the leads. They're . . . *Christ.* *(Pause.)* What am I going to do this month? Oh, *shit* . . . *(Starts for the door.)*

AARONOW: You think they're going to catch . . . where are you going?

ROMA: Down the street.

WILLIAMSON: *(Sticking his head out of the door.)* Where are you going?

ROMA: To the restaura . . . what do you fucking . . . ?

WILLIAMSON: Aren't you going out today?

ROMA: With what? *(Pause.)* With what, John, they took the leads . . .

WILLIAMSON: I have the stuff from last year's . . .

ROMA: Oh. Oh. Oh, your "nostalgia" file, that's fine. No. Swell. 'Cause I don't have to . . .

WILLIAMSON: . . . you want to go out today . . . ?

ROMA: 'Cause I don't have to *eat* this month. No. Okay. *Give* 'em to me . . . *(To himself.)* Fucking Mitch and Murray going to shit a br . . . what am I doing to *do* all . . .

(Williamson starts back into the office. He is accosted by Aaronow.)

AARONOW: Were the leads . . .

ROMA: . . . what am I going to *do* all month . . . ?

AARONOW: Were the leads insured?

WILLIAMSON: I don't know, George, why?

AARONOW: 'Cause, you know, 'cause they weren't, I know that Mitch and Murray uh . . . *(Pause.)*

WILLIAMSON: What?

AARNOW: That they're going to be upset.

WILLIAMSON: That's right. *(Going back into his office. Pause. To Roma.)* You want to go out today . . .?

Walking Papers

Edward F. Miller
1998

Dramatic

Setting: At the Tomb of the Unknown Soldier, Washington, D.C. Lt. Blassie, formerly an unknown Vietnam Vet, has just been identified and must leave the tomb.

Scene: Reveille has just played and WW1 enters, barely getting his pants on.

Of Note: Each soldier speaks and acts appropriately to his own era; thus there are differences in the way the men express themselves.

Nam: Lt. Michael Blassie a solider of the Vietnam War, 20's, deceased.
WW 1: A solider of WWI, 20's deceased.
WW 2: A soldier of WWII, 20's, deceased.
KOR: A soldier of the Korean War, 20's, deceased.

WW 1: Jesus mother and God! What on . . . Jesus, I can barely get these dursed things on.

(WW 2 enters still in his underwear. Slowly getting his clothes on.)

WW 2: Boys, I'm not hearin' what I'm hearin'. Now, I can't believe that those peckerheads got my goddamn ass out of bed. I got in here and I didn't ever want to move again

WW 1: I'm with you, my friend. I've been in here longer than I can remember, and I've never heard anything like that. I mean, I didn't even turn when they put you all in this tomb with me and somehow this shook me to the bone. What's this all about? I'm tired.

WW 2: Why you all dressed up there, Kilroy? Ya goin' somewhere?

KOR: Sir, no sir.

WW 2: Cause if you are, I gotta tell ya . . . You ain't goin' anywhere. This one's a milk run to nowhere.

WW 1: What happened to all those things in you?

NAM: I'm telling you, they just melted away, and were replaced by this new thing.

WW 1: Hmm.

NAM: Don't kid yourself; I am in a situation that I don't want to be in. I was really happy here.

WW 2: Then, stay. Screw those guys. Forget all that shit and stay.

KOR: Yes, stay.

NAM: I can't forget! Those alive won't let me. So, let me go. This is tearin' me apart, man.

(WW 1 Shakes Nam's hand.)

WW 1: It's good to know you. Lt. Blassie.

WW 2: It's a fuckin' raw deal.

KOR: Sir, good luck out there, and thanks for the advice. Do you think there will be someone to replace you? I mean there is an empty bunk. I don't want to be stuck in here alone with those jokers.

NAM: I don't know. I don't think so. If they do, somebody will know him somehow, and it won't be the same for any of you. This was one duty I truly enjoyed having. Good-bye.

(Kor salutes Nam as the lights fade.)

WW 2: All the voices and all the memories seem so random. Just flashes of my own death. They couldn't be all mine; but I embrace them just the same. I can't see how it can be so specific with you. I think it's something you made up just to get out.

NAM: Can you remember being a kid?

WW 2: Yeah.

NAM: Do YOU remember?

WW 2: No.

NAM: Do you remember America at all?

WW 2: Yeah, but it's all random shit all over the place.

NAM: I can remember only one place. I grew up in Missouri. I use to go to the Mississippi and swim in the river. There was a tire swing in this calm chute, and me and my friends would jump in the river for hours. Or we'd go fishing, or play kick ball, and I remember all their names. There was the Corbett brothers, Johnny Johnson, my best friend, and Stewwie, who as a fat kid we'd tease for bein' slow. I mean, do you have any of that?

WW 2: No! But why do you get to leave? I want to leave this place. I hate being restless. I want a history. I want family. I want people to remember me.

NAM: I can't help that. The ticket out of here is a specific history. That's it! If you don't have it, then you stay and have thousands of histories, thousands of lives and memories. I am heartbroken to not have that anymore.

WW 1: In a trench . . . it's wet . . . rats . . . my feet swollen . . . hurt

. . . the stench of death and men and feces and garbage . . . always dark . . . like impending death . . . bored . . . peek up and over out of boredom . . . no helmet . . . wasn't thinking . . . ha . . . and then . . . I don't know, now . . . a general retreat and a wave of pain straifed my back. Then thousands of feet trampling me . . .

NAM: I am Lieutenant Michael J. Blassie. I am an Air Force Pilot, and I was shot down in May 1972 in my A-37 Attack Fighter by ground fire. My plane went down in flames near An Loc, Binh Long Provence. That's it, man.

WW 1: What?

NAM: I am Lieutenant Michael J. Blassie. I am an Air Force Pilot, and I was shot down in May 1972 in my A-37 Attack Fighter by ground fire. My plane went down in flames near An Loc, Binh Long Provence. All that other shit which you got; I ain't got anymore.

WW 1: How can you be so specific?

NAM: I don't know.

WW 1: How? I don't understand this.

NAM: Yeah, It's weird. I mean, yesterday, I had all of this random shit rolling around in me, and when I woke up to reveille, my past solidified.

WW 2: Why don't I have what you have? Why do you get to leave and I don't. I think that you're a fuckin' lyin' asshole.

NAM: I'm not lying. The plane just dovetailed to the right and flamed over, everybody scrambled to get out but the fire knocked out the hydraulics so we punched a whole through the mid gunner door and crawled out . . . chute didn't work.

KOR: And then a destroyer engaging a sub . . . charging for hours lookin' for this gook tub then . . . thud . . . fire . . . smoke . . . thud . . fire . . . smoke . . . water . .

WW 2: It was fucking cold and I was in the water right off the beach and there were bullets and mortar and, a wave crashed our landing craft into a bunker and I was trapped and, out of all the chaos and mortar fire and tracers, I could hear one shell and all of a sudden, a star burst directly behind me, and there was, wait a minute . . . and I was . . .

WW 1: In a plane . . . yes . . . with a bomb between my legs . . . clouds . . . barren land below . . . another plane diving at ten o'clock . . . came out of nowhere . . . did I even hear him? I don't think so.

Pulling up left to face and get above him but too late . . . bullets ripping the wing running across the engine block . . . smoke, fire, boom . . .

KOR: . . . Out . . . to speed like unreal and close to the ground and what seemed like hours like this and up over a hill and smoke, bank left and up and up and turn right and dive hillside down pull-up, straight-out, payload out, boom bank right, hard turn, dive, strafe, strafe, strafe, bank left, up, up, up, float, dive, straight-out, payload out, boom, up, flak, thud, thud, smoke. . .

WW 2: . . . and I was in the south pacific and I was wounded and alone in the jungle and I had a fever . . . or was I in the forest of Ardennes and it was so cold . . . so quiet . . . just fell asleep . . . no, wait, I had a flame thrower and I was on Palermo and a sniper out of nowhere . . . I, no . . .

KOR: . . . smoke to a field of high grass, again running . . . zigzag . . . other men . . . running . . . heavy fire . . . to my left . . . boom . . . limbs flying . . . bear down . . . zig left . . . something, hard under foot . . . then flight . . . maybe can't be sure what's real . . . but then . . .

WW 1: You want a once around with me?

WW 2: Yeah, that's not a bad idea. Now that I'm up, why the hell not.

NAM: HEY! Cool yer jets. There ain't much time, and I got a ton to tell you.

WW 2: Oh, sorry there kiddo.

NAM: Listen, I woke up this morning before the dawn, and I remembered who I am. It all came back to me.

KOR: Your lying.

NAM: It did.

WW 1: Well . . . yes . . . for instance, I was in a field full of soldiers charging at each other with bayonets drawn . . . there was a horse cart off to the right and they kept climbing out of this hole like rats and we responded in kind . . . thousands of men all around me . . . clacking of metal on metal . . . machine gun batter to my right . . . explosions . . . yellow gas . . . I saved my . . . no . . . he saved me? I can't say . . . but . . .

KOR: I charged up some hill like Jonnie Reb . . . insane . . . just runnin' with mortar fire all around . . . just runnin' for my life . . . Christ the hill doesn't even have a name . . . it's some number 53

. . . 47 . . . 32 . . . ? Guy falls to my left . . . tracer fire and then, pishshsh . . .

WW 2: Or when I was in the air and there was flak and we got some but we gave it back too but, we weren't hit. There was an oil leak and Engine #3 gave out.

NAM: Man, I know what you're saying. I've had that feeling and it's scary as all shit. You just gotta be cool. Let those things bleed into and out of you. You can't help it. They'll always be with you. So, just be cool.

KOR: What are you saying to me?

NAM: I'm just saying let those things happen to you. They use to freak me, cause I had a sense that they weren't of me but all around me and going through me. And I use to fight it, or try to keep those images . . . memories as mine. I see them for what they are cause they don't bug me anymore.

(WW 1 and WW 2 enter dressed.)

WW 1: Really now, and how is it you heard it twice and I didn't hear it at all until now?

WW 2: Did I say twice?

WW 1: Yes you did.

WW 2: Oh, what I mean't to say was; I didn't hear reveille at all. What I heard was "Gal From Kalamazoo."

WW1: Now I see what you're saying.

WW 2: Oh you do, do you?

WW 1: You're telling me that you're clueless, carp-headed, slack-jawed, foaming-at-the-mouth idiot.

WW 2: And you're a friggin' asshole.

Hebrew Visions

Anonymous

Reader's Theatre Pieces are designed to be divided up by the speakers in any way deemed appropriate.

It is the beauty of the language and the sweep of the thought that carry the piece, not character or action.

Lines may be spoken in unison, alternatingly, or as an overlapping echo.

Feel free to experiment with the presentation.

Four Men.

1

And Jacob went out from Beersheba and went toward Haran.

And he lighted upon a certain place, and tarried there all night, because the sun was set: and he took hold of the stones of that place and put them for pillows, and lay down in that place to sleep.

And he dreamed, and behold, a ladder set up on the earth, and the top of it reached to heaven: and behold, the angels of God ascending and descending on it.

And behold, the Lord stood above it, and said, I am the Lord God of Abraham thy father, and the God of Isaac: the land whereon thou liest, to thee will I give it, and to thy seed.

And thy seed shall be the dust of the earth; and thou shall spread abroad to the west, and to the east, and to the north, and to the south: and in thee and in thy seed shall all the families of the earth be blessed.

2

The burden of the desert of the sea. As whirlwinds in the south pass through; so it cometh from the desert from a terrible land.

A grievous vision is declared unto me; the treacherous dealer dealeth treacherously, and the spoiler spoileth. Go up, O Elam: besiege, O Media; all the sighing thereof have I made to cease.

Therefore are my loins filled with pain: pangs have taken hold upon me, as the pangs of a woman that travaileth: I was bowed down at the hearing of it; I was dismayed at the seeing of it.

My heart panted, fearfulness affrighted me: the night of my pleasure
    hath he turned into fear unto me.

Prepare the table, watch in the watchtower, eat, drink; arise, ye
    princes, and anoint the shield.

And he saw a chariot with a couple of horsemen, a chariot of asses,
    and a chariot of camels; and he hearkened diligently with much
    heed: and he cried, A lion: My Lord, I stand continually upon the
    watchtower in the day time, and I am set in my ward whole
    nights.

And behold, here cometh a chariot of men, with a couple of horse-
    men. And he answered and said, Babylon is fallen, is fallen; and
    all the graven images of her gods he hath broken unto the
    ground.

O my threshing, and the corn of my floor: that which I have heard of
    the Lord of hosts, the God of Israel, have I declared unto you.

The burden of Dumah. He calleth to me out of Seir, Watchman, what
    of the night? Watchman, what of the night?

The watchman said, the morning cometh, and also the night: if ye will
    inquire, inquire ye: return, come.

The burden of the valley of vision. What aileth thee now, that thou
    art wholly gone up to the house-tops?

Thou that art full of stirs, a tumultuous city, a joyous city: thy slain
    men are not slain with the sword, nor dead in battle.

All the rulers are fled together, they are bound by the archers: all that
    are found in thee are bound together, which have fled from far.

3

And I looked, and behold, a whirlwind came out of the north, a great
    cloud, and a fire infolding itself, and a brightness was about it,
    and out of the midst thereof as the color of amber, out of the
    midst of the fire.

Also out of the midst thereof came the likeness of four living crea-
    tures. And this was their appearance; they had the likeness of a
    man.

And every one had four faces, and every one had four wings.

And their feet were straight feet; and the sole of their feet was like
    the sole of a calf's foot; and they sparkled like the color of bur-
    nished brass.

And they had the hands of a man under their wings on their four
sides; and they had their faces and their wings.

Their wings were joined one to another; they turned not when they
went; they went every one straight forward.

As for the likeness of their faces, they four had the face of a man, and
the face of a lion, on the right side: and they four had the face of
an ox on the left side; they four also had the face of an eagle.

Thus were their faces: and their wings were stretched upward; two
wings of every one were joined one to another, and two covered
their bodies.

And they went every one straight forward: whither the spirit was to
go, they went; and they turned not when they went.

As for the likeness of the living creatures, their appearance was like
burning coals of fire, and like the appearance of lamps: it went
up and down among the living creatures; and the fire was bright,
and out of the fire went forth lightning.

And the living creatures ran and returned as the appearance of a flash
of lightning.

Now as I beheld the living creatures, behold one wheel upon the
earth by the living creatures, with his four faces.

The appearance of the wheels and their work was like unto the color
of a beryl: and they four had one likeness: and their appearance
and their work was as it were a wheel in the middle of a wheel.

When they went, they went upon their four sides: and they turned
not when they went.

As for their rings, they were so high that they were dreadful; and their
rings were full of eyes round about them four.

And when the living creatures went, the wheels went by them: and
when the living creatures were lifted up from the earth, the
wheels were lifted up.

4

And there appeared a great wonder in heaven; a woman clothed with
the sun, and the moon under her feet, and upon her head a
crown of twelve stars:

And she being with child cried, travailing in birth, and pained to be
delivered.

And there appeared another wonder in heaven; and behold a great
red dragon, having

seven heads and ten horns, and seven crowns upon his head.

And his tail drew the third part of the stars of heaven, and did cast them to the earth: and the dragon stood before the woman which was already to be delivered, for to devour her child as soon as it was born.

And she brought forth a man child, who was to rule all nations with a rod of iron: and her child was caught up unto God, and to his throne.

And the woman fled into the wilderness, where she hath a place prepared of God, that they should feed her there a thousand two hundred and three score days.

And there was a war in heaven: Michael and his angels fought against the dragon; and the dragon fought and his angels, and prevailed not; neither was their place found any more in heaven.

And when the dragon saw that he was cast unto the earth, he persecuted the woman which brought forth the man child.

And to the woman were given two wings of a great eagle, that she might fly into the wilderness, into her place, where she is nourished for a time, and times, and half a time, from the face of the serpent.

And the serpent cast out of his mouth water as a flood after the woman, that he might cause her to be carried away of the flood.

And the earth helped the woman, and the earth opened her mouth and swallowed up the flood which the dragon cast out of his mouth.

Night Births
Keaulumoku

Reader's Theatre Pieces are designed to be divided up by the speakers in any way deemed appropriate.

It is the beauty of the language and the sweep of the thought that carry the piece, not character or action.

Lines may be spoken in unison, alternatingly, or as an overlapping echo.

Feel free to experiment with the presentation.

Four men.

At the time when the earth became hot
At the time when the heavens turned about
At the time when the sun was darkened
To cause the moon to shine
The time of the rise of the Pleiades
The slime, this was the source of the earth
The source of the darkness that made darkness
The source of the night that made night
The intense darkness, the deep darkness
Darkness of the sun, darkness of the night
Nothing but night

1
The train of walruses passing by
Milling about in the depths of the sea
The long lines of opule fish
The sea is thick with them
Crabs and hardshelled creatures
They go swallowing on the way
Rising and diving under swiftly and silently
Pimoe lurks behind the horizon
On the long waves, the crested waves
Innumerable the coral ridges
Low, heaped-up, jagged
The little ones seek the dark places

Very dark is the ocean and obscure
A sea of coral like the green heights of Paliuli
The land disappears into them
Covered by the darkness of night
	Still it is night

2
With a dancing motion they go creeping and crawling
The tail swinging its length
Sullenly, sullenly
They go poking about the dunghill
Filth is their food, they devour it
Eat and rest, eat and belch it up
Eating like common people
Distressful is their eating
They move about and become heated
Act as if exhausted
They stagger as they go
Go in the land of crawlers
The family of crawlers born in the night
	Still it is night

3
The parent rats dwell in holes
The little rats huddle together
Those who mark the seasons
Little tolls from the land
Little tolls from the water courses
Trace of the nibblings of these brown-coated ones
With whiskers upstanding
They hide here and there
A rat in the upland, a rat by the sea
A rat running beside the wave
Born to the two, child of the Night-falling-away
Born to the two, child of the Night-creeping-away
The little child creeps as it moves
The little child moves with a spring
Pilfering at the rind
Rind of the 'ohi'a fruit, not a fruit of the upland

A tiny child born as the darkness falls away
A springing child born as the darkness creeps away
Child of the dark and child in the night now here
    Still it is night

4

Fear falls upon me on the mountain top
Fear of the passing night
Fear of the night approaching
Fear of the pregnant night
Fear of the breach of the law
Dread of the place of offering and the narrow trail
Dread of the food and the waste part remaining
Dread of the receding night
Awe of the night approaching
Awe of the dog child of the Night-creeping-away
A dark red dog, a brindled dog
A hairless dog of the hairless ones
A dog as an offering for the oven
Palatable is the sacrifice for supplication
Pitiful in the cold without covering
Pitiful in the heat without a garment
He goes naked on the way to Malama
Where the night ends for the children of night
From the growth and the parching
From the cutting off and the quiet
The driving Hula wind his companion
Younger brother of the naked ones, the 'Olohe
Out from the slime come rootlets
Out from the slime comes young growth
Out from the slime come branching leaves
Out from the slime comes outgrowth
Born in the time when men came from afar
    Still it is night

PART TWO:

SCENES FOR
FOUR WOMEN

Hippolytus
Euripides

Dramatic

Setting: Outside Phaidra's Palace with a statue of the goddess
Aphrodite on one side of the stage and of Artemis on the other.

Scene: Queen Phaidra, in a state of collapse from days of starvation, comes before the women of Troizen with the aid of her
Nurse. She is desperately in love with her step-son Hippolytos
who has sworn his allegiance to Artemis, goddess of the hunt
and of chastity, and turned away from Aphrodite, goddess of
love. Aphrodite's revenge is toward Hippolytos, while using
Phaidra as a pawn in her scheme to destroy him for his slight of
her.

Phaidra: 30's – 40's, wife of King Thêseus.
Nurse: 50's – 60's, Phaidra's servant.
Chorus I: Women of the city of Troizen.
Chorus II: Women of the city of Troizen.

CHORUS I: Mountain
    cliff, mountain
    stream flowing,
    dripping,
    flowing, water from
    Ocean, they
    say, spouting,
    lunging, from
    sheer
    cliff
    face,
    where
    pitchers
    plunge in the
    running
    stream, there,
    there, a
    friend steeped
    crimson robes

in the
stream's
flood, and
lay them,
lay them,
out, lay them
on a rock's
warm
back,
full in the
sun.
CHORUS II: There I heard,
there,
for the first
time,
news,
word of my
queen's,
word of my
mistress'
illness.
CHORUS I: She lies, they
tell me, lies there,
on a bed of
sickness,
inside the house,
never
leaving, never,
wasting,
wasting away,
wasting, on a
bed of sickness,
sickness
sorely afflicted, her
fair head shaded,
shadowed
by fine-spun
fabrics, delicate
cloths.

CHORUS II: Three days now,
    they say,
    three days
    she has
    fasted,
    kept herself
    pure from
    Dêmêter's
    grain, no
    bread,
    pure, no
    bread, passing her
    lips, wishing,
    wishing,
    longing, wishing,
    in her secret
    sorrow,
    secret
    grief, unspoken
    grief, to
    ground the
    craft of her
    life on death's
    unhappy
    shore.
CHORUS I: Is your mind
    wandering, lady,
    wandering
    wildly because,
    Pan,
    Pan, has
    possessed you,
    Pan, or
    Hekate,
    Hekate, or the
    holy
    Korybantes,
    holy, or the
    mountain mother,

great mountain
mother, Kybêlê,
great mother?
CHORUS II: Or has Artemis,
huntress,
Artemis of wild
beasts, has
Artemis been
slighted by
unoffered
offerings,
unoffered, and
now wastes you,
wastes you
away for
offerings not
poured, offerings
unpoured on her
holy
altar?
CHORUS I: For she has
power to
range the
march, range the
sea's dry
land that
stands in the salt
eddies of the sea.
CHORUS II: Or is it your
husband, is it,
is it Thêseus,
Thêseus,
king of Athens,
Thêseus,
nobly
born, who has
taken another
woman, a
woman in the

palace, a
woman who
tends to him
far from your
bed, from your
sight?
CHORUS I: Or has a
sailor from Krete
sailed into our
harbor, our
welcoming
harbor, with
news for the
queen, news of
misfortune that
binds her, binds her
fast to her
bed, powerless,
helpless,
helpless, unable to
act in her
sorrow?
CHORUS II: Woman's
nature is an
uneasy
accord, uneasy
harmony, and a
terrible weary
helplessness
overtakes her,
robbing her of
reason, when the
pangs of
childbirth lay on.
I, too,
I, too, have
felt it's breath
dart through my
womb. But I

called to her,
called, called to the
heavenly one,
Artemis of the
arrows, Artemis,
called, when
labor
approached, and she
always,
always,
by the gods'
grace, gods'
grace,
eases my
pain.
(Phaidra enters supported by her Nurse.)
CHORUS I: But look,
Here's her old nurse in the doorway.
And Phaidra just behind,
Helped by her slaves.
How troubled the nurse looks.
Perhaps now we'll learn the nature
Of our queen's illness—
What eats away at her body
And steals her color.
NURSE: Ah, what a blight of troubles this life is!
What am I to do with you, child? What?
These awful, hateful illnesses! All your
Thought was getting out into the sunlight,
Bringing out your bed, your sickbed,
And that's here, too, now.
And now what? Mm?
As if I didn't know! There it is!
There! Right on cue. The wrinkle of a frown
That tells me a complaint's on the way.
All you talked of was coming outside;
And now you're here, you'll
Soon want to hurry back in,
Back into your bedchamber to hide.

Nothing pleases you. Nothing.
At least not for long. What you have,
You're unhappy with; what you don't have
Is what you want most.
(To the Chorus.)
I'd rather be sick as a dog myself
Than have to tend the sick.
Being sick is a simple proposition.
Tending the sick is not only trouble,
But a grief to the heart as well.
What a mess of pain life is.
Never rest for the weary.

PHAIDRA: Help me—please—
Raise me up—hold my head straight. . .
My poor arms are so weak,
No strength in them anymore—
As if the strings had all loosened—
My delicate arms. . . Raise me . . .
And undo my hair, dear Nurse, won't you?
It's so heavy right now. Let it
Flow to my shoulders . . . let it free. . .
(The Nurse undoes her hair.)

NURSE: Easy does it, my darling.
The less tossing the better, you know.
Relax, now, be calm. It will
Help you to bear up better if you're calm.
Show us a little of that grand nobility of yours.
Everyone has to suffer—
That's what life is.

PHAIDRA: Ohhhh, I want to drink pure water
From a crystal spring, and lie beneath
Black poplars in the uncut meadows!

NURSE: Child, child! What are you saying!
Such crazy words, too! And all these
People here to hear your rantings!
What will they think!

PHAIDRA: The mountains! Oh, the mountains!
Take me there! To the woods,
The pine woods, the hounds and huntsmen,

Oh, dear gods, tracking down their wild prey,
Closing in on the dappled deer, the cries,
The shouting, shouting to the hounds, tossing,
Tossing a spear of Thessaly past my ear,
Clutching the barbed missile in my hand,
Tossing—!
NURSE: My dear, you're delirious!
What's all this hunting and crystal springs?
There's a well-watered hillside
Just by the city walls.
You could drink there.
PHAIDRA: Artemis, mistress of the salt lake,
Mistress of the flats where horses thunder,
How I long to be in your sacred sanctuary
Taming Venetian colts!
NURSE: You're out of your mind!
Chattering nonsense in your madness!
Once you're off to the hills all afire for the hunt,
And now you fancy horses on the waveless sands
Of the seashore! What god
Is making your mind swerve from its course?
PHAIDRA: Oh, no! What have I done!
Lost my senses! What god did this?
I'm ashamed! Ashamed for what I've said!
Nurse, dear Nurse, cover my face again.
Hide me, please. Cover it. Hide my
Tears of shame.
Sanity is pain, but madness is worse.
It's better to die aware of nothing.
NURSE: All right. I'll cover it. There.
But when will death come to cover *my* body?
I haven't lived long to learn little.
And one thing I've learned is this:
That we humans love far too hard.
There should be a limit to our love.
Moderation. Love must never
Pierce to the depths of our souls.
It should be as easily unbound as bound.
(*To the Chorus.*)

What can be worse than suffering pain for two?
Ask me. I know. The grief I suffer
For this woman is almost unbearable. My advice
Is that principles should go only so far
And then give way to reason. Otherwise
You're headed straight for a breakdown.
Satisfaction seldom comes from too rigid a standard.
Besides, it's bad for the health.
—I have little praise for excess,
And much for moderation.
I think the wise will agree.

CHORUS II: Old woman, your faithful care
For our queen is touching. It's clear to us
How sick she really is, what we don't know
Is it's cause. What can you tell us?

NURSE: I question her,
But she tells me nothing.

CHORUS II: Not even how it first began?

NURSE: Nothing. She refuses to speak.

CHORUS II: How feeble she is,
How wasted, poor thing.

NURSE: She hasn't eaten in three days.

CHORUS II: Her madness?
Or does she want to die?

NURSE: I don't know;
But this fast will kill her.

CHORUS I: Yes, but her husband?
Why doesn't he help?

NURSE: She hides her troubles—
Refuses to admit them.

CHORUS II: But can't he see?
Can't he look at her face?

NURSE: He's away from home—
Out of the city.

CHORUS II: But then it's your duty to force her.
Someone has to discover the truth.

Lysistrata

Aristophanes
411 B.C

Setting: Athens, a public square.
Scene: Lysistrata has called a meeting of all the women of Greece.
    She has thought of a way to end war once and for all.

Lysistrata
Kalonike
Myrrhine
Lampito

LYSISTRATA: Women! Who needs them!
    If I'd invited them to an orgy
    Or some lewd bash in honor of Dionysos or Pan,
    Not to mention Aphrodite, for god's sake,
    I'd have to beat them away from my door!
    Traffic would come to a halt,
    Streets clogged with mobs of rowdy revelers,
    Dancing, drums, you name it!
    As it is, there's not a female in sight!
    Ah, well—yes, I guess there's one.
    Spoke too soon, wouldn't you know!
    (Enter Kalonike.)
LYSISTRATA: My next door neighbor. Morning, Kalonike!
KALONIKE: Morning, Lysistrata!
    Gracious, dear, what's the problem?
    Such a frown! Watch it, wrinkles come
    Soon enough by themselves!
LYSISTRATA: Forget the face, Kalonike.
    It's women I'm about.
    You can't trust them. No wonder men say
    The things about us they do.
KALONIKE: And they're probably right.
LYSISTRATA: I mean, really! Here I call a meeting,
    Stressing with everything I've got
    That it's of the utmost importance—
    And what do you think!

Where do you think they are?
At home! Catching a few more winks!

KALONIKE: Easy does it, dear. They'll be along.
Being a woman's no easy matter. First,
You rouse the slaves with a well-aimed
Kick to the butt, then there's a little hubby
Who needs tending to, and the cook,
And bathing a bawling baby, it never ends!

LYSISTRATA: I know, but there are
Things more pressing!

KALONIKE: Pressing? Like what? What's up?

LYSISTRATA: Something big, girl!

KALONIKE: Huge?

LYSISTRATA: Huge enough for us all!

KALONIKE: God, Lysistrata, then why aren't they *here*?

LYSISTRATA: No, Kalonike, not that!
Well, not strictly speaking, that is.
But if it were—ah, *if*—they
Couldn't get here fast enough!
No, but there's something I've been
Toying around with in bed
These last sleepless nights—

KALONIKE: It must be worn to a frazzle by now, dear—

LYSISTRATA: Kalonike, the fate of all the Greece
Lies right square in our hands!
Only we women can save it!

KALONIKE: Some last ditch resort *that* is!
Poor Greece!

LYSISTRATA: The future of Athens
Rests in our hands, girl! First off,
We have to wipe out the Peloponnesians—

KALONIKE: Good! Let's do it!

LYSISTRATA: And then the Boiotians—

KALONIKE: Oh, but just not the eels, dear!
They make such luscious—

LYSISTRATA: Don't worry, it's not
The eels I have in mind. As for Athens,
Well, I really have a hard time saying it—
But you know what just might happen

As well as I do.
	Now, if we could get all the women
	From Thebes and Sparta
	And god know where else
	To meet with us here,
	We could end up the saviors
	Of the entire country!
KALONIKE: Oh, come on, girl! Talk sense!
	Women aren't political animals.
	We're good for keeping around the house
	Like pets. Sitting around all day
	Getting the makeup just right.
	Slinking through the house
	In our best saffron gowns, and, oh,
	Those precious little Persian slippers!
LYSISTRATA: There! You've got it! That's it!
	See-through dresses, scents and blushes,
	Naughty little negligees, and, oh,
	Those precious little Persian slippers!
	That's how we'll do it! That's it!
KALONIKE: What?
LYSISTRATA: Keep our men busy
	From ever hoisting another spear—
KALONIKE: I'll send out a little nothing
	For dyeing tomorrow—
LYSISTRATA: —Or shouldering another shield—
KALONIKE: —And then there's this sexy—
LYSISTRATA: —Or hauling out another sword.
KALONIKE: —And I saw the most dreamy slippers the other—
LYSISTRATA: So where are they, these women
	Who should be here by now?
KALONIKE: They should have *flown*!
	They should have sprouted *wings*,
	Taken *flight*!
LYSISTRATA: No mistaking an Athenian.
	They're always late. But that doesn't excuse
	Those from the Shore or Salamis—
KALONIKE: They've probably been coming
	Since the crack of dawn.

LYSISTRATA: And no one from Acharnai.
    I expected them here hours ago.
KALONIKE: I passed Theagenês' wife having her
    Fortune told; so she's bound to show.
    But here come some of them now!
    Who are they, can you see?
    (Enter Myrrhine and a group of other women.)
LYSISTRATA: They're from Anagyros.
KALONIKE: Wouldn't you know it!
    You can smell their cheap scent a mile off!
MYRRHINE: Oh, golly, Lysistrata, I hope I'm not late!
    —Well, least ways you could say something
    Instead of just scowling.
LYSISTRATA: Don't you ever take anything
    Seriously, Myrrhinê? I mean, not even
    Something this important?
MYRRHINE: Sorry—it was all I could do
    To find my girdle in the dark.
    (Looking around at the others.)
    Well, if it's so important,
    Why are we waiting? Tell us!
LYSISTRATA: The girls from Thebes and Sparta
    Should get here first.
KALONIKE: Good idea. Ah, and here come some now.
    (Enter Lampito, a particularly sturdy woman in a particularly out-
    landish costume, and other women from Sparta.)
LYSISTRATA: Lampito, dear!
    What a ravishing sight!
    How are things in Sparta?
    And the colors! My! How absolutely
    Out-of-doors you look!
    Muscles and all!
    You look ready to strangle a bull!
LAMPITO: Sure could, you know.
    Work out ever' day in the gym.
    And then the fanny-kick dance we do?
    Like this?
    (She demonstrates.)
KALONIKE: And look at the tits!

LAMPITO: Sure'd be nice if you'd
     Keep your hands to yourself.
     Makes me feel like a heifer bein'
     Led to the slaughter.
LYSISTRATA: And this lovely young lady here?
     Where's she from?
LAMPITO: Boiotia. Regular blue-blood type.
LYSISTRATA: Ah, yes Boiotia—
     Spacious skies and amber waves of grain,
     And all that!
KALONIKE: Look close enough, you'll see the grain
     Has just been freshly mown.
LYSISTRATA: And who do we have here?
LAMPITO: Korinth girl. Real special.
KALONIKE: Oh, no doubt!
LAMPITO: So, tell us, whose idea was this little meetin'?
LYSISTRATA: Mine, as a matter of fact.
LAMPITO: So, then, what's up?
MYRRHINE: Right, dear, tell us what's so urgent it can't wait.
LYSISTRATA: Yes, well. But first a small question.
MYRRHINE: So *ask*!
LYSISTRATA: Well, it has to do with your husbands—
     The fathers of your children.
     Wouldn't you rather have them at home
     Than off somewhere fighting?
     I'll bet you not one of you
     Has a husband in the house.
KALONIKE: Mine's been up in Thrace
     For the last five months! Imagine!
     Five months! Keeping an eye
     On that General Eukrates!
MYRRHINE: And mine's been in Pylos for seven!
LAMPITO: Mine no sooner gets a discharge
     Then he just plugs himself right back in.
KALONIKE: And lovers are about as scarce
     As balls on a capon! Ever since those
     Beastly Milesians revolted on Athens
     And cut off the leather trade,
     There hasn't been a decent dildo to be bought!

LYSISTRATA: All right! That's how it is!
    Now! If I can come up with a plan
    To stop this war, who's with me?
MYRRHINE: Count *me* in! I'd pawn
    The shift off my back if I had to.
    Though I might buy a few drinks
    With the proceeds if I got the chance.
KALONIKE: Me, too! And they can
    Split me up the middle like a flounder
    If they have to—for the cause.
LAMPITO: And me! I'd climb on up Mount Taygetos
    On my hands and knees to get at some peace.
LYSISTRATA: All right! Then here it is!
    If we women want our men to give up war,
    If that's what we *really want*—
    I mean if we're serious—
    Then we'll simply have to—
MYRRHINE: Have to—?
KALONIKE: Have to what?
LYSISTRATA: You'll do as I say?
MYRRHINE: Damn straight!
    We'd die for peace!
LYSISTRATA: Then we must give up getting laid by our men.
    (Long silence among the women.)
    So what's the matter? Second thoughts?
    Chickening out so soon?
    Why the long faces, girls? Tears?
    Pale as ghosts? All weepy?
    —Will you or won't you?
    I'm waiting! Yes or no!
MYRRHINE: I—I—I don't think so.
    Maybe it's better the war should just go on—
KALONIKE: Me either. The—the war should—
    Should just better—go on—
LYSISTRATA: Aha! The little flounder,
    Ready to be sliced up the middle for the cause!
KALONIKE: Lysistrata, no! You know
    I'd walk through fire for you!
    I would! But not *that*, dear—
    Not *that*—not *sex*!

Lysistrata

Aristophanes

Comic
Setting: Athens, a public square.
Scene: Lysistrata's plan isn't working. The women keep sneaking off
to have sex with their men. She is very upset.

Lysistrata
First Woman
Second Woman
Third Woman

LYSISTRATA: What is it? I just can't seem
To manage anymore! What's wrong?
They're deserting in droves. Man-crazy,
Every last one of them! I caught
One just now, scraping out a clogged-up
Hole in the wall near Pan's grotto—
Trying to squeeze through.
Another was slithering down the side
Using rope and tackle, and a third
Just outright deserted her sentry post.
And yesterday I even saw one
Mounted on a sparrow's back,
Ready to fly off to the nearest whorehouse.
That one I grabbed by her
Knot of hair and pulled back up.
And the excuses they make!
All just to get back home to their men!
Ah, and there's another.
(To the First Women trying to tiptoe out through the gates.)
You! Halt! I said halt! Where do you
Think you're sneaking off to?
FIRST WOMAN: Sorry! Have to get home!
There's all this gorgeous Milesian
Wool in the house being eaten by moths.
LYSISTRA: Tell me another, dear.
All right, back inside.

FIRST WOMAN: No, I promise, Lysistrata!
   I'll be back! I swear! I'll just
   Run home and spread it all out
   On the bed—so it can breathe.
LYSISTRATA: Afraid not. Your wool
   Will just have to wait. Back to your post.
FIRST WOMAN: But—but it'll all be ruined!
   My fleeces! Wasted!
LYSISTRATA: If that's what it takes—
   (The Second Woman enters running for the gates.)
SECOND WOMAN: Oh, my, oh, my!
   My poor flax is at home!
   My lovely flax from Amorgos!
   Unpeeled!
LYSISTRATA: O god, another one!
   Unpeeled flax this time!
   You! Come back here!
SECOND WOMAN: Once I've got it
   All stripped down, I'll be back!
   By Artemis, I will!
LYSISTRATA: No stripping, dear.
   One stripping leads to another.
   Soon they'll all be stripping.
   (The Third Woman enters trying to look conspicuously pregnant, invoking the goddess.)
THIRD WOMAN: Help me, O help me,
   Holly Eileithyia! Goddess of childbirth,
   Help me! Don't let me drop this
   Baby in this sacred place! It's unlawful!
LYSISTRATA: And what seems to by *your* problem?
THIRD WOMAN: I'm due—it's my time—
   Any second, now! I—
LYSISTRATA: Yesterday you weren't even pregnant.
THIRD WOMAN: Oh, but I am today, Lysistrata!
   Oh, Lysistrata, let me go home!
   I need to call the midwife away!
LYSISTRATA: Oh, come on, dear,
   You can do better than that!
   (Knocking on her stomach and producing a metallic clang.)

Now what could that be, I wonder?
It's hard as a rock.
THIRD WOMAN: Hard? Well, I should hope!
It's—it's a bouncing baby boy—
Or *will* be if I don't hurry!
(Lysistrata taps it once again.)
LYSISTRATA: Bull! It's bronze, and it's hollow!
Let's just have a look at this bambino, shall we?
(She pulls out a large helmet.)
Some baby *that* would have been!
THIRD WOMAN: But I *am* pregnant.
LYSISTRATA: Then explain *this*!
THIRD WOMAN: I, I was afraid
I might start having the baby
While I was still here—and—and I—
I thought if I did, I could just
Drop it in here like—like
Pigeons drop their eggs in a nest—
LYSISTRATA: In the helmet from Athena's statue—
THIRD WOMAN: Well, I—
LYSISTRATA: All right, then— well,
Since this is your baby,
(Taps the helmet.)
I dare say you won't be
Leaving until we've named it,
And that'll be a week and a few days.
THIRD WOMAN: But it's awful!
I just can't sleep in there anymore!
Last night I saw that horrible temple snake!
FIRST WOMAN: Me, too! How can I
Sleep when all it's
Tu-wit-tu-woo-tu-wit-tu-woo
From Athena's goddamn holy owls!
It's a nightmare!
It's driving me batty!
LYSISTRATA: All of you! Stop right there!
—Now, I *know* how much
You miss your husbands. I *know* that.
But how much do you think

They miss *you*? And just imagine
How much worse it is for them.
Their nights don't compare with yours.
Yours are sweet dreams compared with
The agonies *they* endure!
—So let's hang on in there, girls!
Hold out a little bit longer
And victory is ours! It's fated!
I have an oracle here that says so!
Do you want to hear it?

ALL: Read it to us, Lysistrata! Read it!

LYSISTRATA: Quiet! Here it is!
  (She unrolls a scroll and reads.)
  "When swallows do the lusty hoopoes shun
  And spurn their lusty fire-hot desire,
  Then mighty Zeus will end what they've begun,
  And raise the lowly lovely swallow higher."

FIRST WOMAN: Does that mean we get to be
  On top for a change?

LYSISTRATA: "But if the swallows flee the sacred shrine
  And yield to the hoopoes' lusty, ardent flame,
  Then forever accursed away they'll pine,
  Known forever as sex-crazed, to their shame."

THIRD WOMAN: By god, that's pretty
  Clear for an oracle, I'd say.

LYSISTRATA: So, then girls, what'll it be?
  Do we give up or do we go
  Back to our posts? I say
  We keep it going! Back inside, now!
  Think of the disgrace if we gave up!
  How can we fail?
  You heard the oracle!
  (They go off together.)

Ralph Roister Doister

Nicholas Udall
1553

Comic
Setting: Dame Custance's house.
Scene: Dame Custance wants no part of Ralph and she calls forth her domestic staff as allies to arm themselves against the pesky, self-aggrandizing Ralph who is pursuing her despite her engagement to Gawyn Goodluck.

Dame Christian Custance: A beautiful widow being wooed by Ralph, 20's – 30's.
Tibet Talkapace: Her maid, 20's.
Annot Alyface: Her second maid, 20's.
Margery Mumblecrust: Her nurse, 40's – 50's.

(Dame Custance left alone.)
DAME CUSTANCE: So, sirrah! If I should not with him take this way.
　　I should not be rid of him, I think, till doom's day.
　　I will call forth my folks, that, without any mocks.
　　If he comes again, we may give him raps and knocks.
　　Madge Mumblecrust, come forth! and Tibet Talkapace!
　　Yea, and come forth, too, Miss Annot Alyface!
　　(Enter Tibet Talkapace, Annot Alyface, and Margery Mumblecrust.)
ALYFACE: I come.
TALKAPACE: And I am here.
MUMBLECRUST: And I am here too at length.
DAME CUSTANCE: Like warriors, if need be, ye must show your strength.
　　The man that this day hath thus beguiled you
　　Is Ralph Roister Doister, whom ye know well enow,
　　The most lout and dastard that ever on ground trod.
TALKAPACE: I see all folk mock him when he goeth abroad.
DAME CUSTANCE: What, pretty maid! Will ye talk when I speak?
TALKAPACE: No, forsooth, good mistress.
DAME CUSTANCE: Will ye my tale break?
　　He threatened to come hither with all his force to fight;
　　I charge you, if he come, on him with all your might!

MUMBLECRUST: I with my distaff will reach him one rap!
TALKAPACE: And I with my new broom will sweep him one swap,
    And them with our great club I will reach him one rap!
ALYFACE: And I with our skimmer will fling him one flap!
TALKAPACE: The Truepenny's firework will him shrewdly fray,
    And you with the spit may drive him quite away.
DAME CUSTANCE: Go, make all ready, that it may be e'en so.
TALKAPACE: For my part, I shrew them that last about it go!
    (Tibet and Annot Alyface go to arm themselves.)

Tamburlaine

Christopher Marlowe
1587

Dramatic
Setting: Near the battlefields where the Turks and Persians are
    fighting.
Scene: The women bicker and hold much anger toward each other.
    They are on opposing sides but find themselves together wit-
    nessing the battle.

Zabina: Wife to Bajazeth the Turkish Emperor, 30's.
Ebea: Her maid, 20's.
Zenocrate: Daughter of the Sultan of Eygpt, engaged to
    Tamburlaine, 20's.
Anippe: Her maid, 20's.

ZABINA: Base concubine, must thou be plac'd by me
    That am the empress of the mighty Turk?
ZENOCRATE: Disdainful Turkess and unreverend boss,
    Call'st thou me concubine that am betroth'd
    Unto the great and mighty Tamburlaine?
ZABINA: To Tamburlaine, the great Tartarian thief?
ZENOCRATE: Thou wilt repent these lavish words of thine
    When thy great basso-master and thyself
    Must pleased for mercy at his kingly feet,
    And sue to me to be your advocate.
ZABINA: And sue to thee? I tell thee, shameless girl,
    Thou shalt be laundress to my waiting-maid.
    How lik'st thou her, Ebea? Will she serve?
EBEA: Madam, she thinks perhaps she is too fine;
    But I shall turn her into other weeds,
    And make her dainty fingers fall to work.
ZENOCRATE: Hear'st thou, Anippe, how thy drudge doth talk,
    And how my slave, her mistress, menaceth?
    Both for their sauciness shall be employ'd
    To dress the common soldiers' meat and drink;
    For we will scorn they should come near ourselves.
ANIPPE: Yet sometimes let your highness send for them

To do the work my chambermaid disdains.
(They sound the battle within, and stay.)
ZENOCRATE: Ye gods and powers that govern Persia,
And made my lordly love her worthy king,
Now strengthen him against the Turkish Bajazeth,
And let his foes, like flocks of fearful roes
Pursu'd by hunters, fly his angry looks,
That I may see him issue conqueror.
ZABINA: Now, Mahomet, solicit God himself,
And make him rain down murdering shot from heaven,
To dash the Scythians' brains, and strike them dead
That dare to manage arms with him
That offered jewels to thy sacred shrine
When first he warr'd against the Christians.
(To the battle again.)
ZENOCRATE: By this the Turks lie welt'ring in their blood,
And Tamburlaine is lord of Africa.
ZABINA: Thou art deceiv'd. I heard the trumpets sound
As when my emperor overthrew the Greeks,
And led them captive into Africa.
Straight will I use thee as thy pride deserves;
Prepare thyself to live and die my slave.
ZENOCRATE: If Mahomet should come from heaven and swear
My royal lord is slain or conquered,
Yet should he not persuade me otherwise
But that he lives and will be conqueror.

Love's Labour Lost

William Shakespeare
1594

Comic
Setting: In front of the Princess's Pavilion in the King's Park.
Scene: The ladies have all received gifts of love from their suitors
and are being very merry at their expense. The King of Navarre
is wooing the princess and his courtiers, Longaville, Dumain,
and Berowne are wooing the ladies who have all come on a
diplomatic mission from France.

The Princes: Princess of France, 20's.
Her ladies-in-waiting, 20's:
Katharine
Rosaline
Maria

PRINCESS: Sweet hearts, we shall be rich ere we depart,
If fairings come this plentifully in:
A lady wall'd about with diamonds!
Look you what I have from the loving king.
ROSALINE: Madam, came nothing else along with that?
PRINCESS: Nothing but this! Yes, as much love in rime
As would be cramm'd up in a sheet of paper,
Writ o' both sides the leaf, margent and all,
That he was fain to seal on Cupid's name.
ROSALINE: That was the way to make his godhead wax,
For he hath been five thousand years a boy.
KATHARINE: Ay, and a shrewd unhappy gallows too.
ROSALINE: You'll ne'er be friends with him; a' kill'd your sister.
KATHARINE: He made her melancholy, sad, and heavy;
And so she died: had she been light, like you,
Of such a merry, nimble, stirring spirit,
She might ha' been a grandam ere she died:
And so may you; for a light heart lives long.
ROSALINE: What's your dark meaning, mouse, of this light word?
KATHARINE: A light condition in a beauty dark.
ROSALINE: We need more light to find your meaning out.

KATHARINE: You'll mar the light by taking it in snuff;
    Therefore, I'll darkly end the argument.
ROSALINE: Look, what you do, you do it still i' th' dark.
KATHARINE: So do not you, for you are a light wench.
ROSALINE: Indeed I weigh not you, and therefore light.
KATHARINE: You weigh me not? O, that's you care not for me.
ROSALINE: Great reason; for "past cure is still care."
PRINCESS: Well bandied both; a set of wit well play'd.
    But, Rosaline, you have a favour too:
    Who sent it? and what is it?
ROSALINE: I would you knew:
    An if my face were but as fair as yours,
    My favour were as great; be witness this.
    Nay, I have verses too, I thank Berowne:
    The numbers true; and, were the numb'ring too,
    I were the fairest goddess on the ground:
    I am compared to twenty thousand fairs.
    O, he hath drawn my picture in his letter!
PRINCESS: Any thing like?
ROSALINE: Much in the letters; nothing in the praise.
PRINCESS: Beauteous as ink; a good conclusion.
KATHARINE: Fair as a text B in a copy-book.
ROSALINE: 'Ware pencils, ho! Let me not die your debtor,
    My red dominical, my golden letter:
    O that your face were not so full of O's!
PRINCESS: A pox of that jest! And I beshrew all shrows.
    But, Katharine, what was sent to you from fair Dumaine?
KATHRINE: Madam, this glove.
PRINCESS: Did he not send you twain?
KATHARINE: Yes, madam, and moreover
    Some thousand verses of a faithful lover,
    A huge translation of hypocrisy,
    Vilely compiled, profound simplicity.
MARIA: This and these pearls to me sent Longaville:
    The letter is too long by half a mile.
PRINCESS: I think no less. Dost thou not wish in heart
    The chain were longer and the letter short?
MARIA: Ay, or I would these hands might never part.
PRINCESS: We are wise girls to mock our lovers so.

ROSALINE: They are worse fools to purchase mocking so.
    That same Berowne I'll torture ere I go:
    O that I knew he were but in by th' week!
    How I would make him fawn and beg and seek
    And wait the season and observe the times,
    And spend his prodigal wits in bootless rimes,
    And shape his service wholly to my hests,
    And make him proud to make me proud that jests!
    So pertaunt-like would I o'ersway his state
    That he should be my fool and I his fate.
PRINCESS: None are so surely caught, when they are catcht,
    As wit turn'd fool: folly, in wisdom hatcht,
    Hath wisdom's warrant and the help of school
    And wit's own grace to grace a learned fool.
ROSALINE: The blood of youth burns not with such excess
    As gravity's revolt to wantonness.
MARIA: Folly in fools bears not so strong a note
    As foolery in the wise, when wit doth dote;
    Since all the power thereof it doth apply
    To prove, by wit, worth in simplicity.
PRINCESS: Here comes Boyet, and mirth is in his face.

All's Well that Ends Well
William Shakespeare
1602

Comic
Setting: Outside the walls of the city of Florence.
Scene: Florence and Siena are at war and Bertram, who is French, is gaining military experience by fighting with the Florentines. He is in love with Diana but married to Helena who has come to Florence on a religious pilgrimage. Here she meets Diana and her mother who run a hostel for wayfarers and pilgrims. They can hear the tuckets (drums) of the army in the distance and have gone to the walls to observe. The Count's man, Parolles, has previously approached Diana on the Count's behalf.

Diana Capilet: A young lady of Florence, wooed by Bertram the Count of Rossillion.
Old Widow Capilet: Her mother 50's – 60's.
Mariana: Her neighbor and the Widow's friend 40's – 60's.
Helena: A gentlewoman raised by the Countess of Rossillion, Bertram's mother; in love with Bertram and recently married to him.

WIDOW: Nay, come; for if they do approach the city, we shall lose all the sight.
DIANA: They say the French count has done most honourable service.
WIDOW: It is reported that he has taken their greatest commander; and that with his own hand he slew the duke's brother.
(Tucket.) We have lost our labour; they are gone a contrary way: hark! You may know by their trumpets.
MARIANA: Come, let's return again, and suffice ourselves with the report of it. Well, Diana, take heed of this French earl: the honour of a maid is her name; and no legacy is so rich as honesty.
WIDOW: I have told my neighbour how you have been solicited by a gentleman his companion.
MARIANA: I know that knave; hang him! One Parolles: filthy officer he is in those suggestions for the young earl. —Beware of them, Diana; their promises, enticements, oaths, tokens, and all

these engines of lust, are not the things they go under: many a maid hath been seduced by them; and the misery is, example, that so terrible shows in the wrack of maidenhood, cannot for all that dissuade succession, but that they are limed with the twigs that threaten them. I hope I need not to advise you further; but I hope your own grace will keep you where you are, though there were no further danger known but the modesty which is so lost.

DIANA: You shall not need to fear me.

WIDOW: I hope so. Look, here comes a pilgrim: I know she will lie at my house; thither they send one another: I'll question her. *(Enter Helena, in the dress of a pilgrim.)* God save you, pilgrim! Whither are you bound?

HELENA: To Saint Jacques le Grand.
Where do the palmers lodge, I do beseech you?

WIDOW: At the Saint Francis here, beside the port.

HELENA: Is this the way?

WIDOW: Ay, marry, is't. Hark you! They come this way—*(A march afar off.)* If you will tarry, holy pilgrim, but will the troops come by, I will conduct you where you shall be lodged;
The rather, for I think I know your hostess
As ample as myself.

HELENA: Is it yourself?

WIDOW: If you shall please so, pilgrim.

HELENA: I thank you, and will stay upon your leisure.

WIDOW: You came, I think, from France?

HELENA: I did so.

WIDOW: Here you shall see a countryman of yours
That has done worthy service.

HELENA: His name, I pray you.

DIANA: The Count Rousillon: know you such a one?

HELENA: But by the ear, that hears most nobly of him:
His face I know not.

DIANA: Whatsome'er he is,
He's bravely taken here. He stole from France,
As 'tis reported, for the king had married him
Against his liking: think you it is so?

HELENA: Ay, surely, mere the truth: I know his lady.

DIANA: There is a gentleman that serves the count

Reports but coarsely of her.

HELENA: What's his name?

DIANA: Monsieur Parolles.

HELENA: O, I believe with him,
In argument of praise, or to the worth
Of the great count himself, she is too mean
To have her name repeated: all her deserving
Is a reserved honesty, and that
I have not heard examined.

DIANA: Alas, poor lady!
'Tis a hard bondage to become the wife
Of a detesting lord.

WIDOW: I write good creature; wheresoe'er she is,
Her heart weighs sadly: this young maid might do her
A shrewd turn, if she pleased.

HELENA: How do you mean?
May be the amorous count solicits her
In the unlawful purpose.

WIDOW: He does indeed;
And brokes with all that can in such a suit
Corrupt the tender honour of a maid:
But she is arm'd for him, and keeps her guard
In honestest defence.

MARTINA: The gods forbid else!

WIDOW: So, now they come.—

The Clandestine Marriage

David Garrick
1766

Comic

Setting: A room in the Sterling home.

Scene: Miss Sterling, engaged to a wealthy man, is lording it over her sister Fanny. She does not know of Fanny's clandestine marriage because their aunt, Mrs. Heidelberg, holds the purse strings and wants the girls to marry men of "quality". Money rules the world and Mr. Lovewell is not a man of means.

Fanny Sterling: 20's, secretly married (and pregnant) to Mr. Lovewell.
Miss Sterling: Her older sister, 20's.
Mrs. Trusty: The family housekeeper.
Mrs. Heidelberg: The aunt and holder of the family inheritance.

MISS STERL: Oh, my dear sister, say no more! This is downright hypocrisy—You shall never convince me that you don't envy me beyond measure—Well, after all it is extremely natural—It is impossible to be angry with you.

FANNY: Indeed, sister, you have no cause.

MISS STERL: And you really pretend not to envy me?

FANNY: Not in the least.

MISS STERL: And you don't in the least wish that you was just in my situation?

FANNY: No, indeed, I don't. Why should I?

MISS STERL: Why should you? —What, on the brink of marriage, fortune, title. —But I had forgot. —There's that dear sweet creature Mr. Lovewell in the case. —You would not break your faith with your true love now for the world, I warrant you.

FANNY: Mr. Lovewell! —Always Mr. Lovewell! —Lord, what signifies Mr. Lovewell, sister?

MISS STERL: Pretty peevish soul! —Oh, my dear, grave, romantick sister! A perfect philosopher in petticoats! —Love and a cottage! —Eh, Fanny! —Ah, give me indifference and a coach and six!

FANNY: And why not the coach and six without the indifference? —But, pray, when is this happy marriage of yours to be celebrated? —I long to give you joy.

MISS STERL: In a day or two—I can't tell exactly—Oh, my dear sister! I must mortify her a little. *(Aside.)* —I know you have a pretty taste. Pray, give me your opinion of my jewels. —How d'ye like the stile of this esclavage? *(Shewing jewels.)*

FANNY: Extremely handsome indeed, and well fancied.

MISS STERL: What d'ye think of these bracelets? I shall have a miniature of my father, set round with diamonds, to one, and Sir John's to the other.— And this pair of ear-rings! Set transparent! —here, the tops, you see, will take off to wear in a morning, or in an undress—how d'ye like them? *(Shewing jewels.)*

FANNY: Very much, I assure you. Bless me; sister, you have a prodigious quantity of jewels, you'll be the very Queen of Diamonds.

MISS STERL: Ha! ha! ha! very well, my dear! —I shall be as fine as a little queen indeed. —I have a bouquet to come home tomorrow— made up of diamonds, and rubies, and emeralds, and topazes, and amethysts—jewels of all colours, green, red, blue, yellow, intermixt—the prettiest thing you ever saw in your life! —The jeweller says I shall set out with as many diamonds as any body in town, except Lady Brilliant, and Polly *What d'ye-call-it*, Lord Squander's kept mistress.

FANNY: But what are your wedding-cloaths, sister?

MISS STERL: Oh, white and silver to be sure, you know—I bought them at Sir Joseph Lutestring's, and sat above an hour in the parlour behind the shop, consulting Lady Lutestring about gold and silver stuffs, on purpose to mortify her.

FANNY: Fie, sister! How could you be so abominably provoking?

MISS STERL: Oh, I have no patience with the pride of your city-knights' ladies. —Did you never observe the airs of Lady Lutestring drest in the richest brocade out of her husband's shop, playing crown-whist at Haberdasher's-Hall? —While the civil smirking Sir Joseph, with a smug wig trimmed round his broad face as close as a new-cut yew-hedge, and his shoes so black that they shine again, stands all day in his shop, fastened to his counter like a bad shilling?

FANNY: Indeed, indeed, sister, this is too much—If you talk at this rate, you will be absolutely a bye-word in the city—You must never venture on the inside of Temple-Bar again.

MISS STERL: Never do I desire it—never, my dear Fanny, I promise you—Oh, how I long to be transported to the dear regions of

Grosvenor-Square, far, far from the dull districts of Aldersgate, Cheap, Candlewick, and Farringdon Without and Within! My heart goes pit-a-pat at the very idea of being introduced at Court! Gilt chariot! Pyeballed horses! Laced liveries! And then the whispers buzzing round the circle, "Who is that young Lady! Who is she?" "Lady Melvil, Ma'am!" Lady Melvil! My ears tingle at the sound. And then at dinner, instead of my father perpetually asking, "Any news upon 'Change?" to cry, "Well, Sir John! anything new from Arthur's?" Or, to say to some other woman of quality, "Was your Ladyship at the Dutchess of Rubber's last night? Did you call in at Lady Thunder's? In the immensity of croud I swear I did not see you, scarce a soul at the opera last Saturday, shall I see you at Carlisle-House next Thursday?" Oh, the dear Beau-Monde! I was born to move in the sphere of the great world.

FANNY: And so, in the midst of all this happiness, you have no compassion for me, no pity for us poor mortals in common life.

MISS STERL: (Affectedly.) You, you're above pity. You would not change conditions with me, you're over head and ears in love, you know. Nay, for that matter, if Mr. Lovewell and you come together, as I doubt you will, you will live very comfortably, I dare say. He will mind his business, you'll employ yourself in the delightful care of your family, and once in a season perhaps you'll sit together in a front-box at a benefit play, as we used to do at our dancing-master's, you know, and perhaps I may meet you in the summer with some other citizens at Tunbridge. For my part, I shall always entertain a proper regard for my relations. You sha'nt want my countenance, I assure you.

FANNY: Oh, you're too kind, sister!

(Enter Mrs. Heidelberg.)

MRS. HEIDEL: (At entering.) Here this evening! I vow and pertest we shall scarce have time to provide for them, Oh, my dear! (To Miss Sterl.) I am glad to see you're not quite in dishabille. Lord Ogleby and Sir John Melvil will be here tonight.

MISS STERL: Tonight, Ma'am?

MRS. HEIDEL: Yes, my dear, tonight. Do, put on a smarter cap, and change those ordinary ruffles! Lord, I have such a deal to do, I shall scarce have time to slip on my Italian lutestring. Where is this dawdle of a housekeeper? (Enter Mrs. Trusty.) Oh, here, Trusty!

Do you know that people of qualaty are expected here this evening?

TRUSTY: Yes, Ma'am.

MRS. HEIDEL: Well—Do you be sure now that every thing is done in the most genteelest manner, and to the honour of the fammaly.

TRUSTY: Yes, Ma'am.

MRS. HEIDEL: Well, but mind what I say to you.

TRUSTY: Yes, Ma'am.

MRS. HEIDEL: His Lordship is to lie in the chintz bedchamber, d'ye hear? And Sir John in the blue damask room. His Lordship's valet-de-shamb in the opposite.

TRUSTY: But Mr. Lovewell is come down, and you know that's his room, Ma'am.

MRS. HEIDEL: Well, well, Mr. Lovewell may make shift, or get a bed at the George. But hark ye, Trusty!

TRUSTY: Ma'am!

MRS. HEIDEL: Get the great dining-room in order as soon as possible. Unpaper the curtains, take the civers off the couch and the chairs, and put the china on the mantle-piece immediately.

TRUSTY: Yes, Ma'am.

MRS. HEIDEL: Be gone then! Fly, this instant! Where's my brother Sterling.

TRUSTY: Talking to the butler, Ma'am.

MRS. HEIDEL: Very well. *(Exit Trusty.)* Miss Fanny! I pertest I did not see you before, Lord, child, what's the matter with you?

FANNY: With me? Nothing, Ma'am.

MRS. HEIDEL: Bless me! Why your face is as pale, and black, and yellow, of fifty colours, I pertest. And then you have drest yourself as loose and as big, I declare there is not such a thing to be seen now, as a young woman with a fine waist. You all make yourselves as round as Mrs. Deputy Barter. Go, child! You know the qualaty will be here by and by. Go, and make yourself a little ore fit to be seen. *(Exit Fanny.)*

She is gone away in tears, absolutely crying, I vow and pertest. This ridiculous Love! We must put a stop to it. It makes a perfect natural of the girl.

MISS STERL: Poor soul! She can't help it. *(Affectedly.)*

MRS. HEIDEL: Well, my dear! Now I shall have an opportunity of convincing you of the absurdity of what you was telling me concerning Sir John Melvil's behaviour to you.

MISS STERL: Oh, it gives me no manner of uneasiness. But, indeed, Ma'am, I cannot be persuaded but that Sir John is an extremely cold lover. Such distant civility, grave looks, and lukewarm professions of esteem for me and the whole family! I have heard of flames and darts, but Sir John's is a passion of mere ice and snow.

MRS. HEIDEL: Oh, fie, my dear! I am perfectly ashamed of you. That's so like the notions of your poor sister! What you complain of as coldness and indiffarence, is nothing but the extreme gentilaty of his address, an exact pictur of the manners of qualaty.

MISS STERL: Oh, he is the very mirror of complaisance! Full of formal bows and set speeches! I declare, if there was any violent passion on my side, I should be quite jealous of him.

MRS. HEIDEL: I say jealus indeed. Jealus of who, pray?

MISS STERL: My sister Fanny. She seems a much greater favourite than I am, and he prays her infinitely more attention, I assure you.

MRS. HEIDEL: Lord! D'ye think a man of fashion, as he is, can't distinguish between the genteel and the wulgar part of the famaly? Between you and your sister, for instance, or me and my brother? Be advised by me, child! It is all politeness and good breeding. Nobody knows the qualaty better than I do.

MISS STERL: In my mind the old lord, his uncle, has ten times more gallantry about him than Sir John. He is full of attentions to the ladies, and smiles, and grins, and leers, and ogles, and fills every wrinkle in his old wizen face with comical expressions of tenderness. I think he wou'd make an admirable sweetheart.

Overtones

Alice Gerstenberg
1913

Dramatic

Setting: Harriet's fashionable living room. Tea is prepared.

Scene: Harriet has been in love with Margaret's husband for many years, despite having married into wealth and privilege herself. Now the friends meet and their alter egos reflect the true feelings they experience.

Of Note: The alter egos, more primitive and unrepressed, can see the woman, but the woman cannot see the alter egos. The voices of Hetty and Maggie should reflect their more unrestrained selves.

Harriet: 20's – 40's; a cultured and careful woman, married to Charles.
Hetty: Her alter ego.
Margaret: An old friend of Harriet's, 20's – 40's, now married to John an artist whom Harriet once loved.
Maggie: Margaret's alter ego.

HETTY: *(The telephone rings.)* There she is now. *(Hetty hurries to 'phone but Harriet regains her supremacy.)*

HARRIET: *(Authoritatively.)* Wait! I can't let the telephone girl down there hear my real self. It isn't proper. *(At phone.)* Show Mrs. Caldwell up.

HETTY: I'm so excited, my heart's in my mouth.

HARRIET: *(At the mirror.)* A nice state you've put my nerves into.

HETTY: Don't let her see you're nervous.

HARRIET: Quick, put the veil on, or she'll see you shining through me. *(Harriet takes a scarf of chiffon that has been lying over the back of a chair and drapes it on Hetty, covering her face. The chiffon is the same color of their gowns but paler in shade so that it pales Hetty's darker gown to match Harriet's lighter one. As Hetty moves in the following scene the chiffon falls away revealing now and then the gown of deeper dye underneath.)*

HETTY: Tell her Charles is rich and fascinating—boast of our friends, make her feel she needs us.

HARRIET: I'll make her ask John to paint us.

HETTY: That's just my thought—if John paints our portrait—

HARRIET: We can wear an exquisite gown—

HETTY: And make him fall in love again and—

HARRIET: *(Schemingly.)* Yes. *(Margaret parts the portières back center and extends her hand. Margaret is followed by her counterpart Maggie.)* Oh, Margaret, I'm so glad to see you!

HETTY: *(To Maggie.)* That's a lie.

MARGARET: *(In superficial voice throughout.)* It's enchanting to see you Harriet.

MAGGIE: *(In emotional voice throughout.)* I'd bite you, if I dared.

HARRIET: *(To Margaret.)* Wasn't our meeting a stroke of luck?

MARGARET: *(Coming down left of table.)* I've thought of you so often, Harriet; and to come back and find you living in New York.

HARRIET: *(Coming down right of table.)* Mr. Goodrich has many interests here.

MAGGIE: *(To Margaret.)* Flatter her.

MARGARET: I know, Mr. Goodrich is so successful.

HETTY: *(To Harriet.)* Tell her we're rich.

HARRIET: *(To Margaret.)* Won't you sit down?

MARGARET: *(Takes a chair.)* What a beautiful cabinet!

HARRIET: Do you like it? I'm afraid Charles paid an extravagant price.

MAGGIE: *(To Hetty.)* I don't believe it.

MARGARET: *(Sitting down. To Harriet.)* I am sure he must have.

HARRIET: *(Sitting down.)* How well you are looking, Margaret.

HETTY: Yes, you are not. There are circles under your eyes.

MAGGIE: *(To Hetty.)* I haven't eaten since breakfast and I'm hungry.

MARGARET: *(To Harriet.)* How well you are looking, too.

MAGGIE: *(To Hetty.)* You have hard lines about your lips, are you happy?

HETTY: *(To Harriet.)* Don't let her know that I'm unhappy.

HARRIET: *(To Margaret.)* Why shouldn't I look well? My life is full, happy, complete—

MAGGIE: I wonder.

HETTY: *(In Harriet's ear.)* Tell her we have an automobile.

MARGARET: *(To Harriet.)* My life is complete, too.

MAGGIE: My heart is torn with sorrow; my husband cannot make a living. He will kill himself if he does not get an order for a painting.

MARGARET: *(Laughs.)* You must come and see us in our studio. John has been doing some excellent portraits. He cannot begin to fill his orders.

HETTY: *(To Harriet.)* Tell her we have an automobile.

HARRIET: *(To Margaret.)* Do you take lemon in your tea?

MAGGIE: Take cream. It's more filling.

MARGARET: *(Looking nonchalantly at tea things.)* No, cream, if you please. How cozy!

MAGGIE: *(Glaring at tea things.)* Only cakes! I could eat them all!

HARRIET: *(To Margaret.)* How many lumps?

MAGGIE: *(To Margaret.)* Sugar is nourishing.

MARGARET: *(To Harriet.)* Three, please. I used to drink very sweet coffee in Turkey and ever since I've—

HETTY: I don't believe you were ever in Turkey.

MAGGIE: I wasn't, but it is none of your business.

HARRIET: *(Pouring tea.)* Have you been in Turkey? Do tell me about it.

MAGGIE: *(To Margaret.)* Change the subject.

MARGARET: *(To Harriet.)* You must go there. You have so much taste in dress you would enjoy seeing their costumes.

MAGGIE: Isn't she going to pass the cake?

MARGARET: *(To Harriet.)* John painted several portraits there.

HETTY: *(To Harriet.)* Why don't you stop her bragging and tell her we have an automobile?

HARRIET: *(Offers cake across the table to Margaret.)* Cake?

MAGGIE: *(Stands back of Margaret, shadowing her as Hetty shadows Harriet. Maggie reaches claws out for the cake and groans with joy.)* At last! *(But her claws do not touch the cake.)*

MARGARET: *(With a graceful, nonchalant hand places cake upon her plate and bites at it slowly and delicately.)* Thank you.

HETTY: *(To Harriet.)* Automobile!

MAGGIE: *(To Margaret.)* Follow up the costumes with the suggestion that she would make a good model for John. It isn't too early to begin getting what you came for.

MARGARET: *(Ignoring Maggie.)* What delicious cake.

HETTY: *(Excitedly to Harriet.)* There's your chance for the auto.

HARRIET: *(Nonchalantly to Margaret.)* Yes, it is good cake, isn't it? There are always a great many people buying it at Harper's. I sat in my automobile fifteen minutes this morning waiting for my chauffeur to get it.

MAGGIE: *(To Margaret.)* Make her order a portrait.

MARGARET: *(To Harriet.)* If you stopped at Harper's you must have noticed the new gowns at Henderson's. Aren't the shop windows alluring these days?

HARRIET: Even my chauffeur notices them.

MAGGIE: I know you have an automobile, I heard you the first time.

MARGARET: I notice gowns now with an artist's eye as John does. The one you have on, my dear, is very paintable.

HETTY: Don't let her see you're anxious to be painted.

HARRIET: *(Nonchalantly.)* Oh, it's just a little model.

MAGGIE: *(To Margaret.)* Don't seem anxious to get the order.

MARGARET: *(Nonchalantly.)* Perhaps it isn't the gown itself but the way you wear it that pleases the eye. Some people can wear anything with grace.

HETTY: Yes, I'm very graceful.

HARRIET: *(To Margaret.)* You flatter me, my dear.

MARGARET: On the contrary, Harriet, I have an intense admiration for you. I remember how beautiful you were—as a girl. In fact, I was quite jealous when John was paying you so much attention.

HETTY: She is gloating because I lost him.

HARRIET: Those were childhood days in a country town.

MAGGIE: *(To Margaret.)* She's trying to make you feel that John was only a country boy.

MARGARET: Most great men have come from the country. There is a fair chance that John will be added to the list.

HETTY: I know it and I am bitterly jealous of you.

HARRIET: Undoubtedly he owes much of his success to you, Margaret, your experience in economy and your ability to endure hardship. Those first few years in Paris must have been a struggle.

MAGGIE: She is sneering at your poverty.

MARGARET: Yes, we did find life difficult at first, not the luxurious start a girl has who marries wealth.

HETTY: *(To Harriet.)* Deny that you married Charles for his money.
(Harriet deems it wise to ignore Hetty's advice.)

MARGARET: But John and I are so congenial in our tastes, that we were impervious to hardship or unhappiness.

HETTY: *(In anguish.)* Do you love each other? Is it really true?

HARRIET: *(Sweetly.)* Did you have all the romance of starving for his art?

MAGGIE: *(To Margaret.)* She's taunting you. Get even with her.

MARGARET: Not for long. Prince Rier soon discovered John's genius, and introduced him royally to wealthy Parisians who gave him many orders.

HETTY: *(To Maggie.)* Are you telling the truth or are you lying?

HARRIET: If he had so many opportunities there, you must have had great inducements to come back to the States.

MAGGIE: *(To Hetty.)* We did, but not the kind you think.

MARGARET: John became the rage among Americans traveling in France, too, and they simply insisted upon his coming here.

HARRIET: Whom is he going to paint here?

MAGGIE: *(Frightened.)* What names dare I make up?

MARGARET: *(Calmly.)* Just at present Miss Dorothy Ainsworth of Oregon is posing. You may not know the name, but she is the daughter of a wealthy miner who found gold in Alaska.

HARRIET: I dare say there are many Western people we have never heard of.

MARGARET: You must have found social life in New York very interesting, Harriet, after the simplicity of our home town.

HETTY: *(To Maggie.)* There's no need to remind us that our beginnings were the same.

HARRIET: Of course Charles's family make everything delightful for me. They are so well connected.

MAGGIE: *(To Margaret.)* Flatter her.

MARGARET: I heard it mentioned yesterday that you had made yourself very popular. Some one said you were very clever!

HARRIET: *(Pleased.)* Who told you that?

MAGGIE: Nobody!

MARGARET: *(Pleasantly.)* Oh, confidences should be suspected—respected, I mean. They said, too, that you are gaining some reputation as a critic of art.

HARRIET: I make no pretences.

MARGARET: Are you and Mr. Goodrich interested in the same things, too?

HETTY: No!

HARRIET: Yes, indeed, Charles and I are inseparable.

MAGGIE: I wonder.

HARRIET: Do have another cake.

MAGGIE: *(In relief.)* Oh, yes.

    (Again her claws extend but do not touch the cake.)

MARGARET: *(Takes cake delicately.)* I really shouldn't—after my big luncheon. John took me to the Ritz and we are invited to the Bedfords' for dinner—they have such a magnificent house near the drive, I really shouldn't, but the cakes are so good.

MAGGIE: Starving!

HARRIET: *(To Margaret.)* More tea?

MAGGIE: Yes!

MARGARET: No, thank you. How wonderfully life has arranged itself for you. Wealth, position, a happy marriage, every opportunity to enjoy all pleasures; beauty, art—how happy you must be.

HETTY: *(In anguish.)* Don't call me happy. I've never been happy since I gave up John. All these years without him—a future without him—no—no—I shall win him back—away from you—away from you—

HARREIT: *(Does not see Maggie pointing to cream and Margaret stealing some.)* I sometimes think it is unfair for anyone to be as happy as I am. Charles and I are just as much in love now as when we married. To me he is just the dearest man in the world.

MAGGIE: *(Passionately.)* My John is. I love him so much I could die for him. I'm going through hunger and want to make him great and he loves me. He worships me!

MARGARET: *(Leisurely to Harriet.)* I should like to meet Mr. Goodrich. Bring him to our studio. John has some sketches to show. Not many, because all the portraits have been purchased by the subjects. He gets as much as four thousand dollars now.

HETTY: *(To Harriet.)* Don't pay that much.

HARRIET: *(To Margaret.)* As much as that?

MARGARET: It is not really too much when one considers that John is in the foremost ranks of artists today. A picture painted by him now will double and treble in value.

MAGGIE: It's a lie. He is growing weak with despair.

HARRIET: Does he paint all day long?

MAGGIE: No, he draws advertisements for our bread.

MARGARET: *(To Harriet.)* When you and your husband come to see us, telephone first—

MAGGIE: Yes, so we can get the advertisements out of the way.

MARGARET: Otherwise you might arrive while he has a sitter, and John refuses to let me disturb him then.

HETTY: Make her ask for an order.

HARRIET: *(To Margaret.)* Le Grange offered to paint me for a thousand.

MARGARET: Louis Le Grange's reputation isn't worth more than that.

HARRIET: Well, I've heard his work well mentioned.

MAGGIE: Yes, he is doing splendid work.

MARGARET: Oh, dear me, no. He is only praised by the masses. He is accepted not at all by artists themselves.

HETTY: *(Anxiously.)* Must I really pay the full price?

HARRIET: Le Grange thought I would make a good subject.

MAGGIE: *(To Margaret.)* Let her fish for it.

MARGARET: Of course you would. Why don't you let Le Grange paint you, if you *trust* him?

HETTY: She doesn't seem anxious to have John do it.

HARRIET: But if LeGrange isn't accepted by artists, it would be a waste of time to pose for him, wouldn't it?

MARGARET: Yes, I think it would.

MAGGIE: *(Passionately to Hetty across back of table.)* Give us the order. John is so despondent he can't endure much longer. Help us! Help me! Save us!

HETTY: *(To Harriet.)* Don't seem too eager.

Disconcerted States of Mind

Giacomo Balla

1916

Dramatic

Setting: A bare stage.

Of Note: This piece may be performed in unison, as a rondo, a canon, or in any way deemed appropriate.

First person
Second person
Third person
Fourth person

> *(Four people dressed differently. White stage. Begin all together.)*
> *(Spoken in unison:)*

FIRST PERSON: *(Loudly.)* 666 666 666 666
SECOND PERSON: *(Loudly.)* 333 333 333 333
THIRD PERSON: *(Loudly.)* 444 444 444 444
FOURTH PERSON: *(Loudly.)* 999 999 999 999

> *(Pause, always seriously.)*

> *(Spoken in unison:)*

FIRST PERSON: *(Loudly.)* aaa aaa aaa aaa
SECOND PERSON: *(Loudly.)* ttt ttt ttt ttt
THIRD PERSON: *(Loudly.)* sss sss sss sss
FOURTH PERSON: *(Loudly.)* uuu uuu uuu uuu

> *(Always seriously. Spoken in unison:)*

FIRST PERSON: *raises his hat*
SECOND PERSON: *looks at his watch*
THIRD PERSON: *blows his nose*
FOURTH PERSON: *reads a newspaper*

> *(Pause, very expressive. Spoken in unison:)*

FIRST PERSON: *(Loudly.)* sadness—aiaiaiaiaiaiaiaiai
SECOND PERSON: *(Loudly.)* quickness—quickly, quickly
THIRD PERSON: *(Loudly.)* pleasure—si si si si si si
FOURTH PERSON: *(Loudly.)* denial—no no no no no no

> *(Leave the stage, walking rigidly.)*

Yerma

Federico Garcia Lorca
1934

Yerma: A young married woman, childless.
First Old Woman
First Girl: Late teens, early 20's, married woman with a child.
Second Girl: Late teens, early 20's, married women, childless.

FIRST OLD WOMAN: I know what you're going to ask me. Of such
things I cannot speak.
(She rises.)
YERMA: *(Holding her.)* But why not? It has given me confidence to
hear you speak. I've wanted to talk to an old woman for a long
time now. Because I want to know. Yes. And you will tell me. . .
FIRST OLD WOMAN: Tell you what?
YERMA: *(Lowering her voice.)* What you know. Why am I barren?
Must I be left in the prime of my life taking care of little birds, or
putting up tiny pleated curtains in my little windows? No. You
must tell me what I need to do, because I will do anything, even
if you told me to stick needles into the tenderest part of my eyes.
FIRST OLD WOMAN: I? I know nothing. I laid down face up and
started to sing. Children came like water. Oh, who can say this
body you have isn't beautiful? You take a step, and at the end of
the street a horse whinnies. Oh! Leave me now, child, don't make
me talk. I think of many things I'd rather not say out loud.
YERMA: Why not? I talk of nothing else with my husband!
FIRST OLD WOMAN: Listen: does your husband please you?
YERMA: What?
FIRST OLD WOMAN: Do you love him? If you long to be with him . . .
YERMA: I don't know.
FIRST OLD WOMAN: You don't tremble when he comes near you?
Don't you feel a dream come over you when his lips touch yours?
Tell me.
YERMA: No. I've never felt anything.
FIRST OLD WOMAN: Never? Not even when you've danced?
YERMA: *(Remembering.)* Maybe. . .Once. . .Victor.
FIRST OLD WOMAN: Go on.
YERMA: He grabbed me by the waist and I couldn't say a word to

him, because I couldn't talk. Another time this same Victor, when he was fourteen old—he was quite big for his age, he took me in his arms to leap over a ditch and I started shaking so hard my teeth rattled. But I've always been shy.

FIRST OLD WOMAN: And with your husband?

YERMA: My husband is something else. My father gave him to me and I accepted. Happily. That's the absolute truth. Why, from the first day I was engaged to him I started thinking. . .about having children. . .And I would see myself in his eyes. Yes, but only in order to see myself very small, easily handled, as if I was my own daughter.

FIRST OLD WOMAN: It was the opposite with me. Maybe that's why you haven't had a child yet. You've got to take pleasure in men, girl. We have to unbraid our hair and drink water from their very mouths. That's the way the world works.

YERMA: Your world, not mine. I think about a lot of things, and I'm sure that what I think about are things my son will understand. I gave myself to my husband for his sake, and I keep giving myself to him to see if he will be born, but not out of pleasure.

FIRST OLD WOMAN: And so you're barren!

YERMA: Not barren, no, because I'm filling up with hate. Tell me: is it my fault? Should I only look at a man for the man himself and nothing more? Then, what are you to think when he leaves you in bed with your sad eyes looking at the ceiling, and he turns away and goes to sleep? Should I keep thinking of him, or in what could burst from my chest? I don't know, but please tell me, out of charity! *(She kneels.)*

FIRST OLD WOMAN: Oh, what an open flower! What a beautiful child you are. Leave me be. Do not make me speak anymore. I don't want to talk to you. These are matters of honor, and I don't burn anyone's honor. As you well know. Still, you should be less innocent.

YERMA: *(Sadly.)* All doors are closed to girls like me who are raised in the country. Everything turns to half-words, gestures, because they say that these things mustn't be talked about. And you, too, you keep silent as well, and leave with the knowledgeable air, like a doctor, knowing everything, but keeping it from one who is dying of thirst.

FIRST OLD WOMAN: I'll speak to a woman who is calm. But not to you. I'm old, and I know what I say.

YERMA: Then, God help me.

FIRST OLD WOMAN: Not God. I've never liked God. When are people going to realize he doesn't exit? Men are the ones who have to help us.

YERMA: But why do you say this to me? Why?

FIRST OLD WOMAN: *(Leaving.)* Though there should be a God, even if he were tiny, so that he could bring down his lightning on the rotten men who wreck the happiness of the fields.

YERMA: I don't understand what you're trying to tell me.

FIRST OLD WOMAN: Well, I know what I'm saying. Do not suffer. Hope for the best. You're still very young. What do you want to do?

(She leaves. Two Girls appear.)

FIRST GIRL: Everywhere we go we run into people.

YERMA: With all work that needs to be done, the men have to be in the olive groves, and we must bring them food. The only people left in their homes are the old people.

SECOND GIRL: Are you on your way back to the village?

YERMA: That's where I am headed.

FIRST GIRL: I'm in a great hurry. I've left my baby sleeping, and there's no one in the house.

YERMA: Then, hurry up, woman. You can't leave children alone. Are there pigs at your place?

FIRST GIRL: No, but you're right. I should hurry.

YERMA: Go ahead. That's how things happen. Surely, you've locked the door, though.

FIRST GIRL: Naturally,

YERMA: Yes, but even so, we don't understand what a small child really is. Something that seems perfectly harmless to us can destroy him: a tiny needle, a sip of water.

FIRST GIRL: You're right. I'll run on. I don't think of these things.

YERMA: Go on.

SECOND GIRL: If you had four or five, you wouldn't talk like that.

YERMA: Why not? Even if I had forty.

SECOND GIRL: Anyway, you and I, by not having any, live a more peaceful life.

YERMA: Not I.

SECOND GIRL: Well, I do. What a fuss! My mother, on the other had, does nothing but give me herbs so I will have children, and in October we'll go to a saint who they say gives to those who beg to him with fervor. My mother will ask him for me. Not I.

YERMA: Why did you get married?

SECOND GIRL: Because it was arranged. Everyone gets married. If we keep on like this, the only unmarried ones will be little girls. Well, and besides. . .in reality one gets married long before going to church. But the old women keep worrying about all these things. I'm nineteen years old and I don't like to cook or clean. Well, now I spend the entire day doing what I like least. And what for? What needs does my husband have to be my husband? We did the same thing as sweethearts as we do now. It's all just old folks' nonsense.

YERMA: Be quiet. Don't say such things.

SECOND GIRL: You'll be calling me crazy as well. That crazy girl, that crazy girl. *(She laughs.)* I can tell you the only thing I've learned in this life: everyone is stuck inside their houses doing what they don't wish to do. How much better it is to be out on the street! I can go to the river, I can go up to the tower and ring the bells, or I can drink of glass of anisette.

YERMA: You're just a girl.

SECOND GIRL: Yes, but I'm not crazy. *(She laughs.)*

YERMA: Doesn't your mother live up on the highest point of the village?

SECOND GIRL: Yes.

YERMA: In the last house?

SECOND GIRL: Yes.

YERMA: What's her name?

SECOND GIRL: Dolores. Why do you ask?

YERMA: No reason.

SECOND GIRL: You ask for a reason!

YERMA: I don't know. . .I've heard say . . .

SECOND GIRL: Well, that's your concern. . .Look, I'm going to take my husband his food. *(She laughs.)* That's something to see. A pity I can't say he's my sweetheart, isn't it? *(She laughs.)* The crazy girl goes on! *(She leaves, laughing joyfully.)* Good-bye!

VICTOR'S VOICE: *(Singing.)* Shepherd, why do you sleep alone?
    Shepherd, why do you sleep alone?

On my wool blanket
You will sleep so much more.
Shepherd, why do you sleep alone?
YERMA: *(Listening.)* Shepherd, why do you sleep alone?
On my wool blanket
You will sleep so much more.
Your blanket of dark stone,
Shepherd,
And your shirt of frost, Shepherd,
Gray rushes of winter
On the even-tide of your bed.
The oak-roots set their needles
Shepherd,
Under your pillow soft,
Shepherd,
And if you hear a woman's voice
It is the broken voice of the stream.
Shepherd, shepherd.
What does the hill-side want of you?
Shepherd.
Hillside of bitter weeds
What child is killing you?
The thorn of the great broom-tree.

Night Must Fall

Emlyn Williams

1935

Dramatic

Setting: Forest corner—the home of Mrs. Bramson in Essex, England

Scene: An October morning. Mrs. Bramson is in a very bad mood and has found a reason to start an argument. She has discovered that Dora has broken some valuable china plates.

Mrs. Bramson: A fussy, discontented hypochondriac, 55.
Mrs. Terence: The cook—cockney, fearless, 40's.
Dora Parkoe: Pretty, a bit dim, a bit "sluttish", 20's.
Olivia Grayne: Mrs. Bramson's niece, 28, subdued, works for her aunt.

MRS. BRAMSON: Fetch that girl here. This minute.

MRS. TERENCE: Oh, leave the child alone.

MRS. BRAMSON: Leave her alone, the little sneak thief? Fetch her here.

MRS. TERENCE: *(At the top of her voice.)* Dora! *(Opening the front door and calling into the trees.)* Dora!

OLIVIA: What's Dora done now?

MRS. BRAMSON: Broken three of my Crown Derby, that's all. Thought if she planted them in the rose-bed I wouldn't be well enough to see them, I suppose. Well I have seen.

MRS. TERENCE: *(Crossing and calling to the bedroom.)* You're wanted.

DORA'S VOICE: What for?

MRS. TERENCE: She wants to kiss you good morning, what d'you think. . . *(She collects the tablecloth, fetches a vase from the mantelpiece, and goes into the kitchen. Dora enters gingerly from the bedroom carrying a cup and a saucer on a tray.)*

DORA: Did you want me, mum?

MRS. BRAMSON: Crown Derby to you, my girl.

DORA: *(Uncertain.)* Beg pardon, mum?

MRS. BRAMSON: I suppose you think that china came from Marks and Spencer?

DORA: Oh. . . *(Snivelling.)* Oh. . . Oh. . .

OLIVIA: *(Coming between Dora and Mrs. Bramson.)* Come along, Dora, it's not as bad as all that.

DORA: Oh yes, it is. . . Oh. . .

MRS. BRAMSON: You can leave, that's all. You can leave. *(Appalled, Dora drops the tray and breaks the saucer.)* That settles it. Now you'll have to leave.

DORA: *(With a cry.)* Oh, please I. . . *(Kneeling and collecting broken china.)* Oh, ma'am. . . I'm not meself, you see— *(Snivelling.)* I'm in. . . terrible trouble.

MRS. BRAMSON: Have you been stealing?

DORA: *(Shocked.)* Oh, no!

OLIVIA: *(After a pause.)* Are you going to have a baby?

(After a pause, Dora nods.)

DORA: *(Putting the china in her apron.)* The idea of me stealing. . . I do go to Sunday School anyways. . .

MRS. BRAMSON: So that's the game. Wouldn't think butter would melt in her mouth. . . You'll have to go, of course, I can't have that sort of thing in this house—and stop squeaking! You'll bring my heart on again. It's all this modern life. I've always said so. All these films and rubbish.

OLIVIA: My dear auntie, you can't have a baby by just sitting in the pictures.

MRS. BRAMSON: Go away, and don't interfere.

(Olivia goes to the left window. Dora rises.)

MRS. BRAMSON: *(Triumphantly.)* So you're going to have a child. When?

DORA: *(Sniffling.)* Last August Bank Holiday. . .

MRS. BRAMSON: What?. . . Oh!

DORA: I 'aven't got a penny only what I earn—and if I lose my job 'ere—

MRS. BRAMSON: He'll have to marry you.

DORA: Oh, I don't think he's keen. . .

MRS. BRAMSON: I'll *make* him keen. Who is the gentlemen?

DORA: A boy I know; Dan his name is—leas' 'e's not a gentleman. He's a pageboy at the Tallboys.

MRS. BRAMSON: The Tallboys? D'you mean that new-fangled place all awnings and loudspeakers and things?

DORA: That's right. On the by-pass.

MRS. BRAMSON: Just the nice ripe sort of place for mischief, it always looked to me. All those lanterns. . . What's his character, the good-for-nothing scoundrel?

DORA: Oh, he's nice, really. He done the wrong thing by me, but he's all right, if you know what I mean. . .

MRS. BRAMSON: No, I don't. Where does he come from?

DORA: He's sort of Welsh, I think. 'E's been to sea, too. He's funny of course. Ever so open. Baby-face, they call him. Though I never seem to get 'old of what 'e's thinking somehow—

MRS. BRAMSON: I'll get hold of what he's thinking, all right. I've had my knife into that sort ever since I was a girl.

DORA: Oh, mum, if I got him to let you speak to him—d'you think, I could stay on?

MRS. BRAMSON: *(After a pause.)* If he marries you at once.

DORA: Shall I—*(Eagerly.)* As a matter of fact, ma'am, he's gone on a message on his bicycle to Payley Hill this morning, and he said he might pop in to see me on the way back—

MRS. BRAMSON: That's right; nothing like visitors to brighten your mornings, eh? I'll deal with him.

DORA: Yes. . . *(Going, and turning at the kitchen door in impulsive relief.)* Oh, ma'am—

MRS. BRAMSON: And I'll stop the Crown Derby out of your wages.

DORA: *(Crestfallen.)* Oh!

MRS. BRAMSON: What were you going to say?

DORA: Well, ma'am, I *was* going to say I don't know how to thank you for your generosity. . . *(She goes into the kitchen. The clock chimes.)*

MRS. BRAMSON: Olivia!

OLIVIA: Yes, auntie?

MRS. BRAMSON: You've forgotten again. Medicine's overdue. Most important.

(Olivia crosses to the medicine cupboard and fetches the medicine. Mrs. Terence comes in from the kitchen with a vase of flowers and barges between the sofa and the wheelchair.)

MRS. TERENCE: *(Muttering)* All this furniture. . .

MRS. BRAMSON: *(To her.)* Did *you* know she's having a baby?

MRS. TERENCE: *(Coldly.)* She did mention it in conversation.

MRS. BRAMSON: Playing with fire, that's the game nowadays.

MRS. TERENCE: *(Arranging flowers as Olivia gives Mrs. Bramson her medicine.)* Playing with fiddlesticks. We're only young once; that 'ot summer too. She's been a fool, but she's no criminal. And, talking of criminals, there's a p'liceman at the kitchen door.

MRS. BRAMSON: A what?

MRS. TERENCE: A p'liceman. A bobby.

MRS. BRAMSON: What does he want?

MRS. TERENCE: Better ask 'im. I know my conscience is clear; I don't know about other people's

MRS. BRAMSON: But I've never had a policeman coming to see me before!

(Dora runs in from the kitchen.)

DORA: *(Terrified.)* There's a man there! From the p'lice! 'E said something about the Tallboys! 'E—'e 'asnt come about me, 'as 'e?

MRS. TERENCE: Of course, he 'asnt—

MRS. BRAMSON: He may have.

MRS. TERENCE: Don't frighten the girl; she's simple enough now.

MRS. BRAMSON: *(Sharply.)* It's against the law, what she's done, isn't it? *(To Dora.)* Go back in there till he sends for you.

(Dora creeps back into the kitchen.)

OLIVIA: *(At the left window.)* He isn't a policeman, as a matter of fact. He must be a plainclothesman.

MRS. TERENCE: *(Sardonically.)* Scotland Yard, I should think.

(Belsize is seen outside, crossing the left window to the front door.)

MRS. BRAMSON: That place in those detective books? Don't be so silly.

MRS. TERENCE: He says he wants to see you very particular— *(A sharp rat-rat at the front door. Going to the hall.)* On a very particular matter. . . *(Turning on Mrs. Bramson.)* And don't you start callin' *me* silly! *(Going to the front door, and opening it.)* This way, sir. . .

Ladies in Retirement

Denham and Percy
1939

Dramatic

Setting: Mrs. Fiske's home on the Marshes of an estuary of the Thames east of Gravesend, England, 1885.

Scene: Mrs. Fiske feels the two sisters have overstayed their welcome as guests in her home and she has asked Ellen to arrange for their departure. The sisters believe they are going for a ride in the country. At all costs, Ellen will protect her sisters and she has devised a malevolent plan to take possession of the house.

Ellen Creed: 30's, a dark and moody woman, serious—works as a housekeeper and takes care of her adult sisters.

Louisa Creed and Emily Creed: The sisters, 30's – 40's, childlike, somewhat "slow" and very naïve.

Leonora Fiske: Ellen's employer, 50's.

ELLEN: There's nothing to be cooked. I've left everything ready.

LEONORA: *(Gaily.)* Yes, but, as I'm all by myself, I think I shall get up a bottle of that champagne Lord Kenardington sent me for Christmas.

ELLEN: *(Her lips tightening.)* I believe you're going to celebrate my sisters going.

LEONORA: I don't mind telling you, Ellen—I am! This is the first time I shall have been able to call my house my own for months.

ELLEN: *(With an oblique glance.)* It'll be the first time you've slept here alone, too, won't it?

LEONORA: I don't suppose even that will worry me with a pint of Cliquot inside me!

ELLEN: I've made a salad. And there's a cold partridge and some cream cheese from the convent.

LEONORA: A bird! Cream cheese! Champagne! It only wants the right setting. A private room at Kettner's—candlelight—distant music. And someone's foot pressing yours—very lightly—under the table. My goodness, Ellen! What am I talking about? Why haven't you stopped me? I'm in a crazy mood today! *(She is at the kitchen door.)*

(Ellen is by the table on which lies the cashbox.)

ELLEN: *(Quietly.)* You're leaving your money.

LEONORA: *(Darting back.)* Oh, mercy! I really am crazy. *(She puts back the cashbox in the oven and locks the padlock.)* The bell's been stopped some time. Your sisters ought to be back. *(Coming to Ellen.)* Ellen, I believe in your heart you're glad to be rid of them, too. Though, of course, you'll never admit it.

(The front door opens and Louisa and Emily enter. They look very quaint and uncountrified in their outdoor attire. Emily carries a large spray of autumnal "Traveler's Joy.")

LOUISA: I hope we're back in time, Ellen, as you told us. Oh, dear. How nice it is to be indoors again!

LEONORA: What have you got there, Miss Emily?

EMILY: Lucy told me it's called "Traveler's Joy."

LEONORA: H'm—very appropriate, when you're going for a drive.

EMILY: It has white flowers in the summer, I remember when we came the hedges were full of it. Do you think, Ellen, it would keep through the winter like sea lavender and honesty?

ELLEN: I don't know, Emily.

LOUISA: Oh, but I expect you do, Ellen. Only you won't say. *(Sitting down with a little sigh.)* I wish I weren't going for this drive. Do you think I need to, Ellen?

ELLEN: I particularly want you to, darling. I'm giving you a great treat.

LOUISA: Yes, dear, I know. But I'd sooner stay in the house. It's getting quite evening. And I don't like the long shadows.

EMILY: *(Letting the "Traveler's Joy" fall to the ground.)* I'm very glad we're going for a drive. And I'm glad it's late. We shall be able to see the sun disappear behind the river.

ELLEN: A September evening's the most beautiful time of the year. And there's nothing to be afraid of. I'm coming with you.

LOUISA: Is Miss Fiske coming, too?

LEONORA: No. You'll be just by yourselves. *(Rather naughtily.)* That'll be what you like, won't it, Miss Louisa?

LOUISA: Yes. Yes.

EMILY: I think I'll go up and get into an easier pair of boots. These pinch me rather.

ELLEN: No, you sit down. I'll run up and get them.

LOUISA: No, Emily. You mustn't let Ellen wait on you.

ELLEN: It's all right. I've got to go up in any case. I've got to get my own bonnet and cloak.

EMILY: They're in the left-hand corner of the cupboard.

ELLEN: I'll find them, Emily. *(She runs upstairs.)*

LOUISA: Ellen's in one of her bossy moods today, isn't she, Emily?

EMILY: She always orders us about. She won't let us have wills of our own.

LOUISA: I think she's worried about something. I think she's got something on her mind.

LEONORA: Oh, come, Miss Louisa! I don't think that's right. I've noticed nothing different about her.

LOUISA: But then you wouldn't, would you? You're not one of the family. I know Ellen's worried about something. I can tell it.

EMILY: *(Beginning to take off her boots.)* I wonder if we are just going for a drive. I wonder if she's sending us away.

LOUISA: *(In immediate agitation.)* Don't say that, Emily! Oh, I do hope it's not true. But you'd know, Miss Fiske, wouldn't you? You're not both sending us away, are you?

LEONORA: *(Artfully.)* Do you think I *should* know—not being one of the family?

LOUISA: No, no. I suppose that's true. I suppose you wouldn't. Ellen would arrange that by herself, wouldn't she?

EMILY: If Ellen tries to send me away, I shan't go.

LOUISA: Oh, but we must do what Ellen tell us, mustn't we? I don't know what would become of us if we offended Ellen.

EMILY: She might take me to the station, but I wouldn't get into the train.

LEONORA: I think you're both imagining much too much.

LOUISA: Yes. I think we are. I think you're right. I don't think Ellen would deceive us.

EMILY: *(Suddenly, looking towards the window.)* What's become of your telescope, Louisa?

LOUISA: It's on the windowsill, dear.

EMILY: No, it isn't.

LOUISA: *(Rising, agitatedly.)* Isn't it? Where is it? It was here when I went out! I knew I oughtn't to have gone out! I knew something would happen.

LEONORA: It's quite all right, Miss Louisa. Ellen took it out into the kitchen. I think she was going to clean it.

LOUISA: Oh, no, she wasn't. I always do that myself. Why has she taken it into the kitchen? I believe it's been broken! I must get it, I must have it!

LEONORA: I promise you it's not been broken. If you'll wait here, I'll get it for you.

LOUISA: No, *I* wish to get it.

LEONORA: *(Snapping.)* I'm sorry, but you can't!

EMILY: *(Sullenly.)* Why shouldn't Louisa get it herself?

LEONORA: *(Going to the kitchen door.)* Because it happens to be my kitchen and Miss Louisa's my guest.

LOUISA: *(Following her.)* I'm going to get it!

(She feebly seizes Leonora and there is an undignified little struggle at the door, which ends by Leonora forcing Louisa on to the piano stool.)

LEONORA: Please sit down, Miss Louisa. Don't you realize you're making the most ridiculous scene about absolutely nothing? *(She goes quickly out into the kitchen.)*

(Louisa sobs.)

LOUISA: It's broken! I know it's broken!

EMILY: I don't think Ellen broke it. I think *she* broke it. She wasn't really angry when she spoke like that. She was only saying it to cover up something.

LOUISA: Oh, how I hate her!

EMILY: Ellen wouldn't like you to say that. They're friends again—she and Ellen. I think they're in league together.

LOUISA: I wish you wouldn't keep saying things against Ellen, Emily!

EMILY: You think Ellen's perfect, don't you? You'll find out about her one day.

(Ellen comes down the stairs. She is wearing her bonnet and cloak, and carries a pair of lady's elastic-sided boots.)

ELLEN: *(Giving Emily the boots.)* Here are your boots, Emily.

EMILY: Thank you, Ellen.

ELLEN: What's the matter, Louisa darling?

LOUISA: *(Tearfully.)* Ellen! Someone's broken my telescope.

ELLEN: Have they, dear? Oh, no. I don't think they can have.

LOUISA: But why did you take it out into the kitchen.

ELLEN: I didn't.

LOUISA: *(Excitedly.)* There, Emily! She was lying. She was lying.

ELLEN: Who was? Who was lying?

LOUISA: Miss Fiske! She said you'd taken it into the kitchen to clean it. She's gone to fetch it now. I *knew* you wouldn't have.

ELLEN: *(Suddenly remembering that, of course, the telescope is packed.)* Oh? Oh, yes, of course. It's all right, darling. I'd forgotten. I did take it out. It's quite true.

LOUISA: You're only humoring me because you know it's broken.

ELLEN: *(Sharply.)* Nonsense, Louisa. Stop being silly.

EMILY: *(Suddenly.)* These are not my boots, Ellen. They're yours.

ELLEN: Yes, I know, dear. I'm making you a present of them. You always do have my old ones, don't you?

EMILY: Thank you. But I wish you'd brought me my own. My feet ache, and yours always take a little getting accustomed to.

ELLEN: Well, you won't have to do any walking on your drive.
       (Leonora enters from the kitchen in triumph, with the telescope. Emily begins grudgingly to put on the boots Ellen has brought.)

LEONORA: Here we are! You see, Miss Louisa! It's not broken. It's as right as ninepence.

LOUISA: *(Seizing it.)* Oh— thank you. I *am* glad to have it. No—it hasn't been broken. But it hasn't been cleaned.

ELLEN: I haven't had time yet.

LEONORA: *(Laughing.)* Miss Louisa was so agitated I believe she thought I was going to steal it, Ellen.

ELLEN: *(To Louisa, tenderly.)* It was just a lot of fuss about nothing, wasn't it?

LOUISA: Yes, dear. I was very silly. But it's not nothing to me.

LEONORA: *(Going to the stairs.)* Ellen, call me when the fly comes. I'd like to see you all safely off.

EMILY: *(Resentfully.)* There's no need for you to trouble. We shall be back in two hours, shan't we?

LEONORA: *(With almost a wink at Ellen.)* Well, I'd like to make sure you start comfortably. *(She hurries upstairs.)*

LOUISA: Emily says that we're not really going for a drive. That you're sending us away. That we're not coming back. That's not true, is it Ellen?

ELLEN: Of course it's not true. What made you think that, Emily?

EMILY: You see, Miss Fiske doesn't like us. And she's been so different, so friendly. Almost as if she knew she was getting rid of us.

ELLEN: Well, you're both quite wrong. You *are* coming back. I promise you that. And I've always kept my promises to you, haven't I?

LOUISA: Yes, Ellen. You have—always.

EMILY: She seemed very anxious to come and say good-bye to us.

ELLEN: We may be saying good-bye to *her*.

EMILY: What do you mean, Ellen?

ELLEN: I want you to keep a little secret. Will you promise me?

LOUISA: Yes, Ellen. Of course we promise.

ELLEN: And you, too, Emily. You must promise, too.

EMILY: Very well. I promise you, Ellen.

ELLEN: *(She goes to the stairway door and closes it.)* You're very happy here, aren't you? You like this place?

LOUISA: Yes, Ellen.

EMILY: Yes, Ellen. We're very happy.

ELLEN: You'd be happier still, wouldn't you, if we were here just by ourselves?

LOUISA: Oh, yes, Ellen. She spoils everything.

EMILY: But it's her house. How could we be here by ourselves?

ELLEN: That's what I want to tell you. I'm going to try and persuade her to sell it to me.

LOUISA: Oh, how clever, Ellen! Then she could go away and live somewhere else.

EMILY: But supposing she wants too much money for it, Ellen? She may want more than you're prepared to pay.

ELLEN: I'm prepared to pay quite a big price, Emily.

EMILY: I didn't think you had all that much money, Ellen.

ELLEN: Oh, I've saved quite a lot.

LOUISA: *(Trembling with excitement.)* Oh, it will be lovely if it can be ours! I'm so excited, Ellen. When will you know? When will you ask her?

ELLEN: I'm going to ask her today. That's one of the reasons for the drive. I want to get you out of the place. I want to tackle her by myself.

EMILY: But you're coming out with us.

ELLEN: Only as far as the Priory. Then I shall get out and slip back. And you'll go on for your drive round.

LOUISA: Oh, I shall tell the man to hurry! We mustn't be away to long. I shall be so anxious to know.

ELLEN: That's just what I don't want. I want you to give me at least two hours. It's a complicated thing to arrange, you know. It can't be done in five minutes. I want to get it all fixed up before you come back.

EMILY: Buy why should you come with us at all, Ellen?

(Ellen does not answer.)

ELLEN: I want to call at the convent.

LOUISA: Buy why must you call there, Ellen? Father wouldn't have liked your calling at the convent.

ELLEN: *(After a moment.)* I want to get the Reverend Mother on our side. She has great influence with Miss Fiske. I want her to help me persuade her.

LOUISA: Oh, of course. Oh, how clever you are, Ellen! I should never have thought of that.

(Ellen goes to the half-moon table and takes a devotional book from it.)

ELLEN: Now, look here, Louisa. Here's a Bible. I want you to put your hand on it and swear on father's memory that you'll never repeat what I've told you about buying the house as long as you live.

LOUISA: Yes, Ellen. If you wish it, Ellen. But it rather frightens me. What do I say?

ELLEN: Just say "I promise."

LOUISA: I promise.

ELLEN: You, too, Emily.

EMILY: I won't swear on the Bible. It's wicked.

LOUISA: Oh, Emily! You must do what Ellen says.

ELLEN: If you won't promise me, Emily, I shan't buy the house. And I shall send you both back to London.

LOUISA: Oh, Ellen—not that, please. Emily, do be sensible.

EMILY: Very well. But I don't like being made to do things. I promise.

(There comes a sudden rat-tat-tat-tat at the front door.)

LOUISA: Oh, dear! What's that?

ELLEN: *(Looking through the open window.)* It's the man from Rochester with the carriage. *(Calling.)* All right! We'll be out in a minute!

THE MAN'S VOICE: *(Calling back.)* Very good, mum. I'll turn the 'orses. Which way d'ye want to go?

ELLEN: We'll tell you later. *(Leaving the window.)* Now, come along, my darlings.

LOUISA: *(Like an excited child.)* Oh, wouldn't it be lovely if, when we came back, we found that you'd bought the house and she'd gone!

ELLEN: *(Turning on her almost savagely.)* Will you be quiet!

LOUISA: Oh, don't! Don't be cross with me, Ellen!

ELLEN: You've just sworn on the Bible never to mention it again!

LOUISA: *(Awed.)* I'm sorry. I thought it didn't count when we were together.

ELLEN: She might have overhead you and that would have spoilt everything. It's better for us not to discuss it even among ourselves.

LOUISA: *(Meekly.)* Whatever you say, Ellen.

(Leonora enters from the stairway door.)

LEONORA: Did I hear the carriage?

ELLEN: Yes. It's just come. We're going now.

LEONORA: I do hope you all have a nice drive.

LOUISA: I expect we shall come back very hungry.

ELLEN: Now, come along. *(As they go out the front door.)*

LOUISA: Oh, it is a high step, isn't it, from the ground? You'll have to help me, Ellen.

ELLEN: The driver will lift you up.

LOUISA: Oh, that will be fun! Won't it, Emily?

(They disappear. Leonora watches their departure.)

LEONORA: Good-bye. Make the most of it! Have you told the driver which way, Ellen?

ELLEN: *(Calling back.)* He knows.

A Young Lady of Property

Horton Foote

1953

Dramatic

Setting: In the kitchen. Southern United States of America, 1925.

Scene: Aunt Gert has asked the tenants to move out. Wilma's father is remarrying and Wilma is frantic and frightened that she will lose her house to the newlyweds. She and her Aunt have been to see a lawyer, and then Wilma goes alone to confront the future stepmother, Mrs. Leighton. Now she returns triumphant after she and "Sybil" reach an accord.

Wilma Thompson: Dreams of going to Hollywood and being a movie star, 15. Owner of a house left to her by her mother who died years ago. The house has been rented out to tenants.

Arabella Cookenboo: Her best friend and her shadow, 15, shy, gentle, loyal and faithful to Wilma.

Gert Miller: Wilma's Aunt, 50's, with whom she lives.

Minna Boyd: 40's, the family housekeeper, black, stylish, high-spirited.

GERT: Well, we've won.

MINNA: What do you mean?

GERT: I mean just what I say. Lester is not going to sell the house.

MINNA: What happened?

GERT: I don't know what happened. I went over to see Bill and we talked it all through, and he said legally we really had no chance but he'd call up Lester and try to at least bluff him into thinking we had. And when he called Lester he said Lester wasn't home, and so I suggested his calling you know where.

MINNA: No. Where?

GERT: Mrs. Leighton's. And sure enough he was there, and Bill told him why he was calling and Lester said well, it didn't matter as he'd decided not to sell the house after all.

MINNA: You don't meant it?

GERT: Oh, yes, I do. Where's Wilma?

MINNA: She's over there with them.

GERT: Over where with them?

MINNA: At Mrs. Leighton's.

GERT: Why, Minna. . .

MINNA: Now don't holler at me. I told her not to go, but she said she was going and then she ran out the door so fast I couldn't stop her. . .

(Wilma comes running in.)

WILMA: Heard the news? House is mine again.

MINNA: Do you know what happened?

WILMA: Sure. Mrs. Leighton isn't so bad. Boy, I went running over there expecting the worse. . .

GERT: Wilma, what do you mean going to that woman's house, Wilma I declare. . .

WILMA: Oh, she's not so bad. Anyway we've got her to thank for it.

MINNA: Well, what happened? Will somebody please tell me what happened?

WILMA: Well, you know I was sitting here and it came to me. It came to me just like that. See Mrs. Leighton. She's the one to stop it and it's got to be stopped. Well, I was so scared my knees were trembling the whole time going over there, but I made myself do it, walked in on her and she looked more nervous than I did.

GERT: Was your father there?

WILMA: No, ma'am. He came later. Wasn't anybody there but me and Mrs. Leighton. I'm calling her Sibyl now. She asked me to. Did Arabella come yet?

MINNA: Arabella?

WILMA: I called and asked her to come and celebrate. I'm so excited. I just had to have company tonight. I know I won't be able to sleep anyway. I hope you don't mind, Aunt Gert. . .

MINNA: If you don't tell me what happened . . .

WILMA: Well. . . Mrs. Leighton. . . I mean Sibyl. . . *(Arabella comes up to the screen door.)* Oh, come on in, Arabella.

ARABELLA: Hi. I almost didn't get to come. I told my mama it was life or death and so she gave in. But she made me swear we'd be in bed by ten. Did you hear about Mr. Delafonte?

WILMA: No? What?

ARABELLA: He's a crook. It was in the Houston papers tonight. He was operating a business under false pretenses. He had been charging twenty-five dollars for those screen tests and using a camera with no film in it.

WILMA: My goodness.

ARABELLA: It was in all the papers. On the second page. My father said he mustn't have been very much not to even get on the front page. He wasn't a Hollywood director at all. He didn't even know Lila Lee or Betty Compson. . .

WILMA: He didn't?

ARABELLA: No.

MINNA: Wilma, will you get back to your story before I lose my mind?

WILMA: Oh. Yes. . . I got my house back, Arabella.

ARABELLA: You did?

WILMA: Sure. That's why I called you over to spend the night. A kind of celebration.

ARABELLA: Well, that's wonderful. . .

MINNA: Wilma. . .

WILMA: All right. Where was I?

GERT: You were at Mrs. Leighton's?

WILMA: Oh, yes. Sibyl's. I'm calling her Sibyl now, Arabella. She asked me to.

MINNA: Well. . . what happened? Wilma, if you don't tell me. . .

WILMA: Well, I just told her the whole thing.

MINNA: What whole thing?

WILMA: Well, I told her about my mother meaning for the house to always be mine, and how I loved the house, and how I was lonely and the house was lonely and that I had hoped my daddy and I could go there and live some day but knew now we couldn't and I had planned to go to Hollywood and be a movie star but that this afternoon my friend Arabella and I decided we didn't really want to do that, and that I knew then that what I wanted to do really was to live in Harrison and get married and live in my house and have children so that I wouldn't be lonely any more and the house wouldn't. And then she started crying.

GERT: You don't mean it.

WILMA: Yes, ma'am. And I felt real sorry for her and I said I didn't hold anything against her and then Daddy came in and she said why didn't he tell her that was my house, and he said because it wasn't. And then she asked him about what Mother told you, and he said that was true but now I was going to have a better house, and she said I didn't want to have a better house, but my own house and that she wouldn't marry him if he sold this house and she said they both had jobs in Houston and would manage somehow, but I had nothing, so then he said all right.

GERT: Well. Good for her.

MINNA: Sure enough good for her.

WILMA: And then Mr. Bill called and Daddy told him the house was mine again and then she cried and hugged me and asked me to kiss her and I did, and then Daddy cried and I kissed him, and then I cried. And they asked me to the wedding and I said I'd go and that I'd come visit them this summer in Houston. And then I came home.

MINNA: Well. Well, indeed.

GERT: My goodness. So that's how it happened. And you say Mrs. Leighton cried?

WILMA: Twice. We all did. Daddy and Mrs. Leighton and me. . .

GERT: Well, I'm glad, Wilma, it's all worked out.

WILMA: And can I go visit them this summer in Houston?

GERT: If you like.

WILMA: And can I go to the wedding?

GERT: Yes, if you want to.

WILMA: I want to.

MINNA: Now you better have some supper.

WILMA: No. I couldn't eat, I'm still too excited.

MINNA: Miss Gert, she hasn't had a bite on her stomach. . .

GERT: Well, it won't kill her this one time, Minna.

WILMA: Aunt Gert, can Arabella and I go over to my house for just a few minutes and swing? We'll be home by ten. . .

GERT: No, Wilma, it's late.

WILMA: Please. Just to celebrate. I have it coming to me. We'll just stay a few minutes.

GERT: Well. . .

WILMA: Please. . .

GERT: Will you be back here by ten, and not make me have to send Minna over there?

WILMA: Yes, ma'am.

GERT: All right.

WILMA: Oh, thank you. You're the best aunt in the whole world. Come on, Arabella. . .

ARABELLA: All right.

(They start for the screen door. Gert follows after them. They go out the screen door. Gert calls after them.)

GERT: Now remember. Back by ten. Arabella has promised her mother. And you've promised me.

WILMA: *(Calling in distance.)* Yes ma'am. *(Gert comes back into the room.)*

GERT: Well, I'm glad it's ending this way.

MINNA: Yes, ma'am.

GERT: I never thought it would. Well, I said hard things to Lester. I'm sorry I had to, but I felt I had to.

MINNA: Of course you did.

GERT: Well, I'll go to my room. You go on when you're ready.

MINNA: All right. I'm ready now. The excitement has wore me out.

GERT: Me too. Leave the light on for the children. I'll keep away until they come in.

MINNA: Yes'm.

GERT: Good night.

MINNA: Good night.

(Gert goes out, Minna goes to get her hat.)

(Dissolve to: The front yard. Wilma and Arabella are there swinging.)

WILMA: Don't you just love to swing?

ARABELLA: Uh huh.

WILMA: It's a lovely night, isn't it? Listen to that mockingbird. The crazy thing must think it's daytime.

ARABELLA: It's light enough to be.

WILMA: It certainly is.

ARABELLA: Well, it was lucky we decided to give up Hollywood with Mr. Delafonte turning out to be a crook and all.

WILMA: Wasn't it lucky?

ARABELLA: Do you feel lonely now?

WILMA: No, I don't feel nearly so lonely. Now I've got my house and plan to get married. And my daddy and I are going to see each other, and I think Mrs. Leighton is going to make a nice friend. She's crazy about moving pictures.

ARABELLA: Funny how things work out.

WILMA: Very funny.

ARABELLA: Guess who called me on the telephone.

WILMA: Who?

ARABELLA: Tommy. . . Murray.

WILMA: You don't say.

ARABELLA: He asked me for a date next week. Picture show. He said Jay was going to call you.

WILMA: Did he?

ARABELLA: I asked him to tell Jay that you weren't only interested in going out with movie actors.

WILMA: What did he say?

ARABELLA: He said he thought Jay knew that.

(A pause. Wilma jumps out of the swing.)

ARABELLA: Wilma. What's the matter with you? Wilma. . . *(She runs to her.)*

WILMA: I don't know. I felt funny there for a minute. A cloud passed over the moon and I felt lonely. . . and funny. . . and scared. . .

Confessions of a Female Disorder

Susan Miller
1973

Comic
Setting: Ronnie's bedroom.
Scene: Ronnie has just started her menstrual period.

Of Note: All the roles should be played by adult actresses.

Ronnie: In this scene she is about 13 years old.
Cheerleader #1: A friend, 20's – 30's.
Cheerleader #2: A friend, 20's – 30's.
Cheerleader #3: A friend, 20's – 30's.
Brief walk-on of Ronnie's Mother.

CHEERLEADER #1: What are you doing, Ronnie, babe? Gonna stick them in some drawer and let them get all crusty.

CHEERLEADER #2: We caught you red-handed, girl . . . caught you trying to hide it. The place to watch is way down there, kiddo.

RONNIE: What am I going to do?

CHEERLEADER #1: Nothing. Don't ask questions like that. People will look at you funny. You have no business wanting to do anything, Missy. Miss bloody pants.

CHEERLEADER #2: Down, Ronnie. Keep looking down.

CHEERLEADER #3: Everyone else *does unto you* . . . in, on, around, above you.

CHEERLEADER #1: Lady. Little lady.

CHEERLEADER #2: This is a very big day. Dance with me, Ronnie.

RONNIE: I'm bleeding to death.

CHEERLEADER #1: Rinse your pants out in cold water, honey, and relax.

RONNIE: What's going on? What's happening to me?

ALL: *(Forming a dance line.)* The curse . . . cha, cha, cha.

RONNIE: What?

CHEERLEADER #3: The curse.

CHEERLEADER #2: You've just fallen off the roof.

RONNIE: This is so embarrassing. What will I tell my mother?

CHEERLEADER #1: Mama knows.

RONNIE: She does?

CHEERLEADER #2: She comes from a long line of bleeders.

RONNIE: What about my friends, do they know?

CHEERLEADER #2: Some of them. Listen, you look pale. Why don't you lie down.

RONNIE: But I'm still . . . you know.

CHEERLEADER #3: It's nothing, sweetie. Just a little raw baby matter.

RONNIE: (Lying down.) I must have bumped into something. I just don't understand how it could have happened.

CHEERLEADER #1: You little girls are just too much. You've got the stuff dreams are made of, pussycat.

CHEERLEADER #3: You wanna try one of my lipsticks? Heavenly Rose, it's called. You'll feel like a new person.

(Cheerleader practices a cheer. Ronnie's Mother enters. She slaps Ronnie. Then kisses her, hands her a Kotex pad, and walks out.)

RONNIE: Did I do something wrong?

CHEERLEADER #1: What's the matter, didn't you like our little initiation ceremony?

RONNIE: But she never hit me before. My mother's a soft woman.

CHEERLEADER #3: It's a custom; don't knock it.

RONNIE: She slapped me.

CHEERLEADER #1: It was just a warning.

CHEERLEADER #2: Don't you see, she had to haul off and hit you, kid. You've become offensive.

CHEERLEADER #3: And nasty.

CHEERLEADER #1 AND #2: Unclean.

CHEERLEADER #2: But don't worry, babe. You're not the only one.

RONNIE: (Indicating Kotex.) What will I do with this?

CHEERLEADER #1: Shove it between your legs. Like a badge.

CHEERLEADER #2: Be proud of yourself, kiddo.

RONNIE: People will stare at me. They'll know.

CHEERLEADER #1: This is your beginning, baby.

CHEERLEADER #2: Go ahead. Put that thing on. Strut around with it; see how it feels.

RONNIE: I don't think I'm going to like it. It looks uncomfortable.

CHEERLEADER #3: Everything you put down there from now on is going to be uncomfortable. But you'll get used to it.

RONNIE: When does this stop? I mean, when will it go away?

CHEERLEADER #1: *(Amused.)* It used to disappear after forty-five years or so, but now they have these groovy little hormone pills that keep it going.

CHEERLEADER #2: Like an act of faith.

RONNIE: I don't feel so well. I think I'd like to be by myself.

CHEERLEADER #2: Go ahead and moan. We don't mind.

RONNIE: This is the thing they talk about in the lavatories. The older girls. This must be what it is.

CHEERLEADER #1: Well, it isn't a big secret, you know.

RONNIE: I don't want to talk to them anymore . . . those laughing girls. I don't want to look at them.

CHEERLEADER #2: Hey, c'mon. Pretty soon you'll have a pajama party and laugh yourself silly.

RONNIE: I'm white. I'm so white. Isn't it peculiar?

CHEERLEADER #3: I'll get you something to eat. How about a peanut butter and jelly sandwich or something?

RONNIE: I don't have any taste. My stomach's a balloon.

CHEERLEADER #1: But Ronnie, babe, this little number is your meal ticket.

CHEERLEADER #3: You can use it as an excuse for gym. I always do. *(Pause.)* I always do. *(Pause.)* Stiff upper lip, kid.

CHEERLEADER #1: Take a Midol.

CHEERLEADER #2: Here's looking down at you, sweetie.

ALL: *(Doing a cheer.)* C-U-N-T. *Introducing Ron-nie!*

A Late Snow

Jane Chambers
1974

Dramatic

Setting: Ellie's lakeside cabin

Scene: Quincey has unlocked the cabin with her own key, and she and Pat are hauling a big wooden cupboard.

Ellie: 30's, sophisticated, a college professor.

Quincey: 20's, a young writer, pleasant, open and honest, Ellie's lover.

Pat: 30's, attractive, a "charming alcoholic", Ellie's former lover.

Margo: 40's, a famous writer and scholar; attractive, self-contained.

QUINCEY: That cupboard is special.

PAT: It looks like all the others. She wouldn't know the difference. You've walked by before. I've seen you.

QUINCEY: You lived with her for five years. You were an important part of her life.

PAT: *(Satisfied.)* I never should have let her buy me out.

QUINCEY: You made her buy you out!

PAT: She wouldn't let me live here and I needed the money. We laid these floors ourselves—and framed the windows—

QUINCEY: We've got to go now.

PAT: Ellie's mother sent us those drapes.

QUINCEY: It'll be dark soon.

PAT: So what? You said she won't be back until Sunday.

QUINCEY: The conference isn't over until Saturday night. She's flying back on Sunday.

PAT: When we bought this place there was no insulation, no paneling, you could see the ground through the floorboards.

QUINCEY: Please, Pat, let's go.

PAT: She's really got you tied up, hasn't she? Little Miss Step-and-Fetch-It. Ellie loves to give orders. I never took them *(She goes back to bar.)* Are you a teetotaler, too?

QUINCEY: No. Are you going to be able to drive?

PAT: My reputation precedes me.

QUINCEY: Ellie says you have a problem.

PAT: *(Pours them each a drink.)* Ellie says I'm a drunk. She's at a conference?

QUINCEY: In Philadelphia. University department heads.

PAT: She go alone?

QUINCEY: With the university department heads.

PAT: I never knew a conference to end on a Saturday night. *(She hands Quincey a drink.)* Cheers. *(At window.)* When did the ice go this year?

QUINCEY: Sometime last week, I think.

PAT: We used to bet on the day.

QUINCEY: We weren't out here.

PAT: Ever see it go?

QUINCEY: No.

PAT: It starts melting around the edges. For a few days, it's slush for maybe fifteen, twenty feet around the shoreline. Then the circle of ice that's left in the middle of the lake gets gray, then black—then WHOOSH. It goes under in ten seconds. The black lake turns navy, then sky blue. And it's spring. *(She surveys the cabin.)* You a student of Ellie's?

QUINCEY: I was, last year when I was in grad school. I'm a writer.

PAT: Published?

QUINCEY: No.

PAT: How do you earn a living?

QUINCEY: I edit a throwaway.

PAT: What?

QUINCEY: A rag. One of those four-page weekly papers with neighborhood news and a lot of ads that you find in your mailbox.

PAT: I didn't know Ellie was into seducing her students.

QUINCEY: She's not. She didn't seduce me. I pursued her. It wasn't easy. She wasn't over you.

PAT: Oh?

QUINCEY: I lived with your ghost for months.

PAT: She never answered my letters. She hung up when I called her.

QUINCEY: Five years is a long time.

PAT: Yes, it is.

QUINCEY: It takes a while to get over it. She's over it now.

PAT: Chilly in here. Let's start a fire.

QUINCEY: Let's go.

PAT: There's wood in the crib by the fireplace. You know how to start a fire?

QUINCEY: Of course.

PAT: Well, do it. I'm going to take a look upstairs.

QUINCEY: No.

PAT: *(Charming.)* She'll never know.

QUINCEY: No.

PAT: For old times' sake.

QUINCEY: No.

PAT: *(Handing her the starter wood.)* Placate me. Lonely, nearing middle age, with a slight tendency to imbibe, a pitiful figure. . . *(Quincey laughs in spite of herself.)* Good girl.

QUINCEY: Don't take anything!

PAT: *(Going upstairs.)* You can frisk me when I come down.
(Quincey begins to make a fire. We hear a car motor, see lights flash across the kitchen. Quincey looks up quizzically as the key turns in the backdoor.)
(Ellie enters.)

QUINCEY: Oh, shit!

ELLIE: Quincey!

QUINCEY: You're back early!
(Quincey embraces Ellie, who responds perfunctorily, then pulls nervously away. Ellie is dismayed by Quincey's unexpected presence but tries valiantly not to show it.)

QUINCEY: I wanted to surprise you!

ELLIE: You did.
(Quincey pulls Ellie to the cupboard.)

QUINCEY: With this. *(She hugs Ellie.)* Happy First Anniversary!

ELLIE: Quincey, where did you get this?
(At the back door, Margo appears, suitcase in hand. She stands there, unnoticed.)

QUINCEY: *(About the cupboard.)* Surprise!

ELLIE: Where did you get it?

QUINCEY: It's what you wanted!

ELLIE: It's just like the old one.

QUINCEY: It *is* the old one.

MARGO: May I come in?
(Ellie looks from Margo to Quincey, back to Margo. She is flustered.)

QUINCEY: Hello.

MARGO: Hello

ELLIE: *(Recovering.)* This is Quincey Evans, a former student of mine. Quincey, Margo.

QUINCEY: Margo. *The* Margo?

MARGO: The only one I know.

QUINCEY: *A Memory of Autumn, The Last Question, Miller's Breach, Afternoon in . . .*

MARGO: Amazing

QUINCEY: I took a course in you. Ellie teaches a course in you.

ELLIE: It's true.

MARGO: I never thought of myself as a multiple-choice answer.

QUINCEY: You're always an essay. I thought you were retired *(Catches herself.)* —a recluse. I thought you never came out in public.

MARGO: Only after dark.

QUINCEY: I mean you never give interviews or. . . *(Shrugs.)* I'm getting in deeper, aren't I? Sorry. Welcome. *(To Ellie.)* Where did you find her?

ELLIE: Margo was the guest lecturer at the conference. We flew back together.

MARGO: She's trying to coerce me into teaching.

ELLIE: A lecture series. Wouldn't that be a coup?

QUINCEY: Terrific. You're a kind of cult among the undergrads.

MARGO: It terrifies me.

QUINCEY: I have everything you've ever written.

ELLIE: I asked Margo to spend the day here tomorrow—so I can do my sales pitch.

QUINCEY: It's like seeing a legend come to life.

ELLIE: I promised her a quiet day by the lake.

QUINCEY: I hope we'll have time to talk. I have a thousand questions.

ELLIE: I have yet to sell her on the joys of university life.

QUINCEY: I'm a writer, too, you know. Fledgling but good, I think.

MARGO: Ellie, I'm tired. . . and a little uncomfortable. Can I change?

ELLIE: Of course. Upstairs, Excuse us, Quincey.

> *(Ellie picks up Margo's bag, starts up the stairs. She encounters Pat on her way down. Ellie is startled and angry at Pat's presence.)*

PAT: Hi.

ELLIE: What are you doing here?

PAT: I came with the cupboard.

QUINCEY: She insisted: free delivery.

PAT: *(To Ellie.)* Thank you?

ELLIE: Thank you. Excuse us, please.

> *(She leads Margo, bewildered, upstairs. Margo stops at the master bedroom.)*

MARGO: What a cozy room. And a beautiful view of the lake.

ELLIE: Yes. *(Pause.)* Put your things anywhere.

MARGO: But this is your room, isn't it?

ELLIE: It's the nicest room. The guest room is kind of sparse. I'll sleep there.

MARGO: No.

ELLIE: Please. I insist.

MARGO: No. It's your room.

ELLIE: The guest room overlooks the compost heap. Please?

MARGO: All right.

ELLIE: It's the least I can do. *(Pause.)* I'm sorry. I didn't expect anyone to be here.

MARGO: *(Smiles.)* It's a regular party, isn't it?

ELLIE: They'll be leaving soon.

MARGO: It's all right.

ELLIE: It's not all right. I promised you a quiet weekend.

MARGO: They're your friends. I'm sure they're interesting people. *(She starts to undress.)* Aren't they?

ELLIE: *(Ignoring that.)* I know how you feel about meeting strangers.

MARGO: That's my problem. I'm a big girl now. I can take care of myself.

ELLIE: I'm sorry about Quincey. She's young and exuberant. She didn't mean to embarrass you.

MARGO: Embarrass me? I was flattered. Would you hand me that shirt, please?

> *(Downstairs.)*

PAT: *(To Quincey.)* Well, well. Aren't you glad we stuck around?

QUINCEY: Cool it. That's business.

PAT: I'll say.

QUINCEY: Don't you know who she is?

PAT: I heard your eulogy.

QUINCEY: She's like a myth. I've never seen a picture of her. I've read everything she's ever written, but I never knew what she looked like before.

PAT: You won't forget.

QUINCEY: Ellie has many business associates. That's what this is. I know Ellie.

PAT: I guess I don't. I thought she was true-blue-lou.

QUINCEY: She is.

(Upstairs, Ellie is uncomfortable watching Margo.)

ELLIE: They won't stay long.

MARGO: Will you stop worrying?

ELLIE: Sorry. I'll go downstairs and take care of it. *(Pause.)* Are you all right?

MARGO: I'm fine. Just fine.

(Ellie descends the stairs as Pat is pouring another drink.)

ELLIE: Quincey? Thank you. *(She hugs Quincey warmly.)* I'm sorry I was abrupt—I was just stunned to find you here.

QUINCEY: It's all right.

ELLIE: It was an opportunity that I couldn't pass up, honey. Every university in the country has tried to get Margo on faculty. No one's ever succeeded. We seemed to hit it off at the conference. . .

QUINCEY: It's important to you, isn't it?

ELLIE: Honey, she doesn't know. . . I mean, I haven't said anything. So, play it cool?

QUINCEY: I hate doing that.

ELLIE: Please?

PAT: *(Entering their area.)* So, how are you, Ellie?

ELLIE: Fine, Pat. And you?

PAT: Fine.

ELLIE: Good.

PAT: You look well.

ELLIE: So do you.

PAT: The house looks good.

ELLIE: It's a nice house.

PAT: It always was, I miss it.

ELLIE: Don't give me that. You made me buy you out.

PAT: I needed the money.

ELLIE: I didn't have it, if you remember.

PAT: You got it, though. You could always get money if you had to.

ELLIE: Sure. At eight percent interest.

PAT: The pleasures of a good credit rating.

ELLIE: It's been good seeing you, Pat. I appreciate your bringing the cupboard out. You don't mind giving Quincey a ride back to town, do you?

PAT: *(Pause.)* I see.

ELLIE: I have work to do.

QUINCEY: I'd like to stay, Ellie. I'd like to talk to her.

ELLIE: If I get her to sign a contact, you'll have lots of chance to talk to her. *(Pause.)* It wouldn't look good, honey. I'm sorry, Quincey. *(Pat grins. Margo comes down the stairs, sloppy, comfortable.)*

MARGO: This the real person. That other lady is a sham.

PAT: Hi.

ELLIE: Oh, Margo, this is Pat Leonard.

PAT: I've read your work.

MARGO: And?

PAT: You're good.

QUINCEY: Great.

MARGO: You really are a fan, aren't you?

QUINCEY: An admirer. Fan sounds—childish.

PAT: You must be used to adulation.

MARGO: Not at all. I don't see many people. That's one of the things that distress me about Ellie's idea.

QUINCEY: Lecturing?

MARGO: It terrifies me. All those people!

QUINCEY: Adoring you.

MARGO: Why? For what?

QUINCEY: For being one of the best writers in the world.

MARGO: She's tenacious.

PAT: Ellie can testify to that.

ELLIE: I don't know what you're talking about

PAT: Quincey told me about your first meeting.

MARGO: Oh? *(Pause.)* Well?

QUINCEY: It's not a very interesting story. I want to talk to you. If I could have picked any writer in the world to interview, it would have been you: and here you are.

MARGO: I'm overwhelmed. I'm also hungry. I never could eat that airline food. How about some supper?

ELLIE: Pat and Quincey have to get back to town.

MARGO: We bought plenty of food. . . Ellie and I stopped in this marvelous little country store—

PAT: O'Brien's.

MARGO: You know it?

PAT: Well.

MARGO: And I'm cooking.

ELLIE: No.

MARGO: Yes. Does that tempt you?

QUINCEY: Ellie. . . ?

PAT: We'd love to stay.

MARGO: Good!

QUINCEY: We'll leave right after supper.

Crimes of the Heart

Beth Henley
1979

Comic
Setting: In the Kitchen of Lenny's home, the South.
Scene: Babe has just been released on bail after attempting to shoot her husband. Chick has gone to get her. Meg has returned home from California. Lenny and Meg are eating pecans.

Meg: 20's, a singer, home from Hollywood after a not-too-successful stab at fame and fortune.
Lenny: 30's, the oldest sister, sensible and lonely.
Babe: Early 20's, the youngest sister, childlike, needs protecting, married to Zackery, a lawyer.
Chick: Their cousin, late 20's – 30's.

MEG: *(Trying with teeth.)* Ah, where's the sport in a nutcracker? Where's the challenge?
LENNY: It's over here in the utensil drawer. *(As Lenny gets the nutcracker, Meg opens the pecan by stepping on it with her shoe.)*
MEG: There! Open! *(She picks up the crumbled pecan and eats it.)* Mmmm, delicious. Delicious. Where'd you get the fresh pecans?
LENNY: Oh. . . I don't know.
MEG: They sure are tasty.
LENNY: Doc Porter brought them over.
MEG: Doc. What's Doc doing here in town?
LENNY: Well, his father died a couple of months ago. Now he's back home seeing to his property.
MEG: Gosh, the last I heard of Doc, he was in the East painting the walls of houses to earn a living. *(Amused.)* Heard he was living with some Yankee woman who made clay pots.
LENNY: Joan.
MEG: What?
LENNY: Her name's Joan. She came down with him. That's one of her pots. Doc's married to her.
MEG: Married—
LENNY: Uh huh.
MEG: Doc married a Yankee?

LENNY: That's right; and they've got two kids.

MEG: Kids—

LENNY: A boy and a girl.

MEG: God. Then his kids must be half Yankee.

LENNY: I suppose.

MEG: God. That really gets me. I don't know why, but somehow that really gets me.

LENNY: I don't know why it should.

MEG: And what a stupid-looking pot! Who'd buy it, anyway?

LENNY: Wait—I think that's them. Yeah, that's Chick's car! Oh, there's Babe! Hello, Babe! They're home, Meg! They're home.

(Meg hides.)

BABE'S VOICE: Lenny! I'm home! I'm free!

(Babe, twenty-four, enters exuberantly. She has an angelic face and fierce, volatile eyes. She carries a pink pocketbook.)

BABE: I'm home! *(Meg jumps out of hiding.)* Oh, Meg—Look, it's Meg! *(Running to hug her.)* Meg! When did you get home?

MEG: Just now!

BABE: Well, it's so good to see you! I'm so glad you're home! I'm so relieved.

(Chick enters.)

MEG: Why, Chick; hello.

CHICK: Hello, Cousin Margaret. What brings you back to Hazlehurst?

MEG: Oh, I came on home . . . *(Turning to Babe.)* I came on home to see about Babe.

BABE: *(Running to hug Meg.)* Oh, Meg—

MEG: How are things with you, Babe?

CHICK: Well, they are dismal, if you want my opinion. She is refusing to cooperate with her lawyer, that nice-looking young Lloyd boy. She won't tell any of us why she committed this heinous crime, except to say that she didn't like Zackery's looks—

BABE: Oh, look, Lenny brought my suitcase from home! And my saxophone! Thank you! *(She runs over to the cot and gets out her saxophone.)*

CHICK: Now, that young lawyer is coming over here this afternoon, and when he gets here he expects to get some concrete answers! That's what he expects! No more of this nonsense and stubbornness from you, Rebecca McGrath, or they'll put you in jail and throw away the key!

BABE: *(Overlapping to Meg.)* Meg, come look at my new saxophone. I went to Jackson and bought it used. Feel it. It's so heavy.

MEG: *(Overlapping Chick.)* It's beautiful. *(The room goes silent.)*

CHICK: Isn't that right, won't they throw away the key?

LENNY: Well, honestly, I don't know about that—

CHICK: They will! And leave you there to rot. So, Rebecca, what are you going to tell Mr. Lloyd about shooting Zackery when he gets here? What are your reasons going to be?

BABE: *(Glaring.)* That I didn't like his looks! I just didn't like his stinking looks! And I don't like yours much, either, Chick the Stick! So just leave me alone! I mean it! Leave me alone! Oooh! *(She exits up the stairs. There is a long moment of silence.)*

CHICK: Well, I was only trying to warn her that she's going to have to help herself. It's just that she doesn't understand how serious the situation is. Does she? She doesn't have the vaguest idea. Does she, now?

LENNY: Well, it's true, she does seem a little confused.

CHICK: And that's putting it mildly, Lenny honey. That's putting it mighty mild. So, Margaret, how's your singing career going? We keep looking for your picture in the movie magazines. *(Meg moves to light a cigarette.)* You know, you shouldn't smoke. It causes cancer. Cancer of the lungs. They say each cigarette is just a little stick of cancer. A little death stick.

MEG: That's what I like about it, Chick—taking a drag off of death. *(She takes a long, deep drag.)* Mmm! Gives me a sense of controlling my own destiny. What power! What exhilaration! Want a drag?

LENNY: *(Trying to break the tension.)* Ah, Zackery's liver's been saved! His sister called up and said his liver was saved. Isn't that good news?

MEG: Well, yes, that's fine news. Mighty fine news. Why, I've been told that the liver's a powerful important bodily organ. I believe it's used to absorb all of our excess bile.

LENNY: Yes—well—it's been saved. *(The phone rings. Lenny gets it.)*

MEG: So! Did you hear all that good news about the liver, Little Chicken?

CHICK: I heard it. And don't you call me Chicken! *(Meg clucks like a chicken.)* I've told you a hundred times if I've told you once not to call me Chicken. You cannot call me Chicken.

LENNY: . . . Oh, no!. . . Of course, we'll be right over! 'Bye! *(She hangs up the phone.)* That was Annie May—Peekay and Buck Jr. have eaten paint!

CHICK: Oh, no! Are they all right? They're not sick? They're not sick, are they?

LENNY: I don't know. I don't know. Come on. We've got to run on next door.

CHICK: *(Overlapping.)* Oh, God! Oh, please! Please let them be all right! Don't let them die! Please, don't let them die! *(Chick runs off howling, with Lenny following after. Meg sits alone, finishing her cigarette. After a moment, Babe's voice is heard.)*

BABE'S VOICE: Pst—Psst!

(Meg looks around. Babe comes tiptoeing down the stairs.)

BABE: Has she gone?

MEG: She's gone. Peekay and Buck Jr. just ate their paints.

BABE: What idiots.

MEG: Yeah.

BABE: You know, Chick's hated us ever since we had to move here from Vicksburg to live with Old Grandmama and Old Granddaddy.

MEG: She's an idiot.

BABE: Yeah. Do you know what she told me this morning while I was still behind bars and couldn't get away?

MEG: What?

BABE: She told me how embarrassing it was for her all those years ago, you know, when Mama—

MEG: Yeah, down in the cellar.

BABE: She said our mama had shamed the entire family, and we were known notoriously all through Hazlehurst. *(About to cry.)* Then she went on to say how I would now be getting just as much bad publicity, and humiliating her and the family all over again.

MEG: Ah, forget it, Babe. Just forget it.

BABE: I told her, "Mama got national coverage! National!" And if Zackery wasn't a senator from Copiah County, I probably wouldn't even be getting statewide.

MEG: Of course you wouldn't.

BABE: *(After a pause.)* Gosh, sometimes I wonder. . .

MEG: What?

BABE: Why she did it. Why Mama hung herself.

MEG: I don't know. She had a bad day. A real bad day. You know how it feels on a real bad day.

BABE: And that old yellow cat. It was sad about that old cat.

MEG: Yeah.

BABE: I bet if Daddy hadn't of left us, they'd still be alive.

MEG: Oh, I don't know.

BABE: 'Cause it was after he left that she started spending whole days just sitting there and smoking on the back porch steps. She'd sling her ashes down onto the different bugs and ants that'd be passing by.

MEG: Yeah. Well, I'm glad he left.

BABA: That old yellow cat'd stay back there with her. I thought if she felt something for anyone it woulda been that old cat. Guess I musta been mistaken.

MEG: God, he was a bastard. Really, with his white teeth. Daddy was such a bastard.

BABE: Was he? I don't remember.

(Meg blows out a mouthful of smoke.)

BABE: *(After a moment, uneasily.)* I think I'm gonna make some lemonade. You want some?

MEG: Sure. *(Babe cuts lemons, dumps sugar, stirs ice cubes, etc., throughout the following exchange.)* Babe. Why won't you talk? Why won't you tell anyone about shooting Zackery?

BABE: Oooh—

MEG: Why not? You must have had a good reason. Didn't you?

BABE: I guess I did.

MEG: Well, what was it?

BABE: I. . . I can't say.

MEG: Why not? *(Pause.)* Babe, why not? You can tell me.

BABE: 'Cause I'm sort of protecting someone.

MEG: Protecting someone? Oh, Babe, then you really didn't shoot him! I knew you couldn't have done it! I knew it!

BABE: No, I shot him. I shot him all right. I meant to kill him. I was aiming for his heart, but I guess my hands were shaking and I— just got him in the stomach.

MEG: *(Collapsing.)* I see.

BABE: *(Stirring the lemonade.)* So I'm guilty. And I'm just gonna have to take my punishment and go on to jail.

MEG: Oh, Babe—

BABE: Don't worry, Meg, jail's gonna be a relief to me. I can learn to play my new Saxophone. I won't have to live with Zackery anymore. And I won't have his snoopy old sister, Lucille, coming over and pushing me around. Jail will be a relief. Here's your lemonade.

MEG: Thanks.

BABE: It taste okay?

MEG: Perfect.

BABE: I like a lot of sugar in mine. I'm gonna add some more sugar. *(Babe goes to add more sugar to her lemonade as Lenny bursts through the back door in a state of excitement and confusion.)*

LENNY: Well, it looks like the paint is primarily on their arms and faces, but Chick wants me to drive them all over to Dr. Winn's just to make sure. *(She grabs her car keys from the counter, and as she does so, she notices the mess of lemons and sugar.)* Oh, now, Babe, try not to make a mess here; and be careful with this sharp knife. Honestly, all that sugar's gonna get you sick. Well 'bye, 'bye. I'll be back as soon as I can.

MEG: 'Bye, Lenny.

BABE: 'Bye.

(Lenny exits.)

BABE: Boy, I don't know what's happening to Lenny.

MEG: What do you mean?

BABE: "Don't make a mess; don't make yourself sick; don't cut yourself with that sharp knife." She's turning into Old Grandmama.

MEG: You think so?

Catholic School Girls

Casey Kurti
1982

Comic
Setting: St. George's School, the suburbs, 1962.
Scene: It is the first day of first grade and the girls are fussing with
their uniforms and trying to look just right.
Of Note: Parts should be played by adult actresses. This is considered
a "memory" play.

6 years old:
> Elizabeth.
> Wanda.
> Maria Theresa.
> Colleen.

ELIZABETH: I'm ready!
> *(The lights come up quickly. The music stops. It is the first day of
> first grade, 1962.)*
COLLEEN: *(Polishing apple, while watching Maria Theresa crawl under
a desk.)* Where's the teacher? I wanna get started.
WANDA: I saw the teacher in the bathroom. She said to pick a seat.
MARIA THERESA: The teacher's in the bathroom?
> *(Colleen begins to eat the apple.)*
WANDA: She's throwing up.
COLLEEN: Boys are supposed to sit over there. You retarded or some-
thing? What's that?
ELIZABETH: My mother pinned it on me. It's a Holy Medal for the first
day. I live on Remsen Road in an apartment—
COLLEEN: *(To Maria Theresa.)* I live near you.
> *(Overlapping:)*
COLLEEN: You got that white car with the back door off. It's a circus
car right? Right?
ELIZABETH: I have four brothers and two sisters. We ARE going to get
a house—someday.
MARIA THERESA: No!
COLLEEN: You live down by Carvel's. I seen your family there, your
father's fat. . .

WANDA: I know where Carvel's is.

ELIZABETH: *(Crosses to statue.)* Hi, Jesus. Come here, Mr. Gunderson, say hi.

WANDA: Who's Gunderson?

ELIZABETH: My friend, she stays with me. Mr. Gunderson is a girl. She's got a red dress on, with lots of bows. She doesn't like this uniform.

COLLEEN: I don't see her.

ELIZABETH: She's invisible to people.

MARIA THERESA: *(Waves furiously in wrong direction and crawls under desk again.)* My name is Maria Theresa Russo.

ELIZABETH: She has long hair.

MARIA THERESA: I see it.

WANDA: Is she your sister?

ELIZABETH: No she's my friend. I don't talk to my family.

COLLEEN: *(Crosses to front.)* I have my own room. My brothers are slobs. They jump on the couch when my mother is not home. We are the only Catholics on the block, the rest of the families are Jews.

WANDA: I know some Jews.

COLLEEN: Shut up. My second best friend, Kitty, is a Jew. She has a little dollhouse with lights that turn on and off and—

WANDA: There were lots of Jews where we used to live.

COLLEEN: *(Getting furious.)* They go to church on Saturday and they all go to public school.

MARIA THERESA: When is the teacher going to stop throwing up? I don't like it here.

COLLEEN: That's a sin, you have to go on Sunday, right? Right?

ELIZABETH: I don't know.

COLLEEN: Well I do, because I'm going to be a nun. Got a little doll that's a nun. Sister is going to let me try on her bride's veil. . .

MARIA THERESA: Do they have any hair underneath that bride's veil?

WANDA: Oh yes.

COLLEEN: Who says?

WANDA: Mamow—My Mother. She taught me a special hymn for the first day to sing to sister, wanna hear?

COLLEEN: No.

ELIZABETH: Yes.

WANDA: The Ave Maria by Wanda Sluska. . . Zdrowa's Maryo, Laskis Pelna, Panz Toba. . . *(Air-raid siren sounds.)*

COLLEEN: Yuch, stupid name.

MARIA THERESA: Lunchtime, already?

ELIZABETH: That sound means the communists are sending a bomb over here. We have to go home.

WANDA: But we just came here.

COLLEEN: This is Cheez Whiz. What you got? I'll trade you.

MARIA THERESA: I have a meatball hero. I think this is my sister's lunch.

ELIZABETH: There is a bomb shelter in my apartment building. I got to call my grandmother so she can get on the bus and come over to my house before it goes off. She lives in the Bronx. My grandfather isn't coming, he's already dead. You guys can come over and hide, but no boys allowed.

WANDA: We are supposed to hide here.

COLLEEN: Who says?

MARIA THERESA: We have bunk beds. Maria Diana sleeps on top of me. Maria Rose sleeps on top of Maria Ann. Anthony sleeps on top of Salvador Jr. Cosmo sleeps on top of Joseph.

ELIZABETH: Red fiery stuff comes out of that bomb and if it falls on you it could burn your skin right off. *(Maria Theresa pulls out sweater.)* That won't save you. You need a raincoat.

WANDA: I'm getting the teacher. *(Exits.)*

ELIZABETH: This Chinese guy got hit by the bomb the last time while he was riding his bicycle. He got squished right into the ground. You can go over there and see him right now. He is still lying there all flattened out with his bicycle.

COLLEEN: *(Stops eating.)* Is the guy dead?

ELIZABETH: Yes.

COLLEEN: Hey, wait for me.

ELIZABETH: One second. *(She grabs Jesus.)*

MARIA THERESA: I'll get the mother.

COLLEEN: Don't touch the snakes, they could come alive. *(Sister Mary Agnes enters.)*

My Sister in This House

Wendy Kesselman
1982

Dramatic
Setting: The dining room and kitchen of Mme. Danzard's home in Le
    Mans, France. Early 1930's.
Scene: Christine has worked for Mme. Danzard for a while and now
    Lea has come to join her. She is awkward and untrained. Mme.
    Danzard and Isabelle are having a meal, and as always, there is
    friction between them.

Madame Danzard: 50's, a serious woman, owner of the house, Le
    Mans, France.
Isabelle: Her daughter, 20's, spoiled, yet insecure.
Christine: Early 20's, the maid, raised in a convent; serious, a perfec-
    tionist.
Lea: Her younger sister, mid-teen, eager, sweet, has arrived to also
    work as a maid.

MADAME DANZARD: Don't toy with your food, Isabelle. It's to dis-
    agreeable. Always making those little piles.
ISABELLE: I'm not, Maman.
MADAME DANZARD: You mean to tell me I don't see what you're
    doing?
ISABELLE: I'm not toying, Maman.
MADAME DANZARD: *(Coldly.)* Very well, my dear, call it what you will.
    *(She rings a small round bell. Lea and Christine come into the din-
    ing room. Lea is carrying a platter of veal on a tray. She presents
    the platter for Madame Danzard's inspection, as Christine stands
    to the side. Madame Danzard smiles to herself. Lea puts the plat-
    ter down and she and Christine go back into the kitchen.
    Madame Danzard and Isabelle serve themselves and eat in silence
    for a few moments.)*
CHRISTINE: *(Following Lea into the kitchen.)* She liked it. Did you see?
    Did you see her face?
LEA: She likes everything you do.
CHRISTINE: She sees everything.
    (She sits down at the kitchen table and begins to prepare string

beans. Everything Christine does in the kitchen is neat, quick, impeccable. The bowls and plates seem to move like magic beneath her fingers. Lea is clearly a beginner. She sits down beside Christine and begins, clumsily, to help with the beans.)

MADAME DANZARD: *(Savoring the veal.)* This veal is delicious.

ISABELLE: Of course, you love veal. *(She looks at her mother.)*

MADAME DANZARD: Don't you?

ISABELLE: You know I don't. It's too heavy in the middle of the day.

MADAME DANZARD: Not the way she's prepared it. Light as a feather.

ISABELLE: I've heard it ruins the complexion.

MADAME DANZARD: Where did you hear that?

ISABELLE: I read it.

MADAME DANZARD: *(Scornfully.)* Really. Where?

ISABELLE: Somewhere. I don't remember.

MADAME DANZARD: Certain days of the month, my dear, you really are worse than others.

ISABELLE: That shouldn't surprise *you*.

MADAME DANZARD: Isabelle, if you continue in this vein you're going to ruin my meal. *(She eats with a certain relish.)* Wait till the Blanchards come to dinner. I'll have her make her rabbit pâté. Won't that surprise them! The best cook we've had in years.

ISABELLE: Oh I don't know—Marie wasn't so bad.

MADAME DANZARD: Marie? Please. The way she cooked a pot au feu—ahh—it still makes me shudder.

ISABELLE: You exaggerate, Maman.

MADAME DANZARD: Exaggerate? I'm being kind. Marie would have murdered a veal like this. *(Wiping her mouth with her napkin.)* Done to perfection. I hope we never lose her. And she always buys the best.

ISABELLE: I don't know how she does it with the money you give her.

MADAME DANZARD: It's what I've always given them. You have no idea how lucky we are, Isabelle. The servants I've seen in my day. *(She watches Isabelle stuff potatoes into her mouth.)* They eat like birds. *(Looking at Isabelle.)* Always looking so neat, so perfect. You wouldn't think they were maids at all. Though I must admit the younger one gives me trouble—she's so young.

ISABELLE: I like the younger one.

MADAME DANZARD: We'll she's quiet. I'll say that for her.

ISABELLE: *(Mercilessly chewing on the veal.)* Quiet? She never speaks. Neither of them does.

MADAME DANZARD: I guess they must talk between themselves.

ISABELLE: I can't imagine about what.

MADAME DANZARD: *(Looking at Isabelle.)* Well, maybe they pray. *(She laughs.)* That's how it is when you're brought up by the nuns. *(They both laugh.)*

MADAME DANZARD: *(Abruptly stopping the laughter.)* Will you stop it Isabelle. Look at that plate. *(She rings the small round bell. Lea comes into the dining room with a platter of cheese. Madame Danzard and Isabelle are instantly silent. Lea clears away the empty platter of veal and goes back into the kitchen.)* They're so discreet. Not the slightest prying. You can't imagine what it's like to have a prying maid. To have someone going through your things.

ISABELLE: The younger one cleans my shoes so perfectly. And you know, she's almost pretty.

MADAME DANZARD: *(Cleaning her teeth with her tongue.)* When your father and I were first married—she was something that one. But these two are different. Mark my words.

CHRISTINE: *(Rapidly snapping off the ends of the beans.)* How lucky we are, Lea. The other houses I've been, they come into the kitchen and interfere. Madame knows her place.

MADAME DANZARD: They take such pride in the house. Not a speck of dust under the carpet.

CHRISTINE: Madame checks everything. I like that.

LEA: You do? It scares me—the way she checks.

MADAME DANZARD: Not a speck.

CHRISTINE: Oh no, I like it. It's better that way. Believe me. In the end it's better.

MADAME DANZARD: Not under the lamps. Not a ring.

ISABELLE: Really?

MADAME DANZARD: Not one. They're extraordinarily clean.

CHRISTINE: Madame is so precise, so careful. Her lists! Everything down to the last second.

LEA: She doesn't let us get away with a thing.

ISABELLE: Well Maman, let's face it—you don't let them get away with a thing.

MADAME DANZARD: Why should I? I pay them enough.

CHRISTINE: Why should she? She wants the house a certain way.

MADAME DANZARD: This is my house.

ISABELLE: It certainly is.

MADAME DANZARD: Well, it will be yours one day, Isabelle.

CHRISTINE: But she always sees the little things we do right.

MADAME DANZARD: The younger one may be pretty, but it's the older one who fascinates me. I've never had anyone like her.

CHRISTINE: I've never had anyone like Madame before.

MADAME DANZARD: Totally trustworthy. I never have to count the change when she comes back from marketing. Not one sou is missing.

CHRISTINE: *(Holding out the bowl to Lea.)* Put them all in here, Lea.

ISABELLE: They don't seem to have any friends.

MADAME DANZARD: Thank heaven for that.

(Lea spills the beans on the floor.)

CHRISTINE: You're so clumsy. *(She begins picking up the beans. Upset, Lea helps her.)*

MADAME DANZARD: I've seen those people's friends, my dear. Believe me, it's bad enough with that mother of theirs.

ISABELLE: What a horror! It's a lucky thing they have each other.

CHRISTINE: I didn't mean it. You're so silly. What a baby you are.

MADAM DANZARD: And they do love us. They're so devoted to us. You'll see—the whole town will envy us. *(Laughing.)* We have pearls on our hands, Isabelle. Two pearls.

(She rings the small round bell. Isabelle goes over to the sitting room area and takes an evening bag with tiny seed pearls out of a sewing basket. Lea and Christine come into the dining room and begin to clear the dishes. Madame Danzard goes over to the sewing basket and takes out her needlepoint.)

MADAME DANZARD: Let me see, Isabelle. *(Isabelle holds out the evening bag.)* I can't see it from here. *(Isabelle leans closer and hands her the bag. (Christine and Lea work silently together in the kitchen.)* Nice. Very nice. It's coming along. Bit by bit. *(She hands it back to Isabelle, sits down on the couch and begins doing needlepoint.)* You can't rush these things, my dear. Believe me. A bag like that could take you . . . *(She looks at Isabelle laboring with the seed pearls.)* two years. *(Isabelle looks at her.)* Maybe more. But there's no hurry, is there? Nothing to hurry for. You have all the time in the world.

ISABELLE: Yes, Maman.

MADAME DANZARD: All the time. When I was your age I made a bag just like that. Seed pearls too—but mine had a blue background. And when I held it up to the light, it . . .

ISABELLE: It what?

MADAME DANZARD: Shone . . . like little moons. Night after night I worked on that bag. But in the end it was worth it.

ISABELLE: Why, Maman?

MADAME DANZARD: I don't remember. An evening out. A dance.

ISABELLE: Oh, what happened, Maman? Tell me.

MADAME DANZARD: I don't know. Maybe nothing. Maybe nothing ever happened. Listen to that rain. It's been raining like that for a week. A full week. Who knows when it will stop. Do you hear it, Isabelle?

ISABELLE: I hear it.

MADAME DANZARD: It could go on like this for a month. That's all we need. Are you listening to me, Isabelle?

ISABELLE: I'm listening, Maman.

MADAME DANZARD: Last year it went on for three months. Remember?

ISABELLE: That was the year before.

MADAME DANZARD: Was it? Was it really, in Paris it's no better. After all, they're further north.

ISABELLE: Do you really think it rains more in Paris than here?

MADAME DANZARD: More, Isabelle. Much more. I'm sure of it. *(After a pause.)* Maybe we'll go up to Paris this year.

ISABELLE: Oh Maman, could we?

MADAME DANZARD: For a little shopping.

ISABELLE: Oh Maman. When?

MADAME DANZARD: Though I don't know. The things they wear in Paris. And you don't look well in those clothes, Isabelle. You know you don't. Even I don't look well in them. How could one? Hand me the scissors, would you. *(Isabelle looks around.)* There. Right behind you. *(Impatient.)* On the table. *(Isabelle stands up and drops everything.)* What's the matter with you? *(She rings the small round bell. Pulling Isabelle up, as she bends to pick up the seed pearls.)* Really, Isabelle.

(Lea comes in from the kitchen. Madame Danzard points to the floor. Lea kneels and starts collecting the tiny seed pearls that

have fallen. Madame Danzard eyes the floor, making sure every last seed pearl has been picked up.)

MADAME DANZARD: Besides, I don't like to leave the house.

ISABELLE: But why, Maman? What could happen to it?

MADAME DANZARD: A lot can happen to a house when you're not there. And then—going to Paris—such a trip.

ISABELLE: A trip!

MADAME DANZARD: And such an expense. Think of the money. Mmm—Paris.

ISABELLE: Paris!

MADAME DANZARD: Yes, I think we'll just have to skip Paris this year.
(A bell rings. Madame Danzard and Isabelle jump. Lea goes to the door.)

ISABELLE: Who's that?

MADAME DANZARD: Shhh. Let me listen. Who could it be? In this weather.
(Isabelle puts her evening bag back into the sewing basket. She and Madame Danzard sit down on the couch and wait, smiling. Lea comes back with the mail. She puts one letter in her pocket quickly, enters the sitting room with another letter on a tray. She presents the tray to Madame Danzard.)

MADAME DANZARD: Oh! Mail.
(She takes the letter. Lea goes up the stairs.)

ISABELLE: Anything for me, Maman?

MADAME DANZARD: Look at this. Would you look at this, Isabelle. No return address. And look at that handwriting. What do you think it could be? *(She waves the letter toward Isabelle.)*

Shadow of a Man

Cherrie Moraga
1990

Dramatic
Setting: The kitchen.
Scene: A "Novela," a Mexican soap opera, is playing on the television in the kitchen. Hortensia is rolling out tortillas. Lupe and Rosario are watching the TV. Hortensia is upset. Her son Rigo is engaged to marry a "gringa."

Hortensia: The Mother, 40's.
Lupe: The daughter, 12.
Leticia: Hortensia's older daughter, 17.
Rosario: The Aunt, Hortensia's sister, 50's.

HORTENSIA: She can go to hell as far as I'm concern.

ROSARIO: Who, Hortensia?

HORTENSIA: La gringa. They di'nt even get married yet, and she's already got my son where she wants him. Ni lo conozco. He's a stranger. *(She puts the tortilla on the comal, watches it rise.)* The other day, Rigo comes home from the college. Manuel sees him in the door, and a'course he jumps up from the chair para darle un abrazo. And you know what Rigo does? He pushes Manuel away.

ROSARIO: No.

HORTENSIA: And you know what he says?

ROSARIO: Qué?

HORTENSIA: He say, "No, Dad. I'm a man, now. We shake hands."

ROSARIO: No me digas.

HORTENSIA: Te digo. Does that sound like my son to you? *(She sits.)*

ROSARIO: No.

HORTENSIA: And to see the look on Manuel's face. . . *(Pause.)* Y la girl standing there with a smile en la cara.

ROSARIO: ¡Qué barbaridad!

HORTENSIA: It's eating Manuel up. *(She gestures that Manuel has been drinking.)*

ROSARIO: That's not so good, Tencha.

HORTENSIA: *(Intimately.)* Claro que no. ¿Pero qué puedo hacer yo?

LUPE: Miren. Maria's telling Enrique she's pregnant.

ROSARIO: No! ¿De veras? *(They all stop and watch, mesmerized. Muffled voices from the TV, then a commercial.)*

LUPE: ¡Ay! Wait 'til he finds out quién es el padre.

ROSARIO: ¡Híjole!

HORTENSIA: *(Resuming her work.)* But I tell you, one of these days I'm goin' to tell esa gringuita everyt'ing I think of her. She thinks she goin' to keep my son, hold him all to herself? What's it hurt for her husband to stay close to his familia? But, they're a different kin'a peepo, los gringos gente fría. I try to tell Rigo this before they were novios, que iba a tener problemas con ella, pero no me quiso escuchar. So, what could I do! They might fool you with their pecas y ojos azules, but the women are cold.

ROSARIO: I bet her thing down there is frozen up.

HORTENSIA: *(Laughing.)* ¡Ay, Rosario! No digas eso.

ROSARIO: I may be old but my thing is still good 'n hot. ¿Ver-dad, m'ija? Us mexicanas keep our things muy calientes, as hot as that comal allí, no?

LUPE: I dunno, tía.

ROSARIO: ¿No sabes? Tú no sabes, eh? *(Playfully, snatching at Lupe between the legs.)* Is your fuchi fachi hot down there, too?

LUPE: *(Jumping away.)* Stop, tía!

HORTENSIA: ¡Chayo!

ROSARIO: ¡Ay! ¡Tú eres pura gallina! *(Lupe comes up behind Hortensia and takes a warm tortilla from the stack. Hortensia slaps her hand lightly.)*

HORTENSIA: With you around, the stack never gets any bigger.

LUPE: But my panza does. *(She sticks out her stomach.)*

ROSARIO: Now you look like María on the novela. *(Lupe begins to enact "la desesperada" role, when Leticia enters. She is wearing late sixties radical Chicano attire: tight jeans, large looped earrings, an army jacket with a UFW [United Farm Workers] insignia on it, etc.)*

HORTENSIA: Allí viene la política. *(To Leticia.)* I told you I don't want you to wear esa chaqueta.

ROSARIO: Es el estilo, Tencha.

LETICIA: *(Stealing a warm tortilla from the stack.)* Yeah.

HORTENSIA: *(Referring to tortilla.)* ¡Tú también!

LETICIA: *(Rolling up the tortilla.)* How can you stand watching those things? Those novelas are so phony. I mean, c'mon. What do you think the percentage of blondes is in Mexico?

ROSARIO: No sé.

LETICIA: I mean in relation to the whole population?

ROSARIO: No sé.

LETICIA: *(Putting butter on the tortilla.)* One percent? But no, the novelas make it look like half the population is Swedish or something. Even the maids are güeras. But, of course, the son of the patrón falls madly in love with one and they live happily everafter in luxury. Give me a break!

HORTENSIA: Ni modo, I enjoy them.

ROSARIO: Es pura fantansía. Pero, m'ija, they got so many problems, it gets your mind off your own.

LETICIA: I guess that's the idea. *(Offstage a man's heavy labored steps.)*

MANUEL: Hortensia! Hortensia!

HORTENSIA: ¡Ay! Tha' man's goin' to make me crazy. Lupita, go see wha' your papi wan's.

LUPE: Sí, mami,

HORTENSIA: Y si te pide cigarros, don' give him none.

LUPE: Okay. *(She exits.)*

ROSARIO: ¿Todavía 'stá fumando?

LETICA: Like a chimney.

HORTENSIA: Sure! He wan's to kill himself. He's not a'pose to smoke. Es otro día que no trabaja. I don't know what we're goin' to do if he keep missing work.

ROSARIO: He di'nt see el doctor?

LETICIA: Are you kidding?

HORTENSIA: He's scared a death of them. He complain que he pull somet'ing in his arm on the job, que le duele mucho. But I don't believe it. I think it's his heart. The other night he woke up in the middle of the night and he could har'ly breathe. He was burning up. I had to get up to change all the sheets y sus piyamas. . . they were completely soaked. Now he's gottu take the sleeping pills jus' to close his eyes for a few hours. *(Pause.)* Pero vas a ver, tonight he'll go out again.

LETICIA: *(Kissing Hortensia on the cheek.)* Pues, ay te watcho.

HORTENSIA: ¿Adónde vas?

LETICIA: To Irma's.

HORTENSIA: ¿Qué vas a hacer con ésa?

LETICIA: Oh, we're jus' gonna hang out for a while.

HORTENSIA: Well, not on the street, do you hear me?

LETICIA: Aw, mom!

HORTENSIA: Aw, Mom!

ROSARIO: Déjala, Tencha.

HORTENSIA: Pero, no la conoces, es callejera.

LETICIA: Shoot, I'll be graduating in a month.

HORTENSIA: You think graduating makes you una mujer. Eres mujer cuando te cases. Then your husband can worry about you, not me.

LETICIA: Yeah, but Rigo can come and go as he pleases whether he's married or not.

HORTENSIA: Claro. Es hombre.

LETICIA: Es hombre. Es hombre. I'm sick of hearing that. It's not fair.

HORTENSIA: Well, you better get use to things not being fair. Whoever said the world was goin' to be fair?

LETICIA: Well, my world's going to be fair! *(Leticia exits upstage. Rosario and Hortensia stare at the air in silence.)*

HORTENSIA: Te digo, the girl scares me sometimes.

LUPE: *(Entering.)* Papi wants his cigarettes. *(They turn to her. A beat. Then all three simultaneously turn their attention back to the novela. The lights fade to black while the novela continues playing in the darkness.)*

Graces Notes

Rachel Rubin Ladutke

Dramatic
Setting: The kitchen of a farmhouse. December 1966.
Scene: Emily is holding a book but staring into space. Catherine and
Grace are in the middle of an argument. Catherine has just
revealed that she is pregnant.

Grace: 53, speaks her mind, traces remaining of a South Carolina
childhood, genteel, a beauty.
Emily: 16, her daughter.
Catherine: 19, her old daughter.
Molly: 33, her step-daughter, very pregnant.

GRACE: Don't start, Catherine. We have to talk about the future.
What to do afterwards. *(Deep breath.)* I can't think straight. Lord,
how am I going to get dinner ready?
EMILY: Who gives a damn about dinner?
GRACE: I do! Okay. It's Thursday night. We're going to have a nice
quiet meal for a change. The Wards are coming over for cards
later. Tomorrow your father will be home. And on Monday, after
everyone's left, Joseph and you and I are going to sit down and
have a long talk.
CATHERINE: Sure. We can talk about it all you want. I've made my
decision.
GRACE: Nobody's making any decisions right now. Not me, not you.
This is too emotional.
CATHERINE: I'm not emotional, Mama. I'm perfectly calm. I've had a
long time to think about this.
GRACE: Fine, now I'm entitled to the same courtesy. I don't want
either of you to say a word about this tonight. In fact, nobody is
to know until after Christmas. Is that clear?
EMILY: Sure, but why not?
GRACE: Because we're going to have a nice, family holiday. I don't
want anything to ruin it.
CATHERINE: *(Mutters.)* What bullshit.
GRACE: Catherine? Promise me. No big scenes. *(Pause.)* Don't you
think your father deserves to be told next?

CATHERINE: Sure, Mama.

GRACE: Nobody says a word till Monday. Agreed? Emily?

EMILY: I promise.

CATHERINE: Okay. No big scenes.

GRACE: Fine. Who wants to help me with the pies?

EMILY: I don't really feel like it.

CATHERINE: I think I'll go lie down for a while.

GRACE: Catherine? Have you been taking care of yourself?

CATHERINE: Sure. I'm fine, Mama. Just tired, that's all.

GRACE: Eating all right?

CATHERINE: Yes, I said!

EMILY: You want help with your bags?

CATHERINE: Sure. Thanks.

> (They grab the bags and exit. Grace pours herself a drink, sits at the table, and lights a cigarette. Molly enters from the outside.)

MOLLY: Whew, it's really nippy out there! *(Shrugs out of her coat.)*

GRACE: Here, sit down. I'll take that. *(Hangs up Molly's coat. Molly is hugely pregnant.)* Enjoy your walk?

MOLLY: It was wonderful! I'd forgotten how beautiful the trees look when they get covered in snow. In Washington, everything just melts right away. It's been warm so far this winter.

GRACE: Not up here.

MOLLY: I can see that! Abby and Annie. . . ?

GRACE: Last time I checked, they were fast asleep.

MOLLY: Wonderful. *(Grimaces.)* Oh, boy. Sometimes I think this one is twins again. He's so strong. Cath get in all right?

GRACE: I suppose.

MOLLY: Martinis in the afternoon? This looks serious.

GRACE: My funny daughter. *(Pause.)* I was just trying to relax a little.

MOLLY: Grace? Is something wrong?

GRACE: Not a thing. I'm just preoccupied. *(Forcing a smile.)* I've got so much to do.

MOLLY: I could help if you'd let me.

GRACE: No, you won't. One of the main reasons for having you all up here this year is so you wouldn't have to lift a finger. And I meant that. Besides, Emily's a great help to me.

MOLLY: Sure, when she thinks about it. And Cath . . . *(Really looking at her.)* You look kind of drawn out. Are you getting enough sleep?

GRACE: I should be asking you that. *(Gets up.)* Would you like some hot chocolate?

MOLLY: I'd love some! I miss your hot chocolate more than just about anything else on the farm.

GRACE: Flattery will get you everywhere. *(Gets down two mugs.)* I think I'll join you.

MOLLY: Are you *sure* you're feeling all right?

GRACE: Molly, let it go. I'm fine.

MOLLY: Okay, okay. At least let me make the sweet potatoes?

GRACE: Nope. You can help next year.

MOLLY: With *three* kids hanging on me? It'll be a miracle if I get anything done.

GRACE: You love it though.

MOLLY: This one's going to be a boy. I just know it. *(Unable to take anymore, Grace begins to cry.)* Grace? What is it? *(Gets up and embraces Grace.)* I *knew* something was wrong.

GRACE: No. . . *(Grace tries to compose herself. Catherine bursts in.)*

CATHERINE: I'm going to the store. You need anything else?

GRACE: Oh. . . no, I don't think so. I thought you were tired.

MOLLY: Why don't you slow down for a second? Can't you see she's upset?

CATHERINE: Mind your own damn business, Molly! *(To Grace.)* I see you couldn't keep quiet for ten minutes.

MOLLY: Keep quiet about what?

GRACE: Catherine, calm down.

CATHERINE: No, I won't calm down! God, you're such a hypocrite!

GRACE: Catherine. . .

CATHERINE: You said we'd keep this quiet till after Christmas! But the minute I get out of the room, you blab to her! Thanks a lot, Mom.

MOLLY: What are you talking about?

CATHERINE: Come off it, Molly. Don't pretend she didn't tell you I'm pregnant!

MOLLY: *(Stunned.)* You're *what*?

CATHERINE: Some secret, Mom. Thanks a lot.

GRACE: Actually, I didn't tell her.

CATHERINE: Sure. Then what was all that about when I came in? You crying, your precious Molly hugging you. . .

GRACE: I needed a little comfort, that's all! But I didn't tell her why I was upset, Catherine.

CATHERINE: Yeah, right.

MOLLY: She's telling the truth. You just told me yourself. *(Awkward silence.)*

CATHERINE: Oh, man. . . I gotta get out of here for a while. Where's the car keys?

GRACE: Where *are* the car keys? *(Catherine just glares at her.)* Here. *(Hands them to her.)*

CATHERINE: Do you have a couple of bucks? *(Grace hands her some money.)* Thanks. See ya. *(Grabs her coat and slams out.)*

GRACE: *(Trying to joke.)* Car keys, money. . . if I closed my eyes and her voice was a little lower, I'd think Jason was here.

MOLLY: Grace. . . I'm sorry.

GRACE: You didn't do anything wrong, honey. *(Getting tearful again.)* I don't know what to do. How did this happen? I'm scared for her Molly. I'm so scared.

EMILY: Cath! Wait for me! *(Emily bursts in, runs to kitchen door, and stands looking out.)*

MOLLY: She's going to be all right, Mom. Catherine's a survivor. Like you were.

GRACE: I wish I felt that way.

EMILY: She never waits for me! *(Suddenly starts crying.)* She's always running on ahead.

GRACE: It's okay, honey. It's okay. Shh. She just needs some time to herself, that's all. Shh. Everything's going to be fine.

(Grace hugs Emily tight, nearly crying herself. Molly looks on. Lights fade.)

Seventeen Warnings in Search of a Feminist Poem

Erica Jong

Reader's Theater Piece/Poetry

4 Women

1: Beware of the man who denounces ambition;
   his fingers itch under his gloves.
2: Beware of the man who denounces war
    through clenched teeth.
3: Beware of the man who denounces women writers;
   his penis is tiny and he cannot spell.
4: Beware of the man who wants to protect you;
   he will protect you from everything but
   himself.
5: Beware of the man who loves to cook;
   he will fill your kitchen with greasy pots.
6: Beware of the man who loves your soul;
   he is a bullshitter.
7: Beware of the man who denounces his mother;
   he is a son of a bitch.
8: Beware of the man who spells son of a bitch as one word;
   he is a hack.
9: Beware of the man who loves death too well;
   he is taking out insurance.
10: Beware of the man who loves life too well;
    he is a fool.
11: Beware of the man who denounces psychiatrists;
    he is afraid.
12: Beware of the man who trusts psychiatrists;
    he is in hock.
13: Beware of the man who picks your dresses;
    he wants to wear them.
14: Beware of the man you think is harmless;
    he will surprise you.

15: Beware of the man who cares for nothing but books;
   he will run like a trickle of ink.

16: Beware of the man who writes flowery love letters;
   he is preparing for years of silence.

17: Beware of the man who praises liberated women;
   he is planning to quit his job.

PART THREE:

SCENES FOR
TWO MEN/TWO WOMEN

Antigone

Sophocles
442 B.C.

Dramatic

Setting: Outside the Palace.

Scene: Antigone's brother Polyneices led an assault on the city and was killed. Kreon has forbidden his burial and Antigone has defied him in spite of her sister's warnings. Now, Kreon accuses her in front of the citizens.

Antigonê: 20's, daughter of Oedipus, engaged to marry Haimon, son of Creon King of Thebes.

Ismenê: Her sister, 20's.

Kreon: The present King of Thebes who ruled after Oedipus was exiled.

Chorus Leader: An elderly citizen of Thebes.

KREON: You, Antigonê, head bent,
    Eyes to the ground! Look at me!
    Did you or did you not do this?

ANTIGONÊ: How can I deny what I did!
    (Kreon turns to the Sentry.)

KREON: And, you! Leave when you like.
    You're cleared of a very heavy charge.
    (As the Sentry turns to go off left, Kreon continues.)

KREON: Now tell me, and be brief.
    Did you know of my edict forbidding this?

ANTIGONÊ: How could I not? It was public.

KREON: And yet you dared defy these laws?

ANTIGONÊ: Yes, I dared. It wasn't Zeus who made them.
    And Justice dwelling in the underworld
    Makes no such laws for men. Your edict, Kreon,
    For all its strength, is mortal and weak when measured
    Against the laws of the gods, unwritten, unshakable.
    Laws not meant for now, but for ever,
    For no man knows their age; laws that no
    Proud spirit of a man could make me break,
    For one day I must answer to the gods.

I know that I will die. How could I not know?
Even without your edict.
And yet, if I die now, before my time,
How can that be a hardship?
How can one live, as I do, surrounded by evil,
And not greet Death as a friend?

My death isn't important;
And yet, to see my brother lie dead and unburied
Is an agony beyond words. But this is nothing.
If you think me foolish, Kreon, me and my acts,
Perhaps I'm judged a fool by another fool.
CHORUS LEADER: Like father, like daughter,
    Stubborn, unbending:
    Neither learned to yield to adversity.
KREON: The strongest will breaks first. The toughest iron,
    Tempered in white-hot flame, shatters first.
    And wild horses are curbed by the smallest bit.
    Pride in a slave? When the master is nearby?
    This girl is guilty of double impertinence:
    Breaking the law and then boasting of it!
    If this crime goes unpunished, and she's the victor,
    Who's the man here then? She or I?
    No! Sister's child, or closer even
    than anyone who worships at Zeus' altar
    In my own house, she and her sister will pay
    For their crime with death! I hold her sister guilty
    In the same degree in the plotting of this burial!
    (To Attendants.)
    Bring her, someone! I saw her inside just now,
    Distracted and free of her wits. The mind that plots
    Mischief in dark corners often betrays itself
    Before the deed is done. But I hate worse
    The one who acts the crime, then glories in it.
ANTIGONÊ: What more could you want than my death?
KREON: Having that, I have everything.
ANTIGONÊ: Go on, then, kill me. Your words are as hateful to me,
    As mine to you, and I hope they always will be.
    And yet, how could I have greater praise

And glory than by giving the brother I love
A decent and honorable burial?
(To the Chorus.)
And these men agree, if only their lips
Weren't locked in fear of you. But then, of course,
Tyrants have power to do and say what they please!

KREON: You're the only one here thinks so.

ANTIGONÊ: No, they support me. Their tongues are leashed.

KREON: Aren't you ashamed to talk treason!

ANTIGONÊ: Ashamed? Me? Of loving my brother?

KREON: Wasn't Eteoklês your brother, too?

ANTIGONÊ: Yes, by the same mother and father.

KREON: Then how can you dare insult his memory?

ANTIGONÊ: Eteoklês would never say I did that.

KREON: No insult to honor the traitor?

ANTIGONÊ: He was his brother, not some slave!

KREON: He warred on his country; Eteoklês championed it!

ANTIGONÊ: Death demands equal rites for all.

KREON: Equal rites for the wicked and the just?

ANTIGONÊ: Who knows what the gods below call wicked?

KREON: A traitor is a traitor, even in death.

ANTIGONÊ: My nature is to love, not to hate.

KREON: Then share your love with the dead! Go and join them!
While I'm alive no woman rules me!
(Ismenê enters from the palace led on by Guards.)

CHORUS LEADER: But here comes Ismenê, weeping hot tears
For a dear sister, her beauty clouded
By a dark grief.

KREON: Viper! Viper! You, too, Ismenê!
Lurking here in my house, sucking my blood!
Without knowing, I raised two sources of ruin
To topple my throne and power!
Come here! Tell me!
Did you share in this crime, or do you deny it?
Answer me! The burial!

ISMENÊ: I did it, yes, if she lets me say so.
I share the guilt; I share the penalty.

ANTIGONÊ: No! Justice doesn't allow this.
You wanted no part, I gave you none.

ISMENÊ: But now you ship is battered by a stormy sea,
    I'm not ashamed to join in your suffering.
ANTIGONÊ: Words are all you know, Ismenê!
    Death and the dead know what I did.
ISMENÊ: Please, don't deny me the right
    To die with you and honor the dead!
ANTIGONÊ: Why should I share my death with someone
    Who never once raised a hand to help?
ISMENÊ: But what's the use of life without you!
ANTIGONÊ: Ask Kreon. You're always quoting him!
ISMENÊ: You're laughing at me, Antigonê! Why?
ANTIGONÊ: Laughing at you? Yes. But it pains me.
ISMENÊ: I'll do anything, even now.
ANTIGONÊ: Save yourself. I won't envy you.
ISMENÊ: Ah, but why can't I share in your fate?
ANTIGONÊ: You chose life, I chose death.
ISMENÊ: Yes, but not before I warned you!
ANTIGONÊ: Some praised you, others me.
ISMENÊ: Yes, but our offense is the same!
ANTIGONÊ: Be happy, Ismenê: you're alive.
    I gave my life long ago
    When I joined hands to serve the dead.
    (Kreon turns to the Chorus.)
KREON: Gentlemen, it occurs to me
    One of these girls just lost her mind;
    The other never had one.
ISMENÊ: Cruelty unhinges the soundest mind.
KREON: As yours did when you sided with evil.
ISMENÊ: What would life be worth without her?
KREON: Forget she ever lived. She's dead.
ISMENÊ: You'd actually kill your son's bride?
KREON: He'll have other fields to plough!
ISMENÊ: Yes, but what of the love they share?
KREON: My son marry a worthless woman?
ISMENÊ: Oh, Haimon, how your father wrongs you!
KREON: I've heard enough of your marriage babble!
ISMENÊ: You'd steal this girl from your own son?
KREON: No; I'll count on Death for that!
ISMENÊ: It's settled, then? Antigonê dies?

KREON: Settled? Yes! For both of us!
  Guards, take them inside! Hurry!
  They're only women; but even bold men
  Try to escape when Death closes in.
  No running loose.
  (Music begins as the Guards come forward to lead Antigonê and Ismenê into the palace. Kreon remains, as the Chorus at once takes up a new position.)
CHORUS: —Blest are they who have known no evil,
  for once the gods strike
              that house is doomed
      for ever.
  Generation after generation
      falls beneath the blow
              to the end of days,
      like the wave,
  blasting from the black northeast,
      hurling dark sand from the depths
              onto the echoing
      shore.

  —I have seen now from ancient times
      how sorrows pile on sorrows
              for the house of Labdakos
      with no relief from the gods,
  generation after generation;
      and now the last light
              is cut to the root
              by dust,
  by dust offered to the gods below,
  by the folly of a passionate word,
      by frenzy at the heart.

  —Zeus, what human arrogance
  can check your power, Zeus,
  whom neither sleep nor track
      of weariless months of the gods
              can master?
  Ageless you reign in the glistering

mansions of high Olympos,
        and near and far,
        past and future,
your law is fixed forever.
        No greatness ever enters human life,
        but with it comes the curse of Zeus' heaven.

Gammer Gurton's Needle

Mr. S
1560

Comic

Scene: Gammer Gurton has lost her needle somewhere and is very
upset.

Gammer Gurton: A lady, 40's –5 0's.
Hodge: Her servant.
Tib: Her maid.
Cock: Her serving boy.

GAMMER: Alas, Hodge, alas! I may well curse and ban
This day, that I ever saw it, with Gib and the milkpan;
For these and ill luck together, as knoweth Cock, my boy,
Have stuck away my dear neele, and robbed me of my joy,
My fair long straight neele, that was mine only treasure;
The first day of my sorrow is, and last end of my pleasure!
HODGE: Might ha kept it when ye had it! But fools will be fools still.
Lose that is vast in your hands ye need not but ye will.
GAMMER: Go hie thee, Tib, and run thou, whore, to th'end here of
the town!
Didst carry our dust in thy lap; seek where thou pourest it down,
And as thou sawest me roking in the ashes where I mourned,
So see in all the heap of dust thou leave no straw unturned.
TIB: That chall, Gammer, swith and tite, and soon be here again!
GAMMER: Tib, stoop and look down to the ground to it, and take
some pain.
(Exit Tib.)
HODGE: Here is a pretty matter, to see this gear how it goes;
By Gog's soul, I think you would lose your arse an it were loose!
Your neele lost, it is pity you should lack care and endless sorrow.
Gog's death! How shall my breeches be sewed? Shall I go thus
tomorrow?
GAMMER: Ah Hodge, Hodge! if that ich could find my neele, by the
reed,
Chould sew thy breeches, ich promise thee, with full good dou-
ble threed,

And set a patch on either knee should last this months twain.
Now God and good Saint Sithe I pray to send it home again!

HODGE: Whereto served your hands and eyes but this your neele to keep?
What devil had you else to do? Ye kept, ich wot, no sheep!
Cham fain abroad to dig and delve, in water, mire, and clay,
Sossing and possing in the dirt still from day to day.
A hundred things that be abroad cham set to see them weele,
And four of you sit idle at home, and cannot keep a neele!

GAMMER: My neele! Alas! Ich lost it, Hodge, what time ich me up hasted
To save the milk set up for thee, which Gib, our cat, hath wasted.

HODGE: The Devil he burst both Gib and Tib, with all the rest!
Cham always sure of the worst end, whoever have the best!
Where ha you been fidging abroad since you your neele lost?

GAMMER: Within the house, and at the door, sitting by this same post,
Where I was looking a long hour before these folks came here;
But welaway, all was in vain, my neele is never the near!

HODGE: Set me a candle, let me seek, and grope wherever it be.
Gog's heart, ye be so foolish, ich think, you know it not when you it see!

GAMMER: Come hither, Cock; what, Cock, I say!

COCK: How, Gammer?

GAMMER: Go, hie thee soon, and grope behind the old brass pan, which thing when thou has done
There shalt thou find an old shoe, wherein if thou look well,
Thou shalt find lying an inch of a white tallow candell.
Light it, and bring it tite away.

COCK: That shall be done anon.

GAMMER: Nay, tarry, Hodge, till thou hast light, and then we'll seek each one.

HODGE: Come away, ye whoreson boy, are ye asleep? Ye must have a crier!

COCK: Ich cannot get the candle light: here is almost no fire.

HODGE: Chill hold thee a penny chill make thee come, if that ich may catch thine ears!
Art deaf, thou whoreson boy? Cock, I say; why canst not hear's?

GAMMER: Beat him not, Hodge, but help the boy, and come you two
together.
(Exeunt.)

Scene 5
(Gammer, Tib, and Cock, the boy.)
GAMMER: How now, Tib? Quick, let's hear what news thou hast
brought hether!
TIB: Chave tost and tumbled yonder heap over and over again,
And winnowed it through my fingers, as men would winnow
grain;
Not so much as a hen's turd but in pieces I tare it,
Or whatsoever clod or clay I found, I did not spare it,
Looking within and eke without, to find your neele, alas!
But all in vain and without help! Your neele is where it was.
GAMMER: Alas my neele! We shall never meet! Adieu, adieu, for aye!
TIB: Not so, Gammer, we might it find, if we knew where it lay.
COCK: Gog's cross, Gammer, if ye will laugh, look in but at the door,
And see how Hodge lieth tumbling and tossing amidst the flour,
Raking these some fire to find among the ashes dead
Where there is not one spark so big as a pin's head;
At last in a dark corner two sparks he thought he sees
Which were indeed nought else but Gib our cat's two eyes.
"Puff!" quoth Hodge, thinking thereby to have fire without doubt;
With that Gib shut her two eyes, and so the fire was out.
And by and by them opened, even as they were before;
With that the sparks appeared, even as they had done of yore;
And even as Hodge blew the fire (as he did think),
Gib, as she felt the blast, straightway began to wink;
Till Hodge fell of swearing, as came best to his turn,
The fire was sure bewitched, and therefore would not burn.
At last Gib up the stairs, among the old posts and pins,
And Hodge he hied him after, till broke were both his shins;
Cursing and swearing oaths were never of his making,
That Gib would fire the house if that she were not taken.
GAMMER: See, here is all the thought that the foolish urchin taketh!
And Tib, methink, at his elbow almost as merry maketh.
This is all the wit ye have when others make their moan.
Come down, Hodge, where art thou? And let the cat alone!

HODGE: *(From within the house.)* Gog's heart, help and come up!
Gib in her tail hath fire and is like to burn all, if she get a little higher!
Come down, quoth you? Nay, then you might count me a patch.
The house cometh down on your heads, if it take once the thatch.
GAMMER: It is the cat's eyes, fool, that shineth in the dark.
HODGE: Hath the cat, do you think, in every eye a spark?
GAMMER: No, but they shine as like fire as ever man see.
HODGE: By the Mass, an she burn all, yoush bear the blame for me!
GAMMER: Come down and help to seek here our neele, that it were found.
Down, Tib, on the knees, I say! Down, Cock, to the ground!
To God I make avow, and so to good Saint Anne,
A candle shall they have apiece, get it where I can,
If I may my neele find in one place or in other.
HODGE: *(Entering.)* Now a vengeance on Gib light, on Gib and Gib's mother,
And all the generation of cats both far and near!
Look on this ground, whoreson, thinkst thou the neele is here?
COCK: By my troth, Gammer, methought your neele here I saw,
But when my fingers touched it I felt it was a straw.
TIB: See, Hodge, what's this? May it not be within it?
HODGE: Break it, fool, with thy hand, and see an thou canst find it.
TIB: Nay, break it you, Hodge, according to your word.
HODGE: Gog's sides! Fie! It stinks; it is a cat's turd!
It were well done to make thee eat it, by the Mass!
GAMMER: This matter amendeth not; my neele is still where it was.
Our candle is at an end, let us all in quite,
And come another time when we have more light.
(They leave.)

As You Like It

William Shakespeare
1600

Comic
Setting: The lawn before the Duke's palace.
Scene: Charles, the Duke's wrestler, is being challenged by Orlando a young man who is fighting to regain his inheritance. The two cousins are having a merry time as Touchstone enters to report the news.

Rosalind: 20's, daughter of the banished Duke, lively, generous.
Celia: 20'S, her cousin and daughter of the present Duke, devoted to Rosalind.
Touchstone: A clown, a lively, down-to-earth, delightful fellow.
Le Beau: A courtier and attendant of the present Duke.

CELIA: I pray thee, Rosalind, sweet my coz, be merry.
ROSALIND: Dear Celia, I show more mirth than I am mistress of, and would you yet I were merrier? Unless you could teach me to forget a banished father, you must not learn me how to remember any extraordinary pleasure.
CELIA: Herein I see thou lovest me not with the weight that I love thee. If my uncle, thy banished father, had banished thy uncle, the duke my father, so thou hadst been still with me, I could have taught my love to take thy father for mine: so wouldst thou, if the truth of thy love to me were so righteously tempered as mine is to thee.
ROSALIND: Well, I will forget the condition of my estate, to rejoice in yours.
CELIA: You know my father hath no child but I, nor none is like to have; and, truly, when he dies, thou shalt be his heir: for what he hath taken away from thy father perforce, I will render thee again in affection; by mine honour, I will; and when I break that oath, let me turn monster. Therefore, my sweet Rose, my dear Rose, be merry.
ROSALIND: From henceforth I will, coz, and devise sports. Let me see; what think you of falling in love?
CELIA: Marry, I prithee, do, to make sport withal: but love no man in

good earnest; nor no further in sport neither, than with safety of a pure blush thou mayst in honour come off again.

ROSALIND: What shall be our sport then?

CELIA: Let us sit and mock the good housewife Fortune from her wheel, that her gifts may henceforth be bestowed equally.

ROSALIND: I would we could so do, for her benefits are mightily misplaced, and the bountiful blind woman doth most mistake in her gifts to women.

CELIA: 'Tis true; for those that she makes fair she scarce makes honest, and those that she makes honest she makes very ill-favouredly.

ROSALIND: Nay, now thou goest from Fortune's office to Nature's: Fortune reigns in gifts of the world, not in the lineaments of Nature.

(Enter Touchstone.)

CELIA: No? When Nature hath made a fair creature, may she not by Fortune fall into the fire? Though Nature hath given us wit to flout at Fortune, hath not Fortune sent in this fool to cut off the argument?

ROSALIND: Indeed, there is Fortune too hard for Nature, when Fortune makes Nature's natural and cutter-off of Nature's wit.

CELIA: Peradventure this is not Fortune's work neither, but Nature's; who, perceiving our natural wits too dull to reason of such goddesses, hath sent this natural for our whetstone: for always the dullness of the fool is the whetstone of the wits. How now, wit! Whither wander you?

TOUCHSTONE: Mistress, you must come away to your father.

CELIA: Were you made the messenger?

TOUCHSTONE: No, by mine honour; but I was bid to come for you.

ROSALIND: Where learned you that oath, fool?

TOUCHSTONE: Of a certain knight that swore by his honour they were good pancakes, and swore by his honour the mustard was naught. Now, I'll stand to it, the pancakes were naught and the mustard was good, and yet was not the knight forsworn.

CELIA: How prove you that, in the great heap of your knowledge?

ROSALIND: Ay, marry: now unmuzzle your wisdom.

TOUCHSTONE: Stand you both forth now. Stroke your chins, and swear by your beards that I am a knave.

CELIA: By our beards, if we had them, thou art.

TOUCHSTONE: By my knavery, if I had it, then I were; but if you swear by that this is not, you are not forsworn: no more was this knight, swearing by his honour, for he never had any; or if he had, he had sworn it away before ever he saw those pancakes or that mustard.

CELIA: Prithee, who is't that thou meanest?

TOUCHSTONE: One that old Frederick, your father, loves.

CELIA: My father's love is enough to honour him. Enough! Speak no more of him; you'll be whipped for taxation one of these days.

TOUCHSTONE: The more pity that fools may not speak wisely what wise men do foolishly.

CELIA: By my troth, thou sayest true; for since the little wit that fools have was silenced, the little foolery that wise men have makes a great show. Here comes Monsieur Le Beau.

ROSALIND: With his mouth full of news.

CELIA: Which he will put on us, as pigeons feed their young.

ROSALIND: Then we shall be news-cramm'd.

CELIA: All the better; we shall be more marketable. *(Enter Le Beau.)* Bon jour, Monsieur Le Beau. What's the news?

LE BEAU: Fair princess, you have lost much good sport.

CELIA: Sport! Of what colour?

LE BEAU: What colour, madam! How shall I answer you?

ROSALIND: As wit and fortune will.

TOUCHSTONE: Or as the Destinies decree.

CELIA: Well said! That was laid on with a trowel.

TOUCHSTONE: Nay, if I keep not my rank,—

ROSALIND: Thou losest thy old smell.

LE BEAU: You amaze me, ladies. I would have told you of good wrestling, which you have lost sight of.

ROSALIND: Yet tell us the manner of the wrestling.

LE BEAU: I will tell you the beginning; and, if it please your ladyships, you may see the end, for the best is yet to do; and here, where you are, they are coming to perform it.

CELIA: Well, the beginning, that is dead and buried.

LE BEAU: There comes an old man and his three son,—

CELIA: I could match this beginning with an old tale.

LE BEAU: Three proper young men, of excellent growth and presence;—

ROSALIND: With bills on their necks, "Be it know unto all men by these presents."

LE BEAU: The eldest of the three wrestled with Charles, the duke's wrestler; which Charles in a moment threw him and broke three of his ribs, that there is little hope of life in him. So he served the second, and so the third. Yonder they lie; the poor old man, their father, making such pitiful dole over them that all the beholders take his part with weeping.

ROSALIND: Alas!

TOUCHSTONE: But what is the sport, monsieur, that the ladies have lost?

LE BEAU: Why, this that I speak of.

TOUCHSTONE: Thus men may grow wiser every day. It is the first time that ever I heard breaking of ribs was sport for ladies.

CELIA: Or I, I promise thee.

ROSALIND: But is there any else longs to feel this broken music in his sides? Is there yet another dotes upon rib-breaking? Shall we see this wrestling, cousin?

LE BEAU: You must, if you stay here; for here is the place appointed for the wrestling, and they are ready to perform it.

CELIA: Yonder, sure, they are coming. Let us now stay and see it.

Othello

William Shakespeare
1621

Dramatic
Setting: Inside the Palace. Venice.
Scene: Iago's hatred of the Moor for having favored another man to
be his first lieutenant has set in motion a series of events
designed to create suspicion concerning Desdemona's faithful-
ness to Othello. Emilia is questioned concerning Cassio, a young
lieutenant and friend.

Othello: The Moor, General of the Venetian armed forces, 30's – 40's.
Iago: His Lieutenant and confidant, 30's – 40's.
Desdemona: His beautiful young wife, 20's.
Emilia: Iago's wife, 30's, lady, in-waiting to Desdemona.

OTHELLO: You have seen nothing, them?
EMILIA: Nor ever heard, nor ever did suspect.
OTHELLO: Yes, you have seen Cassio and she together.
EMILIA: But then I saw no harm, and then I heard
    Each syllable that breath made up between them.
OTHELLO: What, did they never whisper?
EMILIA: Never, my lord.
OTHELLO: Nor send you out o'th'way?
EMILIA: Never.
OTHELLO: To fetch her fan, her gloves, her mask, nor nothing?
EMILIA: Never, my lord.
OTHELLO: That's strange.
EMILIA: I durst, my lord, to wager she is honest,
    Lay down my soul at stake: if you think other,
    remove your thought,—it doth abuse your bosom.
    If any wretch have put this in your head,
    Let heaven requite it with the serpent's curse!
    For, if she be not honest, chaste, and true,
    There's no man happy; the purest of their wives
    Is foul as slander.
OTHELLO: Bid her come hither: —go. *(Exit Emilia.)*
    She says enough;—yet she's a simple bawd

That cannot say much. This is a subtle whore,
A closet-lock-and-key of villainous secrets:
And yet she'll kneel and pray; I have seen her do't.
(Enter Desdemona with Emilia.)
DESDEMONA: My lord, what is your will?
OTHELLO: Pray, chuck, come hither.
DESDEMONA: What is your pleasure?
OTHELLO: Let me see your eyes; look in my face.
DESDEMONA: What horrible fancy's this?
OTHELLO: *(To Emilia.)* Some of your function, mistress;
    Leave procreants alone, and shut the door;
    Cough, or cry "hem," if any body come:
    Your mystery, your mystery; —nay, dispatch.
    (Exit Emilia.)
DESDEMONA: Upon my knees, what doth your speech import?
    I understand a fury in your words,
    But not the words.
OTHELLO: Why, what art thou?
DESDEMONA: Your wife, my lord; your true
    And loyal wife.
OTHELLO: Come, swear it, damn thyself;
    Lest, being like one of heaven, the devils themselves
    Should fear to seize thee: therefore be double-damn'd—
    Swear thou art honest.
DESDEMONA: Heaven doth truly know it.
OTHELLO: Heaven truly knows that thou art false as hell.
DESDEMONA: To whom, my lord? With whom? How am I false?
OTHELLO: Ah, Desdemona! —Away! Away! Away!
DESDEMONA: Alas the heavy day! —Why do you weep?
    Am I the motive of these tears, my lord?
    If haply you my father do suspect
    An instrument of this your calling back,
    Lay not your blame on me: if you have lost him,
    Why, I have lost him too.
OTHELLO: Had it pleased heaven
    To try me with affliction; had they rain'd
    All kinds of sores and shames on my bare head;
    Steept me in poverty to the very lips;
    Given to captivity me and my utmost hopes;

I should have found in some place of my soul
A drop of patience: But, alas, to make me
A fixed figure for the time of scorn
To point his slow unmoving finger at!—
Yet could I bear that too; well, very well:
But there, where I have garner'd up my heart,
Where either I must live, or bear no life,—
The foundation from the which my current runs,
Or else dries up; to be discarded thence!
Or keep it as a cistern for foul toads
To knot and gender in!—turn thy complexion there,
Patience, thou young and rose-lipt cherubin,—
Ay, there, look grim as hell!

DESDEMONA: I hope my noble lord esteems me honest.

OTHELLO: O, ay; as summer flies are in the shambles,
That quicken even with blowing. O thou weed,
Who are so lovely fair, and smell'st so sweet,
That the sense aches at thee, —would thou hadst ne'er been born!

DESDEMONA: Alas, what ignorant sin have I committed?

OTHELLO: Was this fair paper, this most goodly book,
Made to write 'whore' upon? What committed!
Committed! —O thou public commoner!
I should make very forges of my cheeks,
That would to cinders burn up modesty,
Did I but speak thy deeds. —What committed!—
Heaven stops the nose at it, and the moon winks;
The bawdy wind, that kisses all it meets,
Is husht within the hollow mine of earth,
And will not hear it.—What committed!—
Impudent strumpet!

DESDEMONA: By heaven, you do me wrong.

OTHELLO: Are not you a strumpet?

DESDEMONA: No, as I am a Christian:
If to preserve this vessel for my lord
From any other foul unlawful touch,
Be not to be a strumpet, I am none.

OTHELLO: What, not a whore?

DESDEMONA: No, as I shall be saved.

OTHELLO: Is't possible?

DESDEMONA: O, heaven forgive us!

OTHELLO: I cry you mercy, then:

> I took you for that cunning whore of Venice
> That married with Othello. —You, mistress,
> That have the office opposite to Saint Peter,
> And keep the gate of hell!
> *(Enter Emilia.)*
> You, you, ay, you!
> We have done our course; there's money for your pains:
> I pray you, turn the key, and keep our counsel.
> *(Exit.)*

EMILIA: Alas, what does this gentleman conceive?—

> How do you, madam? how do you, my good lady?

DESDEMONA: Faith, half asleep.

EMILIA: Good madam, what's the matter with my lord?

DESDEMONA: With who?

EMILIA: Why, with my lord, madam.

DESDEMONA: Who is thy lord?

EMILIA: He that is yours, sweet lady.

DESDEMONA: I have none: do not talk to me, Emilia;

> I cannot weep; nor answer have I none,
> But what should go by water. Prithee, tonight
> Lay on my bed my wedding-sheets, —remember;—
> And call thy husband hither.

EMILIA: Here's a change indeed! *(Exit.)*

DESDEMONA: 'Tis meet I should be used so, very meet.

> How have I been behaved, that he might stick
> The small'st opinion on my least misuse?
> *(Enter Emilia with Iago.)*

IAGO: What is your pleasure, madam? How is't with you?

DESDEMONA: I cannot tell. Those that do teach young babes

> Do it with gentle means and easy tasks:
> He might have chid me so; for, in good faith,
> I am a child to chiding.

IAGO: What's the matter, lady?

EMILIA: Alas, Iago, my lord hath so bewhored her,

> Thrown such despite and heavy terms upon her,
> As true hearts cannot bear.

DESDEMONA: Am I that name, Iago?

IAGO: What name, fair lady?

DESDEMONA: Such as she says my lord did say I was.

EMILIA: He call'd her whore: a beggar in his drink
Could not have laid such terms upon his callet.

IAGO: Why did he so?

DESDEMONA: I do not know; I am sure I am none such.

IAGO: Do not weep, do not weep: —alas the day!

EMILIA: Hath she forsook so many noble matches,
Her father, and her country, and her friends,
To be call'd whore? would it not make one weep?

DESDEMONA: It is my wretched fortune.

IAGO: Beshrew him for't!
How comes this trick upon him?

DESDEMONA: Nay, heaven doth know.

EMILIA: I will be hang'd, if some eternal villain,
Some busy and insinuating rogue,
Some cogging, cozening slave, to get some office,
Have not devised this slander; I'll be hang'd else.

IAGO: Fie, there is no such man; it is impossible.

DESDEMONA: If any such there be, heaven pardon him!

EMILIA: A halter pardon him! and hell gnaw his bones!
Why should he call her whore? Who keeps her company?
What place? What time? What form? What likelihood?
The Moor's abused by some most villainous knave,
Some base notorious knave, some scurvy fellow:—
O heaven, that such companions thou'ldst unfold,
And put in every honest hand a whip
To lash the rascals naked through the world
Even from the east to th'west!

IAGO: Speak within door.

EMILIA: O, fie upon them! Some such squire he was
That turn'd your wit the seamy side without,
And made you to suspect me with the Moor.

IAGO: You are a fool; go to.

DESDEMONA: O good Iago,
What shall I do to win my lord again?
Good friend, go to him; for, by this light of heaven,
I know now how I lost him. Here I kneel:—
If e'er my will did trepass 'gainst his love,

Either in discourse of thought or actual deed;
Or that mine eyes, mine ears, or any sense,
Delighted them in any other form;
Or that I do not yet, and never did,
And ever will—though he do shake me off
To beggarly divorcement—love him dearly,
Comfort forswear me! Unkindness may do much;
And his unkindness may defeat my life,
But never taint my love. I cannot say "whore," —
It does abhor me now I speak the word;
To do the act that might the addition earn
Not the world's mass of vanity could make me.

IAGO: I pray, you be content: 'tis but his humour:
The business of the state does him offence,
And he does chide with you.

DESDEMONA: If 'twere no other,—

IAGO: 'Tis but so, I warrant. *(Trumpets within.)*
Hark, how these instruments summon to supper!
The messengers of Venice stay the meat:
Go in, and weep not; all things shall be well.
(Exeunt Desdemona and Emilia.)

The Mulberry Garden

Sir Charles Sedley
1668

Comic

Setting: The Mulberry Garden, a tree-planted pleasure garden on the
 grounds of Buckingham Palace, London.

Scene: Victoria and Olivia Everyoung are two young ladies of fashion
 who are given much opportunity to gad about the town by their
 free-spirited father. They meet Ned and Harry, two men of fashion on a stroll through the gardens.

Victoria and Olivia: Late teens, early 20's, sisters, stylish and free-
 spirited.

Ned Estridge: 20's, fashion conscious and man about town.

Harry Modish: 20's, a man of mode, friend to Ned.

VICT: Sister, whatever the matter is, methinks we don't see half the
 company that used to meet here anights when we were last in
 town.

OLIV: 'Tis true, but methinks 'tis much better than the long walk at
 home. For in my opinion half a score young men and fine ladies
 well dressed, are a greater ornament to a garden than a wilderness of sycamores, orange and lemon trees; and the rustling of
 rich vests and silk petticoats better music than the purling of
 streams, chirping of birds, or any of our country entertainments.
 And *that* I hope the place will afford us yet, as soon as the plays
 are done.

VICT: Sister, what would you give to see Estridge come in now?

OLIV: 'Tis impossible, he would not miss his devotion to the park (for
 all I could give) such an evening as this. Besides the two garni-
 tures he brought out of France are soiled, his feather broke, and
 he has been so out of humour these two days there's no endur-
 ing him. He lost his money too last night I hear, and losing
 gamesters are but ill company.

VICT: Fie sister, you make a saver with a look, and fine in but thinking
 he is so. You deserve not so complete a servant, but I hope you'll
 be as obliging to his face as you are severe to him behind his
 back.

OLIV: The only way to oblige most men is to use 'em thus a little now and then. Even to their faces it gives 'em an opinion of our wit, and is consequently a spur to theirs. The great pleasure of gaming were lost if we saw one another's hands; and of love if we knew one another's hearts. There would be no room for good play in the one, nor for address in the other—which are the refined parts of both. But what would you give to see Horatio?

VICT: To see Horatio, as I knew him once,
I would all other happiness renounce;
But he is now another's, and my aim
Is not to nourish, but to starve my flame:
I dare not hope to captive to regain,
So many charms contribute to his chain.
Althea's slave, let false Horatio live,
Whilst I for freedom, not for empire strive.

OLIV: Fie sister, leave this rhyming at least!

(Enter to them Estridge and Modish.)

EST: Ladies, it is our wonder to find anybody here at this time of day, and no less our happiness to meet with you. All the world is at the park, where we had been ourselves but that we saw your livery at the gate.

VICT: I pray let us not keep you here gentlemen. Your mistresses will curse us and yourselves too, by and by, if the garden should not fill.

EST: If we wish any company, ladies, 'tis for your sakes, not our own.

MOD: For my part I would ne'er desire a garden fuller than this is now. We are two to two, and may be hand to hand when you please.

OLIV: I don't know what you think, but in my mind the more the merrier, especially in these places.

EST: Ay, for show, madam, but it happens in great companies, as at feast, we see a great deal and fall to heartily of nothing and for the most part rise hungry. And 'tis with lovers, madam, as with great-bellied women—if they find what they long for they care not whether there be anything else or no.

VICT: What, in love already? Sure the air of this place is a great softner of men's hearts.

MOD: How can it choose, having so many lovers' sighs daily mixed with it? But 'twere a much better quality in't, madam, if it could incline ladies to believe and look with pity on those flames they raise.

OLIV: 'Tis too early to make love this two hours. "Flames" and "pity" would sound much better in the evening.

MOD: 'Tis not with love, madam, as with meaner arguments. I might entertain you with my passion for an age and yet have as much left for anon as if I had not spoke one word. The sea is easier emptied than a lover's breast!

OLIV: What say you, sir, is this your opinion too?

EST: Yes, faith, madam, and I think a lover can no more say at once what he hath to say to his mistress, than a man can eat at once for his whole lifetime.

OLIV: Nay, if it be so endless, I should beg of my servant, whenever I have one, e'en to keep it to himself for altogether.

EST: There you betray your ignorance—with your pardon, madam. To see the fair Olivia and not love her, is not more impossible than to love her and not tell her on't. Silent lovers you may read of, and in romances too, but heavens forbid you should e'er meet with any.

OLIV: If they knew how little they were like to get by being otherwise I'm confident I should meet with none else.

EST: Well, madam, I perceive love like wine makes our discourse seem extravagant to those that are not wound up to the same height. But had you any spark of what I feel I should have had another answer.

OLIV: Why, what answer?

EST: Nay, I know not, but some pretty one that love would have devised for you; no more to be imagined by you now than what you shall talk of next in your sleep. In the meantime, ladies, will you do us the honour to eat syllabubs?

OLIV: Sister, let's go, so they'll promise to say nothing but what they think to us when we are there.

MOD: You may do what you please, Ned, but 'tis a liberty I dare not use myself to, for fear of an ill habit.

EST: You are very confident of our good opinion, ladies. I believe there are few women in town would accept of our company on these terms.

VICT: Faith, sister, let's bate 'em that circumstance. Truth is a thing merely necessary for witnesses and historians, and in those places doth but curb invention and spoil good company. We will only confine 'em to what's probable.

MOD: Content, and I dare swear 'twill be better for all parties.

(Exeunt.)

The Wild Duck

Henrik Ibsen
1885

Dramatic
Setting: The Ekdal Home. Norway.
Scene: Hedvig's birthday. Gregers has returned home for the marriage of his elderly father, Old Werle, to Mrs. Berte Sorby. He
believes that Gina, who once worked for Old Werle, was pregnant by her employer when she left to marry Hjalmar. His wishes
to reveal this in what he calls the "claim of the ideal," setting
right all old secrets so everyone may live in the light of truth. The
implication is that Hedvig is Old Werle's child, especially since he
sends Hedvig a gift of money every year on her birthday.

Hjalmar Ekdal: 40's, a would-be inventor and portrait photographer
by trade. Self-involved and a procrastinator.
Gina Ekdal: His wife, thrifty, loving, does most of the work.
Hedvig Ekdal: Their daughter, early teens, sweet, innocent, losing her
eyesight gradually.
Gregers Werle: An old friend of Hjalmar, gone for many years working up north at his father's factories. Now returned to "set right"
the lies and secrets of the past.

GREGERS: *(Laying his hands upon his shoulders.)* Dear Hjalmar—wasn't
it good I came.
HJALMAR: Yes.
GREGERS: And that you came to a clear understanding of your situa-
tion—wasn't that good?
HJALMAR: *(A little impatiently.)* Yes, certainly it's good. But there's just
one thing that offends my sense of justice.
GREGERS: What might that be?
HJALMAR: It's just that—well, I don't know if I should speak so frankly
about your father.
GREGERS: Have no scruples on my account.
HJALMAR: Well then. To my mind, you see, there's something offen-
sive in the thought that now the true marriage will be founded
not by me but by him.
GREGERS: No, how can you say such a thing.

HJALMAR: But it's really true. Your father and Mrs. Sorby are entering a marriage founded on total confidence, on complete and unconditional openness on both sides. Nothing swept under the carpet or hidden from each other. They've announced, you could say, a mutual forgiveness of sins.

GREGERS: Well, well, what of it?

HJALMAR: Yes, but *there* it's all been achieved. And just *this* was the great difficulty you said had to be overcome in order to found a true marriage.

GREGERS: But that's in a completely different way, Hjalmar. You're surely not going to compare yourself or her with those two—you understand what I mean.

HJALMAR: But I can't help thinking there's something that hurts and outrages my sense of what's right. It looks exactly as if there was no justice at all guiding the world.

GINA: Oh no, Ekdal, you really shouldn't say things like that.

GREGERS: Hm. Don't let's get into *that* question.

HJALMAR: But then, on the other hand, it's as if I can see distinctly the controlling hand of destiny after all. He's going blind.

GINA: Maybe that's not so certain.

HJALMAR: There's no doubt about it. At least we ought not doubt it: for in just that circumstance lies righteous retribution. In his time he blinded the eyes of a trusting human being—

GREGERS: Unfortunately, he's blinded many.

HJALMAR: And now arrives the inexorable, the unutterable, and demands in turn the old man's eyes.

GINA: Oh no! How can you say something as horrible as that! I'm really frightened.

HJALMAR: It helps to immerse oneself in the night side of existence once in a while. (*Hedvig in hat and coat, enters through the hall door, happy and out of breath.*)

GINA: Back again already?

HEDVIG: Yes, I didn't feel like walking any farther. And that was a good thing; because I just met somebody at the door.

HJALMAR: That would have been Mrs. Sorby.

HEDVIG: Yes.

HJALMAR: (*Pacing the floor.*) I hope you've seen her for the last time. (*Silence. Hedvig looks timidly from one to another, trying to gauge their mood.*)

HEDVIG: *(Moves toward Hjalmar ingratiatingly.)* Father.

HJALMAR: Well—what is it, Hedvig?

HEDVIG: Mrs. Sorby had something for me.

HJALMAR: *(Stopping.)* For you?

HEDVIG: Yes, it's something for tomorrow.

GINA: Berta has always given you a little something for your birthday.

HJALMAR: What is it?

HEDVIG: No, you mustn't know what it is yet, for Mother is to give it to me in bed tomorrow morning.

HJALMAR: Oh, all these secrets I'm being kept out of!

HEDVIG: *(Hurriedly.)* No, you can see it if you want to. It's a big letter. *(Takes the letter from her coat pocket.)*

HJALMAR: A letter, too?

HEDVIG: Yes, it's just the letter. The rest will come later. But think, a letter! I've never had a letter before. And then it has "Miss" written on it. *(Reading.)* "Miss Hedvig Ekdal." Just think—that's me.

HJALMAR: Let me see the letter.

HEDVIG: *(Handing it to him.)* There, you see.

HJALMER: It's Mr. Werle's handwriting.

GINA: Are you sure of that, Ekdal?

HJALMAR: See for yourself.

GINA: How would I know about that?

HJALMAR: Hedvig, may I open the letter and read it?

HEDVIG: Yes, of course you may, if you want to.

GINA: No, not this evening Ekdal. It's meant to be for tomorrow.

HEDVIG: *(Quietly.)* Oh, let him read it! It's sure to be something good, then Father will be happy. And everything will be pleasant again.

HJALMAR: Then I may open it?

HEDVIG: Please do, Father. It'll be lovely to find out what it is.

HJALMAR: Good. *(Opens the envelope, takes out a piece of paper, reads through it and seems bewildered.)* What *is* this—?

GINA: What does it say?

HEDVIG: Oh yes, Father, tell us!

HJALMAR: Quiet! *(Reads the letter once more. He has gone pale but speaks with control.)* It's a deed of gift, Hedvig.

HEDVIG: Just imagine! What do I get?

HJALMAR: Read for yourself. *(Hedvig goes over to the lamp and reads it for a moment.)*

HJALMAR: *(Half-aloud, clenching his fists.)* The eyes! The eyes—and then that letter!

HEDVIG: *(Interrupts her reading.)* Yes, but it looks to me as if it's Grandfather who's getting it.

HJALMAR: *(Taking the letter from her.)* You, Gina. Can you understand this?

GINA: I haven't any idea what it is. Just tell me.

HJALMAR: Mr. Werle writes to Hedvig that her old grandfather doesn't have to trouble himself with copying work anymore but that he can draw one hundred kroner a month from the office.

GREGERS: Aha!

HEDVIG: —a hundred kroner, Mother! I read that.

GINA: That's very good for Grandfather.

HJALMAR: A hundred kroner for as long as he needs it. That means, of course, until he passes on.

GINA: So then he's provided for, poor old man.

HJALMAR: But there's more to follow. You didn't read far enough. Hedvig. Afterwards, this gift goes over to you.

HEDVIG: To me! All of it?

HJALMAR: You're assured the same amount for the rest of your life, he writes. Do you hear, Gina?

GINA: Yes I heard alright.

HEDVIG: Imagine—all the money I'll be getting. *(Shaking him.)* Father, Father—aren't you glad—?

HJALMAR: *(Detaching himself from her.)* Glad! *(Paces about.)* Oh, what vistas—what perspectives open before me. Hedvig—it's her he remembers so generously!

GINA: Yes, because it's Hedvig who has a birthday—

HEDVIG: And you'll get the money in any case, Father! You know I'll give all the money to you and Mother.

HJALMAR: To your mother, yes! That's just it.

GREGERS: Hjalmar, this is a trap being set for you.

HJALMAR: You believe this is yet another trap?

GREGERS: When he was here this morning he told me: "Hjalmar Ekdal isn't the man you imagine him to be."

HJALMAR: Not the man—!

GREGERS: "You'll get to see," he said.

HJLAMAR: Get to see me bought off with money—!

HEDVIG: But Mother, what's this all about?

GINA: Go and take off your coat. *(Hedvig, close to tears, goes out through the kitchen door.)*

GREGERS: Yes, Hjalmar—now you can show if he's right—him or me.

HJALMAR: *(Tears the letter in two and places both pieces on the table, saying.)* Here's my answer.

GREGERS: I knew it.

HJALMER: *(Goes to Gina, who stands by the stove, and speaks in a low voice.)* Let's have no more secrets. If the relationship between him and you was completely over when you—came to fall in love with me, as you put it—why did he arrange it so we could get married?

GINA: He probably thought he could come here when he liked.

HJALMAR: Only *that*: Wasn't he afraid of a certain possibility?

GINA: I don't know what you mean.

HJALMAR: I would like to know whether—your child has the right to live under my roof.

GINA: *(Drawing herself up, her eyes flashing.)* And you can ask *that!*

HJALMAR: You shall answer me this: Does Hedvig belong to me or to—? Well!

GINA: *(Looking at him with cold defiance.)* I don't know.

HJALMAR: *(His voice trembling.)* You don't know!

GINA: How could I know? A woman like me—

HJALMAR: *(Quietly, as he turns from her.)* Then I've nothing more to do in this house.

GREGERS: Think about this, Hjalmar!

HJALMAR: *(Putting on his overcoat.)* For a man like me, there's nothing more to think about.

GREGERS: But there is, inexpressibly much to think about. You three must stay together if you're going to reach a state of forgiving self-sacrifice.

HJALMAR: I don't want to. Never, never! My hat! *(Takes his hat.)* My home lies in ruins around me. *(Bursts into tears.)* Gregers, I have no child!

HEDVIG: *(Who has opened the kitchen door.)* What are you saying. *(She goes to him.)* Father, Father!

GINA: There, there!

HJALMAR: Don't come near me, Hedvig! Get away from me. I can't bear to look at you. Ah, the eyes—! Good-bye. *(Makes for the door.)*

HEDVIG: *(Hanging on to him and crying loudly.)* No, oh no! Don't leave me!

GINA: *(Shouts.)* Look at the child, Ekdal! Look at the child!

HJALMAR: I won't! I can't! I must get out—away from all this! *(He tears himself free from Hedvig and leaves.)*

HEDVIG: *(With despair in her eyes.)* He's leaving us, Mother! He's leaving us! He'll never come back!

GINA: Don't cry, Hedvig. Father will come back.

HEDVIG: *(Throwing herself, sobbing, on the sofa.)* No, no, he'll never come home to us again!

GREGERS: You must believe that I meant everything for the best, Mrs. Ekdal.

GINA: I almost believe you, but God forgive you just the same.

HEDVIG: *(Lying on the sofa.)* I think I shall die from all this! What have I done to him? Mother, you must bring him home again!

GINA: Yes, yes. Just calm down. I'll go out and look for him. *(Puts on her overcoat.)* Perhaps he's gone to Relling's. But you mustn't lie there, crying. Promise me that?

HEDVIG: *(Crying convulsively.)* Yes, I'll stop. As long as Father comes home.

GREGERS: *(To Gina as she leaves.)* Wouldn't it be better if you let him fight his painful battle to the end.

GINA: Oh, he can do that later. First of all we have to calm down the child. *(She goes out through the hall door.)*

HEDVIG: *(Sitting up and drying her tears.)* You have to tell me what is happening. Why doesn't Father want to know me anymore?

GREGERS: You mustn't ask about that until you are big and grown-up.

HEDVIG: *(Sobbing.)* But I can't go around being so horribly unhappy until I'm big and grown-up. I think I know what it is. Maybe I'm not really Father's child.

GREGERS: *(Uneasily.)* How could that be?

HEDVIG: Mother could have found me. And maybe Father's just found out. I've read about such things.

GREGERS: Well, but even if—

HEDVIG: Yes, I think he could love me as much just the same. Even more. The wild duck was sent to us as a present, but all the same I love her ever so much.

GREGERS: *(Diverting her.)* Yes, the wild duck, that's right! Let us talk a bit about the wild duck, Hedvig.

HEDVIG: The poor wild duck. He said he couldn't stand the sight of her, either. Just imagine, he wanted to wring its neck!

GREGERS: Oh, he'd never do that.

HEDVIG: No, but he said he would. And I think it was horrible of Father to say that. For I say a prayer for the wild duck every night, and ask that she be protected from death and everything that's evil.

GREGERS: *(Looking at her.)* Do you usually say prayers at night?

HEDVIG: Oh yes.

GERGERS: Who taught you to?

HEDVIG: I taught myself. Because one time Father was very sick and had leeches on his neck, and he said he was being gripped in the jaws of Death.

GREGERS: Really?

HEDVIG: So I said a prayer for him when I went to bed. And I've gone on doing it ever since.

GREGERS: And now you pray for the wild duck as well?

HEDVIG: I though it best to put in the wild duck because she was so sickly at first.

GREGERS: Do you say morning prayers as well?

HEDVIG: No, I don't do that at all.

GREGERS: Why don't you say morning prayers as well?

HEDVIG: In the morning it's light so that there's nothing to be afraid of any more

GREGERS: And the wild duck that you love so deeply, your father wanted to wring its neck.

HEDVIG: No, he said it would be best for him if he did but that he'd spare it for my sake. And that was very nice of Father.

GREGERS: *(Coming closer.)* But what if you, of your own free will, sacrificed the wild duck for his sake?

HEDVIG: *(Getting up.)* The wild duck!

GREGERS: If you were willing to sacrifice for him the best thing you possess in the whole world.

HEDVIG: Do you believe that would help?

GREGERS: Try it, Hedvig.

HEDVIG: *(Quietly, her eyes shining.)* Yes, I *will* try it.

Mrs. Warren's Profession

George Bernard Shaw
1902

Comic
Setting: A flower-covered cottage in surrey. The Garden.
Scene: Vivie is in the Garden when Mr. Praed introduces himself. They are waiting the arrival of Vivie's mother whom she does not see very often and they are discussing Culture.

Mrs. Kitty Warren: 40's – 50's, dressed flatteringly, charming.
Vivie: Her daughter, 22, sensible, highly educated, plain.
Praed: Past middle-age but with a boyish quality, a friend of Kitty Warren.
Sir George Crofts: 50, fashionable, a man-about-town, an old friend of Kitty Warren and a friend of Praed.

VIVIE: Did you expect to find me an unpractical person?
PRAED: No, no. But surely it's practical to consider not only the work these honors cost, but also the culture they bring.
VIVIE: Culture! My dear Mr. Praed: Do you know what the mathematical tripos means? It means grind, grind, grind, for six to eight hours a day at mathematics, and nothing but mathematics. I'm supposed to know something about science; but I know nothing except the mathematics it involves. I can make calculations for engineers, electricians, insurance companies, and so on; but I know next to nothing about engineering or electricity or insurance. I don't even know arithmetic well. Outside mathematics, lawn-tennis, eating, sleeping, cycling, and walking, I'm a more ignorant barbarian than any woman could possibly be who hadn't gone in for the tripos.
PRAED: *(Revolted.)* What a monstrous, wicked, rascally system! I knew it! I felt at once that it meant destroying all that makes womanhood beautiful.
VIVIE: I don't object to it on that score in the least. I shall turn it to very good account, I assure you.
PRAED: Pooh! In what way?
VIVIE: I shall set up in chambers in the city and work at actuarial calculations and conveyancing. Under cover of that I shall do some

law, with one eye on the Stock Exchange all the time. I've come down here by myself to read law—not for a holiday, as my mother imagines. I hate holidays.

PRAED: You make my blood run cold. Are you to have no romance, no beauty in your life?

VIVIE: I don't care for either, I assure you.

PRAED: You can't mean that.

VIVIE: Oh yes I do. I like working and getting paid for it. When I'm tired of working, I like a comfortable chair, a cigar, a little whisky, and a novel with a good detective story in it.

PRAED: *(In a frenzy of repudiation.)* I don't believe it. I am an artist; and I can't believe it: I refuse to believe it. *(Enthusiastically.)* Ah, my dear Miss Warren, you haven't discovered yet, I see, what a wonderful world art can open up to you.

VIVIE: Yes, I have. Last May I spent six weeks in London with Honoria Fraser. Mamma thought we were doing a round of sight-seeing together; but I was really at Honoria's chambers in Chancery Lane every day, working away at actuarial calculations for her, and helping her as well as a greenhorn could. In the evenings we smoked and talked, and never dreamt of going out except for exercise. And I never enjoyed myself more in my life. I cleared all my expenses and got initiated into the business without a fee into the bargain.

PRAED: But bless my heart and soul, Miss Warren, do you call that trying art?

VIVIE: Wait a bit. That wasn't the beginning. I went up to town on an invitation from some artistic people in Fitzjohn's Avenue: One of the girls was a Newnham chum. They took me to the National Gallery, to the Opera, and to a concert where the band played all the evening, Beethoven and Wagner and so on. I wouldn't go through that experience again for anything you could offer me. I held out for civility's sake until the third day; and then I said, plump out, that I couldn't stand any more of it, and went off to Chancery Lane. Now you know the sort of perfectly splendid modern young lady I am. How do you think I shall get on with my mother?

PRAED: *(Startled.)* Well, I hope—er—

VIVIE: It's not so much what you hope as what you believe, that I want to know.

PRAED: Well, frankly, I am afraid your mother will be a little disappointed. Not from any shortcoming on your part, I don't mean that. But you are so different from her ideal.

VIVIE: What is her ideal like?

PRAED: Well, you must have observed, Miss Warren, that people who are dissatisfied with their own bringing up generally think that the world would be all right if everybody were to be brought up quite differently. Now your mothers' life has been—er—I suppose you know—

VIVIE: I know nothing. *(Praed is appalled. His consternation grows as she continues.)* That's exactly my difficulty. You forget, Mr. Praed, that I hardly know my mother. Since I was a child I have lived in England, at school or college or with people paid to take charge of me. I have been boarded out all my life; and my mother has lived in Brussels or Vienna and never let me go to her. I only see her when she visits England for a few days. I don't complain; it's been very pleasant; for people have been very good to me; and there has always been plenty of money to make things smooth. But don't imagine I know anything about my mother. I know far less than you do.

PRAED: *(Very ill at ease.)* In that case— *(He stops, quite at a loss. Then, with a forced attempt at gaiety.)* But what nonsense we are talking! Of course you and your mother will get on capitally. *(He rises, and looks abroad at the view.)* What a charming little place you have here!

VIVIE: *(Unmoved.)* If you think you are doing anything but confirming my worst suspicions by changing the subject like that, you must take me for a much greater fool than I hope I am.

PRAED: Your worst suspicions! Oh, pray don't say that. Now don't.

VIVIE: Why won't my mother's life bear being talked about?

PRAED: Pray think, Miss Vivie. It is natural that I should have a certain delicacy in talking to my old friend's daughter about her behind her back. You will have plenty of opportunity of talking to her about it when she comes. *(Anxiously.)* I wonder what is keeping her.

VIVIE: No: She won't talk about it either. *(Rising.)* However, I won't press you. Only mind this, Mr. Praed. I strongly suspect there will be a battle royal when my mother hears of my Chancery Lane project.

PRAED: *(Ruefully.)* I'm afraid there will.

VIVIE: I shall win the battle, because I want nothing but my fare to London to start there tomorrow earning my own living by devilling for Honoria. Besides, I have no mysteries to keep up; and it seems she has. I shall use that advantage over her if necessary.

PRAED: *(Greatly shocked.)* Oh, no. No, pray. You'd not do such a thing.

VIVIE: Then tell me why not.

PRAED: I really cannot. I appeal to your good feeling. *(She smiles at his sentimentality.)* Besides, you may be too bold. Your mother is not to be trifled with when she's angry.

VIVIE: You can't frighten me, Mr. Praed. In that month at Chancery Lane I had opportunities of taking the measure of one or two women very like my mother who came to consult Honoria. You may back me to win. But if I hit harder in my ignorance than I need, remember that it is you who refuse to enlighten me. Now let us drop the subject. *(She takes her chair and replaces it near the hammock with the same vigorous swing as before.)*

PRAED: *(Taking a desperate resolution.)* One word, Miss Warren. I had better tell you. It's very difficult; but—

(Mrs. Warren and Sir George Crofts arrive at the gate. Mrs. Warren is a woman between 40 and 50, good-looking, showily dressed in a brilliant hat and a gay blouse fitting tightly over her bust and flanked by fashionable sleeves. Rather spoiled and domineering, but, on the whole, a genial and fairly presentable old blackguard of a woman.

Crofts is a tall, powerfully built man of about 50, fashionably dressed in the style of a young man. Nasal voice, reedier than might be expected from his strong frame. Clean-shaven, bull-dog jaws, large flat ears, and thick neck, gentlemanly combination of the most brutal types of city man, sporting man, and man about town.)

VIVIE: Here they are. *(Coming to them as they enter the garden.)* How do, mater. Mr. Praed's been here this half hour, waiting for you.

MRS. WARREN: Well, if you've been waiting, Praddy, it's your own fault: I thought you'd have had the gumption to know I was coming by the 3:10 train. Vivie, put your hat on, dear: You'll get sunburnt. Oh, forgot to introduce you. Sir George Crofts, my little Vivie.

(Crofts advances to Vivie with his most courtly manner. She nods, but makes no motion to shake hands.)

CROFTS: May I shake hands with a young lady whom I have known by reputation very long as the daughter of one of my oldest friends?

VIVIE: *(Who has been looking him up and down sharply.)* If you like. *(She takes his tenderly proffered hand and gives it a squeeze that makes him open his eyes; then turns away and says to her mother.)* Will you come in, or shall I get a couple more chairs? *(She goes into the porch for the chairs.)*

MRS. WARREN: Well, George, what do you think of her?

CROFTS: *(Ruefully.)* She has a powerful fist. Did you shake hands with her, Praed?

PRAED: Yes: It will pass off presently.

CROFTS: I hope so. *(Vivie reappears with two more chairs. He hurries to her assistance.)* Allow me.

MRS. WARREN: *(Patronizingly.)* Let Sir George help you with the chairs, dear.

VIVIE: *(Almost pitching two into his arms.)* Here you are. *(She dusts her hands and turns to Mrs. Warren.)* You'd like some tea, wouldn't you?

MRS. WARREN: *(Sitting in Praed's chair and fanning herself.)* I'm dying for a drop to drink.

VIVIE: I'll see about it. *(She goes into the cottage. Sir George has by this time managed to unfold a chair and plant it beside Mrs. Warren, on her left. He throws the other on the grass and sits down, looking dejected and rather foolish, with the handle of his stick in his mouth. Praed, still very uneasy, fidgets about the garden on their right.)*

MRS. WARREN: *(To Praed, looking at Crofts.)* Just look at him, Praddy: he looks cheerful, don't he? He's been worrying my life out these three years to have that little girl of mine shewn to him; and now that I've done it, he's quite out of countenance. *(Briskly.)* Come! sit up, George; and take your stick out of your mouth. *(Crofts sulkily obeys.)*

PRAED: I think, you know—if you don't mind my saying so—that we had better get out of the habit of thinking of her as a little girl. You see she has really distinguished herself; and I'm not sure, from what I have seen of her, that she is not older than any of us.

MRS. WARREN: *(Greatly amused.)* Only listen to him, George! Older than any of us! Well, she has been stuffing you nicely with her importance.

PRAED: But young people are particularly sensitive about being treated in that way.

MRS. WARREN: Yes; and young people have to get all that nonsense taken out of them, and a good deal more besides. Don't you interfere, Praddy. I know how to treat my own child as well as you do. *(Praed, with a grave shake of his head, walks up the garden with his hands behind his back. Mrs. Warren pretends to laugh, but looks after him with perceptible concern. Then she whispers to Crofts.)* What's the matter with him? What does he take it like that for?

CROFTS: *(Morosely.)* You're afraid of Praed.

MRS. WARREN: What! Me! Afraid of dear old Praddy! Why, a fly wouldn't be afraid of him.

CROFTS: You're afraid of him.

MRS. WARREN: *(Angry.)* I'll trouble you to mind your own business, and not try any of your sulks on me. I'm not afraid of you, any-how. If you can't make yourself agreeable, you'd better go home. *(She gets up, and, turning her back on him, finds herself face to face with Praed.)* Come, Praddy, I know it was only your tender-heartedness. You're afraid I'll bully her.

PRAED: My dear Kitty: You think I'm offended. Don't imagine that: Pray don't. But you know I often notice things that escape you; and though you never take my advice, you sometimes admit afterwards that you ought to have taken it.

MRS. WARREN: Well, what do you notice now?

PRAED: Only that Vivie is a grown woman. Pray, Kitty, treat her with every respect.

MRS. WARREN: *(With genuine amazement.)* Respect! Treat my own daughter with respect! What next, pray!

VIVIE: *(Appearing at the cottage door and calling to Mrs. Warren.)* Mother: Will you come up to my room and take your bonnet off before tea?

MRS. WARREN: Yes, dearie. *(She laughs indulgently at Praed and pats him on the cheek as she passes him on her way to the porch. She follows Vivie into the cottage.)*

CROFTS: *(Furtively.)* I say, Praed.

PRAED: Yes.

CROFTS: I want to ask you a rather particular question.

PRAED: Certainly. *(He takes Mrs. Warren's chair and sits close to Crofts.)*

CROFTS: That's right: They might hear us from the window. Look here: Did Kitty ever tell you who that girl's father is?

PRAED: Never.

CROFTS: Have you any suspicion of who it might be?

PRAED: None.

CROFTS: *(Not believing him.)* I know, of course, that you perhaps might feel bound not to tell if she had said anything to you. But it's very awkward to be uncertain about it now that we shall be meeting the girl every day. We don't exactly know how we ought to feel towards her.

PRAED: What difference can that make? We take her on her own merits. What does it matter who her father was?

CROFTS: *(Suspiciously.)* Then you know who he was?

PRAED: *(with a touch of temper.)* I said no just now. Did you not hear me?

CROFTS: Look here, Praed. I ask you as a particular favor. If you do know *(Movement of protest from Praed.)*—I only say, if you know, you might at least set my mind at rest about her. The fact is I feel attracted towards her. Oh, don't be alarmed: It's quite an innocent feeling. That's what puzzles me about it. Why, for all I know, *I* might be her father.

PRAED: You! Impossible! Oh, no, nonsense!

CROFTS: *(Catching him up cunningly.)* You know for certain that I'm not?

PRAED: I know nothing about it, I tell you, any more than you. But really, Crofts—oh, no, it's out of the question. There's not the least resemblance.

CROFTS: As to that, there's no resemblance between her and her mother that I can see. I suppose she's not your daughter, is she?

PRAED: *(He meets the question with an indignant stare; then recovers himself with an effort and answers gently and gravely.)* Now listen to me, my dear Crofts. I have nothing to do with that side of Mrs. Warren's life, and never had. She has never spoken to me about it; and of course I have never spoken to her about it. Your delicacy will tell you that a handsome woman needs some friends who are not—well, not on that footing with her. The effect of her own beauty would become a torment to her if she could not escape from it occasionally. You are probably on much more confidential terms with Kitty than I am. Surely you can ask her the question yourself.

CROFTS: *(Rising impatiently.)* I have asked her often enough. But she's so determined to keep the child all to herself that she would deny that it ever had a father if she could. No: There's nothing to be got out of her—nothing that one can believe, anyhow. I'm thoroughly uncomfortable about it, Praed.

PRAED: *(Rising also.)* Well, as you are, at all events, old enough to be her father, I don't mind agreeing that we both regard Miss Vivie in a parental way, as a young girl whom we are bound to protect and help. All the more, as the real father, whoever he was, was probably a blackguard. What do you say?

CROFTS: *(Aggressively.)* I'm no older than you, if you come to that.

PRAED: Yes, you are, my dear fellow: You were born old. I was born a boy: I've never been able to feel the assurance of a grown-up man in my life.

MRS. WARREN: *(Calling from within the cottage.)* Prad-dee! George! Tea-ea-ea-ea!

The City

Clyde Fitch
1090

Dramatic
Setting: The comfortable family home, Middleburg, New York.
Scene: The family is gathering for the return of daughter Teresa who
  has been in Europe. Mr. Rand receives a disturbing letter. The
  family does not know that he is being blackmailed for a past
  indiscretion years ago.

Mrs. Molly Rand: 50's, a housewife.
Mr. George D. Rand: 50's, a businessman and her husband.
Cicely: 17, their younger daughter.
George, Jr:. 27, their son.

RAND: *(Angry.)* Yes, still keeping it up, the young blackguard! *(He
  tears the letter in two, and throws it into the fire without reading
  it.)*
  *(He watches it burn a second, lighting a cigar; then takes his
  papers, makes himself comfortable in his chair before the fire,
  and starts to read. After a second, Mrs. Rand and Cicely, a very
  pretty girl of about seventeen, enter. Mrs. Rand carries a pitcher
  of water, scissors, and a newspaper. Cicely has her arms full of
  yellow tulips and a big bowl.)*
MRS. RAND: Why, father! Aren't you home early? Teresa's train won't
  be in for an hour or so yet. *(Mrs. Rand, filling the bowl with
  water, spreads the newspaper on the table; then cuts off the
  stems, and hands the flowers one by one to Cicely, who arranges
  them.)*
RAND: I felt tired today, Molly. My head bothers me!
MRS. RAND: *(Going to him with affection and solicitude.)* Why don't
  you lie down? *(She lays her hand on his head.)* You haven't any
  fever. *(She kisses his forehead.)* You're just overtired! *(He pats her
  hand affectionately, and holds it.)* When are you going to give up
  business entirely, darling, and leave it all to George?
RAND: Never, I'm afraid, dear. *(Letting go her hand.)* I've tried to face
  the idea, but the idleness appalls me.
CICELY: Mother, have you the scissors?

MRS. RAND: Yes, dear. *(Joins her, and continues with the flowers.)*

RAND: Besides, George is too restless, too discontented yet, for me to trust him with my two banks! He's got the New York bee in his bonnet.

CICELY: *(Glances at her mother before she speaks.)* Oh! We all have that, father—except you.

RAND: And mother!

CICELY: Humph! Mother's just as bad as the rest of us. Only she's afraid to say so. *(Smiling.)* Go on, mother, own up you've got villageitis and cityphobia!

MRS. RAND: *(Smiling.)* I *dare*, only I don't want to bother your father!

RAND: That's the effect of George—and Teresa. I've noticed all the innuendoes in her letters home. Europe's spoiled the girl! The New York school started the idea, but I hoped travel would cure her, and instead—!

MRS. RAND: Wait till you see her. Remember, in spite of letters, what a year may have done for her. Oh, I'm so eager to see her! What a long hour this is! *(The telephone bell rings out in the hall. Mrs. Rand goes out and is heard saying, "Hello! Yes, who is it? Oh, is it you, Katherine?".)*

RAND: *(Reading his paper.)* Who's that talking to your mother?

CICELY: One of Middleburg's Social Queens, Mrs. Mulholland—known in our society as the lady who can wear a décolleté gown, cut in accordance with the Middleburg limit, and not look as if she'd dressed in a hurry and forgotten her collar!
(Rand laughs.)

MRS. RAND: *(Offstage.)* Really! I should think she was much too old to be so advanced in the styles as that!

CICELY: The flowers are lovely all over the house. Father, you ought to see them! They came from a New York florist. *(Mrs. Rand off stage "Good-bye. See you at five.")* Our man here hadn't anything but ferns and aniline-dyed pinks.

MRS. RAND: *(Re-enters.)* Kate Mulholland called up to tell me Mary Carterson's mother-in-law is visiting her from South Norwalk, and went down street this morning wearing one of those new washtub hats—and she's sixty, if she isn't over! She was born in 1846—at least she *used* to be!

RAND: *(still reading.)* When do you expect your crowd to come this afternoon?

CICELY: Crowd? *(She laughs derisively.)* The only thing that can get a crowd in Middleburg is a fire or funeral!

MRS. RAND: As we expect Teresa at four, I asked everybody to come in at five. But you know, father, *"everybody"* in Middleburg isn't *many!*

CICELY: Not many—nor *much!*

RAND: You have the best the town affords, and it's good old stock!

CICELY: I'm afraid Tess'll think it's rather tame for a girl who has been presented at *two European courts!*

MRS. RAND: Yes, I'm afraid she'll find it awfully dull. Don't you think, father, we could go to New York, if only for the winter months?

RAND: Don't tell me *you're* ambitious, too?

MRS. RAND: Well, I've done all, in a social way, a woman can in Middleburg, and I want to do more.

CICELY: You can't tell the difference in Middleburg between a smart afternoon tea and a Mother's Meeting, or a Sunday-school teacher's conclave, or a Lenten Sewing Circle, or a Fair for the Orphan Asylum, or any other like "Event"! It's always the same old people and the same old thing! Oh, Lord, we live in a cemetery!

RAND: Molly, wouldn't you rather be *it* in Middleburg—than *nit* in the City?

MRS. RAND: But with our influence and our friends—we'd take letters—I would soon have the position your wife was entitled to in the City, too.

CICELY: I don't care a darn about the position, if I can only have something to do, and something to see! Who wants to smell new-mown hay if he can breathe in gasoline on Fifty Avenue instead! Think of the theaters! the crowds! *Think* of being able to go out on the street and *see some one you didn't know even by sight!*

RAND: *(Laughs, amused.)* Molly! How can you deceive yourself? A banker from a small country town would give you about as much position as he could afford to pay for on the West Side, above Fifty-ninth Street.

MRS. RAND: But *George* said you'd been asked to join a big corporation in New York, which would make the family's everlasting fortune, and social position beside.

RAND: *(Looks up, angry.)* George had no right telling you that. I told him only in confidence. What is this anyway—a family conspiracy?

CICELY: No, it is the American legation shut up in Peking, longing for a chance to escape from social starvation.

RAND: *(Thoroughly irritated.)* Now listen! This has got to stop, once and for all! So long as I'm the head of this family, it's going to *keep its head* and not lose it! And our home is *here*, and *will be here*, if to hold it I have to die in harness.

MRS. RAND: *(Going to him affectionately.)* Father, don't be angry! You know *your will is law* with all of us. And so long as you want it, we'll stay right here.

CICELY: Giving teas to the wallflower brigade, and dinners to the Bible class! And our cotillion favors will be articles appropriate for the missionaries' boxes! Oh, Lord!

RAND: Mother, Cicely has convinced me of *one thing.*

CICELY: *(Delighted.)* Not really! Good! What?

RAND: *You* go to no *finishing school* in *New York!* You get *finished* all you're going to, right here in Middleburg. New York would completely turn your head!

CICELY: Well, don't worry; Middleburg will *"finish"* me all right! Good and strong! Maybe New York would turn your head, but Middleburg turns my— *(She is going to say "Stomach," but her mother interrupts.)*

MRS. RAND: Cicely!

(Enter George. He is a handsome, clean-cut young American, of about twenty-seven.)

GEORGE: Hello, everybody!

RAND: *(Surprised.)* Hello, George! What's the matter? It's only half past four! Nothing happened in the office?

GEORGE: Nothing! *All day!* That's why I am here. I thought I'd be in good time for Tess; and, so far as missing anything *really doing in the office* is concerned, I could have left at ten this morning— *(Adds half aside.)* or almost any morning, *in this—our city!*

CICELY: Look out! The word *city* is a red rag to a bull with father, today! And it's for good in the graveyard! I'm going to dress. Thank the Lord, I've actually got somebody new to look smart for, if it's only my sister! *(Yawns and starts to go.)*

RAND: Who's coming to your tea party?

CICELY: *(As she goes out.)* All the names are on the tombstones in the two churchyards, plus Miss Carterson's mother-in-law from South Norwalk!

MRS RAND: I must dress, too. *(Going over to Rand.)* Dear, aren't you going to change your coat, and help me?

RAND: Oh, Molly, don't ask me to bore myself with your old frumps!

MRS. RAND: *I have to!* And I don't know that *I* take any more interest than *you* do in what sort of a hat Mary Carterson's mother is wearing! But if it were in New York—

RAND: *(Sneers.)* Stop! I meant what I said—let's drop that!

MRS. RAND: All right—I didn't say anything!

GEORGE: Look here, father—mother's right.

RAND: *(Interrupting.)* No, *you* do the *"looking,"* George, and straight *in my eyes! (He does so.)* Your mother's wrong, but it isn't *her* fault, it's *you* children.

MRS RAND: *(Remonstrating.)* Now, father—

GEORGE: But we're *not children*, and that's the mistake you make! *I'm* twenty-seven.

MRS. RAND: Yes, father, you forget—George is twenty-seven!

GEORGE: I'm no long a *boy!*

RAND: Then why did you tell your mother about this offer I had from New York, when I told you it was absolutely *confidential!* And a man in business knows what the word *"confidential"* means.

MRS. RAND: It was *my* fault; *I* wormed it out of George!

GEORGE: Nonsense, mother! *(To his father.)* I told, because I thought you needed a good, big hump, and I believed, if all of us put our shoulders to it, we could move you.

RAND: Out of Middleburg?

GEORGE: Yes!

RAND: *Into New York?*

GEORGE: Yes!

RAND: Listen, George—

GEORGE: *(Going on.)* What position is there for a fellow like me in a hole like this?

The Doctor's Duty

Luigi Pirandello
1913

Dramatic

Setting: In the Corsi home. Southern Italy.

Scene: Anna's husband has killed the husband of a woman with whom he was having an affair. Anna defends him and her mother villifies him. The lawyer and the doctor have come to see if he can be moved to the jail. Mrs. Reis has taken charge of the children.

Dr. Tito Lecci: A physician, 40's – 50's.
Franco Cimetta: A lawyer, 30's – 50's.
Anna Corsi: 30, a wife, wildly distraught.
Mrs. Reis: Anna's mother, 50's, blunt, angry.

ANNA: It was a hunger for life, that's all. He didn't think.

MRS. REIS: He had no scruples.

ANNA: Yes, put it any way you like. So many times I've tried to judge one of his acts, but he never gave me time to judge, just as he never attached any importance to anything he did. It was useless to call him to account. A shrug of the shoulders, a smile and off he'd go. No matter, what, he had to keep going. No hesitating to weigh right from wrong.

MRS. REIS: Oh, you admit that!

ANNA: But, you see, there was nothing ever really bad in this constant rage for life of his. He was always himself, always happy, everybody's friend. At thirty-eight he was still a boy, able to play like a child with Didi and Federico, even to lose his temper. And after ten years with me he was still—still—No, no. Maybe he did stray once in while, deceive me from time to time. But lie to me, no. Never. He could never lie with those lips, those eyes, that smile that every day used to light up the whole house. Angelica Neri? Do you really expect me to believe that between her and me Tommaso would— Look, it was nothing more than the whim of the moment for him, nothing, merely proof of a weakness perhaps all men share. Nor would you expect him to have any scruples over his friendship with the husband, who knew perfectly well what kind of woman his wife was and how she dishonored him openly with everyone. Even here, I tell you, in our town house, right under my own eyes, she used to try and seduce Tommaso with her sick monkey tricks. Here, right here! I noticed it and so did he. We used to laugh about it, Tommaso and I! Yes, yes, we laughed, we laughed!

(She bursts into hysterical laughter.)

MRS. REIS: Anna! Anna! You're going mad!

ANNA: You're drive me mad! Facts! Facts! The facts are that Neri knew, and not only about Tommaso but about everyone else, and he never gave the slightest hint of caring. At the last minute he decided to create a tragedy, when what he should have done was to kill her like a mad dog! It wouldn't have cost him a thing! The facts . . . Then I suppose they'll claim Tommaso was carrying a gun to kill Neri? He always carried one because of the work he had to do, the business of the leases and so on in the country.

(Lecci and Cimetta enter at this point. The former is tall, stiff, wears thick eyeglasses; the latter is older, with a nearly white pointed beard and long hair that is still black and combed straight back.)

ANNA: Ah, here's the doctor! And you too, Cimetta?

LECCI: Why this sudden call? Anything new?

ANNA: *(Indicating her mother to Cimetta.)* My mother. *(Turning to Lecci.)* Doctor, they're trying to drive me mad. They want to take him away today!

LECCI: Of course not. Who told you that?

ANNA: The policeman out there. Ask him. That's what he said.

LECCI: Oh, we'll put a stop to that, don't you worry. I'll go to the Commissioner myself, right now. Will you come too, Cimetta?

ANNA: Yes, yes, you go too, please!

CIMETTA: Any time you say. Right this minute. It's just down the street.

LECCI: Don't even think about it. Without my consent they can't move him. That would be the last straw, at this point. *(To Cimetta.)* We accomplished a miracle here, my friend, a real miracle.

ANNA: You see, Mother, it's true. They did it in spite of him, against his wishes.

LECCI: *(Without attaching any importance to the matter.)* Yes, that's true. There was some resistance. Perhaps in his delirium. The real trouble, my friend, came from an accumulation of complications, one more serious than the next and all of them quite unforeseen. I was forced to improvise remedies that were quite often opposed to each other, and all so risky that, believe me, they'd have discouraged and stopped anyone else in my place. If I'd allowed myself for a moment to hesitate or doubt even slightly, good-bye! I can tell you that I've never in my whole career had a satisfaction to equal this one.

CIMETTA: *(To Anna.)* You must excuse me, Mrs. Corsi, for not having come to see you earlier. But I was absolutely stunned by this unexpected disaster. It's shocked the whole town. Until today you've needed a doctor. Now that, unfortunately, you're also going to need a lawyer, I came without waiting for you to call me, because I know the confidence Tommaso has always placed in what little ability I have.

LECCI: I asked our dear friend to come here today with me, because I think it's time we started to prepare the patient for some of the hard facts he's going to have to face.

ANNA: It's going to be horrible, Doctor. I don't think he has the slightest idea, up to now. He's like a child. He's easily moved, cries, laughs at nothing. And just this morning he was telling me that, as soon as he's well, he wants to take a month's vacation in the country.

MRS. REIS: Oh, of course! Why shouldn't he have a vacation?

CIMETTA: Poor Tommaso.

LECCI: Let's give him a couple of days. Meanwhile we'll let him see Cimetta. I can't believe he won't eventually realize what's ahead of him.

ANNA: *(To Cimetta.)* How serious is it?

CIMETTA: *(Closing his eyes, spreading his arms.)* My dear Mrs. Corsi . . . *(Anna hides her face in her hands.)*

LECCI: Come, come this is no time to worry about that. For now he's all right. Anything new since last night?

ANNA: No, nothing.

LECCI: Good. Go in there and ask the nurse to help you get him dressed and out of bed. Take your time, eh? And see if, once he's on his feet, you can get him to take a few steps. Meanwhile, Cimetta and I will go see the Commissioner. We'll be back in a few minutes. Come, come, courage, Anna. You've been very brave till now.

ANNA: *(Her face still covered.)* I can't! I can't any more!

CIMETTA: You've got to!

LECCI: Please, Anna.

ANNA: *(Getting control of herself.)* I'm all right. *(Tries to smile.)* How's this? All right? Until later, then. *(Shakes Cimetta's hand. Then, to Lecci.)* Good-bye. And you, Mother?

MRS. REIS: *(Vehemently.)* I'm going, I'm going!

ANNA: I know . . .

MRS. REIS: Good-bye, Anna.

ANNA: The children—kiss them for me. *(Anna exits at rear.)*

CIMETTA: Poor woman, I hardly recognize her.

MRS. REIS: *(Whirling on him.)* Get him out of here right away! Right away! To jail! That murderer! Please, please, for Anna's sake!

LECCI: It's a question of a day or two, Mrs. Reis. If not today, tomorrow. *(To Cimetta.)* It was an extraordinary concession to leave him here under our care until now. Guarded, yes, but with all the freedom and consideration possible. Especially when you remember who the victim was!

CIMETTA: It's incredible! It's a dream, a nightmare! For that woman! A man like Neri, ugly, apathetic, a worm, who used to drag himself around, utterly indifferent to everything! For years he knew his wife betrayed him openly with everybody and he never cared! When he talked, it was all he could do to whine a few words in that mewing voice of his! And all of a sudden—yes, sir!—his blood boils and over whom? Why, poor Tommaso. *(To Mrs. Reis.)* Tell me, how is it, why is it that Tommaso was a friend of his?

MRS. REIS: They met through that judge, the one who was transferred, Judge—what was his name: Làrcan, I think.

CIMETTA: Ah, yes, Làrcan. Judge Làrcan.

MRS. REIS: He lived here, a few houses away. When he was transferred, he wrote a letter of introduction to my son-in-law for Neri, who was taking his place. That's how they met.

CIMETTA: And wasn't Neri also godfather to one of Tommaso's children?

MRS. REIS: Yes, the last one, the one that died.

CIMITTA: *(To Lecci.)* You see? The man was a jinx. And you can be sure that, with his temperament, death must have been a joy for him. And now a whole family into the abyss because of it. *(Anna returns hurriedly.)*

ANNA: Tell me, Doctor, is it safe to let him leave his room for a few minutes? He wants to.

LECCI: If he can, but he mustn't make the slightest effort. See to it. Hold a chair behind him, in case his legs go out from under him. And be careful. *(To Mrs. Reis.)* Are you coming, too, Mrs. Reis?

MRS. REIS: Yes. I'll go ahead. Good-bye, Anna. *(She exits.)*

LECCI: We'll go, too. After you, Cimetta.

CIMETTA: Good-bye, Mrs. Corsi.

ANNA: Good-bye. *(To Lecci.)* Please, Doctor, tell the guard to stay out there.

LECCI: Don't worry. Although, maybe—

ANNA: No! He mustn't see him!

LECCI: Then you try and tell him. No one can do it better than you.

CIMETTA: He's right.

LECCI: When you get a chance.

ANNA: But how? How?

LECCI: Never mind. We'll be back right away. Good-bye. *(They exit. Anna arranges the chair for the patient and exits out the rear, leaving the door open and the curtain drawn aside.)*

The Happy Journey to Trenton and Camden

Thornton Wilder
1931

Comic
Setting: A bare stage, all settings and props are imaginary.
Scene: The Stage Manager is leaning against the proscenium pillar at the side of the stage. Ma Kirby is putting on her hat before an imaginary mirror.

Ma Kirby: 40's – 50's.
Arthur Kirby: A pre-teenager.
Caroline Kirby: Teenager.
Stage Manager: Plays several roles, as himself.

MA: Where's your pa? Why isn't he here? I declare we'll never get started.

ARTHUR: Ma, where's my hat? I guess I don't go if I can't find my hat. *(Still playing marbles.)*

MA: Go out into the hall and see if it isn't there. Where's Caroline gone to now, the plagued child?

ARTHUR: She's out waitin' in the street talkin' to the Jones girls. —I just looked in the hall a thousand times, Ma, and it isn't there. *(He spits for good luck before a difficult shot and mutters.)* Come on, baby.

MA: Go and look again, I say. Look carefully.
(Arthur rises, reluctantly, crosses right, turns around, returns swiftly to his game center, flinging himself on the floor with a terrible impact, and starts shooting an aggie.)

ARTHUR: No, Ma, it's not there.

MA: *(Serenely.)* Well, you don't leave Newark without that hat, make up your mind to that. I don't go on journeys with a hoodlum.

ARTHUR: Aw, Ma!
(Ma comes down right to the footlights, pulls up an imaginary window and talks toward the audience.)

MA: *(Calling.)* Oh, Mrs. Schwartz!

THE STAGE MANAGER: *(Down left. Consulting his script.)* Here I am, Mrs. Kirby. Are you going yet?

MA: I guess we're going in just a minute. How's the baby?

THE STAGE MANAGER: She's all right now. We slapped her on the back and she spat it up.

MA: Isn't that fine! —Well, now, if you'll be good enough to give the cat a saucer of milk in the morning and the evening, Mrs. Schwartz, I'll be ever so grateful to you. —Oh, good afternoon, Mrs. Hobmeyer!

THE STAGE MANAGER: Good afternoon, Mrs. Kirby, I hear you're going away.

MA: *(Modest.)* Oh, just for three days, Mrs. Hobmeyer, to see my married daughter, Beulah, in Camden. Elmer's got his vacation week from the laundry early this year, and he's just the best driver in the world.

(Caroline comes downstage right and stands by her mother.)

THE STAGE MANAGER: Is the whole family going?

MA: Yes, all four of us that's here. The change ought to be good for the children. My married daughter was downright sick a while ago—

THE STAGE MANAGER: Tchk—tchk—tchk! Yes. I remember you tellin' us.

MA: *(With feeling.)* And I just want to go down and see the child. I ain't seen her since then. I just won't rest easy in my mind without I see her. *(To Caroline.)* Can't you say good afternoon to Mrs. Hobmeyer?

CAROLINE: *(Lowers her eyes and says woodenly.)* Good afternoon, Mrs. Hobmeyer.

THE STAGE MANAGER: Good afternoon, dear. —Well, I'll wait and beat these rugs until after you're gone, because I don't want to choke you. I hope you have a good time and find everything all right.

MA: Thank you, Mrs. Hobmeyer, I hope I will. —Well, I guess that milk for the cat is all, Mrs. Schwartz, if you're sure you don't mind. If anything should come up, the key to the back door is hanging by the ice-box.

CAROLINE: Ma! Not so loud.

ARTHUR: Everybody can hear yuh.

MA: Stop pullin' my dress, children. *(In a loud whisper.)* The key to the back door I'll leave hangin' by the ice-box and I'll leave the screen door unhooked.

THE STAGE MANAGER: Now have a good trip, dear, and give my love to Beulah.

MA: I will, and thank you a thousand times. *(She lowers the window, turns upstage, and looks around. Caroline goes left and vigorously rubs her cheeks. Ma occupies herself with the last touches of packing.)* What can be keeping your pa?

ARTHUR: *(Who has not left his marbles.)* I can't find my hat, Ma.

Undercurrent

Fay Ehlert
1938

Dramatic

Setting: The kitchen area of the basement apartment of the Fishyers.
Suppertime. Thursday night.

Scene: The family is waiting for their older daughter, Annie, who
always comes for Thursday night dinner. They believe she is
legally employed by Miss Page in the Morals Court. Annie is late.

Karl Fishyer: 40's – 50's, a big, hard-working man, a janitor.
Mrs. Fishyer: His wife, 40's – 50's.
Emil: Their son, late teens, helps his father with janitorial work.
Miss Page: Special investigator for the Morals Court, 30's – 40's.

(Pa Fishyer enters wearily from corridor.)

FISHYER: *(Throwing his denim jacket over Morris chair.)* Huh! *(He strides over to the sink and begins washing himself.)* Huh! Supper ready?

MA FISHYER: *(At the table.)* A-almost—

FISHYER: *(He growls.)* Almost? Don'tcha know yess or no? *(He pushes up his spectacles and glares at the clock.)* Vere's Annie? It's nearly six already!

MA FISHYER: De c-clock iss a l-little f-fest. *(Walks nervously to window.)*

FISHYER: Fest? Dat clock iss *alvays* right, you hear me? Alvays right!

MA FISHYER: Yess, P-pa!

FISHYER: *(His wrath increasing.)* Vell, vere iss she?

MA FISHYER: *(Busies herself at stove.)* Na, Pa, she'll be h-here eny minute soon! Yuh know h-how de l-lady k-keeps her! *(She glances at the door through which Mrs. Floyd has left.)* And m-maybe—in dis b-bed veather, she kent come at all!

FISHYER: Vat! *(Drying his hands.)*

MA FISHYER: I-I mean—efen in *good* veather, only vunce a veek does she haff a day off.

FISHYER: Dat'll do! *(Throws towel on sink.)* Ve vait till six *(Takes Bible from table and seats himself in Morris chair.)* and den ve eat!

(Groans as he rubs his rheumatic left arm. Emil enters.) Na, Dummy, vat did she vant? *(Points upward.)*

EMIL: *(Timidly.)* She fergot her key and—

FISHYER: . . . and yuh hed to open de door for her! *(He growls.)* Vy don't yuh say dat right avay? *(He begins reading the Bible, following each word with his finger.)*

MA FISHYER: Come, Emil *(She nods warningly in Fishyer's direction.)* and vash yerself.

FISHYER: *(He reads laboriously.)* "Train op a child in de vay he should go" *(Glares at Emil and then repeats.)* "de vay he *should* go!" *(Reads.)* " . . . and ven he iss old" *(Repeats to himself.)* "old—he vill not depart from it—"
(There is a knock at the outer door and Ma Fishyer stands transfixed, her face ashen. Emil, his hands half-washed, looks inquiringly at his father.)

FISHYER: Na, open de door!

EMIL: *(Hurriedly wiping his hands on his trousers, he mounts the steps and opens the door.)* Whatcha want?

MISS PAGE: Good evening! Does Annie Fishyer live here?

EMIL: Yeh— *(He shuffles back to the sink.)* —come on in!

MISS PAGE: *(Descending the stairs.)* Thank you. I wasn't quite sure. *(Kindly to Ma Fishyer.)* You must be Annie's mother and—

FISHYER: I em Karl Fishyer!

MISS PAGE: Ah, yes, Annie's father. *(She smiles her quick, warm smile.)* I don't think you know me. I am Miss Page, a special investigator from the Morals Court!

MA FISHYER: *(Tremulously to Fishyer.)* De lady, Pa, de l-lady vat Annie v-vorks f-for—

FISHYER: So?

MISS PAGE: *(Surprised.)* Works for me?

MA FISHYER: *(Hurriedly.)* Pleese to come and sit down, mis', here on de sofa! *(She deftly dusts the sofa with a swish of her apron and then steps back and looks at Miss Page apprehensively.)*

MISS PAGE: I think you are mistaking me— *(She stops as she sees Ma Fishyer's drawn face.)*

MA FISHYER: *(Indicating the sofa.)* P-pleese, mis'— *(Pa Fishyer meanwhile replaces the Bible on the table. Miss Page sits down without another word.)*

MA FISHYER: *(Quickly.)* Annie a-ain't home yet, b-but—

MISS PAGE: *(Puzzled.)* Isn't home yet? Are you expecting her?

FISHYER: Huh? *(He turns towards them.)* Shure, I expect her to come!

MA FISHYER: Y-yess, she always c-c-comes here on her day off—Pa means!

MISS PAGE: *(Probing gently.)* Her day off?

MA FISHYER: Maybe she n-nefer tells yuh, b-but she alvays c-c-comes here Thursdays. *(She wets her lips.)* D-don't she, Pa?

FISHYER: *(Grudgingly.)* Huh! *(To Miss Page.)* Since she's vid yuh, mis', yess!

MA FISHYER: *(She talks to Miss Page, but her eyes are anxiously on Fishyer.)* And efery cent vat she earns by yuh, she brings to her pa!

MISS PAGE: She—does what? *(Drawing off her gloves.)*

MA FISHYER: E-efery cent she brings to her pa! She iss a fine girl—

FISHYER: *(Cutting her short.)* Vat's dot to brag ofer?

MISS PAGE: *(Soothingly.)* Well, I'm sure Annie is—

MA FISHYER: *(Eagerly.)* Yuh hear, Pa? Efen Mis' Page sez vat a fine Annie ve got.

FISHYER: Huh, she's purty goot *now!* But before she vent mit yuh, mis' *(He clenches his fist in wrath.)* I—her fadder—didn't know vhere she vas for three month efen—*(Miss Page suppresses a start.)*

MA FISHYER: *(Imploringly.)* But, Pa, yuh know *now* vere she vas! *(To Miss Page.)* H-he m-means de time ven she v-vas by yuh in *(She swallows hard.)* de country. *(Miss Page conceals her astonishment.)*

FISHYER: Efen ef she vas—

MA FISHYER: . . . and how vell she looked ven—

FISHYER: . . . she come home agen! *(He paces angrily back and forth.)* I hear dot a million times already, too!

MA FISHYER: But, P-pa—

FISHYER: All I say iss—dot's no vay to treat yur fadder! And efter de strick bringing op I giff de children, dey must remember—alvays—dat I em dere fadder! *I em de boss here! (To Emil, crouching against the wall.)* Yuh hear me?

MA FISHYER: *(Imploringly.)* Pa, pleese, Pa.

FISHYER: *(Glaring at the clock.)* It's six, ve eat now! *(He seats himself at table and begins slicing bread, motions Emil to his seat. Emil sits facing the audience.)*

MISS PAGE: *(She has been watching them attentively.)* Yes, don't let me interrupt you!

FISHYER: I alvays eat at six! *(Turns towards stove.)* Vere iss dot girl? *(Ma comes to table with platter of stew, which she places quickly before him.)* Vat time yuh let her come today, mis'—?

Blood Wedding

Federico Garcia Lorca
1933

Dramatic
Setting: The Bride's House. Rural Spain.
Scene: The Mother and the Bridegroom have come to pay their respects to the fiancée and her father.

The Mother: 50's, a widow.
The Bridegroom: 20's.
The Father of the Bride: Elderly.
The Bride: 20's.

MOTHER: Did you bring your watch?
BRIDEGROOM: Yes.
(He takes it out and looks at it.)
MOTHER: We must be back on time. How far this family lives!
BRIDEGROOM: But they have good land.
MOTHER: Good, yes but desolate. A four-hour ride and not a house or tree have we passed.
BRIDEGROOM: These are dry lands.
MOTHER: Your father would've covered these lands with trees.
BRIDEGROOM: Without water?
MOTHER: He would've found some. The three years we were married he planted ten cherry trees, *(Remembering.)* the three walnut trees by the mill, a whole vineyard, and a plant called Jupiter which would put out a burst of scarlet flowers, and now is dried up. *(Pause.)*
BRIDEGROOM: *(Referring to Bride.)* She must be getting dressed.
(The Father of the Bride enters. He is elderly with a mane of resplendent white hair. His head is bowed. The Mother and the Bridegroom rise. They shake hands in silence.)
FATHER: Was it a long trip?
MOTHER: Four hours.
(They sit down.)
FATHER: You must've come the long way.
MOTHER: I'm too old to be riding along the river cliffs.
BRIDEGROOM: She gets dizzy.

(Pause.)

FATHER: A fine hemp harvest.

BRIDEGROOM: Quite fine.

FATHER: In my day, this land didn't even yield hemp. We've had to punish it, weep for it, so that it would give us something of use.

MOTHER: But now it does. You shouldn't complain. I haven't come here to ask you for anything.

FATHER: *(Smiling.)* You're much richer than I. Your vineyards are worth a fortune. Each young vine a silver coin. What bothers me. . . do you understand? is that we're so far apart. I like everything to be together. There is a thorn in my heart, and it is that tiny orchard over there in the middle of my fields, which they won't sell to me for all the gold in the world.

BRIDEGROOM: That's the way it always is.

FATHER: If we could have twenty teams of oxen bring your vineyards here, and set them down on the hillside, how happy I'd be!

MOTHER: Why?

FATHER: What's mine is hers, and what's yours is his. That's why. To see it all together it would be beautiful!

BRIDEGROOM: And less work.

MOTHER: When I die, sell our lands, and buy some alongside here.

FATHER: Sell, sell? Bah! You buy a daughter, you buy everything. If I would have had sons I would have bought the entire mountainside up to the break of the stream. Because this isn't good land, but with strong arms one can make it good, and since no one comes around here, no one can steal your fruit and you can sleep in peace.

(Pause.)

MOTHER: You know why I am here.

FATHER: Yes.

MOTHER: And?

FATHER: It's fine by me. They've talked it over.

MOTHER: My son has money and knows how to handle it.

FATHER: So does my daughter.

MOTHER: My son is handsome. He's never been with a woman. His honor is as pure as a sheet hung out in the sun to dry.

FATHER: What can I say about my daughter. At three, when the morning star shines, she makes the bread. She never speaks. She's as soft as wool, she embroiders all kinds of fancywork, and she can cut a strong cord with her teeth.

MOTHER: God bless this house.

FATHER: May God bless it.

(The Maid appears with two trays. One with drinks, and the other with sweets.)

MOTHER: *(To her son.)* When do you want this wedding?

BRIDEGROOM: Next Thursday.

FATHER: The day on which she'll be exactly twenty-two years old.

MOTHER: Twenty-two! That would have been my eldest son's age had he lived. Fierce and passionate he was, as befits a man, and would've lived had men not invented knives.

FATHER: You mustn't think about that.

MOTHER: Every minute. With my hand to my heart.

FATHER: Thursday, then? Are we agreed?

BRIDEGROOM: Indeed.

FATHER: We will accompany the bridal couple and take a carriage to the church, which is quite far, and the wedding party will come along on their on carts and horses.

MOTHER: Very well.

FATHER: *(To the Maid who crosses.)* Tell her she can come in now. *(To the Mother.)* How delighted I will be if you like her.

(The Bride appears. Her hands are in a modest pose, and her head is bowed.)

MOTHER: Come here. Are you happy?

BRIDE: Yes, ma'am.

FATHER: You shouldn't be so serious. After all, she's going to be your mother.

BRIDE: I am happy. I've said "yes" because I wanted to.

MOTHER: Naturally. *(She takes her by the chin.)* Look at me.

FATHER: She is the spitting image of my wife.

MOTHER: Really? What a beautiful face! Do you know what it means to be married, child?

BRIDE: *(Seriously.)* I do.

MOTHER: A man, some children and a wall two yards wide for everything else.

BRIDEGROOM: Do you need anything else?

MOTHER: No. May they all live, that's all! Live long!

BRIDE: I'll know to do my duty.

MOTHER: Here are some gifts for you.

BRIDE: Thank you.

FATHER: Shall we have something?

MOTHER: Not for me. *(To her son.)* You?

BRIDEGROOM: I will.

(He takes a sweet from the tray. The Bride takes another.)

FATHER: *(To Bridegroom.)* Wine?

MOTHER: He doesn't touch it.

FATHER: All the better!

(Pause. They are all standing.)

BRIDEGROOM: *(To the Bride.)* I'll come tomorrow.

BRIDE: What time?

BRIDEGROOM: At five.

BRIDE: I'll wait for you.

BRIDEGROOM: When I leave your side I feel such a great emptiness, and something like a knot in my throat. . .

BRIDE: When you are my husband you won't feel that way anymore.

BRIDEGROOM: That's what I tell myself.

MOTHER: Come now. The sun won't wait. *(To the Father.)* Are we agreed on everything?

FATHER: Agreed.

The Crucible

Arthur Miller
1953

Dramatic
Setting: Salem 1692
Scene: Rev. Parriss's daughter Betty had been with the other girls in the woods. Now she lies in bed, inert, claiming bewitchment. He questions Abigail about what went on.
Of Note: Betty lies in bed in a seeming trance—no lines.

Abigail Williams: Teens, a niece to Reverend Parriss, has had an affair with John Proctor, a married man.
Reverend Parriss: 40's, has lived in Salem for three years, his daughter lies ill, raving and believing she can fly.
Mrs. Ann Putnam: 45, worn-out, a neighbor whose daughter also claims to be bewitched.
Thomas Putnam: Her husband, 50, a bitter man filled with grievances.

ABIGAIL: Uncle, we did dance; let you tell them I confessed it—and I'll be whipped if I must be. But they're speakin' of witchcraft. Betty's not witched.

PARRIS: Abigail, I cannot go before the congregation when I know you have not opened with me. What did you do with her in the forest?

ABIGAIL: We did dance, uncle, and when you leaped out of the bush so suddenly, Betty was frightened and then she fainted. And there's the whole of it.

PARRIS: Child. Sit you down.

ABIGAIL: *(Quavering, as she sits.)* I would never hurt Betty. I love her dearly.

PARRIS: Now look you, child, your punishment will come in its time. But if you trafficked with spirits in the forest I must know it now, for surely my enemies will, and they will ruin me with it.

ABIGAIL: But we never conjured spirits.

PARRIS: Then why can she not move herself since midnight? This child is desperate! *(Abigail lowers her eyes.)* It must come out—my enemies will bring it out. Let me know what you done there. Abigail, do you understand that I have many enemies?

ABIGAIL: I have heard of it, uncle.

PARRIS: There is a faction that is sworn to drive me from my pulpit. Do you understand that?

ABIGAIL: I think so, sir.

PARRIS: Now then, in the midst of such disruption, my own household is discovered to be the very center of some obscene practice. Abominations are done in the forest—

ABIGAIL: It were sport, uncle!

PARRIS: *(Pointing at Betty.)* You call this sport? *(She lowers her eyes. He pleads.)* Abigail, if you know something that may help the doctor, for God's sake tell it to me. *(She is silent.)* I saw Tituba waving her arms over the fire when I came on you. Why was she doing that? And I heard a screeching and gibberish coming from her mouth. She were swaying like a dumb beast over that fire!

ABIGAIL: She always sings her Barbados songs, and we dance.

PARRIS: I cannot blink what I saw, Abigail, for my enemies will not blink it. I saw a dress lying on the grass.

ABIGAIL: *(Innocently.)* A dress?

PARRIS: *(It is very hard to say.)* Aye, a dress. And I thought I saw—someone naked running through the trees!

ABIGAIL: *(In terror.)* No one was naked! You mistake yourself, uncle!

PARRIS: *(With anger.)* I saw it! *(He moves from her. Then, resolved.)* Now tell me true, Abigail. And I pray you feel the weight of truth upon you, for now my ministry's at stake, my ministry and perhaps your cousin's life. Whatever abomination you have done, give me all of it now, for I dare not be taken unaware when I go before them down there.

ABIGAIL: There is nothin' more. I swear it, uncle.

PARRIS: *(Studies her, then nods, half convinced.)* Abigail, I have fought here three long years to bend these stiff-necked people to me, and now, just now when some good respect is rising for me in the parish, you compromise my very character. I have given you a home, child, I have put clothes upon your back—now give me upright answer. Your name is the town—it is entirely white, is it not?

ABIGAIL: *(With an edge of resentment.)* Why, I am sure it is, sir. There be no blush about my name.

PARRIS: *(To the point.)* Abigail, is there any other cause than you have told me, for your being discharged from Goody Proctor's service?

I have heard it said, and I tell you as I heard it, that she comes so rarely to the church this year for she will not sit so close to something soiled. What signified that remark?

ABIGAIL: She hates me, uncle, she must, for I would not be her slave. It's a bitter woman, a lying, cold, sniveling woman, and I will not work for such a woman!

PARRIS: She may be. And yet it has troubled me that you are now seven month out of their house, and in all this time no other family has ever called for your service.

ABIGAIL: They want slaves, not such as I. Let them send to Barbados for that. I will not black my face for any of them! *(With ill-concealed resentment at him.)* Do you begrudge my bed, uncle?

PARRIS: No—no.

ABIGAIL: *(In a temper.)* My name is good in the village! I will not have it said my name is soiled! Goody Proctor is a gossiping liar!
(Enter Mrs. Ann Putnam. She is a twisted soul of forty-five, a death-ridden woman, haunted by dreams.)

PARRIS: *(As soon as the door begins to open.)* No—no, I cannot have anyone. *(He sees her, and a certain deference springs into him, although his worry remains.)* Why, Goody Putnam, come in.

MRS. PUTNAM: *(Full of breath, shiny-eyed.)* It is a marvel. It is surely a stroke of hell upon you.

PARRIS: No, Goody Putnam, it is—

MRS. PUTNAM: *(Glancing at Betty.)* How high did she fly, how high?

PARRIS: No, no, she never flew—

MRS. PUTNAM: *(Very pleased with it.)* Why, it's sure she did. Mr. Collins saw her goin' over Ingersoll's barn, and come down light as bird, he says!

PARRIS: Now, look, Goody Putnam, she never— *(Enter Thomas Putnam, a well-to-do, hard-handed landowner, near fifty.)* Oh, good morning, Mr. Putnam.

PUTNAM: It is a providence the thing is out now! It is a providence.
(He goes directly to the bed.)

PARRIS: What's out, sir, what's—
(Mrs. Putnam goes to the bed.)

PUTNAM: *(Looking down at Betty.)* Why, her eyes is closed! Look you, Ann.

MRS. PUTNAM: Why, that's strange. *(To Parris.)* Ours is open.

PARRIS: *(Shocked.)* Your Ruth is sick?

MRS. PUTNAM: *(With vicious certainty.)* I'd not call it sick; the Devil's touch is heavier than sick. It's death, y'know, it's death drivin' into them, forked and hoofed.

PARRIS: Oh, pray not! Why, how does Ruth ail?

MRS. PUTNAM: She ails as she must—she never waked this morning, but her eyes open and she walks, and hears naught, sees naught, and cannot eat. Her soul is taken, surely.

(Parris is struck.)

PUTMAN: *(As though for further details.)* They say you've sent for Reverend Hale of Beverly?

PARRIS: *(With dwindling conviction now.)* A precaution only. He has much experience in all demonic arts, and I—

MRS. PUTNAM: He has indeed; and found a witch in Beverly last year, and let you remember that.

PARRIS: Now, Goody Ann, they only thought that were a witch, and I am certain there be no element of witchcraft here.

PUTNAM: No witchcraft: Now look you, Mr. Parris—

PARRIS: Thomas, Thomas, I pray you, leap not to witchcraft. I know that you—you least of all, Thomas, would ever wish so disastrous a charge laid upon me. We cannot leap to witchcraft. They will howl me out of Salem for such corruption in my house.

PUTNAM: *(At the moment he is intent upon getting Parris, for whom he has only contempt, to move toward the abyss.)* Mr. Parris, I have taken your part in all contention here, and I would continue; but I cannot if you hold back in this. There are hurtful, vengeful spirits layin' hands on these children.

PARRIS: But, Thomas, you cannot—

PUTNAM: Ann! Tell Mr. Parris what you have done.

MRS. PUTNAM: Reverend Parris, I have laid seven babies unbaptized in the earth. Believe me, sir, you never saw more hearty babies born. And yet, each would wither in my arms the very night of their birth. I have spoke nothin' but my heart has clamored intimations. And now, this year, my Ruth, my only, I see her turning strange. A secret child she has become this year, and shrivels like a sucking mouth were pullin' on her life too. And so I thought to send her to your Tituba—

PARRIS: To Tituba! What may Tituba—?

MRS. PUTNAM: Tituba knows how to speak to the dead, Mr. Parris.

PARRIS: Goody Ann, it is a formidable sin to conjure up the dead!

MRS. PUTNAM: I take it on my soul, but who else may surely tell us what person murdered my babies?

PARRIS: *(Horrified.)* Woman!

MRS. PUTNAM: They were murdered, Mr. Parris! And mark this proof! Mark it! Last night my Ruth were ever so close to their little spirits; I know it, sir. For how else is she stuck dumb now except some power of darkness would stop her mouth? It is a marvelous sign, Mr. Parris!

PUTNAM: Don't you understand it, sir? There is a murdering witch among us, bound to keep herself in the dark. *(Parris turns to Betty, a frantic terror rising in him.)* Let your names make of it what they will, you cannot blink it more.

PARRIS: *(To Abigail.)* Then you were conjuring spirits last night.

ABIGAIL: *(Whispering.)* Not I, sir, Tituba and Ruth.

PARRIS: *(Turns now, with new fear, and goes to Betty, looks down at her, and then gazing off.)* Oh, Abigail, what proper payment for my charity! Now I am undone.

PUTNAM: You are not undone! Let you take hold here. Wait for no one to charge you—declare it yourself. You have discovered witchcraft—

PARRIS: In my house? In my house, Thomas? They will topple me with this.

Picnic on the Battlefield

Fernando Arrabal

Comic

Setting: A battlefield, barbed wire, bombs sounding.

Scene: A battle is in full swing, a soldier lies on his stomach, bombs burst, then silence. . .

Zapo: A young soldier, dressed in gray uniform.

M. Tépan: His father.

MME. Tépan: His mother.

Zépo: An enemy soldier, dressed in green uniform.

(A battlefield. The stage is covered with barbed wire and sandbags. The battle is at its height. Rifle shots, exploding bombs, and machine guns can be heard. Zapo is along on the stage, flat on his stomach, hidden among the sandbags. He is very frightened. The sound of the fighting stops. Silence. Zapo takes a ball of wool and some needles out of a canvas workbag and starts knitting a pullover, which is already quite far advanced. The field telephone, which is by his side, suddenly starts ringing.)

ZAPO: Hallo, hallo. . . yes, Captain. . . yes, I'm the sentry of sector 47. . . Nothing new, Captain. . . Excuse me, Captain, but when's the fighting going to start again? And what am I supposed to do with the hand-grenades? Do I chuck them in front of me or behind me?. . . Don't get me wrong, I didn't mean to annoy you. . . Captain, I really feel terribly lonely, couldn't you send me someone to keep me company?. . . Even if it's only a nanny-goat? *(The Captain is obviously severely reprimanding him.)* Whatever you say, Captain, whatever you say.

(Zapo hangs up. He mutters to himself. Silence. Enter Monsieur and Madame Tépan, carrying baskets as it they are going to a picnic. They address their son, who has his back turned and doesn't see them come in.)

MONS. T: *(Ceremoniously.)* Stand up, my son, and kiss you mother on the brow. *(Zapo, surprised, gets up and kisses his mother very respectfully on the forehead. He is about to speak, but his father doesn't give him a chance.)* And now, kiss me.

ZAPO: But, dear Father and dear Mother, how did you dare to come all this way, to such a dangerous place? You must leave at once.

MONS. T: So you think you've got something to teach your father about war and danger, do you? All this is just a game to me. How many times—to take the first example that comes to mind—have I got off an underground train while it was still moving.

MME. T: We thought you must be bored, so we came to pay you a little visit. This war must be a bit tedious, after all.

ZAPO: It all depends.

MONS. T: I know exactly what happens. To start with you're attracted by the novelty of it all. It's fun to kill people, and throw hand-grenades about, and wear uniforms, you feel smart, but in the end you get bored stiff. You'd have found it much more interesting in my day. Wars were much more lively, much more highly coloured. And then, the best thing was that there were horses, plenty of horses. It was a real pleasure; if the Captain ordered us to attack, there we all were immediately, on horseback, in our red uniforms. It was a sight to be seen. And then there were the charges at the gallop, sword in hand, and suddenly you found yourself face-to-face with the enemy, and he was equal to the occasion too—with his horses—there were always horses, lots of horses, with their well-rounded rumps—in his highly-polished boots, and his green uniforms.

MME. T: No no, the enemy uniform wasn't green. It was blue. I remember distinctly that it was blue.

MONS. T: I tell you it was green.

MME. T: When I was little, how many times did I go out on to the balcony to watch the battle and say to the neighbour's little boy: "I bet you a gumdrop the blues win." And the blues were our enemies.

MONS. T: Oh well, you must be right then.

MME. T: I've always liked battles. As a child I always said that when I grew up I wanted to be a Colonel of dragoons. But my mother wouldn't hear of it, you know how she will stick to her principles at all costs.

MONS. T: Your mother's just a half-wit.

ZAPO: I'm sorry, but you really must go. You can't come into a war unless you're a soldier.

MONS. T: I don't give a damn, we came here to have a picnic with you in the country and to enjoy our Sunday.

MME. T: And I've prepared an excellent meal, too. Sausage, hard-boiled eggs—you know how you like them!—ham sandwiches, red wine, salad, and cakes.

ZAPO: All right, let's have it your way. But if the Captain comes he'll be absolutely furious. Because he isn't at all keen on us having visits when we're at the front. He never stops telling us: "Discipline and hand-grenades are what's wanted in a ware, not visits."

MONS. T: Don't worry, I'll have a few words to say to your Captain.

ZAPO: And what if we have to start fighting again?

MONS. T: You needn't think that'll frighten me, it won't be the first fighting I've seen. Now if only it was battles on horseback! Times have changed, you can't understand. *(Pause.)* We came by motor bike. No one said a word to us.

ZAPO: They must have thought you were the referees.

MONS. T: We had enough trouble getting through, though. What with all the tanks and jeeps.

MME. T: And do you remember the bottleneck that cannon caused, just when we got here?

MONS. T: You mustn't be surprised at anything in wartime, everyone knows that.

MME. T: Good, let's start our meal.

MONS. T: You're quite right, I feel as hungry as a hunter. It's the smell of gunpowder.

MME. T: We'll sit on the rug while we're eating.

ZAPO: Can I bring my rifle with me?

MME. T: You leave your rifle alone. It's not good manners to bring your rifle to table with you. *(Pause.)* But you're absolutely filthy, my boy. How on earth did you get into such a state? Let's have a look at your hands.

ZAPO: *(Ashamed, holding out his hands.)* I had to crawl about on the ground during the maneuvers.

MME. T: And what about your ears?

ZAPO: I washed them this morning.

MME. T: Well that's all right, then. And your teeth? *(He shows them.)* Very good. Who's going to give her little boy a great big kiss for cleaning his teeth so nicely? *(To her husband.)* Well, go on, kiss your son for cleaning his teeth so nicely. *(M Tépan kisses his son.)* Because, you know, there's one thing I will not have, and that's making fighting a war an excuse for not washing.

ZAPO: Yes, Mother. *(They eat.)*

MONS. T: Well, my boy, did you make a good score?

ZAPO: When?

MONS. T: In the last few days, of course.

ZAPO: Where?

MONS. T: At the moment, since you're fighting a war.

ZAPO: No, nothing much. I didn't make a good score. Hardly ever scored a bull.

MONS. T: Which are you best at shooting, enemy horses or soldiers?

ZAPO: No, not horses, there aren't any horses any more.

MONS. T: Well, soldiers then?

ZAPO: Could be.

MONS. T: Could be? Aren't you sure?

ZAPO: Well you see, I shoot without taking aim, *(Pause.)* and at the same time I say a Pater Noster for the chap I've shot.

MONS. T: You must be braver than that. Like your father.

MME. T: I'm going to put a record on. *(She puts a record on the gramophone—a pasodoble. All three are sitting on the ground, listening.)*

MONS. T: That really is music. Yes indeed, olé! *(The music continues. Enter an enemy soldier: Zépo. He is dressed like Zapo. The only difference is the colour of their uniforms. Zépo is in green and Zapo is in gray. Zépo listens to the music openmouthed. He is behind the family so they can't see him. The record ends. As he gets up Zapo discovers Zépo. Both put their hands up. M. and MME. Tépan look at them in surprise.)* What's going on? *(Zapo reacts—he hesitates. Finally, looking as if he's make up his mind, he points his rifle at Zépo.)*

ZAPO: Hands up! *(Zépo puts his hands up even higher, looking even more terrified. Zapo doesn't know what to do. Suddenly he goes quickly over to Zépo and touches him gently on the shoulder, like a child playing a game of "tag".)* Got you! *(To his father, very pleased.)* There we are! A prisoner!

MONS. T: Fine. And now what're you going to do with him?

ZAPO: I don't know, but, well, could be—they might make me a corporal.

MONS. T: In the meantime you'd better tie him up.

ZAPO: Tie him up? Why?

MONS. T: Prisoners always get tied up!

ZAPO: How?

MONS. T: Tie up his hands.

MME. T: Yes, there's no doubt about that, you must tie up his hands, I've always seen them do that.

ZAPO: Right. *(To the prisoner.)* Put your hands together, if you please.

ZEPO: Don't hurt me too much.

ZAPO: I won't.

ZEPO: Ow! You're hurting me.

MONS. T: Now now, don't maltreat your prisoner.

MME. T: Is that the way I brought you up? How many times have I told you that we must be considerate to our fellowmen?

ZAPO: I didn't do it on purpose. *(To Zépo.)* And like that, does it hurt?

ZEPO: No, it's all right like that.

MONS. T: Tell him straight out, say what you mean, don't mind us.

ZEPO: It's all right like that.

MONS. T: Now his feet.

ZAPO: His feet as well, whatever next?

MONS. T: Didn't they teach you the rules?

ZAPO: Yes.

MONS. T: Well then!

ZAPO: *(Very politely, to Zépo.)* Would you be good enough to sit on the ground, please?

ZEPO: Yes, but don't hurt me.

MME. T: You'll see, he'll take a dislike to you.

ZAPO: No he won't, no he won't. I'm not hurting you, am I?

ZEPO: No, that's perfect.

ZAPO: Papa, why don't you take a photo of the prisoner on the ground and me with my foot on his stomach?

MONS. T: Oh yes, that'd look good.

ZEPO: Oh no, not that!

MME. T: Say yes, don't be obstinate.

ZEPO: No. I said no, and no it is.

MME. T: But just a little teeny-weeny photo, what harm could that do you? And we could put it in the dining room, next to the life-saving certificate my husband won thirteen years ago.

ZEPO: No—you won't shift me.

ZAPO: But why won't you let us?

ZEPO: I'm engaged. And if she sees the photo one day, she'll say I don't know how to fight a war properly.

ZAPO: No she won't, all you'll need to say is that it isn't you, it's a panther.

MME. T: Come on, do say yes.

ZEPO: All right then. But only to please you.

ZAPO: Lie down flat. *(Zépo lies down. Zapo puts a foot on his stomach and grabs his rifle with a martial air.)*

MME. T: Stick your chest out a bit further.

ZAPO: Like this?

MME. T: Yes, like that, and don't breathe.

MONS. T: Try and look like a hero.

ZAPO: What d'you mean, like a hero?

MONS. T: It's quite simple; try and look like the butcher does when he's boasting about his successes with the girls.

ZAPO: Like this?

MONS. T: Yes, like that.

MME. T: The most important thing is to puff your chest out and not breathe.

ZEPO: Have you nearly finished?

MONS. T: Just be patient a moment. One. . . two. . . three.

ZAPO: I hope I'll come out well.

MME. T: Yes, you looked very martial.

MONS. T: You were fine.

MME. T: It makes me want to have my photo taken with you.

MONS. T: Now there's a good idea.

ZAPO: Right. I'll take it if you like

MME. T: Give me your helmet to make me look like a soldier.

ZEPO: I don't want any more photos. Even one's far too many.

ZAPO: Don't take it like that. After all, what harm can it do you?

ZEPO: It's my last word.

MONS. T: *(To his wife.)* Don't press the point, prisoners are always very sensitive. If we go on he'll get cross and spoil our fun.

ZAPO: Right, what're we going to do with him, then?

MME. T: We could invite him to lunch. What do you say?

MONS. T: I don't see why not.

ZAPO: *(To Zépo.)* Well, will you have lunch with us, then?

ZEPO: Er . . .

MONS. T: We brought a good bottle with us.

ZEPO: Oh well, all right then.

MME. T: Make yourself at home, don't be afraid to ask for anything you want.

ZEPO: All right.

MONS. T: And what about you, did you make a good score?

ZEPO: When?

MONS. T: In the last few days, of course.

ZEPO: Where?

MONS. T: At the moment, since you're fighting a war.

ZEPO: No, nothing much. I didn't make a good score, hardly ever scored a bull.

MONS. T: Which are you best at shooting? Enemy horses or soldiers?

ZEPO: No, not horses, there aren't any horses anymore.

MONS. T: Well, soldiers then?

ZEPO: Could be.

MONS. T: Could be? Aren't you sure?

ZEPO: Well you see. . . I shoot without taking aim *(Pause.)* and at the same time I say an Ave Maria for the chap I've shot.

ZAPO: An Ave Maria? I'd have thought you'd have said a Pater Noster.

ZEPO: No, always an Ave Maria. *(Pause.)* It's shorter.

MONS. T: Come come, my dear fellow, you must be brave.

MME. T: *(To Zépo.)* We can untie you if you like.

ZEPO: No, don't bother, it doesn't matter.

MONS. T: Don't start getting standoffish with us now. If you'd like us to untie you, say so.

MME. T: Make yourself comfortable.

ZEPO: Well, if that's how you feel, you can untie my feet, but it's only to please you.

MONS. T: Zapo, untie him. *(Zapo unties him.)*

MME. T: Well, do you feel better?

ZEPO: Yes, of course. I really am putting you to a lot of inconvenience.

MONS. T: Not at all, just make yourself at home. And if you'd like us to untie your hands you only have to say so.

ZEPO: No, not my hands, I don't want to impose upon you.

MONS. T: No no, my dear chap, no no. I tell you, it's no trouble at all.

ZEPO: Right. . . well then, untie my hands too. But only for lunch, eh? I don't want you to think that you give me an inch and I take a mile.

MONS. T: Untie his hands, son.

MME. T: Well, since our distinguished prisoner is so charming, we're going to have a marvelous day in the country.

ZEPO: Don't call me your distinguished prisoner, just call me your prisoner.

MME. T: Won't that embarrass you?

ZEPO: No no, not at all.

MONS. T: Well, I must say you're modest. *(Noise of aeroplanes.)*

ZAPO: Aeroplanes. They're sure to be coming to bomb us. *(Zapo and Zépo throw themselves on the sandbags and hide.) (To his parents.)* Take cover. The bombs will fall on you. *(The noise of the aeroplanes overpowers all the other noises. Bombs immediately start to fall. Shells explode very near the stage but not on it. A deafening noise. Zapo and Zépo are cowering down between the sandbags. M. Tépan goes on talking calmly to his wife, and she answers in the same unruffled way. We can't hear what they are saying because of the bombing. Mme. Tépan goes over to one of the baskets and takes an umbrella out of it. She opens it. M. and Mme. Tépan shelter under it as if it were raining. They are standing up. They shift rhythmically from one foot to the other and talk about their personal affairs. The bombing continues. Finally the aeroplanes go away. Silence. M. Tépan stretches an arm outside the umbrella to make sure that nothing more is falling from the heavens.)*

MONS. T: *(To his wife.)* You can shut your umbrella. *(Mme. Tépan does so. They both go over to their son and tap him lightly on the behind with the umbrella.)* Come on, out you come. The bombing's over. *(Zapo and Zépo come out of their hiding place.)*

ZAPO: Didn't you get hit?

MONS. T: What d'you think could happen to your father? *(Proudly.)* Little bombs like that! Don't make me laugh!

Impromptu

Tad Mosel
1961

Comic
Setting: A stage set of a nondescript room with odd angles surrounded by dárkness.

Winifred: Any age.
Tony: Any age.
Ernest: Any age.
Lora: Any age.

WINIFRED: Well, we're here. Somebody say something?

TONY: Is the curtain up?

WINIFRED: Yes.

TONY: But we can't see anything. It's like the end instead of the beginning. What's wrong?

ERNEST: That foot stage manager has forgotten to bring up the lights.

WINIFRED: Oh, no, Ernest, he didn't forget. There's something deliberate about this. I don't trust him.

LORA: You've got him wrong, Winifred. He was very nice. He wouldn't play tricks on us. Not him.

ERNEST: Just leave everything to me. I'll go out and talk to him.

TONY: But you can't!

ERNEST: Why not?

TONY: Don't you remember what he said? We're not to leave the stage until we have acted out the play.

ERNEST: He was just trying to be impressive. I've met his kind before. It's time he learned that actors are more important than stage managers.

TONY: He said it as if it were a law.

ERNEST: Well, I won't stand here in the dark. *(Shouting.)* Lights! Hey, you, out there—lights! *(There is a pause.)*

LORA: Maybe we're not as important as you think, Ernest. Let's just be quiet and wait.

TONY: Is there an audience out there?

WINIFRED: Yes, I can hear them soughing.

ERNEST: You can hear them what?

WINIFRED: Soughing, dear. Breathing heavily, as in sleep.

TONY: I feel as if I'm asleep, too.

WINIFRED: If everybody's going to feel things, we won't get anywhere at all. *(Pause.)*

TONY: Yes. Asleep and dreaming. I'm a child again. I can see myself being led into a room full of people. They laugh and tell me to dance. I don't know what to do. I can't dance. So I hop up and down on one foot. Up and down, up and down. Now they're applauding. I'm a great success. Why do I want to cry? *(There is a pause. The lights come on.)*

ERNEST: That's more like it!

LORA: I knew he'd take care of us! I knew it!

WINIFRED: The stage manager said, "Let there be light," and there was light.

TONY: But the lights won't stand still. They seem to be changing! It's worse than it was before.

WINIFRED: Why don't you go off in a corner and have that cry? *(Tony looks at her.)*

ERNEST: And look, Winifred, you were right. There is an audience!

WINIFRED: So there is!

LORA: Isn't it wonderful? Do you see them, Tony?

TONY: Yes, I see them.

ERNEST: They're waiting for us to begin.

TONY: Do they know what we're going to do? Has it been explained to them?

WINIFRED: I defy you to explain anything that is happening on this stage.

TONY: I was just asking a question.

LORA: Don't ask questions, Tony. You'll only make yourself unhappy. Ernest says they're waiting for us to begin. Well, let's begin!

ERNEST: Wait a minute, Lora. Tony may have a point there. I wonder if they do know what we're doing.

TONY: Maybe we ought to tell them.

WINIFRED: All right, then, tell them!

TONY: Me?

WINIFRED: Certainly. It's your bright idea.

ERNEST: I'm sure I could explain everything very lucidly.

WINIFRED: You probably could, Ernest. That's why I want him to do it.

TONY: I wouldn't know what to say.

WINIFRED: I know you wouldn't.

TONY: *(Naively, inquiringly.)* Are you making fun of me. Winifred?

WINIFRED: Whatever gave you that idea? *(She laughs lightly. Tony looks at her a moment, then he steps down to the edge of the stage and addresses the audience.)*

TONY: Ladies and gentlemen, we are here to—they say that every actor has a dream—a recurring dream—and he's on a stage and there's an audience, and—he doesn't know what the play is or what his lines are. That's the way it is with us. This afternoon. Maybe we are dreaming—maybe we're not really here—I don't know—

WINIFRED: You can stop right there! I know that I'm here, thank you. Irrevocably, unwillingly, disgustingly here.

ERNEST: *(With great tolerance.)* You'd better let me do it, Tony. *(To the audience.)* Ladies and gentlemen, an hour ago each of us received a message to report to this theater; there were jobs waiting for us. When we arrived, the stage manager told us we were to go on stage immediately, before an audience, and improvise a play—which we are about to do. *(To Tony.)* You see how easy it is?

TONY: Yes, it's easy to say what happened. You didn't say what it means. Who are we? Why are we here? That's the important thing.

WINIFRED: That young man has rocks in his head.

LORA: Would it help if we told them our names, Tony?

ERNEST: An excellent suggestion, Lora. I was about to think of it myself. *(He turns to the audience.)*

WINIFRED: Here we go!

ERNEST: *(To the audience.)* You have no programs, so you know nothing about us. My name is Ernest. I am returning to the stage after several successful seasons on the West Coast, where I scored personal successes in more than two-score films. Born of a theatrical family, I was reared in stage dressing rooms. At the age of five, I scored a personal success in—

TONY: Ernest, you're not explaining anything!

ERNEST: I'm telling them who I am!

TONY: But it's more than that!

LORA: Be quiet, Tony. This is very interesting. I love hearing about other people.

TONY: All right. I'll be quiet.

LORA: Go on, Ernest. *(Ernest begins to speak.)*

WINIFRED: *(Quickly.)* Why don't you be quiet, too, Ernest.

ERNEST: I haven't finished.

WINIFRED: Surely they know all about you, an actor of your standing. You don't want to bore them by telling them things they know, do you?

ERNEST: Well—no.

WINIFRED: Then sit down. *(He does so.)*

LORA: It's your turn, Winifred.

WINIFRED: *(Shrugs her shoulders, moves down to the edge of the stage, and addresses the audience.)* I'm Winifred. I have had rather a cloudy career as an actress. You may have seen me, but you won't remember. I usually play the leading lady's best friend. I don't like the theater because you can't trust it. This is an example of what I mean. Next. *(Indicating Lora.)*

LORA: *(After thinking a moment.)* My name used to be Loralee, but somebody said a long stage name is bad luck, so I shortened it to Lora. It hasn't helped me much, but I don't really mind. Perhaps I wasn't meant to be an actress. I think that's all. *(She steps back.)*

WINIFRED: Hold tight, everybody. *(With mock seriousness.)* Your turn, Tony.

TONY: I have nothing to say.

LORA: But, Tony, you've got to tell them something about yourself.

TONY: Why? None of you did. It's all so unreal. *(To the audience.)* Who are you? Why are you here? Did you come for escape, for enlightenment, for curiosity? Or were you, too, commanded?

ERNEST: We weren't any of us commanded!

TONY: Then what are we doing here? It's the only explanation! You're a celebrity—surely this is beneath you. Lora wasn't meant to be an actress. Winifred hates the stage.

WINIFRED: *(Cuttingly.)* And you're afraid, aren't you?

TONY: Yes, I'm afraid! There—I've told them something about myself!

WINIFRED: If that's all you've got to say, sit down. You were amusing for a while, but no longer. Soul-searching is the lowest form of entertainment.

ERNEST: I don't see why you're afraid, Tony. You ask what we're doing here, and the answer is simple. We are here to please the audience, and they are here to be pleased.

WINIFRED: Why can't you be like Ernest, Tony? He knows everything.

LORA: The stage manager's not going to like it if we don't do something soon.

ERNEST: Of course, Lora. *(To the audience.)* I hope you will be patient with outbursts of this sort, ladies and gentlemen. Naturally, some of us are a little confused. But don't worry, we're going to begin our play as soon as we've made a few preparations. You see, the stage manager gave us instructions—

WINIFRED: He wrote upon the tables the words of the Covenant—

ERNEST: Shut up, Winifred. *(To the audience.)* And I think it only fair to let you know what they are. First of all, our play will not end until he is completely satisfied with our performance.

WINIFRED: That's a cheerful thing to tell them. *(To the audience.)* He's one of those sour little men who never like anything.

LORA: You'd better stop talking that way about him, Winifred. He's right over there behind that wall; he can hear you. You might offend him.

WINIFRED: That's nothing compared to what he's done to me.

LORA: But he's so important, and, good. I think he's been very kind to us. I have great faith in him.

ERNEST: I thought you wanted to begin, Lora.

LORA: Oh—I'm sorry, Ernest.

ERNEST: *(To the audience.)* Secondly, we are not permitted to leave the stage until the play has ended. And last of all, our play is to be an imitation of life.

TONY: No, that's wrong! *(Ernest looks at him, annoyed.)* Well, it is. He didn't say that.

LORA: Are you sure, Tony?

TONY: I listened very carefully. He didn't say it was to be an imitation of life. It's supposed to be life.

LORA: Oh. I think maybe you're right.

TONY: That's one thing I know.

ERNEST: Ridiculous. Plays can be about life, like life, for life, or against it.

WINIFRED: The best ones are against it.

ERNEST: But they can't be life.

TONY: That's what he said.

LORA: Yes. Those were his very words.

WINIFRED: *(With a laugh.)* Well, Ernest, for once you're wrong. This is an unexpected pleasure.

ERNEST: I'm not wrong! I know that's what he said. I just wanted to
    see if you remembered.
WINIFRED: *(Enjoying herself.)* We did!
ERNEST: All right, all right. let's go.
LORA: What do we do?
WINIFRED: We smile and say brilliant things. *(To Ernest.)* How do you
    do, Lord Fiddle?
ERNEST: *(Catching on.)* How do you do, Lady Faddle?
WINIFRED: How nice of you to come.
ERNEST: How nice of you to let me.
WINIFRED: How nice of you to say so.
ERNEST: How nice!
WINIFRED: How charming!
ERNEST: How delightful!
WINIFRED: Curtain! *(She looks at the curtain, which does not move.)*
    Guess that wasn't enough.

The Odd Couple

Neil Simon
1966

Comic
Setting: Oscar's apartment.
Scene: Felix is staying with Oscar during this time of separation, and
  he and Oscar have invited the Pigeon sisters down for a social
  evening. Felix is chatting with them while Oscar makes the drinks.

Oscar Madison: Divorced, sportswriter, 40's, a slob.
Felix Ungar: Separated from his wife, 40's, neat, fussy, articulate.
Gwendolyn Pigeon: 20's – 30's, British, pert, lively.
Cecily Pigeon: Her sister, 20's – 30's, they share an apartment upstairs
  in the same building, British, cute, fun loving.

FELIX: Yes, I see. *(He laughs. They all laugh. Suddenly he shouts
  toward the kitchen.)* Oscar, where's the drinks?
OSCAR: *(Offstage.)* Coming! coming!
CECILY: What field of endeavor are you engaged in?
FELIX: I write the news for CBS.
CECILY: Oh! Fascinating!
GWENDOLYN: Where do you get your ideas from?
FELIX: *(He looks at her as though she's a Martian.)* From the news.
GWENDOLYN: Oh yes, of course. Silly me. . .
CECILY: Maybe you can mention Gwen and I in one of your news
  reports.
FELIX: Well, if you do something spectacular, maybe I will.
CECILY: Oh, we've done spectacular things but I don't think we'd
  want it spread all over the telly, do you, Gwen? *(They both laugh.)*
FELIX: *(He laughs too, then cries out almost for help.)* Oscar!
OSCAR: *(Offstage.)* Yeah, yeah!
FELIX: *(To the girls.)* It's such a large apartment, sometimes you have
  to shout.
GWENDOLYN: Just you two baches live here?
FELIX: Baches? Oh, bachelors! We're not bachelors. We're divorced.
  That is, Oscar's divorced. I'm *getting* divorced.
CECILY: Oh. Small world. We've cut the dinghy loose too, as they say.

GWENDOLYN: Well, you couldn't have a *better* matched foursome, could you?

FELIX: *(Smiles weakly.)* No, I suppose not.

GWENDOLYN: Although technically I'm a widow. I was divorcing my husband, but he died before the final papers came through.

FELIX: Oh, I'm awfully sorry. *(Sighs.)* It's a terrible thing, isn't it? Divorce.

GWENDOLYN: It can be—if you haven't got the right solicitor.

CECILY: That's true. Sometimes they can drag it out for months. I was lucky. Snip, cut and I was free.

FELIX: I mean it's terrible what it can do to people. After all, what is divorce? It's taking two happy people and tearing their lives completely apart. It's inhuman, don't you think so?

CECILY: Yes, it can be an awful bother.

GWENDOLYN: But of course, that's all water under the bridge now, eh? Er, I'm terribly sorry, but I think I've forgotten your name.

FELIX: Felix.

GWENDOLYN: Oh, yes, Felix.

CECILY: Like the cat. *(Felix takes his wallet from his jacket pocket.)*

GWENDOLYN: Well, the Pigeons will have to beware of the cat, won't they? *(She laughs.)*

CECILY: *(Nibbles on a nut from the dish.)* Mmm, cashews. Lovely.

FELIX: *(Takes a snapshot out of his wallet.)* This is the worst part of breaking up. *(He hands the picture to Cecily.)*

CECILY: *(Looks at it.)* Childhood sweethearts, were you?

FELIX: No, no. That's my little boy and girl. *(Cecily gives the picture to Gwendolyn, takes a pair of glasses from her purse and puts them on.)* He's seven, she's five.

CECILY: *(Looks again.)* Oh! Sweet.

FELIX: They live with their mother.

GWENDOLYN: I imagine you must miss them terribly.

FELIX: *(Takes back the picture and looks at it longingly.)* I can't stand being away from them. *(Shrugs.)* But—that's what happens with divorce.

CECILY: When do you get to see them?

FELIX: Every night. I stop there on my way home! Then I take them on the weekends, and I get them on holidays and July and August.

CECILY: Oh! Well, when is it that you miss them?

FELIX: Whenever I'm not there. If they didn't have to go to school so early, I'd go over and make them breakfast. They love my French toast.

GWENDOLYN: You're certainly a devoted father.

FELIX: It's Frances who's the wonderful one.

CECILY: She's the little girl?

FELIX: No. She's the mother. My wife.

GWENDOLYN: The one you're divorcing?

FELIX: *(Nods.)* Mm! She's done a terrific job bringing them up. They always look so nice. They're so polite. Speak beautifully. Never, "Yeah." Always, "Yes." They're such good kids. And she did it all. She's the kind of woman who,—Ah, what am I saying? You don't want to hear any of this. *(He puts the picture back in his wallet.)*

CECILY: Nonsense. You have a right to be proud. You have two beautiful children and a wonderful ex-wife.

FELIX: *(Containing his emotions.)* I know. I know. *(He hands Cecily another snapshot.)* That's her. Frances.

GWENDOLYN: *(Looking at the picture.)* Oh, she's pretty. Isn't she pretty, Cecy?

CECILY: Oh, yes. Pretty. A pretty girl. Very pretty.

FELIX: *(Takes the picture back.)* Thank you. *(Shows them another snapshot.)* Isn't this nice?

GWENDOLYN: *(Looks.)* There's no one in the picture.

FELIX: I know. It's a picture of our living room. We had a beautiful apartment.

GWENDOLYN: Oh yes. Pretty. Very pretty.

CECILY: Those are lovely lamps.

FELIX: Thank you! *(Takes the picture.)* We bought them in Mexico on our honeymoon. *(He looks at the picture again.)* I used to love to come home at night. *(He's beginning to break.)* That was my whole life. My wife, my kids—and my apartment. *(He breaks down and sobs.)*

CECILY: Does she have the lamps now too?

FELIX: *(Nods.)* I gave her everything. It'll never be like that again. Never! I—I— *(He turns his head away.)* I'm sorry. *(He takes out a handkerchief and dabs his eyes. Gwendolyn and Cecily look at each other with compassion.)* Please forgive me. I didn't mean to get emotional. *(Trying to pull himself together, he picks up a bowl from the side table and offers it to the girls.)* Would you like some potato chips? *(Cecily takes the bowl.)*

GWENDOLYN: You mustn't be ashamed. I think it's a rare quality in a man to be able to cry.

FELIX: *(Puts a hand over his eyes.)* Please. Let's not talk about it.

CECILY: I think it's sweet. Terribly, terribly sweet. *(She takes a potato chip.)*

FELIX: You're just making it worse.

GWENDOLYN: *(Teary-eyed.)* It's so refreshing to hear a man speak so highly of the woman he's divorcing! Oh, dear. *(She takes out her handkerchief.)* Now you've got me thinking about poor Sydney.

CECILY: Oh, Gwen. Please don't. *(She puts the bowl down.)*

GWENDOLYN: It was a good marriage at first. Everyone said so. Didn't they, Cecily? Not like you and George.

CECILY: *(The past returns as she comforts Gwendolyn.)* That's right. George and I were never happy. Not for one single, solitary day. *(She remembers her unhappiness, grabs her handkerchief and dabs her eyes. All three are now sitting with handkerchiefs at their eyes.)*

FELIX: Isn't this ridiculous?

GWENDOLYN: I don't know what brought this on. I was feeling so good a few minutes ago.

CECILY: I haven't cried since I was fourteen.

FELIX: Just let it pour out. It'll make you feel much better. I always do.

GWENDOLYN: Oh, dear; oh, dear; oh, dear. *(All three sit sobbing into their handkerchiefs. Suddenly Oscar bursts happily into the room with a tray full of drinks. He is all smiles.)*

OSCAR: *(Like a corny M.C.)* Is ev-rybuddy happy? *(Then he see the maudlin scene. Felix and the girls quickly try to pull themselves together.)* What the hell happened?

FELIX: Nothing! Nothing! *(He quickly puts his handkerchief away.)*

OSCAR: What do you mean, nothing? I'm gone three minutes and I walk into a funeral parlor. What did you say to them?

FELIX: I didn't say anything. Don't start in again, Oscar.

OSCAR: I can't leave you alone for five seconds. Well, if you really want to cry, go inside and look at your London broil.

FELIX: *(He rushes madly into the kitchen.)* Oh, my gosh! Why didn't you call me? I told you to call me.

OSCAR: *(Giving a drink to Cecily.)* I'm sorry girls. I forgot to warn you about Felix. He's a walking soap opera.

GWENDOLYN: I think he's the dearest thing I ever met.

CECILY: *(Taking the glass.)* He's so sensitive. So fragile. I just want to bundle him up in my arms and take care of him.

OSCAR: *(Holds out Gwendolyn's drink. At this, he puts it back down on the tray and takes a swallow from his own drink.)* Well, I think when he comes out of that kitchen you may have to. *(Sure enough, Felix comes out of the kitchen onto the landing looking like a wounded puppy. With a protective kitchen glove, he holds a pan with the exposed London broil. Black is the color of his true love.)*

FELIX: *(Very calmly.)* I'm going down to the delicatessen. I'll be right back.

OSCAR: *(Going to him.)* Wait a minute. Maybe it's not so bad. Let's see it.

FELIX: *(Show him.)* Here! Look! Nine dollars and thirty-four cents worth of ashes! *(Pulls the pan away. To the girls.)* I'll get some corned beef sandwiches.

OSCAR: *(Trying to get a look at it.)* Give it to me! Maybe we can save some of it.

FELIX: *(Holding it away from Oscar.)* There's nothing to save. It's all black meat. Nobody likes black meat!

OSCAR: Can't I even look at it?

FELIX: No, you can't look at it!

OSCAR: Why can't I look at it?

FELIX: If you looked at your watch before, you wouldn't have to look at the black meat now! Leave it alone! *(He turns to go back into the kitchen.)*

GWENDOLYN: *(Going to him.)* Felix! Can *we* look at it!

CECILY: *(Turning to him, kneeling on the couch.)* Please? *(Felix stops in the kitchen doorway. He hesitates for a moment. He likes them. Then he turns and wordlessly holds the pan out to them. Gwendolyn and Cecily inspect it wordlessly, and then turn away sobbing quietly. To Oscar.)* How about Chinese food!

OSCAR: A wonderful idea.

GWENDOLYN: I've got a better idea. Why don't we just make potluck in the kitchen?

OSCAR: A *much* better idea.

FELIX: I used up all the pots! *(He crosses to the love seat and sits, still holding the pan.)*

CECILY: Well, then we can eat up in *our* place. We have tons of Horn and Hardart's.

OSCAR: *(Gleefully.)* That's the best idea I ever heard.

GWENDOLYN: Of course it's awfully hot up there. You'll have to take off your jackets.

OSCAR: *(Smiling.)* We can always open up a refrigerator.

CECILY: *(Gets her purse from the couch.)* Give us five minutes to get into our cooking things. *(Gwendolyn gets her purse from the couch.)*

OSCAR: Can't you make it four? I'm suddenly starving to death. *(The girls are crossing to the door.)*

GWENDOLPH: Don't forget the wine.

OSCAR: How could I forget the wine?

CECILY: And a corkscrew.

OSCAR: *And* a corkscrew.

GWENDOLPH: And Felix.

OSCAR: No, I won't forget Felix.

CECILY: Ta, ta!

OSCAR: Ta, ta!

GWENDOLYN: Ta, ta!

(The girls exit.)

OSCAR: *(Throws a kiss at the closed door.)* You bet your sweet little crumpets, "Ta, Ta!" *(He wheels around beaming and quickly gathers up the corkscrew from the bar, and picks up the wine and the records.)* Felix, I love you. You've just overcooked us into one hell of a night. Come on, get the ice bucket. Ready or not, here we come. *(He runs to the door.)*

FELIX: *(Sitting motionless.)* I'm not going!

OSCAR: What?

FELIX: I said I'm not going.

OSCAR: *(Crossing to Felix.)* Are you out of your mind? Do you know what's waiting for us up there? You've just been invited to spend the evening in a two-bedroom hothouse with the Coo-Coo Pigeon Sisters! What do you mean you're not going?

FELIX: I don't know how to talk to them. I don't know what to say. I already told them about my brother in Buffalo. I've used up my conversation.

OSCAR: Felix, they're crazy about you. They told me! One of them wants to wrap you up and make a bundle out of you. You're doing better than I am! Get the ice bucket. *(He starts for the door.)*

FELIX: Don't you understand? I cried! I cried in front of two women.

OSCAR: *(Stops.)* And they *loved* it! I'm thinking of getting hysterical. *(Goes to the door.)* Will you get the ice bucket?

FELIX: But why did I cry? Because I felt guilty. Emotionally I'm still tied to Frances and the kids.

OSCAR: Well, untie the knot just for tonight, will you!

'Dentity Crisis

Christopher Durang
1979

Comic
Setting: The Living Room.
Scene: Jane is lying on the couch. First, an offstage voice, then Edith comes home carrying a bag of groceries and a dress, badly stained with blood, in a dry cleaners' plastic bag.

Edith: The mother, fairly insane, 40's.
Jane: The daughter, claims to have attempted suicide—wearing a disheveled bathrobe, late teens.
Robert: The son.
Mr. Summers: Jane's psychologist.

EDITH: No one in our family has ever attempted suicide before now, and no one since either. It's a sign of defeat, and no one should do it. You know what I think? Jane? Jane?

JANE: What?

EDITH: I don't think you ever attempted suicide at all. That's what I think.

JANE: How do you explain the stains then?

EDITH: I don't. *(Laughs merrily.)* I always say stains will explain themselves, and if they don't then there's nothing can be done about it. *(Edith empties the grocery bag on the table. It is filled with loose potato chips, which Edith playfully arranges as if it is some sort of food sculpture.)*

JANE: I did attempt suicide.

EDITH: No, dear, you didn't. A daughter doesn't contradict her mother.

VOICE: Cuckoo, cuckoo.

JANE: Did you hear the voice of my therapist just then?

EDITH: No dear. *(Listens.)* Ah, now I hear it. He's saying what a fine daughter I have.
(Enter Robert.)

ROBERT: Mother! I'm home.

EDITH: Oh, Jane, it's your brother.

(Edith and Robert kiss passionately and long. Jane is very upset and rips up the plastic covering on her dress.)

ROBERT: Darling, darling.

EDITH: Oh, Dwayne, this is mad. We've got to stop meeting like this. Your father will find out.

JANE: I'll tell him!

EDITH: Jane, you'd never do anything like that.

ROBERT: I'm made for you. I find you . . . exciting. *(They kiss.)*

EDITH: *(Looking off.)* Quick, there's the postman. Act busy.
(Robert and Edith smash the potato chips on the table with their fists, then they brush the crushed chips into a wastebasket with a little broom.)

EDITH: There, he's gone.

ROBERT: *(Holding her.)* Oh, why must you taunt me? Let's get married.

EDITH: We have different blood types.

ROBERT: Oh, Mother, I love you. *(They embrace.)*

EDITH: Oh, my god. Here comes your father.
(Robert, with no change of costume—and without exiting or re-entering—becomes the father.)

ROBERT: Edith, what are you doing?

EDITH: Oh, Arthur, I was just finishing off my morning shopping.

ROBERT: And how is our daughter?

JANE: You're not my father.

EDITH: Don't contradict your father. You love your father, Jane.

JANE: He's my brother.

EDITH: Dwayne is your brother, dear.

ROBERT: Has she been seeing that psychologist of hers?

EDITH: Well, not socially.

ROBERT: Good. *(Shouting at Jane.)* I don't ever want to hear of you dating a psychologist again.

JANE: I never have!

EDITH: Of course not, dear. You obey your father. You're a good daughter.

ROBERT: Not like some I could mention.

EDITH: No.

ROBERT: I could mention some.

EDITH: You could.

ROBERT: I could. I will.

EDITH: Now?

ROBERT: Now. Frances, Lucia, Henrietta, Charmant, Dolores, Loretta, and Peggy.

EDITH: Listen to your father, Jane.

ROBERT: No more of this slashing your thighs, young lady. I don't think that psychologist would ever go out with you again if he knew you were slashing your thighs.

JANE: I don't go out with my psychologist.

EDITH: Of course you don't. He has a wife and sixteen children. You're a good girl. You listen to your father.

JANE: *(To Robert.)* You're not my father.

EDITH: Jane, you know he's your father.

JANE: If you're my father, you must be close to fifty.

ROBERT: I am close to fifty.

JANE: Let me see your driver's license.

ROBERT: Here. *(Hands it to her.)*

JANE: *(Reads it.)* This says you're fifty. How did you get them to put that down?

EDITH: The truth is the truth no matter how you look at it, Jane.

JANE: How come you don't look fifty?

EDITH: Your father never looked his age. Most girls would be pleased that their father looked young.

ROBERT: Most girls are pleased.

EDITH: Jane's pleased you look young, aren't you, Jane? Don't you think Arthur looks young for his age, Grandad?

ROBERT: Eh? What?

EDITH: *(Shouting.)* Don't you think Arthur looks young, Grandad!

ROBERT: *(Smiling senilely.)* Yes, yes. Breakfast.

EDITH: Poor Grandad can't hear a thing.

JANE: Where's Father?

EDITH: Isn't he here? That's funny. I didn't hear the door close.

JANE: Grandad, Mother is having an affair with Dwayne!

ROBERT: *(Not hearing.)* What?

EDITH: He can't hear you. Besides you mustn't make up stories. I don't. Oh, listen to the doorbell. *(Bell rings. Enter Mr. Summers, the psychologist and the previous offstage voice.)* Why, Jane, it's your psychologist. *(To Summers.)* I recognized you from your photos. Jane has plastered her walls with your pictures. I don't know why.

SUMMERS: How do you do? You must be Jane's mother.

EDITH: Yes. I'm Edith Fromage. You probably saw my photo in the papers when you were a little boy. I invented cheese in France in the early portion of the century.

SUMMERS: In what way did you invent cheese?

EDITH: In every way. And this is my son, Dwayne Fromage.

ROBERT: How do you do, sir?

SUMMERS: How do you do? I didn't realize Jane's last name was Fromage.

EDITH: It isn't. I had Jane by another husband. A Mr. Carrot.

JANE: My name isn't Carrot.

EDITH: That's right, dear. It's *Jane* Carrot. *(Whispers.)* Jane's very over-wrought today. The stains wouldn't come out of her dress.

SUMMERS: Oh, I'm sorry.

EDITH: You think you're sorry. You should have seen the woman at the cleaners. I thought we'd have to chain her to the floor.

ROBERT: Perhaps Mr. Summers is hungry.

EDITH: Oh, forgive me. *(Offers him wastebasket of crushed chips.)*

SUMMERS: No thank you.

EDITH: Then how about some entertainment? Jane, play the piano for Mr. Summers.

JANE: I don't play the piano.

EDITH: Of course you do. I've heard you many times. You play very well.

JANE: I've never played the piano.

EDITH: Jane, Mr. Summers would enjoy your playing. Please play.

JANE: I don't know how!

EDITH: *(Angry.)* How do you know? Have your ever tried?

JANE: No.

EDITH: There. You see then. *(To Summers.)* Cello is her real instrument, but we never talk about it.

ROBERT: Please play, Jane.

(Jane walks hesitatingly to the piano, sits. Pause. Makes some noise on keyboard, obviously can't play, starts to cry.)

JANE: I don't know how to play piano!

EDITH: But you do! Why else would we have one? No one else in the house plays.

JANE: I don't remember taking lessons.

EDITH: You probably forgot due to all this strain. *(To Summers.)* You talk to her. She seems in a state. *(To Robert.)* Come on, dear. Call me if you want me, Mr. Summers.

(Robert and Edith kiss, then exit.)

JANE: *(At piano.)* I don't *remember* taking piano lessons.

SUMMERS: Maybe you've repressed it. *(Sits.)* My wife gave me the message about your attempting suicide. Why did you do it, Jane?

JANE: I can't stand it. My mother says she's invented cheese and I start to think maybe she has. There's a man living in the house and I'm not sure whether he's my brother or my father or my grandfather. I can't be sure of anything anymore.

SUMMERS: You're talking quite rationally now. And your self-doubts are a sign of health. The truly crazy person never thinks he's crazy. Now explain to me what led up to your attempted suicide.

JANE: Well, a few days ago I woke up and I head this voice saying, "It wasn't enough."

SUMMERS: Did you recognize the voice?

JANE: Not at first. But then it started to come back to me. When I was eight years old, someone brought me to a theater with lots of other children. We had come to see a production of *Peter Pan*. And I remember something seemed wrong with the whole production, odd things kept happening. Like when the children would fly, the ropes would keep breaking and the actors would come thumping to the ground and they'd have to be carried off by the stagehands. There seemed to be an unlimited supply of understudies to take the children's places, and then *they'd* fall to the ground. And then the crocodile that chases Captain Hook seemed to be a real crocodile, it wasn't an actor, and at one point it fell off the stage, crushing several children in the front row.

SUMMERS: What happened to the children?

JANE: Several understudies came and took their places in the audience. And from scene to scene Wendy seemed to get fatter and fatter until finally by the second act she was immobile and had to be moved with a cart.

SUMMERS: Where does the voice fit in?

JANE: The voice belonged to the actress playing Peter Pan. You remember how in the second act Tinkerbell drinks some poison that Peter's about to drink, in order to save him? And then Peter turns to the audience and he says that Tinkerbell's going to die because not enough people believe in fairies, but that if everybody in the audience claps real hard to show that they do believe in fairies, then maybe Tinkerbell won't die. And so then all the children started to clap. We clapped very hard and very long. My palms hurt and even started to bleed I clapped so hard. Then suddenly the actress playing Peter Pan turned to the audience and she said, "That wasn't enough. You didn't clap hard enough. Tinkerbell's dead." Uh . . . well, and . . . then everyone started to cry. The actress stalked offstage and refused to continue with the play, and they finally had to bring down the curtain. No one could see anything through all the tears, and the ushers had to come help the children up the aisles and out into the street. I don't think any of us were ever the same after that experience.

SUMMERS: How do you think this affected you?

JANE: Well it certainly turned me against theater; but more damagingly, I think it's warped my sense of life. You know—nothing seems worth trying if Tinkerbell's just going to die.

SUMMERS: And so you wanted to die like Tinkerbell.

JANE: Yes.

SUMMERS: *(With importance.)* Jane. I have to bring my wife to the hospital briefly this afternoon, so I have to go now. But I want you to hold on, and I'll check back later today. I think you're going to be all right, but I think you need a complete rest; so when I come back we'll talk about putting you somewhere for a while.

JANE: You mean committing me.

SUMMERS: No. This would just be a rest home, a completely temporary thing. Tinkerbell just needs her batteries recharged, that's all. Now you just make your mind a blank, and I'll be back as soon as I can.

JANE: Thank you. I'll try to stay quiet 'til you return.
(Enter Edith.)

EDITH: Oh, you're leaving. Won't you have some of my cheese first?

SUMMERS: Thank you, Mrs. Fromage, but I have to go now. Please see to it that your daughter stays quiet.

EDITH: Oh, you can rely on me.

SUMMERS: *(To Jane.)* Chin up. *(Exits.)*

EDITH: Jane, dear, I've brought you some sheet music. I thought maybe if you got settled on where middle C was, it might all come back to you.

JANE: Please leave me alone.

EDITH: I don't know why you've turned against the piano.

JANE: *(Suddenly sharp.)* Well you know my one love was always the cello.

EDITH: *(Realizing Jane is being devious.)* A good daughter does not speak to her mother in that tone. I'm sure you didn't mean that. When you are ready to play the piano, let me know. Oh, there's the doorbell.

(Bell rings. Enter Robert.)

ROBERT: *(French accent.)* Ah, Madame Fromage.

EDITH: Oh, Count. How nice. I don't think you've met my daughter. Jane, dear, this is the Count de Rochelay, my new benefactor.

ROBERT: How do you do, Mademoiselle? My people and I are most anxious for your mother to make a comeback. All the time, the people of France say, whatever happened to Edith Fromage who gave us cheese? It is time she left her solitude and returned to the spotlight and invented something new. And so I come to your charming Mama and I convince her to answer the call of the people of France.

EDITH: Jane, say hello to the count.

JANE: Hello.

EDITH: *(Whispers.)* You have to forgive her. She's sulking because she's forgotten how to play the piano.

(He embraces her.)

ROBERT: Madame Fromage, I love you!

EDITH: Please! I don't want my son or husband to hear you!

ROBERT: *(Whispers.)* Madame Fromage, I love you. *(Kisses her.)*

EDITH: Not now. First I must invent something new. Have you the ingredients?

(Robert has a paper bag. Edith takes out a family-size loaf of Wonder Bread and makes a stack of six slices. Then she takes a banana from the bag and rams it into the center of the stack of bread.)

ROBERT: Bravo, Madame!

EDITH: Voila! I have invented banana bread.

ROBERT: Bravo! Let us make love to celebrate!

EDITH: Please, my son or husband might hear.

ROBERT: *(Deaf.)* Eh?

EDITH: Shush, Grandad. Go down to the cellar.

ROBERT: Madame Fromage, France will thank you for this.

EDITH: And I will thank France. It is moments like these when I feel most alive.

(Robert carries Edith off.)

ROBERT: Vive Madame Fromage!

(Jane at piano hits middle C several times. Lights dim, slowly to black. As they do, the light of a flashlight flashes about the stage as Tinkerbell.)

EDITH'S VOICE: *(Offstage, as Peter Pan.)* Tink are you all right, Tink? Tinkerbell?

(Light of Tinkerbell starts to blink on and off.)

JANE: Don't die!

(Jane's solitary clapping is heard in darkness. Tinkerbell's light goes off.)

EDITH'S VOICE: *(Off, in darkness.)* That wasn't enough. She's dead. Tinkerbell's dead.

The Sisters Rosensweig

Wendy Wasserstein

1993

Comic

Setting: Sara's apartment in Queen Anne's Gate, London.

Scene: Pfeni enters from her apartment, which is downstairs. Geoffrey follows. She has returned home to help celebrate Sara's birthday.

Pfeni: 40, a journalist and travel writer.
Geoffrey: 40's, her boyfriend, a musical theater director in London.
Merv: A faux furrier, 40's – 50's.
Sara: The eldest sister, 54—a banker in London—brilliant, divorced with a teen-aged daughter.

GEOFFREY: The problem with you, Pfeni darling, is that you just don't like women very much.

PFENI: That's not true.

GEOFFREY: Of course it is, luv. Think about it. Women make you feel competitive and insecure.

PFENI: That's nonsense, Geoffrey.

GEOFFREY: It's all right, darling. You can't like everyone.

PFENI: And I suppose that you, on the other hand, are open to people of all sexes, race, and color.

GEOFFREY: (*Starts to sing.*) "I am everyday people!" Sly and the Family Stone, 1969.

PFENI: Sara says we should stop seeing each other. She says she and I should grow old together.

GEOFFREY: Pfeni my luv, all you've talked about since you've arrived here is Sara. How guilty you feel that she was ill. How guilty you feel that she's alone. How much you love her. How much you can't bear to be around her. How much you want her praise. How little you care for her opinions.

PFENI: That's not true.

GEOFFREY: All I know is that whenever you're around that woman, you tell me we have to stop seeing each other. My darling, we hardly ever do see each other. I'm always in rehearsal and you're in Timbuktu half the year. It's a bloody brilliant relationship. *(Kisses her on the forehead.)*

PFENI: Oh my God, my life is stuck. "I've forgotten the Italian for window."

GEOFFREY: Very good! *Three Sisters*, Act III. Now, Pfeni darling, see how worthwhile it's been knowing me. If not for me, you'd still think that *Uncle Vanya* was a Neil Simon play about his pathetic uncle in the Bronx.

PFENI: And now instead I've had a three-year relationship with an internationally renowned director and bisexual.

GEOFFREY: You left out botanist. I read botany at Cambridge. And I also put that "f" betwixt your name. If not for me, you'd be plain and simple Penny Rosensweig.

PFENI: Thank you. I have your "f" to keep me warm.

GEOFFREY: For Christ's sake, Pfeni, if you want to find unconditional love, have a baby. Adopt a red and fuzzy brood of them. Better yet, have artificial insemination. *(Lifts up a water glass.)* "Hello darling, this is Daddy. Say good morning to your daddy." "Morning Daddy." Or you could become a lesbian. Most of the really interesting women I know are lesbians.

PFENI: Just tell me one thing? What do you still get out of this?

GEOFFREY: T-shirts from all over the world. Would I be sporting Sunset in Penang if not for you? I've been meaning to ask you, darling, where is Penang?

PFENI: Malaysia. Somerset Maugham lived there.

GEOFFREY: This is what's so wonderful about dating a nice American Jewish girl! You're all so well versed in British colonial history. *(Embraces her.)* Pfeni, my luv, trust me. I am still very happy with you.

PFENI: You wouldn't like to meet a nice man?

GEOFFREY: I meet nice men all the time. I'm a director.

PFENI: I mean some nice man for you to come home to.

GEOFFREY: I've already done that, my darling, and he left me for Rum-Tum-Tugger.

PFENI: Who?

GEOFFREY: Jordan left me for that chorus boy from *Cats*.

PFENI: But that was ages ago.

GEOFFREY: Exactly. And then I met you at the ballet, and Jordan became England's hottest flatware designer. He's soon to be knighted "Sir Cutlery."

PFENI: But . . .

GEOFFREY: But what? Do you want to know if I have my eye on any-one in my show? Is it true what they say about *The Scarlet Pimpernel?* My darling, I am committed. I've signed exclusively with you. Have I told you I've been offered an animated *Fawlty Towers?* I could fit it in next season between *The Duchess of Malfi* and *Oklahoma!* On the other hand, my film career is nowhere near where it should be. Unfortunately, movies do mean endur-ing extended time in Los Angeles. Why don't you have your film capital somewhere more civilized, like *Des Moines? (Pronounces it as if it were French.)*

PFENI: Where?

GEOFFREY: Des Moines, Idaho.

PFENI: It's Des Moines. And it's in Iowa. I'll see what I can do.

GEOFFREY: Pfeni, my angel, I wish you knew what a gorgeous person you are.

PFENI: My sister is gorgeous. I'm not.

GEOFFREY: My darling. I can't waste any more time listening to your negativity and self-criticism. You're becoming almost as self-absorbed as I am. Besides, I'm expecting two hundred homeless people who live under Charing Cross Station to arrive here in just a few.

PFENI: To arrive here? At Sara's house?

GEOFFREY: Well, it's not all two hundred of them, actually. It's closer to a small delegation, and I told them to be certain to ring the downstairs bell and not Sara's.

PFENI: That was thoughtful!

GEOFFREY: Tell me what you think, my darling. I have an idea to do this year's homeless benefit at The National as a sort of story the-ater. I want to hear their brilliant voices telling the simple human tale of their survival. The theater's in danger of becoming hope-lessly elitist. *(The bell rings.)* What's that? *(The bell rings again.)*

PFENI: The bell.

GEOFFREY: But that's not the downstairs bell.

PFENI: No.

GEOFFREY: What should we do?

PFENI: Let's invite your delegation to stay for Sara's birthday party.

(The bell rings again.)

GEOFFREY: I can't allow these people into Sara's house. They're desperate. They take things. They deserve to kill us for centuries of oppression.

PFENI: Relax. Go downstairs. I'll tell them to meet you down there.

GEOFFREY: Brilliant.

(Geoffrey exits to the downstairs service entrance. Pfeni answers the door. Merv Kant, a fifty-eight-year-old American in a wrinkled linen suit, stands in the door. He is immediately warm, but surprisingly sexy. He carries a Turnbull & Asser bag.)

MERV: Hi!

PFENI: Mr. Duncan said he'd prefer to meet you and your group downstairs. There's another entrance down the back.

MERV: My group? You mean my combo?

PFENI: You're not English.

MERV: No, and neither are you.

PFENI: Do you live under Charing Cross Station?

MERV: I live over Charing Cross Station, at the Savoy Hotel. May I leave this for Geoff. *(Enters.)*

PFENI: Who?

MERV: I like to call him Geoff. Drives him crazy. He tells me, "Murf, only someone who rhymes with surf can call me Geoff."

PFENI: Your name is "Murf the Surf?"

MERV: How do you do.

PFENI: Pfeni Rosensweig. I'll get him for you.

MERV: And tell him I went to the Turnbull sale and found the purple shirts we've been searching for. Honey, when I saw that shirt, I was kvelling—like I just discovered the double helix. *(Pfeni knocking on the door.)* Murf is here to say he just discovered the double helix.

(Geoffrey comes out.)

MERV: Geoffrey, mazeltov, you've finally come out of the closet.

GEOFFREY: What ho, Sir Murf?

MERV: What ho! *(Begins to sing and dance around the room.)*

I found the shirt at Turnbull's-a-nanny-nanny-no.

I found the purple shirt at Turnbull's-a-nanny-nanny-no.

And I got one for you and I got one for me.

(Gives Geoffrey the package.)

A-nanny-nanny-no. *(Merv and Geoffrey sing and dance.)*

I found the shirts at Turnbull's. A-nanny-nanny-no!

(They finish in a big finale.)

MERV: *(To Pfeni.)* Honey, I would have gotten one for you but I didn't know your size.

GEOFFREY: How did you find me here?

MERV: You left a message to meet you at seven.

GEOFFREY: But what about the homeless?

MERV: What about the homeless?

GEOFFREY: I believe I told them to meet me where I thought I'd be seeing you.

MERV: Where's that?

GEOFFREY: Drinks at the Savoy at seven. *(Grabs his coat.)* Pfeni, offer Sir Murf a drink, and I'll try to head them off. *(Kisses her.)* Much love, angel. *(Exits.)*

MERV: So.

PFENI: So.

MERV: Would I like a drink?

PFENI: Would you?

MERV: Not really. Whose house am I in?

PFENI: My sister, Sara's.

MERV: It's very nice. What does her husband do?

PFENI: My sister is the managing director of the Hong Kong/Shanghai Bank Europe.

MERV: Sounds like a smart girl.

PFENI: How did you meet Geoffrey?

MERV: Mutual friends. How did you meet Geoffrey?

PFENI: I sat next to him at *Giselle*, and he asked me to be the mother of his children.

(Sara enters, wearing an apron over pants and a sweater.)

SARA: Pfeni! Who's here? Hello.

MERV: Hi. Hello. Merv Kant.

PFENI: This is an American friend of Geoffrey's.

MERV: And you must be Pfeni's younger sister.

SARA: Ha ha ha. Are you here on holiday?

MERV: I was in Budapest last week with the American Jewish Congress.

SARA: Yes, well, Budapest seems to be quite popular recently.

MERV: And on Sunday we go to Ireland to have brunch with the Rabbi of Dublin.

SARA: Fascinating! Where's your friend Geoffrey?

MERV: He's stood me up for the homeless under Charing Cross Station.

SARA: Yes, they also seem to be quite popular these days.

PFENI: Well, I'd better go meet Tom and Tessie. Would you like to share a taxi, Merv?

MERV: *(Looks at Sara.)* No, I'm fine.

SARA: Pfeni, if you're only meeting Tessie now, when will you be home?

PFENI: Soon.

SARA: But you're already two hours late.

PFENI: Sara, doll, soon is soon. *(With accent.)* Now that was really New York! *(Exits, leaving the door wide open.)*

(Sara stands by the door, waiting for Merv to exit voluntarily.)

MERV: Your sister was just offering me a drink. Some cold water would be perfect. Thanks. *(Sara goes to get him a drink.)* So you and your sister are from New York?

SARA: My sister is a traveler, and I live right here in Queen Anne's Gate. Here's your water, Mr. Kant.

MERV: Thanks. Your sister tells me you're a brilliant woman.

SARA: I have a few opinions about European common currency. That hardly makes me brilliant.

MERV: Well, you're the first Jewish woman I've met to run a Hong Kong bank.

SARA: I'm the first woman to run a Hong Kong bank, Mr. Kant.

MERV: It used to be Kantlowitz. You're looking at your watch. Would you prefer that I leave?

SARA: I'm just wondering what time my daughter's coming home.

MERV: Relax. I have three children who never came home and they're all fine now. My oldest, Kip, is a semiotics professor at Boston University. That means he screens *Hiroshima, Mon Amour* once a week. The other boy is a radiologist in North Carolina, Chapel Hill, and my baby, Eva, is a forest ranger in Israel. That means she works for the parks department in Haifa. And your daughter?

SARA: We're hoping she'll be up at Oxford next year.

MERV: She wants to stay here for school?

SARA: From what we've heard about the States now, I think it's wise.

MERV: Tell me what "we've heard."

SARA: It's conventional wisdom, really.

MERV: Really?

SARA: Well, obviously what you have is a society in transition. You've got an industrial economy that is rapidly being transformed into a transactional one. And that's exacerbated by a growing disenfranchised class, decaying inner cities, and a bankrupt educational system. Don't misunderstand me, Mr. Kantlowitz. . .

MERV: Kant, like the philosopher.

SARA: In many ways America is a brilliant country. But it's become as class-driven a society as this one.

MERV: So you're a hot-shot Jewish lady banker who's secretly a Marxist.

SARA: This is hardly the time to be a Marxist.

MERV: But your sister's right. You are a brilliant woman!

SARA: Excuse me, Mr. Kant, I really should check on my roast.

MERV: Are we having roast beef and Yorkshire pudding? Blimey, I've been hoping for a good old-fashioned, high-cholesterol English meal. I had a banger for breakfast this morning.

SARA: *(Extends her hand.)* It was lovely to meet you, Mr. Kant.

MERV: Whenever I come here, I treat myself to one blow-out meal at Simpson's in the Strand.

SARA: Only Americans eat there. It's a tourist trap.

MERV: That's why I was so delighted when Geoffrey invited me here for dinner tonight.

SARA: Geoffrey did what?

MERV: And I said to myself, "Merv, this way you can avoid that tourist trap Simpson's in the Strand and have a good old-fashioned Anglo-Saxon Jewish meal."

SARA: How intimate are you with Geoffrey, Mr. Kant?

MERV: I'd say we have a close working relationship.

SARA: Oh?

MERV: When Geoffrey's musical *The Scarlet Pimpernel* came to New York last season, there arose during rehearsal an emergency need for signature chartreuse pelts. And while the British production blithely used dyed scarlet fox, the anti-fur lobby in New York pressed into early action. So my services were recommended by Geoffrey's producer, Mr. Bernard Lasker. And that was the beginning of a very beautiful friendship.

SARA: So you're a show biz furrier.

MERV: I was a show biz and novelty furrier. Now I am the world leader in synthetic animal protective covering. And Sara, to this day my one regret is that while the anti-furries were still picketing I didn't have Geoffrey sign over to me a quarter percent of that Pumpernickel. Next year I could be playing in Tokyo, Reykjavik, and forty-seven other cities worldwide.

SARA: Mr. Kant . . .

MERV: Please call me Merv. You call me Mr. Kant and I think I'm your high school principal. My hunch is we're roughly the same age.

SARA: Mr. Merv, today is my fifty-fourth birthday.

MERV: We are the same age. Roughly.

SARA: My sister Pfeni has flown here from Bombay, and my other sister, Gorgeous, is due in shortly from Newton, Massachusetts.

MERV: That's exactly why I want to come to your birthday party. Sounds like there'll be such interesting people here. I can't believe your father named you Sara and your other sister Gorgeous!

SARA: We're not just having a roast, actually. The roast is part of a cassoulet. That calls for beans, lamb, and duck and pork sausage. I don't recall the rules precisely, but if any of those go against your or the Rabbi of Dublin's religious or dietary regimen, you might want to get to Simpson's in the Strand after all.

MERV: And what will I tell Geoffrey?

SARA: That I behaved rather rudely and scared you away.

MERV: Do you tend to do that with men?

SARA: Are you a psychiatrist in addition to a furrier?

MERV: Shhh! Please, synthetic animal covering.

SARA: In answer to your question, yes, some men find me threatening.

MERV: My daughter tells me men find her threatening. Of course, when my daughter isn't in the Haifa parks, she's a captain in the Israeli army.

SARA: And your wife?

MERV: My wife was a Roslyn housewife. She died three years ago.

SARA: I'm sorry.

MERV: So was I. Her name was Helene and she wasn't very threatening, which is probably why my daughter is in the Israeli army. And you?

SARA: Me what?

MERV: Your husband.

SARA: My second is on his fifth wife. My first I've lost track of, and personally I doubt there will be a third.

MERV: So you've closed shop.

SARA: I'm a very busy woman, Mr. Merv. Would you excuse me? *(Exits.)*

Après Opera

Michael Bigelow Dixon and Valerie Smith
1987

Comic
Setting: A fashionable restaurant with an Opera motif.
Scene: Peter sits at a table for two toying with a box of matches.
Laurel enters and watches as he lights a match and tries to
squeeze out the flame with his fingers.

Peter: 20's, rumpled, sloppy.
Laurel: 20's, the "waitress from Hell."(dressed in a flamboyant opera
costume)
Karen: 20's, stylish, dressed for success.
Duncan: 20's, eager, trying hard.

PETER: Owwwwww-shit! *(Peter sticks his finger and thumb in a glass
of water.)*
LAUREL: Guess we can't all be G. Gordon Liddy.
PETER: What? Oh, no. It's an experiment. I'm testing the limits of my
mind over matter.
LAUREL: That should help with our menu. Here. Can I bring you any-
thing from the bar?
PETER: No thanks. I'll . . . uh . . . wait for my friend, thanks. Oh! Are
you an opera buff?
LAUREL: Sorry. I just work here. I don't love the theme.
PETER: Oh. Would you mind asking someone then, what's the name
of the opera that's playing?
LAUREL: Yeah maybe. If you're good.
PETER: Thanks . . . uh . . Cathy.
LAUREL: It's not Cathy. I just borrowed her outfit.
PETER: Looks good. *(Laurel exits.)* Waitress from hell. *(Peter returns to
matches and tries the same trick with other hand. Same result.)*
Owwwwww-shit! *(Enter Karen, looking for Peter.)*
KAREN: Peter? Is that . . . Oh, god! Peter!
PETER: Hello, Karen.
KAREN: Peter! It's so good to see you. Let's take a look. Tch-tch. You
look terrible.
PETER: I'm OK. You look good, Karen. Real good.

(Duncan enters and hovers unseen nearby.)

KAREN: You know I still think about you. Every time I eat a cookie, really, there's Peter.

DUNCAN: Like Proust.

PETER: Excuse me?

DUNCAN: *Remembrance of Things Past. (Pause.)* The book? *(Pause.)* You know, the teacake?!?

KAREN: Honey, you're trying too hard.

PETER: Do you know this guy?

KAREN: Do I know this guy?! We're getting married on Sunday. Duncan Durbin meet Peter O'Connell.

DUNCAN: Heard an awful lot about you.

PETER: Try to ignore the awful part. Karen exaggerates.

KAREN: I do not. Come on, let's sit down. *(They look at table for two. Pause.)*

DUNCAN: If the music stops, we can play musical chairs.

KAREN: Honey. . .

DUNCAN: I'll go get another chair. *(Duncan exits.)*

KAREN: So how have you been?

PETER: *(Playing with matches.)* Oh, OK. And you?

KAREN: What can I say? I'm getting married. But I've been dying to see you and when Duncan said he'd like to meet you, too—I talk about you all the time, what we did together—and I thought, hey, why not! Let's all get together, you know. My past and my future. We can all just be friends.

PETER: We weren't ever friends.

KAREN: Yes we were.

PETER: We were lovers. It's different.

KAREN: It's semantics. We mean the same thing. Change of topic.
(Duncan arrives with chair and sits.)

DUNCAN: So, Pete, Karen tells me you bake cookies.

PETER: Not exactly.

DUNCAN: That's what you . . .

KAREN: No, Duncan. I told you Peter manages the Cookies Nook in the mall, where they make the best chocolate fudge raisin pecan.

DUNCAN: No kidding. What's your secret?

PETER: Water.

DUNCAN: Really.

PETER: It's a mix.

DUNCAN: Oh . . . interesting.

KAREN: Honey, you're trying too hard again.

DUNCAN: Ahhh-hgth-hgth-hgth-hgth . . . *(Duncan drops face down on the table.)*

PETER: Jesus Christ!

KAREN: Oh dear . . .

PETER: What's the matter?

KAREN: It's all right . . .

PETER: Is he dead?

KAREN: SHHHH. Don't panic. He's OK.

PETER: Oh, sure. He looks great to me!

(Karen periodically attempts to sit Duncan upright and straighten his tie during the next few pages. He always falls back down.)

KAREN: No, really he is. He's just a touch narcoleptic. And every once in awhile he does this, don't you Dunc? See? Breathing normally. Nothing to worry about. Let's just ignore him.

PETER: Ignore him?

KAREN: In a little bit he'll wake up refreshed and everything will be find. Except maybe a bruise on his forehead. I should've moved that fork.

LAUREL: *(Enters.)* What's his problem?

KAREN: Nothing. He's fine. *(Duncan falls forward again.)*

LAUREL: I can do that Heimlicher thing if you want.

KAREN: No thanks.

LAUREL: CPR?

KAREN: No, really.

LAUREL: Just checking. 'Cause sometimes people get embarrassed. And pretend nothing's wrong when there obviously is.

KAREN: It's nothing like that.

LAUREL: *(Rolls eyes.)* OK. does anybody besides me need something to drink?

KAREN: We'll each have a glass of wine.

LAUREL: And for you, perhaps something flaming?

PETER: Very funny. A bourbon and soda.

LAUREL: All right. That's a B&S for the pyromaniac and a wine each for the corpse and the merry widow. *(Laurel exits.)*

KAREN: He does get some strange reactions.

PETER: Look, Karen. When you called last week, out of the blue, I didn't . . .

KAREN: Oh damn!

PETER: What?

KAREN: Duncan goes to this clinic where they chart his brain waves, and they shove these, you know, electrodes into his head. And sometimes they forget to pull them out. *(She yanks a long electrode out.)* Can I borrow your napkin? *(She applies napkin to Duncan's skull.)* Thanks.

PETER: Look, Karen . . .

KAREN: I'm sorry. You keep getting interrupted.

PETER: Well, it's just . . .

DUNCAN: Hrmufllermphf . . .

KAREN: *(After a pause.)* Go on.

PETER: Well, I don't understand why you . . .

DUNCAN: HRMUFFLERMPHFFFFF!!

PETER: Is he all right?

KAREN: Oh sure. He's just dreaming. Want to see something fun? Oh, I'm sorry, you were talking.

PETER: Never mind.

KAREN: No, no. We don't have to . . .

PETER: No, just go on, OK? Please. Go on.

KAREN: OK. Watch this. Duncan? Duncan? You're strolling at night. The wind's blowing—Phewwwou. *(Duncan reacts with muffled sounds and movements at various points in the story.)* You went out for Hostess Ding-Dongs. *(Like bell.)* Ding-Dong. Ding-Dong. But now you're in a cemetery. Suddenly up from a grave reaches a vampire who grabs you by your shoe. An incredibly hideous vampire with one eye, bad breath and no ears. You try to pull free but you can't. He's got you by your shoe, now your calf, now your knees. He's reaching up your thigh, now higher, higher. He's going to bite! *(Duncan gasps and grabs tablecloth in his fists.)* But wait! You grab hold of a vine and you pull yourself up, up, out of the grave until you're almost free. But no! The vine snaps, and you fall back into the grave. Will Duncan escape or will he be eaten by a vampire with hideous breath and no ears? *(To Peter.)* I like to leave the endings to him.

PETER: Oh that's nice.

KAREN: Then when he wakes up he tells what happened. It's kind of our party piece.

PETER: I don't believe this.

KAREN: It's true.

PETER: No this! Him, you, your marriage. You can't be serious about this guy!

KAREN: Peter! I love him. Duncan's very sweet, considerate, and charming.

PETER: When he's awake.

KAREN: Which he is . . . some of the time.

PETER: Karen, he's fucking Rip Van Winkle.

KAREN: I'm not going to sit here and . . .

PETER: What was it, forty years? That's a lot of nights out bowling, Karen

KAREN: One more word, Peter. One more word and I'm leaving! I swear! Change of topic. No better. Let's just shut up for a minute. I'm timing. *(Laurel enters with drinks.)*

LAUREL: Bourbon and soda. And the wine for two comes with a complimentary loaf of bread. You want to order now? *(Pause.)* Is this thing contagious or what? *(Laurel walks away, but spies on them from a doorway as Peter says in sign language, "Sometimes you drive me crazy.")*

KAREN: That's the same as talking. *(Peter repeats signs.)* What are you trying to say?

PETER: *(As he signs.)* Sometimes . . . you . . . drive . . . me . . . crazy!

LAUREL: *Children of a Lesser God!!!* Am I right?

PETER: We're not ready to order yet!!!

LAUREL: WELL OK!! BUT MAYBE THEY DIDN'T HEAR YOU IN THE KITCHEN!!!!! *(Laurel exits.)*

PETER: Look Karen. Before that maniac comes back or Sleeping Beauty wakes up, would you mind telling me one thing, please? *(The following in one breath.)* Would you tell me why, after more than a year, you tracked me down and invited me here? I mean, I really want to know this 'cause you say you love him but then you want to see me which I don't quite understand 'cause I don't want to see you if you're seeing him 'cause I still feel strongly about you and would like you to return these feelings which you say you won't, so I don't want to see you if you won't and you won't so we won't!! So why am I here? *(Breath.)* I'm leaving, OK. Good-bye.

KAREN: All right, Peter. Sit down. I'll tell you why I called, but first you've got to promise you won't laugh.

PETER: I won't laugh.

KAREN: All right. Two month ago my parents died.

PETER: Jesus. I'm sorry.

KAREN: It's not just that. It's this weird string of events that's happening to me, and I just want it to stop. I mean, first you walk out on me after five years . . .

PETER: Well, after you asked me to leave!

KAREN: That's not how I remember it. And then my folks pass away. And it's weird, but all of a sudden everybody who knew me growing up, everybody who knew me as a kid, as a teen, they're all gone. And it's like, sure I remember my past, but there's nobody around to ask if this really happened or am I dreaming that up. You know? It's like, these people are disappearing and part of me is too. And then Duncan. God bless him. I love him. But every time we get close, it's lights out. And so I get left alone again. And I'm starting to get a little lonely, you know.

PETER: Well I've been pretty lonely, too. *(As Peter reaches for Karen's hand, Duncan wakes up with a start.)*

DUNCAN: Get your hands off her.

PETER: What?

KAREN: Honey. . .

DUNCAN: *(Grabbing Peter, then recoiling.)* Ahhh, that breath!!!

KAREN: Duncan . . .

DUNCAN: Back!!! I'm gonna rip those ears right off again!! *(Duncan grabs Peter in a headlock.)*

PETER: Just a min . . . chgl-chgl-chgl . . .

KAREN: Let him go.

DUNCAN: Get away, god damn it! This is gonna get bloody! *(Duncan grabs a knife off the table.)*

KAREN: Duncan stop!!

PETER: Hey! . . . crf-crf-crf . . .

DUNCAN: God damn it, hold still.

KAREN: Listen to me! He's not the vampire in your dreams!!!!

DUNCAN: Huh? He's not?

KAREN: No. Let him go. *(Duncan drops Peter suddenly.)* That's right. You're awake now.

DUNCAN: I'm what? What's that music?

KAREN: Just an opera.

DUNCAN: *(Sees audience.)* Who are they? Oh my God. I'm on stage.

In an opera! *(He tries to sing, but as in a nightmare, can't.)* My voice! My voice!!! *(For first time the taped opera music has stopped.)*

KAREN: No, honey. You're still dreaming. *(Duncan checks out audience.)* Please. It's just a restaurant. You're awake.

DUNCAN: I'm awake. I'm awake! . . . Thank God.

Poetry Reading

John Chandler
1997

Comic

Setting: Fenton and Allegra's dining room.

Scene: Byron has brought Sarah to his parent's home to meet them and have a nice dinner. Dinner is in progress and Allegra has commented that "People enjoy humor so much!"

Byron: 20's, a graduate student in creative writing, shy, dignified.

Sarah: 30's, a nurse who works with crack babies—drinks to forget the pain—talkative and direct.

Fenton: Byron's father, 50's, upper class—loves order, loves his wife.

Allegra: Fenton's wife, Byron's mother—light-hearted, artsy, outspoken.

SARAH: *(Looking around herself, obviously uncomfortable.)* That depends. I don't think a lot of things are funny.

ALLEGRA: Oh, of course, that's why Byron brought you. He's so earnest. We don't know where it comes from. So *that's* what attracts you to each other. But my dear, you're rather lower class, aren't you?

SARAH: *(Offended.)* I've made it on my own, if that's what you mean.

ALLEGRA: Oh my dear, I hope I haven't said anything out of place here. We believe in laying our cards on the table. And besides, anger is such a good stimulus, don't you think? Hasn't it spurred you on in your life?

SARAH: *(With conviction.)* It's all I've had, sometimes. That doesn't mean I like it.

ALLEGRA: I sometimes think, my dear, that I haven't had enough of it. You see, I can *stimulate* it. Fenton, in his softer moments, tells me I am the muse of his inventiveness, with what he likes to call my dithering. *(To husband.)* Don't you, dear?

FENTON: *(In friendly, enthusiastic way to Sarah.)* I must admit, I'm often *seething* by the time I reach my office. Allegra has forced me to view the muse as a somewhat less . . . companionable presence than I might have expected. In the midst of all this . . . comfort . . . she has created chaos. In small ways, my shirts in a different area of the closet, my slippers in back of rather than before my shoes as I left them, making them invisible in the shadows. That's why we have these . . . these topics, you see. We're on a managed household dispute plan. By dinner I feel full of fuel for these discussions.

ALLEGRA: Yes, and you see he appreciates the irritation. We hope you do too. I'm a firm believer that all of us should learn to better appreciate irritation. I even have a little hint of intuition . . . Byron, dear, have you brought Sarah here to irritate us?

BYRON: No, mother.

ALLEGRA: It would be very clever of you, right on the theme of the evening. Conflict.

BYRON: NO, mother, I certainly did not.

ALLEGRA: *(To Sarah.)* Do you think perhaps the motivation was unconscious?

SARAH: *(Coldly.)* I don't know.

ALLEGRA: But I suppose it demonstrates more of a sense of humor than Byron possesses. He's a fine young man, but so humorless.

FENTON: *(Getting Sarah's attention.)* I should add in all fairness that I dream vivid dreams, and Allegra is almost inevitably at their center. The other night I dreamt I was riding on a white horse, a powerful beast with vapor streaming from his nostrils, his legs and body muscular. I rode with great dignity, in armor, my staff held straight up. And on its tip her head. I was desolate at the loss. And to think I was parading it around as some sort of trophy.

ALLEGRA: It came on the morning of our discussion of romance and reality. Perfect.

SARAH: I . . . I think maybe I met you too soon. *(Turns toward Byron.)* I mean . . . I'm not sure *why* I'm meeting them.

BYRON: You . . . I'm . . . Sarah . . . it's

FENTON: Oh, he's a sly one, you must recognize that, Sarah, my dear, if you want to be involved with him. He seems such an innocent, but it's a protection against throwing himself in a great swan dive into the ocean of life. We've tried to bully him out of this rigidity. It's unseemly in a young man. You're older than he, aren't you.

SARAH: I'm twenty-nine.

FENTON: My goodness, he's only 25. This isn't as it should be.

ALLEGRA: And lower class.

FENTON: I recall in my prep school days we had stories, legends, you might call them, about young boys and older women. Initiation. I dare say that's been driven underground by this new feminism, though perhaps it always *was* underground. What do you think of feminism, my dear?

SARAH: Do you have a drink?

ALLEGRA: We don't drink, my dear. We have wine only for cooking.

SARAH: That'll do.

FENTON: *(To wife.)* My dear, you're being less than candid. I suspect you're assuming she has a drinking problem. Lower class, older, drinking problem. What can Byron be thinking? That's what's coursing through your mind. You're not living your credo. Openness, honesty. *(To Sarah.)* The truth is, my dear, we have a rather limited liquor cabinet, for friends who do not release tensions in *our* way. Scotch perhaps?

SARAH: That's fine.

FENTON: Should we serve you, or would you like to get your own? That way you could measure out the dosage you prefer. Yes? *(Sarah rises and as he continues goes to and through the door to the pantry.)* Yes, your instincts are good, right through that swinging door, it's just in the pantry cabinet, second door on your right. Glasses just above. Ice in freezer.

ALLEGRA: *(Calling pleasantly.)* Actually, my dear, it's now on the left. Glasses opposite. Mixes at the far end of the kitchen, right hand cabinet. That's a lot of instructions. Would you like help, my dear?

SARAH: *(Muffled at beginning, as though she may be tilting the bottle to her lips.)* No. thank you.

FENTON: *(Calling.)* You see what I mean, my dear, it's maddening. *(To Byron.)* Well, Byron, we like her. She's a good sport.

ALLEGRA: The truth is, we may not be in unity on this girl—woman. Perhaps we're treating your situation too . . . too lightly.

FENTON: How unlike you once again. You forget yourself. I should not have to remind you that all of life should be conducted in the spirit of fun and experimentation. I mean, my dear, I feel this . . . irregularity in your attitude is drawing me over the line. That's not fair now, is it? I'm the one who thunders and protests, you're the one who appears to concur and then goes and does what she damned well pleases, *(This and the next few words are in a sudden access of anger.)* creates chaos under the appearance of order. *(He recovers himself and seems cheerier than before as the straightens his tie.)* There, that's better. I lost myself there for a moment. *(To Byron.)* Is this one of those initiation sorts of . . . friendships?

BYRON: There's only four years between us, and I'm grown. Mom, Dad, I don't think . . Sarah's had a *very* difficult life. Beyond our imagining. But a strange thing happened when she was telling me. She seemed to . . . light up . . . twice.

FENTON: Flicker and recover, like a brownout?

BYRON: No. On two occasions. Once each. *(Fervently.)* It was as though some fire illuminated her from inside.

ALLEGRA: *Illuminate.* What a word.

BYRON: Something primal, a fire in the midst of darkness. I thought of the first fire, the way prehistoric man must have felt, some reflection of his own soul. And in the fire history, bitter, brittle history was being consumed, intensifying the heat.

FENTON: *(Loudly.)* Bravo Sarah.

BYRON: And I . . . I saw myself as a servant of the fire. I was gathered with ancestors around the fire, I was warmed by the fire that has warmed humans for thousands and thousands of years.

(For a few moments the three of them are silent in acknowledgment.)

FENTON: A neat little reversal there. You the upper class, she the lower, she ignites and the tables turn.

ALLEGRA: This is a wonderful story, dear. You have had a profound experience. Tell us how you met, how you got to know each other. We should begin at the beginning. Besides, if we go over your history Sarah will have more time to drink furtively. How did you meet?

BYRON: *(Looks nervously at pantry door.)* Sarah?

SARAH: Mmnhh?

BYRON: Are you coming out soon?

SARAH: Mmmhmm.

BYRON: *(To parents.)* We met at a poetry reading. A supposed poetry reading.

ALLEGRA: You and poetry. I think it's sweet. But I must tell you your father thinks it retards your development. We laugh about it a little, I mean imagine at 40 introducing yourself as a poet. The next question must be "Who's supporting you?"

BYRON: Allegra, I don't think appreciating beauty is being retarded. I wish you'd stop talking about me that way. Do you have any idea . . .

FENTON: No, no, no. Byron, we're proud of you and your . . . search. We wouldn't be proper parents if we didn't raise these questions. So poetry has brought you together. *(To wife.)* My dear, you're guilty of failure to make distinctions. I said that poetry retards his *economic* development. But when we're discussing the progress of the heart poetry's just the thing. Why, a couple should be united in wonder, wonder at the *otherness* of the other. That's what he was talking about, the recognition of Sarah's utter otherness. And isn't that why we've flourished? How can we say a word about his development when it's clear by whom he's been instructed? *(Takes her hand.)* You know, Byron, if you and Sarah weren't with us tonight, something quite different might begin to happen at this moment. Right here on the floor, in between the chairs, under the old dining table. It's hard to imagine one's parents in amorous abandon, but it does take place. I think sometimes we've done you a disservice by being so proper in your presence. Do you know your mother enjoys saying four letter words? Only at the proper moments, of course, not in company.

BYRON: *(Horrified.)* Is it true?

ALLEGRA: *(Tenderly.)* It is. I think Sarah's presence, or your fire poem . . . Well, it was almost a poem about her, wasn't it? . . . I think the two of you here tonight have sparked something. Our little boy has come of age.

FENTON: It's an initiation.

ALLEGRA: And we are warmed by your fire.

SARAH: *(Stumbling out the door with a full tumbler of scotch.)* I had a little trouble with your directions.

FENTON: Well, welcome back, Sarah. Here's your chair, over here. Yes, perhaps you'd like to put your tumbler down on the table before you seat yourself. Less spillage. One thing I do hope. I hope you didn't refill the bottle with water to give a false reading of the amount you've consumed. Byron did that once when he was in undergraduate school, and two weeks later a guest complained we served twenty proof scotch. Byron's face was ablaze. We joked about it for months.

SARAH: *(Having felt her way to her place like a blind person.)* I don't

do that. I don't play by your rules. I wouldn't give you the satisfaction.

BYRON: Sarah, what's the matter? Why are you drinking? You wanted . . .

ALLEGRA: Why, Byron, she feels out of place, poor thing. She's ill at
ease. The objects around her are alien to her. You're used to ele-
gance, but for her it is an enemy. I'm sorry, my dear, I'm putting
words in your mouth. It's just that as a woman I feel close to you.

SARAH: Sure, sure I feel out of place. You think this is hospitality? You
think this is "Welcome to my humble abode"?

FENTON: We've tried, Sarah. No doubt we've blundered here and
there. It's a difficult situation. A son brings his sweetheart home
for the first time. There are pressures here for all concerned. I
think we should acknowledge how hard we've all tried. And I
think all in all we've done a good job. Every one of us. We're a
strange foursome, wouldn't you say, and as age-old as the situation is it's replete with strains. You're seeing our dear son. In
bringing you to our house he's making a statement even he may
not fully understand, a statement about forging his own way in
life. And of course you are the only one here who is not familiar
with this household and its eccentricities. We're looking at each
other and wondering what the other sees. I think we've done a
good job. Byron told us about your fire, and we congratulate you
on it. I say let's give ourselves a hand. *(He claps, his wife joins him,
Byron uncertainly puts his hands together. Sarah takes a drink.)*

SARAH: *(To the tempo of "This is the Forest Primeval . . .)*
Blah blah blah blah blah blah blah blah
blah blah blah blah blah blah blah

ALLEGRA: Just a moment, I know that one. I've always been good at
these tempo games. It's, it's "This is the forest primeval, the murmuring pines and the hemlocks," am I right?

SARAH: *(Crocked but surprised.)* Yeah, no wait, it's *(Laboriously hitting each accent as if with a hammer.)* "This is my mother's apartment. Her boyfriend molested my sister," *(Laughs, drinks.)* No,
you were right, I was just kidding. Hey, you guys are fun. I mean,
crazy, but fun.

PART FOUR:

SCENES FOR THREE MEN/ ONE WOMAN

The Brothers Menaechmus

Plautus

215 B.C.

Comic
Setting: A street near Erotium's house.
Scene: Sosicles has arrived in search of his long-lost twin brother.

Menaechmus II: 20's – 30's
Messenio: His slave, 20's
Cylindricus: A cook, 30's – 40's.
Erotium: His employer—a Courtesan—elegant and wealthy, 20's.

(Enter Menaechmus II, and his slave Messenio carrying a bag, followed by sailors with luggage.)

MENAECHMUS II: I think, Messenio, that there is no greater joy for sea travelers than sighting land.

MESSENIO: Yes, but it's still better if it's your own land. Why, I ask you, have we come here—why Epidamnus? We might as well be the ocean: We never miss a single island.

MENAECHMUS II: *(Sadly.)* We are searching for my twin brother.

MESSENIO: Is this search ever going to end? It's six years now that we've spent on it. We've seen 'em all—Istrians, Iberians, the people of Marseilles, Illyrians, the whole Adriatic, all of Magna Graecia, the whole Italian seacoast. If you'd been hunting for a needle you'd have found it long ago, if there had been one. We're looking for a dead man among the living; if he were alive you'd have found him long ago.

MENAECHMUS II: If I can find somebody who can prove that, who can say he knows for certain that my brother is dead, then I shall seek no further. But otherwise I shall go on as long as I live; I know how dear he is to my heart.

MESSENIO: You might as well try to find a knot in a bulrush. Let's clear out of here and go home. Or are we going to write a book—*Our Trip around the World*?

MENAECHMUS II: You do what you're told, take what's given you, and keep out of trouble. Don't annoy me. I'm running this, not you.

MESSENIO: *(Aside.)* Hm-m, that puts me in my place all right. Neat, complete; it can't be beat. But just the same, here I go again. *(Aloud.)* Look at our purse, Menaechmus; our money is feeling the heat: It's getting as thin as a summer shirt. If you don't go home, you'll be hunting for that blessed brother of yours without a cent to bless *yourself* with. That's what Epidamnus is like, full of rakes and tremendous drinkers; a lot of swindlers and spongers live here, and everybody knows their women are the most seductive in the whole world. That's why the place is called Epidamnus; scarcely anybody can come here without getting damned.

MENAECHMUS II: I'll take care of that: Just hand the purse over to me.

MESSENIO: What for?

MENAECHMUS II: What you say makes me worried—about you.

MESSENIO: Makes you worried?

MENAECHMUS II: That you may get yourself damned in Epidamnus. You are very fond of the ladies, Messenio, and I have a bad temper and lose it very easily. So if I have the money, you get double protection: Your foot doesn't slip, and my temper doesn't either.

MESSENIO: *(Handing it over.)* Take it, keep it; it's all right with me. *(Enter Cylindrus the cook, with his market basket.)*

CYLINDRUS: *(To himself.)* I've done a good job of marketing—just what I like myself. I'll give the company a fine dinner. —Glory, there's Menaechmus! Now I'm in for it! Here are the guests at the door before I'm back from the market. I'll go up and speak to him. *(To Menaechmus II.)* Good day, Menaechmus.

MENAECHMUS II: Why, thank you. *(To Messenio.)* He seems to know my name. Who is he?

MESSENIO: I don't know.

CYLINDRUS: Where are the other guests?

MENAECHMUS II: What guests?

CYLINDRUS: *(Grinning.)* Your parasite.

MENAECHMUS II: *(To Messenio.)* My parasite? The man's crazy.

MESSENIO: Didn't I tell you there were a lot of swindlers here?. . .

MENAECHMUS II: *(To Cylindrus.)* What do you mean "my parasite," young man?

CYLINDRUS: Why, "Brush."

MESSENIO: *(Peering into the bag.)* Nonsense, I have your brush safe right here in the bag.

CYLINDRUS: You are a little early for dinner, Menaechmus; I'm just back from the market.

MENAECHMUS II: Tell me, young man: How much do pigs cost here? Grade A pigs, for sacrifice.

CYLINDRUS: A drachma.

MENAECHMUS II: Well, here's a drachma; go get yourself cured at my expense. Because you certainly must be crazy, what's-your-name, to be bothering a perfect stranger like me.

CYLINDRUS: "What's-your-name"! Don't you remember me? I'm Cylindrus.

MENAECHMUS II: The devil take you, whether your name is Cylinder or Colander. I don't know you, and I don't want to.

CYLINDRUS: *(Persisting.)* Your name is Menaechmus.

MENAECHMUS II: You're in your right mind when you call me by name anyway. But where did you ever see me before?

CYLINDRUS: Where did I ever see you before—when my mistress, Erotium, is your mistress?

MENAECHMUS II: Confound it, she's not my mistress, and I don't know you, either.

CYLINDRUS: All the drinks I've poured for you in the house here, and you don't know me?

MESSENIO: I wish I had something to break his head with.

MENAECHMUS II: You pour my drinks for me, do you? When I've never set foot in Epidamnus before today and never even seen the place?

CYLINDRUS: You deny it?

MENAECHMUS II: Of course I deny it.

CYLINDRUS: Don't you live in that house over there?

MENAECHMUS II: The devil take the people that do!

CYLINDRUS: *(Aside.)* If he curses himself like this, *he's* crazy. *(Aloud.)* Menaechmus!

MENAECHMUS II: Well?

CYLINDRUS: If you ask me, you ought to take that drachma you promised me a minute ago and order *yourself* a pig, because your head isn't on straight either, you know, if you curse your own self.

MENAECHMUS II: Confound your cheek, you chatterbox! *(Turns away.)*

CYLINDRUS: *(Aside.)* He likes to joke with me like this. Always full of laughs—when his wife's not there! *(To Menaechmus II.)* Well, sir— *(No response.)* Well, sir— *(Menaechmus II turns.)* Is this enough for the three of you—you, the parasite, and the lady—or shall I get some more?

MENAECHMUS II: What "ladies"? What "parasites"?

MESSENIO: *(To Cylindrus.)* Here, what's the matter with you? Why are you pestering the gentlemen?

CYLINDRUS: Who are you, and what's it to you? I'm talking to *him*; he's a friend of mine.

MESSENIO: You're cracked, that's certain.

CYLINDRUS: *(To Menaechmus II.)* I'll get these things into the pot right away, so don't wander off too far from the house. Anything else I can do for you?

MENAECHMUS II: Yes. Go to the devil.

CYLINDRUS: Oh, better that you should—go inside and make your-self comfortable on your couch, while Vulcan is getting violent with the food. I'll go in and tell Erotium that you're here. I know she'd rather take you in than make you wait outside. *(He goes into the house of Erotium.)*

MENAECHMUS II: Is he gone? Good. Whew! I see there was a lot in what you said.

MESSENIO: Yes, but look out. I think one of those fancy women lives here, just as that crackpot said.

MENAECHMUS II: All the same, I wonder how he knew my name.

MESSENIO: Nothing strange in that; it's just the way these women have. They send their maids and slave boys to the harbor; and if a foreign ship comes in, they find out the name of the owner and where he's from, and then, bingo! they fasten onto him and stick to him like glue. If he falls for it, they send him home a ruined man. *(Pointing to house of Erotium.)* Now in that harbor rides a pirate craft, of which we must beware.

MENAECHMUS II: That's good advice.

MESSENIO: Yes, but it's no good unless you take it. *(The door starts to open.)*

MENAECHMUS II: Quiet a minute; I hear the door opening. Let's see who comes out.

MESSENIO: *(Putting down the bag.)* I'll set this down then. You sailors, keep an eye on the luggage.
(Enter Erotium from her house.)

EROTIUM: *(To slaves within.)* Go in, and do not close the door,

I want it left just so.
See what there is to do inside
And do it all—now go.
The couches must be spread, and perfumes burned:
Neatness entices lovers, I have learned.
Splendor to lovers' loss, to our gain is turned.
(Coming forward.)
But where is the man they said was before my door?
Ah, there he is; he's been of use before;
Yet is, as he deserves, my governor.
I'll go and speak to him myself. —My dear,
I am amazed to see you standing here;
My home is always yours when you appear.
Now all you ordered is prepared,
The doors are opened wide,
Your dinner's cooked, and when you like
Come take your place inside.

MENAECHMUS II: *(To Messenio.)* Who's this woman talking to?

EROTIUM: To you!

MENAECHMUS II: But why? We've never—

EROTIUM: Because it is the will of Venus that I exalt you above all others; and so I should, because you're the one who keeps me blooming with your loving favors.

MENAECHMUS II: *(To Messenio.)* This woman is either insane or drunk, Messenio. Such language, to a perfect stranger!

MESSENIO: *(To Menaechmus II.)* Didn't I tell you that was the way here? Why, these are just falling leaves; stay here a couple of days, and there'll be *trees* falling on you. These women look like pick-ups, but they're not; they're just stickups—Let me talk to her. *(To Erotium.)* Listen, lady—

EROTIUM: What?

MESSENIO: Where did you get so familiar with the gentleman?

EROTIUM: In the same place where he got so familiar with me—here, in Epidamnus.

MESSENIO: In Epidamnus? He never set so much as his foot in the place until today.

EROTIUM: Oh, what a ravishing sense of humor! *(To Menaechmus II.)* Menaechmus dear, won't you come in? We can straighten this out so much better inside.

MENAECHMUS II: *(To Messenio.)* And now she calls me by name too. What's going on here?

MESSENIO: *(To Menaechmus II.)* She's got a whiff of that purse of yours.

MENAECHMUS II: *(To Messenio.)* You're probably right. Here, take it. *(Hands him the purse.)* Now I'll see which she loves, me or the money.

EROTIUM: Let's go in to dinner.

MENAECHMUS II: You are very kind, but *(Backing away.)* no, thank you.

EROTIUM: But you just told me to fix a dinner for you.

MENAECHMUS II: I told you to?

EROTIUM: Why, yes, for you and your parasite.

MENAECHMUS II: What parasite, confound it? *(To Messenio.)* She's crazy.

EROTIUM: Brush.

MENAECHMUS II: What is this brush you all keep talking about? You mean my shoe brush?

EROTIUM: No, of course I mean the Brush who came with you when you brought me the dress you had stolen from your wife.

MENAECHMUS II: What? I gave you a dress that I had stolen from my wife? You're out of your mind! *(To Messenio.)* Why, this woman dreams standing up, like a horse.

EROTIUM: Why do you make fun of me, and deny what you did?

MENAECHMUS II: Well, what *did* I do?

EROTIUM: You gave me a dress of your wife's, today.

MENAECHMUS II: I still deny it. I haven't got a wife and I never had one, and I never set foot in this house before. I had dinner on the boat, came ashore, walked by here, and ran into you.

EROTIUM: *(Frightened.)* Oh, my goodness, your boat?

MENAECHMUS II: A wooden boat—oft sprung, oft plugged, oft struck with maul, and peg lies close by peg, as in a furrier's frame.

EROTIUM: Oh, please stop joking and come in.

MENAECHMUS II: But madam, you are looking for somebody else, not me.

EROTIUM: Do you think I don't know Menaechmus, son of Moschus, born of Syracuse in Sicily where Agathocles was king, and then Phintia, and then Liparo, who left it to Hiero, who is king now?

MENAECHMUS II: That's all correct.

MESSENIO: *(To Menaechmus II.)* Good lord, the woman can't be from there herself, can she? She certainly has you down pat.

MENAECHMUS II: *(Weakening.)* You know, I don't see how I can refuse. *(He starts towards the door.)*

MESSENIO: Don't! If you go in there, you're done for!

MENAECHMUS II: Be quiet. Things are going nicely. Whatever she says, I'll agree to it, and see if I can pick up some entertainment! *(To Erotium.)* I've had a reason for contradicting you all this time: I was afraid this man would tell my wife about the dress and the dinner. But now let's go in, anytime you want.

EROTIUM: Are you going to wait for the parasite any longer?

MENAECHMUS II: No! I don't give a rap for him, and if he comes I don't want him let in.

EROTIUM: That's quite all right with me. But there's something I wish you'd do for me, will you?

MENAECHMUS II: Anything; command me.

EROTIUM: That dress you—gave me—just take it to the place where they do that lovely gold embroidery and get them to fix it up and put on some new trimming.

MENAECHMUS II: Splendid idea! And that'll keep my wife from recognizing it, if she sees it on the street.

EROTIUM: You can take it with you when you go.

MENAECHMUS II: I certainly will!

EROTIUM: Let's go in.

MENAECHMUS II: I'll be right with you. I just want to speak to this man a minute. *(Erotium goes into her house.)* Hi there, Messenio, come here.

MESSENIO: What's going on here? Come to your senses!

MENAECHMUS II: What for?

MESSENIO: Because—

MENAECHMUS II: Oh, I know, don't say it.

MESSENIO: So much the worse.

MENAECHMUS II: The booty is as good as in my hands right now; the siege has just begun! *(Pointing to the sailors.)* Come on now, hustle these men off to an inn somewhere, and then come back for me here before sunset.

MESSENIO: Master, you don't know what these women are!

MENAECHMUS II: None of that! If I do anything foolish, it's my loss, not yours. This woman is a silly fool. the way things look so far, there's booty to be had! *(He goes into the house of Erotium.)*

MESSENIO: God help me! *(Calling after Menaechmus II.)* Sir! *(To himself.)* God help him, too! The pirate ship has got the pinnace steered straight on the rocks! But I'm a fool to expect to control my master. He bought me to obey him, not to give him orders. *(To the sailors.)* Come along you, so I can come back and pick him up in time. Orders is orders! *(They depart.)*

The Creation

Anonymous
Fifteenth Century

Dramatic
Setting: Paradise. The Garden of Eden.
Scene: Satan crawls our of the mouth of Hell and approaches Eve in
Paradise.

Satan: A fallen angel.
Adam: The first man.
Eve: His mate.
God

SATAN: Who thought this time had ever been?
    We that such mirth and joy have seen,
    That we should suffer so much woe?
    Whoever would have trusted so?
    Ten orders in heaven have been
    Of angels serving as was seen
    Each in order of degree.
    The tenth part fell down with me;
    For they chose me as their guide,
    And maintained me in their pride;
    But hark now, fellows, what I say:
    The joy that we have lost for ay,
    God has fashioned man his friend,
    To have that bliss without an end,
    The fallen angels' place to fill,
    Which we have left, such is his will.
    And now are they in paradise,
    But thence they shall, if we be wise.

    My content I shall contrive,
    If I might man betray
    His pleasure to deprive,
    That soon I shall assay.
    In a worm's likeness will I wend,
    And lead astray with subtle lying.

(Moves to paradise.)
    Eve, Eve!
EVE: Who is there?
SATAN: I am a friend.
    For thy good I am coming,
    And thee have sought.
    Of all the fruit that ye see hanging
    In paradise, why eat ye nought?
EVE: We may from every one
    Take whate'er we thought,
    But one tree we must shun,
    Or into harm be brought.
SATAN: And why that tree? that would I know,
    more than others standing by?
EVE: For God forbids us near it go
    Nor eat thereof, Adam nor I,
    We leave for fear;
    And if we did we both should die,
    He said, and end our pleasures here.
SATAN: *(Knowingly.)* Sssss! Eve, now be intent
    To heed what thou shalt hear,
    What matter is here meant,
    That he should chill your cheer.
    To eat thereof he you forbad,
    I know it well, this was his will,
    Because he would none other had
    The virtues this tree may instill.
    For wilt thou see,
    Who eats the fruit, of good and ill
    Shall knowledge have as well as he.
EVE: Why what kind of thing art thou,
    That tells this tale to me?
SATAN: A worm that knows well how
    That ye may worshipped be.
EVE: What worship should we win thereby?
    To eat thereof the need is nought;
    Our lordship is in mastery
    Of all things that on earth are wrought.
SATAN: Woman, away!

To greater state ye may be brought,
    If ye will do as I shall say.
EVE: For no need do we long
    That should our good dismay.
SATAN: Nay, indeed it is no wrong,
    Safely to eat ye may.
    Sure, no peril therein lies,
    But worship for the winning.
    For right as God ye shall be wise,
    And peer with him in everything.
    Aye, Gods shall ye be!
    And of good and ill have knowing,
    For to be as wise as he.
EVE: Is this true that thou say?
SATAN: Yea! why trust thou not me?
    I never would in no way
    Tell ought but truth to thee.
EVE: Thy words have won, my doubts are dashed,
    To fetch this fruit for our own food.
    (Eve bites, and Satan writhes in exultation.)
SATAN: Bite on boldly be not abashed,
    And take Adam to amend his mood,
    Also his bliss.
    (Satan withdraws. Adam approaches.)
EVE: Adam! Have here the fruit full good.
ADAM: Alas! Woman, why took thou this?
    Our Lord commanded us both
    To shun this tree of his.
    Thy work will make him wroth,
    Alas! Thou hast done amiss.
EVE: Adam, by grief be nought beset,
    And I shall say the reason why;
    Such wisdom hissed a worm I met,
    We shall as gods be, thou and I,
    If that we ate
    Here of this tree; Adam, deny
    Not such worship for to get.
    For we shall be as wise
    As God that is so great,

And so ourselves may prize;
    So eat and earn that state.
ADAM: To eat it I would not eschew,
    If certain of thy saying.
EVE: Bite on boldly, for it is true,
    As gods we shall know everything.
ADAM: To win that name
    I shall it taste at thy teaching.
    (Adam bites the apple.)
    Alas! What have I done for shame!
    Ill counsel came from thee!
    Ah! Eve, thou art to blame,
    That thus enticed thou me;
    My limbs against me exclaim,
    For I am naked as I think.
EVE: Alas, Adam, right so am I.
ADAM: And for sorrow why might we not sink,
    For we have grieved God almighty
    That made me man,
    Broken his bidding bitterly!
    Alas! That ever we it began!
    This work, Eve, thou hast wrought,
    And made this bad bargain.
EVE: Nay, Adam, chide me nought.
ADAM: Alas, dear Eve, whom then?
EVE: The worm of chiding is most worthy,
    With tales untrue he me betrayed.
ADAM: Alas! I listened to thy story,
    And let with lies thou me persuade.
    So may I bide,
    For that rash act I am repaid,
    For that deed done I curse my pride.
    Our nakedness me grieves,
    Wherewith shall we it hide?
EVE: Let us take these fig-leaves
    Since they grow here beside.
ADAM: Right as thou say so shall it be,
    For we are naked and all bare.
    Full gladly now I would hide me,

From my Lord's sight, I know not where,
So I be not caught.
GOD: *(In his throne.)* Adam! Adam!
ADAM: Lord!
GOD: Where art thou, there?
ADAM: I hear thee, Lord, but see thee nought.
GOD: Say, to whom does it belong,
this work that thou hast wrought?
ADAM: Lord, Eve made me do wrong
And to this plight me brought.
GOD: Say, Eve, why didst thou Adam make
To eat the fruit that should hang still,
Which was commanded none should take?
EVE: A worm, Lord, beguiled my will,
So welaway!
That ever I did that deed so ill!
GOD: Ah! Wicked worm, woe wait on thee for ay,
For thou in this manner
Hast caused such deep dismay;
My malediction have thou here,
With all the might I may.
And on thy belly shalt thou glide.
(Satan grovels on his belly.)
And be ay full of enmity
To all mankind on every side,
And earth thy sustenance shall be
To eat and drink.
Adam and Eve, also ye
From work on earth ye shall not shrink,
But labor for your food.
ADAM: Alas! For sorrow and care,
We that had all world's good,
Now thrust out as I think.

Isaac

Anonymous
Fifteenth Century

Dramatic
Setting: Isaac and Rebecca's home.
Scene: Isaac has only one blessing to give.

Isaac: An elderly man, blind.
Jacob: His son, a farmer.
Esau: His other son, a hunter.
Rebecca: Isaac's wife.

ISAAC: Come here son and kiss me,
    That I may sense the smell of thee;
    The smell of my son is like
    To a field with flowers or honey hive.
    Where are thou, Esau, my son?
JACOB: Here, father, and ask your benison.
ISAAC: The blessing my father gave to me,
    God of heaven and I give thee;
    God thee with great plenty greet,
    Of wine, of oil, and of wheat;
    And grant thy children all
    To worship thee, both great and small;
    Whoso thee blesses, blessed be he;
    Whoso thee curses, cursed be he.
    Now hast thou my great blessing,
    Love thee shall all thine offspring;
    Go now whither thou hast to go.
JACOB: Grant mercy, sir, I will do so.
    (Jacob retires. Esau advances.)
ESAU: Have, eat, father, of my hunting,
    And give me then your blessing.
ISAAC: Who is that?
ESAU: I, your son
    Esau, who brings you venison.
ISAAC: Who was that was right now here,
    And brought me the broth of a deer?

I ate well, and blessed him;
    And he is blessed, in every limb.
ESAU: Alas! I may weep and sob.
ISAAC: Thou art beguiled through Jacob,
    That is born thy very brother.
ESAU: Have ye kept me no other
    Blessing, but gave ye him each one?
ISSAC: Such another have I none;
    God grant that to thy lot may stand
    The dew of heaven and fruit of land;
    Other than this can I not say.
ESAU: Now, alas, and welaway!
    May I with that traitor meet,
    I shall repay this bitter cheat;
    My parents' grief should not away,
    For if we meet I shall him slay.
    (Esau retires. Rebecca advances.)
REBECCA: Isaac, my own life would slip by,
    If thus hated Jacob die.
    I will send him to Aran,
    There my brother dwells, Laban;
    And there may he serve in peace
    Till his brother's wrath will cease.
    Why should I all in a day
    Lose both my sons? Better nay.
ISAAC: Thou sayest sooth, wife; call him hither,
    And let us tell him where and whither
    That he may Esau flee
    Who vows such vengeance shall be.
    (Jacob advances.)
REBECCA: Jacob, son! thy father and I
    Would speak with thee; come, stand us by!
    From the country must thou flee,
    So that Esau slay not thee.
JACOB: Wither should I go from here?
REBECCA: To Mesopotamia; with thine uncle Laban bide,
    Who dwells Jordan's stream beside;
    And there may thou with him live,
    Until Esau, my son, forgive

And forget, and his rage be dead.

JACOB: I will go, father, as is said.

ISSAC: Yea, son, do as thy parents say;
Come kiss us both, and wend thy way.

JACOB: Have good day, sir and dame!
(He kisses father and mother.)

ISSAC: God shield thee, son, from sin and shame!

REBECCA: And give thee grace, good man to be,
And send me glad tidings of thee.
(Jacob goes one way. Isaac and Rebecca the other.)

The Chicken Pie and the Chocolate Cake

Anonymous
15th C

Comic
Setting: A street, then, a house on that street.
Scene: The rogues are cold and complaining about it.

Husband: A pastry cook, any age.
His wife: About the same age as her husband.
Two hungry and clever fellows, any age:
    First Rogue.
    Second Rogue.

FIRST ROGUE: Ay ay ay!
SECOND ROGUE: What's the matter?
FIRST ROGUE: I'm cold, I'm shivering, and I've got nothing but rags over my skin.
SECOND ROGUE: It's a rough time for both of us. Ay ay ay!
FIRST ROGUE: What's the matter?
SECOND ROGUE: I'm cold, I'm shivering.
FIRST ROGUE: Poor beggars are out of luck nowadays. Ay ay ay!
SECOND ROGUE: What's the matter?
FIRST ROGUE: I'm cold, I'm shivering, I'm dressed in rags and shreds.
SECOND ROGUE: What about me?
FIRST ROGUE: I'm worse off than you, because I'm famished and penniless.
SECOND ROGUE: Couldn't you find a way of getting a bite to eat?
FIRST ROGUE: Let's stretch out our hands from door to door.
SECOND ROGUE: We'd better take separate ways, don't you think?
FIRST ROGUE: If you say so. But we'll share and share alike, all right?
    Whether it's meat or bread or butter or eggs.
SECOND ROGUE: Certainly. Shall we start?
    (House.)
HUSBAND: Mary!
WIFE: What is it, Walt?

HUSBAND: I'm dining in town with friends. There's a chicken pie on the table that I want you to send me when I call for it.

WIFE: I will, dear.

(Street.)

FIRST ROGUE: Hey, this sounds like a good deal. Let's start here.

SECOND ROGUE: One of us is enough. I'll go scouting my way and you see what you can grab here. All right?

FIRST ROGUE: All right.

(Exit Second Rogue.)

FIRST ROGUE: *(Knocking at the door.)* May the saints rain blessings on your house. Charity for the poor.

WIFE: *(At the door.)* There's nobody in the house just now, my good man. Come back another time.

(Inside.)

HUSBAND: While I'm thinking about the pie, don't hand it over to anybody unless he gives you a sure sign.

WIFE: Don't worry. I won't give it away if I'm suspicious of the messenger.

HUSBAND: The man I send you will take your little finger like this. Get it?

WIFE: Oh yes.

(Exit the Husband.)

FIRST ROGUE: Am I glad I overhead their conversation! *(He knocks again.)* Merciful lady, won't you take pity on me? I haven't had a crumb to eat in two and a half days.

WIFE: Ask God to help you. *(She goes back inside.)*

FIRST ROGUE: God strike you deaf and dumb!

(Enter the Second Rogue.)

SECOND ROGUE: I'm as hungry as ever and I don't see my pal. I won't stand for it if he tries to cheat me out of my half. Oh, there he is. Any success?

FIRST ROGUE: No success, and I'm fighting mad besides. How about you?

SECOND ROGUE: I couldn't squeeze a nickel out of anybody, as God is my witness.

FIRST ROGUE: Some dinner we're going to have today!

SECOND ROGUE: Can't you think of a trick to find us something to eat?

FIRST ROGUE: I can, if you'll go where I tell you.

SECOND ROGUE: I'm your friend for life! Tell me where.

FIRST ROGUE: Go to the pastrycook's house over there, and ask for a chicken pie. Don't forget to act sure of yourself. Take the wife's little finger like this and tell her, "Your husband wants you to give me this chicken pie." All right?

SECOND ROGUE: But supposing he's come back already? How will I talk me way out?

FIRST ROGUE: I know he hasn't come back, because he left a minute ago.

SECOND ROGUE: Take her finger, eh? All right, here I go. *(He hesitates.)*

FIRST ROGUE: Go on, you blockhead.

SECOND ROGUE: Damn it, I don't want to get walloped if he's there after all.

FIRST ROGUE: Nothing ventured, nothing gained.

SECOND ROGUE: You're right. Off I go. *(He knocks at the door.)* Lady, your husband wants you to send him that chicken pie. How about it?

WIFE: What's the sign, my friend?

SECOND ROGUE: He told me to take your little finger. Give me your hand.

WIFE: That's the sign sure enough. Here's the pie.

SECOND ROGUE: I'll take it to him right away. *(The Wife re-enters the house.)* I've got it! I've got it! What a brain, what genius! Look at it!

FIRST ROGUE: You got the pie?

SECOND ROGUE: Didn't I though! Didn't I though! What do you say?

FIRST ROGUE: You're brilliant. Three could make a feast with this pie! *(Exeunt the Two Rogues. Enter the Husband.)*

HUSBAND: Well, they've stood me up, the jokers, and I'm an ass to have waited so long. Damn them. I'll go eat that chicken pie with my wife. If there's anything I hate, it's being made a fool of. I'm back, Mary! *(He enters the house.)*

WIFE: My goodness, did you have your dinner?

HUSBAND: No I didn't and I'm mad as a wasp. Devil hand them!

WIFE: But then why did you send for the pie, you dummy?

HUSBAND: Who sent?

WIFE: Listen to the man playing dumb!

HUSBAND: What playing dumb? Wait a minute. Don't tell me you gave it to somebody!

WIFE: Of course I did. A man came to the house, took me by the finger, and told me to hand over the pie.

HUSBAND: How hand over? God damn it to hell, is my pie gone?

WIFE: For goodness' sake, it's you who sent for it, with the sign and all.

HUSBAND: You're a liar! I didn't send for it! What did you do with it?

WIFE: That's a good one! I'm telling you, I gave it to the man who came for it a little while ago.

HUSBAND: Fire and brimstone! I need my stick. You ate it!

WIFE: Stop babbling. I gave it to the man you sent.

HUSBAND: You'll pay for this. I won't take it lying down. You ate it!

WIFE: Now I'm beginning to see red.

HUSBAND: Where's that stick? Wait till I tickle your back with it. The truth! What did you do with the chicken pie? *(He whacks her.)*

WIFE: Murder! He's murdering me! You louse, you tramp!

HUSBAND: Where's that pie? I'll knock the stuffings out of you. Did you eat it without me? Where's the pie?

WIFE: Murder! He's murdering me! I gave it to the man you sent with the sign!

HUSBAND: I'm bursting with anger, I'm starved, and there's nothing left to eat!

(Exeunt Husband and Wife. Enter the Two Rogues.)

FIRST ROGUE: What do you say?

SECOND ROGUE: The pie was scrumptious. Now if you wanted to do your bit, we could get our hands on a beautiful chocolate cake I saw in the house.

FIRST ROGUE: Why don't you go yourself? Take the woman's finger again and tell her that her husband sent for the cake.

SECOND ROGUE: Don't talk nonsense. I've done my share of the work. Now it's your turn.

FIRST ROGUE: All right, I'll go, but keep my half of what's left of the pie.

SECOND ROGUE: Who do you take me for? What's yours is yours, and I swear nobody's going to touch this till you return.

FIRST ROGUE: You're a real pal. Well, I'm off. Wait for me here. *(In the house.)*

WIFE: You've beaten me black and blue. Damn that chicken pie.

HUSBAND: I gave your bones a lesson they needed. Enough. I'm off to cut some wood in the shed.

WIFE: The quicker the better.

(Exit the Husband. The First Rogue knocks at the door.)

FIRST ROGUE: Lady! Your husband has sent me for the chocolate cake. He's fit to be tied because you didn't send it along with the chicken pie.

WIFE: Oh, I'm glad you came. Please step inside.

(The Husband pops in.)

HUSBAND: So you're the rascal! Oh I'm going to cuddle you. *(Beating him.)* What did you do with the pie you picked up here?

FIRST ROGUE: Ay ay ay, it wasn't me!

HUSBAND: What did you do with my pie? I'll beat you into the ground!

FIRST ROGUE: Murder!

HUSBAND: What did you do with my pie?

FIRST ROGUE: I'll tell you the whole story if you'll stop hitting me!

HUSBAND: Talk, you rascal, or I'll knock you to kingdom come.

FIRST ROGUE: I'm talking, I'm talking. A while ago I came here to beg, but nobody gave me a penny. Then I overheard you telling your wife about the pie and giving her the sign. My dear kind sir, I was ravenous, so I went back to my buddy who's as sharp as a razor blade. We're loyal to each other, share and share alike, half his, half mine, whatever we earn. I told him about he sign of the little finger, he came here for the pie, and believe me I'm sorry he ever did. After we'd eaten it the devil reminded him there was a cake here too. Then like a fool I walked in to ask for it.

HUSBAND: Now, by God, I'll beat your brains out if you don't swear to make your friend come to me for his share of the cake. Since you split everything between you, he's got a right to the same treat you had.

FIRST ROGUE: I swear I'll send him to you. And be sure to make him feel the end of your stick.

HUSBAND: On our way, and play it natural.

FIRST ROGUE: As God is my witness he'll get what I got. *(He joins the Second Rogue.)*

SECOND ROGUE: How's that? You came back empty-handed?

FIRST ROGUE: Listen, she cut me short and told me she'd give the cake to nobody but the man who came for the pie.

SECOND ROGUE: I'll go right away. God, I can taste it already! Watch me do my ply. *(He goes to the house.)* Hey there!

WIFE: Who is it?

SECOND ROGUE: Lady, let me have the chocolate cake for your husband.

WIFE: Dear me! Come in!

(The husband jumps out.)

HUSBAND: Thief! Traitor! I'll fix you up for the hangman. There, there, there, a hundred knocks for the chicken pie.

SECOND ROGUE: Mercy, mercy!

WIFE: Thump him a hundred times! How does it feel! Because of you I was thrashed till my bones ached.

HUSBAND: One hundred knocks. There, there, there's for the chicken pie.

SECOND ROGUE: Have mercy on me! I'll never do it again! I'm crippled for life! I'm dead!

WIFE: Harder, Walt, harder, let him remember the pie.

HUSBAND: Go to hell now, and I hope somebody wraps your gut around your neck.

(Exeunt Husband and Wife. The Second Rogue joins the first.)

SECOND ROGUE: You double-crossing bastard, you sent me off to be murdered!

FIRST ROGUE: Aren't we supposed to share and share alike, the good as well as the bad? What do you say, you dumb ape? He hit me ten times worse than you.

SECOND ROGUE: If only you'd warned me, I would never have gone. Oh Jesus, I'm one big sore.

FIRST ROGUE: You know what they say—one rogue shouldn't trust another.

SECOND ROGUE: Never mind.
Let's finish the pie and forget about the cake.
We can still stuff ourselves.
What are we, me and you?
Robbers beaten black and blue.

FIRST ROGUE: Though you're right, you needn't shout;
It's not a thing I'd boast about.
Let's take our aching spines away,
And hope the audience liked our play.

(The End.)

Bilora

Angelo Beolco
1527

Comic

Setting: On the street.

Scene: Andronico has stolen Bilora's wife. Now Bilora and Pittaro have a plan to meet on the street and confront him and get Dina to come home. Bilora and Pittaro appear from opposite directions.

Bilora: A peasant.
Pittaro: An old peasant.
Dina: Bilora's wife.
Andronico: From Venice, a gentleman.
Brief appearance of Tonin.

BILORA: Well, I'm damned! How do we two happen to meet here?

PITTARO: Ah well! Have you had a good dinner? The wine isn't bad, is it?

BILORA: Damned if you're not right, Old Pittaro. I tell you I'm so full you could play a tune on my stomach as though it were a drum.

PITTARO: Well now, what do you want me to do? Shall we talk to the old man and find out at once what his intentions are, so we'll know what to count on? I tell you again that the girl will come back to you, whether he allows it or not.

BILORA: That's just what she told me herself. If only she hasn't changed her mind. By nature she's a bit fickle . . . you know what I mean.

PITTARO: I know. But one thing is sure: The quicker we straighten this matter out the better it will be for all of us. Now how do you want me to go about it? Shall I speak for you, or shall both of us speak?

BILORA: No; you do the talking. You know best what to say. But listen! if you notice that he is getting ill-tempered, you tell him that by heaven she has a husband who is a rough customer, and that if he doesn't send her back, her husband will kill him. Tell him I used to be a soldier. That may scare him.

PITTARO: Good. Leave it to me.

BILORA: And listen! Tell him I'm a regular cutthroat, a bad actor; and don't forget to tell him I used to be a soldier, eh?

PITTARO: Now get out of the way so he won't see you. I'm going to pound on the door. Leave it to me. I'll tell him something he'll understand!

BILORA: Do anything you like, so long as you make him give her back to me. And if he refuses, by the blood of the Virgin, I'll shoot him in the rump with an arrow. Yes, I'll knock his breakfast down to his shoe tops!

PITTARO: Just now be quiet! I don't need any more of your boasts. Get out of sight so I can knock at the door. What did you say his name is?

BILORA: Hell, I don't know how they pronounce that name. I think he's called Messire Ardochêne . . . but I'm not very sure . . . Messire Ardo . . . Messire Ardochê . . . that's it; yes, yes!

PITTARO: *(Knocking.)* Yes, yes, that's right. Hello! within there!

DINA: *(At the window.)* Who's knocking?

PITTARO: A friend, young lady. Tell Messire I want a word with him.

DINA: Who are you?

PITTARO: Just say that it's me, and that I want to speak with him. He'll understand.

DINA: He'll be right down.

BILORA: *(Whispering to Pittaro.)* Listen! Tell him I have killed God knows how many men—that there's a price on my head. Will you?

PITTARO: All right, all right! Be quiet! Get back! You bother me.
(Bilora hides again.)

ANDRONICO: *(Appearing at the door.)* What is this anyway? What have you got to say?

PITTARO: Good evening to your Excellency.

ANDRONICO: Good evening, Pittaro. What do you want of me?

PITTARO: I'd like to have a few confidential words with you, Messire, if you don't mind. Just between you and me. If you will step this way a little.

ANDRONICO: What is it? Be quick about it.

PITTARO: I'm telling you now, Messire. There's no use beating around the bush. You know very well that the other day you stole this girl, the wife of that poor fellow, Bilora, who is now almost out of his head. Well then, I must tell you that I have come to beg your Excellency on his behalf to return her to him. Imagine, dear

Messire, imagine for your self how cruel and unnatural it must seem to one to have another steal his wife. And anyway, you should by now have gotten over your desire. You have had plenty of time in which to satisfy your passion for her. And finally, if I may give you a word of advice, this girl is not the skillet for your kitchen. You are old; she is young. Pardon me for speaking so frankly, Messire.

ANDRONICO: Do you want me to speak honestly? Then, I tell you I will do nothing about it, for it would be utterly impossible for me to get along without her. Is that clear? I have decided to spend the rest of my life with her. What the devil do you expect me to do—let that little girl go back to the farm and work for that big coward of a Bilora, who gives her beatings instead of bread. And you expect me to give her up? No, no! By God, no! I am going to protect my own happiness. And another reason why I refuse to give her up is that one of my principles is never to throw pearls to swine. You think I have gone to the trouble of bringing her here just to let her go again at once? I tell you I have girded on the sword and the shield like a veritable St. George, and I stand day and night under arms. I have spent my energy and risked my life in order to get her, and now, my good man, you may tell Bilora that he had best go home and tend to his own business.

PITTARO: But, Messire, this way his business will go to the dogs. I see you don't think much of my plan for helping him.

ANDRONICO: I would never agree to your plan, even if it cost me half my fortune and brought me to my grave.

PITTARO: Damnation! What do you want him to do? Do you want to drive him to despair?

ANDRONICO: I don't care a hang about his despair. So far as I'm concerned he can roast himself on a spit. Listen! What a devil of an idea! He is in despair! Well, what do you want me to do about it? You have already succeeded in boring me, and very quickly you will get my temper up. You can go to the deuce! Enough of this nonsense; I am getting hot under the collar.

PITTARO: No, no, Messire; you mustn't get excited. Listen! Do this much. Call the girl out here and see what she says. If she wants to go back home, let her go. If she doesn't want to, then keep her and get what pleasure you can from her. What do you say?

ANDRONICO: At last you're talking sensibly. But take care you don't regret your suggestion, for I know very well you'll be surprised. We will see who really counts. She has just got through telling me that she would not leave me for all the men in the world. And it's hardly possible that she has changed her mind since then. However, I am willing to oblige you, and besides, I would not have a clear conscience unless I brought the matter to a proof and made certain that she is not merely pretending when she responds so tenderly to my attentions. Hello! Do you hear me? Don't you hear me? Say there, my beautiful, do you hear me?

DINA: *(From within.)* Is it me you are calling, Messire?

ANDRONICO: Yes, my child. Come down here a minute. *(Aside.)* I must admit that women have few brains . . . in fact most women haven't any . . . and if this one has suddenly changed her mind!. . .
(Dina appears.)

PITTARO: Here she is, Messire.

ANDRONICO: Ah there, my beautiful! What do you say?

DINA: About what, Messire? Not knowing, I can't say anything.

ANDRONICO: Listen! This good man has come on behalf of your husband to reclaim you, and we have agreed that if you want to go, I am to allow it, but if you want to stay, you are to do so. You know very well what your life is here with me, and whether or not I let you want for anything, but it is up to you to say what you'd like to do. As for me, I shall say nothing more.

DINA: Whether I should go with my husband? But why should you want me to do that? It would mean my being beaten every day. I should say I don't want to go! By heaven, I wish I had never known him! He's a miserable coward, as truly as bread is good to eat. Great God, no, Messire! I never want to go back to him. When I look at him I think of a wolf.

ANDRONICO: Enough, enough, enough! *(To Pittaro.)* Well, you have heard her. Are you satisfied? I told you she would refuse to go, and you wouldn't believe me!

PITTARO: Let me tell you, Messire, that I am very angry with this little jade, for it wasn't half an hour ago—in fact just before you came home—that she promised Bilora she would go with him, even if you objected.

DINA: What! I said that? I said . . . or rather, I was practically made to say—as the good woman said—I said . . . nothing at all. *(To Andronico.)* Let him rave; he has imagined all this.

ANDRONICO: Then go back up to your room, and we'll stop this argument. *(To Pittaro.)* That will do. Go in peace. What do you think now? For my part I never doubted for an instant that she would stay with me. Do you need any further proof?

PITTARO: No . . . not for me, Messire. What could I demand? But I should warn you that Bilora is a bad man, who is not inclined at all toward decency, and that you will be safer if you return his wife to him.

ANDRONICO: Aha! What does all this mean? It's not very hard to guess. So! You are trying to threaten me! Don't irritate me further, or I swear someone will get his head broken. Without wasting words, I consider you an imbecile. Get out of here quickly, and don't forget that I refuse absolutely to return the girl. Do you understand? When I come back out of the house in a few moments I don't want to find you here. If I do, then you will be . . . But enough! The matter is settled. *(Andronico re-enters his house. Bilora appears.)*

PITTARO: Go to the devil! And I hope I never see you again.

BILORA: By the blood of Dominustecum, you are a fine talker, you are! You didn't even swear at him, nor tell him I was an outlaw, now blaspheme, nor anything! By the blessed blood of a sick bitch, what sort of a damned fool are you anyway? If you had blasphemed, if you had said I was an outlaw, I am sure he would have given me back my wife. What proves it is that when you told him I was a bad man and that I had no inclination toward decency, he began to tremble a little, and could think of nothing but getting himself safe inside the house.

PITTARO: So! Then why didn't you take a hand in the matter, if you're so brave? You'd like to have got me into an even worse mess, wouldn't you?

BILORA: I don't want to get you into any mess, but I owe you so little thanks it's hardly worth mentioning.

PITTARO: That's what I say. All right, all right. Are you coming?

BILORA: No; not me. Go on, then. I can say that you did your best by me.

(Pittaro leaves.)

BILORA: *(Alone.)* By the blood of a limping bitch, but all my schemes have gone topsy-turvy, and I am flat on my back. Ah, yes! It's enough to make him split his breeches laughing. Never mind! The question is, what am I going to do about it? My life is ruined. It is best that I pick up my feet and get away from here. One thing is sure: I'll never be in danger of feeling bored so long as I'm so mad. Meanwhile I know exactly what I'm going to do. When I see him leave the house I'll jump on him all of a sudden and knock him off his legs. He will hit the ground at the first whack. Then I'll beat him up and down and across, and it will be a wonder if I don't scratch out his eyes and kill him. By God, yes, it will be too bad if I can't bully him into letting her go. Besides that, I'll talk to him in the language of a Spanish soldier; he will think there are at least eight men surrounding him. I had better practice a little the way I am going about it. First I will draw my knife. Let's see if it shines. Damned if it's very bright. He won't get much of a scare out of it. Now let's suppose, *verbo gratia*, that he is walking along over there, and that here am I, Bilora, who knows how to get what he wants. First I will commence to blaspheme and to swear by all the Christeleison of Padua, the Virgin Mary and the Dominustecum. A curse on you, son of a dog! Jew, go hang yourself. I know just how to kick the life out of your buttocks, and jerk you and maul you within an inch of death. Then I'll pull him out of his cloak, put it on my own back, undress him from head to foot, and then run away as fast as my legs will carry me, leaving him spread out on the ground like a big piece of filth. After that I will sell his cloak, buy myself a horse, and join the army. After all, I have no desire to go back home. Ah, yes! I know how to handle things! I wish he would show up, and not be so slow about leaving the house. Hush! Is that him coming now? Has he passed the door? Yes! May the worms eat you, old carcass! Suffering Christ, where is he then? No, he hasn't left the house yet. I'm lucky. Maybe he won't come out again at all. Hush! I swear I hear him coming. Yes, here he comes! I won't budge from this spot. Heaven keep me from jumping on him before he closes the door!

(Andronico appears in the door.)

ANDRONICO: Who the devil is this idiot babbling around the streets at this hour? Some drunken sot. May the plague take him, and may he choke in the bargain! It makes my blood boil. I'd give a lot to be captain of the guard and lay hands on him. I'd give him something he'd remember. *(Calling offstage.)* Do you hear me? Hey, my man, don't you hear me?

TONIN: *(In the house.)* Here I am!

ANDRONICO: Don't come. Stay in the house and keep Dina company. But come and get me at four o'clock. And bring along the lantern. Do you understand?

TONIN: I will come as soon as I can. Don't worry.

ANDRONICO: *(Coming forward.)* I had better go this way. If I cross the little bridge down there I will arrive in no time. Tonin, close the door.

BILORA: May the plague choke you, old villain! Take that! And that! *(He strikes him.)*

ANDRONICO: Aha! my brave fellow! Alas! alas! Help! Fire! Fire! Fire! Ah, I am killed! Ha, traitor! Help! Fire! Murder! I am killed!

BILORA: Yes, fire! Fire! I'll set fire to your tail. And now give me back my wife. You should have left her with me in the first place. Hello! I believe he is actually dead. He doesn't so much as move his foot. Ah well, he as paid the piper! Good night, damn you! He has cashed in all right, that fellow. Didn't I give you warning enough?

King Henry the Sixth, Part III

William Shakespeare
1590

Dramatic
Setting: The Palace. London.
Scene: Lady Grey has come before the King to ask that her husband's lands be restored to her and her children.

King Edward: King of England.
Gloster: Duke of Gloster, Richard, brother of Edward.
Clarence: Duke of Clarence, George, brother of Edward.
Lady Grey: Widow whose husband was killed at the battle of St. Alban's, graceful, modest, 30's.

KING EDWARD: Brother of Gloster, at Stain Alban's field
    This lady's husband, Sir Richard Grey, was slain,
    His lands then seized on by the conqueror:
    Her suit is now to repossess those lands;
    Which we in justice cannot well deny,
    Because in quarrel of the house of York
    The worthy gentlemen did lose his life.
DUKE OF GLOSTER: Your highness shall do well to grant her suit;
    It were dishonour to deny it her.
KING EDWARD: It were no less; but yet I'll make a pause.
DUKE OF GLOSTER: *(Aside to Clarence.)* Yea, it is so?
    I see the lady hath a thing to grant,
    Before the king will grant her humble suit.
DUKE OF CLARENCE: *(Aside to Gloster.)* He knows the game: how true he keeps the wind!
DUKE OF GLOSTER: *(Aside to Clarence.)* Silence!
KING EDWARD: Widow, we will consider of your suit;
    And come some other time to know our mind.
LADY GREY: Right gracious lord, I cannot brook delay:
    May't please your highness to resolve me now;
    And what your pleasure is shall satisfy me.
DUKE OF GLOSTER: *(Aside.)* Ay, widow? then I'll warrant you all you lands,
    An if what pleases him shall pleasure you.
    Fight closer, or, good faith, you'll catch a blow.

DUKE OF CLARENCE: *(Aside to Gloster.)* I fear her not, unless she chance to fall.

DUKE OF GLOSTER: *(Aside to Clarence.)* God forbid that! for he'll take vantages.

KING EDWARD: How many children hast thou, widow? tell me.

DUKE OF CLARENCE: *(Aside to Gloster.)* I think he means to beg a child of her.

DUKE OF GLOSTER: *(Aside to Clarence.)* Nay, whip me, then; he'll rather give her two.

LADY GREY: Three, my most gracious lord.

DUKE OF GLOSTER: *(Aside.)* You shall have four, if you'll be ruled by him.

KING EDWARD: 'Twere pity they should lose their father's lands.

LADY GREY: Be pitiful, dread lord, and grant it, then.

KING EDWARD: Lords, give us leave: I'll try this widow's wit.

DUKE OF GLOSTER: *(Aside.)* Ay, good leave have you; for you will have leave,

Till youth take leave, and leave you to the crutch

(Retires with Clarence.)

KING EDWARD: Now tell me, madam, do you love your children?

LADY GREY: Ay, full as dearly as I love myself.

KING EDWARD: And would you not do much to do them good?

LADY GREY: To do them good, I would sustain some harm.

KING EDWARD: Then get your husband's lands, to do them good.

LADY GREY: Therefore I came unto your majesty.

KING EDWARD: I'll tell you how these lands are to be got.

LADY GREY: So shall you bind me to your highness' service.

KING EDWARD: What service wilt thou do me, if I give them?

LADY GREY: What you command, that rests in me to do.

KIND EDWARD: But you will take exceptions to my boon.

LADY GREY: No, gracious lord, except I cannot do it.

KING EDWARD: Ay, but thou canst do what I mean to ask.

LADY GREY: Why, then I will do what your Grace commands.

DUKE OF GLOSTER: *(Aside to Clarence.)* He plies her hard; and much rain wears the marble.

DUKE OF CLARENCE: *(Aside to Gloster.)* As red as fire! nay, then her way must melt.

LADY GREY: Why stops my lord? shall I not hear my task?

KING EDWARD: An easy task; 'tis but to love a king.

LADY GREY: That's soon perform'd, because I am a subject.

KING EDWARD: Why, then, thy husband's lands I freely give thee.

LADY GREY: I take my leave with many thousand thanks.

DUKE OF GLOSTER: *(Aside to Clarence.)* The match is made; she seals
    it with a curt'sy.

KING EDWARD: But stay thee, —'tis the fruits of love I mean.

LADY GREY: The fruits of love I mean, my loving liege.

KING EDWARD: Ay, but, I fear me, in another sense.
    What love, think'st thou, I sue so much to get?

LADY GREY: My love till death, my humble thanks, my prayers;
    That love which virtue begs, and virtue grants.

KING EDWARD: No, by my troth, I did not mean such love.

LADY GREY: Why, then you mean not as I thought you did.

KING EDWARD: But now you partly may perceive my mind.

LADY GREY: My mind will never grant what I perceive
    Your highness aims at, if I aim aright.

KING EDWARD: To tell thee plain, I aim to lie with thee.

LADY GREY: To tell you plain, I had rather lie in prison.

KING EDWARD: Why, then thou shalt not have thy husband's lands.

LADY GREY: Why, then mine honesty shall be my dower;
    For by that I loss I will not purchase them.

KING EDWARD: Therein thou wrong'st thy children mightily.

LADY GREY: Herein your highness wrongs both them and me.
    But, mighty lord, this merry inclination
    Accords not with the sadness of my suit:
    Please you dismiss me, either with "ay" or "no."

KING EDWARD: Ay, if thou wilt say "ay" to my request;
    No, if thou dost say "no" to my demand.

LADY GREY: Then, no, my lord. My suit is at an end.

DUKE OF GLOSTER: *(Aside to Clarence.)* The widow likes him not, she
    knits her brows.

DUKE OF CLARENCE: *(Aside to Gloster.)* He is the bluntest wooer in
    Christendom.

KING EDWARD: *(Aside.)* Her looks do argue her replete with modesty;
    Her words do show her wit incomparable:
    All her perfections challenge sovereignty:
    One way or other, she is for a king;
    And she shall be my love, or else my queen—
    Say that King Edward take thee for his queen?

LADY GREY: 'Tis better said than done, my gracious lord:
    I am a subject fit to jest withal,
    But far unfit to be a sovereign.
KING EDWARD: Sweet widow, by my state I swear to thee
    I speak no more than what my soul intends;
    And that is, to enjoy thee for my love.
LADY GREY: And that is more than I will yield unto:
    I know I am too mean to be your queen,
    And yet too good to be your concubine.
KING EDWARD: You cavil, widow: I did mean, my queen.
LADY GREY: 'Twill grieve your Grace my sons should call you father.
KING EDWARD: No more than when my daughters call thee mother.
    Thou art a widow, and thou hast some children;
    And, by God's mother, I, being but a bachelor,
    Have other some: Why, 'tis a happy thing
    To be the father unto many sons.
    Answer no more, for thou shalt be my queen.
DUKE OF GLOSTER: *(Aside to Clarence.)* The ghostly father now hath
    done his shrift.
DUKE OF CLARENCE: *(Aside to Gloster.)* When he was made a shriver,
    'twas for shift.
KING EDWARD: Brothers, you muse what chat we two have had.
DUKE OF GLOSTER: The widow likes it not, for she looks sad.
KING EDWARD: You'ld think it strange if I should marry her.
DUKE OF CLARENCE: To whom, my lord?
KING EDWARD: Why, Clarence, to myself.
DUKE OF GLOSTER: That would be ten days' wonder at the least
DUKE OF CLARENCE: That's a day longer than a wonder lasts.
DUKE OF GLOSTER: By so much is the wonder in extremes.
KING EDWARD: Well, jest on, brothers: I can tell you both
    Her suit is granted for her husband's lands.

Taming of the Shrew

William Shakespeare
1593

Comic
Setting: On the road toward Padua.
Scene: Petruchio displays his successful conquest of Katharina's head-strong spirit. She is his wife and must obey.

Petruchio: A gentleman of Verona, suitor and then husband to the "Shrew" Katharina.
Katharina: Wild, headstrong, married now to Petruchio, 20's—had a large dowry and a bad disposition.
Hortensio: A suitor to Katharina's sister Bianca, friend to Petruchio.
Vincentio: An old man; Lucentio's father.

PETRUCHIO: Come on, o' God's name; once more toward our father's.
  Good Lord, how bright and goodly shines the moon!
KATHARINA: The moon! the sun: it is not moonlight now.
PETRUCHIO: I say it is the moon that shines so bright.
KATHARINA: I know it is the sun that shines so bright.
PETRUCHIO: Now, by my mother's son, and that's myself,
  It shall be moon, or star, or what I list,
  Or e'er I journey to your father's house—
  Go one, and fetch our horses back again—
  Evermore crost and crost; nothing but crost!
HORTENSIO: *(Aside to Katharina.)* Say as he says, or well shall never go.
KATHARINA: Forward, I pray, since we have come so far,
  And be it moon, or sun, or what you please:
  An if you please to call it a rush-candle,
  Henceforth I vow it shall be so for me.
PETRUCHIO: I say it is the moon.
KATHARINA: I know it is the moon.
PETRUCHIO: Nay, then, you lie: it is the blessed sun.
KATHARINA: Then, God be blest, it is the blessed sun:—
  But sun it is not, when you say it is not;
  And the moon changes, even as your mind.
  What you will have it named, even that it is;
  And so it shall be still for Katharine.

HORTENSIO: *(Aside.)* Petruchio, go thy ways; the field is won.
PETRUCHIO: Well, forward, forward! thus the bowl should run,
     And not unluckily against the bias,
     But, soft! what company is coming here?
     (Enter Vincentio.)
     (To Vincentio.) Good morrow, gentle mistress: where away?
     Tell me, sweet Kate, and tell me truly too,
     Hast thou beheld a fresher gentlewoman?
     Such war of white and red within her cheeks!
     What stars do spangle heaven with such beauty.
     As those two eyes become that heavenly face?—
     Fair lovely maid, once more good day to thee.—
     Sweet Kate, embrace her for her beauty's sake.
HORTENSIO: *(Aside.)* A' will make the man mad, to make a woman of
     him.
KATHARINA: Young budding virgin, fair and fresh and sweet,
     Wither away; or where is thy abode?
     Happy the parents of so fair a child;
     Happier the man whom favourable stars
     Allot thee for his lovely bedfellow!
PETRUCHIO: Why, how now, Kate! I hope thou art not mad:
     This is a man, old, wrinkled, faded, wither'd;
     And not a maiden, as thou say'st he is.
KATHARINA: Pardon, old father, my mistaking eyes,
     That have been so bedazzled with the sun,
     That every thing I look on seemeth green:
     Now I perceive thou art a reverend father;
     Pardon, I pray thee, for my mad mistaking.
PETRUCHIO: Do, good old grandsire; and withal make known
     Which way thou travellest; if along with us,
     We shall be joyful of thy company.
VINCENTIO: Fair sir, and you my merry mistress.
     That with your strange encounter much amazed me,
     My name is call'd Vincentio; my dwelling Pisa;
     And bound I am to Padua; there to visit
     A son of mine, which long I have not seen.
PETRUCHIO: What is his name?
VINCENTIO: Lucentio, gentle sir.
PETRUCHIO: Happily met; the happier for thy son.

And now by law, as well as reverend age,
I may entitle thee my loving father:
The sister to my wife, this gentlewoman,
Thy son by this hath married. Wonder not,
Nor be not grieved: she is of good esteem,
Her dowry wealthy, and of worthy birth;
Beside, so qualified as may beseem
The spouse of any noble gentleman.
Let me embrace with Old Vincentio:
And wander we to see thy honest son,
Who will of the arrival be full joyous.

VINCENTIO: But is this true? or is it else your pleasure,
Like pleasant travellers, to break a jest
Upon the company you overtake?

HORTENSIO: I do assure thee, father, so it is.

PETRUCHIO: Come, go along, and see the truth hereof;
For our first merriment hath made thee jealous.
(Exeunt Petruchio, Katharina, and Vincentio.)

HORTENSIO: Well, Petruchio, this has put me in heart.
Have to my widow! and if she be froward,
Then hast thou taught Hortensio to be untoward.
(Exit.)

The Lady of Pleasure

James Shirley

1635

Comic

Setting: Lord Bornwell's mansion.

Scene: After an altercation with Lady Bornwell concerning her gambling and extravagant spending habits, Lord Bornwell admits two of her gentleman friends who have come to call. He does not know them.

Lord Thomas Bornwell: 30's – 50's, a wealthy country gentleman who has recently moved to London at the behest of his wife.

Lady Aretina Bornwell: 20's – 30's, his wife, spoiled, vain, headstrong, extravagant, competitive, and charming.

Master Alexander Kickshaw: 20's, a wealthy young fop, well-dressed.

Master John Littleworth: 20's, his friend, also a man of mode—foppish and extravagant—carries sweets with him at all times.

BORNWELL: I have to such a height fulfill'd her humor,
 All application's dangerous; these gallants
 Must be received or shee will fall into
 A tempest, and the house be shooke with names
 Of all her kindred. Tis a servitude
 I may in time shake off.
 (Enter Alexander [Kickshaw] and Littleworth.)
KICKSHAW, LITTLEWORTH: Save you, Sir Thomas!
BORNWELL: Save you, gentlemen.
KICKSHAW: I kisse your hand.
BORNWELL: What day is it abroad?
LITTLEWORTH: The morning rises from your Ladies eyes;
 If she looke cleare, we take the happy omen
 Of a faire day.
BORNWELL: Sheele instantly appeare
 To the discredit of your complement,
 But you expresse your wit thus.
KICKSHAW: And you—modestie,
 Not to affect the praises of your owne.
BORNWELL: Leaving this subject, what game's now on foote?

What exercise carries the generall vote

O' th' towne now? Nothing moves without your knowledge.

KICKSHAW: The cocking now has all the noise; Ile have

A hundred peeces of one battle. Oh!

These birds of *Mars!*

LITTLEWORTH: *Venus* is *Mars* his bird too.

KICKSHAW: Why, and the pretty Doves are *Venusses,*

To show that kisses draw the Charriot.

LITTLEWORTH: I am for that skirmish.

BORNWELL: When shall wee have

More Booths and Bag-pipes upon Bansted downes?

No mighty race is expected? —But my Lady returnes.

(Enter Aretina.)

ARETINA: Faire morning to you, gentlemen!

You went not late to bed by your early visit.

You doe me honour.

KICKSHAW: It becomes our service.

ARETINA: What newes abroad? You hold precious intelligence.

LITTLEWORTH: All tongues are so much busie with your praise.

They have not time to frame other discourse.

Will[t] please you, Madam, tast a Sugerplum?

(Aretina accepts the offer.)

BORNWELL: What do's the Goldsmith thinke the Pearle is worth

You borrowed of my Lady?

KICKSHAW: Tis a rich one.

BORNWELL: She has many other toyes whose fashion you

Will like extremely. You have no intention

To buy any of her Jewels?

KICKSHAW: Understand me—

BORNWELL: You had rather sell perhaps. But, leaving this,

I hope you'le dine with us.

KICKSHAW: I came a' purpose.

ARETINA: And where were you last night?

KICKSHAW: I, Madam?

Where I slept not; it had beene sin where so much

Delight and beauty was to keepe me waking.

There is a Lady, Madam, will be worth

Your free societie; my conversation

Ne'er knew so elegant and brave a soule,

With most incomparable flesh and bloud,—
So spirited! so Courtly! speakes the Languages,
Sings, Dances, playes o' th' Lute to admiration!
Is faire and paints not, games too, keepes a table
And talkes most witty Satyre, has a wit
Of a cleane Mercury.

LITTLEWORTH: Is shee married?

KICKSHAW: No.

ARETINA: A Virgin?

KICKSHAW: Neither.

LITTLEWORTH: What, a widow? Something
Of this wide commendation might have beene
Excused. This, such a prodigie?

KICKSHAW: Repent
Before I name her. Shee did never see
yet full sixteene, an age in the opinion
Of wise men not contemptible; she has
Mourned out her yeare too for the honest Knight
That had compassion of her youth, and dy'd
So timely. Such a widow is not common,
And now she shines more fresh and tempting
Than any naturall Virgin.

ARETINA: What's her name?

KICKSHAW: Shee was Christened Celestina. By her husband
The Lady Bellamour. This Ring was hers.

BORNWELL: You borrowed it to coppie out the Posie?

KICKSHAW: Are they not pretty Rubies: 'Twas a grace
she was pleasd to shew me, that I might have one
Made of the same fashion, for I love
All pretty formes.

ARETINA: And is she glorious?

KICKSHAW: She is full of Jewels, Madam, but I am
most taken with the bravery of her minde,
Although her garments have all grace and ornament.

ARETINA: You have beene high in praises.

KICKSHAW: I come short,
No flattery can reach her.

BORNWELL: *(Aside.)* Now my Lady
Is troubled, as she feared to be eclipsd;

This newes will cost me somewhat.

ARETINA: You deserve
    Her favour for this noble character.

KICKSHAW: And I possesse it, by my starres benevolence!

ARETINA: You must bring us acquainted.

BORNWELL: I pray doe, sir,
    I long to see her too. Madam, I have
    Thought upon't and corrected my opinion.
    Pursue what wayes of pleasure your desires
    Incline you too; not onely with my state,
    But with my person I will follow you.
    I see the folly of my thrift, and will
    Repent in Sacke and prodigalitie
    To your owne hearts content.

ARETINA: But doe not mocke.

BORNWELL: Take me to your imbraces, gentlemen,
    And tutor me.

LITTLEWORTH: And will you kisse the Ladies?

BORNWELL: And sing and dance. I long to see this beauty;
    I would faine lose a hundred pounds at dice now;
    Thou sha't have another gowne and petticote.
    Tomorrow will you sell my running horses?
    We have no Greeke wine in the house, I thinke,
    Pray send one of our footemen to the Merchant
    And throw the hogsheads of March-beer into
    The kenell to make roome for Sackes and Clarret!
    What thinke you to be drunke yet before dinner?
    We will have constant musicke and maintaine
    Them and their Fidles in phantasticke liveries;
    Ile tune my voyce to catches. I must have
    My dyning roome enlarg'd to invite Embassadors;
    Weele feast the parish in the fields, and teach
    The Military men new discipline,
    Who shall charge all their new Artillerie
    With Oringes and Lemonds, boy, to play
    All dinner upon our capons.

KICKSHAW: Hee's exalted!

BORNWELL: I will doe anything to please my Lady.
    Let that suffice, and kisse oth' same condition.

I am converted, doe not you dispute
But patiently allow the miracle!
ARETINA: I am glad to heare you, sir, in so good tune.
(Enter Servant.)
SERVANT: Madam, the Painter.
ARETINA: I am to sit this morning.
BORNWELL: Doe, while I give new directions to my Steward.
KICKSHAW: With your favour, we'le waite on you; sitting's but
A melancholy exercise without
Some company to discourse.
ARETINA: It does conclude a Ladies morning worke. We rise, make fine,
Sit for our Picture, and tis time to dine.
LITTLEWORTH: Praying's forgot?
KICKSHAW: Tis out of fashion.
(Exeunt.)

The Barber of Seville

Pierre-Augustin Caron de Beaumarchais
1775

Comic
Setting: Seville.
Scene: The Count caught a glimpse of Rosine in Madrid and has followed her to her home in Seville. Now, he is disguised, using the name Lindor, and he meets Figaro on a street near Rosine and Bartholo's house.

Rosine: A young lady of noble birth, 20's—a sweet, innocent young woman.
Bartholo: A doctor, her guardian, 40's – 50's.
Count: Count Almaviva, a Spanish Nobleman, 20's – 30's—in love with Rosine and in disguise so his true status will not be known.
Figaro: A barber, former valet of Almaviva—loves to sing, 40's, poor and rather fat and flabby.

COUNT: The day is advancing more slowly than I thought. She usually appears at the window much later than this. Never mind; it is better to be too early than to miss that moment of seeing her. If one of my friends at the court guessed that I was a hundred leagues away from Madrid and spending my mornings under the windows of a woman I have never spoken to he would take me for a romantic of Queen Isabella's time. Well, why not? Every man pursues his own happiness. Mine is in the heart of Rosine. But why follow a woman as far as Seville, when Madrid and the court offer such a selection of easy pleasures? Ah, that is exactly why I ran away. I am bored with these unending conquests of women whose motives are self-interest, social climbing, or vanity. It is sweet to be loved for oneself. And if I could be sure that this disguise—damn, an intruder.
(Figaro comes in, wearing a guitar, attached bandolier-fashioned by a wide ribbon. He has a pencil and paper in his hand.)
FIGARO: *(Singing.)*
      Let us not pine.
      It eats us alive.
      But the fire of a good wine

Helps us revive.
Without wine, a man
Is a meaningless loon.
He lives out a gray span
And dies off too soon.
That's not bad. Up to now. What next?
And dies off too soon . . .
Yes, good wine and idleness
Fight for my heart . . .
No, they don't fight, they rule there together, peacefully:
Reign in my heart.
Can you say "reign"? I don't see why not. When you're writing a
comic opera, you can't stop to look at every word. Nowadays, if
a thing isn't worth saying, you sing it.
Yes, good wine and idleness
Reign in my heart . . .
I'd like to end with something beautiful, brilliant, glittering,
something with a kick in it. *(He goes down on one knee and
writes as he sings.)*
Reign in my heart.
If one takes my tenderness,
The other gives me happiness.
No, no. That's flat. That's not it. I need a clash, an antithesis:
If one is my mistress
The other . . .
Yes, perfect:
The other's my tart.
Well done, Figaro. *(He writes as he sings.)*
Yes, good wine and idleness
Reign in my heart.
If one is my mistress,
The other's my tart.
The other's my tart.
The other's my tart.
Just wait until there's an orchestra behind it, and I'll show you
critics if I don't know what I'm talking about. *(He sees the Count.)*
I've seen that reverend somewhere before. *(He stands up.)*
COUNT: *(Aside.)* I'm sure I know that man.
FIGARO: No, he isn't a reverend. That haughtiness, that nobility . . .

COUNT: That grotesque shape . . .

FIGARO: I wasn't wrong: it's Count Almaviva.

COUNT: I believe it's that rogue Figaro.

FIGARO: It certainly is, my lord.

COUNT: Fool, if you say one word . . .

FIGARO: It's you all right, my lord. I recognized you. You always honored me with that kind of friendly greeting.

COUNT: I can't say I recognized you. Look how fat and flabby you are . . .

FIGARO: What do you expect, sir? That's poverty for you.

COUNT: Poor creature. What are you doing in Seville? I gave you references for a job with the government.

FIGARO: I took that job, and don't think I'm not grateful, my lord.

COUNT: Call me Lindor. Can't you see by my disguise that I don't want to be known?

FIGARO: I'll go away.

COUNT: No, stay here. I am waiting for something, and two men standing and talking look less suspicious than one walking about on his own. So pretend we're talking. Now, about the job . . .

FIGARO: The minister took Your Excellency's recommendation into account and, without hesitation, made me assistant medicine-mixer.

COUNT: For all army hospitals?

FIGARO: No, for all the royal stud farms in Andalusia.

COUNT: (Laughing.) A fine beginning.

FIGARO: It wasn't bad. I was in charge of bandages and drugs, and I often sold good horse medicine to men . . .

COUNT: Which killed the king's subjects.

FIGARO: Ah, there's no universal remedy. But sometimes they got over it. They're tough people in Galicia, Catalonia, and Auvergnat.

COUNT: Why did you give it up?

FIGARO: It gave me up. Someone told the government what I was up to: "Crooked-fingered Envy, with pale and livid hue . . . "

COUNT: Spare me that. Do you write poetry too? I saw you kneeling and scribbling and singing over there before.

FIGARO: That was exactly my trouble. When someone reported to the minister that I was composing bouquets of verse—and rather well, if I say so myself—dedicated to Chloris, and that I was sending puzzles and madrigals to the newspapers, and then when he learned that I was suddenly in print—he took a dim view of it and made me give up my job, on the pretext that literature and business don't go together.

COUNT: Good reasoning. But couldn't you make him understand?

FIGARO: I thought it was better for him to forget about me. A great man is doing you enough good when he isn't doing you harm.

COUNT: You're not telling me everything. When you were in my employ, you were a pretty slovenly character.

FIGARO: Well, my lord, you can't expect a poor man to be perfect.

COUNT: Lazy, disorganized . . .

FIGARO: A servant is expected to be as virtuous as his master, my lord, but do you know many masters who are fit to be good servants?

COUNT: *(Laughing.)* A sharp point. And so you retired to this city?

FIGARO: No, not straight away.

COUNT: *(Stopping him.)* One moment. I thought she was . . . Keep talking. I am still listening.

FIGARO: Back in Madrid, I thought I'd try my literary talents out again, and the theater seemed to be the most likely field of honor . . .

COUNT: God save us!

FIGARO: *(During this speech, the Count watches the blind of Rosine's window.)* I can't think why I wasn't the greatest success; I filled the orchestra with solid supporters; they had hands like washboards. I insisted: no gloves or canes—nothing that might deaden the applause—and, on my honor, before the opening, everyone in the café across the street seemed to be on my side. But the critics turned up in force . . .

COUNT: Ah, the critics. And the author's preparations were undermined?

FIGARO: It can happen to anybody. They booed me. But if ever I get that audience together again . . .

COUNT: You'll have your revenge by boring them to death?

FIGARO: I'll have my revenge. I'm saving it for them, by Christ.

COUNT: Are you still angry enough to swear about it? In the Palace of Justice, you know, you have only twenty-four hours to curse your judges.

FIGARO: In the theater you have twenty-four years; a lifetime is too short to get over my kind of resentment.

COUNT: It's good to see how you enjoy your anger. But you haven't told me what made you leave Madrid.

FIGARO: Must have been my good angel, sir, since I've been lucky enough to find my old master again. I say that the men of letters in Madrid were a pack of wolves, always attacking each other. Authors were beset by their cousins, their critics, their book-sellers, their censors, the people who envied them and the people who imitated them—all these insects, these mosquitoes, fastened themselves to the skin of the unfortunate authors and sucked them dry. And so I left Madrid, tired of writing, bored with myself, disgusted with other people; my debts heavy and my pockets light; convinced once and for all that the useful income from a razor is better than the doubtful honors of a pen. I took my baggage on my back and traveled philosophically through the two Castiles, La Mancha, Estremadura, Sierra Morena, and Andalusia, being acclaimed in one town, jailed in another, but always on top of events; praised by these people, denounced by those people; helping out in good times, making do in bad times, taunting all the fools and daunting all the knaves; laughing at my misfortune and clipping every beard I came across. And here I am at last in Seville, where you see me ready to serve Your Excellency in whatever capacity you desire.

COUNT: Who gave you such a joyful philosophy?

FIGARO: Lady Misfortune. I force myself to laugh at everything for fear of being forced to weep at it. What do you keep looking at over there?

COUNT: Let's get away.

FIGARO: Why?

COUNT: Come on, dolt. You'll ruin my plans.

(They go out. The blind on the first floor of the house is pulled back and Bartholo and Rosine appear at the window.)

ROSINE: How delightful to breathe this fresh air! The window is so rarely open.

BARTHOLO: What is that paper you are holding?

ROSINE: Some verses from *The Useless Precaution,* which my singing teacher gave me yesterday.

BARTHOLO: What is *The Useless Precaution?*

ROSINE: It's a new comedy.

BARTHOLO: Another play, eh? More of this modern rubbish?

ROSINE: I don't know.

BARTHOLO: The newspapers and the government are to blame. This is a barbarous century!

ROSINE: You're always abusing our poor century.

BARTHOLO: Pardon the liberty. What has it produced that it should be praised? Every kind of stupidity: freedom of thought, the law of gravity, electricity, religious tolerance, inoculation, quinine, the encyclopedia—and plays that anybody can understand . . .

(The paper falls out of Rosine's hands, into the street.)

ROSINE: Oh, dear. My song! My song fell while I was listening to you. Hurry down after it, sir, hurry; it will blow away.

BARTHOLO: When you're holding something, hold on to it. *(He leaves the balcony.)*

ROSINE: *(Looks back inside and hisses into the street.)* Psst, psst. *(The Count appears.)* Pick up the paper, quickly, and hide. *(The Count bounds forward, picks up the paper, and goes off.)*

BARTHOLO: *(Coming out of the house and looking about.)* Where is it? I can't see anything.

ROSINE: Under the balcony, at the foot of the wall.

BARTHOLO: I can't see a thing. Did anybody else pass by?

ROSINE: Not that I saw.

BARTHOLO: *(To himself.)* And I'm soft enough to look for it. Bartholo, you're an indulgent old fool. This will teach you never to open street windows. *(He goes in again.)*

ROSINE: *(Still on the balcony.)* My plight has driven me to do this: I am alone, trapped, and persecuted by an objectionable man. Is it a crime to escape from slavery?

BARTHOLO: *(Coming on to the balcony.)* Come inside, young lady. I am to blame if your song is lost; it was bad luck but it won't happen again. I promise you. *(He locks the window with a key.)*

(The Count and Figaro re-enter cautiously.)

COUNT: Now that they've gone inside, let's look at this song, which must contain some hidden message. It is a letter.

FIGARO: He asked what *The Useless Precaution* was!

COUNT: *(Reading eagerly.)* "I am curious to know why you are interested in me. As soon as my guardian goes out, sing the tune to these verses, casually, and let me know the name, the rank, and the intentions of the man who seems to be so obstinately concerned with the unfortunate Rosine."

FIGARO: *(Imitating Rosine's voice.)* Oh, dear. My song! My song fell. Hurry down after, it, sir, hurry! *(He laughs.)* These women! Do you want to make the most innocent one deceitful? Then lock her up.

COUNT: My dear Rosine!

FIGARO: Now I understand why you are wearing that disguise, my lord; you're planning to court her.

COUNT: Correct. But if you tattle . . .

FIGARO: Figaro tattle? My lord, I'm not going to pour out those high-falutin phrases about honor and devotion to reassure you; people break them every day. All I want to say is: My self-interest is in your hands; weigh it, balance it, and . . .

COUNT: Good enough. You may as well know that six months ago, on the Prado, I happened to meet a young woman of such beauty—well, you have just seen her. I sent throughout Madrid to find her. No luck. A few days ago I discovered that she is called Rosine, that she is an orphan of noble blood, and that she is married to an old doctor of this city named Bartholo.

FIGARO: A pretty little bird. Not easy to dislodge from the nest. But who told you she was the doctor's wife?

COUNT: Everybody.

FIGARO: That's a story he invented when he got back from Madrid to mislead the young men of Seville and keep them away. She is still only his ward. But before long . . .

COUNT: *(Spiritedly.)* Never! Not after that piece of news! I'd made up my mind to risk everything just to apologize to her, and I find she's free. There isn't a moment to lose. I must get her to love me, and then I must snatch her away from him. How well do you know this guardian?

Candida

George Bernard Shaw
1895

Comic

Setting: St. Dominic's Parsonage. Home to Rev. Morell and Candida Morell.

Scene: In this, the opening scene of the play, Proserpine is at work in the office, as Morell opens the last of his mail and groans.

The Reverend James Mavor Morell: A Christian Socialist clergyman, 40, vigorous, pleasant, energetic. Married to Candida.

Miss Proserpine Garnett: 30, neat, rather abrupt—Morell's typist.

Reverend Alexander Mill (Lexy.): The Curate, assistant to Morell, 20's, fresh from the University.

Mr. Burgess: 60, Candida's father—factory owner, vulgar.

(The Reverend James Mavor Morell is a Christian Socialist clergyman of the Church of England, and an active member of the Guild of St. Matthew and the Christian Social Union. A vigorous, genial, popular man of forty, robust and good-looking, full of energy, with pleasant, hearty, considerate manners, and a sound, unaffected voice, which he uses with the clean, athletic articulation of a practiced orator, and with a wide range and perfect command of expression. He is a first-rate clergyman, able to say what he likes to whom he likes, to lecture people without setting himself up against them, to impose his authority on them without humiliating them, and to interfere in their business without impertinence. His wellspring of spiritual enthusiasm and sympathetic emotion has never run dry for a moment: He still eats and sleeps heartily enough to win the daily battle between exhaustion and recuperation triumphantly. Withal, a great baby, pardonably vain of his powers and unconsciously pleased with himself. He has a healthy complexion, a good forehead, with the brows somewhat blunt, and the eyes bright and eager, a mouth resolute, but not particularly well cut, and a substantial nose, with the mobile, spreading nostrils of the dramatic orator, but, like all his features, void of subtlety.

The typist, Miss Proserpine Garnett, is a brisk little woman of about 30, of the lower middle class, neatly but cheaply dressed in a black merino shirt and a blouse, rather pert and quick of speech, and not very civil in her manner, but sensitive and affectionate. She is clattering away busily at her machine whilst Morell opens the last of his morning's letters. He realizes its contents with a comic groan of despair.)

PROSERPINE: Another lecture?

MORELL: Yes. The Hoxton Freedom Group want me to address them on Sunday morning *(Great emphasis on "Sunday," this being the unreasonable part of the business.)* What are they?

PROSERPINE: Communist Anarchists, I think.

MORELL: Just like Anarchists not to know that they can't have a parson on Sunday! Tell them to come to church if they want to hear me: It will do them good. Say I can only come on Mondays and Thursdays. Have you the diary there?

PROSERPINE: *(Taking up the diary.)* Yes.

MORELL: Have I any lecture on for next Monday?

PROSPERPINE: *(Referring to diary.)* Tower Hamlets Radical Club.

MORELL: Well, Thursday then?

PROSERPINE: English Land Restoration League.

MORELL: What next?

PROSERPINE: Guild of St. Matthew on Monday. Independent Labor Party, Greenwich Branch, on Thursday. Monday, Social-Democratic Federation, Mile End Branch. Thursday, first Confirmation class— *(Impatiently.)* Oh, I'd better tell them you can't come. They're only half a dozen ignorant and conceited costermongers without five shillings between them.

MORELL: *(Amused.)* Ah; but you see they're near relatives of mine, Miss Garnett.

PROSERPINE: *(Staring at him.)* Relatives of yours!

MORELL: Yes: We have the same father—in Heaven.

PROSERPINE: *(Relieved.)* Oh, is that all?

MORELL: *(With a sadness which is a luxury to a man whose voice expresses it so finely.)* Ah, you don't believe it. Everybody says it: Nobody believes it—nobody. *(Briskly, getting back to business.)* Well, well! Come, Miss Proserpine, can't you find a date for the costers? What about the 25th?: That was vacant the day before yesterday.

PROSERPINE: *(Referring to diary.)* Engaged—the Fabian Society.

MORELL: Bother the Fabian Society! Is the 28th gone, too?

PROSERPINE: City dinner. You're invited to dine with the Founder's Company.

MORELL: That'll do; I'll go to the Hoxton Group of Freedom instead. *(She enters the engagement in silence, with implacable disparagement of the Hoxton Anarchists in every line of her face. Morell bursts open the cover of a copy of* The Church Reformer, *which has come by post, and glances through Mr. Stewart Hendlam's leader and the Guild of St. Matthew news. These proceedings are presently enlivened by the appearance of Morell's curate, the Reverend Alexander Mill, a young gentleman gathered by Morell from the nearest University settlement, whither he had come from Oxford to give the east end of London the benefit of his university training. He is a conceitedly well-intentioned, enthusiastic, immature person, with nothing positively unbearable about him except a habit of speaking with his lips carefully closed for half an inch from each corner, a finicking articulation, and a set of horribly corrupt vowels, notably* ow for o, *this being his chief means of bringing Oxford refinement to bear on Hackney vulgarity. Morell, whom he has won over by a doglike devotion, looks up indulgently from* The Church Reformer *as he enters, and remarks.)* Well, Lexy! Late again, as usual.

LEXY: I'm afraid so. I wish I could get up in the morning.

MORELL: *(Exulting in his own energy.)* Ha! ha! *(Whimsically.)* Watch and pray, Lexy: watch and pray.

LEXY: I know. *(Rising wittily to the occasion.)* But how can I watch and pray when I am asleep? Isn't that so, Miss Prossy?

PROSERPINE: *(Sharply.)* Miss Garnett, if you please.

LEXY: I beg your pardon, Miss Garnett.

PROSERPINE: You've got to do all the work today.

LEXY: Why?

PROSERPINE: Never mind why. It will do you good to earn your supper before you eat it, for once in a way, as I do. Come: Don't dawdle. You should have been off on your rounds half an hour ago.

LEXY: *(Perplexed.)* Is she in earnest, Morell?

MORELL: *(In the highest spirits—his eyes dancing.)* Yes. I am going to dawdle today.

LEXY: You! You don't know how.

MORELL: *(Heartily.)* Ha! ha! Don't I? I'm going to have this day all to myself—or at least the forenoon. My wife's coming back: She's due here at 11:45.

LEXY: *(Surprised.)* Coming back already—with the children? I thought they were to stay to the end of the month.

MORELL: So they are: She's only coming up for two days, to get some flannel things for Jimmy, and to see how we're getting on without her.

LEXY: *(Anxiously.)* But, my dear Morell, if what Jimmy and Fluffy had was scarlatina, do you think it wise—

MORELL: Scarlatina!—rubbish, German measles. I brought it into the house myself from the Pycroft Street School. A parson is like a doctor, my boy: He must face infection as a soldier must face bullets. *(He rises and claps Lexy on the shoulder.)* Catch the measles if you can, Lexy: She'll nurse you; and what a piece of luck that will be for you! —eh?

LEXY: *(Smiling uneasily.)* It's so hard to understand you about Mrs. Morell—

MORELL: *(Tenderly.)* Ah, my boy, get married—get married to a good woman; and then you'll understand. That's a foretaste of what will be best in the Kingdom of Heaven we are trying to establish on earth. That will cure you of dawdling. An honest man feels that he must pay Heaven for every hour of happiness with a good spell of hard, unselfish work to make others happy. We have no more right to consume happiness without producing it than to consume wealth without producing it. Get a wife like my Candida; and you'll always be in arrear with your repayment.
(He pats Lexy affectionately on the back, and is leaving the room when Lexy calls to him.)

LEXY: Oh, wait a bit: I forgot. *(Morell halts and turns with the door knob in his hand.)* Your father-in-law is coming round to see you.
(Morell shuts the door again, with a complete change of manner.)

MORELL: *(Surprised and not pleased.)* Mr. Burgess?

LEXY: Yes. I passed him in the park, arguing with somebody. He gave me good day and asked me to let you know that he was coming.

MORELL: *(Half incredulous.)* But he hasn't called here for—I may almost say for years. Are you sure, Lexy? You're not joking, are you?

LEXY: *(Earnestly.)* No, sir, really.

MORELL: *(Thoughtfully.)* Hm! Time for him to take another look at Candida before she grows out of his knowledge. *(He resigns himself to the inevitable, and goes out. Lexy looks after him with beaming, foolish worship.)*

LEXY: What a good man! What a thorough, loving soul he is!
(He takes Morell's place at the table, making himself very comfortable as he takes out a cigarette.)

PROSERPINE: *(Impatiently, pulling the letter she has been working at off the typewriter and folding it.)* Oh, a man ought to be able to be fond of his wife without making a fool of himself about her.

LEXY: *(Shocked.)* Oh, Miss Prossy!

PROSERPINE: *(Rising busily and coming to the stationery case to get an envelope, in which she encloses the letter as she speaks.)* Candida here, and Candida there, and Candida everywhere! *(She licks the envelope.)* It's enough to drive anyone out of their senses *(Thumping the envelope to make it stick.)* to hear a perfectly commonplace woman raved about in that absurd manner merely because she's got good hair, and a tolerable figure.

LEXY: *(With reproachful gravity.)* I think her extremely beautiful, Miss Garnett. *(He takes the photograph up; looks at it; and adds, with even greater impressiveness.)* Extremely beautiful. How fine her eyes are!

PROSERPINE: Her eyes are not a bit better than mine—now! *(He puts down the photograph and stares austerely at her.)* And you know very well that you think me dowdy and second-rate enough.

LEXY: *(Rising majestically.)* Heaven forbid that I should think of any God's creatures in such a way! *(He moves stiffly away from her across the room to the neighbourhood of the bookcase.)*

PROSERPINE: Thank you. That's very nice and comforting,

LEXY: *(Saddened by her depravity.)* I had no idea you had any feeling against Mrs. Morell.

PROSERPINE: *(Indignantly.)* I have no feeling against her. She's very nice, very good-hearted: I'm very fond of her and can appreciate her real qualities far better than any man can. *(He shakes his head sadly and turns to the bookcase, looking along the shelves for a volume. She follows him with intense pepperiness.)* You don't believe me? *(He turns and faces her. She pounces at him with spitfire energy.)* You think I'm jealous. Oh, what a profound knowledge of the human heart you have, Mr. Lexy Mill! How well you know the weaknesses of Woman, don't you! It must be so nice to be a man and have a fine penetrating intellect instead of mere emotions like us, and to know that the reason we don't share your amorous delusions is that we're all jealous of one another! *(She abandons him with a toss of her shoulders, and crosses to the fire to warm her hands.)*

LEXY: Ah, if you women only had the same clue to Man's strength that you have to his weakness, Miss Prossy, there would be no Woman Question.

PROSERPINE: *(Over her shoulder, as she stoops, holding her hands to the blaze.)* Where did you hear Morell say that? You didn't invent it yourself: You're not clever enough.

LEXY: That's quite true. I am not ashamed of owing him that, as I owe him so many other spiritual truths. He said it at the annual conference of the Women's Liberal Federation. Allow me to add that though they didn't appreciate it, I, a mere man, did. *(He turns to the bookcase again, hoping that this may leave her crushed.)*

PROSERPINE: *(Putting her hair straight at the little panel of mirror in the mantelpiece.)* Well, when you talk to me, give me your own ideas, such as they are, and not his. You never cut a poorer figure than when you are trying to imitate him.

LEXY: *(Stung.)* I try to follow his example, not to imitate him.

PROSERPINE: *(Coming at him again on her way back to her work.)* Yes, you do: You imitate him. Why do you tuck your umbrella under your arm instead of carrying it in your hand like anyone else? Why do you walk with your chin stuck out before you, hurrying along with that eager look in your eyes—you, who never get up before half past nine in the morning: Why do you say "knoaledge" in church, though you always say "knolledge" in private conversation! Bah! do you think I don't know? *(She goes back to the typewriter.)* Here, come and set about your work: We've wasted enough time for one morning. Here's a copy of the diary for today. *(She hands him a memorandum.)*

LEXY: *(Deeply offended.)* Thank you. *(He takes it and stands at the table with his back to her, reading it. She begins to transcribe her shorthand notes on the typewriter without troubling herself about his feelings. Mr. Burgess enters unannounced. He is a man of sixty, made coarse and sordid by the compulsory selfishness of petty commerce, and later on softened into sluggish bumptious-*

ness by overfeeding and commercial success. A vulgar, ignorant, guzzling man, offensive and contemptuous to people whose labor is cheap, respectful to wealth and rank, and quite sincere and without rancor or envy in both attitudes. Finding him without talent, the world has offered him no decently paid work except ignoble work, and he has become, in consequence, somewhat hoggish. But he has no suspicion of this himself, and honestly regards his commercial prosperity as the inevitable and socially wholesome triumph of the ability, industry, shrewdness, and experience in business of a man who in private is easygoing, affectionate, and humorously convivial to a fault. Corporeally, he is a podgy man, with a square, clean-shaven face and a square beard under his chin; dust colored, with a patch of grey in the center, and small watery blue eyes with a plaintively sentimental expression, which he transfers easily to his voice by his habit of pompously intoning his sentences.)

BURGESS: *(Stopping on the threshold, and looking round.)* They told me Mr. Morell was here.

PROSERPINE: *(Rising.)* He's upstairs. I'll fetch him for you.

BURGESS: *(Staring boorishly at her.)* You're not the same young lady as hused to typewrite for him?

PROSERPINE: No.

BURGESS: *(Assenting.)* No: She was young-er. *(Miss Garnett stolidly stares at him; then goes out with great dignity. He receives this quite obtusely, and crosses to the hearth-rug, where he turns and spreads himself with his back to the fire.)* Startin' on your rounds, Mr. Mill?

LEXY: *(Folding his paper and pocketing it.)* Yes: I must be off presently.)

BURGESS: *(Momentously.)* Don't let me detain you, Mr. Mill. What I come about is private between me and Mr. Morell.

LEXY: *(Huffily.)* I have no intention of intruding, I am sure, Mr. Burgess. Good morning.

BURGESS: *(Patronizingly.)* Oh, good morning to you. *(Morell returns as Lexy is making for the door.)*

MORELL: *(To Lexy.)* Off to work?

LEXY: Yes, sir.

MORELL: *(Patting him affectionately on the shoulder.)* Take my silk handkerchief and wrap your throat up. There's a cold wind. Away with you.

(Lexy brightens up, and goes out.)

BURGESS: Spoilin' your curates, as usu'l, James. Good mornin'. When I pay a man, an' 'is livin' depen's on me, I keep him in his place.

MORELL: *(Rather shortly.)* I always keep my curates in their places as my helpers and comrades. If you get as much work out of your clerks and warehousemen as I do out of my curates, you must be getting rich pretty fast. Will you take your old chair?

(He points with curt authority to the armchair beside the fire-place; then takes the spare chair from the table and sits down in front of Burgess.)

BURGESS: *(Without moving.)* Just the same as hever, James!

MORELL: When you last called—it was about three years ago, I think—you said the same thing a little more frankly. Your exact words then were: "Just as big a fool as ever, James?"

BURGESS: *(Soothingly.)* Well, perhaps I did; but *(With conciliatory cheerfulness.)* I meant no offense by it. A clorgyman is privileged to be a bit of a fool, you know: it's on'y becomin' in his profession that he should. Anyhow, I come here, not to rake up hold differences, but to let bygones by bygones. *(Suddenly becoming very solemn, and approaching Morell.)* James: Three years ago, you done me a hill turn. You done me hout of a contrac'; an' when I gev you 'arsh words in my nat'ral disappointment, you turned my daughter again me. Well, I've come to act the part of a Cherischin. *(Offering his hand.)* I forgive you, James.

MORELL: *(Starting up.)* Confound your impudence!

BURGESS: *(Retreating, with almost lachrymose deprecation of this treatment.)* Is that becomin' language for a clorgyman, James?—and you so partic'lar, too?

MORELL: *(Hotly.)* No, sir, it is not becoming language for a clergyman. I used the wrong word. I should have said damn your impudence: That's what St. Paul, or any honest priest, would have said to you. Do you think I have forgotten that tender of yours for the contract to supply clothing to the workhouse?

BURGESS: *(In a paroxysm of public spirit.)* I acted in the interest of the ratepayers, James. It was the lowest tender: You can't deny that.

MORELL: Yes, the lowest, because you paid worse wages than any other employer—starvation wages—aye, worse than starvation wages—to the women who made the clothing. Your wages would have driven them to the streets to keep body and soul together. *(Getting angrier and angrier.)* Those women were my parishioners. I shamed the Guardians out of accepting your tender: I shamed the ratepayers out of letting them do it: I shamed everybody but you. *(Boiling over.)* How dare you, sir, come here and offer to forgive me, and talk about your daughter, and—

BURGESS: Easy, James, easy, easy. Don't git hinto a fluster about nothink. I've howned I was wrong.

MORELL: *(Fuming about.)* Have you? I didn't hear you.

BURGESS: Of course I did. I hown it now. Come: I harsk your pardon for the letter I wrote you. Is that enough?

MORELL: *(Snapping his fingers.)* That's nothing. Have you raised the wages?

BURGESS: *(Triumphantly.)* Yes.

MORELL: *(Stopping dead.)* What!

BURGESS: *(Unctuously.)* I've turned a moddle hemployer. I don't hemploy no women now: They're all sacked; and the work is done by machinery. Not a man 'as less than sixpence a *hour*; and the skilled 'ands gits the Trade Union rate. *(Proudly.)* What 'ave you to say to me now?

MORELL: *(Overwhelmed.)* Is it possible! Well, there's more joy in heaven over one sinner that repenteth— *(Going to Burgess with an explosion of apologetic cordiality.)* My dear Burgess, I most heartily beg your pardon for my hard thoughts of you. *(Grasps his hand.)* And now, don't you feel the better for the change? Come, confess, you're happier. You look happier.

BURGESS: *(Ruefully.)* Well, p'raps I do. I s'pose I must, since you notice it. At all events, I git my contrax asseppit [accepted] by the County Council. *(Savagely.)* They dussent 'ave nothink to do with me unless I paid fair wages—curse 'em for a parcel o' meddlin' fools!

MORELL: *(Dropping his hand, utterly discouraged.)* So that was why you raised the wages! *(He sits down moodily.)*

BURGESS: *(Severely, in spreading, mounting tones.)* Why else should I do it? What does it lead to but drink and huppishness in workin' men? *(He seats himself magisterially in the easy chair.)* It's hall very well for you, James: It gits you hinto the papers and makes a great man of you; but you never think of the 'arm you do, puttin' money into the pockets of workin' men that they don't know 'ow to spend, and takin' it from people that might be makin' a good huse on it.

MORELL: *(With a heavy sigh, speaking with cold politeness.)* What is your business with me this morning? I shall not pretend to believe that you are here merely out of family sentiment.

BURGESS: *(Obstinately.)* Yes, I ham—just family sentiment and nothink else.

MORELL: *(With weary calm.)* I don't believe you!

BURGESS: *(Rising threateningly.)* Don't say that to me again, James Mavor Morell.

MORELL: *(Unmoved.)* I'll say it just as often as may be necessary to convince you that it's true. I don't believe you.

BURGESS: *(Collapsing into an abyss of wounded feeling.)* Oh, well, if you're determined to be unfriendly, I s'pose I'd better go. *(He moves reluctantly toward the door. Morell makes no sign. He lingers.)* I didn't hexpect to find a hunforgivin' spirit in you, James.

The Monkey's Paw

W.W. Jacobs
1910

Dramatic

Setting: The living room of the White's home. A fire in the fireplace. Winter. Near London.

Scene: A chess game is in progress.

Mr. White: 60's.

Mrs. White: His wife.

Herbert: His son, late 20's, an electrical engineer for a power company.

Sargeant Major Thomas Morris: A retired soldier, 40's – 50's, left arm is missing.

MR. WHITE: *(Moving at last, and triumphant.)* There, Herbert, my boy! Got you, I think.

HERBERT: Oh, you're a deep 'un, Dad, aren't you?

MRS. WHITE: Mean to say he's beaten you at last?

HERBERT: Lor, no! Why, he's overlooked—

MR. WHITE: *(Very excited.)* I see it! Lemme have that back!

HERBERT: Not much. Rules of the game!

MR. WHITE: *(Disgusted.)* I don't hold with them scientific rules. You turn what ought to be an innocent relaxation—

MRS. WHITE: Don't talk so much, Father. You put him off—

HERBERT: *(Laughing.)* Not he!

MR. WHITE: *(Trying to distract his attention.)* Hark at the wind.

HERBERT: *(Drily.)* Ah! I'm listening. Check.

MR. WHITE: *(Still trying to distract him.)* I should hardly think Sergeant-Major Morris'd come tonight.

HERBERT: Mate. *(Rises.)*

MR. WHITE: *(With an outbreak of disgust and sweeping the chessmen off the board.)* That's the worst of living so far out. Your friends can't come for a quiet chat, and you addle your brains over a confounded—

HERBERT: Now, Father! Morris'll turn up all right.

MR. WHITE: *(Still in a temper.)* Lover's Lane, Fulham! Ho! Of all the beastly, slushy, out-o'-the-way places to live in—! Pathway's a bog, and the road's a torrent. *(To Mrs. White, who has risen, and is at his side.)* What's the County Council thinking of, that's what I want to know? Because this is the only house in the road it doesn't matter if nobody can get near it, I s'pose.

MRS. WHITE: Never mind, dear. Perhaps you'll win tomorrow. *(She moves to the back of table.)*

MR. WHITE: Perhaps I'll—perhaps I'll—! What d'you mean? *(Bursts out laughing.)* There! You always know what's going on inside o' me, don't you, Mother?

MRS. WHITE: Ought to, after thirty years, John. *(She goes to dresser, and busies herself wiping tumblers on tray there. He rises, goes to fireplace and lights pipe.)*

HERBERT: And it's not such a bad place, Dad, after all. One of the few old-fashioned houses left near London. None o' your stucco villas. Home-like, I call it. And so do you, or you wouldn't ha' bought it. *(Rolls a cigarette.)*

MR. WHITE: *(Growling.)* Nice job I made o' that, too! With two hundred pounds owin' on it.

HERBERT: *(On back of chair.)* Why, I shall work that off in no time, Dad. Matter o' three years, with the rise promised me.

MR. WHITE: If you don't get married.

HERBERT: Not me. Not that sort.

MR.S WHITE: I wish you would, Herbert. A good, steady, lad— *(She brings the tray with a bottle of whisky, glasses, a lemon, spoons, buns, and a knife to the table.)*

HERBERT: Lots o' time, Mother. Sufficient for the day—as the sayin' goes. Just now my dynamos don't leave me any time for love-making. Jealous they are, I tell you!

MR. WHITE: *(Chuckling.)* I lay awake o' night often, and think: If Herbert took a nap, and let his what-d'you-call-ums—dynamos, run down, all Fulham would be in darkness. Lord! what a joke!

HERBERT: Joke! And me with the sack! Pretty idea of a joke you've got, I don't think. *(Knock at outer door.)*

MRS. WHITE: Hark! *(Knock repeated, louder.)*

MR. WHITE: *(Going toward door.)* That's him. That's the Sergeant-Major. *(He unlocks door, back.)*

HERBERT: *(Removes chessboard.)* Wonder what yarn he's got for us tonight. *(Places chessboard on piano.)*

MRS. WHITE: *(Goes up right, busies herself putting the other armchair nearer fire, etc.)* Don't let the door slam, John! *(Mr. White opens the door a little, struggling with it. Wind. Sergeant-Major Morris, a veteran with a distinct military appearance—left arm gone—dressed as a commissionaire, is seen to enter. Mr. White helps him off with his coat, which he hangs up in the outer hall.)*

MR. WHITE: *(At the door.)* Slip in quick! It's as much as I can do to hold it against the wind.

SERGEANT: Awful! Awful! *(Busy taking off his cloak, etc.)* And a mile up the road—by the cemetery—it's worse. Enough to blow the hair off your head.

MR. WHITE: Give me your stick.

SERGEANT: If 'twasn't I knew what a welcome I'd get—

MR. WHITE: *(Preceding him into the room.)* Sergeant-Major Morris!

MRS. WHITE: Tut! tut! So cold you must be! Come to the fire; do'ee, now.

SERGEANT: How are you, marm? *(To Herbert.)* How's yourself, laddie? Not on duty yet, eh? Day week, eh?

HERBERT: No sir. Night week. But there's half an hour yet.

SERGEANT: *(Sitting in the armchair above the fire, toward which Mrs. White is motioning him. Mr. White mixes grog for Morris.)* Thank'ee kindly, marm. That's good—hah! That's a sight better than the trenches at Chitral. That's better than settin' in a puddle with the rain pourin' down in buckets, and the natives takin' pot-shots at you.

MRS. WHITE: Didn't you have no umbrellas? *(Corner below fire; kneels before it, stirs it, etc.)*

SERGEANT: Umbrell—? Ho! ho! That's good! Eh, White? That's good. Did ye hear what she said? Umbrellas! —*And* goloshes! *And* hot-water bottles! —Ho, yes! No offence, marm, but it's easy to see you was never a soldier.

HERBERT: *(Rather hurt.)* Mother spoke out o' kindness, sir.

SERGEANT: And well I know it; and no offense intended. No, marm, 'ardship, 'ardship is the soldier's lot. Starvation, fever, and get yourself shot. That's a bit o' my own.

MRS. WHITE: You don't look to've taken much harm—except— *(Indicates his empty sleeve. She takes kettle to table, then returns to fire.)*

SERGEANT: *(Showing a medal hidden under his coat.)* And that I got this for. No, marm. Tough. Thomas Morris is tough. *(Mr. White is holding a glass of grog under the Sergeant's nose.)* And sober. What's this now?

MR. WHITE: Put your nose in it: You'll see.

SERGEANT: Whisky? And hot? And sugar? And a slice o' lemon? No. I said I'd never—but seein' the sort o' night. Well! *(Waving the glass at them.)* Here's another thousand a year!

MR. WHITE: *(Also with a glass.)* Same to you, and many of 'em.

SERGEANT: *(To Herbert, who has no glass.)* What? Not you?

HERBERT: *(Laughing and sitting across chair.)* Oh! 'tisn't for want of being sociable. But my work don't go with it. Not if 'twas ever so little. I've got to keep a cool head, a steady eye, and a still hand. The fly-wheel might gobble me up.

MRS. WHITE: Don't, Herbert. *(Sits in armchair below fire.)*

HERBERT: *(Laughing.)* No fear, Mother.

SERGEANT: Ah! You electricians! —Sort o' magicians, you are. Light! says you—and light it is. And, power! says you—and the trams go whizzin'. And, knowledge! says you, and words go 'ummin' to the ends o' the world. It fair beats me—and I've seen a bit in my time, too.

HERBERT: *(Nudges his father.)* Your Indian magic? All a fake, Governor. The fakir's fake.

SERGEANT: Fake, you call it? I tell you, I've *seen* it.

HERBERT: *(Nudging his father with his foot.)* Oh, come, now! Such as what? Come, now!

SERGEANT: I've seen a cove with no more clothes on than a babby, *(To Mrs. White.)* if you know what I mean—take an empty basket—empty, mind!—as empty as—as this here glass—

MR. WHITE: Hand it over, Morris. *(Hands it to Herbert, who goes quickly behind table and fills it.)*

SERGEANT: Which was not my intentions, but used for illustration.

HERBERT: *(While mixing.)* Oh, *I've* seen the basket trick; and I've read how it was done. Why, I could do it myself, with a bit o' practice. Ladle out something stronger. *(Herbert brings him the glass.)*

SERGEANT: Stronger? —What do you say to an old fakir chuckin' a rope up in the air, in the *air*, mind you! —and swarming up it, same as if it was 'ooked on—and vanishing clean out 'o sight? — I've seen *that. (Herbert goes to table, plunges a knife into a bun and offers it to the Sergeant with exaggerated politeness.)*

SERGEANT: *(Eyeing it with disgust.)* Bun?—What for?

HERBERT: That yarn takes it. *(Mr. and Mrs. White delighted.)*

SERGEANT: Mean to say you doubt my word?

MRS. WHITE: No, no! He's only taking you off. —You shouldn't, Herbert.

MR. WHITE: Herbert always was one for a bit o' fun!
(Herbert puts bun back on table, comes round in front, and moving the chair out of the way, sits cross-legged on the floor at his father's side.)

SERGEANT: But it's true. Why, if I chose, I could tell you things—But there! You don't get no more yarns out o' *me.*

MR. WHITE: Nonsense, old friend. *(Puts down his glass.)* You're not going to get shirty about a bit o' fun. *(Moves his chair nearer Morris's.)* What was that you started telling me the other day about a monkey's paw, or something? *(Nudges Herbert, and winks at Mrs. White.)*

SERGEANT: *(Gravely.)* Nothing. Leastways, nothing worth hearing.

MRS.WHITE: *(With astonished curiosity.)* Monkey's *paw*—?

MR. WHITE: Ah—you was tellin' me—

SERGEANT: Nothing. Don't go on about it. *(Puts his empty glass to his lips, then stares at it.)* What? Empty again? There! When I begin thinkin' o' the paw, it makes me that absent-minded—

MR. WHITE: *(Rises and fills glass.)* You said you always carried it on you.

SERGEANT: So I do, for fear o' what might happen. *(Sunk in thought.)* Ah! —Ay!

MR. WHITE: *(Handing him his glass refilled.)* There. *(Sits again in same chair.)*

MRS. WHITE: What's it for?

SERGEANT: You wouldn't believe me, if I was to tell you.

HERBERT: *I* will, every word.

SERGEANT: Magic, then! Don't you laugh!

HERBERT: I'm not. Got it on you now?

SERGEANT: Of course.

HERBERT: Let's see it. *(Seeing the Sergeant embarrassed with his glass, Mrs. White rises, takes it from him, places it on mantelpiece and remains standing.)*

SERGEANT: Oh, it's nothing to look at. *(Hunting in his pocket.)* Just an ordinary—little paw—dried to a mummy. *(Produces it and holds it toward Mrs. White.)* Here.

MRS. WHITE: *(Who has leant forward eagerly to see it, starts back with a little cry of disgust.)* Oh!

HERBERT: Give us a look. *(Morris passes the paw to Mr. White, from whom Herbert takes it.)* Why, it's all dried up!

SERGEANT: I said so.

(Wind.)

MRS. WHITE: *(With a slight shudder.)* Hark at the wind! *(Sits again in her old place.)*

MR. WHITE: *(Taking the paw from Herbert.)* And what might there be special about it?

SERGEANT: *(Impressively.)* That there paw has had a spell put upon it!

MR. WHITE: No? *(In great alarm he thrusts the paw back into Morris's hand.)*

SERGEANT: *(Pensively, holding the paw in the palm of his hand.)* Ah! By an old fakir. He was a very holy man. He'd sat all doubled up in one spot, goin' on for fifteen year; thinkin' o' things. And he wanted to show that fate ruled people. That everything was cut and dried from the beginning, as you might say. That there warn't no gettin' away from it. And that, if you tried to, you caught it hot. *(Pauses solemnly.)* So he put a spell on this bit of a paw. It might ha' been anything else, but he took the first thing that came handy. Ah! He put a spell on it, and made it so that three people *(Looking at them and with deep meaning.)* could each have three wishes.

(All but Mrs. White laugh rather nervously.)

MRS. WHITE: Ssh! Don't!

SERGEANT: *(More gravely.)* But—! But, mark you, though the wishes was granted, those three people would have cause to wish they *hadn't* been.

MR. WHITE: But how *could* the wishes be granted?

SERGEANT: He didn't say. It would all happen so natural, you might think it a coincidence if so disposed.

HERBERT: Why haven't you tried it, sir?

SERGEANT: *(Gravely, after a pause.)* I have.

HERBERT: *(Eagerly.)* You've had your three wishes?

SERGEANT: *(Gravely.)* Yes.

MRS. WHITE: Were they granted?

SERGEANT: *(Staring at the fire.)* They were. *(A pause.)*

MR. WHITE: Has anybody else wished?

SERGEANT: Yes. The first owner had his three wish— *(Lost in recollection.)* Yes, oh, yes, he had his three wishes all right. I don't know what his first two were, *(Very impressively.)* but the third was for death. *(All shudder.)* That's how I got the paw. *(A pause.)*

HERBERT: *(Cheerfully.)* Well! Seems to me you've only got to wish for things that *can't* have any bad luck about 'em— *(Rises.)*

SERGEANT: *(Shaking his head.)* Ah!

MR. WHITE: *(Tentatively.)* Morris—if you've had your three wishes— it's no good to you, now—what do you keep it for?

SERGEANT: *(Still holding the paw; looking at it.)* Fancy, I s'pose. I did have some idea of selling it, but I don't think I will. It's done mischief enough already. Besides, people won't buy. Some of 'em think it's a fairy tale. And some want to try it first, and pay after. *(Nervous laugh from the others.)*

MRS. WHITE: If you could have another three wishes, would you?

SERGEANT: *(Slowly, weighing the paw in his hand and looking at it.)* I don't know—I don't know— *(Suddenly, with violence, flinging it in the fire.)* No! I'm damned if I would! *(Movement from all.)*

MR. WHITE: *(Rises and quickly snatches it out of the fire.)* What are you doing? *(White goes to the fireplace.)*

SERGEANT: *(Rising and following him and trying to prevent him.)* Let it burn! Let the infernal thing burn!

MRS. WHITE: *(Rises.)* Let it burn, Father!

MR. WHITE: *(Wiping it on his coat sleeve.)* No. If you don't want it, give it to me.

The Doctor's Duty

Luigi Pirandello
1913

Dramatic

Setting: The Corsi Home.

Scene: Tomasso has been seriously wounded in a battle with Neri—
the husband of a woman with whom he had an affair. He has
killed Neri. His loyal wife has stood by him, attributing his cheat-
ing to a spirited nature, but Tomasso has tried several times to re-
open his wounds and is feeling desperate and hopeless. The
doctor and the lawyer have been to see him.

Tomasso Corsi: 30's – 40's, handsome, sweet by nature.
Anna: His wife, 30's.
Dr. Tito Lecci: His physician, 40's – 50's.
Franco Cimetta: His lawyer, 40's – 50's.

TOMASSO: Anna. *(And as Anna turns quickly and bends over him,
her eyes full of tears.)* Why? *(A pause. Then, hesitantly.)* You
still—you still haven't forgiven me? *(He takes her hand and places
it over his eyes. Anna presses her trembling lips together as fresh
tears flow from her eyes and she cannot find her voice to answer
him. He removes her hand from her eyes.)* Have you?

ANNA: *(In anguish, timidly.)* Yes, I have . . . I have . . .

TOMASSO: Well then? *(Taking her face in his hands and drawing it
close to his, very tenderly.)* You understand, you know it's true
when I tell you that never, never in my heart, in my thoughts,
never have you been out of them, my saint, my love.

ANNA: *(Gently drawing away from him and stroking his hair.)* Yes,
yes, but hush now. You'll tire yourself out.

TOMASSO: It was an outrage.

ANNA: Don't please. Don't think about it.

TOMASSO: No, it's better if I tell you.

ANNA: I don't want to hear anything about it. No, don't tell me anything. I know. I know everything.

TOMASSO: Just to clear away every cloud between us.

ANNA: But there aren't any.

TOMASSO: It was an outrage that he should catch me in that shameful, stupid moment.

ANNA: Don't please don't, Tomasso.

TOMASSO: You'll understand, if you really have forgive me.

ANNA: Yes, yes, but please don't go on.

TOMASSO: A stupid mistake, which the fool wanted to compound by trying to kill me, twice.

ANNA: He did? Really?

TOMASSO: Twice. He rushed at me, holding the gun, and fired. He was trying to kill me. I had to, I had to defend myself. He gave me no choice. I couldn't—you understand—I couldn't let myself be killed over her. I couldn't, for your sake. And I told him so. But he was out of his mind, he was all over me. And I couldn't get to my feet, to get out of bed, for—for shame. He fired and the first shot broke the glass in a picture over the bed. I turned and shouted at him, "What are you doing?" I was almost laughing, it seemed so impossible that he couldn't see what an outrage, what madness it was to try and kill me like that, in that very moment, to kill me when I didn't even want to be there. I was there only by accident; she had sent for me, with some excuse.

ANNA: You see, you're getting all excited. Please, Tomasso, that's enough. It's bad for you.

TOMASSO: My whole life was at stake and had nothing to do with what was going on there: you, the children, my business. He shot again, point-blank. Oh, you will, will you? Then take this, you bastard! But I don't remember shooting at him. He sat down with a thud on the floor. Then he rolled over on his face. That was when I noticed I was holding the gun, still hot and smoking, in my hand. I felt something rising in my chest . . . I don't know, something awful, horrible. I looked at the corpse on the floor, at the window through which she had jumped. I heard the noise in the street below and—and with that same weapon I . . .

(Exhausted, he falls back against the pillow.)

ANNA: You see, you see what you're doing, Tomasso? Oh, God!

TOMASSO: It's nothing. I'm a little tired.

ANNA: Do you want to go back to bed?

TOMASSO: No, I'm fine here. It's over now. I'm strong enough. Now I have to get well right away. I just wanted to tell you, how it was and—and that I had to . . .

ANNA: Please, please don't start in again. All this you— *(She is inter-*
rupted by the entrance of Lecci and Cimetta.) Ah, the doctor's
here again. All this you'll tell—you'll tell the judges, and you'll
see, they— *(At these words, Tomasso suddenly leans up on one*
elbow and stares at Lecci and Cimetta as they come forward.)

TOMASSO: But I—oh, yes—the trial . . . *(He turns very pale and falls*
back, exhausted.

LECCI: *(Going to him.)* Come, come, mere formalities!

TOMASSO: *(Under his breath, staring at the ceiling.)* And what more
can they do to me than I've already done with my own hands?

CIMETTA: *(Instinctively, with a sign.)* Ah, my friend, it's not enough.

TOMASSO: *(Noticing him and trying to find a reply.)* Not enough? So
then . . . *(Immediately sinking back again.)* Oh, I see, yes . . .
Would you believe it? I thought it was all over. *(Desperately*
throwing his arms about Anna's neck.) Anna, Anna, I'm lost! I'm
lost!

LECCI: Now, now, of course you aren't! What makes you think so?
Who told you that?

TOMASSO: Lost. The trial. Now they'll arrest me. And how could I
have forgotten? Of course! And it'll be all the worse for me,
won't it, Cimetta, because I didn't kill just anybody, but an assistant district attorney, isn't that so, Cimetta?

CIMETTA: If we could only prove that he knew all about his wife's previous affairs!

ANNA: But there are lots of people who could testify to that.

CIMETTA: Oh, but not Neri himself! And you can't, unfortunately,
summon the dead to testify on their word of honor. The worms,
Mrs. Corsi, feed on the honor of the dead. What weight can
hearsay evidence have against factual proof? We may have
known all about his wife, but the facts indicate the contrary: that
he would not accept his wife's behavior and rebelled against it.
You say, "But if you did not wish to be deprived of this right to
live, then you should not have been caught making love to his
wife. By acting as you did bear in mind now that I'm speaking for
the prosecution—you yourself abrogated your right. You exposed
yourself to a risk and therefore you had no right to react.
Understand? Two counts against you.

TOMASSO: *(Trying to interrupt.)* But I—

CIMETTA: Let me finish. On the first count, the charge of adultery, you should have let yourself be punished by him, by the wronged husband, but instead you killed him.

TOMASSO: I had to! Instinctively! To keep him from killing me!

CIMETTA: But immediately afterward you tried to kill yourself by your own hand!

TOMASSO: And isn't that enough?

CIMETTA: How can it be? In fact, it's another point against you!

TOMASSO: It is? Even that?

CIMETTA: By trying to kill yourself you implicitly acknowledged your guilt.

TOMASSO: Yes. And I punished myself.

CIMETTA: No, Tomasso. You tried to escape your punishment.

TOMASSO: By taking my own life? What more could I have done?

CIMETTA: True enough, but you would have had to die! Since you didn't die . . .

TOMASSO: Oh, so that's my real offense? *(Pushing Anna aside so as to confront Lecci.)* But I would have died if he hadn't decided to save me.

LECCI: *(Amazed at being thus drawn into the discussion.)* What me?

TOMASSO: Yes, you! You! I didn't want your attentions! You insisted in forcing them upon me, in bringing me back to life! Why did you bring me back to life, if now—

LECCI: Easy, keep calm. It's bad for you to get so excited.

TOMASSO: Thank you, Doctor. I see you really are concerned over my health! Listen, Cimetta, I want to get to the bottom of this. Calmly, so we won't upset the good doctor. I killed myself. He came along and saved me. By what right, I want to know?

LECCI: *(Evidently disturbed, though trying to smile.)* Excuse me, but after all, I mean, this is a fine way to thank me.

TOMASSO: Thank you? For what? Didn't you hear what Cimetta just said?

LECCI: What was I supposed to do? Let you die?

TOMASSO: Yes, you should have let me die, if you didn't have the right to dispose of the life I gave up and which you restored to me.

LECCI: What do you mean, dispose? We couldn't simply ignore the law!

TOMASSO: I had gone beyond the law, punishing myself more harshly than even the law provides for! We've abolished the death penalty in this country. And if it hadn't been for you, I would be dead.

LECCI: But I had my professional duty, Corsi. It was my duty to do everything I could to save you.

TOMASSO: To hand me over to the law and have me condemned to prison? And by what right—this is what I want to know—by what right do you perform your duty as a doctor on a man who wanted to die, if in exchange society has not granted you the right to let this man live the life you give back to him?

CIMETTA: But excuse me, what about the crime you committed?

TOMASSO: I washed myself clean of it in my own blood! Isn't that enough? I killed a man and I killed myself. He wouldn't let me die. I fought against his attentions. Three times I tore the bandages away. Now here I am, alive again, thanks to him. A new man! How do you expect me to remain bound by a moment in another life that no longer exists? I'm free of the remorse of that moment; I paid for it in an hour that could have become an eternity! Now I have nothing to pay for any more! I have to live again for my family, to work for my children! How can you expect me to go to jail for a crime I never dreamed of committing, that I never would have committed if I hadn't been dragged into it? While those reap the benefits of your skills, of your duty to keep me alive only to be imprisoned, will now coldly commit the crime of condemning me to spend the rest of my life in enforced, brutish idleness, and condemn my children, my innocent children, to poverty and shame! By what right?

(He raises himself up, driven by a rage that the sense of his own helplessness transforms into fury, screams and tears at his face. Then he flings himself back against the arm of the chair. He tries to sob but cannot. The very futility of this tremendous effort leaves him momentarily stunned, as if suspended in a strange void. The others stare at him in mute horror. His face shows the long red marks of his fingers. Frightened, Anna runs to him. First she raises his head, then, helped by Cimetta, she tries to lift him to his feet, but immediately she recoils with a cry of disgust and terror. His shirt is red with blood from the wound.)

ANNA: Doctor! Doctor!

CIMETTA: The wound's opened again!

LECCI: *(Becoming pale, staring, confused.)* The wound? *(Instinctively he starts for the chair, but is immediately stopped by a hoarse, threatening cry from Corsi. Then, almost in a faint, he lets his arms fall to his side.)* No, no. He's right. Didn't you hear? I can't. I mustn't.

(Curtain.)

The Delicacies

William Carlos Williams
1917

Dramatic
Setting: A party.
A Readers' Theater Piece for four voices

Three men.
One woman.

> The hostess, in pink satin and blond hair—dressed high—shone beautifully in her white slippers against the great silent bald head of her little-eyed husband!
>
> Raising a glass of yellow Rhine wine in the narrow space just beyond the light-varnished woodwork and the decorative column between dining-room and hall, she smiled the smile of water tumbling from one ledge to another.
>
> We began with a herring salad: delicately flavored saltines in scallops of lettuce leaves.
>
> The little owl-eyed and thick-set lady with masses of gray hair has smooth pink cheeks without a wrinkle. She cannot be the daughter of the little red-faced fellow dancing about inviting lion-headed Wolff the druggist to play the piano! But she is. Wolff is a terrific smoker: If the telephone goes off at night, so his curled-haired wife whispers—he rises from bed but cannot answer till he has lighted a cigarette.
>
> Sherry wine in little conical glasses, dull brownish yellow, and tomatoes stuffed with finely cut chicken and mayonnaise!
>
> The tall Irishman in a Prince Albert and the usual striped trousers is going to sing for us. (The piano is in a little alcove with dark curtains.) The hostess's sister—ten years younger than she—in black net and velvet, has hair like some filmy haystack, cloudy about the eyes. She will play for her husband.

My wife is young, yes she is young and pretty when she cares to be—when she is interested in a discussion: It is the little dancing mayor's wife telling her of the Day Nursery in East Rutherford, 'cross the track, divided from us by the railroad—and disputes as to precedence. It is in this town the saloon flourishes, the saloon of my friend on the right whose wife has twice offended with chance words. Her English is atrocious! It is in this town that the saloon is situated, close to the railroad track, close as may be, this side being dry, dry, dry: Two people listening on opposite sides of a wall! —The Day Nursery had sixty-five babies the week before last, so my wife's eyes shine and her cheeks are pink and I cannot see a blemish.

Ice cream in the shape of flowers and domestic objects: a pipe for me since I do not smoke, a doll for you.

The figure of some great bulk of a woman disappearing into the kitchen with a quick look over the shoulder. My friend on the left who has spent the whole day in a car the like of which some old fellow would give to an actress: flower holders, mirrors, curtains, plush seats—my friend on the left who is chairman of the Streets committee of the town council—and who has spent the whole day studying automobile fire engines in neighboring towns in view of purchase—my friend, at the Elks last week at the breaking-up hymn, signalled for them to let Bill—a familiar friend of the saloon-keeper—sing out all alone to the organ—and he did sing!

Salz-rolls, exquisite! and Rhine wine *ad libitum*. A masterly caviare sandwich.

The children flitting about above stairs. The councilman has just bought a National eight—some car!

For heaven's sake I mustn't forget the halves of green peppers stuffed with cream cheese and whole walnuts!

Ceremonies in Dark Old Men

Lonne Edler III
1965

Dramatic
Setting: The home of the Parkers. Evening.
Scene: Adele has come home from work exhausted and refused to make another dinner for the men. She resents being the only breadwinner and is angry with all three of them for not looking harder for work.

Mr. Russell Parker: 50's, owns a one-seat barbershop, a widower.
Theo Parker: Early 20's, his older son.
Bobby Parker: Late teens, early 20's, his younger son.
Adele Parker: 20's, his daughter, has a good job in an office.

MR. PARKER: . . . and you can forget about cooking supper and all of that stuff.

ADELE: *(Breaks away, moves back into shop toward counter.)* Thank you, but I've already given myself the privilege of not cooking your supper tonight.

MR. PARKER: You did?

ADELE: The way I figure it, you should have my dinner waiting for me.

MR. PARKER: But I don't know how to cook.

ADELE: *(Turns sharply.)* You can learn.

MR. PARKER: Now look, Adele, if you got something on your mind, say it, 'cause you know damn well I ain't doin' no cooking.

ADELE: *(Pause.)* All right, I will. A thought came to me today as it does every day, and I'm damn tired of thinking about it—

MR. PARKER: What?

ADELE: . . . and that is, I've been down at the motor-license bureau so long, sometimes I forget the reasons I ever took the job in the first place.

MR. PARKER: Now look, everybody knows you quit college and came home to help your mama out. Everybody knows it! What you want me to do? Write some prayers to you?

(The two boys enter the back room from upstairs.)

ADELE: I just want you to get a job!

(The boys step into shop and stand apart from each other.)

BOBBY: Hey, Adele.

ADELLE: Well! From what cave did you fellows crawl out of? I didn't know you hung around barbershops. . . Want a haircut, boys?

THEO: For your information, this is the first time we been in this barbershop today. We been upstairs thinking.

ADELE: With what?

THEO: With our *minds*, baby!

ADELE: If the two of you found that house upstairs so attractive to keep you in it all day, then I can think of only three things: the telephone, the bed, and the kitchen.

BOBBY: The kitchen, that's it: We been washing dishes all day!

ADELE: I don't like that, Bobby!

THEO: And I don't like your attitude!

ADELE: Do you like it when I go out of here every morning to work?

THEO: There you go again with that same old tired talk: work! Mama understood about us, I don't know why you gotta give everybody a hard time. . .

ADELE: That was one of mama's troubles: understanding everybody.

THEO: Now don't start that junk with me!

ADELE: I have got to start that, *Mr. Theopolis Parker!*

MR. PARKER: Hold on now, there's no need for all this . . . Can't we settle this later on, Adele. . .

ADELE: We settle it now. You got six days left, so you gotta do something, and quick. I got a man coming here tomorrow to change the locks on the door. So for the little time you have left, you'll have to come by me to enter this house.

THEO: Who give you the right to do that?

ADELE: Me, Adele Eloise Parker, black, over twenty-one, and the only working person in this house! *(Pause.)* I am not going to let the three of you drive me into the grave the way you did Mama. And if you really want to know how I feel about that, I'll tell you: Mama killed herself because there was no kind of order in this house. There was nothing but her old-fashion love for a bum like you, Theo—and this one *(Points to Bobby.)* who's got nothing better to do with his time but to shoplift every time he walks into a department store. And you, Daddy, you and those fanciful stories you're always ready to tell, and all the talk of the good old days when you were the big vaudeville star, of hitting the numbers big. How? How, Daddy? The money you spent on the numbers you got from Mama. . . In a way, you let Mama make a bum out of you—you let her kill herself!

MR. PARKER: That's a terrible thing to say, Adele, and I'm not going to let you put that off on me!

ADELE: But the fact remains that in the seven years you've been in this barbershop you haven't earned enough money to buy two hot dogs! Most of your time is spent playing checkers with that damn Mr. Jenkins.

THEO: *(Breaks in.)* Why don't you get married or something! We don't need you—Pop is here, it's HIS HOUSE!

ADELE: You're lucky I don't get married and—

THEO: Nobody wants you, baby!

ADELE: *(Theo's remark stops her for a moment. She resettles herself.)* All right, you just let someone ask me, and I'll leave you with *Pop*, to starve with Pop. Or, there's another way: Why don't the three of you just leave right now and try making it on your own? Why don't we try that!

MR. PARKER: What about my shop?

ADELE: Since I'm the one that has to pay the extra forty dollars a month for you to keep this place, there's going to be no more shop. It was a bad investment and the whole of Harlem knows it!

MR. PARKER: *(Grabbing her by the arm, in desperation.)* I'm fifty-four years old!

ADELE: *(Pulling away.)* Don't touch me!

MR. PARKER: You go ahead and do what you want, but I'm not leaving this shop! *(Crosses away from her.)*

ADELE: Can't you understand, Father? I can't go on forever supporting three grown men! *That ain't right!*
    (Long pause.)

MR. PARKER: *(Shaken by her remarks.)* No, it's not right—it's not right at all.

ADELE: —It's going to be *you* or *me.*

BOBBY: *(After a pause.)* I'll do what I can, Adele.

ADELE: You'll do *more* than you can.

BOBBY: I'll do more than I can.

ADELE: Is that all right by you, Mr. Theopolis?

THEO: Yes.
    (Pause.)

ADELE: That's fine. Out of this house tomorrow morning—before I leave here, or with me—suit your choice. And don't look so mournful *(Gathers up her belongings at the shelf.)*, smile. You're going to be happier than you think, earning a living for a change. *(Moves briskly through the back room and up the stairs.)*

BOBBY: You do look pretty bad, Theo. A job might be just the thing for you.

The Journey of the Fifth Horseman

Ronald Ribman, based on a story by Ivan Turgenev
1967

Comic

Setting: Grubov Publishing House, St. Petersburg, Russia. Late afternoon.

Scene: While Zoditch drapes the portrait of their late employer in black crepe, Rubin trims and tweezes his moustache. Terentievna and her grandson sit in the office clutching a manuscript.

Mr. Zoditch: 35, first reader at the Grubov Publishing Company.

Mr. Rubin: 25, a reader at the same company.

Terentievna: 60's, a peasant woman, housekeeper to the recently deceased Mr. Chulkaturin.

Sergey: 17, her grandson, a simple-minded boy in too-small clothes.

TERENTIEVNA: *(To Zoditch.)* Did you say something, mister?

ZODITCH: No.

TERENTIEVNA: Oh, I thought you said something. I thought you was saying you wanted to read the writing, mister.

ZODITCH: I said nothing, madam. I am hanging the crepe now.

TERENTIEVNA: Because if you want I can let you read the writing now, mister.

ZODITCH: *(Exasperated.)* I cannot read your master's manuscript now, madam. I am hanging the crepe now. You have come at a bad time. There has been a death in the firm; our employer, Mr. Grubov, has passed away.

TERENTIEVNA: Oh, has he?

ZODITCH: Yes.

TERENTIEVNA: That's a sorrow.

ZODITCH: Yes.

TERENTIEVNA: And a sorrow it was when my master died, him being so sadly reduced in fortune.

(Zoditch stares at her for a moment and then resigns himself to the fact that she will not be silenced.)

SERGEY: He didn't have a kopeck what you could call his. And them what he owed money to was fierce.

TERENTIEVNA: There was always the moneylenders banging at the door of the house, but I never let none of them get at the master. I kept the doors locked in their faces I did, and I told them what they could do with their bills receivable. As God is my judge, mister, they woulda pulled the sheets off the bed he was dying on, if I'da let 'em, so vicious they was about getting their monies. What makes people get that way over money, do you suppose, mister?

RUBIN: *(He speaks before Zoditch has a chance to answer. He gestures at the painting of Mr. Grubov.)* Well, what do you think, Mr. Zoditch, have they buried him yet? *(Zoditch, without answering, starts down the ladder.)*

TERENTIEVNA: The master's house was what they called the Chulkaturin family house. *(Zoditch looks at her.)* Chulkaturin, mister. It's a name what nobody gets right, and him, poor soul, being the last of 'em what bore the name, who's to care now what the rights and wrongs of sounding it be?

RUBIN: Now that Mr. Grubov is tucked away, we can expect some changes, wouldn't you say, Mr. Zoditch? *(Zoditch still doesn't answer.)* I'd imagine Mr. Pandalevski would be the man to watch. *(Zoditch sits down and begins adjusting himself. He removes the garters from his arms, pushes down his sleeves, runs his hand through his hair.)*

TERENTIEVNA: And a hard thing it is to say "family house" when all that were near and dear to poor Mr. Chulkaturin, his mama and papa, was already gone and buried.

SERGEY: They was dead, wasn't they? Tell 'em about the rats.

TERENTIEVNA: During the winter I took service with the gentleman, I found the house overrun.

SERGEY: Rats big as horses' heads.

TERENTIEVNA: Not only rats, mister. Moles and other creature things what come burrowing in through the cellar to get in from the snow. He wouldn't let me drive them out, though I could have easy enough without him knowing because by that time he was near finished with this world, but I didn't have the heart to go against his wishes, him being perishing like he was and the doctor telling us to leave him be about the little things.

ZODITCH: Madam, I am not interested in rats, moles, and medical reports.

SERGEY: And the lousy stream? What about that?

RUBIN: Of course the fact that Mr. Pandalevski accompanied Miss Grubov to the cemetery may not mean anything definite, unless it's a step in the right direction. A young girl has to rely on someone when her father's dead, don't you thing? *(Zoditch starts angrily over to Rubin's desk. He slams down a stack of manuscripts on it.)*

ZODITCH: Work. Tweeze on your own time.

TERENTIEVNA: The boy is meaning a stream what belonged to the properties. When the master died the water went particularly bad.

SERGEY: It stank, that's what it did. And the garden had nothing to eat from it.

TERENTIEVNA: It was a flower garden, you see, mister.

SERGEY: Well, ya can't eat flowers, so what's the sense in that?

TERENTIEVNA: The flowers was particular treasured by him. You see, mister, he was a gentleman, which was why he didn't need to plant vegetables. And then after he died the spring came around again and everything was coming up, and that's a sorrow, him dead and everything coming up colorful.

RUBIN: Only who would have thought it would turn out to be Mr. Pandalevski she relied on. My money was on you, but he's a comer, he is. Well, it's all a ladder, Mr. Zoditch. It's up or it's down. We can't be keeping our feet on the same rung.

ZODITCH: Be still. I warn you. I'm the first reader.

TERENTIEVNA: The good Lord has His ways, I know, and none of us can choose the comings and goings of things, but I prayed for him that he would last through the spring so the flowers would give him pleasure.

SERGEY: So why didja pour the soap water on 'em?

ZODITCH: Madam, I have already told you, you have come at a bad time. There has been a death in the firm.

TERENTIEVNA: *(Begins coughing. A very bad cough. She pulls out her handkerchief and spits into it.)* That clears it up, it does. So that's how it is with us, mister. All Mr. Chulkaturin left us in exchange for the cruel months of our services, is what I got here. *(She takes a small parcel from her bag.)* And it's for getting it made into a book with you bookmongers, which is what the gentleman him-self was most insistent on so we could get paid something for our kindnesses to him, that me and the boy came to Petersburg. He didn't pay us a bit of wages so it's a fair thing we're doing now trying to make a little money off his writings, wouldn't you say, mister?

ZODITCH: Yes. Yes. *(Annoyed, he takes the offered parcel.)*

TERENTIEVNA: Not that I begrudge working for the sick. Doing a Christian duty to another fellow creature is doing no more than what Christ expects of us. *(Zoditch starts to unwrap the parcel. Suddenly there is the sound of a bell—the kind of bell that hangs over a door. Then the door slams shut.)*

RUBIN: They're back. *(There is a flurry of motion. Rubin shoves his manicuring equipment into the desk and hurriedly begins reading and taking notes at the same time. Zoditch puts on his coat.)*

ZODITCH: Miss Grubov.

Teibele and her Demon

Isaac Singer and Eve Friedman
1522

Comic
Setting: Tiebele's rooms.
Scene: A thunderstorm rages. Tiebele, plagued by a demonic lover, reads aloud from her prayer book.

Teibele: A young woman, beautiful and educated, 20's.
The Rabbi: An old man, 60's.
First Beadle: Assistant to the Rabbi.
Second Beadle: Assistant to the Rabbi.

TEIBELE: "Father in Heaven, I come before Thy throne of judgment with a broken heart. Frightened by my evil deed, my transgression, and iniquity—A vessel of shame and a disgrace to my holy ancestry—"
(The door opens. Enter the Rabbi, leaning on a cane, and two Beadles carrying with them a ram's horn and a spice box.)

TEIBELE: Rabbi!

RABBI: Sha! Teibele, I have pondered what you told me yesterday about being frightened by a creature of the night and we've come to drive it away.

FIRST BEADLE: With blowing the ram's horn. And black candles.

SECOND BEADLE: With incense and conjuring.

TEIBELE: Whom are you going to drive out? There's no one here now.

RABBI: Once the Evil Powers get their foot in the door they cling like burrs.

TEIBELE: I wasn't told you'd be coming. I'm on my way to bed.

RABBI: Better you didn't know ahead of time. When the Evil One gains dominion in a house he can then read your thoughts.

TEIBELE: I'm a simple woman. What do they want from me?

RABBI: You're not so simple. You can read the sacred books. Besides, you are beautiful. So my wife tells me.

TEIBELE: You think it's because of my reading? *(Suddenly brightening of the compliment.)* Did she really say that?

FIRST BEADLE: Such things don't remain a secret.

SECOND BEADLE: People have eyes.

RABBI: Beauty has a source. It comes from on high. One of the ten attributes of God is the glory of His beauty. Demons, however, are ugly. When they spy a beautiful woman they latch on, and will besmirch her to the end of time. If, God forbid, she gives herself to them, she loses her eternal soul, her health, her very life. Therefore those blessed with beauty are always in mortal danger.

TEIBELE: What good is my beauty? I'm an agunah for life, forsaken by men and God.

RABBI: Men may forsake you but you are not forsaken by God and this is the most important fact in any life. Heed my words. Before we begin, describe to me exactly what took place. First, how many were there? Two? Three, More?

TEIBELE: A few, I think.

RABBI: Males or females?

TEIBELE: I didn't notice. I was petrified.

FIRST BEADLE: Did they have feet of roosters?

TEIBELE: I didn't look at their feet.

SECOND BEADLE: Horns?

TEIBELE: Horns? No.

RABBI: Long hair?

TEIBELE: Really, I don't remember.

RABBI: Did they speak to you?

TEIBELE: What? Yes—no!

RABBI: Teibele you were naturally very confused and upset when I saw you yesterday but if I'm going to help you, you mustn't mix up what happened. Now. Did they say anything to you?

TEIBELE: No.

RABBI: Did they try to ravish you?

TEIBELE: I wouldn't forget that.

RABBI: What did they do?

TEIBELE: Nothing! They just walked around. They frightened me so.

RABBI: Have you asked the scribe to check your mezuzah?

TEIBELE: No. I should have sent for him.

RABBI: *(To Second Beadle.)* Remove the mezuzah.

SECOND BEADLE: Yes, Rabbi.

RABBI: Perhaps a letter has been tampered with. *(Beadle unfurls the parchment and hands it to the Rabbi.)*

RABBI: *(Scanning it.)* Not really invalidated but the letter *daled* from the word *echod* is half faded.

FIRST BEADLE: It's their doing!

SECOND BEADLE: Rabbi, there is not a minute to lose.

RABBI: Open the spice box.

TEIBELE: If the ram's horn is blown, it will wake up the whole town.

RABBI: When there's a clap of thunder we'll give the first blast. No one will hear.

TEIBELE: Yes, Rabbi.

RABBI: In the name of God, the Lord of Hosts, whoever has attempted to step over the threshold of this house, be he demon, ghost, lapitut, goblin, hobgoblin, destroyer, defiler, imp or meddler, we adjure you, with the Holy Name of 28, and the Holy Name of 75, in the name of the Holy Angels, Metatron, Sandalfon, Zakiel, Paniel, Raphael, Gabriel, Michael, Uriel to LEAVE THIS DWELLING—both the room where we are standing, the adjoining rooms, the garret, the cellar, the woodshed, the stable, the privy, the drygoods store and everything which belongs to this household. Depart ye and return nevermore—whether male, female, or eunuch. Leave nothing behind—neither on the bed, nor under the bed, in no nook or cranny. Begone and be scattered to the four winds to a place where birds fly not, grain grows not, where Satan, Asmodeus, Samael, Andrimelech hold dominion— *(A peal of thunder.)* Blast! *(First Beadle plays a long drawn out note. Quickly:)* A broken call! *(First Beadle blows three short blasts.)* A tremulous call! *(First Beadle repeats call nine times. To Teibele.)* Believe me, Teibele, no one heard it. *(Pause.)* I brought you these charms and amulets to hang in all the corners of the house.

TEIBELE: Thank you, Rabbi.

RABBI: Before you hang them repeat the incantation. Kuzu b'mochzas kuzu.

TEIBELE: *(Repeating.)* Kuzu, b'mochzas kuzu.

RABBI: Sleep now, Teibele, in blessed rest.

TEIBELE: Thank you, Rabbi, thank you.

The Next to Longest Day

Beth Campbell Stemple
1995

Comic
Setting: On the street. New London, Connecticut, 1912.
Scene: The family is walking uptown to go to dinner.

Eugene O'Neill: 23 years old.
James O'Neill: His father, 65.
Ella O'Neill: His mother, 54.
Jamie O'Neill: His brother, 34.

(James, Ella, Jamie, and Eugene O'Neill walk along the street. They are dressed for the evening in period costume, but their clothes appear somewhat worn. Eugene lags behind, looking out to the sea.)

ELLA: Eugene! Eugene! Quit dreaming of the sea or you'll catch your death of cold! *(Now tenderly.)* Oh, but my Gene. Why don't you come and help me walk through this wind. *(Hands fluttering through her hair.)* It will tear down all the work I did to look nice and presentable this evening.

EUGENE: Coming, Mama.

JAMES: *(Surveying waterfront.)* Just look at this booming town! The manufacturing! The sailing ships! I picked a fine society for us, I know. *(Then critical.)* Oh, it's a damnable place! If only the fog would roll in, so we could be lulled by the foghorn. *(Or if it is foggy or rainy, have him say, "If only the fog would lift, I can't bear to hear that damnable foghorn!")* But forget that—I'm famished!

JAMIE: Papa, let's stop off at Patrick Shea's before dinner. As you say about whiskey.

JAMES: Ah, yes! I've always found that good whiskey, taken in moderation as an appetizer, is the best of tonics.

ELLA: James, I can't bear another night of you carousing with the boys. I am mortified to be walking *downtown*—I shall take the trolley home—by myself!

EUGENE: Mama, no! Don't go by yourself!

JAMIE: The Kid's right, Mama. Stay with us. We won't go to the saloon. What do I care about this hick burg anyway.

ELLA: Oh, all right, but I feel too fat to eat. *(Then bitterly, to Jamie.)* But you'll go to the taverns after dinner. The Turkish and Russian Bath House. I know. *(Painfully.)* The brothels!

EUGENE: He sure has an appetite for fat tarts, the scoundrel.

JAMES: Ella, you look so much prettier when you're plump. *(Angrily.)* I can't believe the sons of James O'Neill have descended so unspeakably low! I don't insist you become priests, yet you spend every nickel I dole out on wine and women!

JAMIE: Don't forget song, Papa. Wine, women and song. *(Looking north.)* The O'Neill Brothers. . . Did you know there was a saloon named the O'Neill Brothers? How do you like that? *(Then critical.)* Oh, you're a dirty blackguard to say what we can or can't do! If I've drunk a drop, I've drunk a gallon, and I'm still no match for what you can hold!

EUGENE: *(Coughing.)* Jamie, stay off the Old Man, you know he's having trouble with the finances.

JAMIE: That's damned rot! Is that what he told you? Damned old penny-pinching bogtrotter! I'm a fool to argue. Can't change the leopard's spots!

JAMES: If you weren't my son, I'd show you what a man does to settle the score!

EUGENE: The only score you can settle is one that doesn't cost you!

JAMES: Ridicule me? If you weren't ailing—you should show more respect!

ELLA: *(As if fainting.)* Boys, boys! My hands! My hands ache. Can you take me back home, I think I need some of my medicine.

EUGENE: Mama, no! Don't say that! We'll have a nice dinner. We will. You'll feel better after you eat. You don't need to go home.

ELLA: Oh, Gene. You're turning into such a fine young man. After all the difficulty, after the hard labor and the trouble I had with you, I love you, in spite of everything.

EUGENE: Mama, I wish—

JAMES: You lunkhead! Help your mother! Can't you see she's having problems?

EUGENE: I just wish—

JAMES: Oh, but you *are* helping her. You always were the sensitive one. If only Jamie had an ounce of your kindness. Or ambition!

JAMIE: Don't cry to me about ambition! Everything I try, you make sure I fail. Oh, but I'm sorry, Papa. It's not my fault I'm not as talented as you!

JAMES: You can't blame me for your folly! You're a gifted actor, yet you ply your performances on call girls! And no college could hold you! Not enough whisky to keep your attention!

EUGENE: Papa, that's a lie! Jamie has to find his calling! You were lucky to know yours.

JAMES: Lucky? I started out in a machine shop when I was ten. He's over 30 and he can't keep an honest wage. *(Motioning to the docks.)* Why can't you just go over to the Ironworks? You should learn a trade.

JAMIE: If you'd just let go of some of your precious money, I'm sure I could invest it ten times better than you! *(As though performing Monte Cristo:)* "Those who love money, you know, think too much of what they risk to be easily induced to fight a duel."

ELLA: Stop it, both of you! How you can argue like this when Eugene's so pitifully sick? Can you keep up with us, dear?

EUGENE: *(Coughing.)* Mama, I'm fine, it's just a cold. But I wish—

ELLA: Oh, a summer cold makes anyone irritable.

JAMIE: He's not irritable, at least he has a job. That hick town rag knows a good writer when it sees one. Your stuff is special, isn't it, Kid?

EUGENE: Oh, I can write my Laconics column. The rhymes and the little stories. More interesting than every little fire or theft. But it doesn't seem to be enough.

JAMES: I'll hear none if it! For once, I can finally be proud of one of my sons. Of course, it's not a living wage, and you're no Shakespeare. But it's a start.

JAMIE: Papa, shut up! You and your precious Shakespeare! If only you had the talent to perform it, instead of mugging an old cartoon to death.

ELLA: Jamie—you apologize to your father! He was once a brilliant thespian. *(Then romantically.)* I remember the first time I saw him. He was radiant on the stage. I could think of nothing else.

JAMES: Yes, your mother was once beautiful and captivating. And she knew it, too, God bless her. *(To the boys.)* Can we have a meal in public without this damnable quarreling?

JAMIE: It's amazing you're springing for the restaurant, Old Man.

Where's the cheapest one in town? That must be where we're going.

EUGENE: I'd rather go to the shore than uptown to eat. We could have gone to the Lighthouse Inn.

JAMES: Thieving scoundrels! I'll not darken their doorstep again! They water their whiskey, but not as much, perhaps, as Patrick Shea or Joseph McBride. Good Irishmen—but dirty bogtrotters the lot of 'em!

ELLA: Don't you dare take me into one of your billiard rooms. I want to eat beside decent, presentable people. They stand for something. Not sailors. Not actors. *(Bitterly.)* But I've always hated this town and everyone in it! Just take me home!

JAMIE: Mama, we'll find a nice, respectable place to eat. Let's walk up State Street.

ELLA: Perhaps Nathan Peck's, or that lady Rosenthal's, but not the Crocker House.

EUGENE: How do you know about the Crocker House?

ELLA: I read that paper of yours, young man.

JAMES: Any restaurant. Get whatever you want—within reason. *(Optimistically.)* Perhaps we can see a show after dinner. What's playing at the Orpheum? The Empire? I'm sure I can still get us in for free. Oh, but what do these people know about entertaining an audience? I'll have to show them myself!

JAMIE: Or maybe we can shop for shoes—I hear *Economy* Shoes is open evenings.

ELLA: Jamie, you could have followed your father's footsteps so easily. If only you had wanted to. Eugene, did you ever consider acting? You have such sensitivity, and it's a shame to waste it on poetry. Oh, but you deserve to be much more than an actor! What a despicable life, living out of filthy hotels!

JAMES: I gave you the life you said you wanted!

ELLA: I could never complain because I was with you. But if I had become a nun, everything would have been different.

JAMIE: That's all I would need, to have the Kid take up life on the boards! Hasn't he already made me look bad enough? Oh, but don't get the wrong idea, Kid. I love you more than I hate you. You've always made me proud. Even when you were living on the outskirts of Liverpool. I always knew you'd come back.

EUGENE: But come back to what? I want something more, but I can't shake this damnable cold! I just wish—

JAMIE: Well, if you can't be good you can at least be careful. That's what I always say.

EUGENE: No, there's something I want. But I feel like I'm wearing a mask—no one can see through it. I don't know how to take it off!

JAMES: Now that's a new one! Wearing a mask! A damnable laugh!

EUGENE: If you all could shut up for one minute, I could hear myself think! I just wish—

ELLA: Eugene, where did all this come from? I thought you were happy to be home. Yes, I think it really feels like a home this summer.

EUGENE: Yes, Mama, it's good to be home, and it's good that you're home with us, too.

JAMIE: Yes, we're all grand and great. No more sanitoriums—for now!

JAMES: You shut up, you fool! We're gong to have a nice dinner.

ELLA: No, it's miserable! It's not like a home at all. *(To Eugene.)* You were wrong to get married, and even more wrong to bring a child into the world! And you left that poor girl alonge. She wasn't even Catholic, what went through your mind?

EUGENE: I don't know, Mama. I just wish—

ELLA: Now I'm a *grandmother*, sweet Mary Mother of God!

EUGENE: I'm sorry! I'm sorry for everything I've done to everybody! Everything is my fault, I know. But I just wish, I don't know, if I could just have things the way they could have been if—no, that's never the good condition. If it weren't for me, I mean if I had never been born, then, I mean—

JAMES: *(To Eugene.)* Now, for one and for all, could you please tell us what the hell you wish for?

(And for once, they all shut up and stare at Eugene. He is speechless at first, then chooses his words carefully.)

EUGENE: Yes, I have something I wish for. Something secret. But what the hell do you care?

Aurora's Motive

Jamie Pachino
1996

Dramatic
Setting: El Ferrol, Spain. The Family house. 1901
Scene: Aurora's father is entertaining both the General and the
Monsignor, and Aurora has been asked to come in and "show
off" her excellent knowledge. She loves books and loves learning
and spends most of her time in her Father's library.

General Emilio Suarez: 40's – 50's, General in the Spanish Army.
Monsignor Roderigo Diaz: 40's – 60's, a cleric.
Anselmo Rodriguez: 50's, of the wealthy class in Spain.
Aurora: 15, his younger daughter.

ANSELMO: Wait! Wait—one more, one more!
GENERAL: Anselmo, really—!
ANSELMO: *(To Aurora.)* Maceo—tell them about Maceo.
GENERAL: Maceo?!
AURORA: Antonio Maceo. The Cuban revolutionary.
GENERAL: Yes, I know who he is! *(Laughs.)*
ANSELMO: The Cuban revolutionary *who?*
AURORA: Led the freedom fighters.
ANSELMO: And. . . ?
AURORA: . . . started as a private.
DIAZ: Anselmo.
    (Anselmo waves a hand at Diaz, nods to Aurora to continue.)
AURORA: He worked his way to second in command of the Liberation
Army and led an East-West invasion in 1895 considered to be one
of the finest feats in military history.
GENERAL: You are teaching her *battle history?*
ANSELMO: *(Quieting him.)* A hobby. Shh. Go on.
AURORA: He devoted thirty-two years of his life to the independence
of his country.
ANSELMO: And survived. . . ?
AURORA: 900 battles.
ANSELMO: And. . .
AURORA: Twenty-six gun shot wounds.

DIAZ: And he was half colored! *Negro.* The son of an *island* woman. Why are you filling her head with such things?

ANSELMO: She enjoyed it. Isn't she impressive?

AURORA: My head has room for plenty of things.

(The General laughs.)

ANSELMO: Sh-sh-sh. Sit now. *(She sits in the chair.)* I test her. She learns. It's sport. Where's the harm?

DIAZ: You will see, I fear. When it's too late. Filling her head with ideas.

ANSELMO: What's wrong with a woman with an idea?

GENERAL: Your father will be hanged soon.

ANSELMO: For teaching young girls about freedom?

GENERAL: For siding with Cuba in wars against Spain. There are people who expect you to side with your own country Anselmo.

ANSELMO: Bosh. I love this country.

GENERAL: We know that. . .

DIAZ: Of course we know that.

GENERAL and DIAZ: *(To each other.)* "He only wants to see it made right!"

ANSELMO: I only want to see it made right.

(The General and Diaz touch glasses. The General finishes cognac, holds his glass out for more. Aurora goes to the decanter, serves the men.)

ANSELMO: You make fun. But what if it were possible? What if one could make a difference? Take Aurora. She believes, don't you chicken?

AURORA: With God's help, anything is possible.

ANSELMO: You see?

DIAZ: What about the boy?

ANSELMO: What about the boy?

DIAZ: Surely your son has inherited the passion as well?

ANSELMO: Nicolas?

DIAZ: Haven't you fed him with the books?

ANSELMO: Well. . .

AURORA: *(Under.)* Nicolas doesn't even know where the library *is.*

ANSELMO: Aurora. *(To the men.)* Ideas and he don't. . .

GENERAL: What will you do with him?

ANSELMO: Send him to you, probably. The military's the only place for him, I'm afraid. He's. . .

AURORA: Stupid.

ANSELMO: Aurora!

DIAZ: She speaks out a great deal.

ANSELMO: *(Looking at Aurora.)* She knows when it is her turn. *(Aurora returns to her seat, quiets.)*

GENERAL: It's not such a bad life. The military.

ANSELMO: No, no of course not. I suppose I just pictured him differently. How do you picture a son?

GENERAL: Truthfully? Like her.

AURORA: Because just to sit here, I'm changing your minds.

ANSELMO: You see?

DIAZ: It was not a compliment, I think. And you are encouraging it. To keep her here as a child was one thing, but she's—how old now?

AURORA: Fifteen.

DIAZ; Fifteen. She listens. And hears things. To postulate about daughters is one thing, but. . .

ANSELMO: What if there were no difference?

GENERAL: Between sons and daughters?

ANSELMO: Why not?

DIAZ: Why *not?* You mean educating them?

ANSELMO: Look how she learns, given the chance. What can we lose by investigating?

GENERAL: Even I must object here. In war there are theories, hypotheses—strategy sessions held in tents, but when you're on the *field,* it's a different world. It's. . .

ANSELMO: It's a new century. Perhaps you could train women as soldiers too.

GENERAL: Soldiers!

ANSELMO: Strategists.

GENERAL: *Strategists??* (Laughs.) Put the cognac away, child. Your father has had too much!

ANSELMO: Women understand strategy, sacrifice, they know when to surrender, when there can be no surrender. . . They have learned many things, without war.

GENERAL: You go too far! *(To Diaz.)* He goes too far!

ANSELMO: Women have no love affair with battle. They give life. That's what they're good for—they tell us. *(Looks at Diaz.)* Biologically built to.

DIAZ: ". . . and the woman will be saved through childbearing."

AURORA: 1 Timothy 2:15.

ANSELMO: You see, I have not neglected her full education.

GENERAL: But where will you find them, these "soldiers."

AURORA: May I Papa? May I? *(He nods, she stands.)* All you'd have to do is ask! Women would march we would *die* for something we believe in. If you let us, we would kill for it!

DIAZ: *Dios mio!*

AURORA: We can be trained. Our minds are fine. Our hearts are pure.

GENERAL: But your father speaks of *battle*—

AURORA: Haven't you ever seen a mother defend her child?

DIAZ: Anselmo, truly. With all due respect.

AURORA: We're stronger than you know. We can do more than just pray for victory.

ANSELMO: *(To the men.)* Shh. . .

AURORA: We can help you achieve it. So much within us, so much.

ANSELMO: . . . wait.

AURORA: Just waiting to be asked. *(Carried away.)* "For when the truth enters into a fight with the lies of the millennia, we shall have upheavals, a confusion of earthquakes, a moving of mountains and valleys, the like of which as never been dreamed of. I am no man. I am dynamite." Nietzsche. Do you see?
(Stunned moment. Then they laugh.)

DIAZ: Nietzsche! Good grief Anselmo!

ANSELMO: You see? You see!

GENERAL: Good lord! A firecracker, she is! You are right Anselmo! You are right!

ANSELMO: Nietzsche, Darwin, Rousseau, *and the Bible!* She knows them all! Quotes them by heart!

AURORA: *(Under.)* Because I am the boy. In this house. I have been the boy.

GENERAL: Well!

DIAZ: But of course you know what your Nietzsche thought of your gender my dear: "When a woman has scholarly inclinations. . . there is usually something wrong with her sexually." *(The room quiets.)* You must be careful Anselmo, of what you inspire. You never know what will come of it.

ANSELMO: Women are half the world. They should at least be given the chance. For the world to be made right. . .

AURORA: *(Softly.)* And belong to us.

ANSELMO: Good girl. *(Smiles at Aurora.)* Drink to it, pet.
    *(He holds his glass out, looking at the men. Aurora drinks from it,
    savoring. The light narrows in on her.)*
AURORA: Please God, let me follow in the footsteps of my father. Let
    me stand on my own and fight for what is possible. I know I can
    make a difference. Please God. Pretend I am a man. Use me well.

PART FIVE:

SCENES FOR THREE WOMEN/ ONE MAN

Prometheus Bound

Aeschylus
460 B.C.

Scene: Jove has punished Prometheus for stealing fire from the Gods
and giving it to Mankind. The Oceanides offer him whatever
solace and kindness they can. He is secured with huge chains and
it is cold and craggy on the promontory where he is nailed. The
area is imagined as the end of the world.

Prometheus: A Titan, from the race of Giants, now a prisoner of the
God Jove (Zeus). He is chained to a huge boulder in the cold
wastelands of Scythia.

Chorus: *(Should be read by two women.)* The daughters of Oceanus—
divine essences hoping to bring solace to Prometheus, they are
birdlike creatures representing nature.

Io: The daughter of Inachus, king of primeval Argos, who has been
transformed into a cowlike creature by a jealous Queen Hera for
having captured the affections of Jove. She is punished by having
to wander the world plagued by insects.

CHORUS: Do good to men, but do it with discretion.
　　Why shouldst thou harm thyself? Good hope I nurse
　　To see thee soon from these harsh chains unbound,
　　As free, as mighty, as great Jove himself.
PROM: This may not be; the destined course of things
　　Fate must accomplish; I must bend me yet
　　'Neath wrongs on wrongs, ere I may 'scape these bonds.
　　Though Art be strong, Necessity is stronger.
CHORUS: And who is lord of strong Necessity?
PROM: The triform Fates, and the sure-memoried Furies.
CHORUS: And mighty Jove himself must yield to them?
PROM: No more than others Jove can 'scape his doom.
CHORUS: What doom? —No doom hath he but endless sway.
PROM: 'Tis not for thee to know: tempt not the question.
CHORUS: There's some dread mystery in thy chary speech,
　　Close-veiled.
PROM: Urge this no more: the truth thou'lt know
　　In fitting season; now it lies concealed

In deepest darkness! for relenting Jove
Himself must woo this secret from my breast.

CHORAL HYMN
STROPHE I

> Never, O never may Jove,
> Who in Olympus reigns omnipotent lord,
> Plant his high will against my weak opinion!
> Let me approach the gods
> With blood of oxen and with holy feasts,
> By father Ocean's quenchless stream, and pay
> No backward vows:
> Nor let my tongue offend; but in my heart
> Be lowly wisdom graven.

ANTISTROPHE I

> For thus old Wisdom speaks:
> Thy life 'tis sweet to cherish, and while the length
> Of years is thine, thy heart with cheerful hopes
> And lightsome joys to feed.
> But thee, ah me! my blood runs cold to see thee,
> Pierced to the marrow with a thousand pains.
> Not fearing Jove,
> Self-willed thou has respect to man, Prometheus,
> Much more than man deserveth.

STROPHE II

> For what is man? behold!
> Can he requite thy love—child of a day—
> Or help thy extreme need? Hast thou not seen
> The blind and aimless strivings,
> The barren blank endeavour,
> The pithless deeds, of the fleeting dreamlike race?
> Never, O nevermore,
> May mortal wit Jove's ordered plan deceive.

ANTISTROPHE II

> This lore my heart hath learned
> From sight of these, and sharp pains, Prometheus.
> Alas! what diverse strain I sang thee then,
> Around the bridal chamber,
> And around the bridal bath,

When thou my sister fair, Hesione,
Won by rich gifts didst lead
From Ocean's caves thy spousal bed to share.
(Enter Io.)
What land is this?—what race of mortals
Owns this desert? who art thou,
Rock-bound with these wintry fetters,
And for what crime tortured thus?
Worn and weary with far travel,
Tell me where my feet have borne me!
O pain! pain! pain! it strings and goads me again,
The fateful brize!—save me, O Earth!—Avaunt
Thou horrible shadow of the Earth-born Argus!
Count not the grave close up thy hundred eyes,
But thou must come,
Haunting my path with thy suspicious look,
Unhoused from Hades?
Avaunt! avaunt! why wilt thou hound my track,
The famished wanderer of the waste sea-shore?

STROPHE

Pipe not thy sounding wax-compacted reed
With drowsy drone at me! Ah wretched me!
Wandering, still wandering o'er wide Earth, and driven
Where? where? O tell me where?
O Son of Kronos, in what damned sin
Being caught hast thou to misery yoked me thus,
Pricked me to desperation, and my heart
Pierced with thy furious goads?
Blast me with lightnings! bury me in Earth! To the gape
Of greedy sea-monsters Give me! Hear, O hear
My prayer, O King!
Enough, enough, these errant toils have tried me;
And yet no rest I find: nor when, nor where
These woes shall cease may know.

CHORUS: Dost hear the plaint of the ox-horned maid?
PROM: How should I not? the Inachian maid who know not,
Stung by the god-sent brize? the maid who smote
Jove's lustful heart with love: and his harsh spouse
Hounds her o'er Earth with chase interminable.

ANTISTROPHE

 My father's name thou know'st, and my descent!
 Who art thou? god or mortal? Speak! what charm
 Gives wretch like thee, the certain clue to know
 My lamentable fate?
 Aye, and the god-sent plague you know'st; the sting
 That spurs me o'er the far-stretched Earth; the goad
 That mads me sheer, wastes, withers, and consumes,
 A worn and famished maid,
 Whipt by the scourge of jealous Hera's wrath!
 Ah me! ah me! Misery has many shapes,
 But none like mine.
 O thou, who named my Argive home, declare
 What ills await me yet; what end; what hope?
 If hope there be for Io.

CHORUS: I pray thee speak to the weary way-worn maid.

PROM: I'll tell thee all thy wish, not in enigmas
 Tangled and dark, but in plain phrase, as friend
 Should speak to friend. Thou see'st Prometheus, who
 To mortal men gifted immortal fire.

IO: O thou, to man a common blessing given,
 What crime hath bound thee to this wintry rock?

PROM: I have but ceased rehearsing all my wrongs.

IO: And dost thou then refuse the boon I ask?

PROM: What boon? ask what thou wilt, and I will answer.

IO: Say, then, who bound thee to this ragged cliff?

PROM: Stern Jove's decree, and harsh Hephaestus' hand.

IO: And for what crime?

PROM: Let what I've said suffice.

IO: This, too, I ask—what bound hath fate appointed
 To my far-wandering toils?

PROM: This not to know
 Were better than to learn.

IO: Nay, do not hide
 This thing from me!

PROM: If 'tis a boon, believe me,
 I grudge it not.

IO: Then why so slow to answer?

PROM: I would not crush thee with the cruel truth.

IO: Fear not; I choose to hear it.

PROM: Listen then.

CHORUS: Nay, hear me rather. With her own mouth this maid
    Shall first her bygone woes rehearse; next thou
    what yet remains shalt tell.

PROM: Even so. *(To Io.)* Speak thou;
    They are the sisters of thy father, Io;
    And to wail out our griefs, when they who listen
    Our troubles with a willing tear requite, is not without its use.

IO: I will obey,
    And in plain speech my chanceful story tell;
    Though much it grieves me to retrace the source,
    Whence sprung this god-sent pest, and of my shape
    Disfigurement abhorred. Night after night
    Strange dreams around my maiden pillow hovering
    Whispered soft temptings. *"O thrice-blessed maid,*
    Why pin'st thou thus in virgin loneliness,
    When highest wedlock courts thee? Struck by the shaft
    Of fond desire for thee Jove burns, and pants
    To twine his loves with thine. Spurn not, O maid,
    The proffered bed of Jove; but lie thee straight
    To Lerne's bosomed mead, where are the sheep-folds
    And ox-stalls of thy sire, that so the eye
    Of Jove, being filled with thee, may cease from craving."
    Such nightly dreams my restless couch possessed
    Till I, all tears, did force me to unfold
    The portent to my father. He to Pytho
    Sent frequent messengers, and to Dodona,
    Searching the pleasure of the gods; but they
    With various-woven phrase came back, and answers
    More doubtful than the quest. At length, a clear
    And unambiguous voice came to my father,
    Enjoining, with most strict command, to send me
    Far from my home, and from my country far,
    To the extreme bounds of Earth an outcast wanderer,
    Else that the fire-faced bolt of Jove should smite
    Our universal race. By such responses,
    Moved of oracular Loxias, my father
    Reluctant me reluctant drove from home,

and shut the door against me. What he did
he did perforce; Jove's bit was in his mouth.
Forthwith my wit was frenzied, and my form
Assumed the brute. With maniac bound I rushed,
Horned as thou see'st, and with the sharp-mouthed sting
Of gad-fly pricked infuriate to the cliff
Of Lerne, and Cenchréa's limpid wave;
While Argus, Earth-born cow-herd, hundred-eyed,
Followed the winding traces of my path
With sharp observance. Him swift-swooping Fate
Snatched unexpected from his sleepless guard;
But I from land to land still wander on,
Scourged by the wrath of Heaven's relentless Queen.
Thou hast my tale; the sequel, if thou know'st it,
Is thine to tell; but do not seek, I pray thee,
In pity for me, to drop soft lies; for nothing
Is worse than the smooth craft of practised phrase.
CHORUS: Enough, enough! Woe's me that ever
Such voices of strange grief should rend my ear!
That such a tale of woe,
Insults, and wrongs, and horrors, should freeze me through,
As with a two-edged sword!
O destiny! destiny! woes most hard to see,
More hard to bear! Alas! poor maid for thee!
PROM: Thy wails anticipate her woes; restrain
Thy trembling tears till thou hast heard the whole.
CHORUS: Proceed: to know the worst some solace brings
To the vexed heart.

Shakuntala

Kalidasa
400 A.D.

Dramatic
Setting: In a sacred grove.
Scene: The King comes upon the beautiful Shakuntala with her maidens. She appears ill.
Of Note: A Sanskrit classic, the play is written in a poetic, lyrical style: formal and yet passionate.

King Dushyanta: 30's, in love with Shakuntala.
Shakuntala: 20's, a beautiful woman, in love with the King.
Priyamvada: Teen, 20's, her handmaiden.
Anasuya: Teen, 20's, her handmaiden.

(Enter King Dushyanta, with the air of one in love.)
KING: *(Sighing thoughtfully.)* The holy sage posses magic power
    In virtue of his penance; she, his ward,
    Under the shadow of his tutelage
    Rests in security. I know it well;
    Yet sooner shall the rushing cataract
    In foaming eddies re-ascend the steep,
    Than my fond heart turn back from its pursuit.
    God of Love! God of the flowery shafts! we are all of us cruelly
    Deceived by thee, and by the Moon, however deserving of
    Confidence you may both appear.
    For not to us do these thine arrows seem
    Pointed with tender flowerets; not to us
    Doth the pale moon irradiate the earth
    With beams of silver fraught with cooling dews:—
    But on our fevered frames the moon-beams fall
    Like darts on fire, and every flower-tipped shaft
    Of Kama, as it probes our throbbing hearts,
    Seems to be barbed with hardest adamant.
    Adorable god of love! hast thou no pity on me? *(In a tone of anguish.)* How can thy arrows be so sharp when they are pointed with flowers? Ah! I know the reason:
    E'en now in thine unbodied essence lurks

The fire of Shiva's anger, like the flame
That ever hidden in the secret depths
Of ocean, smolders there unseen. How else
Couldst thou, all immaterial as thou art,
Inflame our hearts thus fiercely? thou, whose form
Was scorched to ashes by a sudden flash
From the offended god's terrific eye.
Yet, methinks,
Welcome this anguish, welcome to my heart
These rankling wounds inflicted by the god,
Who on his scutcheon bears the monster-fish
Slain by his prowess: welcome death itself,
So that, commissioned by the lord of love,
This fair one be my executioner.
Adorable divinity! Can I by no reproaches excite your commiseration?
Have I not daily offered by thy shrine
Innumerable vows, the only food
Of thine ethereal essence? Are my prayers
Thus to be slighted? Is it meet that thou
Shouldst aim thy shafts at thy true votary's heart,
Drawing thy bow-string even to thy ear?
(Pacing up and down in a melancholy manner.) Now that the holy men have completed their rites, and have no more need of my services, how shall I dispel my melancholy? *(Sighing.)* I have but one resource. Oh for another sight of the idol of my soul! I will seek her. *(Glancing at the sun.)* In all probability, as the sun's heat is now at its height, Shakuntala is passing her time under the shade of the bowers on the banks of the Malina, attended by her maidens. I will go and look for her there. *(Walking and looking about.)* I suspect the fair one has just passed by this avenue of young trees.
Here, as she tripped along, her fingers plucked
The opening buds: these lacerated plants,
Shorn of their fairest blossoms by her hand,
Seem like dismembered trunks, whose recent wounds
Are still unclosed; while from the bleeding socket
Of many a severed stalk, the milky juice
Still slowly trickles, and betrays her path.
(Feeling a breeze.) What a delicious breeze meets me in this spot!

Here may the zephyr, fragrant with the scent
Of lotuses, and laden with the spray
Caught from the waters of the rippling stream,
Fold in its close embrace my fevered limbs.

(Walking and looking about.) She must be somewhere in the neighborhood of this arbor of overhanging creepers, enclosed by plantations of cane. *(Looking down.)*

For at the entrance here I plainly see
A line of footsteps printed in the sand.
Here are the fresh impressions of her feet;
Their well-known outline faintly marked in front,
More deeply toward the heel; betokening
The graceful undulation of her gait.

I will peep through those branches. *(Walking and looking. With transport.)* Ah! now my eyes are gratified by an entrancing sight. Yonder is the beloved of my heart reclining on a rock strewn with flowers, and attended by her two friends. How fortunate! Concealed behind the leaves, I will listen to their conversation, without raising their suspicions. *(Stands concealed, and gazes at them.)*

(Shakuntala and her two attendants, holding fans in their hands, are discovered as described.)

PRIYAMVADA and ANASUYA: *(Fanning her. In a tone of affection.)* Dearest Shakuntala, is the breeze raised by these broad lotus leaves refreshing to you?

SHAKUNTALA: Dear friends, why should you trouble yourselves to fan me?

(Priyaṃvada and Anasuya look sorrowfully at one another.)

KING: Shakuntala seems indeed to be seriously ill.

(Thoughtfully.) Can it be the intensity of the heat that has affected her? or does my heart suggest the true cause of her malady? *(Gazing at her passionately.)* Why should I doubt it?

The maiden's spotless bosom is o'erspread
With cooling balsam; on her slender arm
Her only bracelet, twined with lotus stalks,
Hangs loose and withered; her recumbent form
Expresses languor. Ne'er could noon-day sun
Inflict such fair disorder on a maid—
No, love, and love alone, is here to blame.

PRIYAMVADA: *(Aside to Anasuya.)* I have observed, Anasuya, that Shakuntala has been indisposed ever since her first interview with King Dushyanta. Depend upon it, her ailment is to be traced to this source.

ANASUYA: The same suspicion, dear Priyamvada, has crossed my mind. but I will at once ask her and ascertain the truth. *(Aloud.)* Dear Shakuntala, I am about to put a question to you. Your indisposition is really very serious.

SHAKUNTALA: *(Half-rising from her couch.)* What were you going to ask?

ANASUYA: We know very little about love-matters, dear Shakuntala; but for all that, I cannot help suspecting your present state to be something similar to that of the lovers we have read about in romances. Tell us frankly what is the cause of your disorder. It is useless to apply a remedy, until the disease be understood.

KING: Anasuya bears me out in my suspicion.

SHAKUNTALA: *(Aside.)* I am, indeed, deeply in love; but cannot rashly disclose my passion to these young girls.

PRIYAMVADA: What Anasuya says, dear Shakuntala, is very just. Why give so little heed to your ailment? Every day you are becoming thinner; though I must confess your complexion is still as beautiful as ever.

KING: Priyamvada speaks most truly.
>Sunk is her velvet cheek; her wasted bosom
>Loses its fulness; e'en her slender waist
>Grows more attenuate; her face is wan,
>Her shoulders droop; as when the vernal blasts
>Sear the young blossoms of the Madhavi
>Blighting their bloom; so mournful is the change,
>Yet in its sadness, fascinating still,
>Inflicted by the mighty lord of love
>On the fair figure of the hermit's daughter.

SHAKUNTALA: Dear friends, to no one would I rather reveal the nature of my malady than to you; but I should only be troubling you.

PRIYAMVADA and ANASUYA: Nay, this is the very point about which we are so solicitous. Sorrow shared with affectionate friends is relieved of half its poignancy.

KING: Pressed by the partners of her joys and griefs,

Her much beloved companions, to reveal
The cherished secret locked within her breast,
She needs must utter it; although her looks
Encourage me to hope, my bosom throbs
As anxiously I listen for her answer.

SHAKUNTALA: Know then, dear friends, that from the first moment the illustrious Prince, who is the guardian of our grove, presented himself to my sight—

(Stops short, and appears confused.)

PRIYAMVADA and ANASUYA: Say on, dear Shakuntala, say on.

SHAKUNTALA: Ever since that happy moment, my heart's affections have been fixed upon him, and my energies of mind and body have all deserted me, as you see.

KING: *(With rapture.)* Her own lips have uttered the words I most longed to hear.
Love lit the flame, and Love himself allays
My burning fever, as when gathering clouds
Rise o'er the earth in summer's dazzling noon,
And grateful showers dispel the morning heat.

SHAKUNTALA: You must consent, then, dear friends, to contrive some means by which I may find favor with the King, or you will have ere long to assist at my funeral.

KING: *(With rapture.)* Enough! These words remove all my doubts.

PRIYAMVADA: *(Aside to Anasuya.)* She is far gone in love, dear Anasuya, and no time ought to be lost. Since she has fixed her affections on a monarch who is the ornament of Puru's line, we need not hesitate for a moment to express our approval.

ANASUYA: I quite agree with you.

PRIYAMVADA: *(Aloud.)* We wish you joy, dear Shakuntala. Your affections are fixed on an object in every respect worthy of you. The noblest river will unite itself to the ocean, and the lovely Madhavi-creeper clings naturally to the mango, the only tree capable of supporting it.

KING: Why need we wonder if the beautiful constellation Vishakha pines to be united with the Moon.

ANASUYA: By what stratagem can we best secure to our friend the accomplishment of her heart's desire, both speedily and secretly?

PRIYAMVADA: The latter point is all we have to think about. As to "speedily," I look upon the whole affair as already settled.

ANASUYA: How so?

PRIYAMVADA: Did you not observe how the King betrayed his liking by the tender manner in which he gazed upon her, and how thin he has become the last few days, as if he had been lying awake thinking of her?

KING: *(Looking at himself.)* Quite true! I certainly am becoming thin from want of sleep:—

As night by night in anxious thought I raise
This wasted arm to rest my sleepless head,
My jeweled bracelet, sullied by the tears
That trickle from my eyes in scalding streams,
Slips toward my elbow from my shriveled wrist.
Oft I replace the bauble, but in vain;
So easily it spans the fleshless limb
That e'en the rough and corrugated skin,
Scarred by the bow-string, will not check its fall.

PRIYAMVADA: *(Thoughtfully.)* An idea strikes me. Anasuya. Let Shakuntala write a love-letter; I will conceal it in a flower, and contrive to drop it in the King's path. He will surely mistake it for the remains of some sacred offering, and will, in all probability, pick it up.

ANASUYA: A very ingenious device! It has my entire approval; but what says Shakuntala?

SHAKUNTALA: I must consider before I can consent to it.

PRIYAMVADA: Could you not, dear Shakuntala, think of some pretty composition in verse, containing a delicate declaration of your love?

SHAKUNTALA: Well, I will do my best; but my heart trembles when I think of the chances of a refusal.

KING: *(With rapture.)* Too timid maid, here stands the man from whom
Thou fearest a repulse; supremely blessed
To call thee all his own. Well might he doubt
His title to thy love; but how couldst thou
Believe thy beauty powerless to subdue him?

PRIYAMVADA and ANASUYA: You undervalue your own merits, dear Shakuntala. What man in his senses would intercept with the skirt of his robe the bright rays of the autumnal moon, which along can allay the fever of his body?

SHAKUNTALA: *(Smiling.)* Then it seems I must do as I am bid.
  (Sits down and appears to be thinking.)
KING: How charming she looks! My very eyes forget to wink, jealous
  of losing even for an instant a sight so enchanting.
  How beautiful the movement of her brow,
  As through her mind love's tender fancies flow!
  And, as she weighs her thoughts, how sweet to trace
  The ardent passion mantling in her face!
SHAKUNTALA: Dear girls, I have thought of a verse, but I have no
  writing-materials at hand.
PRIYAMVADA: Write the letters with your nail on this lotus leaf, which
  is smooth as a parrot's breast.
SHAKUNTALA: *(After writing the verse.)* Listen, dear friends, and tell
  me whether the ideas are appropriately expressed.
PRYAMVADA and ANASUYA: We are all attention.
SHAKUNTALA: *(Reads.)* I know not the secret thy bosom conceals.
  Thy form is not near me to gladden my sight;
  But sad is the tale that my fever reveals,
  Of the love that consumes me by day and by night.
KING: *(Advancing hastily toward her.)* Nay, Love does but warm thee,
  fair maiden—thy frame
  Only droops like the bud in the glare of the noon;
  But me he consumes with a pitiless flame,
  As the beams of the day-star destroy the pale moon.
PRIYAMVADA and ANASUYA: *(Looking at him joyfully, and rising to
  salute him.)* Welcome, the desire of our hearts, that so speedily
  presents itself!
  (Shakuntala makes an effort to rise.)
KING: Nay, trouble not thyself, dear maiden,
  Move not to do me homage; let thy limbs
  Still softly rest upon their flowery couch,
  And gather fragrance from the lotus stalks
  Bruised by the fevered contact of thy frame.
ANASUYA: Deign, gentle Sir, to seat yourself on the rock on which
  our friend is reposing.
  (The King sits down. Shakuntala is confused.)
PRIYAMVADA: Anyone may see at a glance that you are deeply
  attached to each other. But the affection I have for my friend

prompts me to say something of which you hardly require to be informed.

KING: Do not hesitate to speak out, my good girl. If you omit to say what is in your mind, you may be sorry for it afterwards.

PRIYAMVADA: Is it not your special office as a King to remove the suffering of your subjects who are in trouble?

KING: Such is my duty, most assuredly.

PRIYAMVADA: Know, then, that our dear friend has been brought to her present state of suffering entirely through love for you. Her life is in your hands; take pity on her and restore her to health.

KING: Excellent maiden, our attachment is mutual. It is I who am the most honored by it.

Ralph Roister Doister

Nicholas Udall

Comic
Setting: Dame Custance's home.
Scene: Ralph, madly in love with Dame Christian Custance, hides out to watch her serving women and listen to their chatter about his beloved and her household. Margery is spinning, Tibet is sewing.

Margery Mumblecrust: A nurse, 30's – 60's.
Tibet Talkapace: A maid, 20's – 30's.
Ralph Roister Doister: A show-off and a braggart, 20's.
Annot Alyface: Another maid, 20's.

M. MUMBLECRUST: If this distaff were spun, Margery Mumblecrust—
TIB. TALKAPACE: Where good stale ale is, will drink no water, I trust.
M. MUMBLECRUST: Dame Custance hath promised us good ale and white bread—
TIB. TALKAPACE: If she keep not promise I will beshrew her head!
But it will be stark night before I shall have done.
ROISTER DOISTER: I will stand here awhile, and talk with them anon.
I hear them speak of Custance, which doth my heart good;
To hear her name spoken doth even comfort my blood.
M. MUMBLECRUST: Sit down to your work, Tibet, like a good girl.
TIB. TALKAPACE: Nurse, meddle you with your spindle and your whirl!
No haste but good, Madge Mumblecrust; for whip and whur,
The old proverb doth say, never made good fur.
M. MUMBLECRUST: Well, ye will sit down to your work anon, I trust.
TIB. TALKAPACE: Soft fire maketh sweet malt, good Madge Mumblecrust.
M. MUMBLECRUST: And sweet malt maketh jolly good ale for the nones.
TIB. TALKAPACE: Which will slide down the lane without any bones.
(Sings.)
Old brown bread-crusts must have much good mumbling,
But good ale down your throat hath good easy tumbling.
ROISTER DOISTER: The jolliest wench that ere I heard! little mouse!
May I not rejoice that she shall dwell in my house?
TIB. TALKAPACE: So, sirrah, now this gear beginneth for to frame.

M. MUMBLECRUST: Thanks to God, though your work stand still,
    your tongue is not lame!
TIB. TALKAPACE: And, though your teeth be gone, both
    so sharp and so fine,
    Yet your tongue can run on patterns as well as mine.
M. MUMBLECRUST: Ye were not for nought named Tib Talkapace.
TIB. TALKAPACE: Doth my talk grieve you? Alack, God save your
    grace!
M. MUMBLECRUST: I hold a groat ye will drink anon for this gear.
TIB. TALKAPACE: And I will pray you the stripes for me to bear.
M. MUMBLECRUST: I hold a penny, ye will drink without a cup.
TIB. TALKAPACE.: Wherein so e'er ye drink, I wot ye drink all up.
    (Enter Annot Alyface, knitting.)
ANN. ALYFACE: By Cock! and well sewed, my good Tibet Talkapace!
TIB. TALKAPACE: And e'en as well knit, my nown Annot Alyface!
ROISTER DOISTER: See what a sort she keepth that must be my wife.
    Shall not I, when I have her, lead a merry life?
TIB. TALKAPACE: Welcome, my good wench, and sit here by me just.
ANN. ALYFACE: And how doth our old beldame here, Madge
    Mumblecrust?
TIB. TALKAPACE: Chide, and find faults, and threaten to complain.
ANN. ALYFACE: To make us poor girls shent, to her is small gain.
M. MUMBLECRUST: I did neither chide, nor complain, nor threaten.
ROISTER DOISTER: It would grieve my heart to see one of them
    beaten.
M. MUMBLECRUST: I did nothing but bid her work and hold her
    peace.
TIB TALKAPACE: So would I, if you could your clattering cease;
    But the devil cannot make old trot hold her tong.
ANN. ALYFACE: Let all these matters pass, and we three sing a sing!
    So shall we pleasantly both the time beguile now
    And eke dispatch all our works ere we can tell how.
TIB. TALKAPACE: I shrew them that say nay, and that shall not be I.
M. MUMBLECRUST: And I am well content.
TIB. TALKAPACE: Sing on then, by-and-by.
ROISTER DOISTER: And I will not away, but listen to their song,
    Yet Merrygreek and my folks tarry very long.
    (Tib. Talkapace, Ann. Alyface, and Margery, do sing here.)

                    Pipe, merry Annot, & c.
 Trilla, trilla, trillary.
 Work, Tibet; work, Annot; work, Margery!
 Sew, Tibet; knit, Annot; spin, Margery!
 Let us see who shall win the victory.

TIB. TALKAPACE: This sleeve is not willing to be sewed, I trow.
 A small thing might make me all in the ground to throw!
 (Then they sing again.)

                    Pipe, merry Annot, & c.
 Trilla, trilla, trillary.
 What, Tibet? what, Annot? what, Margery?
 Ye sleep, but we do not; that shall we try.
 Your fingers be numbed, our work will not lie.

TIB. TALKAPACE: If ye do so again, well, I would advise you nay.
 In good sooth, one stop more, and I make holiday.
 (They sing the third time.)

                    Pipe, merry Annot, & c.
 Trilla, trilla, trillary.
 Now, Tibet; now, Annot; now, Margery;
 Now whippet apace for the mastery,
 But it will not be, our mouth is so dry.

TIB. TALKAPACE: Ah, each finger is a thumb to-day methink,
 I care not to let all alone, choose it swim or sink.
 (They sing the fourth time.)

                    Pipe, merry Annot, & c.
 Trilla, trilla, trillary.
 When, Tibet: when, Annot? when, Margery?
 I will not! I cannot, no more can I!
 Then give we all over, and there let it lie.
 (Let her cast down her work.)

TIB. TALKAPACE: There it lieth! The worst is but a curried coat,
 Tut, I am used thereto; I care not a groat!

ANN. ALYFACE: Have we done singing since? Then will I in again.
 Here I found you, and here I leave both twain. *(Exit.)*

M. MUMBLECRUST: And I will not be long after. Tib. Talkapace.
 (Spying Roister Doister.)

TIB. TALKAPACE.: What is the matter?

M. MUMBLECRUST: Yond stood a man all this space,
 And hath heard all that ever we spake together.

TIB. TALKAPACE: Marry! the more lout he for his coming hither!
    And the less good he can, to listen maidens' talk!
    I care not an I go bid him hence for to walk.
    It were well done to know what he maketh here away.

ROISTER DOISTER: Now might I speak to them, if I wist what to say.

M. MUMBLECRUST: Nay, we will go both off, and see what he is.

ROISTER DOISTER *(Advancing.)* One that hath heard all your talk and
    singing, iwis.

TIB. TALKAPACE: The more to blame you! a good thrifty husband
    Would elsewhere have had some better matters in hand.

ROISTER DOISTER: I did it for no harm, but for good love I bear
    To your dame mistress Custance, I did your talk hear.
    And, mistress nurse, I will kiss you for acquaintance.

M. MUMBLECRUST: I come anon, sir.

TIB. TALKAPACE: Faith, I would our dame Custance
    Saw this gear!

M. MUMBLECRUST: I must first wipe all clean, yea, I must.

TIB. TALKAPACE: Ill 'chieve it, doting fool, but it must be cust!

M. MUMBLECRUST: God yield you, sir! Chad not so much
    I-chotte not whan,
    Ne'er since chwas bore, chwine, of such a gay gentleman!

ROISTER DOISTER: I will kiss you too, maiden, for the good will I bear you.

TIB. TALKAPACE: No, forsooth, by your leave, ye shall not kiss me!

ROISTER DOISTER: Yes; be not afeared; I do not disdain you a whit.

TIB. TALKAPACE: Why should I fear you? I have not so little wit,
    Ye are but a man, I know very well.

ROISTER DOISTER: Why, then?

TIB. TALKAPACE: Forsooth, for I will not, I use not to kiss men.

ROISTER DOISTER: I would fain kiss you too, good maiden, if I might.

TIB. TALKAPACE: What should that need?

ROISTER DOISTER: But to honour you, by this light!
    I use to kiss all them that I love, to God I vow.

TIB. TALKAPACE: Yea, sir, I pray you, when did ye last kiss your cow?

ROISTER DOISTER: Ye might be proud to kiss me, if ye were wise.

TIB. TALKAPACE: What promotion were therein?

ROISTER DOISTER: Nurse is not so nice.

TIB. TALKAPACE: Well, I have not been taught to kissing and licking.

ROISTER DOISTER: Yet I thank you, mistress nurse, ye made no sticking.

M. MUMBLECRUST: I will not stick for a kiss with such a man as you!

TIB. TALKAPACE: They that lust! I will again to my sewing now.

(Enter Ann. Alyface.)

ANN. ALYFACE: Tidings, ho! tidings! Dame Custance greeteth you well.

ROISTER DOISTER: Whom? me?

ANN ALYFACE: You, sir? No, sir; I do no such tale tell.

ROISTER DOISTER: But, an she knew me here—

ANN. ALYFACE: Tibet Talkapace,
    Your mistress, Custance, and mine, must speak with your grace.

TIB. TALKAPACE: With me?

ANN. ALYFACE: Ye must come in to her, out of all doubts.

TIB. TALKAPACE: And my work not half done! A mischief on all louts!
    (Exeunt Ann. and Tib.)

ROISTER DOISTER: Ah, good sweet nurse!

M. MUMBLECRUST: A good sweet gentleman!

ROISTER DOISTER: What?

M. MUBLECRUST: Nay, I cannot tell, sir; but what thing would you?

ROISTER DOISTER: How doth sweet Custance, my heart of gold, tell
    me how?

M. MUMBLECRUST: She doth very well, sir, and commends me to you.

ROISTER DOISTER: To me?

M. MUMBLECRUST: Yea, to you, sir.

ROISTER DOISTER: To me? Nurse, tell me plain, To me?

M. MUMBLECRUST: Yea.

ROISTER DOISTER: That word maketh me alive again!

M. MUMBLECRUST: She commended me to one last day, whoe'er it was.

ROISTER DOISTER: That was e'en to me and none other, by the Mass.

M. MUMBLECRUST: I cannot tell you surely, but one it was.

ROISTER DOISTER: It was I and none other. This cometh to good pass.
    I promise thee, nurse, I favour her.

M. MUMBLECRUST: E'en so, sir.

ROISTER DOISTER: Bid her sue to me for marriage.

M. MUMBLECRUST: E'en so, sir.

ROISTER DOISTER: And surely for thy sake, she shall speed.

M. MUMBLECRUST: E'en so, sir.

ROISTER DOISTER: I shall be contended to take her.

M. MUMBLECRUST: E'en so, sir.

ROISTER DOISTER: But at thy request, and for thy sake.

M. MUMBLECRUST: E'en so, sir.

ROISTER DOISTER: And, come, hark in thine ear what to say.

M. MUMBLECRUST: E'en so, sir.
    (Here let him tell her a great, long tale in her ear.)

Dido, Queen of Carthage

Christopher Marlowe
1594

Dramatic

Setting: Dido's Palace. Carthage.

Scene: Dido, passionately in love with Aeneas wants always to be with him. Aeneas, a man with a strong sense of duty and honor, is planning to leave Carthage. He feels that the Gods are commanding he return and rebuild the ravaged Troy.

Dido: Queen of Carthage.

Anna: Her sister.

Nurse: An old widow, in charge of Ascanius, the son of Aeneas.

Aeneas: Of Troy, son of Venus, captain of a flotilla of ships, father of Ascanius.

AENEAS: Now will I haste unto Lavinian shore,
    And raise a new foundation to old Troy.
    Witness the gods, and witness heaven and earth,
    How loath I am to leave these Libyan bounds,
    But the eternal Jupiter commands!
    (Enter Dido [with attendants] to Aeneas.)
DIDO: I fear I saw Aeneas' little son
    Led by Achates to the Trojan fleet;"
    If it be so, his father means to fly.
    But here he is; now, Dido, try thy wit
    Aeneas, wherefore go thy men abroad?
    Why are thy ships new rigg'd? Or to what end,
    Launch'd from the haven, lie they in the road?
    Pardon me though I ask; love makes me ask.
AENEAS: O pardon me if I resolve thee why.
    Aeneas will not feign with his dear love.
    I must from hence: this day, swift Mercury,
    When I was laying a platform for these walls,
    Sent from his father Jove, appear'd to me,
    And in his name rebuk'd me bitterly
    For lingering here, neglecting Italy.
DIDO: But yet Aeneas will not leave his love.

AENEAS: I am commanded by immortal Jove
    To leave this town and pass to Italy;
    And therefore must of force.
DIDO: These words proceed not from Aeneas' heart.
AENEAS: Not from my heart, for I can hardly go;
    And yet I may not stay. Dido, farewell.
DIDO: Farewell? Is this the mends for Dido's love?
    Do Trojans use to quit their lovers thus?
    Fare well may Dido, so Aeneas stay;
    I die, if my Aeneas say farewell.
AENEAS: Then let me go, and never say farewell.
DIDO: "Let me go"; "farewell"; "I must from hence."
    These words are poison to poor Dido's soul:
    O speak like my Aeneas, like my love!
    Why look'st thou toward the sea? The time hath been
    When Dido's beauty chain'd thine eyes to her.
    Am I less fair than when thou saw'st me first?
    O then, Aeneas, 'tis for grief of thee.
    Say thou wilt stay in Carthage with thy queen,
    And Dido's beauty will return again.
    Aeneas, say, how canst thou take thy leave?
    Wilt thou kiss Dido? O, thy lips have sworn
    To stay with Dido. Canst thou take her hand?
    Thy hand and mine have plighted mutual faith;
    Therefore, unkind Aeneas, must thou say,
    "Then let me go, and never say farewell"?
AENEAS: O Queen of Carthage, were thou ugly-black,
    Aeneas could not choose but hold thee dear.
    Yet must he not gainsay the gods' behest.
DIDO: The gods? What gods be those that seek my death?
    Wherein have I offended Jupiter,
    That he should take Aeneas from mine arms?
    O no! The gods weigh not what lovers do:
    It is Aeneas calls Aeneas hence,
    And woeful Dido, by these blubb'red cheeks,
    By this right hand, and by our spousal rites,
    Desires Aeneas to remain with her.
    Si bene quid de te merui, fuit aut tibi quidquam
    Dulce meum, miserere domus labentis, et istam

Oro, si quis adhuc precibus locus, exue mentem.
AENEAS: *Desine meque tuis incendere teque querelis;*
   Italiam non sponte sequor.
DIDO: Hast thou forgot how many neighbor kings
   Were up in arms, for making thee my love?
   How Carthage did rebel, Iarbas storm.
   And all the world call me a second Helen
   For being entangled by a stranger's looks?
   So thou wouldst prove as true as Paris did.
   Would, as fair Troy was, Carthage might be sack'd.
   And I be call'd a second Helena!
   Had I a son by thee the grief were less,
   That I might see Aeneas in his face,
   Now if thou go'st, what canst thou leave behind
   But rather will augment than ease my woe?
AENEAS: In vain, my love, thou spend'st thy fainting breath:
   If words might move me, I were overcome.
DIDO: And wilt thou not be mov'd with Dido's words?
   Thy mother was no goddess, perjur'd man,
   Nor Dardanus the author of thy stock;
   But thou art sprung from Scythian Caucasus,
   And tigers from Hyrcania gave thee suck.
   Ah, foolish Dido, to forbear this long!
   Wast thou not wrack'd upon this Libyan shore,
   And cam'st to Dido like a fisher swain?
   Repair'd not I thy ships, made thee a king,
   And all thy needy followers noblemen?
   O serpent, that came creeping from the shore,
   And I for pity harbor'd in my bosom,
   Wilt thou now slay me with thy venomed sting,
   And hiss at Dido for preserving thee?
   Go, go and spare not; seek out Italy;
   I hope that that which love forbids me do,
   The rocks and sea-gulfs will perform at large.
   And thou shalt perish in the billows' ways,
   To whom poor Dido doth bequeath revenge.
   Ay, traitor, and the waves shall cast thee up.
   Where thou and false Achates first set foot;
   Which if it chance, I'll give ye burial,

And weep upon your lifeless carcasses,
Though thou nor he will pity me a whit.
Why star'st thou in my face? If thou wilt stay,
Leap in my arms, mine arms are open wide;
If not, turn from me, and I'll turn from thee;
For though thou hast the heart to say farewell,
I have now power to stay thee.
(Exit Aeneas.)
Is he gone?
Ay, but he'll come again, he cannot go;
He loves me too too well to serve me so:
Yet he that in my sight would not relent,
Will, being absent, be obdurate still.
By this is he got to the water-side;
And see, the sailors take him by the hand,
But he shrinks back; and now, rememb'ring me,
Returns amain: welcome, welcome, my love!
But where's Aeneas? Ah, he's gone, he's gone!
(Enter Anna.)
ANNA: What means my sister thus to rave and cry?
DIDO: O Anna, my Aeneas is aboard,
And, leaving me, will sail to Italy!
Once didst thou go, and he came back again:
Now bring him back, and thou shalt be a queen,
And I will live a private life with him.
ANNA: Wicked Aeneas!
DIDO: Call him not wicked, sister; speak him fair,
And look upon him with a mermaid's eye;
Tell him, I never vow'd at Aulis gulf
The desolation of his native Troy,
Nor sent a thousand ships unto the walls,
Nor ever violated faith to him.
Request him gently, Anna, to return:
I crave but this, he stay a tide or two,
That I may learn to bear it patiently;
If he depart thus suddenly, I die.
Run, Anna, run; stay not to answer me.
ANNA: I go, fair sister: heavens grant good success!
(Enter the Nurse.)

NURSE: O Dido, your little son Ascanius
  Is gone. He lay with me last night,
  And in the morning he was stol'n from me:
  I think some fairies have beguiled me.
DIDO: O cursed hag and false dissembling wretch,
  That slay'st me with thy harsh and hellish tale.
  Thou for some petty gift has let him go,
  And I am thus deluded of my boy.
  Away with her to prison presently,
  Traitoress too keen and cursed sorceress!
NURSE: I know not what you mean by treason, I;
  I am as true as any one of yours.
  (Exeunt the Nurse and Attendants.)
DIDO: Away with her! Suffer her not to speak.
  My sister comes: I like not her sad looks.
  (Enter Anna.)
ANNA: Before I came, Aeneas was aboard.
  And spying me, hois'd up the sails amain;
  But I cried out, "Aeneas, false Aeneas, stay!"
  Then gan he wag his hand, which yet held up,
  Made me suppose he would have heard me speak.
  Then gan they drive into the ocean,
  Which when I view'd, I cried, "Aeneas, stay!"
  Dido, fair Dido wills Aeneas stay!
  Yet he, whose heart of adamant or flint
  My tears nor plaints could mollify a whit.
  Then carelessly I rent my hair for grief,
  Which seen to all, though he beheld me not,
  They gan to move him to redress my ruth,
  And stay a while to hear what I could say;
  But he, clapp'd under hatches, sail'd away.
DIDO: O Anna, Anna, I will follow him!
ANNA: How can ye go when he hath all your fleet?
DIDO: I'll frame me wings of wax like Icarus,
  And o'er his ships will soar unto the sun,
  That they may melt and I fall in his arms;
  Or else I'll make a prayer unto the waves,
  That I may swim to him, like Triton's niece.
  O Anna, fetch Arion's harp,

That I may tice a dolphin to the shore,
And ride upon his back unto my love.
Look, sister, look, lovely Aeneas' ships!
See, see, the billows heave him up to heaven,
And now down falls the keels into the deep.
O sister, sister, take away the rocks,
They'll break his ships, O Proteus, Neptune, Jove,
Save, save Aeneas, Dido's liefest love.
Now is he come on shore, safe without hurt;
But see, Achates will him put to sea,
And all the sailors merry-make for joy;
But he, rememb'ring me, shrinks back again.
See where he comes. Welcome, welcome, my love!

ANNA: Ah, sister, leave these idle fantasies.
Sweet sister, cease; remember who you are.

DIDO: Dido I am, unless I be deceiv'd,
And must I rave thus for a runagate?
Must I make ships for him to sail away?
Nothing can bear me to him but a ship,
And he hath all my fleet. What shall I do,
But die in fury of this oversight?
Ay, I must be the murderer of myself:
No, but I am not; yet I will be straight.
Anna, be glad; now have I found a mean
To rid me from these thoughts of lunacy:
Not far from hence
There is a woman famoused for arts,
Daughter unto the nymphs Hesperides,
Who will'd me sacrifice his ticing relics.
Go, Anna, bid me servants bring me fire.
(Exit Anna.)

The Country Wife

William Wycherly

1675

Comic

Setting: Mr. Pinchwife's home.

Scene: Pinchwife is married to a lovely country woman. He is terribly afraid of having her corrupted by the city women with their loose morals and extravagant ways. Three such damsels come to call on Mrs. Pinchwife to take her to the theatre for the evening.

My Lady Fidget: 20's – 40's.

Dainty Fidget: Her sister-in-law, 20's – 40's.

Mrs. Squeamish: 20's – 40's.

> (All three women are City Matrons, wealthy and vain, interested in gossip and flirtations and extravagant behavior.)

Mr. Pinchwife: 30's – 40's.

LADY FIDG: Your servant, sir. Where is your lady? We are come to wait upon her to the new play.

PINCH: New play!

LADY FIDG: And my husband will wait upon you presently.

PINCH: *(Aside.)* Damn your civility.—Madam, by no means; I will not see sir Jasper here till I have waited upon him at home; nor shall my wife see you till she has waited upon your ladyship at your lodgings.

LADY FIDG: Now we are here, sir . . .

PINCH: No, madam.

DAIN: Pray let us see her.

SQUEAM: We will not stir till we see her.

PINCH: *(Aside.)* A pox on you all! *(Goes to the door, and returns.)* She has locked the door, and is gone aboard.

LADY FIDG: No, you have locked the door, and she's within.

DAIN: They told us below, she was here.

PINCH: *(Aside.)* Will nothing do? Well, it must out then.—To tell you the truth, ladies, which I was afraid to let you know before, least it might endanger your lives, my wife has just now the smallpox come out upon her. Do not be frightened; but pray, be gone, ladies; you shall not stay her in danger of your lives; pray get you gone, ladies.

LADY FIDG: No, no, we have all had 'em.

SQUEAM: Alack, alack!

DAIN: Come, come, we must see how it goes with her; I understand the disease.

LADY FIDG: Come.

PINCH: *(Aside.)* Well, there is no being too hard for women at their own weapon, lying; therefore I'll quit the field.

(Exit Pinchwife.)

SQUEAM: Here's an example of jealousy!

LADY FIDG: Indeed, as the world goes, I wonder there are no more jealous, since wives are so neglected.

DAIN: Pshaw! as the world goes, to what end should they be jealous?

LADY FIDG: Foh! 'tis a nasty world.

SQUEAM: That men of parts, great acquaintance, and quality should take up with and spend themselves and fortunes in keeping little playhouse creatures, foh!

LADY FIDG: Nay, that women of understanding, great acquaintance, and good quality should fall a-keeping too of little creatures, foh!

SQUEAM: Why, 'tis the men of quality's fault. They never visit women of honor and reputation as they used to do; and have not so much as common civility for ladies of our rank, but use us with the same indifferency and ill-breeding as if we were all married to 'em.

LADY FIDG: She says true! 'Tis an arrant shame women of quality should be so slighted. Methinks, birth—birth should go for something. I have known men admired, courted, and followed for their titles only.

SQUEAM: Ay, one would think men of honor should not love, no more than marry, out of their own rank.

DAIN: Fie, fie upon 'em! They are come to think cross-breeding for themselves best, as well as for their dogs and horses.

LADY FIDG: They are dogs, and horses for't!

SQUEAM: One would think, if not for love, for vanity a little.

DAIN: Nay, they do satisfy their vanity upon us sometimes, and are kind to us in their report—tell all the world they lie with us.

LADY FIDG: Damned rascals! That we should be only wronged by 'em. To report a man has. . . had a person, when he has not. . .

had a person, is the greatest wrong in the world that can be. . . done to a person.

SQUEAM: Well, 'tis an arrant shame noble persons should be so wronged and neglected.

LADY FIDG: But still 'tis an arranter shame for a noble person to neglect her own honor, and defame her own noble person with little inconsiderable fellows, foh!

DAIN: I suppose the crime against our honor is the same with a man of quality as with another.

LADY FIDG: How! No, sure, the man of quality is likest one's husband, and therefore the fault should be the less.

DAIN: But then the pleasure should be the less!

LADY FIDG: Fie, fie, fie, for shame, sister! Whither shall we ramble? Be continent in your discourse, or I shall hate you.

DAIN: Besides, an intrigue is so much the more notorious for the man's quality.

SQUEAM: 'Tis true, nobody takes notice of a private man, and therefore with him 'tis more secret, and the crime's the less when 'tis not known.

LADY FIDG: You say true. I'faith, I think you are in the right on't. 'Tis not an injury to a husband till it be an injury to our honors; so that a woman of honor loses no honor with a private person; and to say truth . . .

DAIN: *(Apart to Squeamish.)* So, the *little fellow* is grown a *private person*. . . with her.

LADY FIDG: But still my dear, dear *honor*.
(Enter Sir Jasper, Horner, Dorilant.)

SIR JAS: Ay, my dear, dear of honor, thou hast still so much honor in thy mouth.

HORN: *(Aside.)* That she has none elsewhere.

LADY FIDG: Oh, what d'ye mean to bring in these upon us?

DAIN: Foh! these are as bad as wits.

SQUEAM: Foh!

LADY FIDG: Let us leave the room.

SIR JAS: Stay, stay; faith, to tell you the naked truth . . .

LADY FIDG: Fie, sir Jasper, do not use that word *naked*.

SIR JAS: Well, well, in short, I have business at Whitehall, and cannot go to the play with you, therefore would have you go . . .

LADY FIDG: With those two to a play?

SIR JAS: No, not with t'other, but with Mr. Horner. There can be no more scandal to go with him than with Mr. Tattle, or Master Limberham.

LADY FIDG: With that nasty fellow! No!

SIR JAS: Nay, prithee dear, hear me.

(Whisper to Lady Fidget.)

HORN: Ladies. . .

(Horner, Dorilant drawing near Squeamish and Dainty.)

DAIN: Stand off!

SQUEAM: Do not approach us!

DAIN: You herd with the wits, you are obscenity all over.

SQUEAM: I would as soon look upon a picture of Adam and Eve, without fig leaves, as any of you, if I could help it, therefore keep off, and do not make us sick.

DOR: What a devil are these?

HORN: Why, these are pretenders to honor, as critics to wit, only by censuring others; and as every raw, peevish, out-of-humored affected, dull, tea-drinking, arithmetical fop sets up for a wit, by railing at men of sense, so these for honor by railing at the court and ladies of as great honor as quality

SIR JAS: Come, Mr. Horner, I must desire you to go with these ladies to the play, sir.

HORN: I, sir?

SIR JAS: Ay, ay, come, sir.

HORN: I must beg your pardon, sir, and theirs. I will not be seen in women's company in public again for the world.

SIR JAS: Ha, ha! strange aversion!

SQUEAM: No, he's for women's company in private.

SIR JAS: He—poor man—he! ha, ha, ha!

DAIN: 'Tis a greater shame amongst lewd fellows to be seen in virtuous women's company than for the women to be seen with them.

HORN: Indeed, madam, the time was I only hated virtuous women, but now I hate the other too; I beg your pardon ladies.

LADY FIDG: You are very obliging, sir, because we would not be troubled with you.

SIR JAS: In sober sadness, he shall go.

DOR: Nay, if he wo'not, I am ready to wait upon the ladies; and I think I am the fitter man.

SIR JAS: You, sir, no, I thank you for that—Master Horner is a privileged man amongst the virtuous ladies; 'twill be a great while
before you are so, he, he, he! He's my wife's gallant, he, he, he!
No, pray withdraw, sir, for as I take it, the virtuous ladies have no
business with you.

DOR: And I am sure he can have none with them. 'Tis strange a man
can't come amongst virtuous women now but upon the same
terms as men are admitted into the great Turk's seraglio; but
heaven keep me from being an ombre player with 'em! But
where is Pinchwife?

(Exit Dorilant.)

SIR JAS: Come, come, man; what, avoid the sweet society of woman-
kind?—That sweet, soft, gentle, tame, noble creature, woman,
made for man's companion. . .

The Country Wife

William Wycherly

1675

Comic

Setting: Horner's lodgings. A banquet.

Scene: Each of the women believes Horner has lied to the others and really is in love with her.

My Lady Fidget: 20's – 40's.

Dainty Fidget: Her sister-in-law, 20's – 40's.

Mrs. Squeamish: 20's – 40's.

> *(All three women are City Matrons, wealthy and vain, interested in gossip and flirtations and extravagant behavior.)*

Horner: A wealthy, flirtatious man-about-town who has had a doctor spread the rumor that he is impotent in order to attract ladies without getting their husbands jealous.

HORN: *(Aside.)* A pox! they are come too soon . . . before I have sent back my new mistress.

LADY FIDG: That we may be sure of our welcome, we have brought our entertainment with us, and are resolved to treat thee, dear toad.

DAIN: And that we may be merry to purpose, have left sir Jasper and my old lady Squeamish quarrelling at home at backgammon.

SQUEAM: Therefore, let us make use of our time, lest they should chance to interrupt us.

LADY FIDG: Let us sit then.

HORN: First, that you may be private, let me lock this door and that, and I'll wait upon you presently.

LADY FIDG: No, sir, shut 'em only and your lips for ever, for we must trust you as much as our women.

HORN: You know all vanity's killed in me.—I have no occasion for talking.

LADY FIDG: Now, ladies, supposing we had drank each of us our two bottles, let us speak the truth of our hearts.

DAIN and SQUEAM: Agreed.

LADY FIDG: By this brimmer, for truth is nowhere else to be found. *(Aside to Horner.)* Not in thy heart, false man!

HORN: *(Aside to Lady Fidget.)* You have found me a true man, I'm sure!

LADY FIDG: *(Aside to Horner.)* Not every way.

But let us sit and be merry.

(Lady Fidget sings.)

Why should our damned tyrants oblige us to live
On the pittance of pleasure which they only give?
We must not rejoice,
With wine and with noise.
In vain we must wake in a dull bed alone,
Whilst to our warm rival, the bottle, they're gone.
Then lay aside charms,
And take up these arms.
'Tis wine only give 'em their courage and wit,
Because we live sober, to men we submit.
If for beauties you'd pass,
Take a lick of the glass,
'Twill mend your complexions, and when they are gone,
The best red we have is the red of the grape.
Then, sisters, lay't on,
And damn a good shape.

DAIN: Dear brimmer! Well, in token of our openness and plain-dealing, let us throw our masks over our heads.

HORN: So, 'twill come to the glasses anon.

SQUEAM: Lovely brimmer! Let me enjoy him first.

LADY FIDG: No, I never part with a gallant till I've tried him. Dear brimmer, that mak'st our husbands short-sighted.

DAIN: And our bashful gallants bold.

SQUEAM: And for want of a gallant, the butler lovely in our eyes. Drink eunuch.

LADY FIDG: Drink, thou representative of a husband. Damn a husband!

DAIN: And, as it were a husband, an old keeper.

SQUEAM: And an old grandmother.

HORN: And an English bawd, and a French chirurgion.

LADY FIDG: Ay, we have all reason to curse 'em.

HORN: For my sake, ladies?

LADY FIDG: No, for our own, for the first spoils all young gallants' industry.

DAIN: And the other's art makes 'em bold only with common women.

SQUEAM: And rather run the hazard of the vile distemper amongst them than of a denial amongst us.

DAIN: The filthy toads choose mistresses now as they do stuffs, for having been fancied and worn by others.

SQUEAM: For being common and cheap.

LADY FIDG: Whilst women of quality, like the richest stuffs, lie untumbled and unasked for.

HORN: Ay, neat, and cheap, and new, often they think best.

DAIN: No, sir, the beasts will be known by a mistress longer than by a suit.

SQUEAM: And 'tis not for cheapness neither.

LADY FIDG: No, for the vain fops will take up druggets and embroider 'em. But I wonder at the depraved appetites of witty men; they use to be out of the common road, and hate imitation. Pray tell me, beast, when you were a man, why you rather chose to club with a multitude in a common house for an entertainment than to be the only guest at a good table.

HORN: Why, faith, ceremony and expectation are unsufferable to those that are sharp bent. People always eat with the best stomach at an ordinary, where every man is snatching for the best bit.

LADY FIDG: Though he get a cut over the fingers. . . But I have heard people eat most heartily of another man's meat, that is, what they do not pay for.

HORN: When they are sure of their welcome and freedom, for ceremony in love and eating is as ridiculous as in fighting. Falling on briskly is all should be done in those occasions.

LADY FIDG: Well, then, let me tell you, sir, there is nowhere more freedom than in our houses, and we take freedom from a young person as a sign of good breeding, and a person may be as free as he pleases with us, as frolic, as gamesome, as wild as he will.

HORN: Han't I head you all declaim against wild men?

LADY FIDG: Yes, but for all that, we think wildness in a man as desirable a quality as in a duck or rabbit. A tame man, foh!

HORN: I know not, but your reputations frightened me, as much as your faces invited me.

LADY FIDG: Our reputation! Lord, why should you not think that we women make use of our reputation, as you men of yours, only to deceive the world with less suspicion? Our virtue is like the statesman's religion, the Quaker's word, the gamester's oath, and the great man's honor—but to cheat those that trust us.

SQUEAM: And that demureness, coyness, and modesty that you see in our faces in the boxes at plays is as much a sign of a kind woman as a vizard-mask in the pit.

DAIN: For, I assure you, women are least masked when they have the velvet vizard on.

LADY FIDG: You would have found us modest women in our denials only.

SQUEAM: Our bashfulness is only the reflection of the men's

DAIN: We blush when they are shamefaced.

HORN: I beg your pardon, ladies. I was deceived in you devilishly. But why that mighty pretence to honor?

LADY FIDG: We have told you. But sometimes 'twas for the same reason you men pretend business often, to avoid ill company, to enjoy the better and more privately those you love.

HORN: But why would you ne'er give a friend a wink then?

LADY FIDG: Faith, your reputation frightened us as much as ours did you, you were so notoriously lewd.

HORN: And you so seemingly honest.

LADY FIDG: Was that all that deterred you?

HORN: And so expensive . . . you allow freedom, you say?

LADY FIDG: Ay, ay.

HORN: That I was afraid of losing my little money, as well as my little time, both which my other pleasures required.

LADY FIDG: Money, foh! You talk like a little fellow now. Do such as we expect money?

HORN: I beg your pardon, madam. I must confess, I have heard that great ladies, like great merchants, set but the higher prices upon what they have, because they are not in necessity of taking the first offer.

DAIN: Such as we make sale of our hearts?

SQUEAM: We bribed for our love! Foh!

HORN: With your pardon, ladies, I know, like great men in offices, you seem to exact flattery and attendance only from your followers, but you have receivers about you, and such fees to pay, a man is afraid to pass your grants. Besides, we must let you win at cards, or we lose your hearts. And if you make an assignation, 'tis at a goldsmith's, jeweller's, or china house, where, for your honor you deposit to him, he must pawn his to the punctual cit, and so pay-ing for what you take up, pays for what he takes up.

DAIN: Would you not have us assured of our gallant's love?

SQUEAM: For love is better known by liberality than by jealousy.

LADY FIDG: For one may be dissembled, the other not. *(Aside.)* But my jealousy can be no longer dissembled, and they are telling ripe.—Come, here's to our gallants in waiting, whom we must name, and I'll begin. This is my false rogue.

(Claps him on the back.)

SQUEAM: How!

HORN: *(Aside.)* So, all will out now.

SQUEAM: *(Aside to Horner.)* Did you not tell me, 'twas for my sake only you reported yourself no man?

DAIN: *(Aside to Horner.)* Oh wretch! Did you not swear to me, 'twas for my love and honor you passed for that thing you do?

HORN: So, so.

LADY FIDG: Come, speak ladies; this is my false villain.

SQUEAM: And mine too.

DAIN: And mine.

HORN: Well, then, you are all three my false rogues too, and there's an end on't.

LADY FIDG: Well, then, there's no remedy; sister sharers, let us not fall out, but have a care of our honor. Though we get no presents, no jewels of him, we are savers of our honor, the jewel of most value and use, which shines yet to the world unsuspected, though it be counterfeit.

HORN: Nay, and is e'en good as if were true, provided the world think so; for honor, like beauty now, only depends on the opinion of others.

LADY FIDG: Well, Harry Common, I hope you can be true to three. Swear—but 'tis no purpose to require your oath for you are as often forsworn as you swear to new women.

HORN: Come, faith, madam, let us e'en pardon one another, for all the difference I find betwixt we men and you women, *we* for-swear ourselves at the beginning of an amour, *you* as long as it lasts.

The New York Idea

Landgon Mitchell
1906

Comic
Setting: The home of Mr. Phillip Phillimore. 5 P.M.
Scene: Thomas stands near the tea service. Mrs. Phillimore and her
sister Sarah are preparing for their evening ritual of tea, sherry,
the newspapers, and chitchat.

Mrs. Mary Phillimore: A semi-invalid, refined, fatigued, 50's – 60's.
Miss Grace Phillimore: 20's, her daughter, lively and attractive.
Miss Sarah Heneage: Mary's sister, 60's, large and in control, narrow-
minded.
Thomas: The very un-English butler, 30's – 60's, takes a lively interest
in the affairs of the family.

GRACE: *(Crosses and sits.)* I never in my life walked so far and found
so few people at home. *(Pauses. Takes off gloves. Somewhat
querulously.)* The fact is the nineteenth of May is ridiculously late
to be in town.
(Pause. Thomas comes down L. table.)
MISS HENEAGE: Mr. Phillimore's *Post?*
THOMAS: *(Same business. Pointing to* Evening Post *on tea table.)* The
Post, ma'am.
MISS HENEAGE: *(Indicates cup.)* Miss Phillimore.
*(Thomas takes cup of tea to Grace. Silence. They all sip tea.
Thomas goes back, fills sherry glass, remaining round and about
the tea table. They all drink tea during the following scene.)*
GRACE: The Dudleys were at home. They wished to know when my
brother Philip was to be married, and where and how?
MISS HENEAGE: If the Dudleys were persons of breeding, they'd not
intrude their curiosity upon you.
GRACE: I like Lena Dudley.
MRS. PHILLIMORE: *(Speaks slowly and gently.)* Do I know Miss
Dudley?
GRACE: She knows Philip. She expects an announcement of the wed-
ding.
MRS. PHILLIMORE: I trust you told her that my son, my sister, and

myself are all of the opinion that those who have been divorced should remarry with modesty and without parade.

GRACE: I told the Dudleys Philip's wedding was here, tomorrow.

(Thomas at back of table ready to be of use.)

MISS HENEAGE: *(To Mrs. Phillimore, picking up a sheet of paper which has lain on the table.)* I have spent the afternoon, Mary, in arranging and listing the wedding gifts, and in writing out the announcements of the wedding. I think I have attained a proper form of announcement. *(She takes the sheet of note paper and gives it to Thomas.)* Of course, the announcement Philip himself made was quite out of the question. *(Grace smiles.)* However, there is mine.

(Points to paper. Thomas gives list to Mrs. Phillimore and moves upstage.)

GRACE: I hope you'll send an announcement to the Dudleys.

MRS. PHILLIMORE: *(Reads plaintively, ready to make the best of things.)* Mr. Philip Phillimore and Mrs. Cynthia Dean Karslake announce their marriage, May twentieth, at three o'clock, Nineteen A., Washington Square, New York." *(Replaces paper on Thomas's salver.)* It sounds very nice.

(Thomas hands paper to Miss Heneage.)

MISS HENEAGE: *(Thomas upstage.)* In my opinion it barely escapes sounding nasty. However, it is correct. The only remaining question is—to whom the announcement should not be sent. *(Exit Thomas.)* I consider an announcement of the wedding of two divorced persons to be in the nature of an intimate communication. It not only announces the wedding—it also announces the divorce. *(She returns to her teacup.)* The person I shall ask counsel of is cousin William Sudley. He promised to drop in this afternoon.

GRACE: Oh; we shall hear all about Cairo.

MRS. PHILLIMORE: William is judicious.

(Re-enter Thomas.)

MISS HENEAGE: *(With finality.)* Cousin William will disapprove of the match unless a winter in Cairo has altered his moral tone.

THOMAS: *(Announces.)* Mr. Sudley.

The New York Idea

Landgon Mitchell
1906

Comic
Setting: The home of Mr. Phillip Phillimore.

Mrs. Mary Phillimore: A semi-invalid, refined, fatigued, 50's – 60's.
Miss Grace Phillimore: 20's, her daughter, lively and attractive.
Miss Sarah Heneage: Mary's sister, 60's, large and in control, narrow-minded.
William Sudley: An old gentleman, a man of breeding and self-importance, Grace's cousin.

SUDLEY: *(Shakes hands with Mrs. Phillimore, soberly glad to see them.)* How d'ye do, Mary? *(Same business with Miss Heneage.)* A very warm May you're having, Sarah.
GRACE: *(Comes to him.)* Dear Cousin William!
MISS HENEAGE: Wasn't it warm in Cairo when you left? *(She will have the strict truth, or nothing; still, on account of Sudley's impeccable respectability, she treats him with more than usual leniency.)*
SUDLEY: *(Sits L.)* We left Cairo six weeks ago, Grace, so I've had no news since you wrote in February that Philip was engaged. *(Pause.)* I need not to say I consider Philip's engagement excessively regrettable. He is a judge upon the Supreme Court bench with a divorced wife—and such a divorced wife!
GRACE: Oh, but Philip has succeeded in keeping everything as quiet as possible.
SUDLEY: *(Acidly.)* No, my dear! He has not succeeded in keeping his former wife as quiet as possible. We had not been in Cairo a week when who should turn up but Vida Phillimore. She went everywhere and did everything no woman should!
GRACE: *(Unfeignedly interested.)* Oh, what did she do?
SUDLEY: She "did" Cleopatra at the tableaux at Lord Errington's! She "did" Cleopatra, and she did it robed only in some diaphanous material of a nature so transparent that—in fact she appeared to be draped in moonshine. *(Miss Heneage indicates the presence of Grace. Rises; to C.)* That was only the beginning. As soon as she

heard of Philip's engagement, she gave a dinner in honor of it! Only divorcees were asked! And she had a dummy—yes, my dear, a dummy, at the head of the table. He stood for Philip—that is he sat for Philip!

(Rises, and goes up to the table.)

MISS HENEAGE: *(Irritated and disgusted.)* Ah!

MRS. PHILLIMORE: *(With dismay and pain.)* Dear me!

MISS HENEAGE: *(Confident of the value of her opinion.)* I disapprove of Mrs. Phillimore.

SUDLEY: *(Takes a cigarette.)* Of course you do, but has Philip taken to Egyptian cigarettes in order to celebrate my winter at Cairo?

(Comes below chair.)

GRACE: Those are Cynthia's.

SUDLEY: *(Thinking that no one is worth knowing whom he does not know.)* Who is Cynthia"?

GRACE: Mrs. Karslake—She's staying here, Cousin William. She'll be down in a minute.

SUDLEY: *(Shocked.)* You don't mean to tell me—?!

(To armchair, L.)

MISS HENEAGE: Yes, William, Cynthia is Mrs. Karslake—Mrs. Karslake has no New York house. I disliked the publicity of a hotel in the circumstances, and accordingly when she became engaged to Philip, I invited her here.

SUDLEY: *(Suspicious and distrustful.)* And may I ask *who* Mrs. Karslake is?

MISS HENEAGE: *(With confidence.)* She was a Deane.

SUDLEY: *(Crosses up back of table R., sorry to be obliged to concede good birth to any but his own blood.)* Oh, oh—well, the Deanes are extremely nice people. *(Goes to table.)* Was her father J. William Deane?

MISS HENEAGE: *(Still more secure; nods.)* Yes.

SUDLEY: *(Giving in with difficulty.)* The family is an old one. J. William Deane's daughter? Surely he left a very considerable—

MISS HENEAGE: Oh, fifteen or twenty millions.

SUDLEY: *(Determined not to be dazzled.)* If I remember rightly she was brought up abroad.

MISS HENEAGE: In France and England—and I fancy brought up with a very gay set in very gay places. In fact she is what is called a "sporty" woman.

SUDLEY: *(Always ready to think the worst.)* We might put up with that. But you don't mean to tell me Philip has the—the—the—assurance to marry a woman who has been divorced by—

MISS HENAGE: Not at all. Cynthia Karslake divorced her husband.

SUDLEY: *(Gloomily, since he has less fault to find than he expected.)* She divorced him! Ah!

(Sips his tea.)

MISS HENEAGE: The suit went by default. And, my dear William, there are many palliating circumstances. Cynthia was married to Karslake only seven months. There are no— *(Glances at Grace.)* no hostages to Fortune! Ahem!

SUDLEY: *(Still unwilling to be pleased.)* Ah! What sort of a young woman is she?

(Goes to C.)

GRACE: *(With the superiority of one who is not too popular.)* Men admire her.

MISS HENEAGE: She's not conventional.

MRS. PHILLIMORE: *(Showing a faint sense of justice.)* I am bound to say she has behaved discreetly ever since she arrived in this house.

MISS HENEAGE: Yes, Mary—but I sometimes suspect that she exercises a degree of self-control—

SUDLEY: *(Glad to have something against some one.)* She claps on the lid, eh? And you think that perhaps some day she'll boil over? Well, of course fifteen or twenty millions—but who's Karslake?

GRACE: *(Very superciliously.)* He owns Cynthia K. She's the famous mare.

MISS HENEAGE: He's Henry Karslake's son.

SUDLEY: *(Beginning to make the best of fifteen millions-in-law.)* Oh!—Henry!—Very respectable family. Although I remember his father served a term in the senate. And so the wedding is to be tomorrow?

MRS. PHILLIMORE: *(Assents.)* Tomorrow.

SUDLEY: *(Bored, and his respectability to the front when he thinks of the ceremony; rises. Grace rises.)* Tomorrow. Well, my dear Sarah, a respectable family with some means. We must accept her. But on the whole, I think it will be best for me not to see the young woman. My disapprobation would make itself apparent.

GRACE: *(Whispering to Sudley.)* Cynthia's coming.

Riders to the Sea

John Millington Synge
1904

Dramatic

Setting: A cottage in the Aran Islands, Western Ireland. New white boards lean against the wall for a possible coffin.

Scene: Nora and Cathleen have received a bundl of clothes that have washed up on a rocky shore. They believe it may be the belongings of their brother Michael who is missing from one of the fishing boats and assumed dead. They are trying to hide the bundle from their mother as she enters.

Maurya: An old woman who has lost her husband and all but one of her sons to the Sea.

Cathleen: Her older daughter, 20's.

Nora: Her younger daughter, teens.

Bartley: Her only remaining son, 20's.

NORA: *(In a low voice.)* Where is she?

CATHLEEN: She's lying down, God help her, and may be sleeping, if she's able. *(Nora comes in softly, and takes a bundle from under her shawl.) (Spinning the wheel rapidly.)* What is it you have?

NORA: The young priest is after bringing them. It's a shirt and a plain stocking were got off a drowned man in Donegal. *(Cathleen stops her wheel with a sudden movement, and leans out to listen.)* We're to find out if it's Michael's they are, some time herself will be down looking by the sea.

CATHLEEN: How would they be Michael's, Nora. How would he go the length of that way to the far north?

NORA: The young priest says he's known the like of it. "If it's Michael's they are," says he, "you can tell herself he's got a clean burial by the grace of God, and if they're not his, let no one say a word about them, for she'll be getting her death," says he, "with crying and lamenting."

(The door which Nora half closed is blown open by a gust of wind.)

CATHLEEN: *(Looking out anxiously.)* Did you ask him would he stop Bartley going this day with the horses to the Galway fair?

NORA: "I won't stop him," says he, "but let you not be afraid. Herself does be saying prayers half through the night, and the Almighty God won't leave her destitute," says he, "with no son living."

CATHLEEN: Is the sea bad by the white rocks, Nora?

NORA: Middling bad, God help us. There's a great roaring in the west, and it's worse it'll be getting when the tide's turned to the wind. *(She goes over to the table with the bundle.)* Shall I open it now?

CATHLEEN: Maybe she'd wake up on us, and come in before we'd done. *(Coming to the table.)* It's a long time we'll be, and the two of us crying.

NORA: *(Goes to the inner door and listens.)* She's moving about on the bed. She'll be coming in a minute.

CATHLEEN: Give me the ladder, and I'll put them up in the turf-loft, the way she won't know of them at all, and maybe when the tide turns she'll be going down to see would he be floating from the east.

(They put the ladder against the gable of the chimney; Cathleen goes up a few steps and hides the bundle in the turf-loft. Maurya comes from the inner room.)

MAURYA: *(Looking up at Cathleen and speaking querulously.)* Isn't it turf enough you have for this day and evening?

CATHLEEN: There's a cake baking at the fire for a short space *(Throwing down the turf.)* and Bartley will want it when the tide turns if he goes to Connemara.

(Nora picks up the turf and puts it round the pot-oven.)

MAURYA: *(Sitting down on a stool at the fire.)* He won't go this day with the wind rising from the south and west. He won't go this day, for the young priest will stop him surely.

NORA: He'll not stop him, mother, and I heard Eamon Simon and Stephen Pheety and Colum Shawn saying he would go.

MAURYA: Where is he itself?

NORA: He went down to see would there be another boat sailing in the week, and I'm thinking it won't be long till he's here now, for the tide's turning at the green head, and the hooker's tacking from the east.

CATHLEEN: I hear someone passing the big stones.

NORA: *(Looking out.)* He's coming now, and he in a hurry.

BARTLEY: *(Comes in and looks round the room. Speaking sadly and quietly.)* Where is the bit of new rope, Cathleen, was bought in Connemara?

CATHLEEN: *(Coming down.)* Give it to him, Nora; it's on a nail by the white boards. I hung it up this morning, for the pig with the black feet was eating it.

NORA: *(Giving him a rope.)* Is that it, Bartley?

MAURYA: You'd do right to leave that rope, Bartley, hanging by the boards. *(Bartley takes the rope.)* It will be wanting in this place, I'm telling you, if Michael is washed up tomorrow morning, or the next morning, or any morning in the week, for it's a deep grave we'll make him by the grace of God.

BARTLEY: *(Beginning to work with the rope.)* I've no halter the way I can ride down on the mare, and I must go now quickly. This is the one boat going for two weeks or beyond it, and the fair will be a good fair for horses I heard them saying below.

MAURYA: It's a hard thing they'll be saying below if the body is washed up and there's no man in it to make the coffin, and I after giving a big price for the finest white boards you'd find in Connemara. *(She looks round at the boards.)*

BARTLEY: How would it be washed up, and we after looking each day for nine days, and a strong wind blowing a while back from the west and south?

MAURYA: If it wasn't found itself, that wind is raising the sea, and there was a star up against the moon, and it rising in the night. If it was a hundred horses, or a thousand horses you had itself, what is the price of a thousand horses against a son where there is one only?

BARTLEY: *(Working at the halter, to Cathleen.)* Let you go down each day, and see the sheep aren't jumping in on the rye, and if the jobber comes you can sell the pig with the black feet if there is a good price going.

MAURYA: How would the like of her get a good price for a pig?

BARTLEY: *(To Cathleen.)* If the west wind holds with the last bit of the moon let you and Nora get up weed enough for another cock for the kelp. It's hard set we'll be from this day with no one in it but one man to work.

MAURYA: It's hard set we'll be surely the day you're drown'd with the rest. What way will I live and the girls with me, and I an old woman looking for the grave?

(Bartley lays down the halter, takes off his old coat, and puts on a newer one of the same flannel.)

BARTLEY: *(To Nora.)* Is she coming to the pier?

NORA: *(Looking out.)* She's passing the green head and letting fall her sails.

BARTLEY: *(Getting his purse and tobacco.)* I'll have half an hour to go down, and you'll see me coming again in two days, or in three days, or maybe in four days if the wind is bad.

MAURYA: *(Turning round to the fire, and putting her shawl over her head.)* Isn't it a hard and cruel man won't hear a word from an old woman, and she holding him from the sea?

CATHLEEN: It's the life of a young man to be going on the sea, and who would listen to an old woman with one thing and she saying it over?

BARTLEY: *(Taking the halter.)* I must go now quickly. I'll ride down on the red mare, and the gray pony'll run behind me. . . The blessing of God on you. *(He goes out.)*

MAURYA: *(Crying out as he is in the door.)* He's gone now, God spare us, and we'll not see him again. He's gone now, and when the black night is falling I'll have no son left me in the world.

CATHLEEN: Why wouldn't you give him your blessing and he looking round in the door? Isn't it sorrow enough is on everyone in this house without your sending him out with an unlucky word behind him, and a hard word in his ear?

(Maurya takes up the tongs and begins raking the fire aimlessly without looking round.)

NORA: *(Turning toward her.)* You're taking away the turf from the cake.

CATHLEEN: *(Crying out.)* The Son of God forgive us, Nora, we're after forgetting his bit of bread. *(She comes over to the fire.)*

NORA: And it's destroyed he'll be going till dark night, and he after eating nothing since the sun went up.

CATHLEEN: *(Turning the cake out of the oven.)* It's destroyed he'll be, surely. There's no sense left on any person in a house where an old woman will be talking for ever.

(Maurya sways herself on her stool.)

(Cutting off some of the bread and rolling it in a cloth; to Maurya.) Let you go down now to the spring well and give him this and he passing. You'll see him then and the dark word will

be broken, and you can say "God speed you," the way he'll be easy in his mind.

MAURYA *(Taking the bread.)* Will I be in it as soon as himself?

CATHLEEN: If you go now quickly.

MAURYA: *(Standing up unsteadily.)* It's hard set I am to walk.

CATHLEEN: *(Looking at her anxiously.)* Give her the stick, Nora, or maybe she'll slip on the big stones.

NORA: What, stick?

CATHLEEN: The stick Michael brought from Connemara.

MAURYA: *(Taking a stick Nora gives her.)* In the big world the old people do be leaving things after them for their sons and children, but in this place it is the young men do be leaving things behind for them that do be old. *(She goes out slowly. Nora goes over to the ladder.)*

CATHLEEN: Wait, Nora, maybe she'd turn back quickly. She's that sorry, God help her, you wouldn't know the thing she'd do.

NORA: Is she gone round by the bush?

CATHLEEN: *(Looking out.)* She's gone now. Throw it down quickly, for the Lord knows when she'll be out of it again.

The Stongbox

Carl Sternheim
1912

Comic
Setting: The Krull home.
Scene: Henry and Fanny return from their honeymoon. Lydia and
   Elspeth have hated Fanny for years and feel she stole Henry as
   soon as Lydia's mother died.

Henry Krull: A professor, 47, a widow, now remarried to Fanny.
Fanny Krull: His second wife, 20's, the sister of Henry's first wife.
Lydia Krull: His daughter by his first marriage, 17.
Elspeth True: The spinster aunt who lives with the family.
Emma: The family's servant—brief appearance.

   (Krull and Fanny enter.)
KRULL: Oh, my darlings! Dearest daughter!
LYDIA: *(Runs and throws her arms around him.)* Daddy!
KRULL: And Auntie?
LYDIA: *(Embracing.)* Fanny. Fanny!
EMMA: *(Approaching Krull.)* Professor!
KRULL: Good Emma! And Aunt Elspeth?
EMMA: In her room, Professor.
KRULL: *(In Elspeth True's door.)* Auntie, Auntie dear! *(Disappears into
   her room.)* Beloved Aunt Elspeth!
   (Krull and Elspeth enter.)
ELSPETH: You didn't shave.
KRULL: Of course not! Straight from the train into your arms! Doesn't
   Fanny look enchanting? A little moss rose in bloom! *(Toward
   Fanny.)* My doll!
ELSPETH: *(Stiffly.)* Good day, Fanny.
FANNY: *(Stiffly.)* Good day, Aunt Elspeth.
   (They embrace.)
KRULL: But now the coffee from the stove, Emma! Around the table,
   all of you. *(To Fanny.)* See how we honor the little lady: "A hearty
   welcome!" Bravo! Divine! *(All sit down.)*
KRULL: Children, all's right with God's world on a beautiful spring
   morning! Gliding down German rivers into the valley, proud cas-

tles salute us below. Germania greets you, and the Lorelei, too, until on the brazen horse in Coblenz—

FANNY: In Coblenz we had ourselves photographed on postcards.

KRULL: Ah, Coblenz! Children, Coblenz! We were in seventh heaven. A delicious Walporzheimer wine sent bliss coursing through our veins. A hundred moods enveloped us. Nothing, there's nothing in God's world more resplendent than a morning on the Rhine. *(Emma brings the coffee.)*

KRULL: *(Reading the inscription on the cake.)* "Peace and Blessing upon the Lovers." How refined! *(To Fanny.)* My sweet doll!

ELSPETH: In a word: You had a good time, you were satisfied.

KRULL: If I could but give you half an idea.

ELSPETH: We get it all.

LYDIA: Mr. Silkenband didn't find the photograph from Coblenz in very good taste.

KRULL: A child of caprice must be taken in a comparable spirit. For us it will always conjure up heavenly memories.

LYDIA: But Auntie had her picture taken.

ELSPETH: Hush!

KRULL: Have you actually overcome your old aversion?

ELSPETH: Just a proof. Not the real thing yet.

LYDIA: But a perfect work of art.

FANNY: Let's see your picture.

LYDIA: Do bring it. Father won't believe his eyes. *(Elspeth goes into her room.)*

KRULL: *(To Lydia.)* And what do you think of your new little Mummy? Isn't she beautiful, wrapped in glory? Adorable doll!
(Elspeth returns and hands the picture to Krull.)

KRULL: Aha!
(He hands it, in turn, to Fanny, who breaks out in a fit of laughter.)

ELSPETH: What is it?

FANNY: Schiller's Lady Macbeth all over!

ELSPETH: *(Snatching the picture out of her hands.)* This is really—

FANNY: Like Blücher at Caub—leg on the stool.

ELSPETH: —Tasteless.

LYDIA: Mr. Silkenband is a divinely inspired artist. He called your Coblenz snapshot *kitsch*, shoddy trash—a disgrace to the profession.

KRULL: A caprice, to be taken in a comparable spirit.

FANNY: *(To Elspeth.)* Besides, you look sixty in the picture, five years too many!

KRULL: For goodness' sake hear me out! Let me tell you about Ehrenbreitstein. On top of hilly vineyards stretching down to the Rhine. . .

ELSPETH: All these extravaganzas—Lorelei and Walporzheimer. This trip must have eaten up a lot.

KRULL: By Jove! Does this one fling at pleasure have to be soured with ill-tempered calculations? I even had to borrow two hundred marks from our friends, the Susmichels, in Andernach.

ELSPETH: Awful! How'll you pay them back?

FANNY: Don't worry.

ELSPETH: At the end of March, your bank account showed a balance of 276 marks in favor of the bank.

KRULL: Damn it, how's that possible?

ELSPETH: Trifles for you: the same old story!

KRULL: That would mean 476 marks in the red.

FANNY: Henry bought me another genuine lace kerchief in Cologne. *(To Lydia.)* I brought a light-blue parasol for you.

LYDIA: Where is it?

FANNY: In the trunk. On top. Here's the key.

LYDIA: A million thanks, dear Fanny. I have so many important things to tell you.

(Fanny and Lydia go off quickly to Fanny's room.)

FANNY: *(In the doorway.)* And for you, Aunt—

ELSPETH: No presents for me on borrowed money.

FANNY: That's what I call character!

(She follows Lydia quickly.)

KRULL: A delightful wench, a ray of sunshine! A living doll!

ELSPETH: The twelve hundred marks you borrowed from me must also be paid back. To clean up our affairs at last.

KRULL: Aunt Elspeth, what a wet blanket on our moving in!

ELSPETH: In a word, Lady Macbeth.

KRULL: Banter.

ESPETH: Malice! I know my little niece down to the roots of her hair.

KRULL: *(Laughs.)* Roots of her hair!

ELSPETH: Don't laugh! She and I are both women. Don't make fun. Every greeting from your trip was vile.

KRULL: How often we thought kindly of you. Which reminds me how Fanny toasted you with the seasoned wine at Susmichel's. The goblets tingled with the tone of genuine emotion.

ELSPETH: The Rhine has had an unfavorable effect on your penchant for the cliché. No protestations, no arguments. You owe me money, you grow more obligated to me. I demand respect.

KRULL: Every member of the household will grant you that.

ELSPETH: You want to come into my money.

KRULL: If you love us. We're next of kin.

ELSPETH: That always calls for action.

KRULL: Affection and gratitude guaranteed.

ELSPETH: Greatest courtesy and more. Are you willing? Look me in the eye. You didn't bat an eyelash.

KRULL: *(Laughing convulsively.)* You can look into my heart as into a mirror. *(The bright laughter of women is heard from the adjacent room.)* Listen: how heartily they laugh!

(Elspeth leaves the room without a word.)

KRULL: *(Taking the photograph from the table.)* Excellent. The real Elspeth. *(He sighs.)* Ah, yes . . .

Scene 5

(Fanny enters.)

FANNY: Did she toss around figures?

KRULL: What do I care about such frippery? It'll turn out all right. But be nice to her. Not with feigned love. Simply on this basis: We want to inherit.

FANNY: We shall, in any case. For one thing, there's no other relative, however distant. But then there's her notorious sense of family . . .

KRULL: She means well.

FANNY: With you, perhaps. But enough of her. Her role here is finished, once and for all. On that we are agreed.

KRULL: Completely.

FANNY: I took Sidonie's place at your side on that condition.

KRULL: Certainly. She gets the attention due her—and that's all, *basta*.

FANNY: I must have lost my locket.

KRULL: The gold one with my picture?

FANNY: I felt it in my bosom on the train this morning. *(She unbuttons.)*

KRULL: That would be—

FANNY: Can you reach it?

KRULL: *(Feeling his way.)* I have it! *(He pulls it out.)* Sweet little wife, sweet . . .

FANNY: Henry.

KRULL: The world, ah the world is beautiful! To sink— *(They embrace.) (After a moment.)* How much could she have?

FANNY: Fifty, sixty thousand at least.

KRULL: Sixty thousand. I thought so, too! *(Kisses her.)* Sweetie pie!

FANNY: Dearest!

Fumed Oak

Noel Coward
1935

Comic
Setting: The Gow breakfast room. A rainy morning.
Scene: Mrs. Rockett is seated in a chair doing some mending. There
is a deep silence at the table. Doris is reading the paper. Elsie is
dipping toast into a boiled egg and sniffling loudly. She has a
cold. Henry has just entered and been given tea and a plate of
haddock which he eats in silence. The silence continues until Elsie
speaks.

Elsie: 14, a schoolgirl.
Doris Gow: Her mother, 30's, sour, preoccupied and grumpy.
Mrs. Rockett: Doris's mother, 60's, living with the family.
Henry Gow: Doris's husband, late 30's – 40's, a businessman—in his
own world.

ELSIE: Mum?
DORIS: What?
ELSIE: When can I put my hair up?
DORIS: *(Snappily.)* When you're old enough.
ELSIE: Gladys Pierce is the same age as me and she's got hers up.
DORIS: Never you mind about Gladys Pierce, get on with your break-
fast.
ELSIE: I don't see why I can't have it cut. That would be better than
nothing. *(This remark is ignored.)* Maisie Blake had hers cut last
week and it looks lovely.
DORIS: Never you mind about Maisie Blake neither. She's common.
ELSIE: Miss Pritchard doesn't think so. Miss Pritchard likes Maisie Blake
a lot, she said it looked ever so nice.
DORIS: *(Irritably.)* What?
ELSIE: Her hair.
DORIS: Get on with your breakfast. You'll be late.
ELSIE: *(Petulantly.)* Oh, Mum—
DORIS: And stop sniffling. Sniffle, sniffle, sniffle! Haven't you got a
handkerchief?
ELSIE: Yes, but it's a clean one.

DORIS: Never mind, use it.

MRS. ROCKETT: The child can't help having a cold.

DORIS: She can blow her nose, can't she, even if she has got a cold?

ELSIE: *(Conversationally.)* Dodie Watson's got a terrible cold, she's had it for weeks. It went to her chest and then it went back to her head again.

MRS. ROCKETT: That's the worst of schools, you're always catching something.

ELSIE: Miss Pritchard's awful mean to Dodie Watson, she said she'd had enough of it.

DORIS: Enough of what?

ELSIE: Her cold. *(There is silence again, which is presently shattered by the wailing of a baby in the house next door.)*

MRS. ROCKETT: There's that child again. It kept me awake all night.

DORIS: I'm very sorry, I'm sure. *(She picks up the newspaper.)*

MRS. ROCKETT: *(Fiddling in her workbasket.)* I wasn't blaming you.

DORIS: The night before last it was the hot-water pipes.

MRS. ROCKETT: You ought to have them seen to.

DORIS: You know as well as I do you can't stop them making that noise every now and then.

MRS. ROCKETT: *(Threading a needle.)* I'm sure I don't know why you don't get a plumber in.

DORIA: *(Grandly.)* Because I do not consider it necessary.

MRS. ROCKETT: You would if you slept in my room—gurgle gurgle gurgle all night long—it's all very fine for you, you're at the end of the passage.

DORIS: *(With meaning.)* You don't have to sleep there.

MRS. ROCKETT: What do you mean by that?

DORIS: You know perfectly well what I mean.

MRS. ROCKETT: *(With spirit.)* Listen to me, Doris Gow. I've got a perfect right to complain if I want to, and well you know it. It isn't as if I was staying here for nothing.

DORIS: I really don't know what's the matter with you lately, Mother, you do nothing but grumble.

MRS. ROCKETT: Me, grumble! I like that, I'm sure. That's rich, that is.

DORIS: Well, you do. It gives me a headache.

MRS. ROCKETT: You ought to do something about those headaches of yours. They seem to pop on and off at the least thing.

DORIS: And wish you wouldn't keep passing remarks about not staying here for nothing.

MRS. ROCKETT: Well, it's true, I don't.

DORIS: Anyone would think we was taking advantage of you, to hear you talk.

MRS. ROCKETT: Well, they wouldn't be far wrong.

DORIS: Mother, how can you! You're not paying a penny more than you can afford.

MRS. ROCKETT: I never said I was. It isn't the money, it's the lack of consideration. *(Elsie puts her exercise book away in her satchel.)*

DORIS: Pity you don't go and live with Nora for a change.

MRS. ROCKETT: Nora hasn't got a spare room.

DORIS: Phyllis has, a lovely one, looking out over the railway. I'm sure her hot-water pipes wouldn't keep you awake, there isn't enough hot water in them.

MRS. ROCKETT: Of course, if I'm not wanted here, I can always go to a boarding-house or a private hotel.

DORIS: Catch you!

MRS. ROCKETT: I'm not the sort to outstay my welcome anywhere. . .

DORIS: Oh, for heaven's sake don't start that again. . . *(She bangs the paper down on the table.)*

MRS. ROCKETT: *(Addressing the air.)* It seems as though some of us had got out of bed the wrong side this morning.

ELSIE: Mum, can I have some more toast?

DORIS: No.

ELSIE: I could make it myself over the kitchen fire.

DORIS: No, I tell you. Can't you understand plain English? You've had quite enough and you'll be late for school.

MRS. ROCKETT: Never mind, Elsie, here's twopence. *(Taking it out of her purse.)* You can buy yourself a sponge cake at Barrets.

ELSIE: *(Rising and taking the twopence.)* Thanks, Grandma.

DORIS: You'll do no such thing, Elsie. I'm not going to have a child of mine stuffing herself with cake in the middle of the High Street.

MRS. ROCKETT: *(Sweetly.)* Eat it in the shop, dear.

DORIS: Go on, you'll be late.

ELSIE: Oh, Mum, it's only ten to.

DORIS: Do as I tell you.

ELSIE: Oh, all right. *(She crosses in front of the table and goes sullenly out of the room and can be heard scampering noisily up the stairs.)*

MRS. ROCKETT: *(Irritatingly.)* Poor little soul.

DORIS: I'll trouble you not to spoil Elsie, Mother.

MRS. ROCKETT: Spoil her! I like that. Better than half-starving her.

DORIS: *(Hotly.)* Are you insinuating . . .

MRS. ROCKETT: I'm not insinuating anything. Elsie's getting a big girl, she only had one bit of toast for her breakfast and she used that for her egg. I saw her.

DORIS: *(Rising and putting away the paper in the sideboard drawer.)* It's none of your business, and in future I'd be much obliged if you'd keep your twopences to yourself. *(She returns to her seat at the table.)*

(Henry rises and fetches the paper out.)

MRS. ROCKETT: *(Hurt.)* Very well, of course if I'm to be abused every time I try to bring a little happiness into the child's life . . .

DORIS: Anyone would think I ill-treated her the way you talk.

MRS. ROCKETT: You certainly nag her enough.

DORIS: I don't do any such thing—and I wish you'd leave me to bring up my own child in my own way.

MRS. ROCKETT: That cold's been hanging over her for weeks and a fat lot you care—

DORIS: *(Rising and getting tray from beside the sideboard.)* I've dosed her for it, haven't I? The whole house stinks of Vapex. What more can I do?

MRS. ROCKETT: She ought to have had Doctor Bristow last Saturday when it was so bad. He'd have cleared it up in no time.

DORIS: *(Putting tray on her chair and beginning to clear things onto it.)* You and your Doctor Bristow.

MRS. ROCKETT: Nice thing if it turned to bronchitis. *(Doris throws scraps into the fire.)* Mrs. Henderson's Muriel got bronchitis, all through neglecting a cold; the poor child couldn't breathe, they had to have two kettles going night and day—

DORIS: I suppose your precious Doctor Bristow told you that.

MRS. ROCKETT: Yes, he did, and what's more, he saved the girl's life, you ask Mrs. Henderson.

DORIS: Catch me ask Mrs. Henderson anything, stuck-up thing. . .

MRS. ROCKETT: Mrs. Henderson's a very nice ladylike woman, just because she's quiet and a bit reserved you say she's stuck-up. . .

DORIS: Who does she think she is, anyway, Lady Mountbatten? *(She takes the cruet to the sideboard.)*

MRS. ROCKETT: Really, Doris, you make me tired sometimes, you do really.

DORIS: If you're so fond of Mrs. Henderson it's a pity you don't see more of her. I notice you don't go there often.

MRS. ROCKETT: *(With dignity.)* I go when I am invited.

DORIS: *(Triumphantly.)* Exactly.

MRS. ROCKETT: She's not the kind of woman that likes people popping in and out all the time. We can't all be Amy Fawcetts.

DORIS: What's the matter with Amy Fawcett? *(She takes the teapot to the sideboard.)*

MRS. ROCKETT: Well, she's common for one thing, she dyes her hair for another, and she's a bit too free and easy all round for my taste.

DORIS: She doesn't put on airs, anyway.

MRS. ROCKETT: I should think not, after the sort of life she's led.

DORIS: *(Takes bread to sideboard.)* How do you know what sort of a life she's led?

MRS. ROCKETT: Everybody knows, you only have to look at her; I'm a woman of the world, I am, you can't pull the wool over my eyes— *(Elsie comes into the room wearing a mackintosh and a tam-o'-shanter.)*

ELSIE: Mum, we want a new roll of toilet paper.

DORIS: How many times have I told you ladies don't talk about such things!

ELSIE: *(As she stamps over to the piano and begins to search untidily through a pile of music on it.)* It's right down to the bit of cardboard.

DORIS: *(Scraping the bottom of her cup on the saucer.)* Don't untidy everything like that. What are you looking for?

ELSIE: "The Pixies' Parade," I had it last night.

DORIS: If it's the one with the blue cover it's at the bottom.

ELSIE: It isn't—oh dear, Miss Pritchard will be mad at me if I can't find it.

MRS. ROCKETT: *(Rising.)* Perhaps you put it in your satchel, dear. Here, let me look— *(She opens Elsie's satchel which is hanging over the back of a chair and fumbles in it.)* Is this it?

ELSIE: Oh yes, thanks, Grandma.

DORIS: Go along now, for heaven's sake, you'll be late.

(Mrs. Rockett helps Elsie on with her satchel.)

ELSIE: Oh, all right, Mum. Good-bye, Grandma, good-bye, Dad.

HENRY: Good-bye.

MRS. ROCKETT: Good-bye, dear, give Grandma a kiss. *(Elsie does so.)*

DORIS: *(Pushing Elsie out of the door.)* Don't dawdle on the way home.

ELSIE: Oh, all right, Mum. *(She goes out. The slam of the front door shakes the house.)*

DORIS: *(Irritably.)* There now.

MRS. ROCKETT: *(With studied politeness.)* If you are going down to the shops this morning, would it be troubling you too much to get me a reel of white cotton? *(She sits in the armchair.)*

DORIS: *(Tidying the piano.)* I thought you were coming with me.

MRS. ROCKETT: I really don't feel up to it.

DORIS: I'll put it on my list. *(She takes a piece of paper out of the sideboard drawer and scribbles on it.)*

MRS. ROCKETT: If it's out of your way, please don't trouble. It'll do another time.

DORIS: Henry, it's past nine.

HENRY: *(Without looking up.)* I know.

DORIS: You'll be late.

HENRY: Never mind.

DORIS: That's a nice way to talk, I must say.

MRS. ROCKETT: I'm sure if my Robert had ever lazed about like that in the mornings, I'd have thought the world had come to an end.

DORIS: Henry'll do it once too often, mark my words. *(She crosses behind Henry.)*

MRS. ROCKETT: *(Biting off, her thread.)* Well, that corner's finished. *(She puts away her embroidery and starts to knit.)*

DORIS: *(To Henry.)* You'll have to move now, I've got to clear. *(Taking first his saucer, then his cup, from his hand.)*

(Henry rises absently.)

MRS. ROCKETT: Where's Ethel?

DORIS: Doing the bedroom. *(Henry quietly goes out of the room.)* *(Throwing more scraps on the fire.)* Look at that wicked waste.

MRS. ROCKETT: What's the matter with him?

DORIS: Don't ask me, I'm sure I couldn't tell you.

MRS. ROCKETT: He came in very late last night, I heard him go into the bathroom. *(There is a pause.)* That cistern makes a terrible noise.

DORIS: *(Emptying crumbs from cloth into fire and folding it.)* Does it indeed!

MRS. ROCKETT: Yes, it does.

DORIS: *(Slamming the teapot onto the tray.)* Very sorry, I'm sure.

MRS. ROCKETT: Where's he been?

DORIS: How do I know?

MRS. ROCKETT: Didn't you ask him?

DORIS: I wouldn't demean myself.

MRS. ROCKETT: Been drinking?

DORIS: No.

MRS. ROCKETT: Sounded very like it to me, all that banging about.

DORIS: You know Henry never touches a drop.

MRS. ROCKETT: I know he says he doesn't.

DORIS: Oh, do shut up, Mother, we're not all like Father. *(She puts the cloth in the sideboard drawer, then scrapes grease with her nail from the green cloth on the table.)*

MRS. ROCKETT: You watch your tongue, Doris Gow, don't let me hear you saying anything against the memory of your poor father.

DORIS: I wasn't.

MRS. ROCKETT: *(Belligerently.)* Oh yes, you were, you were insinuating again.

DORIS: *(Hoisting up the tray.)* Father drank and you know it, everybody knew it. *(She moves L.)*

MRS. ROCKETT: You're a wicked woman.

DORIS: It's true.

MRS. ROCKETT: Your father was a gentleman, which is more than your husband will ever be, with all his night-classes and his book reading—night-classes, indeed!

DORIS: *(Poking the fire.)* Who's insinuating now?

MRS. ROCKETT: *(Angrily.)* I am and I'm not afraid to say so.

DORIS: What of it?

MRS. ROCKETT: *(With heavy sarcasm.)* I suppose he was at a night-class last night?

DORIS: *(Loudly.)* Mind your own business.

(Henry comes in, wearing his mackintosh and a bowler hat.)

HENRY: What's up?

DORIS: Where were you last night?

HENRY: Why?

DORIS: Mother wants to know and so do I.

HENRY: I was kept late at the shop and I had a bit of dinner in town.

DORIS: Who with?

HENRY: Charlie Henderson. *(He picks up the paper off the table and goes out. The baby next door bursts into fresh wails.)*

MRS. ROCKETT: There goes that child again. It's my belief it's hungry.

DORIS: Wonder you don't go and give it twopence to buy sponge-cake. *(She pulls the door open with her foot and goes out with the tray as the lights fade on the scene.)*

The Hollow

Agatha Christie
1952

Dramatic

Setting: The garden room of the Angkatell home, The Hollow. A Friday in early September.

Scene: Sir Henry is reading *The Times*. Henrietta is sculpting in clay and frowning.

Henrietta Angkatell: 33, a sculptor, attractive.
Lady Lucy Angkatell: 60, her mother.
Sir Henry Angkatell: 70's, her distinguished father.
Midge Harvey: Sir Henry's cousin, 20's – 30's, sweet nature, badly off financially.

HENRIETTA: *(As she enters.)* Damn and damn and damn!

SIR HENRY: *(Looking up.)* Not going well?

HENRIETTA: *(Taking a cigarette from the box on the coffee table.)* What misery it is to be a sculptor.

SIR HENRY: It must be. I always thought you had to have models for this sort of thing.

HENRIETTA: It's an abstract piece I'm modelling, darling.

SIR HENRY: What— *(He points with distaste to the piece of modern sculpture on the pedestal R.)* like that?

HENRIETTA: *(Crossing to the mantelpiece.)* Anything interesting in *The Times*? *(She lights her cigarette with the table lighter on the mantelpiece.)*

SIR HENRY: Lots of people dead. *(He looks at Henrietta.)* You've got clay on your nose.

HENRIETTA: What?

SIR HENRY: Clay—on your *nose*.

HENRIETTA: *(Looking in the mirror on the mantelpiece; vaguely.)* Oh, so I have. *(She rubs her nose, then her forehead, turns and moves, L.C.)*

SIR HENRY: Now it's all over your face.

HENRIETTA: *(Moving up C.; exasperated.)* Does it matter, darling?

SIR HENRY: Evidently not.

(Henrietta goes on to the terrace up C. and resumes work. Lady

Angkatell enters R. She is a very charming and aristocratic-looking woman aged about sixty, completely vague, but with a lot of personality. She is apparently in the middle of a conversation.

LADY ANGKATELL: *(Crossing above the sofa to the fireplace.)* Oh dear, oh, dear! If it isn't one thing it's another. Did I leave a mole-trap in here? *(She picks up the mole-trap from the mantlepiece and eases C.)* Ah yes—there it is. The worst of moles is—you never know where they are going to pop up next. People are quite right when they say that nature in the mild is seldom raw. *(She crosses below the sofa to R.)* Don't you think I'm right, Henry?

SIR HENRY: I couldn't say, my dear, unless I know what you're talking about.

LADY ANGKATELL: I'm going to pursue them quite ruthlessly—I really am.

(Her voice dies away as she exits R.)

HENRIETTA: *(Looking in through the French window up C.)* What did Lucy say?

SIR HENRY: Nothing much. Just being Lucyish. I say, it's half past six.

HENRIETTA: I'll have to stop and clean myself up. They're all coming by car, I suppose? *(She drapes a damp cloth over her work.)*

SIR HENRY: All except Midge. She's coming by Green Line bus. Ought to be here by now.

HENRIETTA: Darling Midge. She is nice. Heaps nicer than any of us, don't you think? *(She pushes the stand out of sight R. of the terrace.)*

SIR HENRY: I must have notice of that question.

HENRIETTA: *(Moving C.; laughing.)* Well, less eccentric, anyway. There's something very sane about Midge. *(She rubs her hands on her overall.)*

SIR HENRY: *(Indignantly.)* I'm perfectly sane, thank you.

HENRIETTA: *(Removing her overall and looking at Sir Henry.)* Ye-es—perhaps *you* are. *(She puts her overall over the back of the armchair L.C.)*

SIR HENRY: *(Smiling.)* As sane as anyone can be that has to live with Lucy, bless her heart. *(He laughs.)*

(Henrietta laughs, crosses to the mantelpiece and puts her cigarette ash in the ashtray.)

(He puts his newspaper on the coffee table. Worried.) You know, Henrietta, I'm getting worried about Lucy.

HENRIETTA: Worried? Why?

SIR HENRY: Lucy doesn't realize there are certain things she can't do.

HENRIETTA: *(Looking in the mirror.)* I don't think I quite know what you mean. *(She pats her hair.)*

SIR HENRY: She's always got away with things. I don't suppose any other woman in the world could have flouted the traditions of Government House as she did. *(He takes his pipe from his pocket.)* Most Governor's wives have to toe the line of convention. But not Lucy! Oh dear me, no! She played merry hell with precedence at dinner parties—and that, my dear Henrietta, is the blackest of crimes. *(Henrietta turns.)* *(He pats his pockets, feeling for his tobacco pouch.)* She put deadly enemies next to each other. She ran riot over the color question. And instead of setting everyone at loggerheads, I'm damned if she didn't get away with it.*(Henrietta picks up the tobacco jar from the mantelpiece, crosses, and hands it to Sir Henry.)* Oh, thank you. It's that trick of hers—always smiling at people and looking so sweet and helpless. Servants are the same—she gives them any amount of trouble and they simply adore her.

HENRIETTA: I know what you mean. *(She sits on the sofa at the left end.)* Things you wouldn't stand from anyone else, you feel they are quite all right if Lucy does them. What is it? Charm? Hypnotism?

SIR HENRY: *(Filling his pipe.)* I don't know. She's always been the same from a girl. But you know, Henrietta, it's growing on me. She doesn't seem to realize there are limits. I really believe Lucy would feel she could get away with *murder*.

HENRIETTA: *(Rising and picking up the piece of clay from the carpet.)* Darling Henry, you and Lucy are angels letting me make my messes here—treading clay into your carpet. *(She crosses and puts the piece of clay in the wastepaper basket down R. .)* When I had that fire at my studio, I thought it was the end of everything—it was sweet of you to let me move in on you.

SIR HENRY: My dear, we're proud of you. Why, I've just been reading a whole article about you and your show in *The Times*.

HENRIETTA: *(Crossing to the coffee table and picking up* The Times.*)* Where?

SIR HENRY: Top of the page. There, I believe. Of course, I don't profess to know much about it myself.

HENRIETA: *(Reading.)* "The most significant piece of the year." Oh, what gup! I must go and wash.

(She drops the paper on the sofa, crosses, picks up her overall, and exits hurriedly L. Sir Henry rises, puts the papers and tobacco on the coffee table, takes the clay from the table to the waste-paper basket, moves to the drinks table, and picks up the matches. Midge Harvey enters up C. from L. She is small, neatly dressed but obviously badly off. She is a warm-hearted, practical, and very nice young woman, a little younger than Henrietta. She carries a suitcase.)

MIDGE: *(As she enters.)* Hullo, Cousin Henry.

SIR HENRY: *(Turning.)* Midge! *(He moves to R. of her, takes the suitcase from her, and kisses her.)* Nice to see you.

MIDGE: Nice to see you.

SIR HENRY: How are you?

MIDGE: Terribly well.

SIR HENRY: Not been overworking you in that damned dress shop of yours?

MIDGE: *(Moving down C.)* Business is pretty slack at the moment, or I shouldn't have got the weekend off. The bus was absolutely crowded; I've never known it go so slowly. *(She sits on the sofa, puts her bag and gloves beside her and looks towards the window R.)* It's heaven to be here. Who's coming this weekend?

SIR HENRY: *(Putting the suitcase on the floor R. of the armchair L.C.)* Nobody much. The Cristows. You know them, of course.

MIDGE: The Harley Street doctor with a rather dim wife?

SIR HENRY: That's right. Nobody else. Oh yes— *(He strikes a match.)* Edward, of course.

MIDGE: *(Turning to face Sir Henry, suddenly stricken by the sound of the name.)* Edward!

SIR HENRY: *(Lighting his pipe.)* Quite a job to get Edward away from Ainswick these days.

MIDGE: *(Rising.)* Ainswick! Lovely, lovely Ainswick! *(She crosses to the fireplace and gazes up at the picture above it.)*

SIR HENRY: *(Moving down C.)* Yes, it's a beautiful place.

MIDGE: *(Feeling.)* It's the most beautiful place in the world.

SIR HENRY: *(Putting the matchbox on the coffee table.)* Had some happy times there, eh? *(He eases to R. of the armchair L.C.)*

MIDGE: *(Turning.)* All the happy times I've ever had were there.

(Lady Angkatell enters R. She carries a large empty flower-pot.)

LADY ANGKATELL: *(As she enters.)* Would you believe it— *(She crosses above the sofa to R. of Sir Henry)* they've been at it again. They've pushed up a whole row of lovely little lobelias. Ah well, as long as the weather keeps fine—

SIR HENRY: Here's Midge.

LADY ANGKATELL: Where? *(She crosses to Midge and kisses her.)* Oh, darling Midge, I didn't see you, dear. *(To Sir Henry. Confidentially.)* That would help, wouldn't it? What were you both doing when I came in?

SIR HENRY: Talking Ainswick.

LADY ANGKATELL: *(Sitting in the armchair L.C.; with a sudden change of manner.)* Ainswick!

SIR HENRY: *(Patting Lady Angkatell's shoulder.)* There, there, Lucy.

(A little disturbed, he crosses and exits L.)

MIDGE: *(Indicating the flower pot; surprised.)* Now why did you bring that in here, darling?

LADY ANGKATELL: I can't begin to think. Take it away. *(Midge takes the flower pot from Lady Angkatell, crosses, goes on to the terrace up C. and puts the flower pot on the ground out of sight.)* Thank you, darling. As I was saying, at any rate the weather's all right. That's *something*. Because if a lot of discordant personalities are boxed up indoors . . . *(She looks around.)* Where are you? *(Midge moves to R. of the armchair. L.C.)* Ah, there you are. It makes things ten times worse. Don't you agree?

MIDGE: Makes what worse?

LADY ANGKATELL: One can play games, of course—but that would be like last year when I shall never forgive myself about poor Gerda—and the worst of it is that she really is so nice. It's odd that anyone as nice as Gerda should be so devoid of any kind of intelligence. If that is what they mean of the law of compensation I don't think it's at all fair.

MIDGE: What are you talking about, Lucy?

LADY ANGKATELL: This weekend, darling. *(She takes hold of Midge's left hand.)* It's such a relief to talk it over with you, Midge dear, you're so practical.

MIDGE: Yes, but what *are* we talking over?

LADY ANGKATELL: John, of course, is delightful, with that dynamic personality that all really successful doctors seem to have. But as for Gerda, ah well, we must all be very, very kind.

MIDGE: *(Crossing to the fireplace.)* Come now, Gerda Cristow isn't as bad as all that.

LADY ANGKATELL: Darling. Those eyes. Like a puzzled cow. And she never seems to understand a word one says to her.

MIDGE: I don't suppose she understands a word *you* say—and I don't know that I blame her. Your mind goes so fast, Lucy, that to keep pace with it, your conversation has to take the most astonishing leaps—with all the connecting links left out. *(She sits on the pouffe.)*

LADY ANGKATELL: Like monkeys. Fortunately Henrietta is here. She was wonderful last Spring when we played limericks or anagrams—one of those things—we had all finished when we suddenly discovered that poor Gerda hadn't even started. She didn't even know what the game *was.* It was dreadful wasn't it, Midge?

MIDGE: Why anyone ever comes to stay with the Angkatells, I don't know. What with the brainwork and the round games and your peculiar style of conversation, Lucy.

LADY ANGKATELL: I suppose we must be rather trying. *(She rises, moves to the coffee table and picks up the tobacco jar.)* The poor dear looked so bewildered; and John looked so impatient. *(She crosses to the fireplace.)* It was then that I was grateful to Henrietta. *(She puts the jar on the mantelpiece, turns and moves C.)* She turned to Gerda and asked for the pattern of the knitted pullover she was wearing—a dreadful affair in pea green—with little bobbles and pom-poms and things—oh, sordid—but Gerda brightened up at once and looked so pleased. The worst of it is Henrietta had to buy some wool and knit one.

MIDGE: And was it very terrible?

LADY ANGKATELL: Oh, it was ghastly. No—on Henrietta it looked quite charming—which is what I mean when I say that the world is so very very sad. One simply doesn't know *why*. . .

MIDGE: Woah! Don't start rambling again, darling. Let's stick to the weekend. *(Lady Angkatell sits on the sofa.)* I don't see where the worry is. If you manage to keep off round games, and try to be coherent when you're talking to Gerda, and put Henrietta on duty to tide over the awkward moments, where's the difficulty?

LADY ANGKATELL: It would al be perfectly all right if only Edward weren't coming.

MIDGE: *(Reacting at the name.)* Edward? *(She rises and turns to the fireplace.)* Yes, of course. What on earth made you ask Edward for the weekend, Lucy?

LADY ANGKATELL: I didn't ask him. He wired to know if we could have him. You know how sensitive Edward is. If I'd wired back "No," he would never have asked himself again. Edward's like that.

MIDGE: Yes.

LADY ANGKATELL: Dear Edward. If only Henrietta would make up her mind to marry him. *(Midge turns and faces Lady Angkatell.)* She really is quite fond of him. If only they could have been alone this weekend without the Cristows. As it is, John has the most unfortunate effect on Edward. John becomes so much *more* so, and Edward so much *less* so. If you know what I mean. *(Midge nods.)* But I do feel that it's all going to be terribly difficult. *(She picks up the* Daily Graphic.*)*

Thunder on Sycamore Street

Reginald Rose
1954

Dramatic
Setting: The Blake House on Sycamore Street, 1950's.
Scene: Mrs. Carson has come to warn the Blakes that a vigilante mob is forming that evening to force them to leave the neighborhood. Joe gently tells his little daughter to go to her room. Mrs. Blake sits quietly through this whole scene but is very involved and very afraid.

Mrs. Carson: A neighbor on Sycamore Street, 30's – 50's.
Anna Blake: A housewife, 20's – 30's, a good wife and mother.
Mrs. Blake: Her mother-in-law who lives with them, 50's – 60's.
Joe Blake: Anna's husband, who has spent some time in prison, 30's, honest, direct, strong, kind.

(Anna waits till we hear the door close. Joe puts his arms around her.)
JOE: Tell me. What's wrong, Anna?
ANNA *(Almost sobbing.)* Joe! I don't understand it! Mrs. Carson says. . . She . . .
JOE: *(Gently.)* Mrs. Carson says what?
ANNA: *(Breaking down.)* She says . . . Joe. . . they're going to throw us out of our house. Tonight! Right now! What are we going to do?
JOE: *(Softly.)* Well, I don't know. Who's going to throw us out of our house?
(But Anna can't answer. Joe grips her tightly, then releases her and walks to Mrs. Carson who sits stolidly, waiting.)
JOE: Who's going to throw us out, Mrs. Carson? Do you know?
MRS. CARSON: Well, like I told Mrs. Blake there, I suppose it's none of my business, but I'm not the kind that thinks a thing like this ought to happen to people without them getting at least a . . . well, a warning. Know what I mean?
JOE: No, I don't know what you mean, Mrs. Carson. Did someone send you here?
MRS. CARSON: *(Indignantly.)* Well, I should say not! If my husband knew I was here he'd drag me out by the hair. No, I sneaked in

here, if you please, Mr. Blake. I felt it was my Christian duty. A man ought to have the right to run away, I say.

JOE: What do you mean run away, Mrs. Carson?

MRS. CARSON: Well, you know what I mean.

JOE: Who's going to throw us out?

MRS. CARSON: Well, everybody. The people of Sycamore Street. You know. They don't feel you ought to live here, because . . . Now I don't suppose I have to go into that.

JOE: *(Understanding.)* I see.

ANNA: *(Breaking in.)* Joe, I've been waiting and waiting for you to come home. I've been sitting here . . . and waiting. Listen . . .

JOE: *(Quietly.)* Hold it, Anna. *(To Mrs. Carson.)* What time are they coming, Mrs. Carson?

MRS. CARSON: Quarter after seven. That's the plan. *(She looks at her watch and gets up.)* It's near seven now. They're very angry people, Mr. Blake. I don't think it'd be right for anyone to get hurt. That's why I'm here. If you take my advice, you'll just put some stuff together in a hurry and get out. I don't think there's any point in your calling the police either. There's only two of 'em in Eastmont and I don't think they'd do much good against a crowd like this.

JOE: Thank you, Mrs. Carson.

MRS. CARSON: Oh, don't thank me. It's like I said. I don't know you people, but there's no need for anyone getting hurt long as you move out like everybody wants. No sir. I don't want no part nor parcel to any violence where it's not necessary. Know what I mean?

JOE: Yes, I know what you mean.

MRS. CARSON: I don't know why a thing like this has to start up anyway. It's none of my business, but a man like you ought to know better than to come pushing in here . . . a fine old neighborhood like this! After all, right is right.

JOE: *(Controlled.)* Get out, Mrs. Carson.

MRS. CARSON: What? Well I never! You don't seem to know what I've done for you, Mr. Blake.

ANNA: Joe . . .

JOE: Get out of this house. *(He goes to a chair in which lies Mrs. Carson's coat. He picks it up and thrusts it at her. She takes it, indignant and a bit frightened. Joe turns from her. She begins to put her coat on.)*

MRS. CARSON: Well, I should think you'd at least have the decency to thank me. I might've expected this though. People like you!

ANNA: Mrs. Carson, please . . .

JOE: Anna, stop it! *(He strides to the door and holds it open. Mrs. Carson walks out.)*

MRS. CARSON: I think maybe you'll be getting what you deserve, Mr. Blake. Good night! *(She goes out, Joe slams the door.)*

ANNA: It's true. I can't believe it! Joe! Did you hear what she said? *(She goes to Joe, who still stands at the door, shocked.)* Well, what are you standing there for?

JOE: *(Amazed.)* I don't know.

ANNA: Joe, I'm scared. I'm so scared. I'm sick to my stomach. What are we going to do? *(Joe puts his arms around her as she begins to sob. He holds her close till she quiets down. Then he walks her slowly over to his mother.)*

JOE: *(To his mother.)* Will you read to Judy for a few minutes, Mother? It's time for her story. *(Mrs. Blake starts to get up.)* Winnie the Pooh. She'll tell you what page. *(Mrs. Blake nods and gets up and goes into Judy's room.)*

ANNA: What are you doing, Joe? We've only got fifteen minutes . . . Don't you understand?

JOE: *(Quietly.)* What do you want me to do? I can't stop them from coming here. *(She goes to him and looks up at him, pleading now.)*

ANNA: *(Whispering.)* Joe. Let's get out. We've got time. We can throw some things into the car. . .

JOE: Isn't it a remarkable thing? A quiet street like this and people with thunder in their hearts.

ANNA: Listen to me, Joe, please. We can get most of our clothes in the car. We can stop at a motel. I don't care where we go. Anywhere. Joe, you're not listening. *(Loud.)* What's the matter with you?

JOE: We're staying.

ANNA: *(Frightened.)* No!

JOE: Anna, this is our home and we're staying in it. No one can make us get out of our home. No one. That's a guarantee I happen to have since I'm born.

ANNA: *(Sobbing.)* Joe, you can't Do you know what a mob is like? Do you know what they're capable of doing?

JOE: It's something I've never thought of before . . . a mob. I guess they're capable of doing ugly things.

ANNA: Joe, you're talking and talking and the clock is ticking so fast. Please . . . please. . . Joe. We can run. We can go somewhere else to live. It's not so hard.

JOE: It's very hard, Anna, when it's not your own choice.

ANNA: *(Sobbing.)* Stand here and fight them? We're not an army. We're one man and one woman and an old lady and a baby.

JOE: And the floor we stand on belongs to us. Not to anyone else.

ANNA: They don't care about things like that. Joe, listen to me, please. You're not making sense. Listen . . . Judy's inside. She's six years old now and she's only really known you for a few weeks. We waited four years for you, and she didn't remember you when you picked up her up and kissed her hello, but, Joe, she was so happy. What are you gonna tell her when they set fire to her new house?

The Art of Dining

Tina Howe
1978

Comic

Setting: A new restaurant.

Scene: Cal approaches the three friends asking about their preferences in wine.

Herrick Simmons: A woman with a hearty appetite, 30's.
Nessa Vox: A guilty eater, 30's.
Tony Stassio: A noneater who is always on a diet, 30's.
Cal: The waiter and half-owner of the restaurant, 30's.

CAL: A Burgundy or Beaujolais?

NESSA VOX: I'd like a chateau bottled red Bordeaux!

CAL: *(Making suggestions for her.)* Chateau Belgrave . . . Chateau La Lagune . . .

HERRICK SIMMONS: I think a white Burgundy would serve us much better.

CAL: *(Now to Herrick.)* Pouilly Fuissé . . . Puligny-Montrachet . . .

TONY STASSIO: *(Stubborn.)* Nuits St. Georges!

CAL: *(Suggesting more Burgundies to Herrick.)* Corton-Charlemage. . .

TONY STASSIO: Pinot Chardonnay!

HERRICK SIMMONS: *(A tremendous sigh.)* Corton-Charlemagne, that's more like it!

TONY STASSIO: *(Has made up her mind, with stunning authority.)* PULIGNY-FUISSÉ!

CAL: *(Bewildered as no such brand exists.)* Puligny-Fuissé?

HERRICK SIMMONS: *(Trying to correct Tony.)* Puligny-*Montrachet!*

NESSA VOX: *(Likewise.)* Pouilly-Fuissé!

TONY STASSIO: Montrachet-Fuissé!

CAL: Montrachet-*Puligny!*

NESSA VOX: Puligny . . . Pouilly!

HERRICK SIMMONS: Pouilly-Fuissé!

CAL: Pouilly-Montrachet!

HERRICK SIMMONS: Pouilly-Montrachet?

NESSA VOX: Montrachet-Puligné *(Pronounced "Pulignay.")*

CAL: *(Repeating after her.)* Montrachet-Puligné!

HERRICK SIMMONS: *(Correcting his pronunciation.)* Nee!

CAL: *(Quickly, embarrassed.)* Nee!

TONY STASSIO: Montrachet-Romanne!

HERRICK SIMMONS: *(Is looking at the wine list, trying to make up her mind.)* Puligny-Montrachet! *(Hands the list to Nessa.)*

NESSA FOX: *(Scanning it, considering.)* Puligny-Montrachet . . . ?

TONY STASSIO: *(Takes the list from Nessa and points.)* Pinot Chardonnay!

HERRICK SIMMONS: Pinot Chardonnay?

NESSA VOX: *(Takes the list from Tony and announces.)* Chateau de Lascombes!

HERRICK SIMMONS: Spare me! *(A pause.)*

CAL: *(Sensing trouble.)* Could I be of any assistance?

TONY STASSIO: *(Taking the list back from Nessa, makes another choice. She knows nothing about wine.)* Cotes-du-Rhône!

CAL: Would you like a red wine or white?

TONY STASSIO: *(Pointing to another selection, mispronouncing it.)* Chateauneuf-du-Papé!

CAL: *(Correcting her pronunciation.)* Montrachet-Romané, *nay!*

TONY STASSIO: *(Triumphant in her ignorance.)* MONTRACHET-PULIG-NAY!

CAL, HERRICK, and NESSA: Nee, Nee! *(A pause.)*

HERRICK SIMMONS: *(Turns to Cal and gives him their order.)* Montrachet-Puligny!

CAL: *(Dutifully repeats after her.)* Montrachet-Puligny!

TONY STASSIO: *(Realizes they've reversed the order.)* Puligny-Montrachet!

CAL, HERRICK, and TONY: *(All realize she's right and start laughing, repeating after her.)* Puligny-Montrachet! *(And the lights fade on them.)*

My Visits with MGM (my Grandmother Marta)

Edit Villareal
1989

Dramatic
Setting: Texas.
Scene: There has been a fire and Marta Feliz's family home is burned
to the ground. Now she sifts through both the debris and the
memories of her grandmother's life. In this scene her grandma is
a young woman again.

Marta Feliz: Late 20's, American born of Mexican heritage, the narra-
tor of the play.
Marta Grande: Her grandmother, a Mexican refugee.
Florinda: Her aunt, also a Mexican refugee.
Juan: American born, WWI soldier—died when he was in his 20's.

FLORINDA'S VOICE: *(Whisper.)* This house is mine, Marta.
¿M'entiendes? *(Pause.)* ¿M'entiendes? *(Marta Feliz frowns. A bad
memory.)*
FLORINDA'S VOICE: *(Whispers, then rises in anger.)* ¡Sinvergüenza!
¡Necesitas un palazo!
MARTA FELIZ: *(Discovers the remains of a Mexican morral or hemp
bag, the bright striped colors still visible on the bag.)* ¿'Amá?
Where are you? ¿'Amá?
MARTA FELIZ: *(Light rises on Marta Grande, holding a similar bag.)*
Look. It's one of the old ones, 'Amá. It survived the fire.
FLORINDA'S VOICE: *(Whisper.)* You made a will? American whore!
MARTA GRANDE: *(Smiling.)* Your tía! *(Marta Feliz and Marta Grande
giggle at the old memory. Light dims on Marta Grande.)*
MARTA FELIZ: *(To audience.)* After my 'Amá, my grandmother, died, I
threw away clothes. And I stored away photos, green cards, let-
ters, and bills. The only thing I kept for myself was her coin purse.
Fake leather from the five-and-dime with a rusty hinge that still
closed tight.
MARTA GRANDE: In Texas, everything rusts.
MARTA FELIZ: Inside the coin purse were fourteen silver packages.

Bus fares individually wrapped in tinfoil. Exactly the right combination of nickels and dimes for one bus ride to town and back.

MARTA GRANDE: Una semana. One week.

MARTA FELIZ: She never learned to drive. After she ran over a dog learning to back up for the first time, my grandfather wouldn't ever let her have the wheel. But, as she used to say . . .

MARTA GRANDE: Ni modo.

MARTA FELIZ: Even in her eighties, she used to take the bus into town regularly. All the bus drivers knew her by name, Doña Marta. She'd make them stop for her midblock, coming and going. *(Female figures in silhouette appear, all wearing large Mexican rebozos, or shawls, which cover their heads and bodies. A corrido of leave-taking rises, plaintive yet insistent.)* When she came here from Mexico, I guess she looked the part. *(Marta Grande begins to fill her hemp bag with her belongings.)*

MARTA FELIZ: Quiet. Mexican. Patient. Mexican. Long-suffering. Mexican. Dependent. Mexican. But inside she was different. When she left Mexico she was only fifteen. And all she took with her was what she could carry in a few sturdy morrales or hemp bags. *(Marta Grande steps forward, the archetypal Mexican refugee icon wrapped in her rebozo and carrying her morral.)*

MARTA GRANDE: *(As a young girl.)*
Yo salí
Pero los otros se quedaron
Candelaria y José María
Mis padres, ellos se quedaron.

MARTA FELIZ: Her parents wouldn't go. They were too old, they said. But she left anyway.

MARTA GRANDA: ¡Pos, sí! No podría soportarlo

MARTA FELIZ: She couldn't bear it.

MARTA GRANDE:
Pero mis hermanos se quedaron
Lepolodo se quedó,
Maclovio se quedó,
También Erasmo y Jafet,
Hasta Alfredo se quedó.

MARTA FELIZ: Her brothers wouldn't go. It was the Revolution, they said. The Revolution of 1910. But she left anyway.

MARTA GRANDE: ¡Pos, sí! Yo ya no me agnantaba.

MARTA FELIZ: She couldn't stand it one minute longer.

MARTA GRANDE:

Pero mis hermanas se quedaron.

Ella y Soyenda y Flora,

las tres se quedaron.

MARTA FELIZ: Her sisters wouldn't go. Things will get better. And, if not, they can't get worse, they said. But she left anyway.

MARTA GRANDE: ¡Pos, sí! Mándeme Dios, pero yo ya no me aguantaba.

MARTA FELIZ: And so she begged God's forgiveness. And came to Texas.

MARTA GRANDE: Okay! ¡Estoy lista!

MARTA FELIZ: But not alone. She talked one sister . . .

MARTA GRANDE: ¿Florinda?

FLORINDA: *(One of the shawled silhouettes.)* ¿Mande?

MARTA FELIZ: . . . her little sister, into coming with her.

(Exilio/Exile.)

MARTA GRANDE: ¿Florinda? *(FLORINDA, a distinctly different type from Marta Grande, enters.)*

FLORINDA: *(Plaintive.)* ¡Ay, Marta!

MARTA GRANDE: ¡Ay, Marta!

MARTA GRANDE: You want to go to the United States? Or what?

FLORINDA: I don't know. Tengo miedo, Marta.

MARTA GRANDE: Ni miedo. Ni pedo.

FLORINDA: ¡Ay! No hables así.

MARTA GRANDE: ¿Y por qué no?

FLORINDA: *(Plaintive.)* Me da miedo.

MARTA GRANDE: ¿Pos, sabes qué?

FLORINDA: ¿Qué? *(Long pause.)* Qué, what?

MARTA GRANDE: Yo también tengo miedo.

FLORINDA: You're scared?

MARTA GRANDE: Sí.

FLORINDA: ¿Dónde?

MARTA GRANDE: Aquí. *(Points to her head.)*

FLORINDA: ¿En el coco?

MARTA GRANDE: Sí.

FLORINDA: ¿Miedo de qué, hermanita?

MARTA GRANDE: De chingarme. . .

FLORINDA: *(Disgusted.)* ¡Dios mío!

MARTA GRANDE: ¿Aquí entre esta tierra desgraciada y el cielo?

FLORINDA: Y tú, ¿qué sabres?

MARTA GRANDE: Y tú, ¿qué sabres?

FLORINDA: Y tú, señora, ¿qué sabres?

MARTA FELIZ: *(To audience.)* Somehow, my grandmother convinced the Baptist Church into bringing her and her sister, Florinda, to Texas.

FLORINDA: ¡Ni modo! We had to convert.

MARTA GRANDE: We were the first Baptists in a Methodist family. You should have heard the screams. ¡Por toda la frontera!

MARTA FELIZ: In Texas, they were housed in the basement of the Baptist Church.

FLORINDA: ¡Ay, Marta! It's so dark in here. No hay nada aquí en Tejas. Quiero mi familia.

MARTA FELIZ: But Texas, for my tía Florinda, became a kind of torture chamber, I think.

FLORINDA: ¡Quiero mi 'Amá y mi 'Apá! ¡Quiero mis hermanos!

MARTA FELIZ: Some people can leave their families and get by. But for Florinda, things just got worse. One Sunday she switched from the Baptists to the Pentacostals.

MARTA GRANDE: Your tía, Marta Feliz, was always looking for a macho god.

MARTA FELIZ: One of those primitive types who has answers for everything and leaves nothing to choice. Especially yours.

FLORINDA: *(Tight-lipped.)* Bueno.

MARTA FELIZ: But Florinda was not happy as a Holy Roller either. Living in the United States convinced her that here voodoo was necessary. Magic spells and potions. She used to put together some strange brews. My grandmother told me they were worse than piss.

FLORINDA: *(Offering cup of herbal tea to Marta Grande.)* Estafiate, Marta—for your nerves.

MARTA GRANDE: No me engañes con esa mugre.

FLORINDA: Pos . . .

MARTA GRANDE: I drink only café americano now.

FLORINDA: Okay!

MARTA GRANDE: Cuando me pones en el sanatorio . . .

FLORINDA: Okay!

MARTA GRANDE: Me puedes soplar . . .

FLORINDA: ¡Bueno!

MARTA GRANDE: Con esa mugre desgraciada.

FLORINDA: *(Desperately trying to cope.)* Bueno! Okay! Bueno!

MARTA GRANDE: *(To Marta Feliz.)* I didn't like it.

MARTA FELIZ: It's possible my grandmother ruined Florinda's life when she made her leave Mexico.

FLORINDA: *(Still upset.)* ¡Bueno! Okay! ¡Bueno!

MARTA FELIZ: But I'm glad they came to Texas. Because here, my grandmother met my grandfather. And after that, his life, too, was never the same.

JUAN: *(Offstage.)* ¡Marta! *(Juan, dressed in World War I uniform with rifle, enters.)* Ay, Marta! Where have you been?

MARTA GRANDE: Where do you want me, chulo?

FLORINDA: Este fulano no es mexicano.

JUAN: I'm Tex-Mex, honey. American. And proud of it.

MARTA GRANDE: *(To Florinda, indicating the cup of tea.)* Give him the junk.

FLORINDA: *(Giving Juan the herbal tea.)* Estafiate—for your nerves.

JUAN: Ay, gracias. *(Drinks.)*

MARTA GRANDA: It tastes like piss.

JUAN: Marta, the whole world is at war, and I'm going to go fight. Mira mi uniforme. *(Juan performs military rifle drills.)* You like it?

FLORINDA: Dile no.

MARTA GRANDE: No.

JUAN: Will you marry me before I go away?

FLORINDA: Dile no.

MARTA GRANDE: I won't get married, chulo, to a man who cannot dance. Pero Florinda . . .

FLORINDA: *(Simultaneously with Juan. Prudishly.)* Ay, no!

JUAN: *(Simultaneously with Florinda. Passionately.)* ¡Ay, no! *(Continues.)* Pos, Martita, you're the one I want. Will you marry me after the war? *(Juan does a complicated rifle drill.)*

FLORINDA: Dile no.

MARTA GRANDE: Pos, si regresas en un pedazo, payaso.

MARTA FELIZ: After the war, they picked up where my grandmother had dropped him off. But she wanted proof that he had not been hurt.

MARTA GRANDE: He showed me his body.

JUAN: Pero everything?! Now will you marry me?

FLORINDA: Dile no.

MARTA FELIZ: His body was perfect. Except for a moon-shaped scar on his upper back, exactly the size of the shell that crashed into him in France.

JUAN: ¡Soy macho, Marta!

MARTA GRANDE: Pues . . .

MARTA FELIZ: For the rest of his life, he made her laugh by flexing his arm and changing the scar from a moon into a smile.

JUAN: *(Flexing his arm.)* Now will you marry me? Marta?

MARTA FELIZ: Eventually, she said yes.

JUAN: But I have to convert?

MARTA GRANDE: ¡Pos, sí!

JUAN: To what, Marta?

MARTA GRANDE: To the Baptists.

JUAN: ¡Ay, no!

MARTA GRANDE: Pos, they brought me here to Tejas.

FLORINDA: Aquí se dice "Texas," Marta.

JUAN: But we have always been Catholics, Martita.

MARTA GRANDE: Ni modo.

JUAN: Pos. Okay. Yes!

MARTA FELIZ: I think he would have turned Hindu to marry her.

JUAN: ¡Siempre yes! ¡Por toda mi vida, yes!

MARTA FELIZ: The conversion took place in the Rio Grande. He felt happy falling backwards into the river.

JUAN: For you, Marta, anything!

MARTA FELIZ: But when the water from the river crashed against the moon-shaped scar, he felt a pain.

JUAN: The Germans practiced gas warfare, 'manito. In the trenches in France, 'manito. And I breathed it in. All the guys breathed it in. *(Beat.)* The war is over, Marta. Now will you marry me?

MARTA GRANDE: Pos . . . sí.

MARTA FELIZ: And together, with Florinda, they began a new life.

MARTA GRANDE: *(Coquettishly pinning a large red paper rose on her dark shawl.)* ¡Ay, Yonni!

MARTA FELIZ: She always called him Johnny. I guess she thought it was American, like in the movies.

MARTA GRANDE: Necesitan policías—for the bridge.

JUAN: You want me to become a cop, Marta?

MARTA FELIZ: He was a cop. Until he retired at seventy-five.

MARTA GRANDE: You just have to take the aguacates, bananas and oranges away from the people crossing the border.

JUAN: Pues . . .

MARTA GRANDE: After you get a job, we'll buy a house.

JUAN: Of course!

MARTA GRANDE: Con tíerra—for my chickens.

JUAN: Chickens? Qué suave.

MARTA GRANDE: And six children. . .

JUAN: ¡Dios mío!

MARTA GRANDE: Okay, Yonni?

JUAN: *(After a pause and hopelessly in love.)* Pos. Okay! Yes! Siempre, yes! ¡Por toda mi vida, yes! *(Juan and Marta Grande embrace.)*

MARTA FELIZ: But slowly, the pain that began when he crashed backwards into the river on the day of his conversion became stronger and stronger.

JUAN: I got it from the Germans!

MARTA FELIZ: A lifetime after the war, when his Army discharge papers were old and yellow, he was told he had developed cancer. All by himself.

JUAN: When you're in the Army, ¿sabes?, you can't even piss without their permission. But when you get out, you're to blame for everything that ever happened to you. ¡Qué chingazo!

MARTA FELIZ: My grandmother said that in his casket he looked like the young man she had loved all her life.

MARTA GRANDE: We look so young, Marta Feliz, when we die.

JUAN: *(With a salute.)* After the war, Marta, our life! *(Exits.)*

MARTA GRANDE: I want six, Yonni. Six children.

MARTA FELIZ: And the first one was my mother. *(Marta Grande reveals an infant from the depths of her shawl.)*

MARTA GRANDE: Florinda? Mira.

I Hate Hamlet

Paul Rudnick

1991

Comic

Setting: Andrew's newly rented Brownstone apartment in Manhattan.

Scene: Andrew is a Los Angeles–based television star, and he has rented an apartment in Manhattan. He has been asked to play the lead in Hamlet in New York. This is his first look at the apartment, which was rented sight unseen.

Andrew Rally: Late 20's–early 30's, a TV actor—polished, affable.

Deirdre McDavey: 29, appears younger, romantic—Andrew's girlfriend.

Felicia Dantine: 40's, a glossy, high-powered real estate agent in New York City.

Lillian Troy: 70's, elegant, German accent—Andrew's agent.

ANDREW: *(Looking around.)* Oh my God.

FELICIA: Isn't it fabulous? I'm so glad you took it sight unseen. I just knew it was perfect.

ANDREW: It's amazing, but, gee. . . I'm sorry. This isn't what we talked about. I was thinking of, you know, something . . . less.

FELICIA: But it's a landmark! John Barrymore, the legendary star! And now you, Andrew Rally, from *LA Medical*! I loved that show! You were adorable! Why did they cancel it?

ANDREW: Bad time slot, shaky network—I don't think I can live here, this isn't what we discussed.

FELICIA: I know, I know—but honey, I'm not just a broker. I want you to be happy! You belong here.

ANDREW: Don't worry, it's my mistake. I'll move back to my hotel. It's fine.

FELICIA: *(Gesturing to the cartons.)* But your things are here! It's a match! You and Barrymore!

ANDREW: *(Flattered.)* Please, I'm no Barrymore.

FELICIA: Of course you are, Dr. Jim Corman, rookie surgeon! I even love those commercials you do! What is it—Tomboy Chocolate?

ANDREW: Trailburst Nuggets. It's a breakfast cereal.

FELICIA: *(Delighted.)* And . . . ?

ANDREW and FELICIA: *(Singing the jingle.)* "An anytime snack!"

(The doorbell buzzes.)

FELICIA: An anytime snack! I love it! I love that ad! *(She goes to the intercom, which is located in a niche beside the front door and speaks into it.)* Hello? He sure is! *(Passing the receiver to Andrew.)* For you! Your first guest!

ANDREW: *(Into the receiver.)* Hello? Sure . . . come on up. Please! *(To Felicia.)* It's my girlfriend. She can't wait to see the place.

FELICIA: *(Excited.)* Do I know her? Was she on your show?

ANDREW: No, I met Deirdre in New York. But I'm from LA. I like modern things. High tech. Look at this place—I mean, is there a moat?

(There is a knock on the front door, Andrew opens it.)

(Deirdre McDavey is standing outside, clutching a bouquet of roses. Deirdre wears a green wool cape, a long challis skirt, a lacy antique blouse, and pointy, lace-up Victorian boots. Her hair streams down her back, Alice-in-Wonderland style. Deirdre is Andrew's girlfriend; she is twenty-nine years old, but appears much younger. Deirdre is the breathless soul of romantic enthusiasm. She is always on the verge of a swoon; to Deirdre, life is a miracle a minute. Deirdre is irresistibly appealing, a Valley girl imagining herself a Brontë heroine.)

(Deirdre stands in the doorway, trembling and on the verge of tears. Her eyes are clenched shut. She is practically hyperventilating; she speaks in a passionate, strangled whisper.)

DEIRDRE: Andrew . . . ?

ANDREW: *(With amused patience.)* Yes, Deirdre?

DEIRDRE: Andrew . . . am I . . . here?

ANDREW: This is it.

(Deirdre steps into the apartment and opens her eyes. She gasps. As she tours the premises, she removes her cape and hands Andrew the roses and her velvet shoulder bag.)

DEIRDRE: Oh, *Andrew* . . . his walls . . . his floor . . . the staircase to his roof . . . the air he breathed . . . oh Andrew, just being here makes you a part of history!

FELICIA: And I'm the broker!

DEIRDRE: *(To Felicia.)* I worship you!

(The doorbell buzzes again.)

ANDREW: I'll get it!

FELICIA: *(Handing Deirdre her business card.)* Hi. Felicia Dantine.

ANDREW: *(Into the intercom receiver.)* Hello? Come on up.

FELICIA: Isn't this place amazing? The Barrymore thing? The morning it comes on the market, I get Andrew's call.

DEIRDRE: *(Impressed.)* No.

FELICIA: Two famous actors! It's freaky. Are you in the business?

(There is a knock at the door. Andrew opens the door; Lillian Troy is outside.)

(Lillian is a striking, silver-haired woman in her seventies; she wears an elegant mink coat over a simple navy dress and carries a bottle of champagne. She is smoking an unfiltered Camel cigarette. Lillian speaks with a regal German accent and has a no-nonsense manner, combined with a delight at any sort of high jinks. Lillian is Andrew's agent. As the door opens, Lillian is coughing, a real smoker's hack.)

ANDREW: Lillian, Lillian, are you okay?

LILLIAN: *(Finishing her coughing.)* I am fine. *(Passing Andrew the champagne.)* Take it. *(Surveying the premises.)* This is it. As I remember.

ANDREW: What?

LILLIAN: I have been here before. But I had to be certain. *(As Deirdre curtsies.)* Deirdre, you I know. *(To Felicia.)* Hello. I am Lillian Troy. I am Andrew's agent. The scum of the earth.

FELICIA: Hi. Felicia Dantine. Real estate. I win

ANDREW: *(To Lillian.)* What do you mean, you've been here before?

LILLIAN: It was in, oh, the Forties, I imagine. I had just come to America. *(Looking around.)* It was magical. This great window. The cottage on the roof. Fresh flowers everywhere. I had a little fling. Andrew, perhaps you have found my hairpins.

ANDREW: Lillian—you had a fling here?

FELICIA: In this apartment?

DEIRDRE: With whom?

LILLIAN: Whom do you think?

DEIRDRE: *(Awestruck.)* Lillian—you and . . . Barrymore?

FELICIA: Here?

LILLIAN: I am an old lady. The elderly should not discuss romance, it is distasteful. And creates jealousy. And Andrew has such marvelous news, does everyone know?

DEIRDRE: What? What news?

ANDREW: I haven't told because . . . I'm not sure how I feel about it.

DEIRDRE: What? Andrew, what haven't you told me?

ANDREW: Well . . . you know Shakepeare in the Park, right? The open-air theater, by the lake?

FELICIA: I went once. It poured. Right on *Coriolanus*. Didn't help. They kept going.

DEIRDRE: *(To Andrew.)* What? Tell us!

ANDREW: Well, this summer they're doing *All's Well* and . . . another one.

DEIRDRE: Which one?

ANDREW: *(Taking a deep breath.)* *Hamlet*.

DEIRDRE: Oh my God. Wait. Laertes?

ANDREW: Hamlet.

DEIRDRE: The *lead?*

ANDREW: Yeah, Hamlet.

LILLIAN: Ja! Isn't that extraordinary?

DEIRDRE: *(Starting to hyperventilate again, she holds up her hands and backs away from Andrew.)* You . . . are . . . playing . . . Hamlet? My boyfriend is playing Hamlet?

ANDREW: I don't know why they cast me.

LILLIAN: Because you are talented. You auditioned five times. They saw something.

FELICIA: Dr. Jim Corman! You'll pack the place! I'll even come. Is it the real *Hamlet?* Or like, a musical?

ANDREW: The real one. And she's right, of course, I'm sure they only asked me because of the TV Show. I'm a gimmick. I don't know why I said yes.

LILLIAN: Schnookie, we are talking about *Hamlet*.

DEIRDRE: Wouldn't it be great if we could, like, go back in time and tell Barrymore?

FELICIA: Why?

DEIRDRE: I mean, he was the greatest Hamlet of all time—isn't that what people say?

LILLIAN: That is true. And Andrew, you know, he lived here for many years. Perhaps when he played Hamlet.

DEIRDRE: And now you're here—I bet this is all happening for a reason.

FELICIA: 'Cause you were cancelled! *(Looking around, sniffing the air.)* I get this feeling sometimes, in special apartments. About the people who lived there. *(Felicia climbs the staircase to the first landing. She raises her arms, intoning.)* Barrymore, Barrymore! *(In the distance, a bell tolls from a bell tower. Everyone looks up.)*

LILLIAN: What was that?

FELICIA: The church down the street. The clock in the bell tower.

ANDREW: But . . . it's six o'clock. It only struck once.

DEIRDRE: Oh my God. Just like in *Hamlet*. Right before the ghost of Hamlet's father appears. He comes when the clock strikes one.

FELICIA: Which means . . . ?

ANDREW: That we live in New York. Where everything's broken.

DEIRDRE: But what if it's an omen?

FELICIA: Right. Barrymore. Hamlet. The connection. Maybe he's trying to contact us.

ANDREW: *(Pointing to the messy batch of menus that have been slipped under the front door.)* Yeah. Maybe he's the one who's been slipping all these take-out menus under the door.

DEIRDRE: Andrew!

FELICIA: *(Still on the landing.)* Don't joke. Maybe he's . . . around. It's possibly. Totally.

DEIRDRE: Oh my God. What if we could reach out to him across time and space? Wouldn't that be a great idea?

LILLIAN: Don't ask me about great ideas. I am German.

FELICIA: *(Coming down the stairs.)* Wait. Guys. You know—I'm psychic.

DEIRDRE: Oh my God!

LILLIAN: What do you mean?

FELICIA: I've made contact. With the other side. I go into this pre-conscious state, like a trance. And I speak to a spirit guide.

ANDREW: A spirit guide?

FELICIA: Yeah—my mom. We were real close. After she died, I went into such a slump. I tried everything, therapy, encounter groups, you name it. Finally I saw this ad, for a course—"Spiritual Transcom-munication: Beyond the Physical Sphere."

LILLIAN: So you talk to your mother?

FELICIA: Right. Is your mom gone too? Would you like to contact her?

LILLIAN: No. Why break a habit?

DEIRDRE: The clock. This apartment. *Hamlet*. This is preordained. I think we should do it.

ANDREW: Do what?

DEIRDRE: Contact Barrymore. A séance. Right now.

(There is a pause, as everyone looks at each other; the women are all extremely excited at the prospect of a séance, while Andrew has his doubts.)

FELICIA: I've never tried anyone but Ma. But I'm game!

ANDREW: I don't think so.

LILLIAN: But who can tell? Barrymore might return. As he promised me.

DEIRDRE: Lillian, were you really here? With Barrymore?

LILLIAN: Ask him yourself.

ANDREW: No, come on, this is just an apartment. It's not magical and there aren't any ghosts or supernatural phenomena. And we're not having a séance. *(The door to the roof creaks open and then slams shut, all by itself.)* Do we need candles?

FELICIA: Candles are great.

(Andrew rummages through a box to find a candle.)

DEIRDRE: Felicia, what about a table?

FELICIA: Perfect.

(During the next few speeches, Deirdre and Felicia move a card table to center stage and set chairs and crates around it. Lillian supervises.)

DEIRDRE: *(As she moves the table.)* This is just like at the beginning of *Hamlet*, when the guards call out to the ghost *(With gusto.)*
Stay, illusion!
If you hast any sound or use of voice,
Speak to me!

LILLIAN: *(Holding out her arms.)*
If there be any good thing to be done
That may to thee do ease and grace to me
Speak to me!

DEIRDRE: O, speak!

LILLIAN: Stay and speak!

ANDREW: Oh my God. Felicia, is this how you usually operate? Séances? Shakespeare?

FELICIA: Honey, I've been a broker for almost fifteen years. In Greenwich Village. Try human sacrifice. And cheese. *(Surveying the table.)* Okay, everybody sit. How should we do this? I know, first I'll try and contact Ma and then see if she can get a hold of Barrymore.

(By this point, Deirdre, Lillian, and Felicia are all seated around the table.)

LILLIAN: May I smoke? Does anyone mind?

DEIRDRE: Oh Lillian, it's such a terrible thing to do and we all love you so much, do you have to?

LILLIAN: *(Sighing.)* Very well. *(She puts down her cigarette.)* You know, I really must stop.

DEIRDRE: Smoking?

LILLIAN: No—asking.

(Andrew has located a candle and stuck it in a bottle. He sets the bottle on the table.)

FELICIA: *(To Andrew.)* Now hit the lights, okay, hon? I'm gonna enter this trance state, so Andy, think about what you want to ask Barrymore.

DEIRDRE: Has he met Shakespeare?

LILLIAN: Is it hot?

DEIRDRE: Lillian, Barrymore is not in hell. I'm sure Felicia never even deals with people . . . down there.

FELICIA: Well, if I have a legal problem . . . okay everybody, put your hands on the table, palms down, it helps the flow. Now close your eyes. *(By now Andrew has dimmed the lights; the room is lit only by the candle, Andrew has joined the others seated around the table. Everyone joins hands and closes their eyes.)* Now, just clear your minds, totally blank, clean slate. Deep, even breathing. *(Everyone is now breathing in unison, very deeply. Lillian coughs. Everyone continues breathing. Felicia lifts her head. A convulsion shakes Felicia's body; her head drops. As her head rises, she utters a long, guttural, effectively bizarre moan. Finally, as contact is made, Felicia's head pops up and she assumes a cherry brightness, as if talking on the phone. Her eyes remain shut during her conversation with her mother.)* Yeah Ma, it's me . . . fine, fine, you? *(Confidentially, to the group.)* I got her! . . . Ma, listen to me, I need your help. I'm here with Andrew Rally . . . yeah, *LA Medical* . . . Ma, listen, he wants to talk to someone, over there . . . no Ma, he's seeing someone . . . Ma, I think he's having a career crisis, he's gonna do Shakespeare and he needs to talk to Barrymore, right, John Barrymore . . . from the movies . . . okay, okay, hang on . . . *(To Andrew.)* She needs to know, what do you want to ask Barrymore? What's your question?

DEIRDRE: *(Thrilled.)* Andrew, ask!

ANDREW: Ask him what?

DEIRDRE: Ask him about Hamlet!

LILLIAN: Ask him for advice!

ANDREW: But I don't want advice and I don't want to play Hamlet. I mean I don't think I do. I mean, I hate Hamlet!

The Pleasure of Detachment

Perry Souchuk
1990

Dramatic
Setting: A room with a bed, chair and tall windows.
Of Note: The "Voice" may also be played by a male actor.

Women in bed.
Her maid.
A voice.
A young man.

VOICE: Picture this: a long white day with no fuzzy thinking, a hammock in a grove of palm trees. Picture this: a play with no beginning or end, a play that grows from a kind of reverie. *(Lights up to half. Woman stands at windows, looking out.)* First there was the image of the curtains, which, in its stillness, was like a photograph. But what does it signify? Does the stillness of the curtain mean that we are looking at a play where time is frozen? Can time be frozen? If one definition of time is the way thoughts flow, then time can be frozen if we record an idea. The curtain is a reminder of time . . . the way thoughts flow . . . the possibility of freezing an idea in the space and time of a play. *(Woman moves slowly to bed, lies down, slips hands into straps attached to bedposts.)* This is a play about an exercise in limitation, a self-imposed bondage; self-bondage as a meaningful self-test. In her reverie, the woman, her own test subject, discovers the consolation of stillness. When the ritual of self-bondage ends, the mind is again set in motion, then the body, then the world. *(Music fades. Lights up full.)*

WOMAN: *(Leaning forward.)* In order not to move I had to know I couldn't move! Human nature, human nature.
(Maid enters with fresh sheets, etc.)

MAID: How are we doing today?

WOMAN: Pretty well. *(Thoughtfully, rearranging herself in bed.)* Did you know that Toussaint L'Ouverture said that nature speaks in louder tones than philosophy or self-interest?

MAID: *(Humoring her.)* No, I didn't know that. *(Carefully.)* The doctor will be here this afternoon.

WOMAN: But I just saw the doctor yesterday!

MAID: *(Assuringly.)* And he said you are doing very well.

WOMAN: Did he also say that as I was leaving he asked me out for a drink?

(Maid turns, surprised.)

WOMAN: I asked him, "Would you ask me out if I wasn't well?" And he answered, "I don't think so." *(Pause.)* He's my doctor, but he's not my medicine.

(Maid exits.)

VOICE: Some facts about the woman: She led a life not dominated by facts. She was wide-eyed only when alone. She had dreams where all she had to do was turn around to see a different world.

WOMAN: Who doesn't?

VOICE: Her goal was never to be hidden or veiled.

MAID: *(Entering with water pitcher and glass.)* What's on the agenda for today?

WOMAN: I think I'll start my new story today.

MAID: Lovely! *(Pause.)* Am I in it?

WOMAN: *(Pausing, surprise.)* I don't know!

VOICE: How about the story of a woman obsessed with the idea of turning her obsessions into something concrete? Or the story of a woman whose biggest dilemma is an excess of joy? Or a woman who enjoys a certain detachment, a certain pleasure, the pleasure of detachment?

(Young man enters carrying valise. Sees Woman in bed.)

YOUNG MAN: *(Flustered, uneasy.)* Hhhhello. *(Staring at Woman.)* The doctor sent me over to see if you might need anything today.

WOMAN: *(Delighted, curious.)* If I might need anything! Like what?

YOUNG MAN: *(Uneasily.)* I I don't know.

MAID: *(Turning to Young Man.)* I thought the doctor was coming today?

WOMAN: But I don't need the doctor today!

VOICE: No, what the woman *needs* is an answer. She's looking for an answer to a very tricky question.

WOMAN: *(Started.)* Excuse me?

(Maid and Young Man stare at Woman.)

VOICE: The question is: How do you tell the difference between anxiety and desire?

(Pause.)

WOMAN: I give up!

VOICE: The difference between anxiety and desire is that desire is influential. Desire is like a tattoo which only shows when you want it to. You see, a tattoo draws a person in for a closer look. Desire attracts, anxiety repels.

WOMAN: *(Looking at Maid and then at Young Man.)* How do you get rid of a tattoo?

YOUNG MAN: *(Trying to be helpful.)* I read somewhere that you can get rid of a tattoo by rubbing salt into it!

WOMAN: *(To Young Man.)* And what does one do with an unwanted . . . desire?

(Flustered, Young Man turns away from bed.)

VOICE: The unwanted desire becomes an open wound just waiting for a pinch of salt!

WOMAN: Ouch!!

VOICE: Try this: Write down a few ideas. Digest those ideas with the juices of past experience.

YOUNG MAN: *(Moving closer to bed.)* Are you really writing a story?

WOMAN: As we speak!

YOUNG MAN: What's it about?

WOMAN: *(Mysteriously.)* It's . . . kind of a travel book.

VOICE: She plans a trip by reading about different places, and the reading becomes the trip.

WOMAN: *(As a confession, to no one in particular.)* When I travel by train, I say to myself, while I'm on this train every thought is a jumping-off place! *(Pause.)* When I got back from my last trip I could only recall three words: weather, wonder, and what-cha-ma-call-its! I remember . . . I was in a car driving through Missouri. My aunt was with me, and her German welder friend was driving. He was a welder and she was a writer.

VOICE: Oh, so you mean they understood each other?

YOUNG MAN: *(Moving closer to Maid.)* Did you say Missouri or misery? *(Maid ignores Young Man. Still absorbed in Woman's story, she rises and moves closer to bed.)*

WOMAN: He asked me if I liked motorcycles, and I looked at him and said: *(Turning to look at Young Man, self-satisfied.)* It depends who's driving!

(Young Man, shocked, drops into chair.)

VOICE: The woman acquires a certain mystery, simply by the fact that we have come to see her. Who is she? She is an actress who rehearses lines and movements in order to get an idea across. And the audience works to understand the idea. The actress works with a director in order to get the right inflection. The audience's rehearsal is life outside the play. The ideal play is written by the audience and the writer and the actor. The greater the audience's imagination, the greater the play.

WOMAN: *(Twisting to look out windows, hands still in straps.)* I looked out the window and saw a bubble floating by. The sky was an unseeable blue, a depthless blue! A great shimmering lake spread out in front of me. I watched pink and silver fish crisscrossing in the air.

VOICE: *(Gently.)* In telling a story, you must give the listener the feeling of listening. Don't tell me so easily what you know.

WOMAN: Every morning I wake up and feel the world spreading out, starting over. *(Leaning forward.)* I run after ideas like a rabbit without a carrot in front of his nose!

(Woman settles back into bed. Music begins softly under dialogue.)

VOICE: She gazed out the window at the November sky.

WOMAN: *(Startled. Turning away from windows.)* Is it November already?

MAID: *(Soothingly.)* Of course it's November! Now you just relax. *(Maid examines straps, then freezes.)* *(To Young Man.)* I think I've tied the straps too tight! *(She starts to undo strap. Young Man jumps up, unties other strap.)*

(Pause.)

YOUNG MAN: She's bleeding!

VOICE: The talent of blood to coagulate itself, stopping the flow to the outside in order to preserve the flowing on the inside. Not unlike the flowing of mental activity, the talent of the brain to compound the flow, idea upon idea, until the brain has made a kind of story. The writer wills the cells of his body to seek out the nutrition of new ideas. But there is a sadness in translating sensation into words. The writer feels the inadequacies of his expression.

(Woman gets out of bed, goes to windows.) This is a play about the way thoughts flow in and out of stories. Tonight, the woman is looking for her own story.

(Young Man moves to Woman, opens valise.)

YOUNG MAN: *(Fishing around in valise.)* I have a collection of rocks you might like to see. It's a small collection really. *(Pause.)* Actually, I only have one rock. But it's very beautiful. *(Takes out rock, puts it in Woman's hand. Woman holds rock, turns to look out windows. Lights fade to black.)*

564

LYSISTRATA by Aristophanes, translated by Carl Mueller. Copyright ©2000 by Carl Mueller. Reprinted with permission by the Author. All inquiries should be sent to Carl Mueller, UCLA Dept. of Theater, 102 E. Melnitz, Box 961622, Los Angeles, CA 90095-1622.

MY SISTER IN THIS HOUSE by Wendy Kesselman. Copyright ©1982 by Wendy Kesselman. Reprinted with permission by the Author. All inquires should be sent to Samuel French, Inc., Attn: George Lane, 45 W. 25th St., New York, NY 10010.

MY VISITS WITH MGM by Emili Villareal. Copyright ©1989 by Emili Villareal. Reprinted by permission of Linda Garza, Arte Público Press. All inquiries should be sent to Arte Publico Press, Attn: Linda Garza, 4800 Calhoun, Houston, TX 77204-2174.

THE NEXT TO LONGEST DAY by Beth Campbell Stemple. Copyright ©1995 by Beth Campbell Stemple. Reprinted by permission of the Author. All inquiries should be sent to bstemple@uconect.net.

OEDIPUS THE KING by Sophocles, translated by Carl Mueller. Copyright ©2000 by Smith and Kraus. Reprinted with permission by Smith and Kraus. All inquiries should be sent to Smith and Kraus, Inc., P.O. Box 127, Lyme, NH 03768.

PICNIC ON THE BATTLEFIELD by Fernando Arrabal, translated by Barbara Wright. Copyright ©1867 by Calder & Boyars, Ltd. Reprinted with permission by Mary Flower at Grove/Atlantic, Inc. All inquiries should be sent to Grove/Atlantic, Include, 841 Broadway, New York, NY 10003. For performance rights, contact Samuel French, Inc., 45 W. 25th St., New York, NY 10010. Inquiries for all other English language rights should be addressed to Calder Publications Ltd., 126 Cornwall Road, London SE1 8TQ.

POETRY READING by John Chandler. Copyright ©1997 by John Chandler. Reprinted by permission of John Chandler. All inquiries should be sent to John Chandler, 334 Rider Road, Corralitos, CA 95076.

THE SISTERS ROSENSWEIG by Wendy Wasserstein. Copyright ©1993 by Wendy Wasserstein. Reprinted by permission of Harcourt, Inc. All inquiries should be addressed to Harcourt, Inc., 6277 Sea Harbor Drive, 6th Floor, Orlando, FL 32887-6777.

STOPWATCH by Jon Jory. Copyright ©1983. Reprinted with permission by Dramatic Publishing. All inquiries should be sent to Dramatic Publishing, 311 Washington St., Woodstock, IL, 60098.

STREAMERS from PLAYS FOR THE THEATRE by David Rabe. Copyright ©1977 by David Rabe. Reprinted by Permission of Samuel French, Inc. All inquiries should be directed to Samuel French, Inc., 45 W. 25th St., New York, NY 10010.

TEIBLE AND HER DEMON by Isaac Bashevis Singer and Eve Friedman. Copyright ©1984 by Isaac Bashevis Singer and Eve Friedman. Reprinted by permission of Samuel French, Inc. All inquiries should be sent to Samuel French, Inc., 45 W. 25th St., New York, NY 10010.

THUNDER ON SYCAMORE STREET by Reginald Rose. Copyright ©1954 by Reginald Rose. Reprinted by permission of Mitch Douglas at International

8157012